The Good Skiing Guide

D0733243

THE GOOD SKIING GUIDE

Europe's 200 best
winter sports resorts

Edited by **Chris Gill**
Resorts Editor: **Adam Ruck**

Published by Consumers' Association
and Hodder & Stoughton

The Good Skiing Guide is published by
Consumers' Association, 14 Buckingham Street, London WC2N 6DS and
Hodder & Stoughton, 47 Bedford Square, London WC1B 3DP

The Good skiing guide.
  1. Skis and skiing—Europe—Handbooks, manuals, etc.
  I. Gill, Chris II. Ruck, Adam
  796.93'094   GV854.8.E9
  ISBN 0 340 35254 X

Reprinted 1985

Design Patrick Nugent
Maps David Perrott, Machynlleth
Illustrations Jim Robins
Printed and bound in Great Britain by
Pindar Print Ltd, Scarborough

Front cover Seefeld, Tirol, Austria
Back cover (left to right) The Editor of *Which?*, struggling a bit
above Stuben, Vorarlberg, Austria; ice bar at Adelboden, Bernese
Oberland, Switzerland; tobogganing in Switzerland

Contents

Contributors

The *Guide* has in the main been produced by the staff and freelance researchers of *Holiday Which?*, but sections have been contributed by the following specialist writers:

Konrad Bartelski For several years Britain's only world-class downhill racer, now retired from competition

Alan Blackshaw Author of the *Penguin Guide to Mountaineering*

Mark Heller Author of many books about skiing, and ski-resort critic of *The Guardian*

David Goldsmith Freelance journalist, and Equipment Editor of *Ski Survey*, journal of the Ski Club of Great Britain

Nicol Glyn Physical fitness teacher, and author of the Ski Club of Great Britain booklet *Ski-fit*

Iain Peter Mountain guide and ski instructor at Glenmore Lodge National Outdoor Training Centre in Aviemore.

We should like to acknowledge the assistance of the Automobile Association in compiling parts of the Travel facts section.

Last but not least on our list of contributors are the hundreds of individuals – most but not all of them subscribers to *Which?* magazine – who have answered our calls for help over the last two years and sent in their own reports on ski resorts, equipment, insurance claims, ski schools and tour operators. We have made full use of those reports, and are very grateful to have had them. We are doubly grateful to those reporters who have acted as unpaid inspectors while on holiday in the 1984–85 season.

Why this Guide?

This is a guide to holiday skiing. It sets out to explain what's involved in skiing, for the benefit of novices; and it sets out to help all skiers – beginners, 'intermediates' and experts alike – to get the most out of their skiing, with chapters on choosing equipment, get-fit exercises and so on. But the main object of the *Guide* – the reason why we've produced it – is to help you choose your resort.

We start from the belief that making the right choice of resort for a skiing holiday is important; and that getting it right is tricky. We don't expect everyone to agree with us. Good luck with the weather, the snow, the company, the accommodation and the ski-school instructor lottery can make up for a great many deficiencies in a resort itself, and may make you content to pick your resorts with a pin. You may find the choice of resort equally straightforward for the quite different reason that you have already found somewhere that suits you down to the ground, and don't intend to budge from it.

We're not out to tempt contented skiers to venture further afield. If you always have a good holiday regardless of where you go skiing, you earn our unreserved envy. If you have found your perfect resort – and it remains perfect as your skills, abilities and appetites develop or decline – you would clearly be risking disappointment by going elsewhere. But we can't help observing that many skiers are content because they don't know what they're missing.

If you go back year after year to the three familiar runs of Niederbad in Tirol you may never realise what it can mean to ski in Les Trois Alpes, with ten times as much skiing served by a lift system designed for convenience and comfort, and not haphazardly assembled over the years. If you stay repeatedly in the egg-boxes of Luna 2000, you may remain oblivious to the rustic charm to be enjoyed by day and riotous knee-slapping to be enjoyed by night in Söllbach, 5,000 feet lower and 300 miles to the north-east. These are differences which the brochures of tour operators, with one or two honourable exceptions, tend to submerge in a sea of superlatives. This *Guide* is designed to make them as clear as possible.

If you glance through the resort section of the *Guide*, occupying the middle two-thirds of the book, you'll see immediately one way in which we've set about this task: our maps. Virtually all the maps of ski runs and lifts you'll come across elsewhere take the form of an artist's impression of the area, as it might be seen from a helicopter, looking towards the horizon. That sort of map is easy to take in at a glance, but gives no proper indication of distance; runs in the foreground look longer than they are, relative to those in the background; such maps cannot be given a scale, and so cannot be used to compare one ski area with another. And in all but the simplest resorts, the artist is also required to cheat, and bring in to view lifts and runs which in real life would be hidden, thus further distorting the impression you get.

Reading our maps may take a bit more effort, but it pays. Like any conventional map, they take a vertically downward view of the ground, showing its ups and downs by means of contour lines and shading. And throughout the book they are drawn at a consistent scale – so that you can glance at a pair of maps and compare the skiing of one resort with that of the other. If you've been to any of the resorts we've mapped, you'll be able to use them as benchmarks to measure the others.

The maps are purely factual. In the text of our resort reports, on the other hand, we've also gone out of our way to produce clear judgements whenever we can. In doing so, and in simply describing places, we've taken pains to be consistent. Whenever skiers compare notes it soon becomes evident that one man's schuss is another man's precipice; our 'steep wall' or 'long walk' may not be the same as yours, but at least you know that we mean the same thing throughout the book – again, you can use familiar resorts to tune in to our wavelength.

In the interests of consistency we have based our assessments on the work of a small team of inspectors, trained on common ground so that one person's judgements could be related to another's. But we're well aware that some aspects of a resort are not easy to judge on brief working visits; so we have been grateful to have the guidance of the 400 correspondents who have sent in over 1,000 reports giving us the real holiday-maker's view. Future editions of the *Guide* will need similar help; if you're willing to give it, please use our Report Checklist.

A book calling itself *The Good Skiing Guide* ought to be selective, and it is; it might be expected to include 'good' resorts and to exclude 'bad' ones, but it doesn't. There's no such thing as a 'bad' resort. Every ski resort can properly claim to be good for someone; so, as our subtitle suggests, we have included the cream of Europe's resorts. To be more precise, we've included the resorts which we think have the biggest claims on your attention (for a wide range of reasons) if you're choosing a holiday with an open mind. If your favourite resort's not in, write and convince us that it should be.

On the other hand, do pause and reflect before you write to ask why we seem so unenthusiastic about the slopes where you had that wonderful afternoon's skiing in March 1981. Try though we may (and we do), it is inevitable that reports like ours, which aim to find faults where they exist, will seem negative compared with what you might read elsewhere – or compared with what you might write about your own favourite places. We know that skiing is tremendous fun, that the Alps in winter are entrancing and that any ski resort is a fabulous place on the right day. We could have prefaced each resort entry with a statement to that effect; but we hope that saying it once is enough.

The skiing phenomenon

Skiing is a leisure phenomenon without equal – a huge, many-sided industry based, apparently, on a simple passion for sliding down snow-covered slopes on long, elaborately constructed plastic planks. Apparently; in reality the sliding downhill, exhilarating though it can be, is only a part of the appeal of a skiing holiday – and often a smaller part than many skiers will readily admit.

Whatever it is that sells skiing holidays, their sales are huge and so is their impact. In Europe alone, millions make an annual two-week pilgrimage to the Alps. In their name, forests are felled, mountainsides reshaped and draped with machinery to provide easy and efficient skiing; where skiable terrain exists but villages do not, resorts are created from nothing; restaurants are built in impossible positions, so that the creature comforts we're used to on holidays by the sea can also be enjoyed two vertical miles above it; come winter, shepherds and students are transformed into uniformed armies of ski-school *maestri* and *moniteurs*, of fabulous seductive power; come snow, fleets of snow-cats work through the night on the ski-runs to smooth the path of the morning's skiers.

Of course, it was not always so. Although skis have been used for thousands of years as a practical means of travel over snow-bound country, it's only in the past hundred years that skiing has become an end in itself; only in the last fifty that it has become a holiday activity for the British and other lowlanders; and only in the last thirty years that skiing has developed into a multi-billion-pound industry.

As skiing has changed, so have ski resorts – which makes it essential for any would-be connoisseur of resorts to have an appreciation of the evolution of the sport. That evolution is charted here by *Mark Heller*, who in 60 years of skiing has witnessed a good many of the most important developments, and in 40 years of writing has been able to reflect on all of them.

The origins of skiing

The late 1920s and early 1930s have often been called the 'Golden Years' of skiing. Golden they were for the few bright, gifted young British who dominated the sport in their exclusive hideouts of Wengen, Mürren and Villars. They brought to an obscure and exotic activity the gay abandon of the playing fields and often a monumental insensitivity towards the bewildered mountain farmers over whose pastures they flung themselves with unbounded daring. They defied all who opposed them; as far as they were concerned, they were the only skiers in the world and the only skiing worthy of the name was downhill racing.

In fact, they were only the highly visible public blooming of an activity which, as far as anyone can determine, has its roots in the ending of the

Würm Ice Age some ten thousand years ago. Who invented skis, and when, will probably never be known. The earliest hard evidence is the prehistoric ski remains found in Scandinavia, reliably dated at around 2500 BC, by which time skis had evolved into all three possible forms – two long, two short, or one long and one short. In AD 700 the Chinese described them in detail and called them 'Wooden Horses' (MuMa), a fact that thoroughly confused the scholars of the Middle Ages and later.

Although the legends of Scandinavia are full of skiing deeds, skiing raised no wider interest until the great labour migrations from Scandinavia to North America and Australia in the early and middle 19th century. In California they staged some heroic speed skiing races and John A. Thomson (born Jon Thorsteinson Rue) carried the mail over the Sierras from Placerville to Carson Valley – about 145 km – for many years, starting in 1856. A Norwegian introduced skiing to the gold mining community in the Snowy Mountains in Australia and in 1861 formed the first ski club in the world, the Kiandra Club. In 1868, Konrad Wild tried to imitate Norwegian friends by skiing in Mitlödi in Switzerland. But none of these isolated incidents did more than cause local surprise and amusement.

But at about this time, in Norway, an unknown, semi-literate cottager from Morgedal called Sondre Norheim instinctively redesigned the traditional ski. He gave it a waist, reduced the length and invented a binding that held the foot on to the ski. As a result, skis became fully manoeuvrable for the first time, with the help of techniques we would now call the Telemark turn and the Christie stop. Norheim dominated the local ski scene; in 1868 he competed in Oslo in the annual gentlemen's ski competition (now the Holmenkollen championships) and won everything.

The birth of Alpine skiing

The next haphazard step was the Great Exhibition in Paris in 1889. Here an unknown Finnish exhibitor showed and sold skis. How many pairs were sold is unknown, but among the buyers were a number of Germans from the Black Forest and two visitors from the Swiss mountain resort of Davos: a Dr Paulcke (a German physician working there) and a young apprentice called Branger who bought two pairs – one for himself and one for his brother and sister to share.

The instruction leaflet was primitive and incomprehensible – it was, of course, written in Finnish. Dr Paulcke employed a Norwegian valet who was expected to teach his master how to ski. But Paulcke's presumption that all Norwegians are born skiers proved incorrect, and the skis were thrown into the attic where they were eventually discovered by his son, subsequently to become one of the the the great Alpine ski pioneers.

The Brangers, however, realised that their skis would be a lot better for sliding downhill than the beer barrel staves they were accustomed to using, and set about teaching themselves secretly, at night, how to turn and stop. The Brangers became the ski pioneers of Davos and in 1894 achieved fame by taking Conan Doyle over the pass to Arosa.

The Black Forest skiers were even more influential. An eccentric

poet, failed artist and visionary, one Mathias Zdarsky, discovered skis
there (and later again on the Semmering hills outside Vienna) and by
the turn of the century had opened the first real ski school in the world
on his derelict farm property in Lilienfeld near Vienna. He invented the
modern stem turn, devised means of skiing steep Alpine ground and
laid the foundations for Alpine skiing as we know it today.

It's in the early years of this century that, with hindsight, we can now
see the outline of a burgeoning new industry. At first, skiing was still
very much a novelty, pursued by eccentrics. But before long it began to
take root in the first generation of ski resorts. They were all
well-established summer resorts – which meant they had plenty of
accommodation, and were easily reached by railway; and they all had
easy undulating terrain nearby on the high summer grazing meadows –
slopes the skiers could handle with their crude techniques. Several of
these resorts had built up a thriving winter tourist trade before the
advent of skiing; some of these adapted to the new sport much more
readily than others.

Davos was already patronised by several hundred tuberculosis
sufferers and a further thousand or so relatives and friends. There was
skating and lugeing, and there quickly grew up a very active skiing
fraternity. With the primitive guidance of the brothers Branger and
friends, British and Dutch visitors (and a few Germans and
Argentinians) explored much of the terrain around Davos that is skied
today, including the famous Parsenn run to Küblis (accidentally
discovered by two English skiers looking for the pass to Arosa – a little
error of 180 compass degrees). In the Bernese Oberland, skiing
became accepted in Wengen and Mürren, and Vivian Caulfeild's
teaching and writing enjoyed a wide following. Elsewhere in
Switzerland, the Ski Club of Lucerne boasted ski lessons under
Norwegian tutors.

In Austria, skiing was taking hold of visitors to Kitzbühel, and a ski
school was established under Colonel Bilgeri at St Christoph, above St
Anton. In Italy, Adolfo Kind set up a school at Sauze d'Oulx. Meanwhile,
Duhamel fought a losing battle to establish a school at Grenoble, on the
fringes of the French Alps.

By 1921 there was no skiable Alp – no pass, no summit which today
is equipped with lifts and is skied by thousands daily – which did not
carry ski tracks. But the higher tracks were predominantly those of
mountaineers of one sort or another. The visitors to the comfortable
resorts still found they did not need to go beyond the gentle slopes of
the upper grazing meadows to find sport which was more than
sufficiently strenuous and sometimes dangerous.

The Golden Years

During the twenties, skiing tightened its grip on the first-generation
resorts. The trio of resorts below the Jungfrau became British enclaves
which the Swiss claimed they needed a passport to enter. In Wengen,
the skiers persuaded the Jungfrau railway to run up from both Wengen
and Grindelwald as far as Kleine Scheidegg, the col between the two
villages, and thus created the concept of 'downhill only' skiing. The idea

of downhill racing was only a small step further, and a great rivalry developed between Wengen's Downhill Only Club and the Kandahar Club across the valley in Mürren. Meanwhile, over the hill in Grindelwald, the Eagle Club took a different direction, concentrating on skiing the remote passes and glaciers. In Austria, St Anton combined social smartness with improving technique: the Schneider brothers – pupils of Bilgeri – perfected the stem christie turn and crouch, and thus opened up the really steep slopes to continuous, controlled ski-turning.

The British upper crust travelled out to their chosen spots under the auspices of Thomas Cook, Sir Henry Lunn and the Ski Club of Great Britain. They went for three weeks or a month at least, and many for the whole season from December to March. Resorts published weekly guest lists which were eagerly scanned for news of friends, rivals and the grand folk. There was a distinct pecking order of hotels, and within those hotels of the styles of accommodation; bathrooms were a rarity, and even running water something to be advertised. There were fancy-dress evenings and gala evenings, and luggage was swollen by the extra clothes which these essential events demanded. There were excursions by horse-drawn sleigh, barbecues, ice-rink jollities and the daily fashion parade up and down the village main street for those – still in the majority – who were bent on a mixture of 'winter sports' rather than skiing.

The growing enthusiasm for the new sport was by no means confined to the British, or to the famous resorts which they dominated. At weekends in the 1920s the skiers of Switzerland, Austria and Germany began to cram the railway stations and bus depots on their way to invade sleepy mountain villages surrounded by 'good skiing ground' – the gentle pasture which skiers sought out. Almost overnight these villages, unknown to tourists and rarely visited by outsiders other than farmers or commercial travellers, found themselves catering for the strange needs of the even stranger skiers – and found, too, a welcome and unsuspected new source of income. These were the villages which were shortly to become the second generation of ski resorts.

For the skiers whose ambitions went beyond the railways and funiculars of the established resorts (or whose purses would not stretch that far), the day was long and tiring. They left early in the morning; carrying their lunch (packed by the hotel according to an invariable formula) in uncomfortable rucksacks alongside the necessary skiing paraphernalia – sealskins, ski wax, spare gloves, sweaters, bits of string and wire for emergency repairs. After a climb of three, four or even five hours, the food would be consumed on some freezing col or in the shelter of a rock or tree, before the downhill run was started – not without some trepidation.

A run which is today completed by a first-year skier in a matter of minutes could be long, tiring and testing when tackled with the primitive equipment and techniques of the day. It could be wildly exciting and exhilarating – swoop after swoop of unblemished snow, schuss after schuss; or bitterly frustrating, on crusty snow or on the last run of the day, down steep narrow passages until the final, painful, icy woodland path brought into sight the still-distant village, half-hidden in the misty valley, the lights just beginning to show.

The romantic sight of the village – and the prospect it offered of thawing out frozen toes in welcoming hostelries – erased any doubts about the wisdom of having made the climb in the first place. The exertions of the day gave a special tang to 'five o'clock tea' – hot, fuggy rooms crammed with damp skiers, flush-faced and clumpen-booted, shouting, laughing, singing, dancing to a rustic three-piece band, supping hot chocolate or *Glühwein* and devouring cream cakes, united in adventures shared.

Skiing for everyone

With the close of the 1920s, Davos enters the story again. In 1931, the first funicular designed specially for skiers was built there; it went from the town to the Parsenn Weissfluhjoch, thus opening up the huge snowfields of the Parsenn to anyone who cared to take the ride. But the real revolution was still to come. The Parsenn railway, like those of Wengen, Grindelwald, Mürren and Villars, was fine for the experienced skier; but the novice still faced weeks, possibly years of drudgery, plodding repeatedly up the nursery slopes in order to acquire the skills necessary to tackle the longer Alpine runs.

Erich Konstam, an engineer from Zurich, calculated that in every hour on the slopes the average pupil spent only six minutes sliding downhill, and set about devising something to improve matters. What he came up with was the T-bar drag-lift; the first one in the world was opened for business on the Bolgen nursery slopes in Davos on the last day of 1934. The T-bar took half a minute to haul skiers up slopes that had previously taken twenty minutes to climb. Other resorts were not slow to see the potential of ski-lifts, and before long they were being installed not only on the nursery slopes but also on the treeless higher slopes; the peaks and passes that had once been the reward of half a day's climbing could now be skied five times in a morning. What's more, uphill transport now became affordable for villages which would not have dreamt of building a mountain railway.

The stage was thus set for an explosive increase in the number of people skiing, in particular of people learning to ski. Major Ingham and Erna Low started running skiing parties to Austria from Britain, signalling the beginning of the end of the socially exclusive nature of British skiing. It was a very small beginning, to be sure – skiing still required an affluence which was narrowly distributed in those days. But the hills heard the unfamiliar accents of the Midlands and the North; and the Ski Club of Great Britain shuddered.

The expansion of skiing was interrupted, to say the least, by the annexation of Austria and the World War which followed not long afterwards. But the War in its way gave the industry new impetus. In Switzerland, virtually isolated by the hostilities, skiing became much more popular as a result of a campaign to conserve fuel by encouraging outdoor sports; the slogan was *Ein ganzes Volk fahrt Ski* – 'A whole nation skis'. The impact on Austria was quite different but more profound. Under the Marshall plan, designed to finance the reconstruction of Europe's devastated industries, Austria chose to refurbish and develop its tourist villages. Before the War, places such as Söll, Sölden and Saalbach had responded slowly to the demands of skiers, despite their evidently plentiful supply of 'good skiing country'. The post-War plan was to install ski-lifts and build hotels, and to set about capturing the European ski market. The butcher, the baker and the farmer's boy could ski, and were prepared to teach others how to. And when they weren't skiing they would turn their hand to devising après-ski amusements to match anything seen in the grander resorts before the War.

In Britain Thomas Cook, Lunn, Ingham, Erna Low, Clarkson and others stood ready to package these wares and sell them to an entirely new generation and (more importantly) new class of skier – the ordinary inhabitants of Britain, liberated from the confines of a summer week in Blackpool or Margate, and no longer afraid of foreign places. Not surprisingly, the established skiing fraternity didn't go along with any of this, but returned to its traditional haunts and travelled to them by traditional means. The idea grew that the ski-fields of Austria – which certainly were in the main lower and less extensive than those of Switzerland – were also easier, and less worthy of the real skier's attention. This mattered not at all to the new generation, who wholeheartedly took to the uninhibited hospitality of the Austrian villages and have never looked back.

Against this background, France stepped in with the next and probably final revolution in skiing habits and skiing ambience. There had been very little skiing development before World War II – Megève was the principal exception – and the French Alps were thus a clean canvas awaiting bold strokes. Under the patronage of President de Gaulle and the uncompromising dictatorship of Engineer Michaud, an old dream became reality. On skifields of an immensity hard to envisage, M Michaud constructed Courchevel and the incomparable 'Three Valleys' ski-drome. It was closely followed by La Plagne, Val d'Isère, Les Deux-Alpes, L'Alpe d'Huez, Les Arcs and a dozen more 'green-field' ski sites. This was the birth of the third generation of ski centres, where the 'village' was no more than a service station for skiers. There were few hotels but many apartments (a neat financial twist to make the owners finance their own ski resort) and the lifts left from the apartment door. Après-ski, a term originally coined by the French fashion press to sell a new kind of leisure wear, died – the skiers retired to their self-catering apartments and only resort staff crowded the ridiculously expensive discos and bars. Covered arcades replaced village streets, boutiques took the place of the village shop and the ambience was uniform and grey. But the skiing, around which everything was planned, was magnificent. The runs were planned where no skiers had been before, their surface engineered and graded, difficulties categorised and planned for every level of performance, nursery areas carefully segregated from the hurly burly of piste life. These new resorts presented the old ski villages with a dangerous challenge which, on pure skiing terms, they were quite unable to meet then and which all but a few are still unable to meet now.

Developments elsewhere

The story of Alpine skiing is seen unfolding most clearly in Switzerland, Austria and France, but it is of course not confined to those countries. What of the Italians, who absorb a good proportion of Britain's skiers each year? Before World War II they had, from time to time, made some heroic appearances on the scene, but to no great effect. In 1934 the Agnelli family, the Fiat founders, had built the world's first 'green-field' resort, a futuristic little village near Turin called Sestriere. There were two daring cable-cars and, on paper, the skiing was magnificent. For reasons defying logic, it failed totally to capture the ski world's imagination. Cervinia, then still called Breuil, was developed in order to fulfil Mussolini's dream of building the highest, longest cable-car in the world. Three links from the newly-built village to the 11,000-foot col, called variously the Theodul Pass or Plateau Rosa or Testa Grigia, were completed with surprising speed by 1939 and linked Cervinia with Zermatt. Zermatt was not amused and, war intervening, the cable-car was not publicly opened until 1946.

Cervinia was created for the Italians, in particular for the weekend entertainment of the inhabitants of Turin and Milan – and so have been most Italian ski resorts. In the years after World War II, all along the Italian face of the Alps, resorts sprang up and flourished at weekends while on weekdays they were deserted except for the bored Italian grass (snow?) widows and their offspring, banished to these massive apartment blocks and residential grand hotels until their husbands returned for their Friday to Monday weekends. But some resorts – notably Sauze d'Oulx – played unashamedly to the British tour operator market. At the other end of the Alps, the resorts of the Dolomites were and are conveniently placed for invasion by car-borne Germans – and linguistically suited to receiving them, having been part of Austria until 1919. In a bold move to underline their appeal, a mass of Dolomite resorts combined to form what was in 1970 and remains today the largest single lift-pass area in the world, the Super-Dolomiti. This was a considerable achievement: Italian resorts have traditionally suffered from having several distinct lift companies, each requiring the skier to hold a separate pass.

Spanish skiing resorts, on the other hand, were a pure exercise in speculative development. Apart from La Molina there was no serious ski development (not least because of the uncertain snow cover and very moody weather) until the massive financial investment in the Spanish coastal areas began to show healthy profits. Parallel investment was then available for the grudging development of such subsequently popular resorts as Formigal. Today there are about thirty ski centres, ranging from the tiny two-lift one-hotel Picos Europa ski 'region' to the super-smart Baqueira on the French frontier.

Both Italy and Spain, though suffering from poor ski planning and even poorer trail maintenance and haphazard ski instruction, have profited greatly from a weak currency and comparatively cheap ski holiday prices. Andorra, a tiny independent state on the Spanish side of the Pyrenees has also made low prices a sure part of its appeal by managing to levy no taxes – and Soldeu in particular has benefitted by encouraging British instructors to operate there.

Surprisingly, perhaps, the vast mountain territories of North America contributed little to the early Alpine ski development except for one technical innovation that has swept all ski countries – the chair-lift. It was invented in 1936 at Sun Valley in Idaho. Here the Union Pacific company created a ski resort, based by Hollywood architects on second-hand accounts of Austrian villages. It became the model for all succeeding North American ski centres when, after World War II, serious attempts were made to propagate the European ski success story. The problems were very different from those of the Alps. Not only were distances immeasurably greater, but also there were no convenient farming villages upon which the ski resort could be grafted. The emerging pattern has remained unchanged. A 'mountain' was leased from State or Federal Forestry Agencies, permits were obtained to clear trees to make ski trails and planning permission obtained to construct a base service area which might or might not include residential facilities. The mountain and the 'village' real estate are mostly separate financial entities. On account of the very much higher tree-line of the West Coast's Rocky Mountain areas (where the bulk of the development has taken place), the runs are down very wide clearings and, with the very special consistency of West Coast snow, the skiing surface is a revelation to the European skier. And so, for that matter are the discipline, lift queuing (if any), piste preparation, marking and maintenance and the friendly, polite ambience. Whether by accident or design, American ski centres seem to have taken note of all the errors and unpleasantnesses to be found in Europe and eradicated them. The result may well be, to our eyes, almost synthetic, but there is no denying that the experience, even allowing for the relatively short runs and high altitude, is a revelation and dangerously addictive. Regrettably, there is little or nothing that can be imported to the Alps without simultaneously requiring quite unattainable alterations in law, custom and circumstances.

There has, however, been one North American development which, inevitably, will find its way into the Alps. A few years ago, a skier sued a ski resort for massive damages for injury sustained while skiing one of its trails. He claimed that the trail was ill-prepared and not in accordance with the publicly advertised snow conditions. He won. Now all American ski resorts have had to carry massive third-party insurance against future similar claims while, at the same time, spending further millions on extra special 'snow farming' (rolling, grooming, mogul bashing and covering with man-made snow).

The strangest recent development in both the Alpine countries and in North America is the re-emergence of cross-country skiing as a major recreation, paralleling the spread of fitness cults. It is the latest headache to irk the resorts. Quite apart from the cost of planning, preparing, maintaining and marking the special trails (for which payment can not easily be extracted from the skier), they are now faced with such strange problems as the control of dogs fouling the tracks, the rescue of overweight incompetent participants who collapse far from base, and the organisation of a complete teaching service for a recreation which, in theory, is supposed to be a simple, back-to-nature occupation.

Visitors to Norway are very soon put to rights about the how and why and where of this earliest, simplest, most athletic and most enjoyable form of skiing. Despite the growth of 'slalom skiing' in Scandinavia, only two Norwegian resorts offer much in the way of downhill runs – Geilo and Voss. The other hundred or more tiny, well-appointed mountain hotels are still faithful to the old traditions; the guests depart after an ample serve-yourself breakfast to ski the hundreds of miles of marked routes that take them through wondrous forests or out on to the highlands where horizon and sky meet seemingly at the end of the world. The evenings are restful and quiet and 'old-fashioned', with talk of trails travelled, animals seen and tomorrow's expedition. Once you've experienced the freedom of the true, ancient ski sport, the boredom of machine-prepared tracks up and down a valley is unacceptable.

Two other ski areas deserve a little more than a passing reference. Scotland, the only practical venue for skiing in the British Isles, has in its own and not always quiet way paralleled the British interest in skiing in the Alps. The detailed history is convoluted, fraught with local and national politics and prejudices and a continuing, unwinnable fight against weather and poor snow cover. Three principal areas have survived (and new ones are being planned) since the earliest skiing efforts in Scotland in 1892. Glencoe was the private dream and development of Philip Rankin who, despite every obstacle deliberately put in his way, produced what many consider the best skiing venue in Scotland – even if access is not easy and the lift system discontinuous. Aviemore in the Cairngorms is a serious, all-season holiday centre which is today the nearest in scope and facilities to a serious, although minor, Alpine ski resort (a comparison they deeply resent!). Glenshee, largely the work of enthusiasts from Dundee, is a friendly club-orientated ski area of considerable potential but suffering from inadequate accommodation. But just as important as the problems of weather and distance from metropolitan England is the fundamental and inescapable fact that Aviemore and Glenshee and Lecht and Glencoe are not the Alps; and, silly as it may be, skiers prefer their thirst to be quenched by *Glühwein* in a *Stube* rather than tea in a cafeteria.

Skiing in Eastern Europe also suffers from a comparable psychological disadvantage. In Poland, Czechoslovakia, Romania, Bulgaria and Yugoslavia they too have known skiing for as long as have the Alps and, by 1939, there was every sign that it was to become a major tourist attraction. But, unfair as it may seem, it would appear that Alpine skiing is not considered a 'serious' occupation in Eastern bloc countries and the activity still carries with it overtones of an anti-social, suspect activity.

On the other hand, for anyone willing to accept slightly haphazard ski organisation and a lengthy journey, the enthusiasm, friendliness and cheapness to be found in Eastern Europe may be worth the possible disadvantages of slightly limited ski terrain, often primitive uplift and (in Zakopane, for example) inordinate waiting time for the quite inadequate capacity of the cable-car. It remains to be seen how far the very successful Olympic games in Sarajevo in 1984 will produce a renewed interest in skiing in any of the more than 40 ski centres that are available.

Looking forward

A mere 80 years since modern skiing first tentatively made its appearance in Switzerland, there are now more than 3,000 ski resorts catering for a world-wide market of more than 30 million skiers. They may not all be skiing at the same time, but the ski area open to them is finite and the crowding is becoming such that the future must inevitably look somewhat bleak. There is little more that can be invented or developed that will extend the available ski-fields or reduce the queues and the collisions on pistes which now accommodate ten times the number of skiers they were designed for, skiing twice as fast.

In many ways the skiing circle has almost closed. Once again the downhill skiers are discovering the pleasures of the slow climb, the deserved rest on a sun-dazzled summit and the savoured, well-earned run home. Soon the new converts to cross-country skiing will be demanding the untamed trails of Norway. If there is a fourth generation of resorts to come, perhaps it will be the composite ideal – the Austrian hamlet with ski-fields like those in Aspen or Vail, a lift system of French thoroughness, and the après-ski life of the Oberland of the late 1920s. An impossible dream? Probably. But then so was Alpine skiing to Mathias Zdarsky, and look where that dream led to.

A Skiing Primer

Going on a skiing holiday isn't like taking a conventional summer holiday or winter break. For a start, choosing the holiday itself is only half the battle, and accounts for only half the bills. You've still got to arrange special clothes and equipment, special insurance, skiing lessons and a pass or ticket for transport uphill so that you can concentrate your efforts on sliding back down. Then there's the risk that you'll hate the whole business – that after a couple of days the pain of your boots, the ferocity of the weather, the unpleasantness of the lift queues, the indifference of your instructor, the impossibly slippery surface of the ski-runs or the frustration of your own incompetence will drive you off the slopes and into the bars, never to set foot on skis again.

That risk is very small. What's much more likely is that you'll be hooked – that you'll develop a perennial craving to be in the mountains. By December each year you may find yourself irresistibly drawn to spending Saturday mornings stretching your credit limit in ski shops and Sunday afternoons glued to BBC2's *Ski Sunday*, eager to gain some second-hand sensation of being back amid the snow.

The addictive power of skiing holidays is only partly explained by the exhilaration of skiing itself. What's just as important is that to go skiing is to be transported from the damp greyness of winter at home to a quite different world. It isn't only that the snow turns all but the most desperate of resorts into a magically sparkling place. It's also a world where you can dress as colourfully as you like without risking ridicule; where, for the price of a cable-car ride, skiers and non-skiers alike can get to places and see panoramas which were once the province of a few mountaineers; where the sun can toast your face even if the air is so cold that you have to be kitted out as for a moonwalk; where indulgence in food and drink is made respectable by your exertions on the slopes; where you can enjoy the rare treat of immersing yourself for weeks at a time in learning or polishing skills of no practical value; where the business of making new friends or rubbing along with old ones is lubricated by the common interest in skiing; and from which you return looking (and possibly feeling) wonderfully healthy. You have been warned.

If you haven't been skiing, there's a lot to learn about the kinds of resorts you can go to, about the kinds of holiday to be had in them, about the equipment you'll need – and of course about skiing itself. Even if you now go by the name 'intermediate' (that is, you're neither beginner nor expert), you're unlikely to have amassed a very wide range of skiing experience. This chapter covers the basics. Later chapters look in more detail at the choice of equipment, clothing, insurance – and, of course, the choice of a resort.

The season

One thing that virtually all skiing holidays have in common is that they happen in winter – though there is such a thing as summer skiing, which takes place on the permanent snowfields and glaciers found in the Alps at heights above sea level of over 3,000 metres or so.

In most ski resorts, the season starts with Christmas – the first big holiday period of the winter. That's not to say you can't go skiing before then, but if you do you must choose your resort with care to be confident of finding the lifts open and a good covering of snow on the runs. Christmas and (particularly) New Year in the Alps can be very jolly – but are not a good time for serious skiing, because of the crowds.

January is low season and not traditionally a Continental holiday time. Although there should be plenty of snow on the runs, the blizzards that often bring it can also mean skiing without being able to see where you're going, and getting miserably cold. Resorts popular with package holiday-makers from Britain are half-alive, populated only by people taking advantage of low package prices. Other resorts may be practically deserted until a bright weekend follows a week of snow, when the nearby city dwellers come out to play. The other side of the coin, however, is that queues are minimal, so you can get a lot of skiing in – and the weather can often turn out surprisingly well. It's simply that it's more of a lottery than later in the season.

February sees the beginning of the high season, with correspondingly high prices. It's the best compromise between winter and spring: snow should have accumulated on the runs, and the weather should be improving to the point where the chances of a bronzed face are pretty good. As spring approaches, sunshine becomes more reliable and snow less so – and even in March some of the more vulnerable resorts are regularly in danger of losing much of their skiing. Easter, whenever it falls, is the final peak in the skiing season, but if it's late in the spring the number of resorts able to capitalise on it may be very few.

Purely from the skiing point of view there is something to be said for each of the periods of the season *except* Christmas and Easter, and in any large group of skiers you will find advocates of every particular week in the skiing calendar. If we had to come off the fence with a recommendation for beginners it would be for early March, when the odds are against consistently bad weather; everyone skis better in sunshine, but novices can be transformed by it – and if you throw in the towel you can at least hope to revel in the intense spring sun.

The strength of the sun catches many first-time skiers off-guard; at high altitudes the sun's rays have to penetrate less air than they meet on the way to lower spots such as London or Liverpool, with the result that less of their original strength is lost in the process. And their effect is greatly intensified by the reflected glare from snow. As the season progresses, skiers need to take more careful precautions against getting burnt or blinded *and* against finding themselves on unskiable slopes as the sun begins to affect the snow.

Ski resorts

The range of places in which you can base yourself for a skiing holiday is vast. Neither the ancient city of Innsbruck in the Austrian Tirol nor the pair of buildings called Super Nendaz in the Swiss Valais can properly be called ski resorts, but you can have a skiing holiday in either. Even within the narrower range of places which *are* thought of as resorts, there is chalk and cheese. Many of the differences are explained in our chapter on 'The skiing phenomenon', which identifies three broad 'generations' of resort – the long-established railway-based resorts, where skiing began; the smaller village resorts, stemming from the period between the two World Wars when skiing began to expand, but developed most spectacularly since the second War; and the entirely new resorts, purpose-built since World War II. The three generations of resorts are classically (though not exclusively) to be found in Switzerland, Austria and France respectively.

Resorts vary in how much skiing terrain they offer, and how much charm. These are perhaps the two most basic variables, but there are many others. Some resorts are built on main roads, while others are car-free; some are small and tightly knit, while others are big and sprawling; in some you can expect snow on the streets (though there are no guarantees), while in others it would be a freak occurrence; some have few visitors from other countries, while others are over-run by incomers (and some resorts are dominated by the British); some resorts are the province of dedicated skiers, while in others ankle-length mink coats outnumber anoraks; some are deserted in the daytime because the skiers quit the village to spend the day up the mountain, while others are the hub of activity.

You might with some justification expect that one thing ski resorts would have in common is altitude; but you'd be wrong. There are a lot of resorts (in Austria, particularly) which are in or close to major valleys, at heights above sea level of no more than 600 metres (2,000ft). The skiing around these places is largely on clearings through the forests, and may go no higher than 1,800m or 2,000m (6,500ft). At the other extreme are resorts where even the 'village' – the point from which the skiing goes up – is higher than that. Val Thorens at 2,300m (7,000ft) is the highest resort in Europe; there are quite a few over 1,800m. These resorts have most or all of their skiing on open slopes above the tree-line (the altitude above which trees can't survive the cold).

Altitude is an important consideration when choosing a resort. All other things being equal, you get more snow falling at higher altitudes; and because the air generally gets cooler the higher you go, the snow stays longer, and stays in good skiing condition longer. But, of course, all other things are not equal. The 600m-high resorts of Austria, for example, get much better snow than communities at that same altitude in France, where virtually all resorts are above 1,000 metres.

Even if you count the queuing for lifts and the riding on them, the time you spend actually skiing is unlikely to amount to half your waking hours in the resort. If you mould your skiing to ski-school hours you may do no more than two hours in the morning and two in the afternoon. If on the other hand you ski from when the lifts start to when they stop you could probably double that.

But to do that you'd have to miss out lunch. One of the delights of skiing – indeed, one of its main attractions for some people – is lunch 'on the mountain'. It may come as a bit of a surprise to discover that (in many but not all ski areas) the mountains are dotted with hostelries of one sort and another where food and drink can be had in abundance. In many resorts some of the restaurants are accessible to non-skiers, too. You won't find *haute cuisine*, but you won't care. The simplest of meals becomes intensely satisfying when consumed on a sun-terrace at 2,500m after a morning's skiing; or in an atmospheric mountain hut while a blizzard rages outside. (If, like many skiers, you lubricate lunch with beer, wine or schnapps, you may find you ski better afterwards. This isn't necessarily self-deception: some skiers do indeed benefit from an artificial boost to their confidence. But moderation is vital: there is increasing concern in the ski world about accidents – to themselves and to others – caused by drunken skiers.)

The skiing day ends with sunset – most lifts will stop running at around 4pm to 4.30pm in the depths of winter, perhaps as late as 5.30pm in spring. And when skiing ends, après-ski begins – at least in theory. Resorts vary widely in what après-ski activity they provide – and it's not always very much. But after a long, hard day's skiing you may find the key question is not whether there is life in your resort, but whether there is life in your legs.

Perhaps because fatigue tends to set in so early, it is traditional for skiers to combine the evening's musical entertainment with tea, one of the most important meals of the day. The clomping ski-booted tea-dance is still alive, and kicking, whether it be to the accompaniment of yodelling tunes, Edelweiss and the March of the Mods on the concertina, zither and rhythm machine or to old pop songs pumped out just as mechanically by Brylcreem-and-leather live bands. In more sophisticated traditional resorts the tea-dance has evolved into tea with background music, or simply tea. Hotels in many long-established Swiss resorts may organise chess and bridge games.

Later evening entertainment ranges from further live music (in many places the same band continues after a break of an hour or two) with higher prices, to discothèques (much like discothèques anywhere) and bars, sometimes styled (especially in France) as pubs or piano bars. Some of the latter do have live piano players, but often the musical background is pre-recorded. Most resorts have a cinema (films in English are rare); a few have casinos.

In a resort popular with package holiday-makers, the chances are that organised evenings out on the town, or out on the mountain, will be offered by the tour operators' local representatives. Typical activities include meals in restaurants or fondue parties, meals or drinking sessions in a mountain restaurant followed by toboggan rides, disco evenings with specially negotiated prices, Tyrolean evenings (local dances and costumes), and bowling (the last two typical of Austria). In some resorts, especially where accommodation is in staffed chalets, the personnel may organise drinks parties and, if the clients give the nod (Heaven help them if they don't) real parties. The livelier club-chalet operators organise fancy dress and drag beauty contests and so on, much as they do in summer.

In these popular package resorts the beat goes on through the peaks and troughs of the season – and whatever else you may think about organised nightlife, it does have the advantage that you can count on a lively atmosphere in at least one establishment, even in low season. In contrast, the resorts with a reputation for chic, which do undoubtedly pull in the sophisticated night owls at certain times, can be entirely lifeless in low season.

Many resorts come to life at weekends, when discothèques are packed and charge much higher prices than during the week. This is particularly true of Italian resorts, even ones which are remote from big towns; those which aren't much used by tour operators wake up from apparent mid-week hibernation, and those which are, such as Sauze and Cervinia, take on a different atmosphere.

With a handful of exceptions, French ski resorts tend to be particularly short on commercial nightlife. There isn't much of the traditional cheek-to-cheek live music that provides an alternative to discothèques in many Austrian and Swiss hotels. Discothèque prices are higher than most skiers care to pay, and people staying in apartments and chalets are inclined to stay in at night. The fact that most people are not staying in hotels, coupled with the fact of being in France, means that there is normally a reasonable range of restaurants, whereas in all but the biggest Swiss and Austrian resorts eating out means eating in hotel dining rooms – or indulging in a typical Alpine evening with fondue in an old (or 'old') chalet/barn.

Skiing and après-skiing aren't the only things you can do in a ski resort. Many skiers (particularly those on holiday for a fortnight or more) like to take a day off now and again and do other things; or they like to mix skiing with other activities – perhaps swimming or skating in the early evening; and not everyone who goes to a ski resort is a skier. So resorts normally parade a long list of sporting and other activities you can do. Swimming and skating are pretty standard, though not universal. There may be curling, tobogganing, horse-riding, sleigh rides, hot-air balloons, cleared paths for mountain walks, and so on. From some resorts there are excursions to nearby (or not so nearby) places of cultural or commercial interest; naturally, the location of the resort determines above all else what is available.

Cross-country skiing (from which downhill skiing evolved) is enjoying a distinct revival, and most resorts now have prepared tracks on which you can practise the basic skills required. Cross-country skiers use much lighter equipment than downhill skiers, and travel over (that is, up as well as down) gentler hills, or across completely flat countryside. Serious cross-country skiers in your party will want to consider their choice of resort just as carefully as the downhillers; a few Alpine resorts offer a reasonable small-scale simulation of the real Scandinavian thing, while most do not approach it, offering little more than a flat loop a couple of kilometres long.

The skiing

For downhill skiing you need snow, and slopes. Not all mountain **slopes** are suitable for skiing. In the early days, skiers roamed over areas which in summer were pasture for cattle – generally undulating slopes, smooth and grassy, and needing only a thin covering of snow to be skiable. A great many resorts still depend on pasture-land for their ski-fields – and it can be something of a surprise to go to such a resort in summer to find cattle contentedly munching on your favourite run, to the cacophony of their huge necklace-bells. But that surprise is nothing compared with the shock of seeing in summer the rocky terrain which forms the ski-fields of the higher resorts – and the obvious extent of the bulldozing which often goes on in order to form skiable runs.

Virtually every resort has nursery slopes in or close to the village itself, where beginners spend their first day or two coming to terms with the treacherous new extensions to their anatomy. Ideally, a nursery slope should slope very gently indeed, finishing up in a part which is completely flat; many come close to this ideal, but some fall a good way short. In some resorts, the nursery slopes are not at the village level but higher up the mountain; this may be dictated by the lie of the land – some resorts sit on a completely flat valley bottom enclosed by ferociously steep valley sides – or it may reflect a general lack of snow at village level, particularly if that level is low. Some resorts have village nursery slopes *and* higher slopes, to which beginners can be taken if the snow lower down is too poor.

The main runs of the resort, similarly, may reach down to the resort or stop short, or may depend on snow conditions. If the valley sides close to the village are steep, runs which go down more-or-less directly will be fairly (or even very) difficult. In these circumstances beginners will usually be able to get a lift down the mountain as well as up it, or they will be able to wend their way down a gentle but narrow zig-zag track through the forest. These woodland paths are thought by many to have little appeal, being boring, often dangerously overcrowded, hazardous if icy, and (at least for a beginner) surprisingly hard work. There are exceptions, but generally this is not skiing for fun, it is skiing to get home. Skiing for fun happens mainly on two kinds of run – on broad swathes cut through less precipitous areas of forest or on wide open mountainsides above the tree-line.

In the beginning, skiers just found a suitable piece of mountainside and skied down it. People still do much the same, and are said to be skiing 'off-piste'; 'piste' is the French for trail, and has worked its way into skiing English. It's used slightly differently from the word 'run', which simply indicates an identifiable route which skiers take, whereas a piste is a run which is marked and patrolled; it is thus possible to speak of an 'off-piste run'.

Pistes have several advantages for inexpert skiers. They are staked out, so that you know you're following a recognised route to somewhere – particularly important in poor visibility; they're identified, so that you should be able to work out whether a particular piste goes where you want to go; they (usually) have defined edges, which should mean that you don't stray on to ground which is unsuitable for skiing; their surface is normally kept fairly smooth and unbroken by piste-bashing machines, making the skiing easier; they're patrolled by safety monitors who should mark any dangerous parts and if necessary close the piste altogether in poor conditions or if there is a danger of avalanche; and they're almost always graded, so that (in theory at least) you can predict how difficult each run is.

Most resorts grade their runs by means of a colour-code which is used (with varying degrees of clarity) on signposts and maps of the ski-area. Most use three colours: black for the most difficult, red for medium-difficult and blue for easier ones; some add a green category, at the 'easiest' end of the scale. The precise definition attached to the three or four gradings varies from resort to resort – red will be described as 'difficult' in one resort (and black 'very difficult') whereas it will be described as 'medium' in another. These discrepancies might be of some concern were they not completely overwhelmed by the much more pronounced variations in *real* meaning. The sad fact is that you cannot rely on a resort's piste gradings to indicate more than relative steepness within that resort – the black will be steeper than the red, and so on. When it comes to judging how easy or difficult one ski area is and comparing it with another, the piste gradings are of very little use. Every resort will contrive to have at least one 'black' run regardless of the unalterably horizontal tendency of its skiing terrain; and every resort will be sure to show on its piste map a sprinkling of both blues and reds, even if the runs are indistinguishable in practice. It's important to remember that any given piste will be considerably more or less difficult to ski at different times. Crowds of people, for example, can make a moderate slope distinctly tricky; but what matters above all else is the state of the snow. Good snow on a black run, for example, may make it easier to ski than a blue run in an icy condition.

The first requirement of the **snow** is that it should entirely cover the slopes. This may sound elementary, but it is a lucky pair of skis which spend a week on the slopes without encountering grass, earth or rocks poking through the snow at least once. Because a good covering of snow is the first essential, and because many skiers who live in the Alpine countries (and a few who live elsewhere) can tailor their skiing plans to suit the conditions, most resorts measure the depth of snow lying on the lower and upper slopes, and the results are widely published. To the innocent eye the figures look very impressive. Recorded depths of between one and two metres are common, at least on the upper slopes, and depths of below 50cm (or about 20 inches) are cause for concern. Surely that's enough to ski on? Well, yes it is – more than enough, on a perfectly smooth piste. But in practice, even when the tourist office is quoting a measured depth of snow in excess of a metre, there will be uneven areas where the scraping action of hundreds of skis has exposed some of the bumps in the ground.

The other key thing about snow is what condition it's in. The state of the snow can vary enormously, requiring different levels of skill and effort for safe and dignified progress. The easiest sort of fresh snow to ski is the tiny light flakes which fall in very cold conditions, called powder. Experienced skiers dream about powder – the expert will dream of skiing off-piste, skis hidden in deep powder, the less expert of skiing on-piste in a shallow layer of powder in which the most incompetent and half-hearted turns will work perfectly. Most of the time, you have to dream, and ski on something else.

The something else may be heavier fresh snow, which can be murderously tiring and even dangerous for the average skier; or older snow which will have been compacted either by skiers or by bashers. It is now standard practice for fresh snow on the pistes to be 'bashed' by caterpillar tractors towing rollers and/or blades. This is partly to prolong the life of the snow, but also because skiers these days are accustomed to skiing on snow which has already been flattened by the passage of other skiers, and many can't cope with virgin snow if it's more than a few inches deep. The bashing is designed to give the first skiers of the day as smooth a ride as the last.

In fact, the first skiers of the day often get a smoother ride than the last, because they get a uniformly flat surface; later in the day, slopes which are steep and long enough to cause skiers to do lots of turns on the way down become covered with *moguls* – mounds of snow created by skiers themselves in the simple process of following in one another's tracks. Where the skis run and turn, the snow is compacted and to some extent scraped away; in between, it accumulates in uncompacted piles. Some steep runs in a resort may be bashed rarely or not at all, partly because they're difficult to bash, and partly because some skiers prefer to ski unprepared snow – either deep fresh snow or the moguls which eventually form.

Bashing apart, the snow's condition will depend above all else on what the weather has done since it fell. If it's consistently fairly cold, snow can maintain a pleasant powdery surface for some time, even though it is firmly compacted. If it's very cold the snow will tend to go hard; if the air becomes warm during the day or if the sun is strong (not always the same thing) the snow will tend to soften – and if this is followed by low temperatures at night the result the next morning will be very hard indeed; at the extreme, and as a matter of routine when winter gives way to spring, the snow at lower altitudes does actually melt and become slush – and in that case what you get the next morning is not very hard snow but rock-hard, rutted ice. This is at best unpleasant and at worst highly dangerous. At higher altitudes, off-piste skiers hope to find 'corn' or 'spring' snow – a thin layer of sugar-like crystals on a hard base, which gives excellent pre-lunch skiing.

In a resort of any size, there will (at least late in the season) be sharp variations in the snow conditions on different runs, according to how high they are, how much sun they get (and when they get it), and how much they get skied. The essential message for beginners is not to labour on icy lower slopes in the belief that the higher ones will be more difficult. As a general rule, the snow at altitude will be better for skiing. Of course, you need to take account of how difficult the runs themselves are, as well – they may be just as gentle as those low down, or they may not be.

The lifts

What comes down must first go up. Although a few people like to get up their chosen mountain under their own steam, and some people can afford to be deposited on the summit by helicopter, most skiers use lifts built on the mountainside (or, very occasionally, built within it).

Most resorts have a variety of types of lift, though individual resorts and indeed whole countries, display bias towards particular forms. The study of lifts is an important discipline for serious skiers and resort managers alike. You may very well want your choice of resort to be influenced by the kinds of lift you'll be required to use; if you're keen on skiing you'll certainly want to be alert to the competing merits of the different lifts, so as to spend as little time as possible queuing and riding, and as much time as possible skiing.

Lift queues are a fact of skiing life – a resort with sufficient lift capacity to eliminate queues at peak times would be hopelessly uneconomic for most of the season. There are however resorts at one extreme where serious queues are exceptional, and at the other extreme resorts where they are the norm. Bad queues normally arise where a lift is a bottleneck in a haphazardly constructed system. Often, these come about where the main way out of a substantial resort is either a **funicular railway** or a **cable-car**. In concept, the two are very similar – two cars or small trains linked by a wire, so that the one descending helps to pull the other one up. The rate at which either sort of lift can get a crowd up the mountain depends on the capacity of each car and the length of the ride. The big new cable-car at Courchevel, for example, can shift over 1,500 people an hour; 500 would be more normal.

What distinguishes the cable-car is that the fixed cable along which the car runs takes it to spectacular heights above the ground. This makes all the difference to the sensations given to passengers, and some difference to the safety record: neither is very reassuring. On the other hand, neither should put you off; the safety record is rather like that of aircraft – too patchy to make any statistical sense. There is a widespread feeling that cable-cars in Italy are more suspect than those elsewhere – perhaps because there are quite a lot of elderly ones springing from Mussolini's era. It is true that the most serious crash happened in Italy (at Cavalese, in the Dolomites) in 1976, when 42 people died. But there have been serious accidents in France and Switzerland, too.

For certain sorts of job – lifting moderate numbers of skiers over precipitous ground – the cable-car is still the right tool; the recently built cable-car at Val Thorens is a good example. But for getting skiers out of their resort and up on to the main slopes the modern solution is a **gondola**, more graphically described by the Americans as a bubble lift. The basic characteristic of the gondola is that a fast-moving wire carries a series of small cabins (with seats) which are detached from the wire and brought to a snail's pace at each end of the ride, so that you can easily get in or out. Some older cabins seat only two people; many more seat four, and most modern ones seat six, and may shift over

2,000 people an hour. They go at a fair speed – so not only does the queue move quickly but also you are transported to the top quickly.

Railways, cable-cars and gondolas are generally big-time lifts, for major uphill leaps in major resorts. In such resorts they are almost always supplemented by smaller-scale lifts – chair-lifts and drag-lifts – and small resorts are often equipped entirely with such lifts. **Chair-lifts** transport you in mid-air, but without the need to take your skis off. Most are slow-moving, and offer little or no protection against the wind – which can be appreciably more biting a few metres above ground level. Most chairs take people two at a time, but there are single chairs, which on a cold day are pure misery; and there are 3- and 4-seaters (usually with special mechanisms – see below).

Drag-lifts propel you along the ground on your skis. The simplest form of drag-lift is the rope tow, which has a continuously moving rope to which handles are firmly attached. You grab a handle as it goes by, at considerable risk to your arms and shoulders. Fortunately, the tow is used only in a few resorts, and on very gentle, short slopes. The two more common forms of drag are physically less taxing because they don't so much pull you as push you along from behind – the **button** lift, taking one person at a time (sometimes called a Poma, after the main maker); and the **T-bar**, taking two.

Drags are standard equipment on nursery slopes – because they're cheap to build, not because they're easy for beginners to ride. On the contrary, drags can be something of a nightmare for beginners, who find that skiing uphill requires a set of skills quite different from those they're starting to develop for skiing down. In your first few days and weeks of skiing, falls on drag-lifts are only to be expected. On the nursery slopes you're unlikely to injure anything more than your pride; but some longer drags take you over hilly terrain, well away from any piste, where you can get into considerable difficulties if you fall. As we explain on the facing page, the T-bar is generally reckoned to be the greater of the two evils, and it is not surprising that many skiers, especially those brought up in France, where nearly all drag-lifts are buttons, reckon that the abundance of T-bars is a major drawback to skiing in Austria, where they are the norm. At least one Austrian resort now grades its drag-lifts as well as its pistes, in a laudable attempt to deter inexperienced skiers from taking unnecessary risks.

The distinctions between these types of lift are becoming more and more blurred. Les Deux Alpes is installing a gondola-style lift where each of the cabins is like a small cable-car – holding 20 people, with no seats. A number of resorts now have chair-lifts which employ a gondola-style mechanism to detach the chairs from the wire while you waddle on and off. This does away with problems of skiing away at the top; much more importantly, it also makes it possible for the chairs to move at a much higher speed, shortening the time you spend dangling in freezing mid-air. Four-seat chair-lifts of this kind have the highest theoretical carrying capacity of any existing lifts – as many as 2,800 people an hour. Sadly, no resort has yet found a way of forcing skiers to fill the available seats – so this capacity is not achieved in practice.

There are various ways of paying for lifts. In any one resort you're

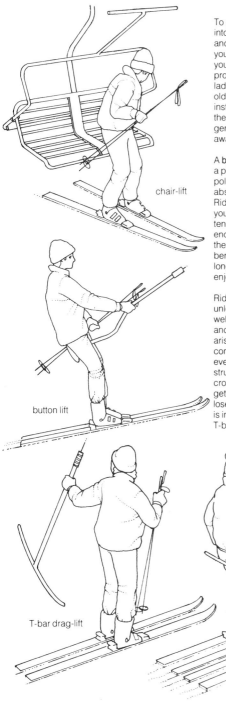

chair-lift

button lift

T-bar drag-lift

To get on to a **chair-lift**, you shuffle into position ahead of a moving chair and sit down as it thumps the back of your calf. As the chair proceeds to lift you into the air you pull down a protective bar and heave your ski-laden feet on to a foot rest. (Some old single-seat chairs have a chain instead of a bar, and no foot rest.) At the top, you're delivered on to a gently sloping ramp and accelerate away from the chair on your skis.

A **button** lift propels you by means of a plate-sized disc on the end of a pole which is attached (via a shock-absorbing spring) to a moving wire. Riding a button is not difficult, once you learn to relax and overcome the tendency to sit down. You learn soon enough to steer round the hazards of the track – dips, bumps, rocks, bends, fallen skiers – and before long you may even find that you enjoy the ride.

Riding a **T-bar** is quite a lot trickier: unless the two of you are physically well-matched, the ride will be tiring and uncomfortable; when obstacles arise, there's immense scope for confusion about how to avoid them; even without obstacles, it's a bit of a struggle to prevent your skis crossing or your boot clips from getting locked together; if the duet loses its collective balance, recovery is impossible. Travelling alone on a T-bar is very uncomfortable.

able to use two or three of the possible means. Most skiers who have graduated from the nursery slopes will use a **lift pass** – a 'rover' ticket allowing unlimited rides for the duration of its validity, which may be anything from the whole season downwards. Some resorts don't issue passes for less than a day; many which issue half-day passes do so only for the afternoon. A welcome development in a few resorts is the pass on which you can get a refund depending on what time of day you hand it in (and what time you bought it). Normally, you cannot get a refund on a lift pass by handing it in, or if you lose it. The circumstances in which you *can* get a refund will be defined in small print on the pass, or the form you fill in to get one, or in the ticket office; usually, all the lifts in the ski area have to be closed – a state of affairs which the lift companies naturally strive to avoid. Buying a lift pass for more than a day, therefore, is in principle a bit of a gamble. But in practice, prices are such that a week or a fortnight's pass is normally a worthwhile buy in spite of the risk that you may not get full use out of it. If the weather forecast is a week of blizzards, that's different. A pass is also much more convenient than the alternatives.

But it would clearly be unreasonable to expect beginners to buy full-price passes. On your first day you may not use a lift at all, and in the first week as a whole you may use very few if you have a cautious instructor. Different resorts deal differently with this. A common arrangement is to sell **coupons** or **points-cards**; each lift has a 'value', and to use it you hand over so many coupons or get so many points punched off your card. This is a good arrangement not only for beginners but also for skiers who want to stray widely over the mountain but not to do a great deal of skiing on any one day. The other possible arrangements aren't nearly so good for that sort of skier. One is to have a cheap beginner's pass, which gets you on to certain lifts serving easy pistes, but not others; and the other is to have some lifts which are free. Paying **cash** for individual rides is normally possible for major lifts – particularly for long cable-cars, gondolas and railways which non-skiers might like to go up for the view, or to meet skiers for lunch. In some resorts you can pay cash for smaller lifts, too.

In many resorts there is a further choice of lift passes even when you've decided on the duration you want. Normally the choice will be between a pass for the local lifts only, or a more expensive one also covering the lifts of neighbouring resorts. These are usually resorts you can get to on skis: there are now a number of areas in the Alps where the skiing of different resorts has been linked together so that you can ski a huge variety of interconnected runs – sometimes crossing national boundaries. Where you face this kind of choice, inexperienced skiers need to take advice – and find out whether you can buy a basic pass and get an extension for the one day you decide to go over the other side of the hill. Anyone joining ski school should find out where their instructors are likely to take them.

In Italian resorts the choice may be between different passes within the one resort, because different sets of lifts are operated by different companies; if they're on speaking terms there will be a joint pass available, but that isn't always how it is.

Equipment

Skiers take any amount of equipment with them up the mountain to deal with this or that eventuality. But there are three items (or rather pairs of items) which are indispensable: ski boots – monstrous plastic affairs which make walking a comical misery; skis, fitted with bindings to secure them to the boots; and poles, which have all sorts of uses.

In the beginning, skiers used **boots** not unlike those used by mountain walkers. Modern ski boots are designed specifically for skiing; as a result they give much better control of the skis, but are useless for anything else, including walking. A boot consists of a rigid outer shell made of plastic, and a padded inner lining. The inner is designed to cushion the rigid support of the shell and spread the pressure comfortably over your ankle and foot. The boot must fit well enough to anchor your heel firmly in the back of the boot but allow free movement of your toes. Ski boots are no longer tightened with laces; although there are lots of fancy alternatives, most modern boots employ buckles or clips instead – so they're sometimes called clip boots. Comfortable yet effective boots are vitally important if you're to enjoy your skiing.

The first thing a **ski** has to do is slide on the snow, so it has a smooth plastic sole. This sole is easily damaged by skiing over things other than snow, and substantial gouges in it will make the ski slide much less easily; so it's important to keep the sole in good repair. To make it really slippery, the sole should also have a very thin layer of wax applied. You may think that slippery skis are the last thing you want, since your main problem is keeping your speed down rather than keeping it up. But a smooth, waxed ski makes turning less effort; and on many runs there are level sections where slippery soles make the difference between coasting along and having to walk.

But the ski spends very little time flat on its sole. The most frequently used techniques in skiing – traversing, turning and slide-slipping – all involve tilting the ski so that its edge bites into the snow, and so controls your speed and direction. The steeper the slope, the more the ski is being used on its edge; and the harder the snow, the more important it is that the metal strip which forms the edge should present a clean, sharp right-angle.

The condition of the ski's sole and edges is all the inexperienced skier needs to worry about. More expert skiers may be sensitive to other aspects of a ski's performance; the outline shape of the ski and the subtleties of its internal construction will determine how the ski bends and twists, and what snow conditions and styles of skiing it suits. General-purpose skis are a compromise which will cope adequately with all conditions.

The length of ski you should use is a matter of continuing debate, in which fashion holds as much sway as logic. For many years, the 'proper' length of ski for an individual to use, beginner or not, was defined by how high you could reach with your hands. A few years ago there was a big drive to put beginners on short ('compact') skis, which are easier to turn; many more advanced skiers joined them – the cry was that skiing is for fun, and short skis give more fun for less effort. More recently, the view has gained ground that compact skis are slow, and difficult to control in a straight downhill run – so intermediate skiers are now encouraged to buy 'mid-length' skis. Compact skis are still the best bet for first-year skiers and are still available in rental shops, but are not normally found on sale.

The most important function of **bindings** is not to bind the boots to the skis but to separate them automatically when your legs are in danger. A good pair of modern bindings, carefully adjusted, will give you excellent protection from leg injury. The few unfortunates who hobble home with a leg in plaster are nearly always the victims of obsolete or wrongly adjusted bindings.

The bindings will need adjusting to suit the length of your boot; this setting must be exactly right – too tight and the boot will be dangerously jammed, too far apart and the boot will wobble on the ski. There's another adjustment to cope with slight variations in the thickness of the boot's front and back flanges. Once the bindings have been adjusted to accommodate your boots, they must be set to release under appropriate forces. The mechanism and springs inside a binding are designed to 'sense' the forces on your leg while you're skiing and absorb any safe shocks that occur during a normal run – you shouldn't eject from the binding unless you really need to. If you fall, and a leg is subjected to twisting or pulling forces, the binding should let you out before there is any chance of injury.

It sounds simple enough, but it's not. Obviously, a frail skier could be injured by a fall which would not harm a stronger one; vigorous skiers will want to stay in their bindings in circumstances where timid skiers would welcome a release. The binding manufacturers have come up with elaborate charts which you can use to work out your 'ideal' setting taking into account the size of your boots, your skiing ability, your age, and either your weight or the thickness of your leg bones – a dimension which only a few shops are equipped to measure, but which is a much better guide than your weight.

When you come out of your bindings it's essential that your skis don't career off down the mountain on their own. They could do a lot of harm to anyone who got in the way, and the walk down the mountain wouldn't do you any good. The traditional precaution was to have safety straps linking your ankles to your heel bindings. But they're a real nuisance to put on and off, and mean that you stay in uncomfortably close touch with your skis when you have a fall. On modern bindings, the traditional straps have been replaced by brakes, which spring into action as soon as your boot is released. Usually, the ski comes to a halt further up the hill than you do. But straps are still the better bet for skiing in soft, deep snow, where a loose ski can nose-dive and prove extremely hard to find – or be lost altogether until spring.

It is possible to ski without them, but almost any skiing movement is more easily executed if you have **poles** to help you balance or to lean on. There's more about poles, and the other items of equipment, in 'Getting equipped' on page 391.

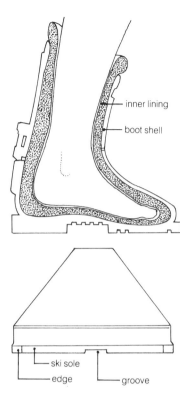

inner lining

boot shell

The **boot** helps you control and steer your skis by preventing sideways movement of your ankle joint. As you push your knee to the left or the right the ski tilts on to the same edge – a fundamental part of the techniques of turning and stopping. The boot also resists the forward and backward bending of your ankle. When you push your knee forwards or backwards, your shin or calf presses against the boot, and your weight is transmitted to the front or back part of the ski.

The **ski** has a core (often of wood or foam plastic) sandwiched between various layers of glass-fibre and other materials. The sole often has a groove along its length, meant to help straight running. To make the edges bite on really hard snow, they're made of steel, and are ground or filed to form a clean, sharp right-angle.

ski sole

edge   groove

Most **bindings** hold your boots between separate toe and heel units which you step into (they're sometimes called 'step-in' bindings). Boots have projections front and back specially shaped to fit. Either unit can release your boot, according to the kind of tumble you take. In a forward fall the heel unit should open. In a twisting fall (which means most falls) the toe unit should open – particularly important because strains and breakages will otherwise result.

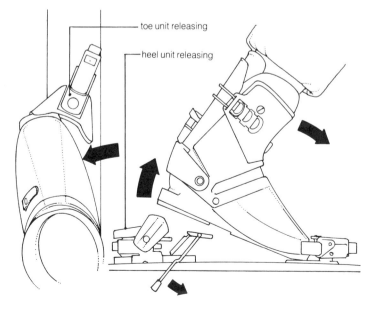

toe unit releasing

heel unit releasing

Clothes

Like most outdoor sporting activities, skiing is undoubtedly a more comfortable business when done in clothes designed to deal with the conditions, which can be savage but vary widely. You may be sitting motionless on a chair-lift for half an hour in temperatures ten or twenty degrees below freezing and in winds which make the effective temperature even lower (the wind-chill factor); you may be skiing energetically in strong sun and air temperatures ten degrees above freezing; you may get drenched in wet snow (either because it is falling or you are) or even (horror of horrors) rain. What sets skiing somewhat apart from otherwise comparable activities – sailing or mountaineering, say – is that the clothing industry it has spawned is in general much more concerned with fashion than with function. The result is that the unwary can easily spend a small fortune on ski clothes which look wonderful but which are not particularly effective.

Most people find specially made **trousers** well worth having. They provide much better insulation against the cold than normal trousers, and even if they're not really waterproof (which most are not), they won't get soaked by wet snow – and subsequently frozen solid – in the way that jeans do (for example). There are two main sorts of trousers – fairly loose-fitting, padded dungarees called salopettes, and tighter-fitting ski-pants (sometimes called racing pants) which may reach well above the waist and be supported by braces (just like salopettes) or may have an elasticated waistband.

Special skiing **jackets** are just as widely used, despite the fact that most of the ones sold at moderate prices do a mediocre job. They'll generally keep you warm in fine weather, and allow you to brush off snow as long as it's dryish. But few jackets offer more than token resistance to rain or wet snow, or deal particularly well with the sweat you produce when working hard, or have effective arrangements for sealing your wrists against snow. In other words, they offer little practical advantage over an ordinary anorak, worn over sweaters. Some people find a padded **waistcoat**, or 'gilet', a useful garment – if you are skiing in very cold weather a waistcoat can go on top of a jacket, while in hot weather you can simply wear it over a sweater; but since you're still going to need a jacket it has to be seen as an extra expense, and not one to which we would give a high priority. If you want to buy only one outer garment, but like the idea of a waistcoat, you can buy a jacket with sleeves which are attached by zip and are easily removed to produce a waistcoat.

Instead of a separate jacket and trousers, you can get a **one-piece suit**. There's nothing like it for keeping out the snow around your middle, but there are drawbacks: you can cope with differing weather conditions only by adding layers to it – you can't remove a layer, unless the suit actually consists of a jacket and trousers which zip together (and most do not). Even if the suit is of the zip-together variety, the top bit is unlikely to make much sense as a jacket on its own – so it won't be much use when you're not skiing.

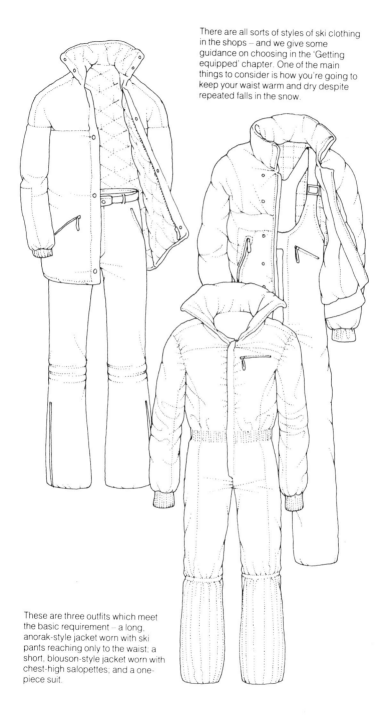

There are all sorts of styles of ski clothing in the shops – and we give some guidance on choosing in the 'Getting equipped' chapter. One of the main things to consider is how you're going to keep your waist warm and dry despite repeated falls in the snow.

These are three outfits which meet the basic requirement – a long, anorak-style jacket worn with ski pants reaching only to the waist; a short, blouson-style jacket worn with chest-high salopettes; and a one-piece suit.

Ski clothes have traditionally made very full use of the spectrum of colours. These days they are by no means uniformly bright in colour – pastels and military drabs are just as popular. Followers of fashion must look elsewhere for guidance, but there are some practical considerations. The first is safety: the brighter the clothes you wear, the more easily you'll be seen by others. This can be important in all sorts of circumstances, but is particularly relevant if you have an accident or get caught in an avalanche. White is to be avoided absolutely – it makes you invisible against the snow. Secondly, bear in mind that if you have to wear the same clothes for two weeks (and many people do) they can get very dirty if they're a pale colour: lifts can be oily – and brightly dyed new gloves tend to stain everything they touch when they get wet.

In cold weather, all but the warmest jackets need supplementing by one or more **sweaters**. Ski shops sell smart, bright ones at very high prices, but (except for the very fashion conscious) any old sweater will do. A stock of several thinnish sweaters is more versatile than one or two very thick ones. And you'll need sweaters for the evening, too (again how dressy and fashionable depends on the resort – and the weather).

Opinions differ in the matter of **shirts**. The 'proper' equipment – except in hot weather late in the season – is a cotton polo-neck shirt, which will keep the chill wind from your neck. But many people ski in ordinary shirts; one advantage of this arrangement is that your tan is less likely to terminate abruptly just below the chin (though you can now get polos with a zip-up neck).

You can of course make adjustment to the thermal insulation of your outfit by installing **underclothes** under your clothes. There's no particular reason why you should, if your 'over' clothes are chosen carefully. But it certainly is true that a pair of trousers which are adequate in March may be not up to the challenge of January, when warm tights/long johns would be a sensible addition.

Racing aces, we are told, do without **socks**, which would impair the precise control they have to exert over their skis by introducing a spongey layer between the foot and the boot. Even for ordinary skiers the trend is towards having socks as thin as possible; very thick socks are neither necessary nor desirable in a modern boot. You can buy special ski socks, usually with a smooth outside and a fluffy inside, but any socks will do, as long as they reach above the top of the boot – otherwise you may find the top digging into your shins. You can get special thermal socks, meant to be warmer than ordinary ones. Using identical socks throughout the holiday will make it easier to get your boot adjustments consistently right.

On the other hand, special ski **gloves** or **mittens** are a luxury you can't do without. They are expensive, and easily lost, and they wear out; but they don't fall apart half as quickly as ordinary gloves, and they do a reasonable job in difficult circumstances of keeping your fingers warm – an important matter. Insulating inner gloves can be worn if you find one layer isn't enough. Mittens are warmer than gloves; but you're more likely to have to take them off to do up your jacket or get out your lift pass, which rather defeats the object. Leather lasts longer than plastic and is generally to be recommended; but it is not waterproof unless treated with some water-repelling agent (you can buy sprays).

You will need a **hat**. It's advisable to carry one with you even in good weather because the weather can change very quickly – and sitting on a long chair-lift, particularly late in the afternoon or in the shade, can be cold even on a sunny day. Ears can get very cold, so make sure your hat pulls down over them and keeps out the wind; alternatively, you can get special headbands which fit snugly over the ears. A **scarf** is useful to give protection to your neck or chin – which you're likely to need on a very cold day unless you have a jacket with a high collar which zips right to your nose (but don't wear a long, dangling scarf which could get caught on a ski-lift). A balaclava isn't a bad idea.

In most resorts you will need very little in the way of special **après-ski** clothes. Few hotels or night-clubs impose jacket-and-tie rules, and you're unlikely to feel out of place when dressed casually. A ski jacket will normally do for trips out in the evening – but if you take only one bear in mind that the exertions of the day may leave it damp and/or smelly. Most people wear special après-ski boots – often huge, highly insulated ones known (after one of the brand leaders) as Moonboots, or furry ones which give the impression that the occupant is being assaulted by two small dogs. In cold, dry conditions such boots are fine – they usually have soles which grip as well as can be expected on icy roads, and they'll keep your feet warm (though possibly sweaty, too). But not all such boots deal happily with water and slushy snow, for which there is nothing to beat wellingtons (provided they're big enough for thick socks).

Bits and pieces

Whenever you go skiing it's almost certain that you'll need some form of protection for your eyes. Cold air alone may make your eyes water when you're on the move, and glare from snow can be uncomfortably strong even when the sun's not out. When the weather's bad the wind and snow can be blinding unless you are able to retreat behind **goggles**, usually with yellow or pink lenses. There's a fair chance that you'll have trouble with goggles misting up on the inside – although there will be some ventilation of the space inside the goggles, it is necessarily limited. Misting is a lot less of a problem with goggles equipped with double-glazing – two lenses instead of one, with a small air gap between. Spectacle wearers have a particularly miserable time with goggles – keeping four surfaces free of snow and mist is a constant struggle. Contact lenses are worth buying for skiing even if you've no inclination to use them for anything else – provided you get a type which you can easily adapt to in a few days before each holiday.

You can get goggles with much darker lenses meant for skiing in sunshine, and many makes of goggles come with interchangeable lenses so that you can use the same basic pair in different conditions. But in good weather most people prefer to use **sunglasses** to cut out glare from the snow – particularly late in the season when it's sunny most of the time, and the glare off the snow is very strong.

Run-of-the-mill sunglasses that you use at home can be used, but they may not be strong enough for snow glare. Make sure sunglasses fit tightly or are tied on with elastic or string – they're easily lost in a fall in fresh snow. If possible, always use plastic rather than glass lenses – in a fall you could not only cut your face badly but also severely damage the eye.

Any bits of skin which this assembly of paraphernalia leaves exposed will need protection from both the cold, dry air and the sun's rays. You'll need a sun-screen with a high protection factor, and lip salve to prevent your lips cracking.

If you keep to a minimum the bits and pieces you take with you on the mountain, you may be able to cram it all into your jacket pockets. But the stuff mounts up, particularly if you (very sensibly) travel prepared for any change in the weather; and jackets are all too rarely equipped with decent-sized pockets. The alternative is to use a small pack. **Bumbags** go round the waist, like a belt; they don't hold much and if you fall over a lot, or travel on chair-lifts, the contents are liable to get squashed, unless you wear the bag in front of you. **Back-packs** alleviate some of these problems; you can get special small ones for skiing. There are now some small bumbags on the market which convert into a back-pack when needed.

Rent or buy?

The major items of equipment and clothing don't have to be bought – they can be hired from a shop at home or in the resort, or through a tour operator – who will probably have a deal with a local shop.

Expert and frequent skiers invariably conclude that they're better off from most points of view owning their own **skis** and **boots** – even if snow conditions sometimes lead them to hire another pair of skis for one reason or another. For the absolute beginner, on the other hand, it's equally clear that buying is folly – and that renting at home doesn't make much sense either. When you're just starting, it's impossible for you to judge in the shop whether a boot is the right size and shape for your foot, so you're quite likely to have to change the boots you first accept; if you take to skiing quickly you may want to progress to more 'advanced' skis and boots; if on the other hand you don't take to it at all you'll want to cut your losses by handing in what you hired.

It's for the people in between – 'intermediate' skiers, particularly those who don't do much skiing in a year – that the decision to rent or buy is less straightforward. The first consideration for most people will be the **cost**. Whether buying or renting is cheaper depends on a number of things. If you managed to keep a single set of cheapish kit for ten years, and spent only a small amount each year on maintenance, the cost would be lower than that of renting in all but the very cheapest resorts – assuming you do a fortnight's skiing each year. But can you expect to keep it that long? You may come to believe that you've 'outgrown' your skis, or that your boots no longer give the support they once did (or the support the latest designs promise). You may be encouraged to trade up by the belief that your old gear has a second-hand value; no doubt it does, but it won't be much. If in the ten years you get through three pairs of boots and two pairs of skis instead of one, your average annual cost can climb to the point where it exceeds the cost of renting in all but the poshest resorts.

Many skiers buy their own equipment not because of cost but because of **convenience**. The shorter your skiing trips, the more this matters: with your own equipment there's no time wasted in ski shops when you could be skiing; no going back in search of boots you can live with. But carrying skis and boots does make travel more of a hassle.

The **quality** of what you get enters into the equation, too. In most major resorts you can expect to find a choice of shops offering well maintained, modern equipment. But you can't bank on that everywhere; in high season, the better equipment may run out and an unscrupulous hire shop may be tempted to retrieve old skis from the scrap-heap rather than start adding new ones to their hire stock. If there's a choice of shop, you can go elsewhere; but if you've pre-paid through your tour operator, or if you're in a tiny Italian village, there may be no choice. Buying your own equipment or hiring in the UK gets around these worries.

Good well-fitting boots are such a priority for an enjoyable ski holiday that many skiers buy a pair before they even think about buying skis. Buyers get a lot more attention in ski shops than renters and once you've found a comfortable pair of boots you can look forward to agony-free skiing for years to come. There are two ways to go about finding such boots: buy a pair that you've tried out by renting, or buy from a UK shop which offers a 'comfort guarantee'. If you rent boots in the resort, do not hesitate to change them if you experience cramp or pressure points in the first day or two; don't put up with pain in the hope that things will improve. If the shop is unsympathetic, or has run out of alternatives, call the deal off and go to another shop.

Pay particular attention to the condition of rented skis and bindings. The soles should be smooth and the edges should be reasonably sharp. It's very important to be sure that your binding adjustment has been carried out properly. See 'Getting equipped'.

You can also hire ski **jackets** and **trousers**. Once you're hooked on skiing holidays, the idea of renting clothes doesn't have much appeal. Your main problem is likely to be that of resisting the temptation to splash out on completely unnecessary additions to your skiing wardrobe every winter. But the first-timer who buys lots of special clothes risks wasting money. You may decide that once is enough, and your special clothes – designed to keep you warm in sub-zero temperatures – won't be much use in the warm, wet climate of home.

An alternative strategy for beginners is to concentrate on choosing a jacket for which you can envisage some use other than skiing, and a pair of trousers which are cheap. But the best thing to do is beg or borrow as much as you can from any skiing friends. You may be surprised at how easy this is.

Learning

Every skier has to learn to ski; but you can approach learning in a variety of ways. For some holiday skiers, skiing and learning are one and the same – they check in to ski school year after year, and rarely go skiing except with an instructor. Other people regard learning as a process to be got out of the way so that they can then get on with actually skiing; others again regard it as yet another extra expense, to be cut out at the first opportunity. Neither extreme is to be recommended. Eternal pupils probably do less skiing than independent skiers, and may never learn to find their own way around the mountains. Skiers who go without instruction after year two, on the other hand, run the risk of finding that their skills never develop beyond the level necessary to ski good pistes in good conditions. Resolve, then, to steer a middle course.

Every ski resort worthy of the name – and certainly every resort covered by this *Guide* – has a ski-school. Traditionally, resorts have had just one – generally an 'official' school, administered by the resort authorities, and either affiliated to or actually a part of a national ski-teaching organisation. It's now increasingly common, particularly in French resorts, to find two schools. The second may be much like the first, or it may adopt some distinguishing attitude or practices – it may claim to make learning more fun, or may work with smaller class sizes, for example; or it may aim at visitors from abroad, calling itself International and providing instructors with appropriate languages. Choosing between two schools is not easy unless you can get some evidence locally about what actually goes on in each school.

Classes work on a weekly cycle, and usually last six days. In some places they're mornings only, in others both morning and afternoon. The general idea is that you join a class at the beginning of the week and stick with it. You turn up at the school meeting point at the appointed hour, and first of all get sifted into the right group. If you're a complete beginner, that may be all the school needs to know. If not, slotting you into the right class is trickier, and really requires a test. Some schools apply a test of aptitude (or perhaps attitude) even to complete beginners. With or without a test, mix-ups can occur – but if you're wrongly classified at first you can move later.

In a resort with a substantial British trade, you should be able to join a class consisting entirely of English-speaking pupils, and you can expect an instructor with a more than basic grasp of English. Of course, you may judge that your French/German/Italian is good enough for you to seek integration with the locals instead. In other resorts you may have no alternative, and if your grasp of the local language is not good this is very undesirable; even an instructor who can speak English will get bored with repeating everything, and you will miss the often useful observations made on other people's technique.

The basic idea of ski classes is that everyone in the class carries out the same exercises one after the other. Some things you do in turn, each person performing under the gaze of the instructor, witnessed in superior calm by those who have already done it and in increasing anxiety by those still to come. The obvious drawback is that the more people there are in the group, the less time you spend actually skiing (and, more importantly, getting feedback on your skiing). When everyone in the group has grasped the basics of a particular movement, the instructor will lead the whole group down the slope in a continuous snake; the idea is that the whole snake follows exactly the route and pace of the instructor, and learns to mimic him. In practice, it's usually only the one or two skiers immediately behind the instructor who get much out of this – so it's important that everyone takes turns at the front (although everyone in the snake benefits from the confidence of knowing that the terrain ahead holds no unseen terrors).

The class process as a whole suffers from the further disadvantage that the quick learners are held up by the slow, and the slow feel shown up by the quick. The instructor should be prepared to move people out of the class into other classes as the week progresses; if you think this is necessary (particularly if you think you're too good for your present class) be prepared to insist on a move – it may be in the instructor's financial interest to keep the class as big as possible. But classes do have two great attractions. They're cheap – the cost should not put anyone off. And they can be great fun – particularly if you're not skiing with a party of friends, your ski-class can become the focus of your holiday.

Individual lessons, with an instructor all to yourself or shared with one or two friends, are of course much more expensive. They are also more purposeful – not simply because the smaller group means less time spent watching others, but because you tend to sense the francs/schillings/lire clocking up if any time is wasted fooling around or stopping for a schnapps. But you can make real progress in an hour, particularly if you hit upon an interested instructor. Unfortunately, in some resorts your hour may have to be squeezed into the instructor's schedule before the morning classes (which from experience we wouldn't recommend) or during the lunch break.

You don't have to go to a proper school in order to learn to ski. If you have friends who are competent, patient and willing, you can get the benefit of personal tuition at zero cost; but unless you're very lucky, the tuition is unlikely to be of the first quality, and there is a risk that it may on the contrary be highly unreliable and misleading. There is the further possibility of buying instruction from an unofficial source. In many resorts there are good English-speaking skiers who tout around the resort for skiers dissatisfied with the ski school. Although they don't come free, these 'ski-bums' do cost quite a lot less than individual lessons with an official instructor; like friends, they may lack teaching skills, but at least most of them ski well enough to be worth mimicking, and you don't have to devote half your energy to preserving good relations as you may have to with a friend.

A great deal of effort is these days put into the business of standardising ski tuition – which means not only ensuring that instructors know how to ski and how to teach, but also that what is taught in one place is consistent with what is taught in another.

Skiers who spend one holiday in Méribel and the next in St Anton should not now find, as they once did, that they are asked to do quite different things to achieve the same result. You will still find variations in emphasis, but these are as likely to be variations between individual instructors as they are to be the result of different regional or national philosophies of ski teaching.

The most fundamental departure from convention in ski teaching is the now well-established method of *ski evolutif*, known in the USA as the Graduated Length Method. It carries to extremes the widely accepted notion that beginners should not be encumbered with skis as long as those used by experts: you start on very short skis indeed, and having mastered them move on in stages to longer and longer ones. The French resort of Les Arcs is the home of *evolutif*, and the only place where it is universally employed – though it is available in some other French resorts and a few Swiss ones. We sent a researcher out to try it; on the facing page are some extracts from her diary. As you'll see, *evolutif* doesn't take the misery out of learning to ski; but if at the end of your first week you're starting to feel like a real skier, skiing long runs and experimenting with steep slopes and off-piste skiing, you're not doing badly.

Preparation

If you want to practise skiing before you get to the snow, you can do so on a number of artificial or **dry ski slopes** dotted around Britain. The slopes are covered with a mat of plastic bristles – some of them fairly fine, like a scrubbing brush, others much coarser and stiffer, like the teeth of a comb.

If you wanted to, you could learn enough on a dry slope to become a competent piste skier without ever seeing snow; and if you were to do so you would find most varieties of snow a good bit easier to ski on than plastic. But there's the rub: plastic isn't easy to ski on, and learning on it can be a demoralising business – not helped by the fact that falls which might be amusing on snow become distinctly painful. You run the risk that far from arriving in the Alps skilled and confident you'll arrive there convinced of your own incompetence – or with a thumb in plaster.

This is not to say that you should not try dry skiing – you should. Complete beginners generally find that a session or two with an instructor at a dry slope gives them a very valuable head start on their first skiing holiday. You become familiar with the boots and skis, and get used to standing and walking with them on; and if you persevere you can acquire the basic skiing skills. But don't be surprised if you don't enjoy it much; console yourself with thoughts of real snow.

One thing you can't expect to get out of a few hours' dry skiing is **fitness** for skiing – for that you have to do exercises. Skiers are very good at convincing themselves that they don't need to get fit before going skiing, and most people have very happy holidays without doing so. But there's no doubt (as we explain later) that getting fit pays dividends in a number of ways.

Ski evolutif: the diary of an evolving skier

Day 1

Struggle with unyielding boots, and then a few precarious slides down the nearest slope on our stunted, metre-long skis. It's quite easy to fall over backwards, because they stop just behind your heel. We assemble to be grouped into classes by making a trial run down a gentle slope towards a wall of instructors. We end up in five or six groups of about a dozen.

PM Our instructor, Jean-Paul, shows us the basic stance to adopt – skis and knees together, bent knees. First exercise – side-slipping; facing across a slope, keeping your skis together, slip down sideways and stop. Lots of uncontrollable sliding downwards and frantic digging of sticks into the snow.

Next, cautious wide turns, after JP demonstrates how to do it with exaggerated movements. In the middle of the turn you are meant to change your weight on to the outer ski, theoretically without the skis parting company. At first it is very difficult to keep the skis together and prevent the points colliding as you make the turn. As you lean into the turn it's easy to lean over too far and topple over sideways. We all do.

JP starts to add an elegant little jump at the end of the turn to bring the weight back equally on to each ski. We try to copy his neat jump; hopeless – we fall over continually. But never mind: if at first...

Day 2

Higher up the mountain for more side-slipping and turning practice. JP plants his sticks in the snow and skis off without them. We follow suit with flailing arms – and soon fall down as our legs begin to flail too. Convinced that sticks are vital for balance, we are now taught how to plant them properly as part of the turn, not as a last resort to avoid falling.

Day 3

Getting up isn't easy; we ease tender feet into lumpy boots and limp towards the slopes like weary commuters. Is this really a holiday? Going through the familiar turning routines we are now relatively steady on our skis; but JP takes us on to short turns, for which you need to have much tighter control. One by one we grotesquely imitate JP, looking as if we're trying to keep an invisible hula hoop in motion, and land one after another near his feet.

PM We change to longer skis (1.3 metres), and confidence wanes as we struggle to control them. We follow JP on longish runs and several people have difficulty keeping up. One girl sits down, removes her skis and starts to trudge down the hill until P cajoles her into persevering.

Day 4

We explore new pistes, with breaks when JP makes each of us perform a series of turns for him to comment on. The pace quickens and JP expects us to follow him from the top to the bottom of long runs. When it goes well it's exhilarating – the better skiers jockey for a place at the front of the line and people dashingly cut across each other. But others are still rather nervous and cautious, anxious not to fall over and hold the rest of the class up – one man is demoted to the class below because he's doing just that.

Day 5

On to even longer skis – 1.6 metres. This time the adjustment doesn't take so long. We just carry on skiing long runs, tackling different and steeper pistes and beginning to experiment with moguls. We feel like real skiers, at home on our skis – not able to go fast on steep and icy slopes, but at least able to try them.

Day 6

Heavy snow overnight. JP takes us through woods for some off-piste skiing, more for his own amusement than for our benefit. In the deep soft snow we fall over constantly, tumbling over snow drifts and each other. But at least it's fairly comfortable.

Day 7

Time to go home. Looking back, for the last three days of the course most of us had been skiing quite competently and enjoying it. Sometimes we could even reach the end of a piste without having fallen over once, and most of the aches and bruises of the first few days had worn off. It's been hard work – we rarely felt fit enough to go out in the evenings and certainly not to stay out late. But no one in our group gave up.

The risks

Skiing can be a hazardous sport: it's an unfortunate fact that some of the people who do it get hurt, some seriously. But the risks are often exaggerated – only a small percentage of those who go skiing suffer any injury at all, and (contrary to popular belief) very few of them have broken legs. Improvements in release bindings and boots have reduced the number of broken legs and ankles very considerably, and now injuries to arms, knees and heads are more common.

Most mishaps on the slopes are unlikely to prevent your getting back to the resort under your own steam. But of course skiers with broken limbs or other serious injuries are in need of **rescue**. If you're skiing on a recognised piste this shouldn't present too many problems. First, stick a pair of skis upright in the snow so as to form an X; this is a recognised sign to alert other skiers and routine safety patrols to the fact that someone is hurt. Patrols should cover all the pistes at the end of the day in any resort, and periodically during the day in a well-organised one. If a patrol happens along, they will be able to summon help by radio: otherwise, you'll need to get someone to go and make contact with the rescue service. In some resorts this will involve looking out for an SOS phone, which you're likely to find at the bottom of a major lift or run; in others, all the lift attendants are equipped with phones with which they can summon help. In due course the injured skier will be loaded into a stretcher-sledge (which British skiers with characteristic delicacy tend to call 'the blood wagon') and steered down to the resort or to a lift giving access to it. There will be a charge for such a rescue in some resorts, but it will not be large.

Most major resorts have a clinic or small hospital where fractures, sprains and other injuries can be diagnosed and treated. In smaller resorts you may have to be taken to a nearby town.

When skiing in Scotland, the UK's National Health Service will provide treatment, regardless of the fact that your injuries are self-inflicted. Abroad, you can often call on reciprocal medical care deals in which the UK is a partner. But, as *Holiday Which?* never tires of observing, the bureaucracy surrounding that system (even in its recently simplified form) is a big hurdle to have to get over – and most ski-resort clinics are in any case privately run, which means that reciprocal care deals are worthless. Also, medical attention isn't the only cost which can arise on a skiing trip. Some of the risks you run may be covered by a policy you have already taken out – loss of luggage, for example – but others are most unlikely to be covered. Your travel plans may have to be changed; you may break or lose your skis; and as we've said you may have to pay for a rescue. As a result, you need winter sports **insurance**.

Most tour operators have their own policies arranged direct with an insurance company. Many insist that you take out their policy (so making life easier from an administrative point of view – both in the office and in the resort when claims arise) and its cost is often included in the package holiday price. This means that if you don't like the policy, you have to buy another and effectively pay a second premium. All tour operators publish insurance details in the brochure but they are often rather scanty. The only way to find out what you're actually covered for is to ask for a copy of the actual policy before you book your holiday.

If your tour operator's policy is not compulsory or if you are not travelling with a tour operator, you can take out an independent policy through your travel agent, or through a source of insurance in general – an insurance company or a broker. There are a few specialist ski insurance policies, but most of those offered by travel agents are simply variants of regular holiday policies. These normally exclude winter sports but payment of a higher premium – usually double the normal one – gets you the extra cover.

When you have bought your insurance, keep the policy (or confirmation of booking) in a safe place and take it with you when you go on holiday. This can save time and complications should you, or one of your party, injure yourself. The procedure when a claim arises will vary with the circumstances.

How to go

When Henry Lunn hit on the idea of organising holidays to the Alps, in the last winter of the nineteenth century, he ran into the problem that his market was not too keen on the idea of packaged tourism. So he called his operation the Public Schools Alpine Sports Club, which proved immediately acceptable. The package tour has since come to dominate the British winter sports market, and although a few operators still style their wares to woo skiers who normally would not dream of taking organised holidays, most of them sell on price.

The arguments in favour of the package are compelling; for the great majority of skiers the package offers the same holiday you might arrange for yourself, at a significant saving of money, time, and worry. Most skiers are happy to stay in one place for the duration of their holiday, and don't really need their own transport. The number of highly recommendable resorts where you can't get a package is small. Going on a package doesn't mean you're confined to a single style of large characterless hotel, providing monotonous food: in most resorts, packages cover most of the range of accommodation – from b&b to Ritzy, from places entirely taken over by UK tour operators to places mainly used by individual visitors. Tour operators will normally lay on organised activities during the holiday, but you're not obliged to take part in them. The resort representative can in theory give valuable help when things go wrong. And a growing number of tour operators are helping their clients to get the most out of their skiing by providing ski-guides to show you around the slopes.

Accommodation
When choosing skiing accommodation priorities are not exactly the same as for other holidays. The most important thing for many skiers is location; ski-boots are not made for walking, and a long walk morning

and afternoon is a very unpleasant routine. Nearly all resorts produce street plans with hotels and apartment blocks marked on them, obtainable by post from the local tourist office if the national tourist office in the UK can't provide one. From these maps, even the crudest of them, it is usually possible to get an idea of how conveniently placed any hotel really is (very wiggly streets indicate a hill, straight ones are probably flat, and so on).

The **hotel** holiday, whether it be in a winter palace or a simple guest-house, is the norm in all but the most recently built resorts. Hotels in the Alps are not fundamentally different from hotels elsewhere. There are straightforward package hotels which, particularly in parts of Italy, may be best thought of mainly as a dormitory. There are a few exceptionally good places, and a great many pleasant, middle-of-the-road hotels. Austria and the Italian Dolomites deserve special mention in this respect, because of the great many modern hotels and guest-houses which have been built to high standards with traditional trimmings. Even the simplest places in these areas are generally reliable.

Board terms vary from full board to bed and breakfast. Half board (breakfast and an evening meal) is the usual arrangement, and suits most skiers best – particularly in resorts well equipped with mountain restaurants. Full board usually represents very good value (it's usually only about £15 to £25 a week more than half board), and in the right sort of resort it may not be too inconvenient. Most hotels will offer their full-board residents packed lunches, but these can be more trouble than they're worth. Bed and breakfast usually costs £20 to £50 a week less than half board for comparable accommodation; the attraction is not that you save money, but that you're free to eat in different places every night – more fun in some resorts than others. Some operators offer half- and full-board terms in the form of meal vouchers valid in specified mountain and resort restaurants.

Baths are a vital ingredient of a skiing holiday, and everyone wants to bath at the same time. Money spent on a room with private facilities, even if it adds significantly to the cost of a holiday (usually about £2 to £4, sometimes £5 a day), is money which few skiers will regret spending. A bath to yourself is one of the great advantages of the hotel holiday over most chalets and apartments – provided the hotel hot water supply is up to the demand.

In all Alpine resorts there are second homes (flats and chalets) which are let out for much of the winter season through an international letting agency (eg Interhome) or through local ones (information from local tourist offices). **Self-catering** packages are offered by British operators to a much more limited number of places, principally new French resorts where there are plenty of 'compact studios' (ie cramped flats) and very little other accommodation.

Saving money is one of the main attractions of the self-catering holiday – you can get a week in a top-rate resort for as little as £100, travel included. Local shops and supermarkets, especially in the high resorts which have the most self-catering accommodation, tend to be very expensive; but eating costs will still be modest by hotel/restaurant standards, especially if you self-cater as a group. If you drive out to ski, which doesn't exclude taking a package holiday, you can fill the car up with provisions to cut costs even further.

The other great attractions of a self-catering holiday are the privacy and freedom it offers. You can eat what you like, when it suits you and where it suits you; if your children are a nuisance they inconvenience only you; if you want to eat out on the town at night you can simply use the flat as a cheap dormitory; if you take with you no clothes other than ski clothes, no one need ever know. The drawbacks are obvious (you have to cater for yourself) but perhaps easily underestimated. After a day's skiing, not many people feel like trudging round the supermarket and then cooking and washing up. Less enthusiastic skiers and non-skiers may be quite happy to do this, and indeed there may be little else to occupy their time in many self-catering resorts.

It is very important to establish not only how conveniently situated an apartment is (in many new resorts the main problem is having to queue for the lift to and from the umpteenth floor), but also what its dimensions are. This information is usually easy to get hold of, and should be studied carefully; if 20 sounds quite a few square metres, take a moment to think it through. Do not assume if the flat is described as being for six that it would be extravagant not to fill it with six people. The additional cost per person of sharing such a flat between only four people will not be enormous – perhaps £20 or £40 per week – but in terms of enjoyment can make the difference between success or failure of the self-catering idea, and of the holiday as a whole. It can be the difference between friends and ex-friends.

Living space is in very many flats made to serve as sleeping space for (at least) two people. This means that two people have to get up first and go to bed last, and that anyone going to the bathroom may have to climb over them. Their privacy suffers and the living space inevitably does as well. If a hotel room is poky you can usually go and sit in the hotel bar or sitting room, and do no more than sleep in your bedroom. If a flat has inadequate living space you'll be driven out into the bars and restaurants of the resort, where you will spend money.

Stacking time for access to bathroom facilities, morning and evening, is very important; four is really the largest number of people who can happily share a ski holiday bathroom, and that is far from ideal. Think about how you'll want to lie and soak as soon as you get in from skiing. Think about how you'll want to be out on the slopes early in the morning, and how frustrated you may be if you have to wait for 20 minutes before you can shave; it often means the difference between strolling on to the cable-car and a half-hour scrum.

The packaged **chalet** holiday is a peculiarly British phenomenon: tour operators rent all or part of a house for the season, and staff it with British or colonial girls who clean up and cook and turn the chalet into a home. It all started as a swinging '60s London thing, combining the delights of metropolitan cocktail gatherings and country house-parties. Gals who were more used to being waited on than waiting boned up on Cordon Bleu cookery and dashed off to spend a winter or two in resorts like Méribel, Verbier and Val d'Isère. To underline the excitement of the venture, the young socialites in charge decreed that no one should be allowed over the threshold under the age of consent or past the distant milestone of one score years and ten that defines the natural course of man's life.

Although there may still be a hint of social exclusiveness about chalet holidays, they reach a much wider public these days, and the girls are as likely to come from New Zealand as from Knightsbridge. The bosses themselves have found that there is life after thirty, and that the arrival of children does not preclude the possibility of enjoying the chalet formula. There is still a flexible rule that senior citizens and young children are not welcome except as part of a whole-chalet group. But there are now chalets which cater especially for families with young children. A real sign of the times is that middle-of-the-road Thomson Holidays is now offering chalet parties in Verbier.

The term 'chalet' indicates the style of holiday more precisely than the style of building – though you are normally accommodated in small-scale buildings in traditional Alpine style. Similar holidays are now offered in ordinary modern flats – in which case the inhabitants of several flats will be herded together under one roof for meals. Chalets are rarely to be found right in the centre of a resort, as a hotel might be, and many are on the outskirts. On the other hand, some are very well placed for skiing from and to the front door.

A big chalet will normally be marketed as several separate units – often on separate floors. These units normally take from 8 to 20 people, mostly in the upper end of that range. You can take over a whole unit and fill it with family or friends, and make yourself very much at home. Or you can go on your own or in small numbers and join other such people to fill the place – the operators claim to strive to make up compatible groups, though they are clearly not in a position to guarantee success. Chalet life pivots informally around the living/eating room, where you can relax, drink your duty-free Scotch and play cards or whatever. There's rarely more than one 'common' room, and so no prospect of escape from being sociable. This may involve tolerating invasions by the residents of other chalets or the friends of your chalet girls, as well as the inmates. You shouldn't bank on retreating to your bedroom, which is likely to be cramped and poorly furnished – and to have paper-thin walls. Bathroom facilities, too, are often inadequate in one way or another – even if there are enough baths and showers you'll be lucky to find constant hot water.

You are usually well fed, and heartily – from eggs and porridge at breakfast, through bread and jam (and cakes if you're lucky) at tea-time to a three-course dinner with wine included. The budgets on which the girls cook are not large, but most seem to manage to construct appetising meals in an anglicised bistro/trattoria style. Most people reckon the meals one of the plus-points of a chalet holiday.

Naturally a lot depends on the temperament and competence of the chalet girls. At best they can be extremely good cooks, very useful guides to the skiing and resort life, sympathetic to whatever style of holiday you want to adopt, and fun. Not all chalet girls are such paragons, and it's important to be alert to the possibility that some will consider their social lives more important than your holiday.

Some operators have developed the chalet idea into something rather different – the 'club' chalet. These are sizeable hotels or other holiday institutions run in chalet style – that is to say with English-speaking staff cooking and cleaning up. These jumbo chalets typically suit small groups, couples or individuals looking for a gregarious, sociable holiday, but really haven't got much to do with the original chalet idea. The large numbers of staff in these places usually keep themselves to themselves much more than chalet girls do. The accommodation – particularly the bedrooms – is often markedly better than that of the typical chalet.

Travel

Most people get to the Alps by **air**. The flight to Geneva, Milan, Munich or wherever generally takes only an hour or two, but is of course preceded by three or four hours' struggle at this end and is followed by anything up to eight hours on a coach winding its way into the Alps. Door to door, you rarely get much change out of a day – only if your flight leaves before dawn are you likely to get any skiing in on day one. The journey is not only long, but also fragmented – and the transitions from one stage to another are wearying, particularly if you're lugging skis and boots with you as well as a normal amount of holiday luggage.

For all the hassles, air travel is the most common means of transport from Britain to the Alps, and usually the quickest. If you live far from London (or, rather, far from Gatwick Airport) the availability of holidays from a convenient UK departure airport is bound to be a consideration when choosing a holiday – a number of tour operators use midland, northern and Scottish airports as well as London ones. You should also look carefully at the destination airport, especially when travelling to Italy, because operators don't always use the most convenient one. For Sauze d'Oulx and other Milky Way resorts, for example, some operators use Milan instead of Turin, which means a much longer transfer than is necessary.

If you are taking equipment with you, wrap it up well – a ski bag and boot bag are well worth investing in for protection and ease of carrying; don't wear your ski-boots (or après-ski boots unless you know your feet can take a Turkish bath). A few operators charge extra to carry skis, but most allow you a pair in addition to the usual baggage limit.

Travel by **coach** has only recently been offered on a large scale by operators. It has proved very popular, and it's not difficult to see why. For one thing it is very cheap – about £40 less than going by plane. For another, you get on the coach in London (or Birmingham or Manchester) and apart from the Channel crossing you don't have to move until you are in the resort; what's more, your luggage doesn't have to move at all. It takes longer than flying, but many people find it much less of a strain. Then there's the fact that the travelling is usually arranged so that you get one more day's skiing (7 days on the slopes for a week, 14 for a fortnight) than holiday-makers going by air. The disadvantages are that you have to put up with 24 hours on a coach, and that you may have to take all or part of Friday off work (especially if you're starting from the north). Most of the coaches used are reasonably comfortable for short people, and loos and videos are usually provided; but the arrangements (where there are any) for transforming the coaches into double-decker dormitories do not suit everyone.

Not so long ago air travel was reserved for the privileged few, and the Snowsports Special **train** from Victoria to Austria was the way everyone else went on their winter-sports packages. Now that flying is cheaper than going by train, few tour operators even offer rail travel as an option. But it has its attractions – it's more restful than flying, particularly if you're going to a resort which is on a main line (St Anton is the classical example). Many operators give their clients the option of driving out, and these arrangements can in most cases be tailored to include rail travel instead.

Getting to the Alps by **car** can work out cheaper than flying, and for self-caterers there is the added saving of being able to take cheap coffee and cans of beans. Naturally the economics of driving out depend on how full you fill your car; but they also depend on the extras involved in travelling out (motorway tolls, overnight stops, meals and drinks en route), and whether you count the cost of the essential service and preparation of the car for winter conditions, wear and tear from salty Alpine roads (not to mention wear and tear from encounters with Post Buses and snowploughs), snow chains, ski racks, breakdown insurance for the car, and a Green Card to extend your ordinary insurance for Continental use. It's far too simple to take the cost of a ferry and the cost of petrol over 650 miles and think that driving looks cheap.

But there are non-economic advantages too – principally that if you have a car you broaden the possibilities of a ski holiday enormously. You can meander out and back and enjoy the pleasures of travelling through France or Germany; a night in Paris perhaps, or an afternoon's wine tasting in Burgundy. If your accommodation isn't ideally placed in the resort you can be free of the overcrowded bus service and save leg-work. You can take off for some sightseeing or shopping in the local town, to ski in another resort, or to have a evening out in different surroundings. There's no doubt that taking a car is also the most convenient, least exhausting way of getting your luggage to the resort.

The disadvantages are basically the effort and the worry. Driving can be very tiring, slow and difficult, in April as well as January. Anything going wrong with the car is very time-consuming even if you're insured to the hilt. And there's no denying that driving on snow is hazardous and tricky – though there are plenty of resorts where snow on the access roads is the exception rather than the rule. In general front-wheel drive is better than rear, except in cars (old VW, Porsche) with the engine weight over the driving rear wheels. A good part of our 'Travel facts' chapter is devoted to information for motorists.

Choosing your resort

Choice of resort may not be the most important reason for the success or failure of a holiday – luck with the weather and snow, and perhaps with companions, is probably more decisive – but it is one aspect of the holiday over which you have some control. Every ski resort is somebody's ideal resort; on the other hand, none suits everyone. In this chapter our aim is mainly to provoke thought about what constitutes your own ideal – so that with the help of the main resorts section of the *Guide* you can arrive at your own short-list. But we also offer a short-cut to that short-list: at the beginning of the resorts section is a four-page comparative chart summarising our verdicts on all the major resorts covered by the *Guide*.

The time-of-year factor
The general pros and cons of different skiing months are outlined in 'A Skiing Primer'. The shifting patterns of weather and crowds affect resorts in different ways: timing of a holiday should weigh heavily in the balance when choosing your resort.

Going skiing **before Christmas** means going before the skiing season is properly under way. Choose a large, well-known resort popular with good skiers. Val d'Isère has a famous pre-Christmas downhill race, is lively and as reliable for snow as anywhere. A few resorts (Verbier and St Anton are the best known examples) are popular places for pre-season ski courses known as Wedelkurse or Cours de Godille. The resorts offer all-in packages of accommodation, lift pass and ski school just as they do at other low-season periods. There is an undeserved mystique about these courses, which are in fact no more than an intensive course of ski school which can be undertaken by fit skiers of all standards.

If you are going skiing over **Christmas/New Year** mainly in order to be away from home for the festivities, then resort charm and specific choice of hotel count for a lot. Little Austrian resorts such as Alpbach and Serfaus have a delightfully festive atmosphere at this time of year and are justifiably popular, despite their limited skiing. In general, lower resorts which have a permanent as well as a casual population are attractively Christmassy. Skiers who have had snowless skiing over the holiday in the last couple of years will be tempted to aim high. They shouldn't be surprised to find bleak, low-visibility conditions if the weather is more normal for the time of year. They must also be prepared to find not much of a Yuletide atmosphere – though a jovial chalet party can do a lot to make up for that. One clear advantage of a high, purpose-built resort is that you can expect queues to be less severe, because of better-organised lifts.

Some long-established Swiss resorts have a special appeal; the

British have been spending Christmas in resorts such as Wengen and Mürren for over half a century, and there's still nowhere more suitable for living out your own Christmas-card idyll – beautiful old log-cabin chalets, no cars, and magnificent scenery.

Continental skiers stay at home in **January**, unless tempted on to the slopes by good weather at the weekend. Keen British skiers, lured to the Alps by keen British package prices, should go to places with a big British trade – such as Val d'Isère, Sauze d'Oulx, Verbier and Söll – if they want to be sure of finding much life in the resort.

Although recent winters have not conformed to the pattern, January is normally expected to bring more than a fair share of blizzards. In these conditions, medium-altitude resorts with plenty of skiing below the tree-line come into their own, because visibility is better among trees and the slopes are sheltered from wind – so lifts are less likely to be closed. In general the Alpine tree-line is at about 1800 to 2000m; resorts such as Kitzbühel and Söll in the Austrian Tirol offer a full 1000 metres of skiing (measured vertically) in more-or-less friendly woodland surroundings. Chair-lifts and drag-lifts are less prone to closure than cable-cars, but riding them can be bitterly cold. The ideal is to have a choice of kinds of lift.

January is a tempting time to visit big-name resorts notorious for their lift queues. If you have a week of good weather, you'll get very fit and be an immediate convert to January holidays. With a car, you could even sample several such resorts in one trip, fixing up hotel or guest-house accommodation as you go – you'll have no trouble finding a bed.

You can hope to find decent skiing wherever you go in **February**; but you must expect crowds. The French, Swiss and Germans have holidays during the month. The concentration of French holidays is particularly heavy, and although the French resorts are better able to cope than most, the roads leading to them (the Tarentaise resorts in particular) are not. The national tourist office can tell you which particular weeks to avoid each year.

For a holiday in **early March**, it is advisable to choose a resort with plenty of skiing above 2000m on slopes facing north and east. In high resorts you can be pretty sure of snow and reasonably hopeful of good snow; conditions are often excellent for exploring off-piste. (Many Austrian resorts, on the other hand, offer low-season prices for March, because they are regarded as increasingly risky for snow as the month progresses.)

To be confident of finding decent skiing in **late March** or **April** you have to go high – as a rule of thumb, you need slopes in the range 2500m to 3500m, and probably north-facing. The resorts which can provide such slopes are few, with the result that skiers are concentrated in those resorts and the crowds at Easter are the worst of the season – particularly in France, where many of the reliable resorts are to be found.

The tail end of the season in the Alps is often the time when conditions are at their best in Scotland; in the depth of winter the weather is often discouragingly bad, while in spring the sun is not so strong as to ruin the snow.

The ability factor

It's important that your choice of resort takes account of the kind of skier you are. We've called this the ability factor, but it's actually rather broader, embracing your skiing appetite as well as aptitude.

The first requirement of a resort for **beginners** is that it should have a gentle nursery slope on which to take those first faltering steps on skis. It should ideally not be much of a slope at all (part of it should be completely flat); it should be big enough to cope with however many beginners there are, and it should not be part of a piste used by other skiers on their way down the mountain. It should have a gentle, slow lift, not one which non-nursery skiers are tempted to use. It should get some sunshine, and there should be a bar close by.

Most resorts have such slopes beside the village, at the foot of the main ski slopes. If the nursery slopes are high up, beginners face the cost of getting to and from them each day. On the other hand, high-level nursery slopes are usually sunnier than village ones; they are usually more convenient for mid-day meetings with other skiers; and they are extremely valuable if snow is in short supply in the village – the lower the resort is, the more likely this is, especially late in the season. Many purpose-built resorts have achieved the best of both worlds by siting themselves high up, with excellent wide-open nursery areas immediately at hand. Alpe d'Huez, Sestriere and Isola 2000 are spectacularly good in this respect.

Nursery slopes are for the first few days only. For a painless graduation to real skiing, you need easy, unthreatening pistes – graded green in those resorts which sensibly adopt four categories of run – on which to build up confidence. Many resorts which have perfectly good nursery areas – Selva, for example – are very uncomfortable places for a near-beginner because they lack such runs. It is equally important to bear in mind that not all beginners are dedicated piste-bashers by the end of their first week. Some don't take to skiing at all, and throw in the towel (and their crippling hired boots); others find skiing all day a bit exhausting, and like to mix skiing with other things. So it's important to consider the charm factor, and the non-skiing factor – dealt with later in the chapter.

Fashionable resorts with enormous ski areas, where lift passes and ski hire are expensive, are wasted on most beginners. Affluent beginners – or beginners joining parties of more experienced skiers – need not avoid them altogether. But some big-name resorts which appeal strongly to good skiers are best avoided for your first trip – see our comparative chart.

We know of only one resort where **intermediate** skiers will not find skiing suitable for their ability: La Grâve, in the southern French Alps, has a gondola lift which serves 1500m vertical of totally unprepared, unpatrolled, unmaintained and steep mountainside. In all other resorts most of the pistes will be negotiable under good snow conditions by plucky (and that does not mean fearless or reckless) intermediates. Plenty of them ski around the toughest skiing resorts in the Alps without a qualm. These resorts do not provide very much scope for relaxing, flattering skiing – you have to enjoy a challenge, and be prepared to take a lift down if you're not up to it.

Many intermediate skiers are keen and adventurous without relishing the challenge of difficult skiing, and the modern resorts with big ski areas have bred a species of skier for whom variety in skiing is very much the spice of life. These piste-freaks look for resorts where 'you can ski for a week without doing the same piste twice'; and provided you're not too literal about it there is now quite a range of resorts which conform to the specification. Many are modern French resorts in the Tarentaise or the northern Alps. Piste tourism at its most beautiful is to be found in the majestic scenery around the Sella Group in the Dolomites. In all these areas, no very difficult runs have to be skied in the course of skiing from resort to resort. Our comparative chart identifies several other traditional resorts with extensive skiing areas where intermediates can cover lots of ground without terrifying themselves. And the Guide's piste maps are in a way tailor-made for the intermediate piste-basher, who can now see at a glance what a resort means when it claims to possess 'le plus grand domaine skiable du monde'.

We hesitate to prescribe what the **expert** skier should look for in a resort – we imagine that anyone who is expert at negotiating steep slopes will also have become expert at identifying them, and at figuring out what other resort characteristics are desirable. But our comparative chart shows which resorts we would turn to first for tough skiing and for off-piste skiing.

Any grade of skier may have an interest in the quality of the **ski-school**. In the Guide's resort assessments, we have drawn what conclusions what we can about individual ski schools from our reporters' experiences, but it is impossible to generalise except in a few respects. First, standards within any one school are likely to vary widely, and schools with long-standing reputations (such as those of Kitzbühel and St Anton) are no exception to this. Secondly, it's important for most skiers that they are taught in English; this means not only that the instructor must speak English well, but also that there must be enough English-speakers wanting tuition to justify the creation of an English-speaking class – and that means going to a resort with a big UK holiday trade. Thirdly, it doesn't matter how skilled the instructor is if there are 20 people in the class – your progress will be slow, or nil. We've paid particular attention to class size in our resort reports but, as you'll see, there are precious few resorts which do not at some time or another permit classes of ludicrous sizes.

The access factor

Holiday-makers who are used to a 30-minute ride from package airport to package hotel in their summer resorts get a bit of a shock when they first go skiing. Coach transfers of less than two hours are exceptional. Most of the very easily accessible resorts are in two areas – close to Geneva, where France, Switzerland and Italy meet, or in the eastern Austrian Tirol, within easy reach of Munich airport by motorway. Resorts in Western Austria and Eastern Switzerland are all much further away from either Munich or Zurich. Most Italian resorts involve very long airport transfers – some as long as eight hours, even without delays; the exceptions are the resorts in the extreme west of the country, which are about two hours from Turin. Enthusiastic supporters of resorts in the Tarentaise region of the French Alps – Méribel, Val d'Isère and so on – admit that the transfers are a drawback. In theory the journey from Geneva takes four hours or so, culminating in tortuous climbs from the valley to the high resorts. But the real problem is weekend traffic jams, which can result in a doubling of the theoretical journey times.

If you're going by car, don't pay too much attention to slight differences in distance to resorts; winter weather (in the Channel as well as the Alps) and holiday traffic are more likely to determine how long the journey takes. But some of the differences are not slight: it's an appreciably longer-than-average journey to Italian resorts east of Milan, to St Moritz, and to southern French resorts – especially Isola 2000 and its neighbours, which are best reached via Nice.

In the 'Travel facts' chapter we list the major resorts which have railway stations. Many can be reached with only one or two changes of train, and some can be reached with no changes at all – Aviemore, Badgastein and St Anton, which is outstanding in this respect: you can board a train at Victoria after lunch, and disembark next morning about 100 yards from the cable-car station which gives direct access to some of the best skiing in the world.

The convenience factor

Most skiers would like to have ski lifts going up from their front door and pistes coming back down to it. Most would also like to spend their holiday in a community rather than a holiday camp. But it is very rare to find a village or town which is ideally placed as a skiing base *and* has grown up naturally for some other reason. St Anton is one example – a travellers' rest at the foot of the Arlberg Pass, and coincidentally at the foot of excellent ski slopes. Its village centre is a very convenient base for skiers. Obergurgl is another – a high village which might have been purpose-built, but didn't need to be. In most other traditional resorts, you need to choose your location with care, and with one eye firmly on the public transport system.

If the convenience factor really matters, though, you will almost certainly be better off choosing a modern resort which has been designed solely for skiers. Convenience is not just a question of getting around; planned resorts, provided they are sufficiently remote, can in theory achieve an approximate balance between the supply of uphill transport and the demand for it. Although resort developers make no money out of blissfully uncongested lifts, many purpose-built resorts have managed to put this theory into reasonably effective practice; what's more, many have also managed to plan lift and piste networks so as to avoid bottlenecks.

Skiing convenience dictates a style of building and a resort layout which have little in common with real communities. In most ski areas there is one situation which makes a more convenient base than any other, and the logical plan is one which concentrates skiers there. The landmarks of the first purpose-built resort, Sestriere, show the logic in action: tall, round towers full of very cramped accommodation.

Some small resorts – Puy St Vincent, Isola 2000 – consist of little more than one single-building complex, with flats, shops, bars, restaurants and resort offices under one roof. The walking you have to do is along carpeted corridors, the lift queues are to get to and from the 32nd floor. They're a bit like ocean liners – except that low standards of finish and maintenance have made them more like troop ships than the QE2. But a single such unit cannot simply be expanded to accommodate any number of skiers, or to service any size of ski-area. Thus, in the much larger resort of La Plagne (which claims to sell more lift passes than any other resort), half a dozen clusters of buildings are scattered far and wide, high and low, around an enormous skiing area – including a couple of old hamlets far below the main resort centres which stand high up in the wide snow-fields above the tree line.

There is no shortage of skiers who welcome the effortlessness of holidays in these new resorts. There are keen skiers who are obliged to take their holidays in high season, when many resorts cannot handle the crowds; they ski hard, value the lift system which enables them to do so, and are not too bothered about après-ski or sleigh rides. Then there are skiing families, who find that the freedom and economy of the apartment formula suits them and their pockets well, and that many of the new resorts (especially in France) are the most relaxing places to take children.

Needless to say, resorts such as these do not suit everyone; one man's convenience food is another man's junk. Non-skiing activities (day-time and night-time) are rarely as fully developed as in traditional resorts. What they lack more than anything else is life, the feeling of being a community, which by definition they are not. Hoteliers, shop-keepers and ski instructors are foreigners hired for the season or commuters from the valley, who leaving the place deserted in the evening except for holiday-makers at a loose end, who may search in vain for a café with some local atmosphere.

Other big resorts have been developed differently, to have some resemblance to a real village – in overall structure even if not in style. It is no coincidence that these resorts – of which Méribel is the clearest example – are ones where you need to take care about where in the village you stay, just as you do in traditional resorts.

It may not be possible to give a new resort the vitality of an established community, but it is possible to build one which is both convenient and appealing – provided it is not also required to be large. That, at least, is the conclusion we draw from the example of Valmorel, recently developed not far from the Three Valleys. Its designers have obviously set out to synthesise an Alpine village atmosphere, and if the buildings mature rather than decay as they age, that objective seems likely to be achieved.

In many ways the most successful of the big purpose-built resorts is one of the first – Courchevel. It is no beauty, but under snow its ugliness is not obtrusive and it is much less shoddy than many younger resorts. It has a lively centre, with comfortable hotels (it pre-dates the great self-catering boom), restaurants and varied nightlife. Chalets and more hotels are spread round the mountainside in a broad horseshoe so that nearly everyone can get to and from home on skis. The terrain is such that the skiing around the resort itself is spacious and very easy, and snow is usually reliable at resort level. For bad weather there is good skiing below the resort among the woods. Queues build up at the main lift departure point, but there are alternative ways into the system. The only thing it isn't easy to do in Courchevel is economise.

The crowds factor

You don't have to be a super-keen skier to prefer skiing in a resort which is relatively free of lift queues; they are boring, tiring, often stressful, and disruptive of the best-laid plans. Tourist offices like to produce statistics giving the ratio of resort beds to lift capacity in persons per hour, but these figures rarely tell you what you need to know about queues – and can be highly misleading. The *Guide's* resort reports contain what concrete information we have about queues in recent seasons, but it is also helpful to have an appreciation of what makes a resort more likely or less likely to suffer from bad queues in high season.

   A resort will be relatively queue-free if it is small (relative to its skiing area) and remote from centres of population; or if it has a lift system without bottlenecks (a shortage of lifts leaving the resort is the usual problem – and most of the resorts which don't suffer from bottlenecks are purpose-built ones); or if it attracts a high proportion of non-skiers and cross-country skiers; or if it doesn't attract many people at all. A few examples will serve to show how these factors operate in practice.

   Obergurgl is very popular, and its lift system which depends on single-seater chair-lifts is not the ultimate in efficiency; it often has good snow when other places are short. But it very rarely has lift queues, because it is a very small place and, equally important, it is remote. Valmorel is small and rarely gets crowded; other resorts in its neighbourhood are much more powerful magnets. Val d'Isère is large and very popular, but remote and very well served by four main lifts from the valley floor – three of them double lifts. Queues are rarely bad, except when the weather is bad and higher lifts are closed. Ischgl is not a huge resort, and overall its lift system is impressively large. But queues can be very bad, because the lifts out of the resort are inadequate, and a lot of skiers come by bus or car for the day from nearby villages.

   Famous, large resorts which provide inefficient access to excellent skiing areas normally have substantial queues. In the Engadine (St Moritz and area) the ratio of beds to lift capacity, and especially lift capacity from the resorts, is typically discouraging. But queues are usually not serious, because so many people do things other than skiing, and because many skiers are late starters in the morning.

   The queueing for lifts in most of the long-established resorts is in fact not the problem it used to be, now that new lifts have relieved their notorious bottlenecks. But the result of all this efficiency is that the pistes in many resorts are becoming crowded, instead of the lifts; this is just as unpleasant and much more dangerous. At least in the Chamonix Valley (where the hostility of terrain and ecologists have for years combined to frustrate initiatives to alleviate the queueing problem), when you do get to the top of the mountain you don't have to ski all the way down in a crowd, as you often do on the Grande Motte in Tignes.

The accommodation factor

Most skiers choose the style of their holiday accommodation before considering where to look for it – indeed many skiers go to the same sort of accommodation year after year. Such single-mindedness predetermines to some extent your choice of resort.

Nearly all package holidays in Italy and Austria employ **hotel** accommodation. In most Italian resorts there are plenty of cheap, mostly very simple hotels and guest-houses, which make other forms of accommodation look expensive. Cheap as they are, not all these places represent good value, unless your requirements are minimal. The Pensione Turistica in Courmayeur, for example, features one bath and one shower for 26 beds. Most of our reporters' disappointment with hotels came from Italian holidays. Most Italian resorts have one or two large, comfortable hotels; few of these are stylish or cheaper than comfortable hotels in other countries.

In Austria (and in most of the Dolomite resorts – which are in many ways more Austrian than Italian) the standard of hotel accommodation is high and uniform. Not only are most hotels well-kept, clean and comfortable, they also tend to be attractive (outside and in) and welcoming. For many of our reporters, the attraction of a particular hotel is a powerful reason to return to an Austrian resort which they might otherwise desert. Lots of not-very-luxurious Austrian hotels have saunas and pools. In (and near) the largest and most famous resorts, such as Kitzbühel and St Anton, many package operators offer cheap holidays in simple bed-and-breakfast accommodation (the prefix 'Haus' indicates this); even the simplest are usually attractive and adequately comfortable. In most skiing regions of Austria there are lots of small villages within easy driving distance of skiing, where almost every family takes in bed-and-breakfast guests.

In traditional Swiss and French resorts there is a much greater variety of style, standard and price of hotel accommodation, ranging from very simple boarding houses, where ski-bums cram several to a room and live very cheaply, to simple family hotels and (mostly in Switzerland) large, expensive palaces which are almost self-sufficient resorts in themselves. In the new purpose-built resorts there are usually few hotels, and not much of a range of comfort and cost. Courchevel is one of the few purpose-built French resorts with a lot of hotels, some of them very comfortable and expensive.

There are **self-catering** chalets and apartments for rent in most resorts, but the majority of self-catering package holidays are in French resorts, mostly purpose-built. Shopping facilities, more important for self-caterers than other skiers, are usually good and convenient, but demand for them in the early evening is heavy, and prices are of course higher than in valley-bottom *hypermarchés*. It is quite possible to arrange self-catering holidays in other resorts – write to the local tourist offices for information, and get hold of the Interhome brochure for the country you're looking at; if nothing else, it will give you a clear idea of the possibilities.

Verbier and the French Tarentaise resorts are the great homes of the **chalet** holiday, and now of the **club chalet** which has sprung off from the original animal; all are very fashionable among gregarious young and not-so-young keen skiers who like the staffed chalet formula. Chalets are also to be found in a few other Swiss and Italian (mainly Dolomite) resorts, and in a very few Austrian ones. The cost of chalet holidays doesn't vary much from country to country, which makes them a particularly attractive way to holiday in Switzerland and not very attractive in Italy.

The charm factor

Keen skiers who piste-bash themselves to exhaustion every day may well scorn the idea that the style, looks and diversions of a ski resort could make any difference to them. But for most people the very word 'Alpine' has connotations of Christmas-card charm, and an Alpine holiday with no trees, no log cabins, no jingle bells, and no skaters – only bare rock and snow and concrete – adds up to a sadly incomplete holiday. Resort charm has seven major ingredients.

A year-round community – probably a village, but sometimes a town, with a life independent of skiing; preferably farming buildings and hamlets dotted around the valley and hillsides. This is most easily found in Austria, where many ski resorts have grown out of farming communities, at relatively low altitude. It is not a matter of prettiness, more a matter of people – a sense of place, of character.

A picturesque setting – not too enclosed, with some woodland. The beauty of the mountain scenery is a major contribution, for example, to the appeal of Zermatt and St Moritz. It is an even greater element of the appeal of the Dolomites. Not all high mountain scenery is particularly beautiful – on the contrary, it is often merely bleak, hostile and monotonous. Resorts in balcony settings half way up the flanks of wide, deep valleys benefit from broader, longer views and usually more sunshine than resorts at the bottom of valleys, which may be better placed for multi-directional skiing; examples are Crans-Montana, Sauze d'Oulx, Wengen and Mürren – surely the most beautifully set ski resort of all.

Absence of cars – or at least an absence of busy through-routes; preferably snowy streets. Here most high, remote resorts naturally have the advantage. Most purpose-built resorts restrict or banish cars; and most car-free resorts are purpose-built – the main exceptions are Zermatt, Saas Fee, Mürren, Wengen and Serfaus.

Traditional winter sports activities – horses and sleighs, walkers, outdoor skating and curling, tobogganers, cross-country skiers to give the place something other than the brutal downhill atmosphere. Most often found in long-established winter sports resorts, mainly in Switzerland (St Moritz and Arosa among others). Seefeld is a departure from the pattern – in Austria, and mainly of recent development.

Decent mountain restaurants – plentiful in number, with outside terraces for good weather and mountain-refuge-style (rather than cafeteria-style) interiors for bad weather. Long-established resorts, and especially ones popular for summer walking, tend to be well and attractively catered for – Klosters, Zermatt, Courmayeur, the Dolomites, Gstaad, even Sauze d'Oulx.

Dignified clientele – resort not dominated by rowdy international youth. Undoubtedly the popularity of resorts such as Sauze d'Oulx, Mayrhofen, Söll, Val d'Isère, St Anton with rowdy young people, not necessarily British, spoils the atmosphere for others.

Chalet-style buildings – with balconies and pitched roofs. In Austria, not only are many resorts attractive old villages, they have also been developed in a carefully pseudo-traditional style; very few – not even resorts which grew from almost nothing, such as Obergurgl and Zürs – are eyesores. Not all 'traditional' resorts can claim this, especially in Switzerland: Davos, Arosa, Crans-Montana, even St Moritz, can rival any purpose-built resort for architectural bleakness.

The non-skiing factor

The needs of non-skiers are largely covered under the charm factor. For variety of spectacle as well as variety of activity, there is no beating the Engadine (St Moritz and its surroundings); part of its great appeal is the scope it offers for escaping the paraphernalia and mechanics of a modern ski resort to explore beautiful wooded valleys where no skiers (or at least no Alpine piste skiers) venture.

Many people like to get out of the resort for a day to go shopping or sightseeing, or simply for a change. Resorts near Innsbruck are the very good for this, with plentiful day-trips to Innsbruck and to the various places of interest, cultural and material, over the Brenner Pass in Italy. Non-skiers in the Dolomites not only have these interesting excursions within reach, they can also do their own Sella Ronda spectacular by public bus and can just about fit in visits to Venice or Verona. By contrast, a non-skier in one of the resorts of the French Tarentaise region – Val d'Isère or Méribel, say – is there for the duration of the holiday.

The family factor

Properly speaking, there is not a separate family factor. If you are taking children skiing, you will want to take account of the matters we have considered under charm, convenience, ability, access (long coach transfers can be a nightmare with children), non-skiing and accommodation. But there remains the distinct question of how resorts actually look after children. In general, the most recent generation of purpose-built resorts aims for family business, and the skiing requirements of beginners, and especially junior beginners, are very well looked after. Parents can dump their offspring for the day or half-day in trained hands and enjoy their own skiing. See our comparative chart at the beginning of the resorts section. Consider also where you will want to spend your skiing day, and how far away it is from the nursery areas.

The snow factor

Good snow is an important element in a satisfactory skiing holiday; in general, where you should go to find it varies with the time of year, and that factor is dealt with at the beginning of the chapter. But with most resorts there is always a risk that the snow at a normally dependable time of year will turn out to be disappointing, and if you're prepared to travel out of high season it's tempting to think that you can avoid this risk by fixing your holiday at the last moment and going to a resort which is doing well in the snow reports published in the newspapers.

There are two kinds of published snow reports. Resort tourist offices issue figures for the depth of snow on the upper and lower slopes; even if these figures were reliable (which they are not) they would give only a crude idea of the snow cover. Much more valuable are the reports sent by the Ski Club of Great Britain's representatives (based in about 30 Alpine resorts). These incorporate the figures, but add brief comments which are very illuminating once you learn to read between the words. The Club has to tread carefully in order to provide helpful information while meeting its obligation to the resorts, which sponsor the reps in the expectation that having a rep in town will attract British skiers. So the comments (which are often telexed by the tourist office) have to be delicately written if conditions are poor: 'Good skiing above 2,500 metres' and 'Good skiing on upper slopes' are favourite ways of describing wash-out conditions on the lower slopes.

Naturally, reps vary in how they handle these difficulties, and in how they perceive snow conditions. Some resort officials take a much closer interest in the reports than others, too. So resort-to-resort comparisons are unlikely to tell you much. But you can certainly use the reports to build up a general picture of which broad areas of the Alps are in favour with the great snowmaker in the sky, and which are out.

A further problem is the inevitable delays involved in getting the reports published. At best, a snow report can tell you where you ought to have been yesterday. Even if you decide on a week-end departure on the basis of a report in Friday's paper, the report may well relate to conditions early in the week, which means that by the time you are on skis the report will be nearly a week old. In a week snow conditions can change dramatically – particularly late in the season.

The cost factor

For most people, the cost of a skiing holiday can be broken down into three parts – your package of transport, accommodation and perhaps meals; your skiing 'overheads' (equipment, lift pass, tuition); and incidentals (drinks, meals other than those included in the package).

Our studies of **package** prices lead us to the conclusion that it is difficult to generalise about which resorts or which countries are cheap and which expensive, and still more difficult to generalise about which places offer good and bad value for what you pay. So much depends on the particular deal assembled by the tour operator that even such plausible assertions as 'Italy is less expensive than Switzerland' are questionable – one of our reporters had a week in a catered chalet in a respectable Swiss resort in high season 1985 for £130 (including flight), which is difficult to beat.

Our reports on major resorts cover the **skiing overheads** in detail – we give the prices for equipment hire, lift pass and ski school for a six-day holiday. There are striking variations, but the differences are as pronounced between resorts as they are between countries. Big resorts which attract lots of keen skiers are able to get away with prices considerably higher than those of smaller places which are less in vogue.

Our reporters have assiduously noted all sorts of incidental costs in the resorts they visited in 1985. Comparisons are complicated by the fact that different countries are cheap and expensive in different ways, and a lot depends on how you adapt to local circumstances. If you insist on drinking a lot of wine in Switzerland, for example, you'll pay the price; and if you don't take to pasta in Italy you won't find the country nearly so cheap as those who do. Nevertheless, the overall picture (in 1985, using February 1985 exchange rates) is fairly clear: Austria and Italy are a lot cheaper than Switzerland and France – with Switzerland (just the most expensive) as much as 40 per cent dearer than Austria (the cheapest, by a small margin). Although comparisons with Britain are even more tricky, it's also pretty clear that prices at home come somewhere between the extremes, and nearer to France than to Italy.

THE 200 BEST SKI RESORTS IN EUROPE

For full **resort index** see pages 387–8

The heart of the *Guide* starts here. In this 330-page section, we describe and assess the 200 or so ski resorts in Europe which, one way or another, have the biggest claims on your attention – either because of their own qualities or because they give access to excellent skiing belonging to neighbouring resorts.

We have arranged the resorts geographically, without regard to nations or the alphabet. We're aware that some people like to decide first which country to go to, and then to choose within it – and our geographical order *will* be a bit painful if you're committed to pasta and Chianti. But countries other than Italy form almost solid blocks of the book, and the geographical order has the great advantage that it allows us to deal sensibly with the several shared ski areas which cross boundaries both alphabetical and national – chief among them the Portes du Soleil (France/Switzerland), the Milky Way (France/Italy) and the Matterhorn area, between Zermatt (Switzerland) and Cervinia (Italy). Even where there is not shared skiing, there is sense in choosing your resort in the knowledge of what other resorts nearby have to offer. The skier who likes to explore can easily run up against borders – from the Chamonix valley in France, for example, the sunny slopes of Courmayeur in Italy lie only half an hour away through the Mont Blanc Tunnel. If you want to know what lies over the hill, you need only look over the page.

There are several ways to find the resorts you might want to read about. Over the page, resorts are listed by chapter, in the order they appear. Then there's a series of maps – of Europe in general, and (in more detail) of the Alpine countries. After the maps, and immediately before the resorts themselves, comes a four-page chart summarising our verdicts on the major resorts we've covered. And finally, right at the end of the resorts section on page 387, is an alphabetical index.

Resorts chapter by chapter

The resorts are grouped into short chapters, which are ordered geographically, starting in north-east Italy and going through the Alps in an anti-clockwise sweep via Austria and Switzerland to France. Then comes Scotland, and finally the Pyrenees.

Major resorts – those which attract a lot of British visitors or which have undeniably major ski areas – are covered in detail, with information on lift passes, ski school and so on, as well as a full description of (and judgements on) the resort; the names of these resorts are printed in **bold type** below. Minor resorts, which are summarised in a few lines (or even a few words), appear in ordinary type below. The skiing of each major resort – and of most minor resorts linked in to a major area – is described in detail, and shown on a map; the key to these maps is on page 76.

The two final resort chapters, on Scotland and the Pyrenees, do not fit the same pattern. Each contains a general review of the style of resort to be found in those areas; in the Pyrenees we have concentrated on the specialised attractions of the duty-free state of Andorra, while the Scotland chapter inevitably consists mainly of an assessment of Aviemore, the only fully fledged Scottish ski resort.

In the list below, recognised names of ski areas are given in *italic type* after the resort names.

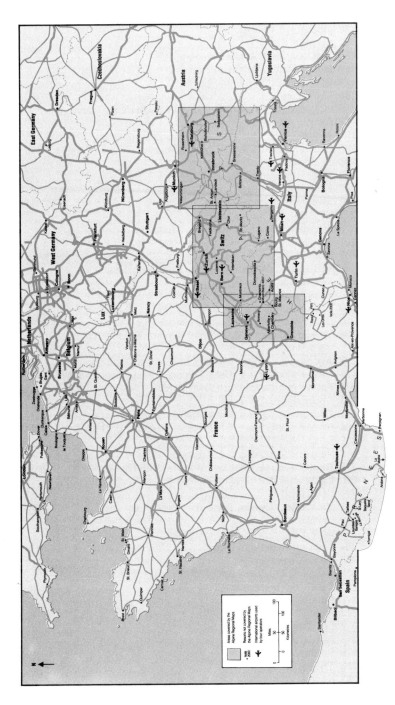

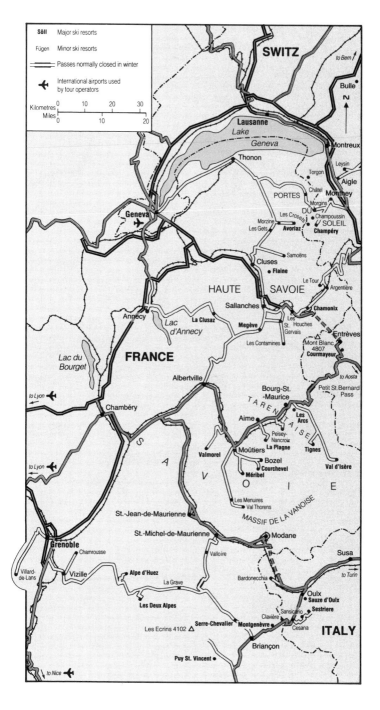

Legend

Söll — Major ski resorts

Fügen — Minor ski resorts

Passes normally closed in winter

International airports used by tour operators

Kilometres 0   10   20   30
Miles 0   10   20

SWITZ

to Bern

Bulle

N

Lausanne
Lake
Geneva

Montreux

Thonon

Leysin

Torgon

Aigle

Châtel

Monthey

PORTES

DU

Morgins

Les Crosets

Champoussin

SOLEIL

Morzine

Les Gets

Avoriaz

Champéry

Geneva

Samoëns

Cluses

• Flaine

Le Tour

Argentière

HAUTE   SAVOIE

Sallanches

Chamonix

Annecy

La Clusaz

Megève

Les
Houches

Entrèves

Lac
d'Annecy

St.
Gervais

Mont Blanc
4807

Les Contamines

Courmayeur

Lac du
Bourget

FRANCE

to Aosta

Albertville

Bourg-St.
-Maurice

Petit St.Bernard
Pass

to Lyon

Chambéry

T A R E N
Aime

Les
Arcs

Peisey-
Nancroix

S

Valmorel

Moûtiers

La Plagne

T A I S E

Tignes

to Lyon

Bozel

Courchevel

Val d'Isère

A

Méribel

V

Les Menuires

O   I   E

Val Thorens

St.-Jean-de-Maurienne

MASSIF DE LA VANOISE

St.-Michel-de-Maurienne

Modane

Grenoble

Chamrousse

Valloire

Susa

Villard-
de-Lans

Vizille

Alpe d'Huez

to Turin

La Grave

Bardonecchia

Les Deux Alpes

Oulx

Sauze d'Oulx

Sestriere

Sansicario

Clavière

Cesana

Les Ecrins 4102

Serre-Chevalier

Montgenèvre

ITALY

Briançon

to Nice

Puy St. Vincent

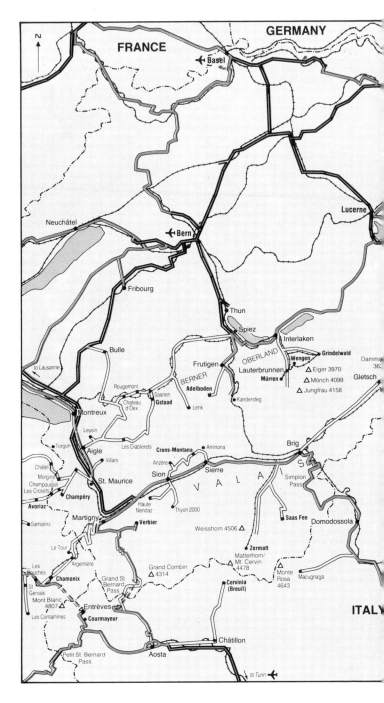

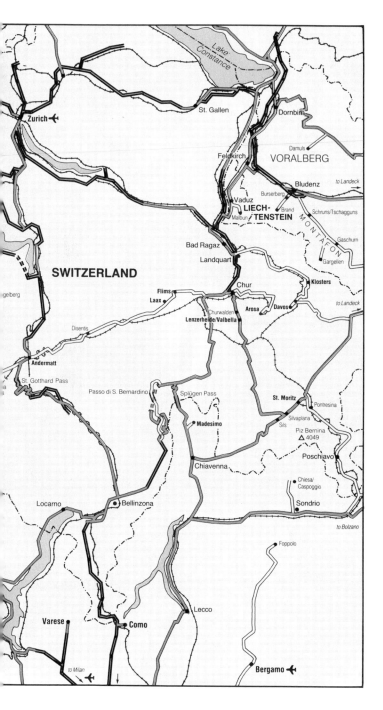

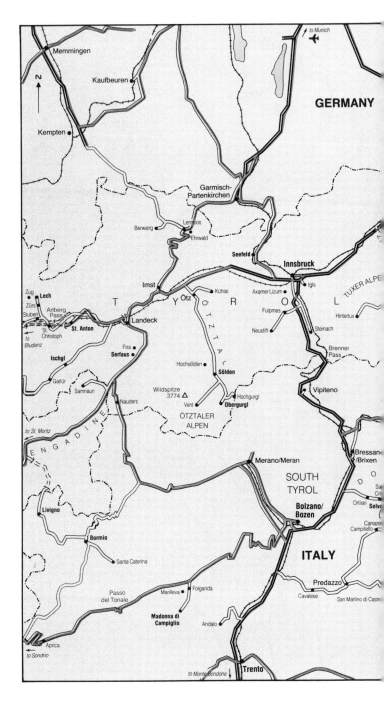

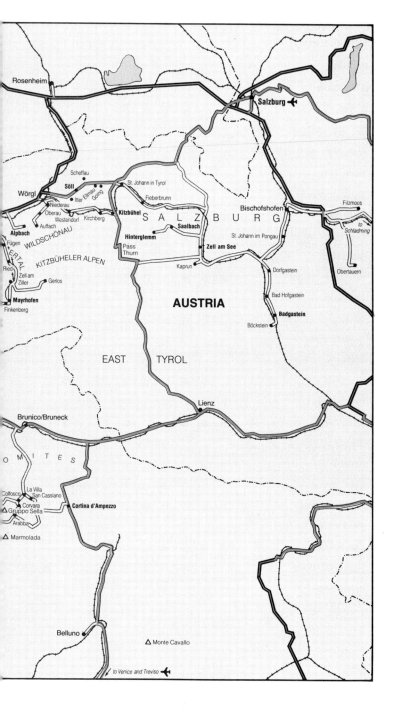

MAJOR RESORTS IN SUMMARY

- ⬤ (grey) Good
- ○ Adequate
- ● Bad

RESORT VERDICTS

Legend: **G** = Good, **○** = Adequate, **●** = Bad

	ALPBACH	ALPE D'HUEZ	ANDERMATT	LES ARCS	AROSA	AVORIAZ	BADGASTEIN	BORMIO	CERVINIA	CHAMONIX
Nursery slopes	○	G	●	○	G	G	●	○	G	●
Easy skiing	G	G	●	○	○	○	●	○	G	●
Big skiing area			G		G		G	G		G
Tough skiing	●	G	G	G	●	○	G	●	●	G
Off-piste skiing			G	G						G
Ski touring			G		G				G	G
Skiing convenience	●	●	●		●	G	●	●	●	●
Lift queues	○	○	●	G	○	○	●	●	●	●
Mountain restaurants	○	●	●	●	○	●	○	○	●	●
Beautiful scenery				G						G
Cross-country skiing					G					
Not skiing	○	●	●	●	G	●	G	G	●	○
Family skiing	G	G		G	G	G				
Alpine charm	G	●	G	●	○	●	●	○	●	○
Freedom from cars				G		G				
Après-ski	G	○	○	●	○	●	G	○	○	G
Short transfers	G	○	○	●	○	G	○	●	○	G
Easy road access	G	G	○	●	●	○	○	●	○	G
Rail access			G				G			G
Late holidays	●	G	○	G	○	○	○	●	G	G
Resort-level snow	○	G	G	G	G	G	●	●	G	●
Sunny skiing		G		G					G	
Self-catering				G		G				G
Chalet holidays										
Cheap alcohol										

Note In some categories, we use only the 'Good' rating – to pick out resorts which have something special to offer in that respect.

LA CLUSAZ	CORTINA D'AMPEZZO	COURCHEVEL	COURMAYEUR	CRANS-MONTANA	DAVOS	LES DEUX ALPES	FLAINE	FLIMS	GSTAAD	ISCHGL	ISOLA 2000	KITZBUHEL	KLOSTERS	LECH	LENZERHEIDE	LIVIGNO
○	◐	◐	●	◐	○	○	◐	○	○	●	◐	○	○	◐	○	◐
○	○	◐	●	○	○	○	◐	○	◐	●	○	○	○	◐	○	◐
	◐	◐			◐	◐	◐	◐		◐			◐	◐	◐	◐
●	●	○	●	●	○	◐	●	●	●	○	●	●	○	●	●	●
			◐		◐	◐										
			◐		◐											
●	●	◐	●	○	●	○	◐	●	●	○	◐	●	●	○	●	●
○	○	○	○	◐	●	○	○	○	○	●	○	●	●	●	○	●
○	◐	○	◐	○	○	●	●	○	◐	○	○	◐	◐	●	○	●
	◐	◐		◐	◐	◐				◐	◐		◐		◐	
○	◐	●	◐	◐	◐	●	●	◐	◐	○	●	◐	◐	○	◐	●
				◐		◐				◐			◐			
○	◐	●	○	●	●	●	●	○	◐	◐	●	◐	◐	◐	●	●
				◐			◐			●						
○	◐	◐	◐	◐	○	◐	●	●	○	◐	●	◐	●	○	●	○
◐	●	●	◐	○	○	○	◐	○	○	●	○	◐	○	○	○	●
◐	●	●	◐	○	○	◐	◐	○	○	○	●	◐	○	●	○	●
				◐	◐							◐	◐			
●	●	○	○	●	○	◐	◐	●	●	○	◐	●	○	○	○	◐
○	○	◐	○	●	○	◐	◐	●	○	○	◐	●	○	○	○	◐
				◐	◐			◐						◐	◐	◐
							◐			◐						
		◐														
										◐						◐

MAJOR RESORTS IN SUMMARY

● Good
○ Adequate
● Bad

Legend used below: **G** = Good, **A** = Adequate, **B** = Bad

RESORT VERDICTS

	MADESIMO	MADONNA DI CAMPIGLIO	MAYRHOFEN	MEGEVE	MERIBEL	MONTGENEVRE	OBERGURGL	LA PLAGNE	SAALBACH	SAAS FEE
Nursery slopes	B	G	G	A	B	A	A	G	A	G
Easy skiing	B	G	G	G	A	A	A	G	G	A
Big skiing area		G		G	G	G		G	G	
Tough skiing	G	B	B	B	A	A	B	B	B	A
Off-piste skiing								G		
Ski touring							G			
Skiing convenience	A	A	B	B	A	G	A	G	A	B
Lift queues	A	G	B	A	G	A	G	A	A	A
Mountain restaurants	A	G	A	G	A	A	A	B	A	A
Beautiful scenery		G		G						G
Cross-country skiing				G						
Not skiing	B	B	G	G	B	B	B	B	A	A
Family skiing		G						G		G
Alpine charm	B	A	G	G	A	A	G	B	A	G
Freedom from cars								G		G
Après-ski	B	A	G	G	B	B	G	B	G	B
Short transfers	B	B	A	G	B	A	B	B	A	B
Easy road access	B	B	G	G	A	A	B	B	A	B
Rail access			G							
Late holidays	A	B	A	B	A	B	G	G	A	G
Resort-level snow	A	A	B	B	A	A	G	G	A	A
Sunny skiing				G	G				G	
Self-catering					G			G		
Chalet holidays					G					
Cheap alcohol										

Note In some categories, we use only the 'Good' rating – to pick out resorts which have something special to offer in that respect.

ST ANTON	ST MORITZ	SAUZE D'OULX	SEEFELD	SELVA	SERFAUS	SERRE-CHEVALIER	SESTRIERE	SOLDEN	SOLL	TIGNES	VAL D'ISERE	VALMOREL	VERBIER	WENGEN	ZELL AM SEE	ZERMATT
●	●	○	○	◐	◐	○	◐	●	○	○	◐	◐	○	◐	●	●
●	○	○	○	○	◐	○	○	○	○	○	◐	○	●	◐	◐	○
◐	◐	◐		◐			◐	◐		◐	◐	◐		◐	◐	
◐	○	○	○	●	●	○	●	○	●	○	◐	●	◐	●	○	
●							◐				◐	◐		◐		◐
					◐								◐			◐
●	●	●	●	●	◐	○	◐	○	●	◐	○	◐	●	○	●	●
●	○	○	○	●	○	○	○	●	●	◐	◐		●	○	○	○
○	○	◐	○	◐	○	○	●	○	○	●	●	○	○	○	◐	◐
	◐			◐									◐	◐		◐
	◐		◐	◐	◐	◐										
●	◐	●	◐	○	○	●	●	●	○	●	●	●	●	◐	◐	○
					◐					◐		◐		◐		
○	○	●	○	●	◐	●	●	○	○	●	●	◐	○		○	◐
					◐								◐			◐
◐	◐	◐	○	◐	○	○	○	◐	◐	●	◐	●	◐	○		
○	●	○	◐	●	○	●	○	●	◐	●	●	○	○	●	○	●
◐	●	○	◐	●	●	●	○	○	◐	●	●	○	●	○	◐	●
◐	◐		◐										◐	◐	◐	◐
●	○	●	○	●	○	○	○	○	●	◐	◐	○	○	●	●	◐
○	◐	●	○	●	◐	●	◐	●	●	◐	◐	○	○	◐	●	○
◐	◐	◐											◐		◐	
										◐	◐		◐			
◐				◐							◐		◐	◐		◐

Reading a resort entry

Resorts in the Guide are divided into 'major' resorts and 'minor' ones.
These categories are not meant to indicate the size or the absolute
worth of any resort. Alpbach, although small, is a 'major' resort because
it attracts a great number of British skiers for very good reasons; Les
Menuires, which has much bigger and better skiing, is a 'minor' resort
because it has a very limited appeal.

In the first chapter, starting on the facing page, Selva is the major
resort. Its name is picked out in large type, and is followed by a list of
verdicts – the things it is 'good for' and 'bad for'. The summary chart on
the preceding pages compares the verdicts for different resorts.

Below the verdicts is list of minor resorts covered by the chapter, and
then a general summary of the area. Then follows a detailed description
of the major ski area, including the skiing of minor resorts provided it is
part of (or at least linked to) the major area. After that comes a
description of the major resort village or villages, with details of ski
school and so on. Finally there are brief descriptions of the significant
minor resort villages in the area; if their skiing is separate from that of
the major resort, this is where it will be described.

The skiing area of each major resort (and linked minor resorts) is
shown on a map. These maps are specially drawn to a consistent
scale, and use colour tints to show height above sea level – see the key
below. The arrows on the runs indicate the resorts' own gradings, not
our assessment of difficulty. The maps are meant to help you compare
resorts, not to find your way around the mountains.

Both the text and the maps are based on the 1984–85 ski season; but
where a new lift is virtually certain to be in place for the 1985–86
season, we have included it.

Two final points of clarification. When we say a resort is good for lift
queues, we don't mean that it's a resort where queues are easy to find;
we mean that from the queueing point of view it's a good resort. When
we talk about a run of 1600m vertical, we don't mean a mile-high
precipice; we mean that the bottom is 1600m lower than the top.

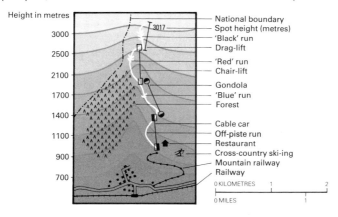

Super-scenery Dolomiti

Selva Italy 1550m

Good for *Big ski area, beautiful scenery, nursery slopes, cross-country skiing, mountain restaurants, après-ski, chalet holidays*
Bad for *Skiing convenience, Alpine charm, tough skiing, resort-level snow, late holidays, short airport transfers, lift queues, easy road access*

Linked resorts: Ortisei, Corvara, Canazei, San Cassiano, Arabba, Colfosco, Campitello, Santa Cristina, La Villa

For most British skiers, skiing in the Dolomites means skiing in the area around the massive Gruppo Sella, Europe's Table Mountain. The Sella Ronda is the name of the trip round the mountain. It is piste tourism at its most spectacular, with as much of the enjoyment coming from the dramatic spectacle of the changing landscape, like an Ice Age Grand Canyon, as from the skiing itself.

The Dolomites typically have gentle lower slopes surmounted by vertical cliffs, which means a large proportion of easy runs and a few extremely steep, narrow chutes between towers of rock, with few runs between the two extremes. Although the peaks are high, not much skiing takes place near the tops, and the range of altitude is not great. A more important reservation is that the Dolomites have an extremely erratic snow record. The area seems to inspire extremes of love and hate, and luck with the snow is probably the main reason.

Although the Sella region is entirely in Italy, holidays there have very little Italian about them. Much of the area was Austrian until 1918 (many villages have dual names as a result) and the area as a whole is dominated by car-borne visitors from Germany. Nightlife consists of beer-swilling and tea-dances to the sound of zither and squeeze-box. Standing slightly apart from most of the German-speaking Dolomites is the Val Gardena (Gröden), and particularly its main town of Ortisei, where the Ladin dialect and traditional crafts are proudly perpetuated.

It is not an area of big resorts. Accommodation is spread widely round the valleys in hamlets at the foot of the slopes or in complete isolation – clean, simple b&b houses and new chalet-style hotels. The Val Gardena does have two large resorts. Ortisei (St Ulrich) is a long-established town of considerable charm which is off the main Sella Ronda circuit. The major resort is Selva (Wolkenstein), a disappointingly ugly and characterless place, with no centre and no style; it is inconveniently arranged, but is a good base for exploring the region. There are lots of long and challenging runs on the local slopes, and both après-ski and accommodation are plentiful and varied. Unfortunately snow conditions on Selva's rocky, windswept slopes are all too often highly unpleasant, making it a less convenient base for moderate skiers than Corvara, the most major of the minor resorts encircling the

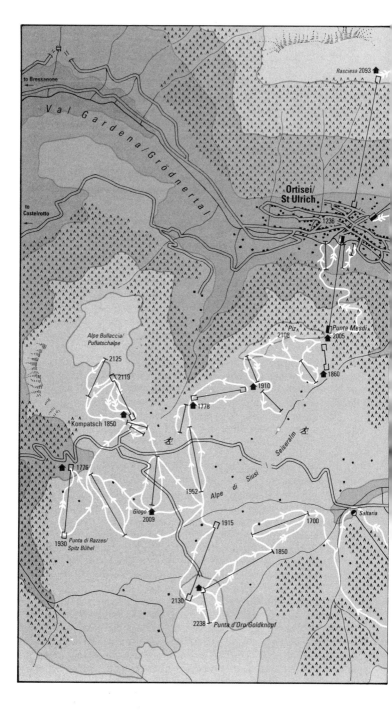

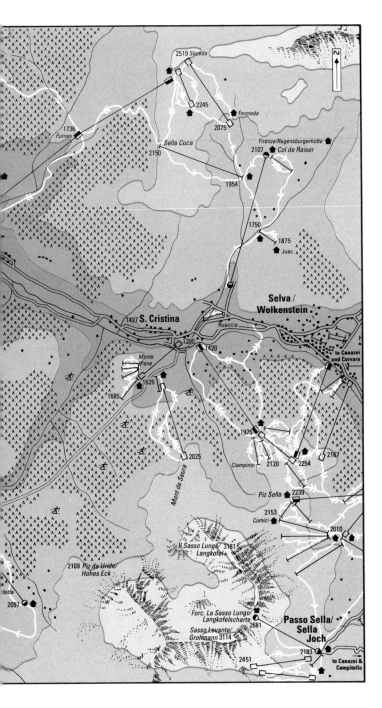

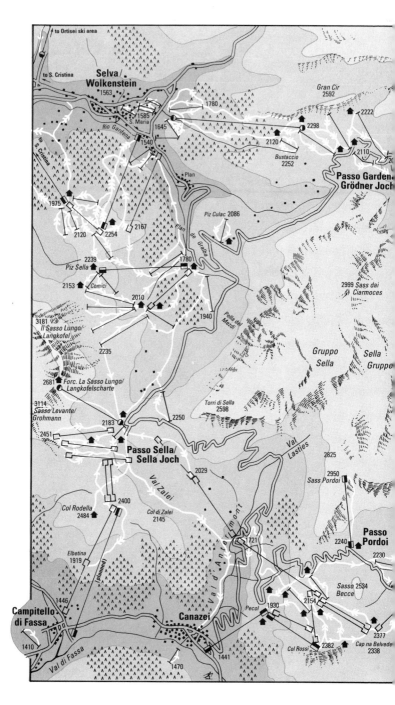

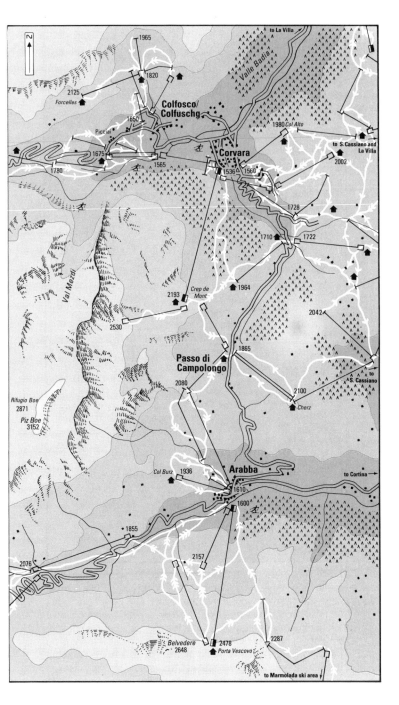

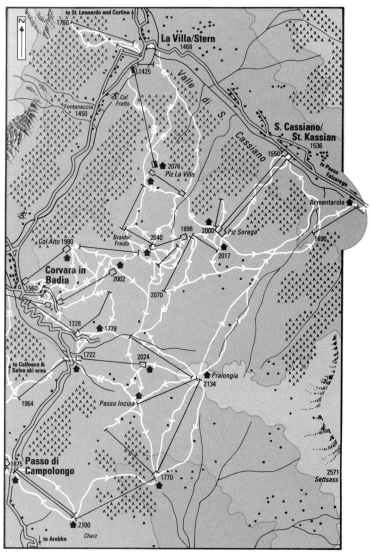

Alta Badia region, with its infinity of blue runs. For good skiers the choice destination is Arabba, which has skiing on a big, steep, north-facing mountain looming above the resort.

The Sella Ronda can now be skied in either direction. Either way, it consists predominantly of easy blue runs; the red sections are not very severe, but poor snow conditions may make them difficult – there is no escaping south-facing slopes at some stage. The tour involves about 20km of uphill transport, and 26km and 4000m vertical of skiing. It takes about five hours, not allowing for queues or rests.

The skiing top 2950m bottom 1225m

Ortisei: Alpe di Siusi A cable-car from the southern edge of the town scales a very steep wooded mountainside. The only run down is an unpleasant red-graded track engineered into the face, with netting to protect skiers from long drops. The cable-car delivers you to Punta Mesdi (2006m), on the rim of the remarkable Alpe di Siusi (Seiseralm) – a broad, high, gently-sloping basin which claims to be the biggest alp (in its sense of high pasture) in the Alps. Behind Punta Mesdi there is an extensive, confusing and incompletely linked arrangement of short drags and chair-lifts which make it just about possible to ski down to a collection of hotels at 1850m and join up with some longer lifts on the other side of the basin with a top station of 2238m. Nearly all the skiing is extremely gentle, and getting from lift to lift involves walking, or at least strenuous skating and poling.

The Alpe di Siusi is an idyllic area for the under-confident and for those who enjoy pottering around in beautiful mountain surroundings, with sleigh rides, extensive cross-country trails, walking paths and dozens of hotels and restaurants dotted around the spacious sunny slopes. From the top of the gondola, beneath the towering silhouette of the double-barrelled Sasso Lungo, it is possible to ski across through the woods to Monte Pana above S Cristina.

Ortisei/Santa Cristina: Seceda Two lifts from the edge of the town give access to south and south-west facing slopes with runs which are long by Dolomite standards, but which very often lack snow and are little skied. The long two-stage cable-car to Seceda may involve long waits for a quorum to assemble, even in high season. The top section scales an impressive cliff to the main skiing area – south-facing slopes above the Col Raiser and S Cristina offering open intermediate skiing and advanced sunbathing, with several very welcoming restaurant chalets. Below Col Raiser there is a single easy run down to the edge of S Cristina; it is also possible to ski (off-piste) to the edge of Selva. There is one long run back to Ortisei, skirting the rock face with a narrow path and running on through the woods easily and very prettily.

Santa Cristina: Monte Pana This small community of hotels and restaurants is reached by road or chair-lift from S Cristina, with a fan of nursery lifts and a stand-up bucket lift which serves two short woodland runs (black and red) which in themselves hardly merit a detour. There is no marked run down to S Cristina.

Santa Cristina/Selva: Ciampinoi Cable-cars from the edge of S Cristina and the centre of Selva (and a less busy chair-lift) give access to this splendid skiing mountain – one of the best in the Dolomites, with a spray of broad, long, challenging north-facing runs cut through the woods below its bald, rounded peak. Unfortunately, the top is often windswept and presents a treacherous combination of ice and stones. There is no easy way down, except on the top half of the S Cristina run. From Ciampinoi and from Piz Sella at the top of the Plan de Gralba skiing it is possible to ski round to Monte Pana. Although signposted at the top, this pleasant ski-ramble is not easy to follow.

Selva: Plan de Gralba/Passo Sella Plan de Gralba (1780m) can be reached either by bus in a few minutes from Selva, or via Ciampinoi. The skiing route gets a lot of sun, is rarely in good condition, and is usually crowded, which adds to the difficulty of negotiating the ice and stones and roots. It is quite steep enough for long falls. Plan de Gralba is a roadside skiing service area with one network of short, easy intermediate runs linked to another higher, bleak and windswept one above the Sella Pass between 2200 and 2500m. The landscape above Plan de Gralba is pleasantly wooded, with restaurants and an outdoor ice bar. Unfortunately the peaks of the Sasso Lungo block out the sun early in the afternoon. There is a very easy run beside the road to Selva, skirting the Ciampinoi mountain. The link from Plan de Gralba to Passo Sella is called Rock City or the Moon Walk – a track through a chaos of enormous boulders and does indeed involve some walking. It finishes at the foot of the Sasso Lungo bucket lift which climbs to a refuge in a narrow breach between two of the pinnacles of the jagged mountain. The notorious run back down is a steep, narrow slope – not exceedingly difficult in good snow, but a dangerous slope on which to fall. Much less often skied and less steep is the wild and beautiful run down behind the mountain to Monte Pana. Lifts have recently been installed, to complete the link in both directions between Passo Sella and the Canazei skiing area at Pecol via Lupo Bianco (1721m), a roadside restaurant.

Selva: Dantercepies The Dantercepies gondola goes from the top end of Selva to 2298m above Passo Gardena, serving a couple of long and satisfying red runs back to Selva and a more challenging narrow unofficial run between the pylons. This is splendid skiing in good snow conditions.

Colfosco From the top of the Dantercepies lift a very long, very gentle run drops down to the lifts and pistes of Colfosco, much of it a straight schuss. The last kilometre to Corvara is almost flat; many skiers take the chair-lift in both directions. Set apart from this main skiing thoroughfare, the little village of Colfosco has its own nursery area and a few attractive runs above it between 2125m and 1650m, served by a series of drag-lifts. This is a secluded ski area with enjoyable intermediate runs and a particularly delightful sun-soaked bar among the trees at the top. We saw no sign of a black run down from the top to the road above Colfosco, as indicated on some maps.

Corvara: Boe On the western side of the road over Passo Campolongo a chain of lifts provides connections to and from Arabba, which are quick unless there are morning queues for the Boe cable-car at Corvara. The runs to Arabba face south and tend to be icy in the mornings; apart from this there is no great difficulty about the skiing, although most of it is graded red. The long run down to Corvara beneath the Boe cable-car is wide and fast. The blackness of the run down from the top chair is mainly to do with its being unprepared.

Corvara: Alta Badia The bulk of Corvara's skiing is the wide area east of the Campolongo road which Corvara shares with the smaller villages of La Villa and San Cassiano. The not very high, round-topped, wooded mountain is covered with little drags and chair-lifts and what seems like an endless number of very gentle runs, individually short but adding up to a great deal of skiing. The main problem is that in a number of places the pistes have to be walked. The great exception is the excellent north-facing black run above La Villa of nearly 700m vertical – there is also a challenging red variant. At the other end of the web of lifts and runs, the area around Pralongia and Cherz is always uncrowded. This provides an alternative, slower way to and from Arabba.

Arabba The attraction of this small area is a series of long, steep, north-facing runs on a wide, fragmented mountainside served by a cable-car which climbs nearly 900m from the village to the Porta Vescovo (2478m). Arabba tends to get very crowded, especially when conditions elsewhere are generally poor. A two-stage chair-lift has been installed to relieve the cable-car and to enable moderate skiers to proceed towards Pordoi without tackling the slightly daunting slope, often icy and stony, at the top of the cable-car. The grading of the various runs to Arabba varies from map to map. They are in practice all excellent, challenging descents, black or stiff red in difficulty. The top station of the cable-car commands a magnificent view southwards to the grand, glacier-covered northern flank of the highest mountain in the Dolomites, the Marmolada (3344m), which provides a huge area of late-season and summer skiing. A new chain of lifts gives access via Passo Padon to the sunny slopes above Marmolada's resort, Malga Ciapela. They are covered by the lift pass, but the Marmolada isn't.

Passo Pordoi As well as being the link between Arabba and Canazei, Pordoi has a cable-car which climbs very steeply up to 2950m. This is the only lift which penetrates the fortifications of the mighty Gruppo Sella. It serves no pistes, but several notorious runs. The obvious one is the Forcella, under the cable-car. This faces due south and includes a narrow, very steep top section which must very often be dangerously icy or bare, as we found it. Longer off-piste routes include the Val Lasties down to the near the Lupo Bianco restaurant and lifts; and the Val de Mesdi, the great adventure which involves a 45-minute walk across the massif, before entering a very long, enclosed north-facing valley which drops, steeply in parts, down towards Colfosco.

Canazei The local skiing is confined to the open, not very large, north-west-facing bowl above Pecol (1933m), reached either by road or by cable-car. The top of the skiing is 2426m, so runs served by the fan of lifts up to the rim of the bowl are not long. They are mostly of intermediate difficulty with a couple of short nursery lifts. There is a long, gentle but often unskiable descent to Canazei via Lupo Bianco.

   Nursery slopes in Selva itself are excellent, provided snow conditions are good – a wide open area near the resort centre and beneath the Dantercepies lifts. Unfortunately the slopes and lifts are often busy with skiers in transit. Alpe de Siusi is ideal for inexperienced skiers as is the Alta Badia area as a whole.

   Mountain restaurants are one of the great joys of skiing in the Dolomites. There are plenty of them, the views are beautiful, most of them are very welcoming and prices are generally reasonable. The Alta Badia and Val Gardena are better provided with restaurants than the Val di Fassa and Arabba.

Lifts

Passes All lifts covered by the Superski Dolomiti pass, but no bus services. Various local passes are available.	**Cost** 6-day Superski Dolomiti L136,000. 20% off in low season. **Beginners** Coupons. **Children** 30% off under 14.

The worst lift bottle-necks are at Selva (Ciampinoi cable-car and Dantercepies gondola), S Cristina (Ruaccia cable-car) and Corvara (Boe cable-car) where morning queues of at least half an hour are common in season. The Porta Vescovo at Arabba gets particularly crowded in the late morning and early afternoon, especially when conditions elsewhere in the region are poor. The return from Corvara to Selva is a very tedious series of lifts, often with queues for each.

The resort

Selva is a long shapeless village which suffers from having grown along the road. From the centre it extends far down towards S Cristina with an interrupted succession of shops and hotels and a spread of chalets set back from the road. It has no very obvious village character and there are hardly any old buildings, but when full in winter it is a lively place. Snow permitting, it is possible to ski back from Ciampinoi and Dantercepies to within easy reach of most parts of the village.

Accommodation is mainly in modern comfortable hotels, none of them very stylish, and simple b&b houses; staffed chalet accommodation is offered by a few companies. The Aaritz (𝒪 75011) and Antares (𝒪 75400) are comfortable, expensive hotels near the Ciampinoi lift. Even better placed for access to both Ciampinoi and the Costabella chair-lift (for lazy access to Dantercepies) are the comfortable, functional Laurin (𝒪 75105) and the Genziana (𝒪 75187) and, more cheaply, the large and fairly simple Stella (𝒪 75162). The Posta (𝒪 75174) is one of the most attractive and oldest hotels, and one of the least conveniently situated.

Après-ski is one of Selva's main advantages over the other mostly small and peaceful resorts in the Sella area. There are several discothèques (reporters recommend the Club Stella), one or two places with live music, and plenty of bars and inexpensive restaurants.

Ski school

Classes 3hr, mornings only. **Cost** 6 days L95,000. Private lessons L21,000/hr.	**Children** Ski kindergarten, ages 4–12, 10.00–6.00, 6 days with lunch L160,000. Non-ski kindergarten, ages 2–4, 10.00–4.00, 6 days L120,000.

Other activities

Cross-country 12km trail in Vallunga with abbreviations to create shorter trails. 2km easy trail at La Selva (on edge of resort). **Not skiing** Natural ice rink, swimming/	sauna/solaria (hotels open to non-residents), sleigh rides, curling, bowling alley, extensive walking paths around Selva and above S Cristina and Ortisei, ski-bob permitted on most runs.

Selva lacks the charm factor, but in most respects the Val Gardena as a whole is excellent for cross-country and non-skiers.

Travel

Airport Munich or Milan; transfers about 5hr.
Road Via Munich, Brenner, Bressanone; chains occasionally needed.

Railway Chiusa (27km); frequent buses.
Reachable resorts Cortina is within day-trip range, particularly from Arabba.

Skiers have to make full use of the valley bus services – frequent between Ortisei and Selva and Plan de Gralba, less so up to the passes to link up with services in other valleys. The competition for places is tough. There are no evening services. Driving from one place to another is usually not much quicker than travelling on skis.

Miscellaneous

Tourist office ✆ (471) 75122. Tx 400359.
Medical Fracture clinic, doctors, chemists in resort; dentist at Ortisei, hospital at Bolzano (42km).
Package holidays CW, JM, SMW.

Equipment hire 6 days skis L30,000–90,000, boots L12,000–21,000, X-C L36,000.
Resort beds 4,000 in hotels, 3,500 in apartments.

Minor resorts

Ortisei 1240m

The main town in the Val Gardena is charming but not convenient as a base for keen Alpine skiers, and is neglected in winter, at least by the British. But the Alpe di Siusi, reached either by road from Castelrotto or by cable-car from Ortisei, is unbeatable for beautiful walks, sleigh rides and cross-country skiing at high altitude. Ortisei is also well-placed for excursions to the Adige Valley reaching as far as Verona. There is a local museum as well as a display of religious wood-carving for which the valley is famous. Another tradition which adds to the charm of the village streets is ice sculpture.

The town centre is by-passed by the main valley road, but this busy highway still has to be crossed on foot to get to and from the ice rink and Alpe di Siusi cable-car. The main street is a long one and includes a short, fairly steep hill between the church and main square and bus terminal. As in Selva, staying in Ortisei usually involves quite a lot of tiresome walking. Ortisei nightlife is less lively than Selva's but there are some good bars and restaurants, especially the delightful Zur Traube/all'Uva, and a discothèque. A local passion is ice hockey; there are often evening league matches. Most of the many hotels in the centre of the resort are simple, except for the smart and expensive Adler (✆ 76203). Opposite it is the Posta (✆ 76392), a large, solid, central old village hotel. The Snaltnerhof (✆ 76746) is simple, inexpensive and welcoming, and very well placed beside the main bus stop. The Alpe di Siusi offers varying degrees of retreat. The main community is Kompatsch, at the top of the road up from Castelrotto, where there are several hotels, a ski school with kindergarten and a skating rink. Two large, comfortable and secluded hotels are the Floralpina (✆ 72907) at the S Cristina end, and the Sonne (✆ 76377) near the top of the cable-car from Ortisei.

Tourist office ✆ (471) 76328. Tx 400305.

Arabba 1600m

A small village which is the best resort in the area for good skiers, unless they want a choice of après-ski as well. There is nothing much to do except ski, eat and sleep, apart from one discothèque ('small, friendly, plenty of atmosphere', according to one reporter who visited in low season). Most British visitors stay in chalets; there are a few hotels (none of them very expensive) and a number of b&b houses. Getting to and from ski-lifts never involves much walking. The Sport Hotel Arabba (∅ 79158) is about the most comfortable hotel. The Posta (∅ 79105) is simpler, cheaper, older and more friendly.

Tourist Office ∅ (436) 79130. Tx 440823. Package holidays SMW.

Corvara 1550m

The main resort of the Alta Badia area and probably the best location on the Sella Ronda for skiers who want a lot of open skiing and the best chance of good snow conditions close at hand. Selva and Arabba are easily reached and the most remote segment of the available skiing (Canazei) is the least interesting for intermediate skiers.

The village is a characterless sprawl of modern chalets and chalet-style hotels large and small, spread across a large area beside the roads down from the Gardena and Campolongo passes. The centre and most convenient place to stay is near the Col Alto chair-lift (for access to the Alta Badia which is a manageable walk from the Boe cable-car (for Arabba) and the scene of most of Corvara's limited après-ski. This usually includes dancing (at tea-time and in the evening) at the Posta (∅ 83175), the biggest, smartest and most central of the hotels (pool and sauna). The Veneranda (∅ 83127) and Fortuna (∅ 83043) are much smaller and less expensive and are also very conveniently placed. There is a short cross-country track between the Boe cable-car and Colfosco and an ice rink with facilities for curling on the edge of the village.

Tourist office ∅ (471) 83176.

Colfosco 1650m

A small holiday village which has grown up beside the road between Corvara and the Gardena Pass with easy access to Selva and Corvara and a small skiing area of its own (including a good nursery area) beside the village. There are a couple of plush, modern, expensive hotels at the top of the village of which one, the Kolfuschgerhof (∅ 83188), boasts a swimming pool and squash court. Most hotels are more modest; the Centrale (∅ 83118) is large and comfortable and, as it sounds, well placed for skiing and also for après-ski.

Tourist office ∅ (471) 83145. Package holidays SCG, SMW.

San Cassiano 1537m

A small roadside village in typical Dolomite style with a lot of mostly new chalet buildings, largely consisting of hotels and b&b houses. San Cassiano has some of the best of the local skiing for beginners and timid skiers who can enjoy the very long, easy runs down to the village itself from Pralongia and from Piz Sorega before venturing further afield. The Rosa Alpina (✆ 84500) is a large, comfortable, modern hotel (with pool) at the centre of the village and the focus of après-ski (live bands afternoon and evening). There are some cross-country possibilities at Armentarola, a cluster of quiet hotels and restaurants about 1km east. Cortina is less than an hour away via Valparola and Falzarego passes – a spectacular drive through a rocky wilderness.

Tourist office ✆ (471) 84422. Package holidays SMW.

Canazei 1440m

Canazei is a large, noisy village with the busy main Val di Fassa road running through the middle of it. It is the only real alternative to the Val Gardena for skiers wanting varied off-slope activities and plenty of nightlife. Its local skiing is inconvenient and limited, but once on the slopes (only by the cable-car, which is a long walk from the resort centre, and often crowded), it doesn't take long to reach Arabba.

The village centre is an attractive jumble of busy narrow streets with some rustic old buildings as well as new hotels and shopping precincts which have sprung up with the Dolomites' tourist boom. There are plenty of bars, restaurants and evening entertainment (mostly hotel-oriented), with discos and jokey contests. There is a large public pool/sauna, a natural ice rink beside an attractive wooded playground in the centre, and a long chain of cross-country trails (mostly easy) along the shady side of the river. The Val di Fassa hosts a 70km X-C marathon (the Marcialongo) between Canazei and Cavalese; some stretches of the course are open only at the time of the race.

In the centre, the Croce Bianca (✆ 61111) is a long-established hotel, substantial and comfortably redecorated. The Bellevue (✆ 61104) is better placed for the cable-car. The Laurin (✆ 61286) is on the wrong side of town for skiing purposes, but is otherwise attractive.

Two hotels offer greater skiing convenience. The Bellavista (✆ 61165) is at Pecol, near the top of the Canazei cable-car – a comfortable and friendly hotel. Higher up (2100m), the inexpensive 80-year-old Pordoi (✆ 61115) is somewhat spartan. A new self-catering annexe with pool and sauna has recently been opened.

Tourist office ✆ (462) 61113.

Campitello 1440m

Canazei's close neighbour is a quieter and much smaller village, its centre set back from the main road, an attractive collection of old buildings beside a stream running down into the main river. Its main ski-lift is the slow two-stage chair-lift to Col Rodella above the Sella Pass, soon to be replaced by a cable-car. For the time being the Monti Pallidi (✆ 61139) is the most convenient place to stay, at the top of the village beside the chair-lift. There are adequate shopping facilities in the village, and we are informed that there is nightlife too, in the Fummelbunker, which roughly translated means the Grope Hole. There are secluded nursery slopes in the valley, conditions permitting. There are no pistes down to Campitello; returning via the chair-lift is much more relaxing than the struggle back through Canazei.

Tourist office ✆ (462) 61137.

Ageing beauty

Cortina d'Ampezzo Italy 1230m

Good for *Nursery slopes, big ski area, mountain restaurants, beautiful scenery, après-ski, cross-country skiing, not skiing*
Bad for *Tough skiing, skiing convenience, late holidays, short airport transfers, easy road access, local transport*

Cortina is Italy's most fashionable ski resort and, unlike many Dolomite resorts, thoroughly Italian in atmosphere and style. It is one of the most remote resorts for visitors from north and west, and although it is very cosmopolitan the bulk of its clientèle is cosmopolitan Italians. It hosted the 1956 winter Olympics and ranks with St Moritz and Chamonix as one of the most complete wintersports resorts in the world. Its downhill skiing is excellent, with some of the best nursery slopes anywhere and some long, challenging runs for good skiers, all in dramatically beautiful scenery. Much of the most recent development of the resort was generated by the Olympics, and it is showing its age. It is a large sunny town in a wide valley with separate skiing areas spread around the surrounding mountains, and travelling between them is tiresome.

Cortina has a very glamorous reputation which may deter skiers who look to Italy for informal, cheap holidays. For a short high season (New Year and mid-February) there are plenty of beautiful people to match the shop windows, but it is not an exclusive or uniformly expensive resort: there are plenty of small, attractive, not outrageously expensive hotels, and simple, friendly bars full of character as well as the expensive restaurants and nightclubs.

The skiing top 2930m bottom 1220m

The skiing is typical of the Dolomites in being broken up by cliff faces. There are excellent open fields of very easy runs and a few steep and narrow gullies which verge on the extreme. Between the two there is a variety of intermediate skiing, and longer runs than in any of the other Dolomite resorts. The main Tofana skiing area is west of the town, served by two stages of a three-stage cable-car. On the other side of the large resort the Staunies and Faloria areas are just about linked, despite the road between them. They provide a few interesting runs, but do not add up to a very satisfactory network. A long way out of town, by the Passo Falzarego, are several lifts which do not add greatly to the quantity of skiing available, but are well worth visiting for a change of spectacular scenery.

The bottom station of the **Tofana** cable-car is a long walk from the centre of the resort. Between the resort and Col Druscie (1774m) the cable-car goes over gentle woodlands and open fields with wide, easy trails complicated only by several danger points where piste crosses

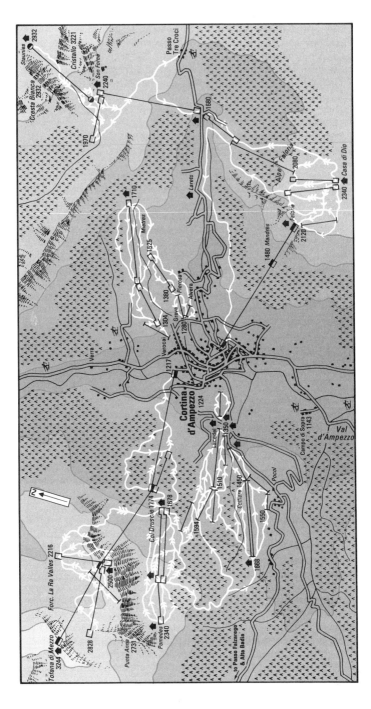

rough roads with unobtrusive warnings for skiers and drivers which are easily missed. Snow conditions often make these home runs more difficult than they are graded (blue/green). The second stage of the cable-car climbs an impressively steep and rocky mountain side to Ra Valles in the middle of an excellent sheltered bowl of intermediate runs between 2828m (the top of the skiing on this side of the valley) and 2216m. The top section of the cable-car serves no skiing but is popular for sun-bathing and limitless views. Near the bottom of the bowl there is a breach in the rock which allows skiers a narrow path down; there is a fairly steep south-facing stretch in the middle of this, and timid skiers should take the cable-car down in poor conditions. The run ends up at the bottom of the Pomedes chair-lifts, about 100m lower than Col Druscei, which is set on a little peak. You get up to it by skiing on down to another chair-lift which itself has an interesting short black run underneath it. The Pomedes chair-lifts, which can usually be reached by car, add an excellent variety of more or less direct runs underneath the lifts (mostly red but with blackish bits), including the spectacular downhill race-course which starts down a narrow *canalone* between massive pillars of rock. There is also a very long circuitous blue trail from the middle station. The Pomedes runs and lifts link up with the splendid open skiing above Pocol and Lacedel, a vast area of very easy and nursery slopes, usually referred to by the general name of Socrepes. This area is hardly ever plagued by fast skiers.

A slow cable-car goes up to **Faloria** from the ring road, the first stage over flat ground, the second over a cliff to 2120m. There are no runs under the cable-car, but an area of short intermediate runs beyond it, including several challenging pitches. You can ski through attractive woods to the Tre Croci road at Rio Gere, either directly from Faloria, or with less effort by means of a little-used red run from Tondi.

On the other side of the Tre Croci road the south-facing slopes at the foot of the **Staunies** are are served by a slow and long chair-lift up to the foot of the cliffs of the Cristallo massif. The run back down is wide and easy. A gondola lift goes up to Staunies, one of the dramatic, steep chutes which are so characteristic of the Dolomites. The run starts narrowly and steeply, faces south and is often unskiable. Its beauty is rather spoilt by lift pylons. The way back to Cortina is a long, easy piste beside the Tre Croci road. There is no link with the extensive area of easy runs served by a number of lifts beneath **Mietres**.

An isolated two-stage chair-lift (1900–2400m) beside the road up to Falzarego serves the intermediate runs of **Cinque Torri**, either side amid beautiful scenery; the slopes face north and are little skied, so snow conditions are usually good.

One of the Dolomites' extremely dramatic cable-cars soars up a cliff face from the Falzarego Pass (2105m) to **Lagazuoi** (2746m). The run back down is mostly blueish in difficulty with a short red section in the middle. Much more worthwhile is the run down the back to Armentarola, near San Cassiano in the Alta Badia (see the previous chapter). This is an 11km run of no great technical difficulty, but wild and exceedingly beautiful, and punctuated by restaurants. There are occasional buses from Cortina and Armentarola to Falzarego.

Nursery slopes (and long green runs for early post-nursery stages) are excellent. Most beginners use the very extensive Socrepes area above the Falzarego road. Pierosa and Mietres area is equally broad and gentle and even more secluded – not linked with any other ski area and not served by bus.

Mountain restaurants are plentiful in all the skiing areas, mostly excellent and not particularly expensive. There are particularly delightful restaurants in the Pomedes/Col Druscie area and above Faloria. There are several expensive restaurants for serious gastronomic lunches near the Socrepes lifts, notably El Camineto.

Lifts

Passes Superski Dolomiti Pass covers all lifts. Local pass for Cortina area available. Passes include ski bus but no other bus services.

Cost 6-day Superski pass L136,000. 20% off in low season.
Children 30% off up to 14.
Beginners Coupons.

Cortina's skiing is very far from being a unified system, and getting from one place to another can be extremely time-consuming. That apart, there are no major problems. In particular, high-season morning queues for the Tofana cable-car are not as serious as you might expect. Cortina skiers are notorious late risers. The Faloria cable-car is inefficient, but there is not much demand for it.

The resort

Cortina is a handsome small town of 8,500 inhabitants set in a beautiful broad bowl. The centre is a crossroads, not of very major routes, but there is plenty of through, as well as local, traffic. The attractive main street, Corso Italia, is sheltered from this as a pedestrian precinct, and traffic streams round a central one-way circuit. There are lots of very stylish shop windows and elegant people strolling up and down in the early evening. Outside the centre the resort spreads widely up and down the valley, with comfortable chalets beside the main road out towards Dobbiaco, and some development across the river on the hill which climbs more steeply up towards Falzarego.

Accommodation consists of a great variety of hotels from international conference comfort to very simple, and large numbers of private apartments and chalets, usually empty. The most attractive hotel is the absolutely central, comfortable Poste (∅ 4271), right at the heart of fashionable Cortina life. Also comfortable, central and stylish, but cheaper, is the Parc Victoria (∅ 3246). Two small, attractive chalet hotels within walking distance of the main cable-car are the Capannina (∅ 2950), with a well reputed restaurant, and the inexpensive Barisetti (∅ 2491). Although its position is not convenient, the Menardi (∅ 2400) is highly recommended – attractive, friendly, medium price; the ski-bus passes within easy walking distance. The Montana (∅ 3366) is one of the cheapest and most central b&b hotels. The Fiames (∅ 2366) is a very simple hotel, placed conveniently for the cross-country trails.

Après-ski is very varied, but evenings are generally quiet outside high season. There are a dozen discothèques, and numerous bars with a lot of character – the Poste hotel bar being the smartest rendezvous in the early evening. There are also several excellent restaurants outside hotels, notably the Meloncino, and the very expensive Toula, both beside the road up towards Falzarego, and in hotels (the Capannina and the Da Beppe Sello). Occasionally there is an ice disco on the Olympic rink, and evening bobsleigh practice to watch.

Ski school

Classes 9.15–noon, noon–2.00, or 2.00–4.30.
Cost 6 days (mornings only) L100,000.

Private lessons L26,000/hr.
Children Ski kindergarten at Pierosa nursery area – no non-ski kindergarten.

This is the main ski school with an office in the centre of the resort, and a meeting place for adult beginners at the Socrepes lift. There is a smaller ski school (the Azzurra Cortina) with an office at the foot of the Faloria cable-car. Prices are similar, classes are mornings only.

Other activities

Cross-country Extensive trails, total length 74km, of varying difficulty (graded green, red and black) in the valley north of Cortina, with a base and ski school and equipment rental facilities

at Fiames (3km from Cortina).
Not skiing Artificial ice-rink (skating/curling), swimming, tennis, saunas, sleigh rides, riding, ski-bobbing, 6km walking paths.

The cross-country trails are long and beautiful and varied, although Fiames is a long way from central Cortina and the trails do not link with any of the Alpine skiing areas. About half of the 74km of trails consists of the run to Dobbiaco, following the old railway track. There is a marathon in early February, ending in the Corso Italia. There are good walks along the valley and to restaurants in the skiing area. Excursions are easily arranged around the Dolomites and to Venice. The resort is varied, interesting and colourful, with an excellent skating rink.

Travel

Airport Venice; transfer 3hr.
Railway Calalzo (30km) or Dobbiaco (32km); frequent buses.

Road Via Munich, Brenner, Dobbiaco; chains occasionally needed.
Reachable resorts The Sella Ronda resorts are within reach for day-trips.

The ski-bus service consists of two buses circling anti-clockwise continuously between the two cable-cars. The service is reported to be erratic, stops for lunch and leaves many parts of the resort unserved. Other bus services from the centre have to be paid for, apart from the morning bus up to Pocol for ski school. Having a car is extremely useful, although parking in the centre is difficult.

Miscellaneous

Tourist office ✆ (436) 3231. Tx 440004.
Equipment hire 6 days skis L60,000, boots L30,000, X-C L36,000.
Resort beds 4,500 in hotels; 18,000 in apartments.

Medical Hospital at Calalzo (30km); fracture clinic, doctors, chemists, dentists in resort.
Package holidays CI.

Dolomite backwater

San Martino di Castrozza
Italy 1450m

San Martino, one of the largest and southernmost Dolomite resorts, is comparable to Cortina in many ways. It has a chic reputation which is now quite unfounded, and is an attractive, all-Italian resort, neglected internationally but far from negligible in terms of skiing and entertainment value. Our two reporters found that the friendliness of the resort outweighed its disadvantages, notably the layout – it is built along the road which descends steeply to the south of Passo Rolle. The setting is open and sunny, amid forests beneath the towering pinnacles of the Pale di San Martino – outstandingly beautiful even by Dolomite standards. The village is neither offensive nor charming. Around the church and river bridge is a cluster of shops, bars and hotels – many of the older ones distinctly dowdy.

There are four ski areas, of which only one is within walking distance of the centre. At the top of the village, where there are good nursery slopes and a kindergarten, a chair-lift to **Col Verde** (1930m) serves blue and red runs back to the resort. The spectacular cable-car to **Rosetta** (2639m) serves an adventure run down to Col Verde.

Tognola, below the resort, is the most popular area, and the long gondola from Fratazza (1400m) to the splendid sunny belvedere of Alpe di Tognola (2165m) is often crowded, as are the runs through the woods – long, broad and satisfying trails, ranging from meandering blue to direct, not very severe black. Behind Alpe di Tognola is a wide open basin of gentle skiing (1900m to 2200m) served by several drags.

Ces is a quiet area to the west. A slow chair-lift leads to Malga Ces (1617m), a clearing with a couple of nursery lifts, also accessible by car. A second chair-lift, to Punta Ces (2231m), serves the main slope, which offers some good varied skiing, on and off the piste, open and wooded. The pistes (red and black) are not very difficult for their categories. The café terrace at Punta Ces enjoys splendid views of the opposing peaks.

Passo Rolle is 9km from San Martino, a high, open and sunny area of mostly easy intermediate runs on both sides of the pass between 1880m and 2300m. The steep Paradiso drag-lift serves a variety of more challenging runs down more or less directly beside it.

Pleasant and varied as it is, the local skiing is unlikely to satisfy good, keen skiers for more than a few days, and San Martino is too far from the rest of the Dolomite skiing for excursions to be practical. There is an easy cross-country circuit at San Martino and good long trails at Passo Rolle. The resort is well suited to non-skiers: beautiful walks, ice rink, riding. Bowling, swimming and sauna were advertised but not in evidence. The ski-bus service is essential, adequate, and free to lift pass holders. Après-ski is mostly confined to hotel bars, and the discothèques, little patronised except at weekends.

Tourist office ✆ (439) 62124.

White Madonna

Madonna di Campiglio Italy 1510m

Good for Beautiful scenery, mountain restaurants, nursery slopes, easy skiing, big ski area, sunny skiing
Bad for Tough skiing, late holidays, easy road access, not skiing

Linked resorts: Marilleva, Folgarida

Madonna di Campiglio is a large, comfortable, fairly quiet modern resort in the western Dolomites which attracts well-heeled Italian skiers, few from abroad and hardly any from Britain. The building style is inoffensive and harmonious, which is rare for an Italian ski resort, as is the high standard of accommodation. Its setting among thick pine woods beneath the jagged turrets of the Brenta mountains is a splendid one, familiar to 'Ski Sunday' viewers who are periodically treated to the spectacle of slalom races on the steep slopes of Tre Tre. Most of Madonna's skiing is different – it is a typical of the Dolomites in taking skiers over long distances through beautiful scenery, past tempting refuges, on gentle runs with a limited range of altitude (there is little skiing above 2000m). Lift queues are rarely a problem except at weekends and when snow is scarce, and there is a good nursery area.

Marilleva and Folgarida do attract some British custom. Despite lower prices, they are much less attractive than Madonna, sharing neither the beauty of its surroundings nor its freedom from queues. Skiing home, especially to Marilleva 900, is often impossible.

The skiing top 2510m bottom 1512m

Madonna's skiing is mostly on broad, well-prepared avenues between trees. Most of it is sheltered, sunny and spectacular. Snow on the runs down to the village is not very reliable. There are four main lift departures, three of them within walking distance of the centre.

The **Pradalago** lifts open up the widest area of skiing, linking up with Folgarida and Marilleva. Access is either from the resort via the Pradalago cable-car (soon to be doubled up with a chair-lift) or by roadside chair-lift starting a little way north. There are no marked runs below the cable-car, but there are several back down the route of the chair-lifts. The link to Marilleva and Folgarida consists of straightforward up and down skiing in the woods past the Lago delle Malghette to Monte Vigo, which is the parting of the ways to the other resorts. The **Marilleva** side offers more skiing, including three linked, not very fearsome black runs from over 2000m down through the woods to the bottom station of the Pian del Grum gondola. The bottom section, from 1400m to 900m, is more often than not bare. There is a less direct blue alternative to the black down to 1400. On the **Folgarida** side there is one short black among a profusion of green and blue runs, with one red section under part of the Genzianella chair-lift. There is no difficulty about the runs back to Madonna but they end about five minutes' walk from the resort.

Of the other three ski areas, the largest is **Groste**, reached indirectly from the village via the Spinale cable-car or directly by two-stage cable-car starting opposite the Pradalgo chair. The top station is the departure point for three touring routes (and famous summer walks along the narrow ledges round the rock faces of the Brenta). The runs are beautiful, easy, open and long, with a gentle blue-green route all the way from the top to the Campo Carlo Magno. Several reporters found that the path back to the resort was not skiable.

Monte Spinale can be reached either by cable-car and parallel chair-lift from near the ice rink, or by drag and chair from Campo Carlo Magno. Runs back down to the resort are tough and unreliable for snow, but there are gentler north-facing runs down through the woods to Carlo Magno and an easy red link with the mid-station of the Groste cable-car. The **Cinque Laghi** skiing, Madonna's racing hill, is served by cable-car from the western side of the resort. A short red run down from the cable-car top station links to the Tre Tre chair-lift serving the slalom course – an impressive slope of 600m vertical, not exactly jet black, but providing plenty of challenge. The gradient of the slope is consistent, and there are no easy ways down. The area is very useful for avoiding queues on busy days.

Nursery slopes in Madonna and around the mountains are numerous and generally good, provided there is enough snow at resort level. The best area is Campo Carlo Magno, near the road from Madonna to Folgarida. It is pleasant, spacious, sunny and quiet, unlike the smaller nursery slopes in the centre of the resort. For times of snow shortage there is a small nursery area at Groste.

Madonna and its linked resorts are very well supplied with **mountain restaurants** which add greatly to the joys of skiing around the hills. Many of them are proper restaurants with table cloths and waiters, and real kitchens with chefs. The Nube d'Oro below Spinale, the Rifugio Giorgio Graffer at Groste, and the Panciana above Marilleva are recommended. The Rifugio Spinale is not.

Lifts

Passes 'Skirama' pass covers all Madonna, Folgarida, Marilleva lifts except Carlo Magno nursery lifts, but not buses. Day and half-day passes available, and passes for local sectors. **Cost** 6-day pass L122,000. **Children** 5% off, under 1m30 tall. **Beginners** Payment by the ride.

The lift system works well, with plenty of alternative entrances to the ski areas from the resort, and few bottlenecks except at weekends and when snow conditions restrict the skiing available, when Groste becomes crowded. Folgarida and Marilleva share a local lift pass and in the afternoon the lifts up to Monte Vigo from both resorts are crowded with returning commuters. The cable-cars are prone to closure by wind, but all are duplicated by other lifts. The piste map, complete with contour lines, is excellent.

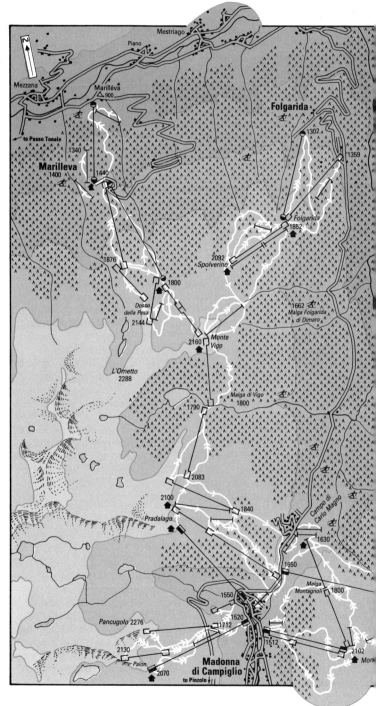

The resort

Madonna stands among pine woods on gently sloping ground just to the south of the Passo Campo Carlo Magno with beautiful long views across to the neighbouring peaks of Brenta and Cima Tosa (3174m) which catch the evening sun to great effect. There is a lively central square near the frozen lake (reported to be used for motor-cycle races) and a one-way system which gets seriously congested at weekends. Shopping is smart but not very varied, and contributes to the atmosphere of quiet elegance rather than high fashion or picturesque mountain charm.

Accommodation is mostly in private apartments and numerous hotels, many of them comfortable and modern. Lift departures are from the northern end of the village, and this is the place to be. Particularly well-located are the Majestic ($\oslash$ 41080), the St Hubertus ($\oslash$ 41144), the Oberosler ($\oslash$ 41136) and the Spinale ($\oslash$ 41116); the last is inexpensive and simple, and recommended for 'copious food and friendly hard-working staff'. The Miramonte ($\oslash$ 41021) is expensive and good – 'excellent food; resident pianist'. The Ideal ($\oslash$ 41016) is less than ideally situated but very welcoming.

Après-ski is varied, with tearooms, bars and several expensive discos, but the evenings are generally subdued. There are many enticing restaurants and even a pub selling expensive bitter.

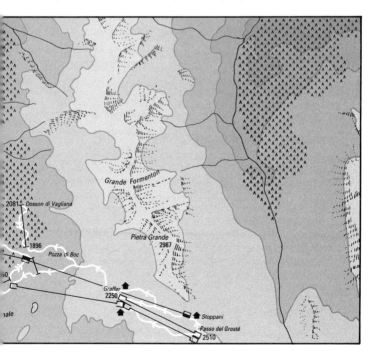

Ski school

Classes 2hr/day, 9.00–11.00 or 11.00–
1.00.
Cost 6 days L72,000–L84,000. Private
lessons L22,000/hr.

Children No ski or non-ski
kindergarten.
Special courses Helicopter skiing,
touring.

There are 9 ski schools, all officially accredited, and with standard
hours and prices. Location of school for accommodation is probably the
most important criterion. The only report we have is of a drunken torchlit
descent from Pradalago – 'the highlight of the holiday'.

Other activities

Cross-country Trails at Campo Carlo
Magno, easy-moderate, 5km and 10km.

Not-skiing Skating, bowling.

The resort does not offer much for non-skiers. Excursions to Venice,
Innsbruck and Lake Garda are advertised. Cross-country trails in the
woods around Campo Carlo Magno are very pretty, but scope is
limited.

Travel

Airport Verona; transfer 3hr; Milan
about 5hr.
Railway Male; bus to resort.

Road Via Innsbruck, Brennner,
Bolzano; chains may be needed.
Reachable resorts Passo Tonale.

A car is useful in the resort if your hotel is at the wrong end, but
otherwise inessential. A ski-bus (not included on the lift pass) links the
bottom lifts stations including Campo Carlo Magno every 20 minutes. It
is reported to be unreliable. There are buses to Marilleva and Folgarida.
Passo Tonale is worth a visit if snow at Madonna is poor.

Miscellaneous

Tourist office ✆ (465) 41026.
Tx 400882.
Medical Hospital in Tione (30km);
doctor, fracture clinic, chemist in resort;
dentist in Pinzolo (13km).

Equipment hire 6 days skis L28,000,
boots L12,000, X-C L32,000.
Resort beds 4,000 in hotels, 26,000 in
apartments.
Package holidays PQ.

Marilleva 900–1400m Folgarida 1300m

Marilleva 900, in the main valley near the Tonale road, has a few hotels,
a nursery lift and ski school at the foot of frequently bare slopes and the
gondola link to Marilleva 1400. This is a purpose-built resort in the
French style, with one huge concrete block very close to the ski-lifts,
and hotels and apartment complexes, swimming pool, sauna,
restaurants and bars, mostly under the same roof. Folgarida is an older
resort, with over 20 hotels, most of them simple and inexpensive.
Unlike Marilleva it is set beside the road to Madonna which makes it a
much better starting point for skiing and après-ski excursions.

Tourist office Marilleva ✆ (463) 77134; Folgarida ✆ (463) 96113
Package holidays Marilleva HM, PQ, STY; Folgarida HM.

Lombard North Central

Bormio Italy 1225m

Good for Not skiing, summer skiing
Bad for Tough skiing, skiing convenience, lift queues, resort-level snow, late holidays, easy road access, short airport transfers

Separate resort: Santa Caterina

Bormio, host of the 1985 skiing World Championships, is a small town in a remote corner of Lombardy at the foot of the Stelvio pass which separates Italian Italy from Germanic Dolomite Italy and serves some of the best summer skiing in the Alps. Bormio's history as a spa goes back to Roman times, and although it is hardly charming (it is spoilt by noisy traffic) the old centre has a lot more character and interest than most ski resorts. The skiing that matters is on one wide mountainside which can provide enormously long, mostly intermediate runs when there is snow on the lower slopes, but as often as not there is very little skiing below 2000m, making the ski area small and often very crowded. Bormio is often presented as a resort for advanced skiers and as a pretty little mountain village; those who go with those expectations will be disappointed.

The lift pass covers Santa Caterina, a pretty nearby village with more reliable snow, less queuing and an area of intermediate skiing which is a match for Bormio's when snow low-down is poor.

The skiing top 3012m bottom 1225m

The north-facing slopes of the tall Monte Vallecetta rise evenly from the riverside near Bormio to its 3148m summit just above the top of a two-stage cable-car from the edge of town. The middle station is Bormio 2000, an upper mini-resort, usually accessible by car (a car park annoyingly separates the two stages of cable-car). An alternative access route is by gondola to Ciuk, followed by chair-lifts. When conditions permit there are very long runs from top to bottom, nearly 1800m vertical in all, with runs of up to 14km – sustained intermediate skiing which is a bit tough for skiers just off the nursery slopes but a bit gentle for skiers with a taste for adventure and a challenge. On the open top half alone the runs are long and satisfying, which is fortunate considering how often there is little skiing below Bormio 2000. A single run is graded black, and this does not justify its grading.

There are more numerous and varied runs on the upper slopes than below Bormio 2000, but the two main runs through the woods below Ciuk are good wide undulating trails. The men's downhill course starts (very steeply) at 2273m just above the top of the La Rocca chair and runs down past Ciuk to near the bottom of the gondola 1000m lower.

For the World Championships 9km of these lower pistes were equipped with snow-making cannons, which could make a big difference to Bormio's holiday skiing if they are used – we have no reports.

There is good summer skiing at the Stelvio pass, although the run down beneath the first cable-car (to 3000m) is not always skiable. This high ski area is not open in winter.

Nursery slopes are at Ciuk and Bormio 2000, the first being larger and more tranquil, but sometimes short of snow. These are good areas, but the lack of village nursery slopes is a disadvantage. There is not much very easy skiing for the post-nursery stages.

Mountain restaurants are plentiful, considering the limited size of the ski area, and several reporters commented on good food, even in the self-service restaurant at Bormio 2000.

Lifts

Passes Area pass (2, 6 or more days) covers Bormio, Santa Caterina, Livigno. Day and half-day pass for Bormio only. **Beginners** Coupons or lift pass. **Cost** 6-day pass L100,000. 25% off in low season. **Children** 20% off, under 10. **Summer skiing** Extensive area at Stelvio Pass (20km), 2760m to 3420m.

At peak times and weekends there are long queues to go up both stages of the cable-car, and in poor snow even longer ones to go down. The main chair and drag-lift above Bormio 2000 may also be crowded. The cable-cars and Cimino chair-lift are vulnerable to wind closure.

The resort

Bormio is an attractively ordinary place, with a greater variety of everyday shops, cafés and restaurants tucked away in the back-streets than in most ski resorts, and good open-air markets. On the other side of the river there is a more modern development of hotels along the road at the foot of the slopes between cable-car and gondola station. This is the most convenient location for skiers' **accommodation**, within 10 or 15 minutes' walk of the old centre. Of the hotels near the cable-car, the Ambassador ($\emptyset$ 904625) is the most friendly and welcoming. The Aurora ($\emptyset$ 901052), the Larice Bianco ($\emptyset$ 904693) and the Funivia ($\emptyset$ 901065) are also very convenient. The Cima Bianca ($\emptyset$ 901449) is an inexpensive, attractive and convenient b&b hotel. In the centre the Posta ($\emptyset$ 904753) and Astoria ($\emptyset$ 904541) are both comfortable and attractive. A reporter who stayed at the Genzianella ($\emptyset$ 904485) at Bormio 2000 enjoyed being able to take advantage of cheap full board terms and miss the queues up from and down to the resort.

Après-ski is generally quiet, but there are a few discos and a wide range of restaurants outside hotels. One reporter enjoyed the meal of her life at the Baiona restaurant 'for £8 a head; phone up to book and the chef picks you up in his jeep'. Many skiers enjoy après-ski inactivity easing the joints in the public thermal baths.

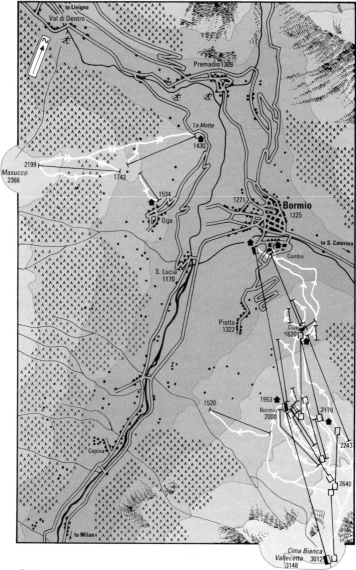

Ski school

Classes 2hr or 4hr per day.
Cost 6 days (12hrs) L62,000. Private lessons L20,000/hr.
Children Prices as adults. No kindergartens.

Special courses Racing, ski touring, helicopter skiing.

There are five schools, all officially recognised. English-speaking instructors are numerous. Several reporters commented on the helicopter excursion to the Vallecetta and off-piste run to S Caterina.

Other activities

Cross-country Trails at Isolaccia (8km) and S Caterina; none in resort.
Not-skiing Two museums, library, cinema, thermal baths, swimming, sauna, sports hall, indoor tennis, clay pigeon shooting, mini-golf, ski-bob, skating, toboggan run.

Bormio offers a lot to the non-skier, with new facilities generated by the World Championships, and is itself interesting. Reporters recommend the excursions to Livigno and St Moritz. The ice rink is unreliable, as are the long X-C trails in the valley.

Travel

Airport Milan (200km); transfers 4½hr.
Railway Tirano (40km); regular buses.
Road Via Mont Blanc Tunnel, Milan, Sondrio; chains rarely needed.
Reachable resorts Livigno, Santa Caterina, St Moritz, Aprica.

There is a free ski-bus round the town and regular buses to Santa Caterina and Livigno. Having a car is hardly essential but makes it possible to avoid queues and easy to explore the other skiing areas. The road to Livigno is long, slow and often difficult; chains are very likely to be needed.

Miscellaneous

Tourist office ✆ (342) 903300.
Tx 314389.
Medical Hospital, doctors, chemists, dentists in resort.
Equipment hire 6 days skis L24,000, boots L10,000, X-C L25,000.
Resort beds 3,500 in hotels; 12,500 in apartments.
Package holidays BS, CI, EN, GL, HO, IG, IT, NE, NT, PQ, SCG, TH..

Santa Caterina 1750m

S Caterina is a quiet little resort in the pretty, wooded Valfurva at the foot of one of the most dramatic drives in the Alps (the Gavia pass), but the end of the road in winter. Busy Bormio, 15km away and 500m lower, is served by regular buses and covered by the area lift pass. In good snow conditions Bormio is quite an attraction for adventurous skiers who may run out of scope at S Caterina, but often the commuter traffic flows the other way because of S Caterina's better snow conditions, and weekend queues can occur. The local skiing is on the north-east-facing slopes of the Sobretta between the village and a top station of 2725m. The higher slopes are fairly steep and graded black, but most of the skiing is intermediate, with a beautiful long run round the mountain behind Cresta Sobretta, and good wide woodland trails including the women's World Championship downhill course. There is a good but often overcrowded nursery area with restaurants above the woods and an easy way home via the Gavia road. There is some attractive cross-country (up to 10km) in quiet surroundings beyond the resort, but not much to do apart from ski or skate on the natural rink. Night-life is limited. Santa Caterina attracts British school groups, not too noisy according to reporters.

Tourist office ✆ (0342) 935598. Package holidays CI, GL, NE, SCB.

High skiing, low spirits

Livigno Italy 1820m
*

Good for *Nursery slopes, easy skiing, resort-level snow, late holidays, sunny skiing, cheap alcohol*
Bad for *Skiing convenience, tough skiing, lift queues, Alpine charm, short airport transfers, easy road access*

Livigno is an unattractive and awkwardly strung-out series of villages in a long, wide, high and exceedingly remote valley – a lost world to which the easiest access from mother Italy is the 2290m pass from Bormio, 45km and nearly two hours' drive away. British skiers face airport transfers of over six hours in which to build up a thirst for Livigno's much-vaunted duty-free drink. The high and wide slopes along both sides of the valley above the resort provide a lot of uncomplicated intermediate skiing for a long winter season. In good weather and good snow it must be splendid, with lots of off-piste scope; in bad weather it is extremely bleak. Whatever the weather, the lift system is very poorly conceived and skiing usually involves a lot of legwork.

The skiing top 2800m bottom 1816m

The skiing is in two areas, now covered by a shared pass. Although there are many more lifts on the east-facing Livitur side of the valley, most of them are short nursery drags and the north- and west-facing Mottolino slopes above the winding road to Bormio offer a similar amount of skiing. Most of the skiing is above the tree-line, and only one lift is enclosed.

The two-stage Lago Salin gondola from the southern end of town spans the longest slopes in the ski area, with several possible variations of the run back down, none of them severe. Behind the top station is a quiet area of short runs beside the Federia drag-lifts, with beautiful views of Switzerland. A very long and gentle blue run northwards along the mountain ridge links up with the Costaccia chair-lifts above the northern end of the resort (S Maria), which serve a small area of shorter wooded runs, mostly easy.

The Mottolino skiing, reached by one drag-lift from the edge of the resort (with bridges over the road for lift and pistes) or by another from the new roadside development above it, is mostly uncomplicated intermediate runs, including a ridiculously over-graded black. Lifts are inadequate, but there is plenty of space and usually good snow on the higher runs, most of which face north.

We have no information about off-piste skiing, and Livigno attracts few ace skiers, but the lie of the land looks very promising. No one could complain that the slopes are over-mechanised.

Nursery slopes and lifts cover a large expanse of the lower slopes

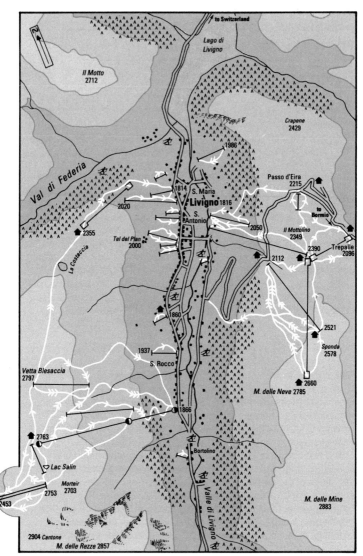

on the Livitur side of the resort. They are open and gentle and easily accessible, with bars close at hand, including the Bar Scuola, the lively headquarters of the main ski school. **Mountain restaurants** are (for Italy) disappointingly scarce.

Lifts

Passes General pass covers all lifts, but no buses, at Livigno, Bormio and S Caterina, except for day-pass (Livigno only). Limited passes available.

Cost 6-day pass L95000. 20% off in low season.
Children 25% off, under 12.
Beginners Coupons.

The system is poorly linked and short of capacity, particularly on the Mottolino side. The undignified scramble (after a long wait) to leap aboard the old Lago Salin bucket ('the most entertaining lift queue in the Alps') is reported to be ended by the installation of a real gondola.

The resort

Livigno is little more than a three-mile straggle of modern hotels, bars and liquor-stores, with a main focus of activity at the San Antonio road junction in the middle. Understandably, many German, Swiss, and Italian skiers take cars, and the main street, which is a busy through-route between Switzerland and Italy, is often very congested. Spirits cost £3 to £4 a litre, petrol is about half the normal Italian price.

   Accommodation is mostly in small, functional hotels along the main road. The Sport (∅ 996186) is reasonably comfortable, well-placed for the Lago Salin lifts at the quiet end of town. There is a cluster of larger, newer hotels near the Sponda drag on the way out to Bormio.

   Après-ski is bar-oriented, inexpensive and lively, but far from riotous. There are not many restaurants other than in hotels and only a few discothèques. The most amusing nightspot is Mario's Pub (restaurant, bar and live music) in San Rocco.

Ski school

Classes 2hr/day, 9.00–11.00 or 11.00–1.00.
Cost 6 days L48,000. Private lessons L18,000/hr.
Children No kindergartens.
Special courses Racing, video.

There are four ski schools, all officially recognised, and all operating at similar times and prices.

Other activities

Cross-country 30km green and 10km red trails along valley floor.
Not skiing Skating, swimming, sauna, squash, ice driving, two cinemas.

There are few diversions except regular excursions to St Moritz and Bormio. The X-C trails are snow-sure but very unpicturesque.

Travel

Airport Zurich (230km) is most easily reached, but most packages use Milan (245km); transfers 6hr plus.
Railway Tirano; bus to resort 3hr.
Road Via Munich, Innsbruck, Landeck, Zernez; chains may be needed; toll tunnel open 8am to 8pm. Alternative route via Bormio; chains often needed.
Reachable resorts Bormio, Santa Caterina, St Moritz.

There is a daytime ski-bus, elusive in the middle of the day and not covered by the lift pass, and regular buses to Bormio and St Moritz. Road access via Austria is not difficult, but the Bormio route is.

Miscellaneous

Tourist office ∅ (342) 996402. Tx 312103.
Medical Doctor, dentist, chemist in resort; hospital at Bormio (45km).
Equipment hire 6 days skis L26,000, boots L14,000, X-C L31,000.
Resort beds 4,000 in hotels, 2,000 in apartments.
Package holidays BS, GL, HO, IG, IT, SNW.

Tonally deficient skiing

Passo Tonale Italy 1882m

Passo Tonale is a small and ugly modern development which has grown up beside the road at a high, bleak pass between the Alps and the Dolomites west of Madonna di Campiglio. Down below, 10km to the west, is Ponte di Legno (1260m), a larger and more sheltered resort with a small ski area of its own and a regular bus service to Tonale; the two resorts share their lift pass.

Tonale's main skiing attraction is the Presena Glacier on the southern side of the resort, beneath the 3069m-peak of Cima Presena. The glacier is reached by cable-car up to Passo del Paradiso (2585m), a breach in the steep, rocky mountains immediately above the resort. It is hardly the gateway to a skier's paradise but there are wide open easy slopes beyond, with a chair-lift over almost flat ground to the foot of the glacier at 2738m. There are five drags above this with a top station of 3016m, a small summer skiing area. The slopes of the glacier are quite gentle and even, and there is a long moderate red from the top station down to Alveo (2210m) with a chair-lift link back up to the top of the cable-car which makes it possible to avoid the flat run back from the glacier. The slopes beneath the cable-car are steep and the self-explanatory 'Direttissima' down to Tonale is an uncompromisingly fierce and genuinely black chute.

On the gentle, south-facing slopes to the north of the resort lie no fewer than 18 short lifts including one reserved for sledges and one sequence of three that reaches 2530m. The runs here are almost all gentle blue and make a splendid nursery area in fine weather. From the bottom of the system a blue run descends gently to Ponte di Legno, following the road to start with before dropping more directly down to join cross-country runs in a narrow valley near the lower resort. Ponte di Legno's own skiing is served by three chair-lifts and a drag, on north-west facing slopes between 2117m and the edge of the resort.

Tonale is a small resort which can be exhausted in a weekend even by moderate skiers. It is most attractive as a day-trip from Aprica or Madonna at times of general snow shortage in these lower resorts. Unfortunately the lift system to the glacier is tailor-made for bottle-necks, and the resort attracts large numbers when good snow is at a premium. At other times Tonale is quiet almost to the point of being deserted. We were unable to ski the glacier, as the lifts were closed for repairs apparently associated with shifting glacier. Before making an excursion to Tonale with the intention of skiing the glacier, it is advisable to telephone the cable-car station (✆ 91355) to find out if the lifts are operating. The tourist office is more likely to speak English, but less likely to know the answer.

Tonale is quiet in the evenings. There is an ice rink, a swimming pool in one hotel, and no less than five different ski schools.

Tourist office ✆ (364) 91343. Package holidays SCB, SCP, STY.

Expensive, at the price

Aprica Italy 1181m

Aprica at its best can offer some good intermediate skiing with runs of over 1400m vertical from top to bottom. But by all accounts it is not very often at its best, and the reports we have received make depressing reading. 'Our trip was cheap – and nasty' wrote one dissatisfied customer, summing up the general impression of standards lower than prices. Most of the disadvantages of Italian skiing are here gathered together, with few redeeming features.

The arrangement of the resort, which extends for about a mile along a road pass east of Sondrio, is unappealing, and there is no attractive old centre. There are two neighbouring ski areas on the same mountainside, but they are not linked and there is neither a general lift pass nor a ski-bus. Accommodation is mostly very drab: we have a report of collapsed beds, exposed and dangerous wiring and food 'quite appalling even by boarding school standards'. Several reporters were surprised to find that the locals were unfriendly and uninterested in foreign visitors. Other reports complained of primitive sanitation in the mountain restaurant and a very low standard of equipment for hire (and refusal to repair hire equipment without payment). The resort is relatively accessible for weekenders from Milan, Como and other towns, and alternates between being overcrowded and deserted.

The skiing, on the south side of the road, mostly consists of trails through woods, intermediate in standard (including the black runs). There is a string of short lifts on the lower slopes above the village which are useful for getting from one end of the resort to the other. The Baradello lift system, at the eastern end of the resort, consists of only three lifts, a cable-car followed by a pair of drags up to 2200m. The runs, graded green to black, exaggerate the variety of the skiing. You can ski across the lower slopes using the nursery lifts, or off-piste from the top station, to the bigger and more interesting Palabione lift system.

The Palabione system attracts most of the weekend crowds. A combination of cable-car, chair-lifts and drags (in three stages) reach a top station of 2600m, with the chance of long runs down to the village when snow conditions are good. One run from the top to bottom is graded black, but does not come close to being as difficult as the grading suggests. Most of the skiing is pleasantly undemanding, with occasional narrow and crowded sections through the trees. The Palabione system shares its lift pass with the Magnolta lifts at the western end of the resort – a cable-car and chair-lift to Monte Filone (2300m). The run down to the mid-station is graded green, the one below it black; the slopes are not so contrasting in reality.

There is a good indoor swimming pool, a natural ice rink, and a cross-country trail across the pass from the Alpine skiing area. Tour operators usually organise day-trips to St Moritz and Livigno.

Tourist office ✆ (342) 746113. Package holidays BS, HM, SCB, SCP, TH.

No rest cure

Badgastein Austria 1000m

Good for *Big ski area, tough skiing, après-ski, not skiing, rail access*
Bad for *Skiing convenience, easy skiing, lift queues, Alpine charm, nursery slopes, resort-level snow*

Linked resort: Bad Hofgastein
Separate resort: Dorfgastein

Badgastein is one of three widely differing resorts in a long and beautiful valley in western Salzburgerland. Dorfgastein, just inside the narrow gateway into the valley, is an unspoilt rustic village near a lot of pleasant intermediate skiing. A few miles upstream, Bad Hofgastein is a spacious and comfortable spa without any grandiose pretensions. Badgastein itself is one of the most ponderously grand of spa resorts, but in a remarkable setting – stacked on a steep hillside at the head of the valley. The river cascades down between the hotel blocks at the heart of the resort, which is still rather sedate and formal, though now more dependent on the conference than the *Kur* business. A second Badgastein has grown up for skiers – a sprawl of hotels and apartment buildings beside the railway station and main ski-lift departure. It is not at all beautiful, but practical and increasingly full of young people, and lively in the evenings.

Lift links between Badgastein and Bad Hofgastein have created one of Austria's major ski areas – big and varied, with very long and mainly challenging runs from top to bottom. Although a few blue trails wind across the slopes, these mountains are in general best suited to experienced skiers. Problems are not confined to the pistes: the drag-lifts are graded blue, red and black according to the gradient, and the blacks often take you well away from the piste, where a fall would be most unpleasant.

The skiing top 2686m bottom 850m

In addition to the main ski area on the western side of the valley between Badgastein and Bad Hofgastein, there are three other separate areas, all less crowded and in different ways very attractive. The Graukogel slopes above Badgastein are few, but long and satisfying for good skiers. Sportgastein has some good runs in a very different style from the main Gastein valley: high altitude, open ground and no resort development at all. And Dorfgastein's friendly skiing adds greatly to the appeal of the region for leisurely skiers.

From a milling concourse of car park, ski school meeting-place and nursery area squeezed between the steep mountain and Badgastein station, a two-stage gondola climbs to the **Stubnerkogel** (2246m), a tangled junction of lift arrivals at the top of a long, narrow ridge. The alternative chair and drag-lift route is less congested but slow and steep. The east-facing runs to Badgastein provide good, tough skiing with a mixture of open ground above half-way and woods below – red or black in difficulty, depending on the conditions. There is a blue run winding down the mountain, but this too is often icy and crowded. The open top half of the slope gives plenty of opportunity for skiing off-piste between the runs. The west-facing back side of the ridge is broken ground with some impressive rocky drops and gullies, and skiing options down to Jungeralm are limited; the piste tends to be crowded. There is more space and some good off-piste skiing beside the steep Hochleiten drag-lift. The north-facing runs down into the Angertal provide some of the best skiing in the region. From Jungeralm a long, undulating black run drops directly through the woods. The alternatives are to traverse laboriously to and fro on the 'Skiweg' from Jungeralm, or take the famous and much more satisfying red run from Stubnerkogel.

From the Angertal, a chair and drag-lift go up over south-facing slopes to the **Schlossalm** skiing – also accessible by funicular railway starting a long walk from Bad Hofgastein. This is a very spacious basin above the tree-line providing a lot of similar intermediate runs, not very long and mostly easier than on the Stubnerkogel. For good skiers the main interest is the beautiful long run round the back of the mountains, reached either from Hohe Scharte (2300m) or from Kleine Scharte (2050m). In good snow the run goes to the bottom of the railway, an 8km descent of 1450m vertical. There are no very easy ways down to the bottom of the mountain, and snow conditions are often poor on the lower slopes and on the south-facing runs down into the Angertal.

The thickly wooded, north-west-facing slopes of **Graukogel** are served by a slow two-stage chair-lift. This is the local racing hill and, apart from one easy run round the top of the mountain, all the trails are challenging variants of the direct descent under the chairs of 900m vertical. Not all of them are prepared. Snow conditions are as good as you'll find locally, and the surroundings and views are delightful.

Sportgastein is a valuable asset if snow elsewhere in the valley is poor – when (unusually) it can become crowded. The high, narrow, dead-end valley is empty and undeveloped save for a couple of restaurants. A chair and then a drag go up from 1600m to Kreuzkogel at 2686m, most of it above the trees and facing west. The top half may be exposed and cold, but usually has good snow on its gentle runs. The great attraction to good skiers is the long north-facing off-piste run over the back down to the tollgate above Böckstein (where you catch a bus). The slopes beneath the chair-lift are steeper, with some good off-piste skiing among the thinly scattered trees as well as a stiff red run.

A long and very slow chain of lifts (chairs and drags) links the skiing of **Dorfgastein** and **Grossarl** via two neighbouring hilltops, Fulseck (2033m) and another Kreuzkogel, which give runs of over 1000m vertical. Although most of the runs are classed red, this is basically friendly terrain and few of the runs are steep, except the black direct descent to Dorfgastein. The Grossarl side is mostly gentle with long, wide runs through the woods and some easy off-piste skiing among the

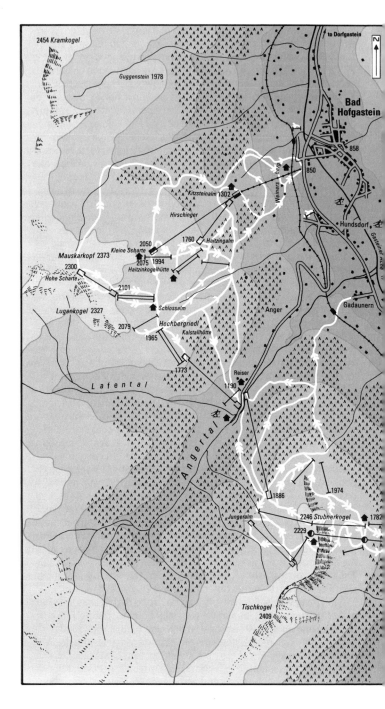

trees. After the crowded and often icy slopes of Stubnerkogel, intermediate skiers may welcome this attractive pastoral landscape.

Nursery slopes at the foot of the Stubnerkogel, Angertal and Bad Hofgastein lifts are rather cramped, and there are not many runs suitable for skiers making the transition from nursery slopes to pistes. The area as a whole is not good for beginners.

Mountain restaurants are plentiful and generally pleasant; there are in most places charming alternatives to the big cafeterias at the main lift stations. There are several very attractive huts on the lower slopes of the Stubnerkogel and of the Schlossalm. Although most piste maps do not seem to mark them, there are restaurants dotted around the slopes above Dorfgastein and Grossarl.

Lifts

Passes Gastein Superski pass covers all lifts, buses and trains. Half-day and day tickets available.
Children 40% off under 14.

Cost 6-day pass AS 1,230; 18% off in low season.
Beginners Coupons, and some limited passes for a few nursery lifts.

At peak times queues, especially for the Stubnerkogel gondola and Bad Hofgastein funicular, can be well over half an hour. To avoid them, drive or catch a bus to the Angertal lifts. On the Stubnerkogel the alternative drag-lifts are steep.

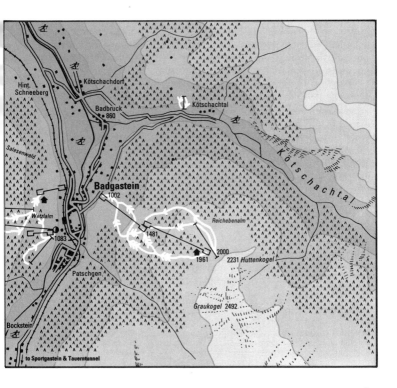

The resort

Badgastein is built in a cramped, claustrophobic position on the steep wooded slopes which abruptly close the southern end of the Gastein Valley. The main road and railway by-pass the resort centre, which is more simply negotiated by the steep footpaths and staircases than by car. The focus of the resort is a smart new complex including hotel, shopping precinct, casino and conference hall projecting from the hillside beside the waterfall. In the vicinity there are shop windows, coiffeurs and tea shops for those with expensive tastes.

The upper level of Badgastein (a steep but short walk away) is a rather ordinary collection of unfashionable spa hotels, which attract skiers in winter because of their convenient location, and newer accommodation which has grown up there for the same reason. Space here is limited by steep slopes on either side; as the skiing part of Badgastein grows, it is spreading along the road south.

Accommodation is mostly in hotels, of which there are hundreds in the valley, many of them with hot and cold running radioactive water. Among the hotels at the top of the resort, within easy walking distance of the Stubnerkogel lifts the new Bärenhof (∅ 3366) is the most comfortable and expensive. The Krone (∅ 2330) and the Goethehof (∅ 2717) are ideally placed but very uninspiring middle-range hotels. Much more charming and in a quieter position is the simple Fischerwirt (∅ 2231). In the centre the Straubinger (∅ 2012) is not in the grand league but handsomely traditional; the map of Europe was redrawn in room 7, so they say. The Grüner Baum hotel (∅ 2516) or Hoteldorf deserves special mention – an idyllic, self-contained tourist colony in the beautifully secluded setting of the Kötschachtal, with accommodation of varying comfort in a number of buildings.

Après-ski is very varied. In the centre there are quiet tea rooms, plush hotel bars with formal dancing, and a casino. The big hotels put on live shows (fashion displays, beauty contests, cabaret). For less formal entertainment, there is a handful of discothèques, and a number of pubs, simple bars and restaurants, mostly around the station. Lots of young and old go out at night, and the atmosphere is usually lively.

Ski school

Classes 2hr morning and afternoon. **Cost** 6 days AS870. Private lessons AS320/hr.

Children Ski kindergarten, ages 2–3, 6 days AS900. Non-ski kindergarten, ages 2–3, 9.00–5.00, 6 days AS900.

There are ski school offices near the main lift stations at Badgastein (Stubnerkogel), Bad Hofgastein and Dorfgastein. Reports are mixed.

Other activities

Cross-country Trails of varying length and difficulty along the main valley floor between Bad Hofgastein and Badbruck (over 20km), around Dorfgastein (12.5km) and Sportgastein (over 20km); also at Böckstein, Angertal and Kötschachtal.

Not skiing Natural ice rinks (skating/curling), swimming/sauna/gym, thermal baths, sleigh rides, riding, toboggan runs, ski bob, tennis, squash, bridge, chess, bowling, casino, museum, theatre, concerts.

Although Badgastein itself is not an ideal base, the valley as a whole has an excellent amount and variety of X-C. are graded. There is lots for non-skiers to do apart from inhale radon; there are long and beautiful walks in the woods above Badgastein and along the eastern flank of the valley towards Bad Hofgastein.

Travel

Airport Salzburg; transfer about 2hr. Also Munich.
Railway Main-line station in resort.

Road Via Munich; chains rarely needed.
Reachable resorts Zell am See, Kaprun and Saalbach are within day-trip range.

Bus services link the village centres and main lift stations reasonably efficiently, but no evening services. In Badgastein, car parking space is inadequate and driving is hazardous, but having a car is very useful for making the most of the skiing and après-ski.

Miscellaneous

Tourist office ✆ (6434) 2531. Tx 67520.
Resort beds 6,000 in hotels, 1,000 in apartments.
Package holidays AU, CB, SCB, SCP, SCG.

Medical Hospital at Schwarzach (25km); numerous doctors, dentists, chemists in resort.
Equipment hire 6 days skis AS480, boots AS240, X-C AS480.

Bad Hofgastein

Bad Hofgastein has neither the inconveniently steep and dark setting nor the stodgy grandeur of Badgastein; it is smaller but still a sizeable resort, spread along the broadest part of the valley. The Kitzstein funicular is inconveniently distant, and the resort is not very ski-oriented: it attracts lots of non-skiing visitors who potter about in the very agreeable, spacious sunny surroundings. It is a good base for the valley's walks and cross-country trails, and busy skating and curling rinks complete the winter scene. There is an outdoor, naturally-heated swimming pool, and a new sports centre (tennis and squash). Evenings are quiet. The most convenient hotels for skiers are the mostly new ones lining the road from the centre to the river. The Kärnten (✆ 711) is well-placed, large and comfortable. Less convenient are the simpler and prettier hotels on the village square – Zum Boten (✆ 416) and Kaiser Franz (✆ 742).

Tourist office ✆ (6432) 4820 **Package holidays** AU, CB.

Dorfgastein

Dorfgastein is a charming, villagey resort, untouched by the depressing influence of spa-hood. Horses and carts clatter along the narrow, arcaded main street past the old church, more often taking local folk about their business than taking tourists for jaunts. There are several well-kept, friendly and comfortable medium-priced hotels in the centre; the Steindlwirt (✆ 2190) and Kirchenwirt (✆ 251) are two of the larger hotels, typically comfortable although without much character. The ski-lift departure is at least a 5-minute walk from the village; the Gasthof Schihäusl (✆ 248) stands at the foot of the slopes. Dorfgastein does not lack bars, music and animation in the evening.

Tourist office ✆ (6433) 277

Downhill all the way

Schladming Austria 750m

Schladming is a world-famous ski racing town which became familiar to Sunday afternoon television viewers before it started attracting British holiday skiers – a process which is sure to gather momentum, to judge by the enthusiasm of our reporters.

Schladming is the furthest east of Austria's major skiing centres and the only one in Styria. It is popular with Viennese and other Austrian skiers, and not full of Germans and British. It also differs from the Austrian norm in giving the attractive impression of being an ordinary old town with a life of its own, independent of tourism; as well as wooden chalets with painted shutters there are sober old stone buildings, including a splendid medieval town gate.

The town lies in the middle of a broad valley on a main east-west road and rail route. The setting is rather like Söll's, with skiing on medium-rise, wooded mountains on one side of the valley facing north towards much higher mountains which make a spectacular backcloth. These are the peaks of the Dachstein, the highest in the eastern Alps, with summer skiing (Alpine and cross-country) on the very gentle expanse of glacier on the northern side of the mountain, reached by cable-car over the sheer southern wall towering above the village of Ramsau, which also has more limited skiing at lower levels. There are more substantial (but more distant) additional areas of skiing at high, purpose-built Obertauern and the resorts in the valleys around St Johann im Pongau, all of it covered along with Schladming's skiing by what is claimed to be the most extensive lift-pass in Austria. But few of our reporters found the need to stray outside the local skiing during their stay in Schladming.

The foothills of the Tauern mountains to the south of the Ennstal provide four self-contained ski areas. (The ski-bus service is essential for adventurous skiers without cars; it is covered by the lift pass.) All face north, with some added skiing on the east and west-facing flanks, and offer long, broad runs through woods from around 2000m to the valley at 750m. At this altitude, good snow from top to bottom cannot be guaranteed, but snow falls and stays at lower altitudes in these parts than in the southern and western Alps. There is very little skiing above the tree-line, not much scope for off-piste skiing, and no very difficult runs; but there is plenty of scope and even variety in the blue and red categories, and the direct descents, which include the famous men's downhill course (4.3 km long, 1006m vertical) down to Schladming itself and the women's one at Haus, offer a sustained challenge to satisfy any skier. Mountain restaurants are adequate in number and generally attractive.

For skiers based in Schladming, the closest skiing is on the **Planai**, served by two-stage gondola to 1894m from the edge of town, a manageable walk from the centre. The lift is often crowded at peak times and weekends (a higher-capacity replacement is planned for 1985–86). The middle station (Kessleralm) of the gondola can be reached by car; a chair-lift runs in parallel with the top half of the gondola. There are snow-making machines on the lower slopes of the Planai, but all the same these slopes are often icy as well as steep. The skiing on the **Hauser Kaibling** (2115m) lies the other side of a narrow valley; there are lifts on the Planai side but the obvious link between the two areas is not yet complete. The main access is by means of a small and inefficient cable-car from the top of the quiet village of Haus, and a newer one (which is often closed) from the bottom of the women's downhill course beside the main road. Motorists can drive up to the eastern edge of the system (Knappl, 1100m) to avoid queues. Both of these mountains offer predominantly intermediate runs, with little in the way of nursery slopes.

Several of our reporters have stayed in or near Rohrmoos, a straggling community beside the road from Schladming to the foot of the **Hochwurzen** mountain, which offers several long red runs between 1100m and 1850m served by two steep drags and a chair-lift, and an extensive network of easy and beginners' slopes around the village and below it down to the western edge of Schladming, where there is a lift link to Planai. Hochwurzen is separated from Planai by a deep and beautiful valley, excellent territory for cross-country skiing, walking and sleigh rides. There is a long toboggan run from top to bottom of the Hochwurzen, on an icy hairpin road alternately reserved for buses and toboggans. Be sure your watch is set to local time.

The westernmost of the four local ski areas is the **Reiteralm**, with skiing from 1860m to the banks of the Enns over 1000m below. Access is either by gondola from the edge of Gleiming village or by chair-lift from an isolated riverside lift station, more convenient for motorists. The skiing is spread over a wide area and similar to Planai and Haus – long woodland trails, with more red than blue runs.

Rohrmoos commends itself to any skiers requiring nursery slopes, and has the added attraction of skiing to most hotel doorsteps. We have favourable reports of the ski school, the kindergarten and even the lift attendants. Schladming is the most convenient base for exploring the whole area, and the place for energetic après-skiers; members report that it is better for tea and early evening après-ski (it has a number of attractive bars and restaurants) than in the small hours, although there are one or two discothèques, and live music in some of the bars. Other activities include bowling, swimming, table tennis, sauna and fitness training, sleigh rides (day and evening), and skating. Excursions to Salzburg by train are easily arranged.

The lift pass arrangements are simple but inflexible, and include a reduction of nearly 40% for children (under 16). There do not appear to be any arrangements for limited passes or coupon payment for lifts.

Tourist office ✆ (87) 22268. **Package holidays** HO, NE, SCB, SCP, TH.

Beside the seaside

Zell am See Austria 750m

Good for *Easy skiing, sunny skiing, not skiing, mountain restaurants, après-ski, rail access, easy road access*
Bad for *Nursery slopes, skiing convenience, resort-level snow, late holidays*

Linked resort: Schüttdorf
Separate resort: Kaprun

Zell am See enjoys a fine setting for a major Alpine summer resort – on a gentle promontory formed, in geography text book style, where a stream flows into the Zellersee. It is a less appropriate setting for a ski resort: the mountains where the stream gathers its waters are a mile or two distant from the resort, and normally reached by bus. The skiing, once reached, is of an unusual kind: much of it is easy, some of it is difficult, and not much of it comes between the two. It is a pleasant, traditional town, car-free in the centre (although with a busy road separating the centre and the mountains); there is plenty to do apart from ski (night and day), and excursions are easy. But whereas most ski resorts bloom in winter, Zell has the air of a place awaiting the return of summer. Those who go skiing partly to savour the mountains will find Zell lacking in Alpine atmosphere.

At the southern extremity of the Zellersee, Schüttdorf is a sprawling suburban dormitory, linked into the skiing at one end of the horseshoe. The more distant village of Kaprun has its own area of easy-intermediate skiing, but is of more interest as the closest resort to the glacier skiing below the Kitzsteinhorn.

The skiing top 1965m bottom 750m

The skiing is on an east-facing semicircular mountain bowl which slopes gently away from the 2000m Schmittenhöhe at its midpoint, giving easy skiing particularly along the southern limb. The steeper skiing is on runs down into the wooded interior of the bowl.

From close to the resort centre a gondola goes up to the southern limb of the horseshoe, and from Schüttdorf a chair-lift does likewise. The main lift station is at the very centre of the bowl, about 2km from the centre of Zell. One of the two cable-cars from here goes directly to (indeed into) the Schmittenhöhe Berghotel, where an elevator delivers you to the sunny summit plateau. Over the back of the summit is a small area of pleasant intermediate runs, of varying difficulty.

Turning right at the summit takes you along a flattish ridge to an area of sunny intermediate skiing, also reachable by the other cable-car from the main lift station to Sonnalm. None of the skiing here is at all

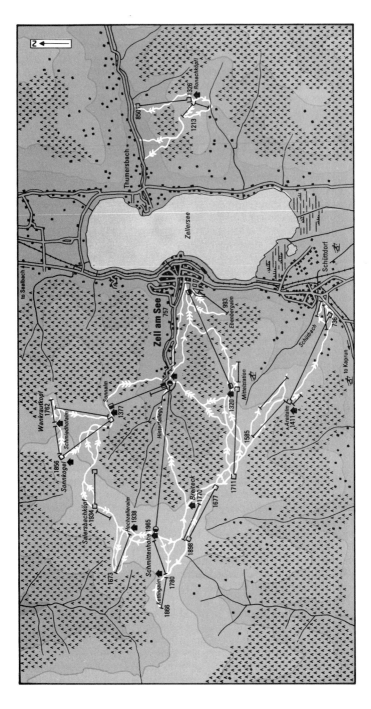

difficult, and the black run from Sonnalm down to the bottom of the cable-car does not merit its grading – but it does get very worn and slushy. Lifts and pistes link Sonnalm with Schmittenhöhe.

South of Schmittenhöhe there is a succession of gentle, broad, sunny pistes along the horseshoe ridge. A right fork takes you to Areitalm, where the chair-lift from Schüttdorf arrives; the pleasant intermediate piste on down to Schüttdorf doesn't keep its snow for long. Taking the left fork brings you to the top of the gondola from Zell. At two points on the horseshoe, black pistes branch off into the bowl. These soon steepen into fine long runs, challenging but not too intimidating for adventurous intermediates. Other runs to the bottom lift stations are less steep, but get more sun and can be very hard at the end of the day.

There are **nursery slopes** at the bottom cable-car station and more at Schüttdorf, but the snow is often in poor condition. Beginners then go up by gondola or chair to higher nursery lifts.

There are quite a number of **mountain restaurants** around the ski area, most of them in pleasant surroundings and sunny positions.

Lifts

Passes Area pass covers all lifts in Zell and Kaprun, and buses between. Available for periods of four days or more. Local passes also available, including half-day and day passes.

Cost 6 days AS1,180. 15% off in low season.
Children 50% off, under 15.
Beginners Coupons, or limited pass.

The reliance on cable-cars for the most direct access to the main runs inevitably causes peak-period queues in the morning – up to an hour at times. Queues for the lifts above the cable-car at Sonnalm should no longer be problem now that Sonnkogel is served by a triple chair-lift.

The resort

Zell is a small lakeside resort, the centre of which is confined between the lake and a busy through-road. It is a sizeable place, a town rather than a village, with shops catering for the needs of residents and the whims of summer tourists rather than just for skiers. In the centre is a pedestrian area around the old church, with curling close by.

Accommodation is in hotels, some in the centre, others in the quieter streets towards the lake and the north end of the town. For après-ski the centre is the best base. The Traube ($\emptyset$ 2368) is a comfortable, friendly small hotel in the pedestrian zone, with an atmospheric bar/restaurant. A long way up-market is the very smooth Neue Post ($\emptyset$ 3773). Most people will find better value in the charming and inexpensive Alte Post ($\emptyset$ 2422), close to the gondola station. For skiing purposes there is much to be said for staying close to the cable-car station. The Schwebebahn ($\emptyset$ 2461), just above it, is the obvious choice if you can afford it. Staying in Schüttdorf puts you close to cross-country trails, tennis and riding facilities.

There is plenty of **après-ski**, at least in season. There are restaurants at every price level, bars, discos, *Weinstüberl*, tea-dancing, and the standard 'evenings' – Tyrolean, fondue, zither.

Ski school

Classes 2hr, morning and afternoon.
Cost 6 days AS870. Private lessons
AS300/hr.
Children Ski kindergarten, ages 4–10,

10.00–4.00, 6 days with meals AS650.
Non-ski kindergarten, ages 4–11, 6 days
AS480.
Special courses Ski-bob

Other activities

Cross-country Easy and medium loops
totalling 42km on the valley floor north
and south of the lake, and 2.3km at
middle station of Zellerbergbahn. Also
very long linked trails along the Salzach

valley east and west of Kaprun.
Not skiing Swimming, sauna, solarium,
riding, tennis, skating, fitness centre,
toboggan runs, bowling, plane flights.

The extent of X-C trails in the valleys around Zell is enormous; Kaprun
hosts a famous marathon race. There is lots for non-skiers to do, with
very good sports facilities, and easy access by train to Salzburg. When
the lake is frozen, there may be fun and games upon it; but at 750m it's
hardly in the St Moritz league.

Travel

Airport Salzburg is closest, Munich
more commonly used by operators;
transfer about 2½hr.
Railway Station in resort.

Road Via Munich; chains rarely needed.
Reachable resorts Saalbach is very
close, Pass Thurn (above Kitzbühel) and
Badgastein within day-trip range.

Post buses run regularly though not very frequently between the lift
stations and the centre, and to Thumersbach and Kaprun.

Miscellaneous

Tourist office ✆ (6542) 2600. Tx 6/6617
Medical Doctors, chemists, dentist,
fracture clinic in resort.
Equipment hire 6 days skis AS420,
boots AS 150, X-C AS300.

Resort beds 8,200 in hotels, 800 in
apartments.
Package holidays AU, BL, BS, CB, CH,
CL, IT, NE, PS, SKW, SNP, SPT, TC, TT.

Kaprun 770m

Kaprun is a pleasant, unremarkable holiday village with all the
necessary ingredients – splendid sports centre, a range of après-ski,
kindergarten, necessary shops. The local skiing on the Maiskogel
consists of easy-intermediate runs (facing roughly east) served by a
chain of drag-lifts starting near the village and a cable-car starting quite
a way out. A further couple of drags going up to 1737m serve less
straightforward north-facing runs at the top. The Kitzsteinhorn skiing
(2450m–3029m) is reached by cable-car or funicular starting several
miles up the valley. It is an exposed area of predominantly easy-
intermediate skiing, without great variety of terrain but with some
slopes which push the limits of their blue gradings. The most interesting
run is the red to the middle station of the underground funicular, but the
price you pay is an endless push along the plastic floor of a virtually flat
tunnel to the station. Expect long queues (up and down) when snow at
lower levels is poor.

Tourist office ✆ (6547) 8643 Tx 6/6763. **Package holidays** CH, IG.

Circular argument

Saalbach Austria 1000m

Good for *Easy skiing, big ski area, sunny skiing, après ski*
Bad for *Tough skiing*

Linked resort: Hinterglemm

The essentially friendly mountains of the Kitzbühel Alps are familiar territory to British skiers, who have long formed a large part of the winter clientele of such resorts as Alpbach, Niederau, Söll and Kitzbühel. The eastern extremity of the range, beyond Kitzbühel, is not so well known. The two resorts of the east-west Glemm valley seem to deserve greater popularity, combining as they do a fairly successful replication of Austrian Alpine village charm, an extensive network of easy and intermediate skiing which links the two resorts and the two sides of the valley with almost French efficiency, and adequately varied non-skiing diversions – and all this amid pleasant though unspectacular scenery. But the qualifications – 'fairly', 'almost', 'adequately' – may indicate that Saalbach and Hinterglemm represent too much of a compromise for many skiers. The two villages are 4km apart. Saalbach, the first you come to, is considerably more established and rounded as a resort, as well as bigger and more sophisticated.

The skiing top 2096m bottom 929m

Spread along both sides of the valley, the interlinking lifts enable you to ski comfortably from either village to the other, or indeed to perform a complete circuit of the valley. Hence the area's voguish claim to be a 'Ski Circus'. The south-facing slopes are mostly open and undemanding, but can deteriorate rapidly in good weather, especially on the lower slopes. The north-facing slopes provide a few more challenging runs, but also some pleasant intermediate skiing.

A cable-car from the centre of Saalbach rises 1000m to the eastern summit of the **Schattberg**. Behind the peak is some fairly easy skiing on the sunny slopes served by two drag-lifts and a beginners' lift, and below the cable car is a fine 4km black north-facing run to the village which is never excessively steep, and can be tackled by adventurous intermediates. The easy alternative is a delightful long round-the-mountain blue run through the woods to Jausern. The third option is to turn right towards a connecting lift up to Schattberg West, at 2096m the top of the lift system. The black grading of the runs between the two summits is misleading: this crucial link in the circus holds no terrors. There is then a testing 5km run down to Hinterglemm, partly open and partly wooded, and often pretty busy. The run emerges above the Hinterglemm nursery slopes near the village centre; a new two-stage double chair-lift goes back up to Schattberg.

From nearby, parallel double and single chair-lifts rise over 1000m in two stages to the summit of **Zwölferfkogel** at 1984m. There are two-drag lifts and some fairly easy skiing on the open south-east facing slopes near the top. The main run back to Hinterglemm is a broad intermediate piste facing north-east, with steeper and easier variants. The alternative is to take an unpatrolled back-of-the mountain route directly into the Glemm valley, which presents no serious difficulties until the steep final section where most skiers stick to a narrow zig-zag path. This route connects with the **Hochalm** lifts on the north side of the valley, serving a range of broad, smooth pistes, all graded red, though only the more direct runs justify the grading. From the top you can traverse across to Hinterglemm, or use the series of drags north of the village to progress along the valley. You can also traverse in the opposite direction from Hasenauer to Hochalm. This whole area has wide intersecting pistes of varying steepness suitable for most intermediates, but with little in the way of a challenge. Eventually, via Reiterkogel and Bernkogel, you come to a long straightforward blue run to Saalbach.

There are lifts from Saalbach back up these south-facing slopes on Bernkogel, and onward to Kohlmaiskopf, embarking on another area criss-crossed by intersecting pistes and paths, with some worthwhile intermediate runs, eventually bringing you to Wildenkarkogel. This is also accessible from near Jausern, where the easy run from Schattberg finishes. From the top you can traverse westwards towards Saalbach, or take a connecting lift to the Leogang ski area, on the north side of the ridge. The upper Leogang slopes have wide, open pistes ideal for most intermediates, and the runs down to the village are also fairly straightforward. The return ascent requires four lifts.

Mountain restaurants are profusely distributed around the slopes. Particularly attractive or good value ones include the Westgipfel Alm, the Panorama Alm and the Turner Alm.

The **nursery slopes** at Saalbach are central and gentle but south-facing, and deteriorate badly as the season progresses. Beginners must then use the open slopes on Bernkogel or Schattberg (at the cost of a lift ticket).

Lifts

Passes Single pass covers all local lifts, those for 2 days or more also cover Leogang. 'Hourly' tickets are available which give a refund when you hand them in early, as well as conventional half-day passes.

Cost 6-day pass AS1,320. 25% off in low season.
Children 37% off under 16, 52% off under 11.

Moderate queues develop in the morning peak period on the main exits from Saalbach – up to a half-hour wait for the cable-car. Queues at Hinterglemm are usually shorter. Minor bottlenecks can occur on the connecting lifts on the south-facing slopes, especially when the lower slopes are in poor condition.

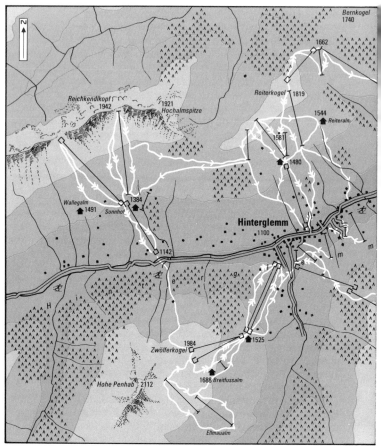

The resort

An attractive grouping of chalet-style buildings clustered around an onion-domed church gives Saalbach the look of a traditional Austrian village. But you don't have to look very hard to tell that present-day Saalbach is almost entirely a post-war development. The traffic-free central zone is pleasantly compact, with shops, restaurants and hotels lining the steepish, narrow main street leading past the church and square. All three main lifts, as well as the nursery slopes, are close by. The atmosphere is lively and friendly, though certainly not rowdy. Both resorts are popular with Germans, Dutch and Scandinavians.

Accommodation includes a mixture of stylish, modern hotels (chalet-style rather than concrete blocks) and cheaper guest-houses, many of which straggle out along the main road on either side of the village. It's well worth staying near the centre if you can, close to the lifts and the main life of the village, and in many cases you can ski right

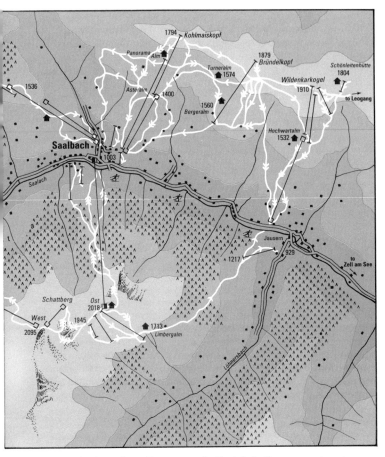

back to the front door. Recommended hotels in the upper price range include the Alpenhotel for plushness and comfort (✆ 666), the Saalbacher Hof for all-round service (✆ 7111) and the Neuhaus for proximity to lifts and value for money (✆ 7151).

Après-ski is lively from late afternoon onwards. Several hotels and bars have tea dancing and are usually packed. The Hinterhag Alm is one lively and popular spot. There's plenty to do in the evenings too, with a variety of discos, live bands and traditional Austrian music.

Ski school

Classes 2hr morning and afternoon.
Cost 6 days AS870. Private lessons AS320/hr, AS1,280/day.
Special courses Racing, Alpine touring.

Children Same times and prices as for adults; lunchtime care/meal for ages 4 up, AS80/day. Ski kindergarten, age 3 up, 10.00–4.00, 6 days with lunch AS1,200.

Reports on the ski school have been mostly favourable, though we've also heard of some inexperienced and indifferent instructors and over-used nursery slopes. Classes can be large (12–14) and you may find yourself in a non-English speaking group. A small breakaway group of instructors now operate as the Saalbacher Ski-Guides, taking non-beginners around the slopes and showing them the best snow conditions, off-piste areas, etc. No formal tuition is given and prices are pitched about 10% below those of the ski school. We've had one enthusiastic report of this service.

Other activities

Cross-country 8km trail from Saalbach to Jausern, 10km trail from Hinterglemm to Lengau.

Not skiing Swimming (free for holders of 6-day or longer lift passes), sauna, solarium, tennis, togogganing, bowling.

Both cross-country trails are along the flat floor of the valley and are overshadowed by the Schattberg and Zwölferkogel respectively. More extensive cross-country opportunities can be found by taking a 35-minute bus ride to Zell am See. Many hotels have their own swimming pools and saunas.

Travel

Airport Munich; transfer about 3hr.
Railway Zell am See; regular buses.
Road Via Munich; chains rarely needed.

Reachable resorts Zell am See and Kaprun are close, Badgastein and Kitzbühel within reach.

Day-time buses run every 20 minutes (and more frequently at morning and afternoon peaks) betwen Jausern, Saalbach and Hinterglemm, supplementing the much less frequent Post bus. There are plenty of taxis to cope with the post-skiing queue overflows and for evening transport along the valley. A car is no great advantage unless you're planning trips outside the valley or staying in the outskirts of the village, and parking in central Saalbach is a problem only partly alleviated by a multi-storey park on the edge of the village.

Miscellaneous

Tourist office ✆ (6541) 7272. Tx 66507.
Medical Doctor and dentist in resort, hospital in Zell am See (18km).
Equipment hire 6 days skis AS420, boots 150, X-C 360.

Resort beds 14,000 in hotels, 2,000 in apartments.
Package holidays AU, BL, HO, IG, IT, NE, SKW.

Hinterglemm 1100m

Although Hinterglemm has also stuck to the proper Alpine style in most of its development, it has achieved a less satisfactory result than Saalbach. The road along the valley runs through the centre, and even though it goes nowhere it interferes with both safety and atmosphere. There are big apartment blocks at the west end of the village, which are rather out of things. The nursery slopes are extensive, north-facing and free from passing traffic; they have the advantage of staying in good condition for longer, but the disadvantage of getting relatively little midwinter sun.

Tourist office As Saalbach. **Package holidays** AU, HO, IG, IT.

Place of Streif

Kitzbühel Austria 760m

Good for *Big ski area, mountain restaurants, après-ski, Alpine charm, not skiing, easy road access, rail access, short airport transfers*
Bad for *Tough skiing, lift queues, skiing convenience, late holidays, resort-level snow*

Linked resorts: Kirchberg, Jochberg, Pass Thurn

Linking lifts and runs to form a ski 'circus' is no longer the novelty it was when they first created one at Kitzbühel. As modern circuses go this one is low, with the result that its lower slopes are often icy, and washed out long before spring; and it suffers from lift bottlenecks – not least in Kitzbühel itself, where the queues are some of the worst (and worst-behaved) in the Alps. But with those provisos it is a very attractive skiing area, possessing a delightful mixture of friendly woodlands (with chalet restaurants playing jolly Tyrolean tunes) and open upper slopes commanding huge and magnificent views – which may come as a surprise, considering the altitude. The snow is often good, and the shared skiing of Kitzbühel and Kirchberg makes an impressive ski region by all but the most testing standards – though the so-called Ski Safari route linking with the skiing of Jochberg and Pass Thurn can hardly be called big game. Most of the skiing is not particularly taxing; as one of our most widely travelled reporters put it, 'without wishing to overstate my skill, I would have welcomed a few more challenging runs'.

Kitzbühel is a substantial town on a main road and rail thoroughfare. It is one of the oldest and most famous of Austrian ski resorts, and along with Lech and Zürs one of the most fashionable. Unlike the other two it is large and not exclusive, and attracts large numbers of British skiers. Slopes and town are very attractive, provided you aren't put off by traffic and teeming humanity. Getting an après-ski drink can involve a renewal of national hostilities which officially ended in 1945. Still, the skiing world would be dull indeed if every resort were quiet, remote and smooth-running, and if you go to Kitz you accept the hubbub that goes with a major international resort. Kitzbühel is a scintillating place, never more so than when the ski-racing world's inhabitants descend on it in their Range Rovers and Porsches for the most famous downhill in the World Cup calendar, on the icy slopes of the Streif.

There are several quieter villages which give the chance to enjoy the skiing, without having to submit to the tumult of the town – Kirchberg most important among them. Although rustic by Kitzbühel's standards, it is nevertheless a large, busy resort. If you want a haven of tranquillity, Kirchberg is not it. But it is certainly more attractive as a base than bargain hotels 'near' Kitzbühel, which in terms of skiing and après-skiing convenience are a long way from anywhere.

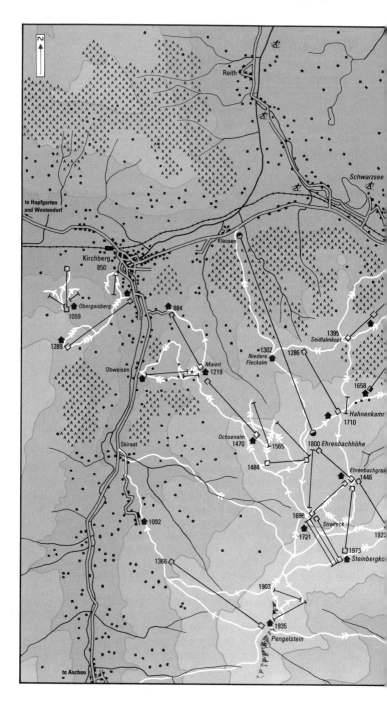

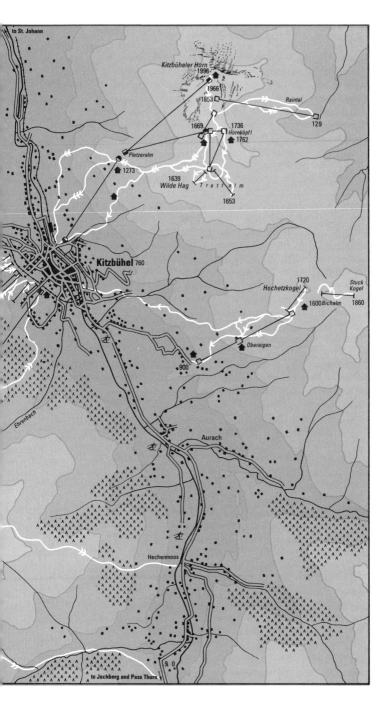

The skiing top 1995m bottom 760m

The skiing is in three main areas. Kitzbühel separates two of them –
Horn and Hahnenkamm (which links Kitzbühel with Kirchberg). The
third, above Jochberg and Pass Thurn, can almost be reached on skis
from the Hahnenkamm – via the 'Ski Safari'.

The **Kitzbüheler Horn** is a big and beautiful mountain, its peak rising
over 1200m from the valley floor and giving tremendous top-of-the-
world views. For the skier, it's less good than it looks: the runs are
rather limited, and much easier than they are graded except when
conditions are bad – which towards the bottom means quite often, since
they face mostly south-west. The skiing is reached (after a long walk
from the town centre across main road, rivers and railway) by a lengthy
combination of gondola and cable-cars – one to the Horn itself, the
other towards the lower Hornköpfl, nearby.

Most flanks of the Horn are steep and rocky, which explains the lack
of a lift link with nearby St Johann. At the top there's no obvious
alternative to the single piste, which soon branches to give access to
the Raintal bowl on the back of the mountain. Although the runs are
black and red, there isn't much to this area (the red is almost a schuss).
Beyond a briefly dense network of short lifts and mostly easy runs
around the Trattalm (a good post-nursery area), the run back down to
Kitzbühel dutifully splits into black, red and blue. The black isn't steep,
but may present a stern test of skating ability. The red is exhaustingly
flat for a long way at the bottom.

Just along the hill, an isolated chain of little-used lifts above the
hamlet of Aurach serves limited straight-up-and-down pistes facing
south-west, and an off-piste route to Fieberbrunn.

The **Hahnenkamm** is the site of the world's most feared downhill
race, but most of the runs are easily managed by intermediates, as long
as the snow is good. It is more easily reached from the centre than the
Horn, but is still quite a walk. Direct access is by cable-car over a steep
wooded mountainside to an open ridge about 900m above. The
preferable alternative in all but the worst weather is to take the two
Streifalm chair-lifts, thus avoiding not only the cable-car queue but also
some plodding at the top. There are a couple of good, long,
northish-facing runs back to the town from the Streifalm, the most direct
being the downhill race-course, described elsewhere in the *Guide* (by
someone who should know) as the ultimate test of a racer's
commitment and sanity. For a brief period after the race the course can
easily be identified and less easily skied.

The Hahnenkamm gives access to the heart of the skiing which
Kitzbühel shares with Kirchberg, a few miles round the mountain. It
offers lots of variety, some good off-piste runs, and some very long and
beautiful pistes – down one flank to the valley between Kitzbühel and
Pass Thurn, and down the other to points either side of Kirchberg.

There's an easy run down into the Ehrenbachgraben dip where more
queues build up for the four chair-lifts which fan out from here (it is very
easy to get in the wrong queue). The skiing here, beneath
Steinbergkogel, is the most challenging in the region – a genuinely

black 500m drop, facing north, with a number of variants and often big moguls. From the top of the ridge there are apparently good off-piste runs, a long run down through the woods to Hechenmoos and an easy connection to the Pengelstein. From Pengelstein there is a long easy run down to a bus stop beyond **Kirchberg** and an unpatrolled route (which involves some initial walking) down to Aschau (bus back to Kirchberg). The Kirchberg lifts are some way from the village, and few Kitzbühel-based skiers bother with the walk across to the Gaisberg single chair-lift which serves a black run dropping 450m. We didn't, either.

Above Kirchberg the Ehrenbachhöhe is a busy meeting place, with several hotels and restaurants around the summit (there's quite a bit of walking). There are easy connections to and from Hahnenkamm skiing, and long runs down north-west-facing slopes back to Kirchberg (mostly gentle) and the north-facing slope to Klausen (with more scope for challenge and off-piste adventure), now served by a 6-seater gondola.

A very long, easy run from Pengelstein forms the main link in the Ski Safari chain; the bottom half goes along a road through woods – very slow, but beautiful. Then it's about 5 or 10 minutes' walk up to the lifts at **Jochberg** (920m to 1728m), of which you have to take nine in order to complete your Safari to the slopes above **Pass Thurn** (1265m to 1995m). A simple network, mostly of drag-lifts but with a couple of double chairs, serves mostly easy, wide open skiing with beautiful views from the top lifts up the valley towards the distant Kitzbüheler Horn and with one stiff mogul-field to provide a change from all the gentle cruising. The return to Kitzbühel from Pass Thurn has be made by bus, a ride of nearly 20km.

Mountain restaurants are liberally scattered around the slopes and peaks of the area; they're not much more expensive than the national average, and in several cases attractive, welcoming and sunny.

The **nursery slopes**, across a broad area at the bottom of the Hahnenkamm, are no more than adequate – rather a thoroughfare, and often short of snow. Both mountains have easy runs to move on to.

Lifts

Passes Kitzbühel, Kirchberg, Jochberg, Pass Thurn, Aschau and Aurach lifts (and linking buses) are covered by one pass. Day passes are cheaper the later you buy them. Also 'hourly' tickets, for which you get a refund when you hand them in, and passes for any 5 days in 7, and 10 in 14. **Cost** 6-day pass AS1,240. 18% off in low-season (includes late March). **Beginners** Coupons (not on all lifts). **Children** 50% off under 15. Also cheap coupons.

Kitzbühel is large, easy to get to, and fashionable. The result is lift queues wherein, as one reporter put it, 'you really feel your capital outlay trickling away'. Exits from the town (especially the Horn gondola) are the main (but by no means the only) bottlenecks, with waits of over an hour not uncommon; the new 6-seater gondola at Klausen has not reduced the Hahnenkamm queues but does offer an easy way to avoid them. Returning to Klausen entails long queues for the lifts back to Ehrenbachhöhe. Queues at Jochberg and Pass Thurn are by comparison negligible.

The resort

Kitzbühel is set splendidly between its main ski areas, spreading across a wide and busy junction of valleys. It is a large and colourful old town enclosed by walls and, less prettily, by main roads and a loop in the railway. The old town with its twin-towered church, cobbled streets and gaily painted houses is one of the few ski resorts you might choose to visit just for a look. The centre is, by day at least, traffic-free, but only at the cost of a complicated and nearly always congested one-way ring-road system, which doesn't prevent traffic seriously impairing the quality of Kitzbühel life throughout the season – for drivers and pedestrians alike. Getting from the centre of town to either ski area involves crossing the railway line and a long walk or slow bus ride.

The resort centre is picturesque and full of tightly packed, beautifully painted buildings and people – many of them Germans, but also large numbers of British and others from further afield. Lots of tour operators take skiers on modest budgets and it is by no means an exclusive resort. Several members commented on how friendly they found local people. Shopping is sophisticated and international.

Accommodation consists equally of hotels large, comfortable and expensive, and guest-houses cheap and simple, with little in between. The town has spread far beyond the old core, and because of the far-reaching coverage of the lift pass lots of (mostly cheap) accommodation which is a long way from Kitzbühel itself is sold under its name. Because skiing on the Horn is of secondary interest, the best location is either in the old centre (certainly the most attractive place to stay) or near the Hahnenkamm lifts, most people's starting point for the skiing, and where the nursery slopes are. Central, attractive but expensive hotels are not hard to find. The Haselsberger (✆2866) is cheaper than most and ideally placed for skiers; one regular visitor recommended the Mühlbergerhof (✆2835) ('very friendly, old fashioned, family-run'), on the ring-road some way from the centre but not far from the main skiing.

Après-ski from late afternoon until the small hours is extremely lively and varied, from the horrifically crowded Londoner pub to the Casino (jacket, tie and passport). There are plenty of tea bars, a tea-dance in the Tenne, discothèques, smoky dives, and more traditional musical venues. Organised evening outings. Restaurants are many and varied.

Ski school

Classes 2hr morning and afternoon.
Children Ski school for ages 3 upwards same times and price as for adults; lunchtime care/meal available.

Cost 6 days AS870. Private lessons about AS300/hr.
Special courses Wedel and others, December and March.

We've had mixed reports, over recent years, of the famous Red Devils – with tales of very large classes and of instructors more interested in skiing than teaching. In 1985, reports were almost entirely favourable – though classes as large as 24 have been spotted.

Other activities

Cross-country 14km trail to and from Hechenmoos (medium), 20km of loops around Reith (mixed), 3km at Schwarzsee (easy). Instruction and free guided excursions (thrice weekly) available.

Not skiing Local museum, open-air ice rink (curling/skating), swimming (free to holders of lift-passes), sauna, solarium, riding, sleigh rides, wildlife park, tennis, squash, fitness centre, toboggan run, ski bobs.

Although Kitzbühel is low and its surroundings rather built up, its X-C trails are good and the guided excursions recommended. Non-skiers will find a great variety of things to do. Operators organise regular excursions to Innsbruck, Salzburg, Kufstein and Italy.

Travel

Airport Munich; transfer about 2hr. Daily public buses.
Road Via Munich; chains rarely needed.

Railway Main-line station in resort.
Reachable resorts The Grossraum ski region (Söll etc) is next door.

The day-time buses around the resort and to other villages in the ski area are efficiently organised, though stretched at peak times. The service is complicated by the one-way system and hampered by the traffic. For the evening, there are plenty of taxis. Taking a car has the undoubted benefit of being independent of the bus system, but this may be outweighed by the hellish difficulty of driving and parking.

Miscellaneous

Tourist office ✆ (5356) 2155. Tx 5118413.
Medical Hospital, doctors (including specialists), chemists, dentists in resort.
Equipment hire 6 days skis AS360–480, boots AS180–270, X-C AS450–540.

Resort beds 7,000 in hotels, 1,000 in apartments.
Package holidays AU, BS, BT, CH, CL, ED, EN, GL, HA, HM, HO, HU, IG, IT, NE, NT, PS, SVL, TC, TH, TT.

Kirchberg 850m

Kirchberg is a busy village 5km from Kitzbühel, centred on a road junction, with river and railway nearby. It shares some of its more interesting neighbour's problems, as well as its skiing – it is full of traffic, and its lifts are an inconvenient 5 or 10 minutes from the centre. The idea that you can do Kitzbühel on the cheap by staying in Kirchberg is misguided, but it is an attractively lively resort in its own right, and has long been popular among British skiers with no taste for the glamour of Kitzbühel. As well as some 7,000 beds (mostly in hotels), 175 farms, 1,500 cows, 300 sheep and 75 horses, it has plenty of good traditional Tyrolean nightlife, good facilities for cross-country, walking, toboganing, skating, sleigh rides, swimming and plenty of organised excursions. Most of the hotels and guest-houses are in the centre, though there are a handful by the main lift departure for Ehrenbachhöhe. There are nursery slopes at that same place, and both skiing and non-skiing kindergartens. We have one recent report comprehensively in favour of the ski-school, and none against.

Tourist office ✆ (5357) 2309. Tx 51371.
Package holidays BS, EN, IT, NE, PS, SKW, SLV, TT.

Grossraum: space available

Söll Austria 700m

Good for *Short airport transfers, après-ski, easy road access, big ski area*
Bad for *Tough skiing, late holidays, skiing convenience, lift queues, resort-level snow*

Linked resorts: Scheffau, Going, Ellmau, Brixen, Hopfgarten
Separate resort: Westendorf

Like nearby Kitzbühel, Söll shares with several less well-known neighbours a broad ski area which is spread around a pleasantly wooded, mostly round-topped ridge – more hilly than mountainous in Alpine terms. The area's name is Grossraum, which means big space, and it is a fair summary. The skiing is friendly in general, with lots of villages dotted along the broad low valleys below. Söll is the main centre, particularly for British visitors: although still definitely a village, it attracts very large numbers of package holiday-makers from the UK, with the result that the proportion of British visitors is very high – probably the highest in the Alps. It attracts especially (to quote one reporter) 'the young singles fraternity for whom skiing is secondary to nightlife' and whose nightlife usually ends up with a lot of noise in the village streets at an hour when skiers ought to be allowed some sleep. But the skiing is more extensive and more varied than it is often given credit for.

The skiing top 1827m bottom 621m

The Grossraum ski region is spread around broad, medium-altitude mountains separating two wide valleys. One side consists of north-facing slopes above Söll, Scheffau, Ellmau and Going, the other of south-facing ones accessible from Hopfgarten and Brixen im Thale. Itter, between Söll and Hopfgarten, has a few short lifts for beginners, but these do not give access to the rest of the skiing. Söll has the highest and steepest skiing, on the Hohe Salve (1829m). But this is a mixed blessing; the runs linking with other parts of the area are tricky at the best of times, and often treacherous, and in bad weather the Hohe Salve chair-lift often doesn't operate. Scheffau's skiing, although less immediately impressive, is better connected, and a better starting point for intermediates wanting to make the most of the Grossraum.

For most people, **Söll**'s skiing starts with a long walk from the village centre to the lifts (there are ski-buses, but few and far between). The two chairs go up to Salvenmoos, an open but not very flat shelf, with a few short drag-lifts on the easier slopes at the foot of the impressively steep Hohe Salve, reached by chair-lift. Runs down from this beautiful, panoramic peak (with church and restaurant on top) are not easy and include a genuinely black run down the face. Apart from these the most interesting runs are the long descents through the trees from Salvenmoos to Söll, an excellent red and a more roundabout 'family run' blue, both of which can be treacherous or unskiable when icy.

Connecting runs from the Hohe Salve to the rest of the Grossraum skiing involve tackling sunny slopes which although not necessarily steep are often unpleasantly icy or bare, or taking a chair-lift down to Rigi above Hopfgarten. The easiest runs follow this chair-lift down and in good conditions can be extended a long way (1200m vertical) down to Hopfgarten itself. From Rigi there are easy runs round to Salvenmoos and a run down to Itter. The more difficult run from Hohe Salve (not a piste) goes directly down the south-facing flank to a wide area of almost flat lifts and runs around Filzalm above Brixen, with easy links to and from Hopfgarten. The runs (including a black) down to Brixen are excellent, given good snow; but don't count on it.

From Filzalm there are easy although time-consuming connections over gently-rounded knolls (Zinsberg and Eiberg) into the top of the valley which divides Söll's skiing from Scheffau's, and up the other side to Brandstadl. Runs down to Scheffau are long open trails through the woods, steep enough to be a challenge and fast, but wide enough to be easily manageable. The alternative is to ski further along the ridge to Hartkaiser, or even Astberg, for runs down to Ellmau and Going. Getting back to Söll from these places means retracing your steps. Many skiers prefer to ski these parts of the system (distant on skis but close by road) by taking the Scheffau–Hopfgarten bus in the morning or the evening. Several reporters found that Scheffau had better snow conditions than Söll, and was worth the trip.

Söll's **nursery slopes** are beside the chair-lift departure – open fields between the bottom of the wooded mountain and the village. They are splendidly wide and near-horizontal, but often short (or devoid) of snow, when the gentle slopes at Salvenmoos have to be used. There are always lots of people around, and often lift queues.

Mountain restaurants were generally considered by reporters to be adequate but not exciting. Those at Salvenmoos are often crowded.

Lifts

Passes Grossraum pass covers all lifts, and the Scheffau–Hopfgarten bus. Day and half-day passes, and limited area passes (eg Söll only) available.

Cost 6-day pass AS960.
Beginners Coupons.
Children 25% off, under 15.

The main problems with the Söll lift system are the limitations of the link with the other Grossraum resorts (often closed in bad weather and awkward in bad conditions) and the time it takes to get to nearby Scheffau on skis. New lifts planned for 1985–86 are the solution. A persistent irritant is the amount of walking between lifts, especially from the top of the double chair-lift out of Söll. Queues are reported as often bad for the main Söll lifts (about half-hour waits common). Afternoon queues can make the journey back from the Scheffau a long one. A new gondola has replaced the old, slow chair-lifts up from Scheffau.

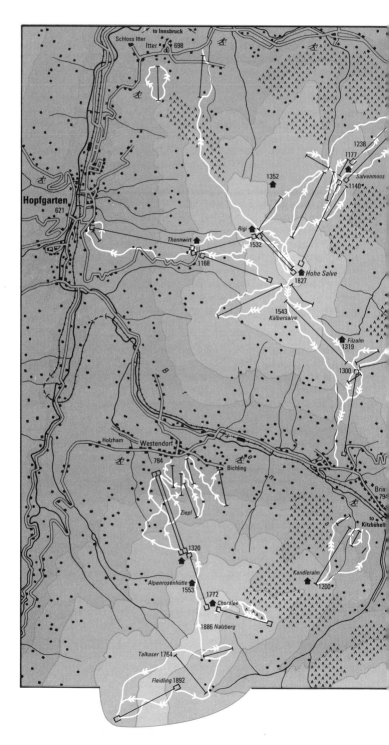

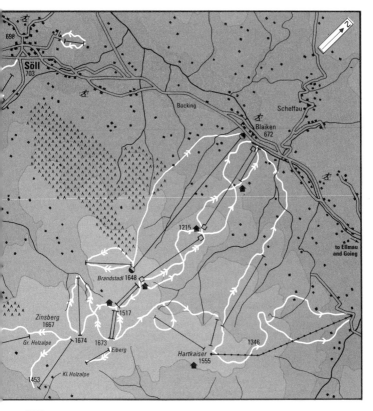

The resort

Söll is not a very large village but it has spread considerably across its
wide valley. The buildings are attractive, in a neat neo-Tyrolean way,
but do not add up convincingly to a village with any real character. A
main road by-passes the village, between it and the ski slopes.

Accommodation is in hotels, mostly simple but satisfactory. The
Post (∅ 5221) is an attractive old hotel right in the centre (of the nightlife
as well as the village). The Eggerwirt (∅ 5236) and Austria (∅ 5213)
are quieter central alternatives. (Several reporters were in central
hotels on full board terms, and regretted it.) There are several hotels
lining the nursery slopes; the Ingeborg (∅ 5223) and Eisenmann (∅
5258) have received favourable reports. Hotels neither in the centre nor
near the skiing appear to have little to recommend them.

With so many young British around, **après-ski** activity is predictably
lively (nearly all reporters remarked on the very crowded thrice-weekly
folk-singing evenings at the Hotel Post and on the Whisky Mühle disco
for up-to-date chart sounds). There are all sorts of organised evening
amusements, from bowling to zither performances.

Ski school

Classes 2hr morning and afternoon.
Cost 6 days AS870. Private lessons
AS280/hr.

Children Ski kindergarten, ages 5–15,
9.30 to 4.15, 6 days with lunch AS1,290.
Special courses Guided Grossraum tours.

We have approving reports of numerous colonial instructors with
better-than-Austrian English (though one reporter recommended the
Austrians, for a more serious attitude).

Other activities

Cross-country 30km easy runs
between Söll, Scheffau and Itter.
Instruction available.

Not skiing Swimming, sauna, solarium,
natural ice rink (skating, curling), riding,
sleigh rides, toboggan run.

The trails, on the valley floor, look satisfactory to our untutored eye, but
one X-C reporter pronounces them uninteresting. The resort is not very
exciting for non-skiers, but the swimming pool (with a heated outdoor
section) is highly recommended. Lots of organised excursions.

Travel

Airport Munich; transfer about 2hr.
Railway Kufstein (15km); bus to resort.
Road Via Munich; chains rarely
needed.

Reachable resorts Kitzbühel is only a
few miles to the east, the Zillertal
(Mayrhofen, Zell, Hintertux) rather further
away to the west.

Set low, and beside a main road very near the motorway system, Söll is
admirably accessible both for motorists and for air travellers. Having a
car can be very valuable for interesting skiing excursions and for going
to glacier areas (Stubai, Hintertux) when local conditions are poor.
Operators sometimes organise similar excursions by coach.

Miscellaneous

Tourist office ✆ (5333) 5216. Tx 51216.
Resort beds 1,400 in hotels, 2,800
other.
Package holidays BS, BT, CH, ED, EN,
GL, HO, IG, IT, NE, NT, TH.

Medical Fracture clinic at Kitzbühel,
hospital at Wörgl (11km), doctor, dentist,
chemist in resort.
Equipment hire 6 days skis AS310,
boots AS185, X-C AS340.

Westendorf   790m

Westendorf is a small village in the Brixental near Kitzbühel and within
sight of the Grossraum skiing, but separate from it. The skiing is a small
area of mostly easy runs, mainly served by a long double chair-lift from
the edge of the village (about 5 minutes' gentle walk from the centre). It
is pretty skiing on broad, mostly woodland pistes and snow-covered
roads, and suits first- and second-time skiers very well. There are good
broad nursery slopes beside the main lift departure point.

Westendorf attracts numerous British skiers, but even more Dutch,
which met with the approval of several reporters. In general it is a very
friendly village, with plenty of nightlife, contemporary (Andy's Tavern)
and traditional, good excursion possibilities, and some excellent hotels
– the Schermer and Jakobwirt both highly recommended by reporters.

Tourist office ✆ (5334) 6230. Tx 51237.
Package holidays BS, EN, GL, HO, IG, IT, NE, NT, TC, TH.

Wildschönau und Schneewinkel

East Tirol: small resorts

Wildschönau sounds savage, but is actually an area of mainly amiable skiing on low, mostly wooded mountains south of the Inn valley, between Alpbach and Söll. The area embraces several villages. Cross-country trails along the valley link the villages, and there are plenty of marked paths. There are nursery slopes at each village, but the rest of the skiing is concentrated above two of them. **Niederau** (830m) is spread out on a gentle north-facing slope, its modern hotels and guest-houses built in traditional style but without any central focus. Chair-lifts (which are not always up to the demand) to two separate ski areas, each with short drags above up to 1600m and 1500m, serving easy open runs. There is some variety in the intermediate runs to the village, the more challenging ones being unprepared routes rather than pistes. Small though it is, the village does not lack lively après-ski in its cafés, bars and discos, largely based in hotels. Our reporters have no complaint with their accommodation. Apart from the big VIP Clubhotel (one of two hotels atop the main lift), top dog is the central Austria ($\emptyset$ 8188). A few yards closer to the lift is the neat, modern Brunner ($\emptyset$ 8218) – simpler and cheaper. The Vicky ($\emptyset$ 8282) is one of the pivots of the nightlife.

The valley road climbs past a natural skating rink to a low col on which sits Oberau, a more established village with its own nursery slopes and an attractive community atmosphere. Beyond it the road drops to Mühltal, and then up a side valley is **Auffach** (870m), a tiny unspoilt but growing village with a chair-lift leading to a succession of drags serving easy and intermediate pistes on the open east-facing slopes of the Schatzberg (1901m).

The resorts which sell their shared lift pass under the *Schneewinkel* name are supposed to have a particularly snowy climate which compensates for their lack of altitude. Reports suggest that the magic may be wearing off. The main resorts, at least as far as British visitors are concerned are just over the hill from Kitzbühel. The hill is the Kitzbühelerhorn, and the easy-intermediate skiing of **St Johann** (660m) fans out over a north-facing wooded shoulder of it, from 1700m down to the edge of the resort. St Johann is a substantial valley town with a pleasant old centre and a lot of non-skiing activities. A few miles south-east is **Fieberbrunn** (800m), a pleasant roadside village with a fair range of easy and intermediate skiing on the Lärchfilzkogel (1655m). There is good ski touring around the Wildseeloder (2117m) to the south. The village has good non-skiing facilities, including swimming and skating, and does not lack traditional après-ski.

Tourist offices Wildschönau $\emptyset$ (5389) 8255, Tx 51139; Fieberbrunn $\emptyset$ (5354) 6304, Tx 51249; St Johann $\emptyset$ (5352) 2218, Tx 51-24117.
Package holidays Niederau: EN, GL, HO, IG, IT, NH, TH. Auffach: IG, STY. St Johann: AU, CH, EN, IT, NH, NT, PS, TH, TT, WM. Fieberbrunn: AU, GL, HO, IG, SNP.

Is love at first sight blind?

Alpbach Austria 1000m

Good for *Alpine charm, easy skiing, family skiing, après-ski, easy road access, short airport transfers*
Bad for *Tough skiing, late holidays, skiing convenience*

Alpbach is a small village in attractive although unspectacular mountainous country between Kitzbühel and Innsbruck. Its skiing area is inconveniently located, and is limited in extent, variety and challenge. Yet Alpbach is one of the best-loved of Austrian resorts, with a special corner in the affections of many British skiers who return year after year to meet their friends, both locals and regular visitors like themselves. Among so many picturesque little Tyrolean villages, Alpbach stands out as one of the prettiest of them all, and it wins visitors over from the moment they arrive. It is a particularly good place for a family holiday at Christmas, and for beginners, who stand to benefit more than most skiers from its welcoming, charming atmosphere.

The skiing top 1890m bottom 830m

Apart from a small nursery area beside the village, all Alpbach's skiing is on the slopes of the Wiedersbergerhorn, which means a short bus ride to and from the resort at either end of the day (and at lunch time for anyone with a village rendezvous). The usual starting point is the Achenwirt lift station beside the road up from Brixlegg. Two stages of chair-lift climb wooded north-facing slopes. There are broad trails down either side to the Kriegalm half-way station, including a race course marked black, and on down to the bottom to give an excellent long, fast course of over 1000m vertical – used by British racing clubs for annual competitions. Around Hornboden the views are splendid, the terrain is open and gentle with several short drag-lifts suitable for near-beginners. There is an easy blue run (mostly pathway) down as far as Kriegalm, but no further. Lifts from Inneralpbach join up with the skiing above Hornboden and serve a long, not very tough red run back down.

A single off-piste route is marked on the lift map, from the top of the Brandegg drag to Inneralpbach. Conditions are not off-piste for long, and neither this nor the added possibility of skiing over the hill to Hygna (buses back) make Alpbach a resort for ski adventurers.

There are several **mountain restaurants**; the self-service ones at Kriegalm and Hornboden are the most popular, but are often crowded; better prospects are to be found at Achenwirt and Inneralpbach.

The **nursery slopes** close to the village centre are very good, being sunny and offering a variety of terrain from flat to slightly challenging. When snow is short, beginners are taken up to Hornboden.

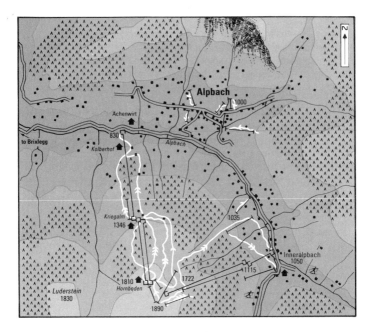

Lifts

Passes Covers all lifts and ski-bus from
Alpbach. 10% off in low season. Day and half-
day passes available.

Cost 6-day pass AS790.
Beginners Coupons.
Children 25% off under 15.

The chair-lifts up from Achenwirt to Hornboden are cold and crowded in
the mornings (half an hour's wait is not unusual) but not unbearably so;
most reporters preferred this to the risk of falling off the long, steep
drag-lift on the Inneralpbach side – amid dense woods with no easy
access to pistes (but now supplemented by a chair-lift).

The resort

Alpbach is a small village in a sunny position set on a hill, but compact
enough for that not to matter too much, even in ski boots. At the heart of
the village is its spotlessly clean green-and-white church, surrounded
by traditional chalet buildings large and small. Tradition is a very
evident part of Alpbach life, especially at Christmas and New Year,
which is when many of Alpbach's family regulars prefer to visit. A good
many such regulars are British; there is even a British ski club, the
Alpbach Visitors, based in the resort. Shopping is limited; one reporter
on a self-catering holiday regretted the lack of a butcher.

   Accommodation is mostly in hotels, with a wide variety of comfort
and cost between simple B&B houses and spacious, very comfortable

hotels. The centre of the village is the most convenient for the ski bus, but location isn't a serious worry. The most comfortable hotels are the expensive Böglerhof ($\wp$ 5227) and Alphof ($\wp$ 5371), both with swimming pools – the Böglerhof ideally placed for ski bus and nursery slopes, the Alphof quite a walk from the village centre. Among less expensive, more informal hotels, reporters recommend the Post ($\wp$ 5203), Messnerwirt ($\wp$ 5212) and Jakoberwirt ($\wp$ 5223) – all very friendly and central. Keen skiers may prefer to stay in Inneralpbach, but if you're that keen you probably shouldn't be considering Alpbach at all.

Après-ski is not very varied but has typically Tyrolean ingredients – notably the Tyrolean Evening itself, plus sleigh rides, skating and curling, very lively tea-time bars in central hotels, and a couple of discothèques. Reporters on B&B found little variety of restaurants.

Ski school

Classes 2hr morning and afternoon.
Cost 6 days AS870. Private lessons AS280/hr.
Children Ski kindergarten, ages 4–12

9.00–4.30, 6 days with lunch AS1,370. Non-ski kindergarten, ages 3–6, 9.30–4.15, 6 days with lunch AS960.

We have generally favourable reports on the ski school. Guides are available for day ski tours (with skins).

Other activities

Cross-country 17km of trails near Inneralpbach. Instruction available.
Not skiing 20km of cleared paths,

swimming, skating, curling, sauna/massage, sleigh rides, toboggan run.

X-C skiers should stay in Inneralpbach. The trails are low, but very attractive. Non-skiers can enjoy plenty of attractive walks, although not much within rendezvous range of skiers, and a wide choice of interesting excursions (Salzburg, Kitzbühel, Innsbruck, Vipiteno). The public pool is good, but a long walk from the village, as is the ice rink.

Travel

Airport Munich; transfer about 2hr.
Road Via Munich; chains rarely needed.

Railway Brixlegg; frequent buses.
Reachable resorts Kitzbühel, Söll, Mayrhofen are within day-trip range.

Having a car in Alpbach seems rather anti-social, but it does help you get to and from skiing, both locally and further afield. If staying in Inneralpbach a car is very useful for après-ski purposes. The bus to Achenwirt runs frequently enough for the needs of the small village; that to Inneralpbach is less frequent.

Miscellaneous

Tourist office $\wp$ (05336) 5211.
Tx 51380.
Equipment hire 6 days skis AS360–480, boots AS150–180, X-C AS390–480.
Resort beds 2,000 in hotels, 300 in apartments.

Medical Chemist and doctor in resort, dentist at Reith (6km), hospital at Wörgl (28km).
Package holidays AA, BS, EN, GL, HA, IG, NT, TH.

Skiing worth waiting for?

Mayrhofen Austria 630m

Good for *Nursery slopes, family skiing, easy skiing, Alpine charm, not skiing, après-ski, easy road access, rail access*
Bad for *Tough skiing, lift queues, skiing convenience, resort-level snow*

Separate resorts: Zell am Ziller, Hintertux

The Zillertal is a long-established summer and winter tourist region. It is a broad, straight, flat-bottomed valley, with a number of villages along the river and narrow-gauge railway. Fügen and Kaltenbach have some skiing but attract few British skiers; Zell am Ziller is a larger village and a bit of a resort; but its larger neighbour Mayrhofen is the main tourist centre, and one of the great British favourites in Austria. Beyond Mayrhofen the Zillertal splits into three small glacier valleys and the Tuxertal – a high, narrow, very rural valley in sharp contrast to the busy Zillertal, leading to Hintertux at the foot of some of Austria's best glacier skiing. Just beyond Mayrhofen, on the way up to Hintertux, Finkenberg is already linked up with Mayrhofen skiing; the more distant rustic village of Lanersbach has projects to join the main ski area, but hasn't yet got much skiing of its own. An overall area lift pass now covers the skiing in all these places and a few others (notably Gerlos, at a pass on the minor road which leads east from Zell am Ziller), but most skiers still go to Mayrhofen, and stay there to ski, with occasional sorties to Hintertux when the weather is good and the snow is bad.

Mayrhofen is a large, towny resort, only fairly attractive; but it enjoys a beautiful setting, its hotels are friendly, clean and comfortable and it is very jolly in the evenings. Its popularity must rest on these things (and on the reputation of the ski school, particularly its caring for young children), because its skiing is far from ideal – being too limited in variety for experienced skiers and yet awkward for the inexperienced, who have to take cable-cars (which means paying, and queuing) not only to get up to the skiing in the morning but also to get down from it in the afternoon. These are important drawbacks in the era of purpose-built resorts, and Mayrhofen has made improvements in the hope of maintaining its popularity – new lifts, and an area lift pass giving Mayrhofen skiers access to different skiing. Despite this, our numerous reporters were almost unanimous in recommending Mayrhofen only to inexperienced skiers, and nearly all of them remarked on the unpleasant length of the lift queues. Mayrhofen does not suffer the snow problems of other low Tyrolean resorts, because most skiers have to spend most of their time up on the sunny slopes at the top of the ski area; bad conditions between 700 and 1500m affect only a couple of runs, and the few experienced skiers who might expect to tackle them.

The skiing top 2278m bottom 640m

Mayrhofen skiing is on two separate mountains enclosing the Zillertal with their steep, wooded walls. The main skiing is on the Penken, reached by cable-car from the edge of town or by the Horberg gondola from Schwendau (a bus-ride away to the north) or, in the other direction, by the long double chair-lift from Finkenberg. The Ahorn on the other side of Mayrhofen is accessible only by cable-car from a point which is more than a walk from the edge of the village. For all these lifts (except Finkenberg's) there is a regular but often over-subscribed ski-bus shuttle service.

The **Ahorn** faces mainly north, but so gentle are the slopes around the top of the cable-car that orientation doesn't matter much. This is an excellent open, spacious beginners' area, with a broad and beautiful panorama. There is one run down from the upper slopes to the bottom which is graded red.

For most skiers, Mayrhofen skiing means the **Penken**. The notoriously crowded cable-car climbs over an unskiable wooded mountainside to a shelf at the top of the trees; chair-lifts starting an awkward distance from the top of the cable-car then go up to Penkenjoch. From Penken there is an unpatrolled run round the mountain, down a north-facing slope and through the woods with increasing difficulty to Schwendau, ending up near the Horberg gondola station. This is an excellent run for good skiers in good snow. Above Penken is a band of open, lightly wooded slopes of mostly intermediate difficulty, around the east-, north- and south-facing slopes of the Penkenjoch ridge. The south-facing side of the ridge is the **Finkenberg** ski area. There are several runs of intermediate standard down towards Finkenberg as far as the trees, but, as in so many places along this narrow, steep-sided valley, the major part of the available mountain – the 1000m vertical from from the middle station of the chair-lift to the village – provides only one run, and that is mostly a path through the woods. On the Mayrhofen side of the Penkenjoch, the most interesting runs are those facing north (the Nordhang), some of which have steep and mogulled stretches where the snow is usually good. The longest runs down to the bottom of the Lärchwald give about 400m vertical drop. A new chair-lift and drag have recently been opened up on the other side of the Horbergtal to Gerent, at 2278m the top of Mayrhofen's skiing. There is only one run down from this point and half of it consists of an uninteresting path across the mountain from the bottom of the Gerent drag-lift to the top of the Horberg gondola. However, the Gerent lifts do (we are told) open up some new off-piste skiing possibilities, and the top half of the run down is impressively steep, often mogulled.

Nursery slopes on the Ahorn are excellent – sunny, high, and pleasantly free from bombers on skis. One beginner complained at the walk from the top of the cable-car to the easiest part of the slopes, for absolute beginners not yet initiated into the mysteries of drag-lifts. There is a small nursery area on the Penken, often used by the adult ski

school; this is more convenient for meeting up with other skiers.

The Penken is also better equipped with **mountain restaurants**, which are plentiful, sunny and good, though often crowded after ski school. Crowds are even more of a problem on the Ahorn, where there is only one restaurant. Going down to the resort for lunch is not something you want to do if you can avoid it.

Lifts

Passes The Zillertal Super Ski pass covers all lifts in Mayrhofen, Finkenberg Hintertux, Lanersbach, Zell am Ziller, Gerlos, Ramsau, Fügen, Hochfügen, Kaltenbach, plus Post buses and the Mayrhofen to Jenbach railway, and is available for periods of over 4 days. The Mayrhofen lift pass covers Penken, Horberg and Ahorn lifts but not Finkenberg ones, and is available for periods from half a day.

Cost 6-day Zillertal pass AS1,000. 20% off in low season.

Beginners Lift pass needed.

Children 33% off under 14.

Summer skiing Extensive at Hintertux.

Reporters tell us that at peak seasons (New Year and February) queues for both cable-cars are very long, both going up in the morning and coming down in the evening. The Horberg gondola is usually much quicker, even taking account of the bus ride. The Finkenberg chair-lift can also be a shorter route to the Penken than the cable-car – though we hear of two-hour queues there at New Year. Tour operator reps may advise against getting the area lift pass; we recommend it strongly for all but beginners, both early and late in the season. Apart from anything else, it enables you to ski the Finkenberg side of the Penkenjoch.

The resort

Mayrhofen is set in the middle of some of Austria's best-loved scenery, at the junction of Zillertal and Tuxertal with very steep wooded mountains climbing to the east, south and west. It is attractively traditional in style and not totally given over to tourism, although its long main street between the market place near the station and the Penken cable-car is busy and touristy. The village is spread out on flat ground beside the river. The main valley road by-passes the resort centre and although there are always plenty of cars around, congestion isn't unpleasant.

Accommodation is mostly in very attractive, traditionally-styled hotels (with traditionally-clad staff), and nearly all reports we have are favourable. One reporter had stayed in four different cheap B&B houses and found them all excellent. There are a couple of hotels by the Penken cable-car station – the Sporthotel (℘ 2205) is large and comfortable and very full of British tourists (residents and evening revellers). The large Neuhaus (℘ 2203) was generally rated by reporters as the best hotel in the resort, within easy reach of the ski-bus. We particularly liked the Kramerwirt (℘ 2615) a refurbished old hotel with lots of charm, and the new, very attractive Elisabeth (℘ 2929) just off the main street. The Neuhaus and Elisabeth both have their own pools, as does the St Georg (℘ 2793), also recommended by one reporter who stayed there.

Après-ski is very lively. There are venues for traditional live music as well as deafening discothèques, and Tyrolean, tobogganing and sleigh-riding evenings are regularly organised by operators. Hotel bars see most of the après-skiing custom, though they are not very atmospheric; the Sporthotel's is packed from early evening.

Ski school

Classes 2hr morning and afternoon.
Cost 6 days AS840. Private lessons
AS270/hr.

Children Ski kindergarten, ages 4–12,
9.15–4.00, 6 days with lunch AS1,200.
Special courses Ski touring trips.

The ski school is Mayrhofen's pride and joy – especially the ski
kindergarten, started by a local and international racing family (Spiess)
in the late 1950s, when it was the first of its kind. Arrangements for
children are excellent – they are looked after all day, and jump the
queue for the cable-car to Ahorn, which is basically a huge skiing
playground. Reports on adult ski school are generally favourable
(English spoken, serious attitude), but large class sizes were
mentioned. The piste map shows some of the possibilities for the local
tours – dotted descents from the surrounding peaks, far beyond the
reach of the ski-lift network. According to the ski school few of the
climbs are more than two to four hours, going slowly, and a proper stem
turn is good enough for the descents.

Other activities

Cross-country 21km of easy trails
along valley floor to Zell am Ziller.
Instruction available.

Not skiing Natural ice rink, bowling,
riding, sleigh rides, swimming, sauna,
jacuzzi, 45km cleared paths.

One X-C skiing reporter was well pleased with the long valley floor
trails, mostly easy. They are not very reliable for snow cover.
Mayrhofen is a good place for non-skiers, although the pool is small
and the natural ice unreliable. Walks are good, and there are plenty of
attractive excursions, within the local area and further afield to
Innsbruck, Salzburg, and Italy (Cortina and Vipiteno). Non-skiers can
reach sunny mountain restaurants on both sides. The valley train is an
attraction in itself, especially for children.

Travel

Airport Munich; transfer about 2½hr.
Railway Jenbach; local train to resort.
Road Via Munich; chains rarely
needed.

Reachable resorts The Grossraum
skiing (Söll etc) and Kitzbühel are within
easy day-trip range.

The local buses round Mayrhofen and serving the main lifts are free to
holders of visitors' cards. There is no evening public transport. A car is
very useful for getting around the Zillertal lift pass area, and for
day-trips. Reporters who attempted Hochfügen for a day's skiing
remarked on how long it took to reach from Fügen, and how infrequent
the buses were.

Miscellaneous

Tourist office ✆ (5285) 2305. Tx 53850.
Medical Hospital at Schwarz (40km);
doctors, dentists, chemist in resort.
Equipment hire 6 days skis AS400,
boots AS150.

Resort beds 7,700, mostly in hotels
and pensions.
Package holidays BS, BT, CL, ED, EN,
GL, HA, HO, IG, IT, NE, NT, SPT, SUS,
TC, TH, TT.

Zell am Ziller

Like Mayrhofen, Zell is a large village in the main valley where life and tourism are not wholly ski-oriented. It is a fairly unremarkable, traditional village, lent some charm by the little steam train running through its centre and the Ziller round the edge, and by the interesting, ornately decorated Baroque church. It is a much quieter place than Mayrhofen, and several reporters remarked that nightlife consisted either of discos or hotel lounges without any cosy atmosphere. As at Mayrhofen the general standard of the accommodation and of hotel food is high, and the warmth of welcome exceptional. Reporters highly recommend the simple Neuwirt (℘ 2209) and the more comfortable Zellerhof (℘ 2612).

Zell's two skiing areas, Kreuzjoch and Gerlosstein, are both inconveniently distant from the resort; the ski-bus is essential, and there may be long queues to get the bus as well as the lifts. The Kreuzjoch skiing faces mainly west and south-west, and chiefly consists of open, easy intermediate runs over slopes spotted with trees between the Rosenalm restaurant and nursery area (1760m) and the top of the skiing (Karspitze, 2260m). There is one woodland run down to Wiesenalm (1309m), but no pistes down to the resort even when the snow is good. There are often queues to go up and down. This is a limited but sunny and attractive skiing area, suited to mixed groups of intermediates and beginners.

The Gerlosstein skiing is even further from Zell, reached either from the road up to Gerlos or from Ramsau, the next village up the valley towards Mayrhofen. The skiing goes only up to 1850m but there are long runs all the way down to the bottom on both sides of the mountain, and snow conditions are usually good (the slopes face north and are less crowded than the Kreuzjoch). One reporter who visited Zell in March after a very warm spell found better snow than at Mayrhofen.

Reports on the ski school and ski kindergarten are favourable.

Tourist office ℘ (5282) 2281. Package holidays BT, EN, HA, IT, NE,
Tx 53650. NT, PQ, SPT, TC.

Hintertux

Hintertux is a small village at the head of the Tuxertal some 10 miles from Mayrhofen (¾hr by bus). Its glacier skiing between 2600m and 3280m attracts serious racers for summer training sessions. In winter the village is a bit bleak and remote, and the skiing on the Gefrorne Wand can be chilly in the extreme. Most skiers go up for the day or the afternoon from the lower resorts, particularly late in the season if the rest of the Zillertal is turning to slush and ice. We were surprised in March to find the glacier almost as uncrowded as Mayrhofen, and impressed by the skiing. On the main glacier area there are long intermediate runs and shorter ones beneath the Tuxerjoch; lower down the runs get increasingly steep, narrow and mogulled. Inexperienced skiers can take gondolas down.

Tourist office ℘ (5287) 207. Package holidays SCP, SNP.

Olympic fame

Innsbruck Austria 575m

This historic city at the cross-roads of western Austria is not what most European skiers expect of a ski resort but, having twice hosted the Olympics, Innsbruck is a thoroughly equipped wintersports town, with an interesting range of downhill and cross-country skiing within easy commuting range, and good free bus services for commuters. This is a familiar routine for American skiers, many of whom come to Innsbruck to enjoy the monuments and the charm of the unspoilt city centre as well as the skiing. Innsbruck is an excellent base for non-skiing excursions (notably to Italy), and evening entertainment is more varied and less contrived than in most mountain villages.

There are steep and often very unfriendly south-facing slopes served by the cable-cars from the edge of Innsbruck, but most of the skiing is on the south side of the valley, above small resorts covered by a joint lift pass. **Igls** (893m) is traditionally the most popular, with sedate hotels and tea shops (where groups of young British skiers may strike a noisy false note), beautiful walks, and the Olympic bob-run which is open to fearless members of the public. The skiing mainly consists of the downhill race-course where Klammer skied himself into legend, a nicely varied north-facing red run beneath the Patscherkofel (2247m). There are easier variants and some off-piste skiing among the trees.

On the other side of the Brenner motorway, **Axamer Lizum** (1600m) is a characterless ski station – a couple of hotels and a huge car park – in the middle of the most interesting local skiing, beneath the neighbouring peaks of Hoadl (2343m) and Pleisen (2236m). Weekend queues for the lifts can be a problem, but the skiing is extensive and varied, mostly above the trees, and includes a splendid long easy black off the Pleisen down to Axams (874m). On the other side of the narrow valley, a chair serves a not-too-severe black run and links up with the long, easy, sunny pistes above the charming, unspoilt old village of **Mutters** (830m).

Slightly further away, with a separate lift pass, the long Stubaital has two main ski areas. Above the small resort of **Fulpmes** (937m), but not immediately accessible from it, there is some excellent skiing in a sheltered bowl between Sennjoch (2224m) and the Schlickeralm (1616m) including some tough and unpisted runs and a small, sunny nursery area. The access chair-lifts are slow and often crowded, and the run down to the car park is often worn bare. 18km beyond the jolly village of **Neustift** (993m) is a large area of glacier skiing, with lifts from Mutterbergalm (1728m) up to 3200m, open all year. In winter there are long runs, not all of them easy, down to the mid-station at 2300m, and a tough, unpisted route down to the base station. When snow elsewhere is in short supply, queues for the Stubai lifts are long.

Innsbruck tourist office ✆ (5222) 25715.
Package holidays AU, IG, NE, NH, RA, TC, TH.

Take your time

Seefeld Austria 1200m

Good for *Cross-country skiing, not skiing, rail access, easy road access, short airport transfers*
Bad for *Downhill skiing, skiing convenience*

Skiers who go to Seefeld fall into three categories. Two groups – cross-country skiers, who have learnt that it is one of the best places in the Alps for their sport, and people (often downhill beginners) who are looking for a complete winter holiday – come away satisfied. The third group – downhillers wanting the variety and challenge a resort of this size normally offers – are disappointed. The plain fact is that the terrain around Seefeld is admirably suited to the Nordic sport, and less to the Alpine one. It provides some pleasant skiing for beginners and for undemanding intermediates who are content with a limited skiing terrain set in attractive scenery. There are a couple of black off-piste runs to tempt the adventurous but these seem almost out of character here. It wouldn't take more than a day or two to exhaust the downhill possibilities. But the resort complements its skiing attractions with a range of non-skiing facilities second to none, and has thus secured its popularity with affluent elderly Germans. If such facilities are among your priorities, Seefeld may sensibly be included in your short-list – provided you are not also looking for genuine (as opposed to synthetic) Alpine charm or for fashionable companions on the slopes. Seefeld is not Kitzbühel: it has been very deliberately developed over recent decades in typically thorough Tyrolean style for a particular purpose, which it meets admirably. Several reporters have thought prices high by Austrian standards.

The skiing top 2074m bottom 1180m

There are two quite separate skiing areas. The Rosshütte to the east is for the more serious skier, while the Gschwandtkopf is a low conical peak south of the village centre, used principally by the ski school. The two are connected to each other, and to other points in the village, by a free circular ski-bus service in each direction, starting at 9.30am. Seefeld disdains the dawn rush for the slopes common to many resorts, and anyone on the slopes much before 10am is something of an early bird.

The skiing at **Gschwandtkopf** is chiefly concentrated on a broad, north-facing slope which rises for 300m between thick woods, starting from just beyond the sports centre. Of the two parallel chair-lifts rising up the centre of the slope only the left-hand one goes to the top, but the summit can also be reached by a combination of shorter lifts – there are three T-bars besides the chairs, all more or less parallel. The runs back

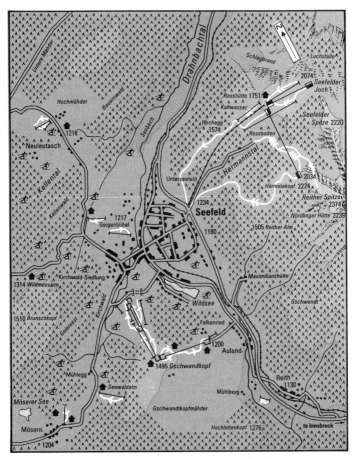

down form a single slope on which even the most timid intermediate can happily find a safe course, but on which steeper sections can be found. On one side of the slope you can test your skill on a coin-in-the-slot timed slalom course. The summit of the Gschwandtkopf can also be reached by a chair-lift from the neighbouring village of Reith on the eastern side of the mountain. The single run down this side is very pleasant and slightly more demanding.

The starting point for the **Rosshütte** ski area is on the eastern edge of the village beside the by-pass, about 1km from the centre. A mountain railway follows a fairly gentle gradient for about 3km up to the Rosshütte (1750m). Queuing is not usually a problem here, but outside peak hours the service may be no better than half-hourly. There are some easy blue runs served by a couple of drag-lifts on the wide area of piste around Rosshütte, or you can take a short cable-car to the summit of the Seefelder Joch (2074m) with some fine views at the top. A parallel drag-lift also goes almost to the top. A couple of good, though shortish, red runs bring you back to Rosshütte. From here the long path back through the woods to the foot of the railway is an almost flat, straight schuss. Adventurous skiers will want to take the small cable-car from Rosshütte which travels high across the Hermannstal valley to a shoulder of the Harmelekopf at 2000m. A short climb to the left then gives access to a couple of steep off-piste runs straight down the sides of the valley until you're forced to follow the flat valley floor back to the railway. The conventional route down from the Harmelekopf descends the shoulder as a nice open red run (watch for worn areas near the top) until it reaches the trees when it duplicates the flat schuss of the path from Rosshütte which it meets at the bottom.

There are short beginners' lifts at the foot of the Gschwandtkopf slopes, but the **nursery slopes** proper are on either side of a separate little hill, Geigenbühel, on the north-east fringe of the village. They have a bit more variety of gradient than many, including very gentle bits.

There are adequate **mountain restaurants** at top and bottom of the Gschwandtkopf, and at Rosshütte. There are plenty of sun-terraces, as much for the benefit of non-skiers as skiers – though you have to pay for a seat. The Rosshütte is particularly popular for basking.

Lifts

Passes Area pass covering all lifts is for minimum of three days. Limited day passes also available.

Cost 6-day pass AS1,160. 15% off in low season.
Beginners Day passes or coupons.
Children 25% off under 14.

The lift system presents no particular problems apart from its basically limited nature. Expect weekend invasions from Munich in good weather, with queues for the nursery lifts as well as the funicular.

The resort

Seefeld spreads across a broad plateau a few hundred metres above (and a few km to the north of) the Inn valley. There are wooded hills (they can hardly be called mountains) to the south and west, and the more pronounced peaks of the Seefelder Spitze and Reither Spitze to the east. Much of the resort's area is rather suburban-feeling, and the village centre proper is entirely to the south-west of the railway station. The streets forming the central cross-roads are traffic-free, and lined by comfortable, neat hotels and by tourist shops of a kind unseen in more purposeful ski resorts. Because skiing does not dominate the lives of visitors, there are always plenty of people about – but the place remains calm and quiet, with voices never raised above a murmur. The human traffic is most concentrated in the street leading to the splendid sports centre on the south-west edge of the town, where there are countless curling and skating rinks.

There is all sorts of **accommodation** in abundance. Location should be considered with some care, according to how you plan to spend your time. The central area is convenient for the sports centre, and it's only a short walk out to the ski-bus route. Right on the central crossroads is the friendly old Tiroler Weinstube (℗ 2208), more affordable than the Post and the smart Alpenhotel Lamm nearby. There are several hotels between the crossroads and the sports centre. If money is no object, the big Klosterbrau (℗ 2621) has most of the facilities you could want under one roof. Further along, the Sonneck (b&b only, ℗ 2387) and next-door Batzenhäusl (℗ 2285) are a quarter the price. The suburbs to the west are better placed for cross-country than those to the east, between the railway and the by-pass. There is an attractive enclave of exclusive hotels (Astoria, Lärchenhof, Schlosshotel) to the north of the centre, close to the Geigenbühel nursery slopes. It's neither easy nor particularly relevant to find accommodation close to the main ski-lifts; if that's the way you're thinking, go elsewhere.

There's quite a good variety of **après-ski**, from tea-dancing to discothèques and a casino which one report calls 'stuffy'. But it is not a boisterous resort; young Brits who wish it was are to be found making the best of it in a simulated pub.

Ski school

Classes 2hr morning and afternoon.
Cost 6 days AS870. Private lessons AS280/hr.
Children Ski kindergarten, ages 4 up, 10.00–16.00, 6 days without meals

AS870. Non-ski kindergarten, ages 3 up, 9.30–13.00, 5 days without meals AS350. Private arrangements can be made for whole-day care.

Reports of the school are uniformly favourable, with some glowing comments on standards of X-C teaching.

Other activities

Cross-country Many trails and loops from the Lenerwiese (2.5km, easy) to the Olympia (25km, difficult).

Not skiing Swimming, 60km of cleared paths, toboggan run, curling, skating and sleigh rides.

X-C can't really be put under 'Other activities' in Seefeld – with thousands of skiers striding along scores of trails, ranging from eight-lane motorways across the plateau to stiff forest tracks, it's the major activity. Or is it? Quite possibly more people spend their time skating to Strauss, or curling, or wallowing in the 'fantastic' pool, or taking long walks. The resort is well placed for excursions to Innsbruck (45min by train) and further afield (over the Brenner to Italy).

Travel

Airport Munich; transfer about 2hr.
Railway Main-line station in resort.
Road Via Munich; chains rarely needed.

Reachable resorts All the outlying ski areas of Innsbruck are within easy striking distance.

The circular ski-bus service works well enough, though it is not very frequent. A car is no great advantage except for long excursions.

Miscellaneous

Tourist office ℗ (5212) 2313. Tx 53452.
Medical Doctor, dentist, chemist in resort; hospital at Innsbruck (20km).
Equipment hire 6 days skis AS480, boots AS150, X-C AS360.

Resort beds 4,500 in hotels, 1,500 in apartments.
Package holidays AU, BS, CL, DE, EN, HO, IG, IT, STY, TC, TH, WM.

Not sold on it

Sölden Austria 1380m

Good for *Après-ski, summer skiing*
Bad for *Lift queues, nursery slopes, not skiing, short airport transfers, resort-level snow*

Sölden is a long established, large and lively resort for which we find it hard to work up much enthusiasm, despite its undoubted qualities. The skiing area is extensive and varied, spread along the high (and in places steep) western wall of the Ötztal, and on paper is impressive – Austria's highest cable-car to over 3000m, and two large glacier areas which offer some very good summer skiing. The reality is a disappointment: the glacier areas do not open until the rest of the skiing starts to melt away in spring, and the skiing served by the cable-car is limited (at least for most people, most of the time). The rest of the skiing is not so outstanding that Sölden can be counted among the really good skiers' resorts, nor so outstanding that it outweighs the disadvantages of the resort itself – a long, main-road straggle with no charm, redeemed only by vibrant nightlife (in high season, at least). Tiny, high-altitude Hochsölden (2090m) shares the skiing but is otherwise quite different – a good choice for skiers who want peace and quiet and ease of access to slopes.

The skiing top 3056m bottom 1377m

Sölden's skiing area is in two linked sectors, south and north, split by the deep Rettenbachtal (where the road up to the summer ski fields has been built). Although both sectors are directly accessible from the edges of Sölden (served by a regular ski-bus), the northern area is usually referred to as the Hochsölden ski area, the southern one as Sölden's skiing. The skiing is extensive, with a healthy vertical drop of about 1600m from the cable-car top station, 1350m from the top above Hochsölden. It is varied, with long runs of varying difficulty down through the trees to Sölden and a fair extent of skiing above the trees, mostly suitable for intermediate skiers. There are some wide open, easy slopes above Hochsölden and a few black runs but these are hardly worthy of the name. Most of the slopes are east-facing, and sunny in the morning (slightly longer at Hochsölden).

   The **Sölden** skiing area is reached by cable-car from the southern end of the resort, where there is a large but not always adequate car-park. There are open slopes around the middle station with a couple of drag-lifts, one of them taking you to a beautiful, long and usually empty run down to the Gaislachalm (where there are several restaurants) and on down a gentle woodland trail to rejoin the main piste to Sölden at Innerwald. The main run down from the middle

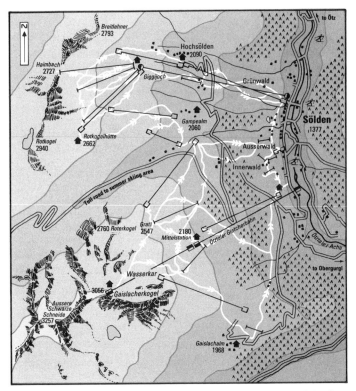

station is red, can be icy, and tends to be crowded at the end of the day. Once you get to know the lower slopes it's usually possible to find a route down through the back gardens to most parts of the village. Roads are a hazard.

The top section of the cable-car climbs over 850 metres steeply to the rocky Gaislacherkogel peak, where there is a round panoramic restaurant. The bowl underneath the cable-car is very steep and has no marked piste, only a 'wilde abfahrt' which must be very exciting when conditions are right. (It was closed when we visited and we have no reports from others.) The normal run from the top station gives beautiful views, but only at the top does it justify its red grading.

Of the two pistes down into the Rettenbachtal to link up with Hochsölden, the one from the middle cable-car station is an easy path and can be pursued as far as Sölden. The run down beside the long Stabele chair-lift is more difficult, and being north-facing often has very good snow. There are some good off-piste possibilities around here, but the underlying terrain is rocky. From the Rettenbachtal there is a more difficult run down to Innerwald and Sölden.

From the northern edge of Sölden a long chair-lift (over 20 minutes) climbs directly to **Hochsölden**, and a gondola which is the most popular way in the mornings goes slightly higher to the Giggijoch. Above this gondola there is a wide open expanse of gentle mountainside. There is a steeper area between Hochsölden and the Haimbach, but the runs marked black on the map are not fierce.

From the Rotkogelhütte there are superb views over to the glacier skiing areas and a beautiful, sunny long run down to the Rettenbachtal via the Gampealm restaurant. This run may be a bit much for inexperienced skiers; if so they will not be able to get across to the Sölden skiing, nor down to Sölden, except via the blue to the gondola station. The black next to that blue is another over-rated run.

There are several large, not very attractive **mountain restaurants** in the obvious places, and a few more charming ones, notably at Gaislachalm, the Gampealm and the Rotkogelhütte.

Nursery slopes are not very satisfactory. Innerwald, a short chair-lift ride from Sölden, has a nursery area which goes without sun for much of the day, and often has poor snow conditions. Most beginners are taken to the slopes above the Giggijoch gondola, which are better. Unfortunately, this ledge drops rather more steeply down to Hochsölden, and one reporter has expressed the view that the immediate vicinity of Hochsölden is 'heavy going' for a beginner.

Lifts

Passes All lifts and the ski-bus are covered by the general lift pass. Day passes available, and 'hourly' cards with refunds when you hand them in.
Cost 6-day pass AS1,380. 15% off in low season.

Beginners Coupons.
Children 40% off, under 14.
Summer skiing Large area up to 3250m, 10 lifts. Season starts when winter skiing stops.

The main problem with the system is serious high-season queues for the two main lifts out of Sölden. At other times, and in most other places, the system works well – though if the cable-car is operating intermittently there will be queues of people wanting to take it.

The resort

Sölden stretches for miles (literally) along the Ötztal valley floor, and the river and the main road run through the village. Although most buildings are traditional in style, the long, wide main street has no particular character or focus. There is usually a lot of traffic and a lot of people – incomers from smaller villages in addition to Sölden residents. Visitors come from many countries, the majority being German.

Hochsölden, reached by road or chair-lift from Sölden, stands over 700 metres higher, above the trees. It is little more than a cluster of hotels, but they are close-knit and there is more of a village atmosphere than in many such resort satellites. There are hardly any shops, no bank, no more bars and restaurants than there are hotels, and in the evening there is almost nowhere to go. But you don't have to go anywhere to have a party, and the regulars of the Hotel Hochsölden make very merry from around 5pm onwards.

Accommodation in Sölden is nearly all hotels and guest-houses. Skiers should choose to stay at either end of the town; the northern end is a better choice for inexperienced skiers who are more likely to enjoy Hochsölden skiing. You could hardly wish for a more attractive hideaway than any of the simple hotels up at Gaislachalm, but peace and quiet will be shattered nightly by tobogganing revellers from Sölden. Location of accommodation in Hochsölden is unimportant. The hotels there are traditional and fairly simple.

In season there is a wide variety of lively **après-ski** action (cafés, live bands, discothèques) and lots of packaged evening outings. After skiing there is a disco (yes, a disco) at Innerwald in the Café Philip until 6pm, when the chair-lift down to Sölden closes. The most popular organised event is a jeep ride from the Alpenland up to the Gaislachalm for Glühwein, dancing and/or dinner, followed by a 6km toboggan ride back to Sölden.

Ski school

Classes 2hr morning and afternoon. Cost 6 days AS870. Private lessons AS450/hr.

Children Ski kindergartens at Sölden and Hochsölden, ages 3–8, 9.00-4.30. 6 days with lunch AS1,200.

Reports suggest that instruction is good but often too widely shared – in groups of as many as 17. The kindergarten is said (by an onlooker) to be 'fun, instructive and safe'.

Other activities

Cross-country Trails along valley floor near Sölden and at Zwieselstein on road towards Obergurgl (15km, easy).

Not skiing Sauna, solarium, swimming, fitness centre, skating, curling, bowling, toboggan run, organised excursions.

The main valley is not very attractive for X-C. Although there are some sporting facilities, it is not really a non-skiers resort either, and there are no cleared mountain paths for walkers.

Travel

Airport Munich; transfers at least 4hr. Railway Ötz (36km): frequent buses. Reachable resorts Obergurgl.

Road Via Ulm, Munich or Basel; the road from Ötz rarely requires chains.

Motorists can by-pass queues by driving to Innerwald or even Hochsölden, and can easily make excursions to Obergurgl. But parking is often a problem along the main road and in lift car-parks. As well as the ski-bus, there are two buses daily from Sölden to Hochsölden and back (last bus and chair-lift from Sölden to Hochsölden at 6pm). Daily buses to Obergurgl (45 mins), Ötz and Innsbruck.

Miscellaneous

Tourist office ✆ (5254) 2212. Tx 53247. Package holidays (H) indicates accommodation in Hochsölden as well as Sölden. BL, BS, GL, HA, HO(H), IG(H), IT(H), NE, TH.

Medical Hospital at Innsbruck; dentist, doctor and chemist in resort. Equipment hire 6 days skis AS300-540, boots AS120-240, X-C AS210-360. Resort beds 3,700 in hotels, 200 in apartments.

Proud relic

Obergurgl Austria 1930m

Good for *Late holidays, Alpine charm, après-ski, ski touring, lift queues, resort-level snow*
Bad for *Tough skiing, short airport transfers, easy road access, not skiing*

Obergurgl is a tiny, high village with an awkward, bitty network of old chair-lifts and drag-lifts which don't add up to a large skiing area, even when you count neighbouring Hochgurgl. It became famous in the days when skiing was much closer to what we now call ski touring; for that purpose, the top of the Ötztal with its 21 glaciers is, as it has always been, a superlative area. Not surprisingly, given the altitude, the immediate surroundings of the resort are bleak; but the resort has charm; it has not gone for growth and it is a real, inhabited village, and not merely a mountainside service area for skiers – which is exactly what Hochgurgl is, and what most resorts at this sort of height are. All visitors agree that Obergurgl is a very friendly place, with a jolly evening atmosphere; you can't help seeing the same faces each day, and to a degree each year. The combination of snow reliability, village charm and lack of crowds puts Austria's highest parish closer to paradise than other ski resorts in more ways than one.

The skiing top 3035m bottom 1911m

The skiing areas of Obergurgl and its satellite Hochgurgl together cover a high, wide, north-west-facing area of the southern end of the Ötztal, and can usually be relied on to have good snow from early December to late April. But not always; for one thing, high winds can make the top slopes unskiable by stripping off fresh snow (or closing the lifts). The skiing is practically all above the tree line and nearly all intermediate in difficulty. There are three small ski areas split up by the valleys beneath peaks and glaciers. Hochgurgl's one area offers the greatest vertical drop, and has the extra variety of a wooded hillside between Hochgurgl and Untergurgl. Obergurgl's two sectors have greater off-piste potential and steeper runs (none of them long) near the top of the lifts. Unfortunately, they are often closed because of avalanche danger, or unpleasantly windswept and bare.

From the middle of Obergurgl, an old single chair takes you over gentle slopes to the **Gaisberg** area – attractive short intermediate runs (categorised red but not difficult) among a scattering of trees, down to the popular Steinmann restaurant, and a couple of short, steeper gullies under the Nederlift. The long single chair-lift to Hohe Mut has an attractive restaurant and sun terrace at the top, and magnificent views out over the glaciers. The only run down is officially off-piste. In good

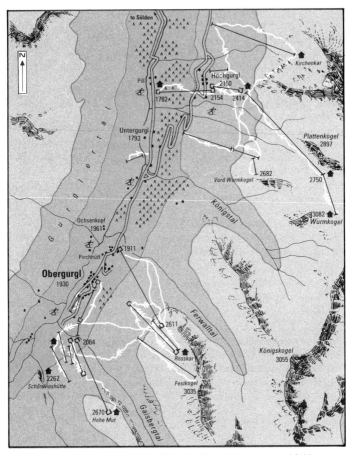

conditions it is not exceedingly difficult, although narrow and fairly
steep in places, but the terrain is rocky and when we visited it was
dangerously lacking snow cover, without any warnings.

The **Festkogel** chair-lift starts from the cluster of hotels at the
entrance to Obergurgl, a long walk from the centre although reachable
(with some poling) on skis from the upper part of the village by the ice
rink. This lift climbs in the shade of a steep wall to a plateau with a new
restaurant and short practice drag-lift and a longer drag up to the
highest point of Obergurgl's skiing. The only runs down to the bottom
are another two off-piste marked routes of moderate difficulty – good
long runs down the flank of a beautiful valley. There are several pistes
under the long twin Rosskar chair-lift – none of them particularly severe
– and an easily manageable run across to Gaisberg.

The skiing of **Hochgurgl** is mostly very gentle, on a broad, open
mountainside above the station; there is a short drag-lift on the glacier
at the very top with a black run, but it merits no more than red. On the
south side of the system is a long drag-lift with a short second section

above it, serving the most interesting of Hochgurgl's pistes for good skiers – correctly marked red on the mountain (black on the piste map), and by the standards of this area long and varied, with moguls on the bottom half in the woods leading down to a car park on the road up to Hochgurgl. There is another good, fast piste through the woods under the chair-lift from Untergurgl which is the main way into the Hochgurgl skiing for visitors.

There are few **mountain restaurants**, and most skiers lunch in the village, where there are hotels with sun terraces. Of the restaurants on-piste, the Hohe Mut does not open until late in the season and the attractive Steinmann is usually very crowded. At Hochgurgl there are several restaurants near the top of the system. The Wurmkogel hut is friendly, attractive and warming, with marvellous views into Italy. the Schönwieshütte, a 20-minute ski and walk from the top of the Sattellift, is heartily recommended by one reporter ('another world').

There is a wide, flat **nursery slope** in the village with a small tow beside it, and plenty of scope for après-nursery skiing, especially above Hochgurgl, so even beginners should make reasonable use of a lift pass.

Lifts

Passes One pass covers all lifts, and local ski-bus. Day passes available.	**Cost** 6-day pass AS1,300. 15% off in low season.
Beginners Lift pass or coupons.	**Children** About 40% off, under 14.

Because Obergurgl is so small and remote, queues are hardly ever a problem except at ski-school departure time; but exposure to inclement elements can be very unpleasant – no lifts offer shelter. Most chairs are single-seaters. Queues for lift passes are bad on Monday mornings. The main limitation of the lift system is the lack of links between the three areas. For a small and not very efficiently mechanised ski area, the lift pass may seem expensive.

The resort

Although traditional in style, Obergurgl is not a picturesque, colourfully painted Tyrolean charmer. A 19th-century guidebook refers to 'a hamlet composed of wretched cowherds' huts, with a church on an eminence'; things have not changed much, except that the hamlet is now composed not of wretched huts but hotels – some comfortable, others simple – offering a not insignificant 3,000 beds. The clientele is predominantly German, with a minority of faithful British visitors.

For a small village, Obergurgl is not compact, and location of **accommodation** is important. There are basically three clusters of buildings. The first is at the entrance to the village – convenient for the Festkogel lift, but otherwise unappealing. Clustered above the old village around the skating rink are comfortable, modern and quite expensive hotels – the Austria (✆ 282) is the most attractive of them, with sauna, jacuzzi, turkish bath and massage. These hotels are easy enough to ski back to, but it is a stiff walk up from the village centre –

'exhausting, long and dangerous' says one report. In the centre there's more of a mixture; the dominant building is the Edelweiss (∅ 223) – a comfortable hotel, but according to one report prone to overbooking. Most UK tour operators use the cheaper, smaller guest-houses. The Wiesenthal is about the cheapest of them – friendly, lively and well-placed (∅ 263). So too, although slightly less cheap, are the Gampen (∅ 238), the Josl (∅ 205), the Fender (∅ 316) and the Jenewein (∅ 203). Of these, only the Gampen does not have a sauna. Hochgurgl has precious little to recommend it as an alternative to the main village.

Après-ski is very jolly in a traditional Tyrolean way, ('... great – we did the conga through the hotel'), mostly bar and hotel-keller oriented. But the dedicated disco piste-basher will soon tire of the lack of variety. In the old centre there are several bars, animated at tea-time (sometimes with tea-dancing) and later, some of them with live music. Reports are generally enthusiastic.

Ski school

Classes 2hr morning and afternoon. **Cost** 6 days AS870. Private lessons (two people) AS1,450/day. **Special courses** Ski touring.

Children Ski kindergarten, ages 6–10, and non-ski kindergarten, ages 3–5, 9.30–12.30, 1.30–4.30, 6 days AS710. No lunchtime care.

Reports on the ski school are generally though not entirely favourable. Many very beautiful and not too arduous day-trips can be made at any time in the season, and from March onwards tourers can undertake the famous Ötztal Rundtour, which takes about a week. Information from the ski school or its leader Herr Giacomelli (∅ 251).

Other activities

Cross-country 10km trail between Obergurgl and Untergurgl. Small loop at Hochgurgl. Instruction available.

Not skiing Natural ice rink (open in the evenings) and hotel pools, saunas, whirlpools; bowling.

The Gurgls are generally very unsuitable for cross-country skiers and non-skiers, and excursion possibilities are limited.

Travel

Airport Munich; transfers about 4½hr. **Reachable resorts** Sölden is very easily reached.

Railway Ötz (48km); regular buses. **Road** Via Ulm, Munich or Basel; chains often necessary.

The road up from Sölden is slow and narrow and prone to closure – though less so than it used to be, thanks to new avalanche barriers. Long delays are reported. A car is of no great advantage except for excursions to Sölden; the bus to and from Untergurgl (for Hochgurgl skiing) is quite efficient.

Miscellaneous

Tourist office ∅ (5256) 258/353. **Medical** Doctor in resort; chemist, dentist in Sölden; hospital at Innsbruck. **Equipment hire** 6 days skis AS360–600, boots AS180, X-C AS420–500.

Resort beds 2,800 in hotels, 90 in apartments. **Package holidays** BL, BS, CB, GL, HA, HO, IG, NE, SUS, TH.

Let the train take the strain

Serfaus Austria 1430m

Good for *Alpine charm, easy skiing, nursery slopes, family skiing, ski touring, freedom from cars, cross-country skiing*
Bad for *Tough skiing, easy road access, skiing convenience*

Separate resort: Fiss

Serfaus works hard to be a family-favourite resort, with all the qualities of charm and friendliness that are associated with winter in the Tyrol. The village is attractive, with a mixture of traditional chalet-style buildings old and (mostly) new, and the accommodation is nearly all of a high standard. It claims to be the only traffic-free ski resort in Austria. There is plenty of après-ski and the skiing, although devoid of challenge to the expert, is high and extensive for a charming Austrian village. The separate ski area of Fiss, a much more ordinary skiing village for local weekenders just down the road, is every bit as good – in some ways better – than that of Serfaus.

The skiing top 2745m bottom 1427m

The skiing extends in a chain of lifts up and down a series of treeless ridges to the west of the resort. The slopes face east and west, with no really long runs, despite the fact that the top of the skiing area is 1300m above Serfaus.

There are three lifts up the wooded hill behind Serfaus to the sunny plateau beside the Alpkopf – a gondola and a small cable-car to a large restaurant building at Kölner Haus and a chair-lift directly to the Alpkopf. The plateau is a good open area for sunbathing, with short drag-lifts for near-beginners. There are several good, long, not very difficult runs through the trees back to Serfaus. From just below Kölner Haus a chair-lift climbs quite steeply to Lazid, serving Serfaus's two most difficult runs. There are a couple of drag-lifts serving fairly easy slopes either side Lazid, which is also the point of departure for the rest of the skiing – down into, and up out of, two further high, shallow valleys. There is no particularly exciting skiing unless you're prepared to climb, but it is a splendid trip from the scenic point of view. The way the lift system is arranged means that it is difficult to ski off-piste and stay within it.

Serfaus is good for beginners and especially children, with a delightful **nursery slope/playground** area in the village itself. There is also a good, high beginners' area around Kölner Haus.

Mountain restaurants are adequate and sunny; two at Kölner Haus (accessible to non-skiers) and two others up at the end of the ski area at Masneralp. One of them is a mountain refuge off the piste.

Lifts

Passes Serfaus only (separate pass
needed for Fiss). Day and afternoon
pass available. Non-consecutive 3- and
10-day passes.

Cost 6-day pass AS1,220. About 20%
off in low season.
Children About 40% off, under 15.
Beginners Coupons.

When the resort is full (at New Year and in February) there are morning
queues for the various lifts leaving the top of the village and at Kölner
Haus. Beyond this, cold is the main problem – none of the high lifts are
enclosed. Skis can be left free of charge at the main lift station.

The resort

Serfaus sits on an open, sunny ledge looking out south-eastwards over
the Inn Valley south of Landeck. The village is small, and although built
along two parallel streets it isn't too much of a straggle, with the skating
rink, church and nursery area in the centre. But it is a bit of a hike up the
hill to the main ski lifts unless you stay along the road, which has been
built up. A new underground railway has replaced the ski-bus serving
the lifts from the car park on the edge of the village where all cars must
be left.

Nearly all the **accommodation** is in modern, attractive, chalet-style
hotels with balconies and the general standard and cost is high. The
Cervosa (∅ 6211) with pool, and the Maximilian (∅ 6255) are about the
most spacious and comfortable hotels, neighbours ideally placed
above the nursery area. The Alte Schmiede (∅ 6492) is less expensive,
attractively decorated, friendly and within easy walking range of the
lifts; there is a cosy, woody bar downstairs.

Après-ski is lively, attractive in setting and mostly traditional in style.
After skiing the Postbar is full (tea-dancing is rumoured), and later on it
is the setting for dancing to traditional Alpine music. For a younger
atmosphere the best places are the bars and discos under the Hotels
Rex and Astoria.

Ski school

Classes 2hr morning and afternoon.
Cost 6 days AS870. Private lessons
AS360/hr.
Special courses One- and two-day ski
tours.

Children Ski kindergarten, ages 4–14,
9.00–5.00, 6 days AS1190. Non-ski
kindergarten, ages 3–6, 9.00–4.30, 6
days with meals AS840.

We have no recent reports on the ski school, but it seems reasonable to
expect some difficulty in finding good English-speaking instruction.

Other activities

Cross-country About 30km of marked
and graded trails (blue and red) in two
main areas, including easy 1km loop at
entrance to village and moderately easy
2½ km loop near Kölnerhaus. Longest

trail 13km. Instruction available.
Not skiing Natural ice rink, public pools
in three hotels, sauna, solarium, sleigh
rides, tobogganing. Cable-car runs one
evening a week for toboggan riders.

The X-C runs between Serfaus and Fiss are not convenient for
rendezvous with other skiers, but the longer wooded runs around
Alpkopf are; this area is secluded and gives beautiful views.

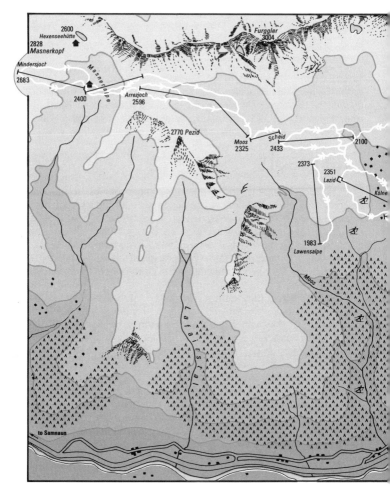

Travel

Airport Munich; transfers about 4hr.
Road Via Munich and Garmisch, or via Ulm or Basel and Feldkirch; chains occasionally necessary.

Railway Landeck (30km); daily buses.
Reachable resorts Fiss is next door. Samnaun (sharing Ischgl's skiing) is not far, and the Arlberg resorts within reach.

Having a car is of no great value in car-free Serfaus unless you want to go on excursions to other resorts. Going to Samnaun is a very attractive idea, since it gives relatively queue-free access to the very good skiing shared with Ischgl. There are frequent buses to Fiss.

Miscellaneous

Tourist office (5476) 6332. Tx 58154.
Medical Doctor in resort, chemist and dentist in Ried (14km), hospital in Landeck (30km).

Equipment hire 6 days skis AS600, boots AS240, X-C AS450
Resort beds 1,000 in hotels, about 500 in apartments.

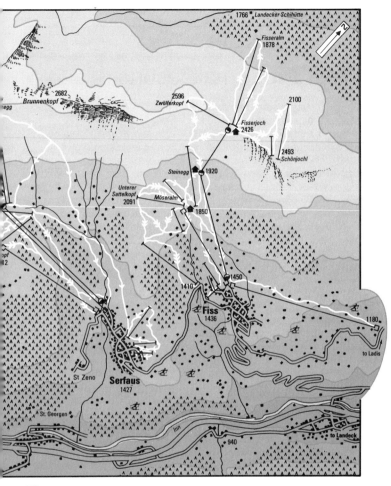

Fiss 1440m

From Fiss you don't travel so far on skis, but in other ways the skiing, spread round a bowl and over the back of its rim, offers more satisfying pistes. They are mostly south-facing, and good snow conditions tend not to last as long as at Serfaus. The main bowl is not particularly large, with a top station of 2426m (the Fisser Joch), but there are some good open runs down to the village from here giving 1000m vertical, and they are in general steeper than at Serfaus. There is also a very good run down through the woods under the Waldlift. From the western side of the Fiss skiing area it is possible to ski down to Serfaus.

Unlike Serfaus, Fiss is expanding its lift system all the time to cope with its increasing number of visitors. There are a number of new lifts behind the Fisser Joch with intermediate north-facing runs, and skiers who embark on the long unprepared descent to Ladis (1180m) can return by a two-stage chair-lift.

Unpackaged tours

West Tirol: small resorts

Among the many small resorts west of Innsbruck not covered in other chapters, a handful are worth describing briefly.

Vent is a small village high up (1900m) in its own beautiful valley, which branches off the Ötztal between Sölden and Obergurgl. As a base for ski touring, it is excellent – it is one of the terminal points of the Ötztal Rundtour. For downhill skiers there is only a chair-lift followed by a drag with wide open intermediate skiing on either side of the lifts back down to the village. There are also two beginners' lifts. Vent is a friendly little place, with one discothèque and a couple of other bars.

Kühtai is also very high (1966m), also close to the Ötztal, and also mainly of interest for the access it gives to ski tours (in particular, excellent day-tours), not in the Ötztal Alps but in the Stubai Alps, which stretch away to the south. There are seven small lifts but the ski area served by them has a vertical drop less than 500 metres, and holds no particular interest apart from the altitude of its base.

Nauders (1400m) is a spacious, traditionally styled village in a remote setting where Austria, Switzerland and Italy meet. Here, too, there is plenty of scope for short ski-tours, but there is more extensive downhill skiing as well. Apart from an excellent open nursery area near the village, the skiing is far enough away for the ski bus to be essential. The main area is high and spread widely round an impressive circus of mountains (facing north and west), but offers surprisingly few good runs. There are short, easy intermediate at altitude, and an exposed but otherwise enjoyable red run served by a chair-lift to 2700m. There are wide, easy paths back to the bottom, and some off-piste skiing in the woods under the gondola. Across the road to Italy, a slow chair-lift serves the wooded Mutzkopf (1812m) – a pretty knoll with a long gentle 'Familienabfahrt'. There is good cross-country skiing, with nearly 30 km of varied trails, some linking up with trails in Italy, and including a small loop in the woods near the top of the main gondola. Non-skiing facilities include indoor tennis, swimming and sauna at several hotels, and coach excursions to St Moritz and Italy (Merano). Après-ski is typically Tyrolean, with live bands in several hotels.

Lermoos (995m) is north of the Inn valley, in an unusual basin encircled by mountains – one of them the Zugspitze, towering 2000m above flat pastures and forming the border with Germany. In the right conditions there is a superb 20km run from the summit to the pretty village of Ehrwald at the foot of the mountain, but most of the downhill skiing in the area is much more limited. Lermoos itself, a pleasant but undistinguished village, has the biggest local installation, with easy and intermediate runs of over 1200m vertical on the Grubigstein. There is abundant cross-country skiing on the floor of the basin and the connecting valleys, cleared walks, a good sports centre/ pool at Ehrwald and plenty of the usual Tyrolean entertainments.

Eldorado for skiers?

Ischgl Austria 1400m

Good for *Big ski area, après-ski, cheap alcohol*

Bad for *Nursery slopes, easy skiing, lift queues, short airport transfers*

Linked resort: Samnaun
Separate resort: Galtür

The recipe for a perfect resort might mix the skiing of Val d'Isère and Tignes with the village charm of Alpbach – the best aspects of French and Austrian skiing – with the drinks prices of Livigno thrown in for good measure. Ischgl, in the Silvretta range which separates Austria and Switzerland, comes closer than most resorts to fitting this recipe. It is an old Tyrolean village high in the remote and beautiful Paznaun valley at the foot of a vast skiing area. And it has the good measure thrown in – you can ski to duty-free Samnaun and back for bargain shopping whenever the drinks cupboard runs dry. Despite these powerful claims on our attention, Ischgl is not widely packaged or well known in Britain; but it is far from undiscovered, and teems with German and Swedish skiers (and après-skiers) throughout the season. Most of the few British who do come to this area end up in Galtür, now something of an outpost for the poor relations. It is an acceptable indignity, perhaps even preferable to the real thing for some traditionalists, but not for keen skiers – the skiing is a small separate area, a little way from Galtür itself. Kappl, a small village a few miles below Ischgl, has south-facing slopes which are, for the time being at least, more extensive and interesting than Galtür's.

Ischgl's skiing contains few severe runs, but plenty are difficult enough for most skiers and satisfyingly long and varied; several sectors are suitable for off-piste skiing. If the area has one great drawback, it is lift queues. You can travel round the shared ski circus only in one direction, and as very few skiers are based in Samnaun there are long queues to get out of Ischgl in the morning and Samnaun in the early afternoon, and congestion on pistes down to Ischgl at the end of the day. An alternative route round the circus is planned, but the problem is an inherent one. The only solution is to start from Samnaun.

The skiing top 2872m bottom 1250m

The Silvretta 'skidorado' consists principally of the splendid slopes above Ischgl; long descents through woods to the village and a series of high, rocky bowls above with plenty of open, easy pistes. A long mountain crest which forms the Austro-Swiss border is reached by lift and easily breached on skis in a number of places, opening up a less

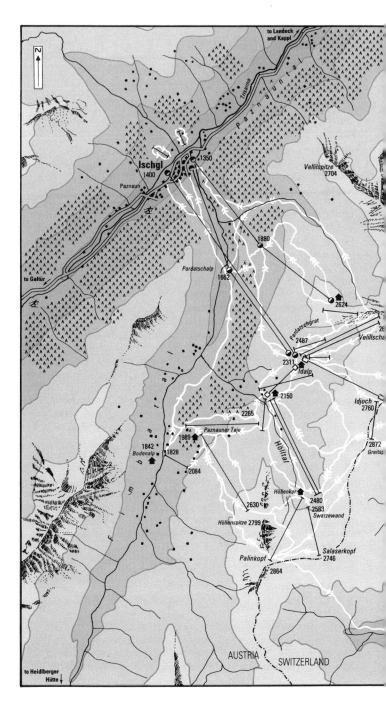

extensive but no less beautiful Swiss ski area above Samnaun. The slopes on the Ischgl side face north-west and west; on the Samnaun side mainly south and east.

From **Ischgl** there are lift departures at both ends of the village, to Idalpe, a broad, sunny, open plateau with a ski school, restaurants, hotel and nursery slopes, and to the Pardatscher Grat above Idalpe with runs back down to Ischgl or an easy connection with the rest of the lift system via Idalpe.

The runs down to either end of Ischgl, especially from Pardatscher Grat, are about the best in the area for good skiers, some of them giving an uninterrupted and demanding 1200m vertical across open slopes and then through woodland. Splendid as these runs are, it is unfortunate that there are none graded easier than red. In the late afternoon they are very crowded and when they are as icy as they were when we skied them, the lower parts of these runs can be extremely hazardous and unpleasant.

On the Idalpe there are lots of lifts going all over the place round a fairly shallow, unevenly shelving, rocky bowl with good, easy runs

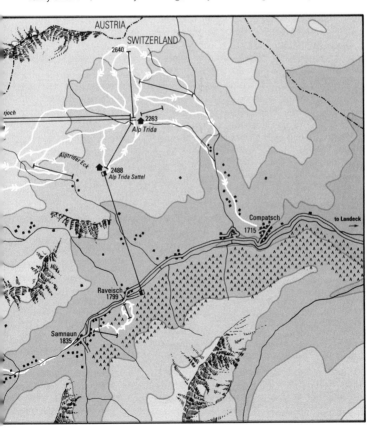

including a few nursery slopes. For better skiers this is not a place to linger, but a staging post with links to other areas. From the Vellilscharte there is one of the most beautiful and least skied of all the descents to Ischgl, down a valley of its own. From Idjoch, there are easy runs down into the sunny Swiss Alp Trida and a more difficult traverse and descent into the narrow Hölltal beside Idalpe. The lifts up the Hölltal serve a variety of short, fairly steep runs, and also give access to some of the best skiing in the region. Behind the Paulinerkopf (the high point of the system) there is some excellent open skiing with runs marked black – not indicating extreme difficulty but a lack of grooming – and the best local off-piste possibilities. This sector is particularly beautiful – sunny in the afternoon, with two very attractive restaurants.

From the top of the Schwarzewand drag-lift above Hölltal, the superb long run down and round to **Samnaun** starts off with a fairly steep, south-facing ice-prone pitch but after that the only problem is crowding at the occasional narrow bottlenecks. The area is to be developed with new lifts which will ease the traffic.

From Samnaun, after a visit to the duty-free shops (which helpfully sell small backpacks) it is a slightly awkward ski beside the road to the cable-car at Raveisch. The cable-car arrives at the southern upper rim of the beautiful Alp Trida basin, with its wide open, easy and intermediate skiing, both on- and off-piste. There is no piste back to the bottom of the cable-car, only a difficult and not reliably safe off-piste descent. The run down from the Alp Trida restaurant ends up at Compatsch, which is more than a walk down the road from Raveisch. From Alp Trida a double T-bar links up with Idalpe and Ischgl, but even this cannot prevent late-afternoon queues.

There are two very attractive, sunny **mountain restaurants** around Bodenalp; otherwise merely adequate, large, new restaurants in most obvious places. Alp Trida is a huge sun trap and its large restaurant has an outdoor bar. Prices are in Swiss francs but schillings pass; duty-free prices don't have much effect in the restaurants. There are several places for lunch in Samnaun itself.

Nursery slopes are at Idalpe – open, sunny, with refreshments close at hand. In general though there are much better places than Ischgl for beginners (Galtür is one), especially given the cost, the queues and the awkwardness of runs down to the resort.

Lifts

Passes The Silvretta pass covers Ischgl, Kappl, See and Samnaun lifts, and local buses and swimming pool entrance.

Cost 6-day pass AS1,290. 15% off in low season.
Children 35% off, under 15.
Beginners Lift pass.

The trouble with the system is that everyone is in the same place at the same time. It is a seasonal problem, and the worst may be over – the Ischgl cable-car has already been replaced by a gondola. The lifts are smart and modern, far superior to the Austrian norm and many more are planned, both to relieve congestion and open up huge new ski areas currently reserved for ski tourers.

The resort

Ischgl is an old village which has developed in a smart and harmonious way with a high standard of new building and accommodation. The centre is by-passed by the main road and is tightly packed, bustling with activity in the early evening. The village has grown up in the shadow at the foot of the steep, wooded mountainsides which are now the ski slopes. Parts of it are hilly and there are several staircases and steep paths which can be very hazardous. Ischgl as a whole is now quite large, and some **accommodation** offered by UK operators is not at all conveniently placed for either of the main lift departures. Most hotels though are reasonably placed for the pistes and lifts, and the general standard of accommodation is high and expensive. The Solaria (∅ 5205) is about the nicest of all, with a beautiful wooden interior and good facilities for residents (squash, sauna). The Sonne (∅ 5302) and the Post (∅ 5233) are both very central – the Sonne with a favourite après-ski bar and an attractive restaurant above the hubbub.

Après-ski is excellent, with a good choice of traditional zither music and tea dancing, sophisticated live music shows, and several very contemporary discothèques of the kind which are found wherever young Swedes go. Fondue expeditions to the Heidelberger Hütte are organised most evenings.

Ski school

Classes 2hr morning and afternoon.
Cost 6 days AS870, private lesson AS280/hr.
Special courses Wedel course; off-piste courses.

Children Ski kindergarten, ages 4–15, 10.30-4.00, 6 days with lunch AS1,200. Non-ski kindergarten at Idalpe, ages 3–6, 9.30-3.45, 6 days with lunch AS540.

Other activities

Cross-country 25km Ischgl/Galtür/Wirl graded blue. Instruction available.
Not skiing 24km cleared walks, swimming (Galtür and some hotels),

skating, curling, sleigh rides, toboggan/mini-bob runs, sauna/solaria, local museum (in Mathon).

The X-C along the dark valley floor is not very interesting, inconvenient for meeting up with others, and quite often interrupted because of avalanche danger. We saw X-C activity in the much more attractive upper section of the Fimbertal reached by gondola to the Pardatscher Alpe, or on foot. There is plenty for non-skiers to do, with very good fair weather walks (up to the mountain restaurants at Bodenalp and beyond), and good non-skiing sports facilities (mostly at Galtür). Excursions to Innsbruck are often organised.

Travel

Airport Munich; transfer about 4½ hr. Also Zurich.
Railway Landeck (30km); frequent buses.

Road Via Basel or Ulm, then Feldkirch. The road up from Landeck is not difficult, but chains may be needed.
Reachable resorts St Anton.

Having a car is no great advantage in the resort, and parking by the lifts is often difficult. There is an underground car park. The Silvretta Pass (to the Montafon) is always closed in winter. Public transport consists of the bus service between Ischgl and Galtür which runs approximately hourly but not in the evening. There are also regular buses to Landeck and points between (including Kappl).

Miscellaneous

Tourist office ✆ (5444) 5266/5318.
Tx 58148.
Medical Hospital at Zams (near Landeck), doctor, dentist, chemist in resort.

Equipment hire 6 days skis AS720, boots AS300, X-C AS900.
Resort beds 5,500 in hotels, 300 in apartments.
Package holidays TH.

Samnaun 1840m

Samnaun is one of those anomalous communities in high, remote, dead-end corners of a country (in this case Switzerland) which has stayed alive thanks to duty-free status. It is not exactly booming – little more than a large cluster of shops and hotels with no more vitality than a supermarket – and it is hardly the place for a winter holiday unless the price of spirits (SF10 to 15 a litre) is an all-important consideration. But it has the advantage that you can ski the Ischgl circus without the rush-hour for lifts and crowds on-piste.

Galtür 1590m

Compared to Ischgl, Galtür is a peaceful little mountain village. It enjoys a sunnier position at the head of the valley. There are hotels both in Galtür and beside the lifts at Wirl. Galtür and Wirl do not throb, as Ischgl does, to the latest hot disco sounds after dark, but there is no shortage of more traditional musical entertainment. Galtür is a good base for X-C skiers, has an ice rink and a surprising smart new sports centre (swimming pool, squash, tennis, bowling) open till midnight.

Galtür's skiing is a small-scale affair, served by a single chair and a few drag-lifts, offering only about 500m vertical drop. Some of the runs (mostly east-facing) are moderately steep, but the greatest appeal of the skiing is to beginners who find wide open slopes round the village itself, and at Wirl, the main ski area (a long walk or short bus ride away).
Package holidays TH.

Alpine watershed

St Anton Austria 1300m

Good for *Tough skiing, big ski area, sunny skiing, off-piste skiing, easy road access, rail access, après-ski, chalet holidays*
Bad for *Easy skiing, lift queues, nursery slopes, skiing convenience, not skiing, late holidays*

Linked resorts: St Christoph, Stuben

The Arlberg is not a province or a mountain but a pass, the only natural route into the bottleneck of western Austria and the point of division of the waters of western Europe (the Rhine) from those of the eastern Danube. In this century the Arlberg has given its name to a once-revolutionary style of skiing and the ski school which taught it, and to a magnificent ski region spread on both sides of the pass. On the western (Vorarlberg) side, Lech and Zürs are Austria's two most exclusive resorts – so exclusive that often no one can get in (or out) for days on end in the winter. On the Tyrolean side, St Anton is a teeming thoroughfare with a privileged place in skiing history, and a place where many a proud skier, flattered by other, gentler ski-fields, discovers that there is more to the sport after all. Although it is possible to ski from one area into the other, they are for practical purposes separate. Lech and Zürs are the subject of the next chapter.

Austrian resorts are renowned for village charm and warmth of welcome rather than extent and challenge of skiing. St Anton stands out as the exception – a big-time resort with slopes to rival the biggest and best of France and Switzerland. As the home of Hannes Schneider's famous Arlberg ski school (now run by the great champion Karl Schranz), St Anton has the image of a resort for the dedicated technical perfectionist. Its ski runs, to which the pioneers of the sport devoted hours of climbing, still offer what is arguably the greatest variety of difficult skiing, on and off the piste, of any resort. That is the great attraction – many would say the only attraction – of what seems the antithesis of a Tyrolean skiing resort. The village has lost most of its charm under the influence of the hordes of young who swarm in from all over the world. Although lift queues and heavy traffic have been diminished by a new road tunnel and a new chair-lift, there are still as many who abhor St Anton as adore it. But it should be judged against the places with which it competes for business – Val d'Isère, Verbier and the like – and not against pretty Tyrolean villages. It then emerges as inconvenient in many ways, but full of character, far from unattractive, and very good fun after dark. It does lack the very high ski-fields of many of the most famous resorts, and many of its slopes get a lot of sun. The Arlberg's reputation for exceptionally abundant (and light) snow is some compensation but, all the same, January probably offers the best chance of avoiding icy pistes and long queues.

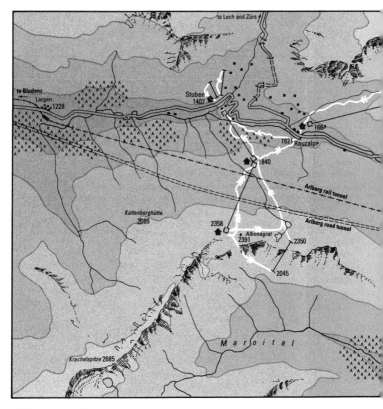

The skiing top 2650m bottom 1304m

Skiing at St Anton means skiing in the aura of the famous Valluga (2811m), a fine peak to the north of the village. There are many separate slopes of mountain, facing mainly south-east and west, and numerous ridges, bowls and subsidiary valleys. Many of the pistes are steep and challenging, and whereas many resorts have to invent black runs to appeal to good skiers, St Anton has to contrive blue runs in order not to discourage the timid. On the other side of the main road, facing the Valluga, St Anton has a separate ski area – the Rendel, which is sunny and not too difficult. A third area – the Albona, above Stuben on the other side of the Arlberg Pass – is (unlike Rendel) reachable on skis from the Valluga; the slopes are bleak, steep and sunless, but often have better snow conditions than anywhere else.

St Anton is a connoisseur's area for off-piste skiing, and every descent variant, however rarely skiable, has its name. It is an area which improves as you get to know it, which you can do via the ski school and the Ski Club of Great Britain. Many of the main runs above St Anton get a lot of sun, and tend to be icy in the mornings during clear, cold weather; always challenging, they can become treacherous.

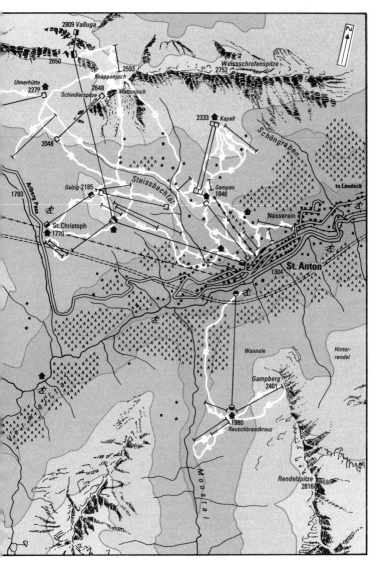

The long **Rendel** gondola starts an awkward distance from the resort
centre – further than a gentle stroll, but not so far that it really seems
worth shoving to get on the village bus, as you often have to. The
gondola and a few short drag-lifts around its top station are set on a
west-facing slope below a rocky ridge. Benefiting from sunny
afternoons, the Rendel and its restaurant terrace get very full on a fine
day. A second stage of the gondola is planned to give access to the
slopes of the Rendelspitze (2816m), but for the moment the top station
of the area is Gampberg. The runs on the top half of the mountain are

open, mostly not very long and suitable for intermediate skiers. There is only one main run down to St Anton – a long red run, good in the right conditions, but which gets very crowded in the late afternoon, and is often icy and/or worn as well. For good skiers the Rendel offers much more excitement off-piste than on; there is a lot of space on the open shoulder of the ridge below Gampberg, and a very alluring secluded bowl behind it; the awkward woodland path out of the bowl is easy to miss, and crucial.

Valluga and Kapall are the two aspects of the main skiing area to the north of St Anton, either side of the long Steissbachtal, which provides an easy (blue) run down to St Anton from each mid-station. **Kapall** is the smaller and less crowded. It is mostly sunny and south-facing. Most of the runs are intermediate and graded red or blue. The blue runs, for example under the chairs from Kapall to Gampen, may unpleasantly surprise intermediates, and the most direct descent to the resort is the famous Kandahar Downhill course, first used in 1928. The bottom half is often icy and slushy, or earthy; but in good conditions there are some good bump sections down through the trees. The run to the Rodelhütte and Nasserein is one of the most interesting, but not well signposted. Beside Kapall, facing east and often keeping better snow than elsewhere, is the short Schöngraben drag-lift with fairly easy pistes beside it, and off-piste runs into the Schöngraben valley – some of the most beautiful, least terrifying and most skied in the area.

The **Valluga** is one of the big names in skiing. The first stage of lifts from both St Anton and St Christoph is to the rounded knoll of Galzig (2185m), with pistes down in all directions and a maze of chairs, cable-cars and tows arriving at different points of the hilltop. There are drag-lifts at the top with easy runs beside them, and a very easy run suitable for near-beginners down to St Christoph. The rest of the slopes of Galzig are steep, and provide some very challenging skiing, notably the Osthang – a long, steep mogul-field through trees down to St Anton. There are all sorts of mostly short, steep off-piste variants down to St Christoph, St Anton and points between. The second section of the cable-car from Galzig takes a spectacular course, high above one bowl, across one ridge, down over another bowl and up to a second ridge, which is still not the Valluga itself, but a shoulder below it – the Vallugagrat. From here a miniature cable-car ferries a few people at a time up to the rocky peak. Skis are not allowed up unless you are with a guide; the descent into the Pazieltal starts very perilously.

The direct descents from Vallugagrat are stern, south-facing slopes down into the Steissbachtal, with two famous unprepared pistes – Mattun, which is steep, and Schindlerkar, which is steeper. Both consist of large moguls which seem to go on and on. They get a lot of sun, and after a cold night should be left well alone until the ice softens up. There are numerous off-piste variations. The most exciting off-piste skiing can be seen below the cable-car and the Schindlergrat chair-lift, and a glance on the way up will be enough to put most skiers off.

For most skiers the beginning of skiing from the Valluga is the easy cruise from the Vallugagrat to a small drag-lift. The easier runs are round the back – no more than a moderately difficult run down to the the

Ulmerhütte, and from there either easily round to the Steissbachtal and to St Anton, or on to Rauz, over the road and down to Stuben. Rauz is no more than a chair-lift station beside the road, but a very useful one as a backdoor to the Valluga, often resorted to by St Anton skiers and day-trippers from Lech/Zürs as a Galzig by-pass. It links up with the new Schindlergrat chair-lift, which takes you to much the same skiing as the Valluga cable-car.

From **Stuben** a long and cold two-stage chair-lift climbs the steep north-facing slopes of the Albona. Wind often makes it unpleasant, but in the right conditions there is some exhilarating steep powder and piste skiing. At the top you can restore circulation in the bar, or beside the short Sonnleiten south-facing drag-lift. There is one run suitable for intermediates down to Rauz, and a steep off-piste descent to St Christoph. A great excursion is the run down to Langen – unmarked except by the warning sign at the outset and not easy to follow, but a beautiful mixture of terrain. Equally beautiful and often more sheltered is the run via the Maroital (much of it through thick woodlands) ending up at a restaurant in the Verwalltal, a long walk from St Anton.

Nursery slopes are not very good, and even if they were, St Anton would be no place for a beginner. Nasserein is the usual place where learners are confined, and there are small nursery lifts at Galzig and Gampen and on the Rendel.

Mountain restaurants are adequately spread around the slopes, and there are a few memorable ones, notably the Krazy Kanguruh just above the resort, the Rodelhütte above Nasserein, and the Ulmerhütte, one of the oldest mountain restaurants in the Alps, one of the most malodorously plumbed, and one of the best for sunset panoramas. They get extremely crowded, and service is often without a smile.

Lifts

Passes Arlberg Pass covers all St Anton, Lech and Zürs lifts and buses within St Anton. Area day and half-day passes available.
Children 40% off, under 15.

Cost 6-day pass AS1,430. 15% off in low season.
Beginners Day and half-day passes valid only for certain lifts – one for beginners, one with greater scope.

Thanks to the Schindlergrat chair-lift, skiing the Valluga is no longer the nightmare it used to be, but long queues still build up for the Galzig cable-car in the morning. The most effective way of avoiding them is to catch a bus to Rauz, where the chair-lift is rarely crowded. Lifts and pistes in the Steissbachtal also get very crowded. Stuben lifts are notoriously cold and slow.

The resort

St Anton is a natural staging post at the bottom of the Arlberg pass road; mountains drop steeply down to the village from both north and south sides. There is room for the village to be by-passed by the main road – but only just, and a number of St Anton's hotels are in effect roadside ones. This main road is not as busy as it used to be, now that the Arlberg tunnel has been constructed, but it is still noisy. Squashed uncomfortably between road and railway is the long, narrow resort centre. It is not particularly beautiful – a mixture of hotel buildings old and new, cafés, shops and hot-dog stalls – but it is always bustling. The village has grown into an inconvenient straggle, with chalets and hotels lining the road down to neighbouring villages. Nasserein is a not very convenient suburb where where many UK operators send their clients. St Anton is emphatically a young people's resort and has bars, discos and fast food to cater for their tastes and, to a certain extent, their budgets: it is not a cheap place to stay, but there are ways of living, and living it up, more cheaply than in many Austrian resorts.

Accommodation is varied in comfort, style, cost and desirability of location. The last is important and skiers lucky enough to stay in the attractive, expensive Post ($\emptyset$ 2213) and Alte Post ($\emptyset$ 2553) or the numerous more down-to-earth central b&b hotels will be the envy of the less privileged stuck halfway between resort centre and Nasserein or up above the resort on the steep hill down from the Arlberg Pass. Other central hotels often used by UK operators are the Rosanna ($\emptyset$ 2400), the Sporthotel ($\emptyset$ 2911), the very attractive Schwarzer Adler ($\emptyset$ 2244) and the less expensive Kristall ($\emptyset$ 2848). Eastwards along the valley there is ample scope (except in peak season) for skiers with a car to stay within range of St Anton, often very cheaply and comfortably. Chalet accommodation in and (mostly) around St Anton is also easily available. Several reporters found that being able to deposit skis and boots at the bottom of the Galzig lift took a lot of the discomfort out of the daily march to and from skiing.

Après-ski is extremely lively and varied, with mountain restaurants where skiers linger until dark; bowling; meals round the fire and tobogganing down from the Rodelhütte; lots of bars and tea rooms along the main street full to bursting from late afternoon (tea-dancing can usually be found) until late; lots of restaurants and cheap snack bars; live bands, noisy pick-up joints and discothèques. Several reporters commented unfavourably on the presence of large numbers of rowdy young Swedes. Nasserein has a few bars and restaurants.

Ski school

Classes 2hr morning and afternoon.
Cost 6 days AS870. Private lesson AS1,450/day (4hr).
Special courses Wedel courses, off-piste, helicopter skiing.

Children Ski kindergarten, ages 5–14, 9.00–4.30, 6 days with lunch AS1,520. Non-ski kindergarten, ages 3–14, same times and price.

St Anton's ski school has a reputation second to none and many keen, proficient skiers who would scorn instruction anywhere else come to St Anton for this reason. Instructors often stay with classes over lunch, acting as guides to bars and restaurants. Whether the school's reputation is still justified is a controversial issue; there are certainly plenty of critics, suggesting that the school is more sensitive to the needs of strong skiers than the fears of timid ones.

Other activities

Cross-country About 35km of trails along main valley from St Anton to and beyond St Jakob, and in Verwalltal. Marked but not graded. Instruction available.

Not skiing 20km of cleared walks, hotel swimming pools/sauna/massage, tennis, squash, artifical rink for skating /curling, sleigh rides, historical museum, tobogganing, ski bob.

Although there are long X-C trails (the Verwalltal is much prettier than the main valley trail beside main road and railway), and lots of non-skiing activities, St Anton is emphatically a resort for keen skiers only.

Travel

Airport Zurich; transfer about 3½hr. Also Munich.
Reachable resorts Zürs and Lech are only a few miles away, over the Arlberg pass.

Railway Main-line station in resort.
Road Via Basel or Ulm, then Feldkirch. The Arlberg Pass is often closed and routinely requires chains; the toll road tunnel rarely presents difficulties.

St Anton has far too many cars, and parking near the centre is always difficult; but a car is handy for making the most of the Arlberg skiing, and for après-ski if you aren't staying centrally. There are buses between St Anton centre and St Jakob via Nasserein, and in the other direction to Mooser Kreuz, at the top of the resort. They are often overcrowded, especially between the centre and the Rendel lift station. There is no evening service. Post buses go to St Christoph, Lech, Stuben and Langen.

Miscellaneous

Tourist office ∅ (5446) 22690/24630. Tx 5817525.
Equipment hire 6 days skis AS600, boots AS180, X-C AS400.
Resort beds 5,200 in hotels, 700 in apartments.

Medical Hospital in Zams (20km); fracture clinic, doctors, dentists, chemist in resort.
Package holidays BL, BS, CW, HA, IG, IT, JM, MM, SCG, SKW, SNP, SUP, SUS, TH

Stuben 1410m

Stuben is a very small village beside the road from Langen. It is dark, cold and windy, but one of the most convenient places to stay for getting around the Arlberg skiing, especially if you have a car. Rauz is nearby, for queue-free access to St Anton skiing, and Lech/Zürs are also close. There are buses in each direction. Stuben has its own skiing, described above, and also some excellent sunny nursery slopes on the other side of the road from the village (a drawback for toddlers). The village is quiet but does boast some traditional nightlife and has a few friendly hotel bars and restaurants.

St Christoph 1780m

A few yards on the Tyrolean side of the Arlberg Pass, St Christoph is no more than a few hotels and restaurants beside the road, among them the massive, smartly renovated old Hospiz. It is a bleak place to be when the blizzards howl, and is not recommended as a holiday base despite direct access to the Valluga by means of the little cable-car which carries a modest 250 skiers an hour to Galzig.

Get stuck in

Lech Austria 1450m

Good for *Easy skiing, nursery slopes, big ski area, Alpine charm, sunny skiing, family skiing, getting marooned*
Bad for *Lift queues, tough skiing, easy road access, mountain restaurants, getting marooned*

Linked resort: Zürs

The deep, steep bowl which divides the Arlberg's two major ski areas could be spanned, but has not been. No doubt this is in order to keep the St Anton riffraff out of the high seclusion of Lech and Zürs – the smart, expensive, showy winter hideaways of rich and royal, with a national split (for Lech) of 60% German visitors, 20% Austrian, 2% British, and at least 95% swathed in furs. The two resorts share a skiing area which is varied, extensive and open but not well mechanised and not (despite piste maps peppered with black runs) as suitable for good skiers as for intermediates and beginners. Liberal use of artificial snow means the slopes are as immaculately groomed as the visitors.

Of the two resorts, Lech is older, larger, livelier and more attractive by far – a complete winter sports resort with good cross-country skiing, delightful walks and other sports facilities, lively but not uproarious in the evenings. Zürs is little more than a large group of expensive modern hotels above the tree-line along the road to Lech.

Lech has an upland suburb, Oberlech, a car-free scattering of chalets and hotels in the middle of sunny, gentle ski-fields above the resort – an attractive base for families with small children. It has more accommodation than Zug, a very picturesque hamlet a mile or two up a dead-end road from Lech which is a delightful place for lunch, as well as an excellent goal for cross-country skiing, walking, sleigh-riding and après-skiing excursions.

Lech and Zürs are not on a major road or railway line. Until the turn of the century, they could be reached from the Arlberg Pass road only by a narrow and hazardous path, and were cut off all winter. Even now there are times when the Flexenpass is blocked for days on end.

The skiing top 2450m bottom 1445m

Lech and Zürs share a skiing area spread over three mountains; you can get around all three on skis, but only clockwise, which means crowds of people all going the same way. Although the valleys are not wide, the lift connections are not perfect. Zürs is high, with all its skiing above the tree-line while Lech has a more attractive arrangement of gentle lower slopes among woodland and open ground above. Zürs is particularly well known for off-piste skiing, for which there are large

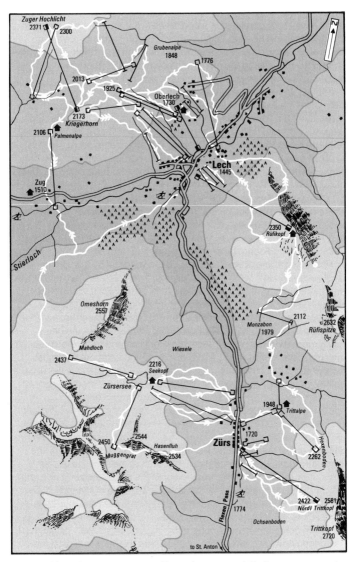

reasonably safe open spaces, although no especially fearsome runs to compare with St Anton.

The **Rüfikopf** cable-car scales an impressive wall from the centre of Lech, too steep to be skied directly but with long, beautiful and difficult unprepared runs, often closed, in several directions either down to Lech via the Wöstertäli or down the shoulder of the Rüfikopf to the woods by the road from Zürs. The only normal pistes are little more than long, beautiful traverses to get to Hexenboden skiing above Zürs.

Lech's main skiing area, on the other side of the river, is contrastingly open and mostly gentle, with a confusing array of lifts serving a maze of short, mostly intermediate pistes. From different parts of the village several lifts serve the slopes between Lech and **Oberlech**, with snow machines installed on the main runs down to make good any inadequacies of nature (the slopes face south-east).

Above Oberlech, lifts and pistes are spread in a wide, fragmented basin below the peaks of the Kriegerhorn and the Zuger Hochlicht, the two linked by a spectacular cable-car. There are easy and intermediate motorway pistes in all directions, but also some tough runs, especially from the Kriegerhorn – a couple of short, steep pistes down towards Lech and to the Steinmähder chairs, and a beautiful long south-facing slope down to Zug, where new snow soon deteriorates. Off-piste skiers can traverse for miles from the Zuger Hochlicht to ski down either to Oberlech or Stubenbach or even Warth; most itineraries involve a lot of walking between bits of skiing. In the other direction the open slopes beside the Steinmähder chair-lift are much favoured after a new snowfall. From the bottom a beautiful long gulley schuss (often closed because of avalanche danger) leads round to Zug.

The skiing above Zürs is also split into two areas by the village. The west-facing slopes, which are accessible from Lech via the Rüfikopf, are themselves split except at the bottom. The two major lifts start at either end of Zürs. The long **Hexenboden** chair-lift serves fairly ordinary intermediate pistes with plenty of off-piste opportunties when the snow is right. The **Trittkopf** cable-car climbs higher and offers much more demanding runs with some difficult and renowned off-piste descents reached by long traverses from the top station. The most difficult to reach is the run down to Stuben, which involves skiing over a gallery which protects the road. Beside Hexenboden there is a link lift for skiers coming from Lech or for those who have skied the north-facing off-piste slopes from Hexenboden down into the Pazieltal.

The east-facing **Seekopf** slopes are served by a long drag-lift from above the centre of the village near the Zürserhof, and a road-side chair-lift out of the village. At the north end of the sector there is one long, fairly easy run down to the village with some off-piste descents accessible by a short climb, ending up on the road between Lech and Zürs. On the other side of the lift there are a couple of more difficult pistes, graded red and, as elsewhere, off-piste variants around the hillside. From Zürsersee (just below the Seekopf) a chair-lift climbs a secluded north-facing bowl behind the Hasenfluh; its easy piste usually has good snow. The alternative is to go over the back and drop down into a steep bowl and on to a beautiful out-of-the-way run, manageable for intermediates, back to Zürs. The other lift from Zürsersee is the Mahdloch chair-lift, which gives access to some superb long runs behind the Omeshorn to Lech and Zug, on and off the piste. This area has perhaps the best moderate and difficult piste skiing that Lech and Zürs has to offer – lots of space, beautiful mountains and no machinery. The more difficult Zug run ends up at the chair-lift to Palmenalpe.

Lech's **nursery slopes** are at Oberlech and are in all respects excellent. Once off the nursery slopes inexperienced skiers will find plenty of scope for building up speed and confidence. Zürs has adequate nursery lifts near the bottom of the Trittkopf cable-car.

Mountain restaurants are surprisingly inadequate for such long-established and fashionable resorts. The Palmenalpe restaurant above Zug gets very crowded. The best places for lunch are Zug (several restaurants, mostly quite a walk from the pistes), and Oberlech, where again there is plenty of choice. The old (14th-century) Goldener Berg restaurant is usually packed at midday and evening. In Zürs there is little alternative to eating in the resort, at a price.

Lifts

Passes Arlberg pass covers all St Anton, Lech, Zürs lifts but not buses. Passes available for day, half-day, and four non-consecutive half-days. **Children** 40% off, under 15.	**Cost** 6-day pass AS1,430. 15% off in low season. **Beginners** Limited pass covering a few lifts, by the day. Adventurous second-week skiers will need an area pass.

The lift system has bottlenecks when the resorts are full, as they are for most of the season. The Rüfikopf cable-car is usually the worst and lots of skiers use the bus to get to Zürs; long waits are also to be expected for the Trittkopf, Seekopf, Palmenalpe and Steinmähder lifts at various times of day as skiers make their way round the circuit and (in Zürs) follow the sun. In contrast to St Anton you can't avoid the Lech/Zürs queues by clever tactics. There are several piste maps in circulation with a confusing variety of pistes and routes.

The resort

Lech is a pleasant, sunny village with a church in the middle, and a covered wooden bridge over the water where sleigh horses take shelter from the elements. There are trees and old buildings and the modern expansion of the resort has been unobtrusive; chalet-style hotels line the main street, next to the river, and smaller chalets are dotted around the gentle lower slopes.

Accommodation is mostly in comfortable and expensive hotels; Lech is compact and the location of accommodation is not very important, except for the very lazy. To do Lech in style the hotels to choose are the Post (℘ 2206), a beautiful traditional hotel in the centre; the Arlberg (℘ 2134), modern, plush, central and spacious; or the Tannbergerhof (℘ 2202), the centre of Lech's gaudy social life. There are numerous less formal hotels, and some rented chalet accommodation, but nowhere is cheap. Rooms are often very hard to come by in high season.

Oberlech has several comfortable hotels near the cable-car station and chalets spread widely around the hillside. The attraction of staying here rather than in Lech is avoiding crowds for the Schlegelkopf lifts. But they soon catch up with you.

Après-ski is a serious and dignified business. Lech après-skiers prefer to put their hair up than to let it down and here, more than in most ski resorts, smart is the order of the day (or rather evening). The tea-dance at the Tannbergerhof is an institution and there is live music later on, here and in several other hotels. Discothèques do not get much custom. Dining and dancing out at Zug (by sleigh) and Oberlech (cable-car up, toboggan or walk down if you miss the last cable-car at 1am) are popular. Eating out is mostly in hotel restaurants.

Ski school

Classes 2hr morning and afternoon.	Children Ski kindergarten, age 6
Cost 6 days AS1,030. Private lessons	upwards, 9.00–4.30, 6 days with meals
AS1,400/day.	AS1,140. Non-ski kindergarten, age 2
Special courses Helicopter drops,	upwards, 9.00–4.30, 6 days with meals
guided off-piste skiing.	AS1,260.

We lack recent reports of teaching standards in the ski school.

Other activities

Cross-country 15km of trails along	Not skiing 25km of cleared paths,
valley to Zug and beyond. Graded easy.	toboggan run (Oberlech), natural ice rink
Instruction available.	(skating/curling), sleigh rides, tennis,
	squash, hotel swimming pool, saunas.

Lech is an attractive place for cross-country and non-skiers mainly because it is so pretty. Walks and X-C trails are not very extensive but are very well suited to those wanting to meet up with skiers.

Travel

Airport Zurich; transfer about 3½hr.	Railway Langen (15km); buses
Road Via Ulm or Basel, then Feldkirch;	connect with international trains.
chains are routinely needed, and the	Reachable resorts St Anton and
Flexenpass is liable to closure.	outposts.

Parking is difficult, restricted and vigorously policed. Having a car is a great help for good skiers who are likely to be drawn to St Anton, but otherwise not necessary. There are regular but not frequent post buses connecting Lech, Zug, Zürs, Stuben, Langen and St Anton.

Miscellaneous

Tourist office ✆ (05583) 2161.	Equipment hire 6 days boots AS700,
Tx 052 39123.	skis AS300, X-C AS500.
Medical Hospital in Bludenz (40km),	Resort beds 5,750 in hotels, 250 in
fracture clinic, doctor, chemist in resort;	apartments.
dentist in St Anton (15km).	Tour operators BL, JM, MM, SUP.

Zürs 1720m

Zürs has grown up (solely for skiing – in summer it is shut) along the road near the Flexenpass. The setting is high, bleak and treeless; the resort conforms to traditional architectural style and is not the eyesore such a place would be in the French Alps, but apart from the broad snow-fields above the resort and the elegant visitors, there is nothing attractive about it. There are few shops and nothing much ever seems to be going on outside the precincts of the many comfortable hotels, and a few bars and restaurants. Zürs is not even a particularly convenient place – although it is small, the lift departure points are awkwardly dotted around; one reporter complained of 'constantly tramping about the village from one lift terminal to another'. A car isn't much help because parking is so difficult.

Tourist office ✆ (5583) 2245, Tx 5239111. Tour operators BL, MM.

Montafon multiplier

Schruns, Tschagguns, St Gallenkirch, Gaschurn, Gargellen Austria 700m–1430m

The Montafon is a large skiing region south of Bludenz in the Austrian
Vorarlberg, based on the long, flat and populous Ill Valley, a popular
tourist thoroughfare in summer but a dead end in winter. The many
villages along the valley have got together to share a lift pass covering
all the local skiing and public transport between the scattered areas.
Pretty little Gargellen, tucked away in a secluded side valley, joins in
the arrangement which has transformed the Montafon from a bitty
region of limited appeal except to ski tourers and German weekenders
into a bitty region of considerable appeal to skiers who want varied
intermediate skiing and don't mind taking buses to get to it.
   Even more than most Austrian resorts, the Montafon is dominated by
Germans, especially the ski areas most accessible to day-trippers
(Schruns and Tschagguns). Gargellen was a great favourite in the early
days of package tours to Austria, but now the area attracts few British
skiers, and we have had few reports. The few have recommended the
area for its broad, open, well-mechanised intermediate skiing with the
chance of long runs down to the valley when the snow is good at these
low levels. Reporters also appreciated the friendliness of the villages,
by no means the most picturesque in Austria (they all straggle), but less
affected by tourism than most. Schruns is the most convenient base for
those relying on buses to get around, as the two relevant bus services
are Schruns–Partenen (the village at the end of the road in winter) and
Schruns–Gargellen. Close scrutiny of the timetables is needed if you're
planning day-trips between Gargellen and Gaschurn/St Gallenkirch,
but they can be managed. Gaschurn and Gargellen are the most
charming resorts, and the least subject to the weekend influx.
   The main resort in the valley is **Schruns** (700m), a busy little market
town and spa beside the river, accessible by train from Bludenz.
Schruns' skiing is the Hochjoch, reached by a long two-stage cable-car
from near the town centre over wooded slopes to Kappell (1850m),
where a good nursery area is cordoned off from other skiers. Above
Kappell a chain of chair-lifts opens up a large area of open easy skiing
beneath rocky crests behind the Kreuzjoch (2350m). There are some
more taxing runs down to Kappell including a possible 11km run for
nearly 1700m vertical if snow is good enough to ski down to the base
station. Slopes face north and north-west. The centre of Schruns is
car-free and shopping is attractively varied. There is plenty for
non-skiers to do, including skating and curling, a local museum, a
reading room, sleigh rides, and indoor tennis and swimming at the
large, central Hotel Löwe (℘ 3141) which is also the focus of Schruns
après-ski.
   Schruns almost merges with its smaller neighbour **Tschagguns**, on
the other side of the valley. There are two small ski areas, neither of

them immediately accessible from the village. The larger is Golm (1000m to 2085m), which has some entertaining open intermediate skiing, including a friendly women's downhill course, above the mid-station of a quaint open-topped funicular.

Higher up the valley, skiing consists of the M-shaped Silvretta Nova system, created by the integration of the north-east-facing slopes above the neighbouring villages of **St Gallenkirch** (880m) and **Gaschurn** (1000m) via the Novatal which divides them. There is lots of space and lots of easy ground to cover on the broad slopes. Lifts reach 2200m at both ends of the system, with a couple of tougher runs and some good off-piste above Gaschurn. Busy lifts have been duplicated in most places, but there are queues for the inefficient single chair-lift from Gaschurn (a replacement is planned). There is an easy (but over-used and often worn) run down to the valley at Gaschurn. St Gallenkirch has access lifts at either end of the long village, but the only pistes down to the valley are under the Garfrescha chairs at the southern end. Reporters commented that the Gaschurn hotels used by British operators are inconveniently placed, so far from the skiing that the bus is essential.

Gargellen (1430m) is a miniature resort (it has only 750 guest beds) tucked away beneath the Madrisa in a secluded side valley away from the main Montafon thoroughfare. It is an old British family favourite, mainly thanks to the very high standard and the friendliness of the Hotel Madrisa (∅ 6331), the main village institution, now expensively modernised but still very handsome. It is the centre of Gargellen après-ski, has a good nursery slope in the back garden, a ski hire shop, swimming pool, fitness room and children's play area.

Gargellen's skiing on the north-east-facing Schafberg is small but attractively varied. There are easy open slopes at the top of the system between 2000m and 2300m, a beautiful long easy run round the mountain from the top to the Gargellenalp mid-station restaurant (1733m), a short blackish route under the chairs to the same point, and some good off-piste skiing nearby. Runs down through the woods to the edge of the straggling village are friendly, and snow at resort-level is much more reliable than in the main valley.

The Montafon has long been famous as an excellent base for ski tours in the beautiful Silvretta and Rätikon mountains which separate Austria and Switzerland. Tourers strike out from the top of the lifts above Gaschurn, Tschagguns and Gargellen, where the favourite and least arduous excursion is over to Switzerland via the Antönierjoch and down into the beautiful, notoriously avalanche-prone valley of St Antönien. This is only a short bus and train ride away from Klosters whose Madrisa lifts lead back towards Gargellen via the Schlappinerjoch. The skiing is not difficult, the uphill sections are not long, and the resorts honour one another's lift passes. The Silvrettasee (1950m) above Partenen is the best starting point for more serious tours in the Silvretta peaks.

Tourist offices Gaschurn ∅ (5558) 201 Schruns ∅ (5556) 2166 Tschagguns ∅ (5556) 2457 St Gallenkirch ∅ (5557) 6234 Gargellen ∅ (5557) 6303.
Package holidays Schruns/Tschagguns SNP, IG; Gaschurn TH; Gargellen IG, MM.

Brand loyalty

Brand Austria 1040m

Brand is a straggling village near Bludenz in a beautiful valley beneath the mighty Scesaplana. Its skiing is of minor interest, and by Austrian standards the village is not particularly charming – it has no real centre, and its layout is not ideal for skiing. Nevertheless Brand is firmly established on the British market. Many beginners, timid intermediates and children enjoy the skiing; some excellent hotels offer good value for money, and although there isn't a great range of nightlife, the atmosphere is friendly and lively.

Chair-lifts from two extremities of the village climb over steep, unskiable wooded slopes to an area of open, sunny, easy skiing between 1600 and 1900m, with a small nursery slope and several restaurants. The only long runs are down from Palüdhütte to the top end of the village (snow cover unreliable), and the beautiful Lorenzital run, reached from the top station, occasionally closed because of avalanche danger. Snow conditions permitting, you can prolong the Lorenzital all the way down to the bottom of the Niggenkopf chair-lift, giving 900m vertical. The north facing flank of the Lorenzital offers some good off-piste skiing. There is a good nursery slope facing north on the other side of the village, a long walk from the rest of the skiing.

Valley-floor cross-country runs are good. There are shorter loops in the Lorenzital at about 1500m, accessible from the Niggenkopf, and a strenuous off-piste cross-country tour (up to 15 km) from the Lorenzital. There is a small natural ice rink, swimming pools and saunas in several hotels, indoor tennis courts, bowling, and 10km of cleared walks. Three mountain restaurants are accessible to non-skiers. Bludenz and Feldkirch, a very attractive old town, are easy to get to.

Après-ski is in hotels, except the self-explanatory Britannia Pub (darts and Saturday's football scores chalked on a blackboard). The Scesaplana is about the only dance spot, at tea-time and later. Its buffet evenings are recommended by reporters.

Welcoming and comfortable hotels is one of the things which takes visitors back to Brand. The Hämmerle (℅ 213) is attractive, comfortable and well placed, not far from the Niggenkopf lift. Reporters enjoyed excellent food, including a buffet breakfast, and very good service (fruit in the bedroom and a bottle of wine for the return journey). The Lagant (℅ 285) is also close to the Niggenkopf – 'pool, views, food all excellent'. The Sporthotel Beck (℅ 306) is a better compromise location for those wanting access to the nursery slopes, and has a good pool/sauna, charming service, and hearty food.

The nearby hamlet of **Bürserberg** has few lifts (only a chair and three drags) but they serve a worthwhile extent of mostly easy, mostly wooded, skiable mountain between 900 and 1800m; it is covered by the Brand lift pass and linked by bus several times a day.

Tourist office ℅ (5559) 201. Tx 052470. **Package holidays** BS, ED, IT, SUS, TH.

Ski-running in the old-fashioned way

Davos Switzerland 1550m

Good for *Big ski area, off-piste skiing, ski touring, cross-country skiing, not skiing, sunny skiing, rail access*
Bad for *Alpine charm, lift queues, skiing convenience*

Klosters Switzerland 1130m

Good for *Big ski area, Alpine charm, mountain restaurants, cross-country skiing, not skiing, rail access*
Bad for *Lift queues, après-ski, skiing convenience*

If skiing has its magic mountain, it is the Parsennalp above Davos, where the ski pioneers of the 19th century discovered a large range of long and beautiful descents in all directions. These runs have not changed, and have not been bettered. For skiers with a taste for long, leisurely outings involving frequent stops at mountain huts and a train-ride home, the Parsenn is in a league of its own. Those who have become used to systematic lift arrangements may well be disappointed – though you may find consolation on one of the four or five less crowded ski areas scattered around this extensive region.

The two resorts which share the Parsenn have little else in common, apart from affluence and long-standing British connections. Davos is one of the big towns of Alpine skiing, and with its square, block buildings it is no beauty; for Swiss Alpine charm, look elsewhere. Already established as a health resort before recreational skiing was invented, it took to the new sport quickly. It was in Davos that a funicular railway was first built especially to carry skiers and it was here that the first drag-lift was installed. Ironically, that invention has in the long term helped other resorts to develop new Parsenns which have eclipsed the original – leaving Davos to look increasingly to cross-country skiers and conference delegates for its business.

Thanks to visits from the bachelor Prince Charles, Klosters has an exclusive image. It is quite attractive, smaller and quieter than Davos – a place to spend months of the winter in the seclusion of your chalet. Its skiing is curious, with exciting and very beautiful runs spread across an enormous north-facing mountain, yet hardly any lifts.

The skiing top 2844m bottom 813m

The core of the skiing is the Parsenn/Weissfluh area above Davos Dorf, which links up with Strela above Davos Platz and the Gotschna area above Klosters Platz. Most of the lifts are on the Davos side of the mountain, but Klosters has the north-facing slopes and more than its

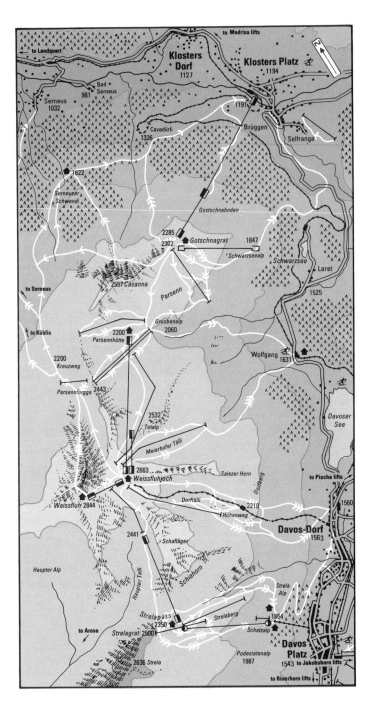

to Madrisa lifts

Klosters Dorf 1127

Klosters Platz 1194

← to Landquart

981 Bad Serneus

Serneus 1032

1191

Brüggen

Selfrange

Cavadürli 1326

1622

Serneuser Schwendi

Gostschnaboden

2285 **Gotschnagrat** 1847
2302

Schwarzseealp

Schwarzsee

Laret

1525

to Serneus →

2557 *Casanna*

Parsenn

to Küblis →

Gruobenalp 2060

2200
Parsennhütte

Wolfgang 1631

2200 *Kreuzweg*

2443 *Parsennfurgga*

2532 *Totalp*

Meierhofer Tälli

Davoser See

2663
Weissfluhjoch

Salezer Horn

to Pischa lifts →

Weissfluh 2844

Dorfberg

Dorftälli

2219

1560

Höhenweg

Davos-Dorf 1563

2441

Schafläger

Haupter Alp

Haupter Tälli

Schiahorn

Strela Alp

Strelapass 2350

Strelaberg

1864

Strelagrat 2500

Schatzalp

to Arosa →

2636 *Strela*

Podestatenalp 1987

Davos Platz 1543

to Jakobshorn lifts

to Rinerhorn lifts →

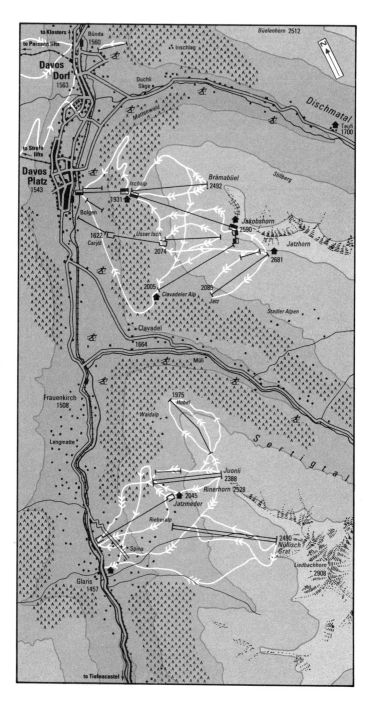

fair share of good skiing. There are four other separate ski-areas which offer excellent skiing with much less crowding. The Jakobshorn, the other side of Davos, has excellent challenging runs and very good off-piste skiing when conditions are right. The recently opened Rinerhorn, above Glaris, is out of the way and uncrowded, with a good range of skiing giving a drop of over 1000m. The other two areas are off our maps: Madrisa, above Klosters Dorf, is excellent for sunshine, uncomplicated skiing and tours over to Austria and back; Pischa is a little-skied open flank of mountainside with good off-piste potential.

From Davos Platz the **Strela** skiing is reached by a steep funicular to the sunny Schatzalp, where there is a large and comfortable old hotel. From here, there is a toboggan run down to Platz, a path for walkers and skiers down to Dorf and off-piste skiing for adventurers. Above the Schatzalp, the east-facing open bowl below the Strela Pass consists of mainly easy skiing down the middle, and some steeper runs. These lifts are used less for the skiing they serve directly than for access to many famous old ski-tours – both on the Davos/Glaris side of the range and down to Arosa over the other side – and as a back-door way into the Parsenn ski area, via a cable-car and drag-lift to Weissfluhjoch.

This is the major lift junction above Davos and the point of arrival of the **Parsenn** railway from Davos Dorf. There are enormous skiing possibilities in three directions: first, back towards Davos Dorf – south-east facing slopes, gentle on the top half, steeper and often icier lower down. Secondly, the extensive wide-open, mostly easy motorway pistes behind the Weissfluhjoch, the heart of Parsenn skiing. For good skiers there is an excellent run, steep in places, from the Meierhoftälli drag-lift to the railway at Wolfgang. And thirdly, there are tremendously long runs, open at first and then wooded, to the villages of Klosters, Serneus, Saas, Küblis and even beyond, to Landquart. Unless you take the cable-car to the top of the Weissfluh none of the runs is particularly difficult – easiest is a simple blue via Cavadürli to Klosters, trickiest is a moderate red to Serneus. But they are all extremely long (precisely how long depends on who you ask – to Küblis it's about 13km), and once you've started there is no turning back. There are signposts to the different villages when the runs split, but they are easily missed. The mountain is basically north-facing and snow is pretty reliable, though the lower slopes may well be bare or patchy. In between the various runs, there is some tough off-piste skiing in the woods.

The two-stage **Gotschnagrat** cable-car from near Klosters Platz railway station is the only lift to the Parsenn from Klosters. The run back down to the Gotschnaboden mid-station is the notorious Gotschnawang or simply Wang – a slope of awesome steepness, dropping about 500m, which Prince Charles is no doubt pleased to have put behind him; mercifully, it is rarely open. The alternative descents from the top station are black, red or blue. The most direct is the magnificent Drostobel black run – long, steep, but nothing like as intimidating as the Wang and much safer. There is an easy traverse across to the Parsennhütte and some very easy runs beside the Parsennmeder drag-lift. Underneath the neighbouring Schwarzsee chair-lift is a black run which often consists of formidable moguls. The red run from the bottom of the chair-lift takes you through the woods and to a not very convenient fringe of Klosters Platz.

The very sunny, south-west facing **Madrisa** bowl above the Saaseralp (1880m), is reached by gondola from Klosters Dorf. Most of the skiing is above the tree-line, and includes a good nursery area near the Saaseralp and some long runs from the top of the Madrisa lift (2542m), including an unprepared black run to Saaseralp, and the beautiful Schlappin run all the way down a wooded valley to the village, marked black but not difficult. This run is joined by a similar black going down directly from Saaseralp, but the wooded lower slopes below Saaseralp are otherwise not skied, and timid intermediates take the lift down. From this area you can make a day-tour round the Madrisa, over to Gargellen in Austria via the Schlappinerjoch (2202m) and back via the St Antonierjoch (2379m) and down to St Antonien (1400m), to catch a bus down to Küblis. The skiing is not particularly difficult, but a guide is recommended (as well as a passport).

Pischa is a small, out-of-the-way ski area worth a visit when the crowds are bad in the more popular areas. A cable-car serves the whole south-west-facing slope (1800m to 2485m). There is a simple array of parallel drag-lifts above the tree-line with very sunny, mostly intermediate runs beside them, and some more difficult descents through the trees. There is easy off-piste skiing beside the runs and some much more adventurous possibilities behind the Pischahorn and along the shoulder down to the Klosters road at Laret.

Jakobshorn is the most extensive alternative to the Parsenn/ Weissfluh skiing, and the most handy from Davos with access from near Platz station. Above the tree-line there is a wide range of long, mostly intermediate runs facing roughly west below the peaks of Jakobshorn and Bramabuel. Both are fairly steep at the top, but things are made easier by a path across the slope behind the Jakobshorn, giving access to gentle skiing in the sunny, west-facing bowl above Clavadeleralp. The woodland paths back to Davos Platz are not appealing, but there's always the cable-car. The steep, north-facing descent from the Jakobshorn to Teufi in the Dischmatal (nearly 900m below) is one of the best off-piste runs in the area. If you tackle it, take advice, and a bus timetable.

Rinerhorn is a small area of west- and north-west-facing slopes above Glaris, a short train-ride from Davos. There are no enclosed lifts, and in the morning the shaded chair-lift up over the woods to Jatzmeder, and the drag-lifts beyond, can be very cold. There is nothing very special about the pistes above the trees, but there are enough runs down to the valley to make this a good area in poor visibility. We can't confirm claims that this area is a powder-snow paradise. About 20 minutes' climbing gives access to the steep, north-facing side of the Sertigtal. There is some less extensive off-piste skiing between the two sets of drag-lifts above Jatzmeder, and a long run down to Glaris, reached from the Nüllischgrat drag-lift.

Although Davos is not really an ideal place for beginners, the **nursery slopes** beside Davos Platz at the bottom of the Jakobshorn are adequate. Klosters has a good sunny nursery area on the Madrisa at Saaseralp, and a few small lifts beside Klosters Dorf.

There is an adequate number of **mountain restaurants**, but most of the high ones, notably at the top of the Jakobshorn and at Weissfluhjoch, are very cheerless. Outstandingly attractive are the delightful *schwendis* in the woods on the way down to Klosters and nearby villages, and a number of restaurants in the valleys around Davos (at Teufi, Clavadell, Sertig, Glaris and at the bottom of Pischa), which fit in well with many skiers' itineraries.

Lifts

Passes General pass covers all Klosters and Davos lifts and railway between Kublis and Glaris (but not buses, irritatingly). Also valid in Gargellen (Austria). Available only for 3 days or more. Also a confusing variety of passes for areas or combinations of them, with or without railway, for half-day and longer periods – some with an option of 8 non-consecutive days.
Cost 6-day pass SF178.
Children 25% off, under 16.
Beginners Coupons. Free lift for ski school pupils at Klosters Dorf.

Davos gets very crowded in peak season (notably the Parsenn railway), as does Klosters; the Gotschnagrat suffers from awful queues, up to 1½ hr at peak times. A gondola from Serneus is planned but not imminent. Apart from the cluster of lifts behind the Weissfluhjoch there is a general shortage of transport in the main Parsenn area, and most of the skiing involves a lot of trips down to the valley, followed by bus or train rides. This is particularly frustrating when snow is poor at lower levels.

The resorts

Davos

Davos is set in a spacious, flat-bottomed junction of valleys beside a lake. The town is a through-route, and often unpleasantly congested with traffic. Buildings are square, grey, concrete and mostly undecorated. Platz is perhaps slightly uglier than Dorf, but has the better shopping and après-ski. Fortunately there is plenty of space nearby where you can find peace and quiet in beautiful surroundings, and a few outlying hamlets with accommodation and easy access to the railway (Wolfgang and Glaris).

Accommodation is in hotels large and small, simple and luxurious, throughout Platz and Dorf. Central Platz is more convenient – an easy walk to the station, and to the lifts for Strela and the Jakobshorn. The Belvedere (℗ 21281) is the traditional grand hotel, these days part of a chain and more expensive than stylish. Of the well-placed hotels, the Alte Post (℗ 35403) is cheerful and reasonable in price. In Davos Dorf, the Seehof (℗ 61201) is very expensive, attractive and comfortable, and well-placed for the Parsenn railway. The Meisser (℗ 52333) is less expensive and as well-placed, with the attraction of being off the main road through the resort.

Après-ski is not particularly chic, but there is a variety of bars, restaurants and well-attended dance spots. Some of the most attractive and least expensive eating places are outside Davos – evenings at

Teufi (reached by car or sleigh) and Schatzalp (last train down at 11pm) are particularly recommended. There is evening skating several times a week at Dorf; Platz has hockey matches, cinemas, and occasional cultural events at the conference centre.

Ski school

Classes 2hr morning and afternoon.
Cost 6 days SF118. Private lessons SF35/hr.
Children Ski kindergarten, Davos Dorf, ages 3–10, 9.00–5.00, 6 days with lunch

SF116. Non-ski kindergarten, Davos Platz, ages 3–10, 9.00–4.30, 6 days with lunch SF135.
Special courses Off-piste, ski-tours.

Davos is a celebrated area for short ski-tours, and the ski school organises group excursions according to conditions and demand from February onwards.

Other activities

Cross-country About 75km of trails along the main valley between Glaris and Wolfgang, and up the Flüela, Dischma and Sertig valleys. Dogs allowed between Davos Platz and Glaris; small illuminated loop between Platz and Dorf. Runs graded easy or medium.

Not skiing Over 60km cleared walks mostly at valley level, natural and artifical ice rinks, curling, fitness centre, swimming pool, sauna, toboggan run, riding, hang-gliding, sleigh rides, cinema, museums.

Although not a picturesque resort, Davos is large and well equipped with sports facilities, including an enormous natural rink – 'the equivalent of several football pitches' according to one reporter. Cross-country is very popular, with excellent long and very attractive valley runs. Gentle walks were the order of the day for the consumptives who first patronised Davos, and it is still an excellent place for walkers – quiet valleys with attractive restaurants, and a few higher paths.

Travel

Airport Zurich; transfer about 3hr.
Railway Station in resort centre.
Road Via Basel/Zurich; chains may be needed from Klosters.

Reachable resorts St Moritz and Lenzerheide-Valbella within range for day-trips, Arosa and Gargellen reachable on skis.

Frequent buses (oversubscribed in high season) link Dorf and Platz from early morning until late in the evening, with more occasional services running Wolfgang–Parsennbahn, Platz–Teufi and Dorf–Pischa. Trains run along the main valley serving all the ski areas except Pischa. A car is an asset for après-ski and for making the most of the ski area, though driving is often slow and parking near the lifts difficult – and many runs end up a long way from the point of departure.

Miscellaneous

Tourist office ✆ (83) 35951. Tx 74326.
Medical Hospital, chemists, dentists, doctors in resort.
Equipment hire 6 days skis SF80, boots SF 40, X-C SF60.

Resort beds 6,000 in hotels, 12,000 in apartments.
Package holidays BL, IG, KU, MM, PS, SGW, SWT.

Klosters

In Klosters, Platz and Dorf are separate villages, Platz very much the centre of skiing and social life – a recognisable village centre, with a number of hotels and shops. Both villages are spread along beside the busy through-road and railway, enclosed in a narrowing wooded valley which admits little sunlight in midwinter.

Accommodation consists mostly of private chalets, with some hotels in both villages. Platz is the more convenient base, with a number of comfortable and expensive hotels around the main street near the station and cable-car. The Alpina Aparthotel (∅ 41233) is a very smart neo-rustic chalet, the Chesa Grischuna (∅ 42222) is smaller, older and more attractive and very desirable. The small Wynegg (∅ 41340) is warm, welcoming and about as cheap you'll find, but its situation on the road towards Davos is not ideal.

Après-ski is quiet. The most attractive places for tea are up the mountain, though in Platz there are several congenial bars. More sophisticated visitors gravitate to the piano bar below the Chesa Grischuna or the Casa Antica – about the only recognisable disco. In Dorf the Madrisa Bar is nice for traditional music, dancing and décor. For eating out the Chesa Grischuna is the most attractive place, the Wynegg has the best atmosphere – by appointment to HRH PoW.

Ski school

Classes 2¼hr morning and afternoon. Cost 6 days SF135. Private lessons SF160/day. Special courses Ski touring.	Children Ski kindergarten, ages 3–6. Non-ski kindergarten, ages 2–5. Both 9.15–4.30, 6 days with lunch SF125.

Guides are available for ski-tours, most usual being the excursion to Gargellen from the Madrisa area.

Other activities

Cross-country About 60km of trails, between Serneus and Dorf, and in the Vereinatal above Platz. Near Platz a small loop for X-C with dogs, illuminated one evening a week.	Not skiing Natural ice rink (night skating once a week), saunas, pools in hotels, squash/fitness centre, sleigh rides, toboggan run, 34km of cleared walks (mostly at valley level).

Klosters is an attractive place for walkers and X-C skiers although the scope is less than at Davos, and the straggling lay-out along the road is a bit of a drawback – though you can get away up the Vereinatal.

Travel

As for Davos except a short half-hour closer to Chur and Zurich. Daytime buses every half hour serve Gotschna	and Madrisa lifts and points between. There are buses from Serneus about every hour, frequent trains to Davos.

Miscellaneous

Tourist office ∅ (83) 41877. Tx 74372. Medical Hospital in Davos. Doctors, chemists, dentist in resort. Package holidays BL, MM, SCG.	Equipment hire 6 days skis SF80, boots SF40, X-C (7 days) SF70. Resort beds 2,000 in hotels, 6,600 in apartments.

Where not to ski?

Arosa Switzerland 1775m

Good for *Not skiing, cross-country skiing, ski touring, nursery slopes, family skiing, sunny skiing, resort-level snow, rail access*
Bad for *Tough skiing, skiing convenience, easy road access*

Of the large, traditional winter sports centres of Switzerland, Arosa is one of the less well known and for dedicated skiers one of the less interesting. The pistes are not particularly extensive, and neither the village nor the winter clientele is particularly beautiful. Nevertheless it commands the loyalty of many regular visitors (a few British, but mostly Swiss and German), and of its kind it is a very good resort. It is an excellent place to do things other than downhill skiing, with some of the most beautiful mountain walks, cross-country trails, and sleigh rides in the Alps, and very good ice rinks. Nearly half Arosa's visitors don't ski, which means queues are rare for those who do – and being high but south-facing it offers a good compromise between snow reliability and skiing in the sun. But there are drawbacks: the very awkward lay-out in two separate parts – the main centre (Obersee) and the higher old village of Innerarosa – plus development along the steep road linking the two; and the ugliness of Obersee's grey blocks.

The skiing top 2653m bottom 1745m

Arosa's ski area is not large for a sizeable resort. It consists of two facets of the bowl at the head of the valley which, although linked by a lift, seem separate because of the distance between the main departure points at opposite ends of the resort, and because of the gullies that split up the mountainside. Pistes descend to each end of the resort. An unusual feature of the skiing in Arosa is crossing paths with non-skiers. There are runs for ski-bobs and toboggans, cleared walking trails across most of the ski area, and sleighs carrying tourists from Maran up to Tschuggen and down to Innerarosa. On a fine day the ski-fields present a rare and attractive picture of a traditional wintersports recreation area.

From Obersee, a two stage cable-car climbs from behind the station and lake to Tschuggen – a broad, sunny plateau above the tree line, also accessible by chair and tow from Innerarosa – and on to the impressive **Weisshorn** (2653m), which has the steepest slopes in the ski area. One run from the top is black, but not very severe except when the south-facing slopes have frozen overnight, and there are some short steep off-piste pitches between the rocky outcrops down the flanks of the Horn. The other pistes are mostly intermediate and easy. Off-piste skiing is limited to brief forays between the trails except for the steep (and in some cases very difficult) runs off the back and the sides

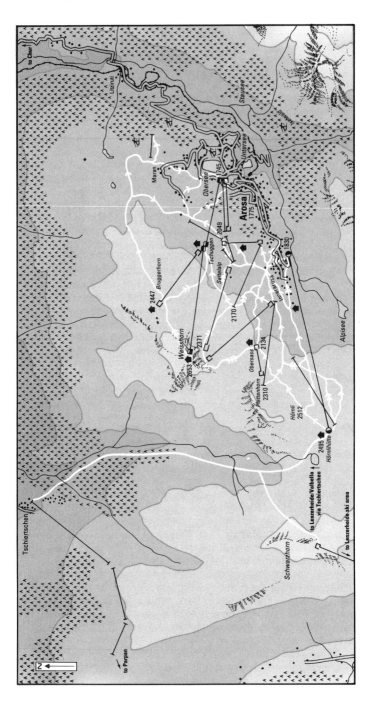

of the Weisshorn, which involve long excursions – to Tschiertschen, Litziruti and Chur. From the top of the Bruggenhorn chair-lift, a long motorway run flanks the mountain and descends to Maran, an uphill suburb of Arosa. Below Tschuggen is the only part of the Arosa ski area which is wooded; there are two runs to Obersee, one directly under the lift, the other easier and more roundabout, via Maran.

You can also ski from Tschuggen to Innerarosa and link up with the **Hörnli** side by means of the Plattenhorn drag lift (the adjacent Bankli chair-lift assures the connection the other way round). The east-facing slopes of the Hörnli are mainly served by a long gondola which starts an inconvenient distance from Innerarosa. The pistes are open, wide and undemanding. From the restaurant on the ridge at the top you look down into an inviting bowl and hidden valley. It is a beautiful ski excursion with a marked but not groomed run of no great difficulty down to the woods and along the flank of the mountainside to the little ski village of Tschiertschen. Provided you set out early you can go on from there to Lenzerheide, and ski back either via the Hörnli or down the beautiful, remote off-piste run past Älplisee.

Mountain restaurants are adequate. The sunny restaurant at the top of the Hörnli has a friendly atmosphere, and being accessible on foot is a popular target for non-skiing hikers and their dogs when the weather is fine. As Tschuggen there is a restaurant and open-air bar.

Nursery slopes are adequate. Tschuggen is a broad sunny plateau with refreshment close at hand, and good for meeting up with other skiers. There is another nursery area at Maran.

Lifts

Passes Area pass covers all lifts and bus. Half-day and day passes available.	**Beginners** Coupons. Free baby-lift at Innerarosa.
Cost 6-day pass SF135.	**Children** 30% off, under 16.

Although limited, the lift system is rarely subject to heavy crowds; 15–30min waits for Weisshorn and Hörnli lifts can occur at peak times; queues which have been a problem at the foot of the lifts linking the two sectors should now be relieved by a recently completed additional lift.

The resort

Arosa is remotely set at the head of a beautiful steep wooded valley at the end of a long, winding 20 miles from Chur. At the bottom, the main centre of the resort is built, in very plain style, around a small lake (Obersee) with the railway and Weisshorn lift station nearby. From here the village climbs along, above and below the road, for about a mile to Innerarosa, which is the old village up in the sunny pastures, much more attractive than Obersee, but with no central focus. There isn't much traffic (there is a midnight-to-6am car curfew), but the road is often very icy and hazardous for walkers.

Accommodation is mostly in hotels varying widely in size and degree of comfort. Obersee is the best location for resort facilities; well-placed hotels include the quiet, comfortable Derby (⌀ 311027), the large Posthotel (*℄* 310121), and the very simple, friendly Vetter (*℄* 311702). Innerarosa is better for access to the skiing and is more open, sunny, and attractive. The Hold (*℄* 311408) is very conveniently placed at Innerarosa; simpler and much less expensive than its palatial neighbour the Kulm (*℄* 310131). Lots of hotels are along the road between the two centres, which has little to recommend it.

Après-ski is varied (floodlit langlauf, evening bus for tobogganers, chess competitions after tea in the Cristallo, ice hockey matches to watch), but far from uproarious for dancers. The Kursaal is the liveliest, most youthful disco. Most restaurants are in hotels; a very cheerful exception is the Waldeck – the ice-hockey team's local.

Ski school

Classes 2hr morning and afternoon.
Cost 6 days SF128. Private lesson SF40/hr.
Special courses Ski touring.

Children Ski kindergarten (Pinocchio Club), ages 3 to 8, 6 full days SF128. Non-ski kindergarten at Hotel Park for ages 3 to 6, 9.00–5.00, 6 days SF144.

There is a great variety of day tours to Davos, Klosters and Lenzerheide, which can be arranged through the ski school.

Other activities

Cross-country 7½ and 5½km trails at Isla, 8km at Prätschalp plus 6km extension, 2 x 2km loops at Maran, 1km at Obersee. 2km loop floodlit until 9.00. Instruction and off-trail guided excursions.

Not skiing Sleigh rides, 29km of cleared walks, riding, artificial and natural skating and curling rinks, ski-bob and toboggan runs, swimming, sauna, massage, tennis, squash, bridge, chess, bowling, fitness centre.

Arosa is very good for cross-country and non-skiers. X-C trails are in two areas, the easy runs and longer Prätschalp one starting from the main X-C centre at Maran; Isla runs are in the woods below Obersee across the railway. Dogs are allowed on the beginners' loop on the lake. There are buses from Obersee to Maran and Isla. Runs are mostly for serious X-C skiers, with lots of hilly woodland trails. There isn't much scope for meeting up with downhill skiers. The high-level cleared paths (with benches) are outstanding.

Travel

Airport Zurich; transfer 3hr by rail.
Road Via Basel, Zurich and Chur. The last 30km is narrow, tortuous and difficult; chains often necessary.

Railway Station in resort (Obersee).
Reachable resorts Lenzerheide and Flims are within striking distance, Davos and Klosters a bit further.

Parking and driving in Arosa is strictly controlled and difficult, and a car isn't much use. Buses run between Innerarosa; Obersee and Maran. Hourly service at night (until 2am).

Miscellaneous

Tourist office *℄* (81) 311621. Tx 74271.
Medical Hospital at Chur (30km); doctors, dentist, chemist, fracture clinic in resort.

Equipment hire 6 days skis SF79, boots SF31, X-C SF71.
Resort beds 6,000 in hotels, 6,200 in apartments.
Package holidays KU, MM, SCG, SWT

If you're passing through...

Lenzerheide-Valbella
Switzerland 1500m

Good for *Not skiing, cross-country skiing, big ski area, sunny skiing*
Bad for *Après-ski, Alpine charm, tough skiing, skiing convenience*

Linked resort: Churwalden

If you haven't heard of Lenzerheide and Valbella, do not fear: you are not alone. Although they share a large skiing area in a famous skiing region, and are popular with the Swiss as a family resort, they have largely escaped international attention. On paper, the area has considerable attractions – as well as the extent of the skiing, it can fairly claim excellent cross-country possibilities, no shortage of non-skiing activities, and a civilised atmosphere. But the extent of the skiing area cannot disguise (in fact it rather emphasises) its lack of variety. And the villages themselves are neither attractive nor convenient.

The originally distinct villages lie at either end of a lake in a wide, attractively wooded pass running north–south, with high mountains oneither side. The road linking them is an important thoroughfare, which in itself reduces the area's appeal for people with small children and which has encouraged the two villages to spread along the valley until they have almost merged. Their comfortable chalets sprawl across the valley too; and the result is a straggling, lifeless sort of place with more of the feel of a suburb than of a living village or a jolly resort.

Two other smaller villages come into the ski area, both used mainly by weekend visitors. Parpan is hardly more than an old hamlet beside the road up from Chur, Churwalden a larger village appreciably lower down, with its own little ski area.

The skiing top 2865m bottom 1230m

The skiing is in separate areas on either side of the inconveniently wide pass. Both have about half woodland and half open skiing terrain; the Danis/ Stätzerhorn area to the west is more extensive, and gets the sun in the morning; the Rothorn to the east is higher, more beautiful, more interesting but more crowded, and gets sun in the afternoon. There are no particularly difficult pistes, although the Rothorn cable-car opens up some off-piste skiing. Runs down to the two villages (or as near to them as they go) are in general gentler than the higher slopes, and suitable for inexperienced skiers, except in poor snow conditions – which are said to be not unusual.

The essential components of the **Rothorn** skiing are the two stages of the large cable-car which climbs from a point beside the lake, well away from both villages, to the peak about 1400m above. The panorama from the top is magnificent; the Rothorn drops away in awesome rocky faces, limiting the skiing possibilities to one main piste behind the main crest, through a wooden gallery, then over a ridge giving a choice of descents (red and not-very-severe black) to the lifts above Parpan and back to the cable-car mid-station at Scharmoin. In terms of length or difficulty there is nothing very special about this run, but it does make a change from the local straight-up-and-down pistes.

From Scharmoin there is a choice of several gentle, winding descents through the woods taking you back either to the bottom station or to the edge of Valbella or Lenzerheide. There are several drags around Scharmoin, the longest linking with the sunny Schwarzhorn chair-lift, high above Parpan. If tempted by the open, not very steep unpisted hillsides below the chair-lift, be warned that you risk ending up stranded somewhere between Parpan and Churwalden.

The best off-piste run goes from the Rothorn to Lenzerheide via the beautiful Alp Sanaspans; it is long and demanding, with no escape once begun except the variant back to the middle station which involves a steep and exposed drop over a rocky ridge separating Sanaspans from the main skiing area.

Various excursions are possible from the Rothorn area into the next valley. You can embark on an enormous circuit via Arosa and Tschiertschen by skiing from the Rothorn via Älplisee (a serious off-piste run) or by first walking round the narrow bowl which divides the top of the Schwarzhorn from Arosa's Hörnli. But most skiers opt for the direct run down from the Schwarzhorn to Tschiertschen – a very beautiful, easily identified, and usually easy semi-piste. Lifts bring you back to the slopes above Churwalden. From here it's a long and almost flat traverse to reach Parpan (for a lift back up on the Rothorn side) or down to Churwalden (for a lift up the other side of the valley). In either case you've only paths to follow.

Compared with the Rothorn and its neighbour the Lenzerhorn, the **Scalottas/ Danis/ Stätzerhorn/ Pradaschier** peaks are not impressive, but the rather featureless open hillsides below them have been easy to develop for skiers: a long network of parallel drag lifts makes it possible to cover a lot of ground, even if there is precious little difference between one piste and another. Conditions permitting, you can ski just about anywhere – so you can have fun when the snow is fresh. The skiing is mostly intermediate, and the couple of runs categorised black are not particularly terrifying. Runs home through the trees are mostly straightforward, but aiming for Lenzerheide from Scalottas you can end up in back gardens or on gritted roads.

The skiing of **Churwalden** is separated from the rest by a steep, densely wooded north-facing hillside, which is not easily skiable. A long, cold, chair-lift makes the connection with Parpan, and good skiers have fun off-piste under it. The other way round is the gentle path which skirts the bottom of the hill from Parpan, beside the road. Churwalden's other lifts provide a descent of 1005 metres back to the village. But from the top the great excursion is to head off northwards along the hill tops for about 2km, to the Dreibundenstein (2174m), at the top of a chain of lifts up from the substantial town of Chur, and then ski down as far as

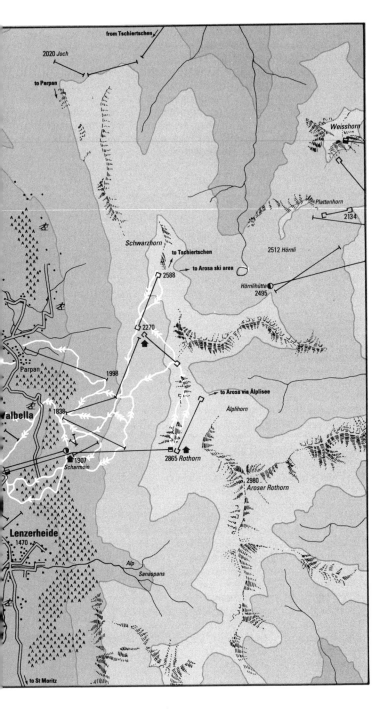

from Tschiertschen

2020 *Joch*

to Parpan

Weisshorn

Plattenhorn

2134

Schwarzhorn

to Tschiertschen

to Arosa ski area

2512 *Hörnli*

2588

Hörnlihütte
2495

2270

1998

to Arosa via Älplisee

Parpan

Älplihorn

Valbella

1838

2865 *Rothorn*

1907
Scharmoin

2980
Aroser Rothorn

Lenzerheide
1470

Alp
Sanaspans

to St Moritz

snow permits. At 595m, Chur is very low; but there is a cable-car up to 1170m, so you can get down to the town even when snow conditions don't allow you to do it on skis.

There are several adequate **nursery slopes**, all at the bottom of the mountains (except for two baby lifts beside the Rothorn middle station). The best area is the gentle lower slope at Churwalden.

There is a good range of sunny **mountain restaurants** on the Danis side, all (except the refuge at the top of Scalottas) about half-way up, around the tree-line. On the Rothorn side there are adequate facilities at half-way and top stations of the cable-car.

Lifts

Passes Available for whole ski area (including buses, but not Arosa, Chur or Tschiertschen lifts) or for separate parts of it (inconveniently split).	**Cost** 6-day pass SF176. **Children** 15% off, under 16. **Beginners** Coupons. One free lift at Scharmoin.

The lift system relies too heavily on short drag-lifts, making access to the Danis side in particular slow and tiresome; and lift departures are sited to keep weekenders out of Lenzerheide, not to make life convenient for Lenzerheiders. Long queues build up for Rothorn lifts especially at weekends. The Scalottas drag-lift is very long and steep.

The resort

Lenzerheide is the major centre of development, and consists of a long main street (the main through-road) at the foot of the Rothorn slopes, with some style-less modern development below the road to the west. On the main street there are some attractive old buildings, but as a whole the place has no particular charm. Valbella has even less identity than Lenzerheide, being no more than a large community of hotels and holiday homes, but it is in some ways a better base; it is less of a roadside strip, and gives direct access to the western ski area at least.

Accommodation consists of apartments and hotels in both villages. The most attractive and best-situated of the numerous hotels in the centre of Lenzerheide is the simplest and cheapest – the friendly Danis (✆ 341117), where people come to drink and play cards in the evening. From the hotel you can walk up to the Dieschen lift and from there ski down to the Rothorn cable-car station. Out of the resort the Guarda Val (✆ 342214) is outstanding – a splendid old building, expensive and comfortable and with a good restaurant, but remote. La Palanca (✆ 343131) is attractive and well placed for the Scalottas lifts. The Dieschen (✆ 341222) is simple and friendly, with a good restaurant; you can ski down to the Rothorn lift station directly from the hotel. In Valbella the best choice is the Chesa Rustica (✆ 343078) close to the Danis lifts and just off the main road.

Après-ski is very quiet, even in Lenzerheide – a couple of tea-rooms, a few restaurants, a disco and some cheek-to-cheek live music in one hotel that we observed.

Ski school

Classes Swiss Ski Schools in Lenzerheide and Valbella. Independent Caselva School in Valbella. All 2hr morning and afternoon.
Cost 5½ days SF125, with 7-day lift-pass SF250. Private lessons SF40/hr.
Children Caselva Ski kindergarten, age 4 upwards, timetable as for adults, SF108/week; non-skiing kindergarten, age up to 7, at Hotel Valbella Inn and Schweizerhof (Lenzerheide), 9.00–6.00 with meal SF126/week.
Special courses Off-piste, racing, freestyle, cross-country and ski-tours.

One reporter went on a pre-season wedel course and was very disappointed by it.

Other activities

Cross-country 42km of trails of all grades including those at Lantsch and Parpan. The Luziuswiese (1km) and Kleinersee (1km) at Lenzerheide are floodlit from 7.00–9.45. Tours and instruction at all three centres.

Not skiing 30km of cleared walks, toboggan runs (one floodlit), sleigh rides, skating (floodlit), curling, swimming pool, fitness centre, sauna, tennis, squash, ski-bob pistes.

Cross-country trails are very good – long, mostly fairly easy, in 3 linked sectors along the pass through attractive woods and round the lake; excellent scope for more adventurous excursions on wide open slopes above Parpan and Churwalden on the eastern side, and in the Danis Alpine skiing area – good for restaurant access. Non-skiers are well provided for, especially for skating and curling (a free lesson is offered). There is a smart sports centre at Dieschen.

Travel

Airport Zurich; transfer about 2½hr.
Railway Chur; frequent buses.
Road Via Zurich; chains may be required.

Reachable resorts St Moritz, Arosa, Laax-Flims, Davos and Klosters are all within day-trip range.

There are buses effectively linking the villages and lifts, and you need them for crossing from one side of the skiing to the other; they run on time, according to one reporter very impressed by this (and little else). No service after tea-time or during lunch. Having a car is not essential, but handy for getting to and from skiing, and for evening entertainment; it also gives the chance of some excellent day-trips.

Miscellaneous

Tourist office ✆ (81) 341588. Tx 74173.
Medical Hospital at Chur (17km); doctors, dentist, chemists, fracture clinic in resort.

Equipment hire 6 days skis SF85, boots SF35, X-C SF70.
Resort beds 2,700 in hotels, 11,000 in apartments.
Package holidays CM, KU, MM.

In with the Inn-crowd

St Moritz Switzerland 1800m

Good for *Beautiful scenery, big ski area, resort-level snow, not skiing, cross-country skiing, après-ski, rail access, sunny skiing*
Bad for *Skiing convenience, nursery slopes, easy road access*

Separate resort: Pontresina

The official line is that you don't have to be rich to enjoy St Moritz. You certainly don't have to be much richer than you do to enjoy other large, fashionable Swiss resorts, and many skiers who never give St Moritz consideration are making a mistake. The scenery is wonderful – the infant river Inn fills a succession of beautiful lakes against a backdrop of 4000-metre peaks with glaciers draped on their shoulders; the non-skier and cross-country skier are better catered for than almost anywhere else; and for a resort which became fashionable because of its scenery and climate, the skiing is surprisingly excellent. And the undisputed queen of wintersports resorts is still a fascinating place for seeing the idle rich on display and the not-so-idle rich at play.

The British began wintering in St Moritz before skiing became a sport, and the resort still revolves as much round tobogganing and riding on the frozen lake as it does around skiing – despite being among the highest of Alpine resorts, with excellent late winter skiing, its real season ends in February because the ice starts to thin and the toboggan runs close. Old hands say that St Moritz has lost its style, as the original core of well-to-do British has been replaced by Continentals and Americans, trying to behave in the same way but succeeding only in behaving wealthily. Certainly the Palace, most expensive of the luxury hotels, seems merely flashy. But the Carlton and the Kulm still have the quiet formality, the card tables, the worn leather and the heavy jowls of London clubs. Although the president of St Moritz Tobogganing Club is now Gunter Sachs, the organisation of the Club's activities is still as defiantly British as a prep school sports day.

The skiing top 3304m bottom 1720m

The upper Engadine skiing is spread widely around the two valleys which meet at Celerina just below St Moritz. There are wide open sunny slopes to flatter and entertain tan-conscious intermediates; steep and gentle descents through woods; long, steep pitches with walls and bumps; excellent glacier skiing with superb views; and lots of scope for long off-piste excursions which few skiers exploit. But these different kinds of skiing are to be found on four widely separated mountains, making decision-making and rendezvous difficult for mixed groups.

Corviglia is the sunny south-facing mountain which demands the least effort of St Moritz residents. The railway from the top of Dorf and the cable-car from the edge of Bad arrive above steep wooded slopes and give access to very wide and open, not very varied slopes with a series of parallel drag-lifts serving a maze of intermediate runs, the most direct of them moderately challenging. There are few runs down to the valley, the only clear piste being the blue run down from Signal to the cable-car station at Bad. The cable-car up to Piz Nair gives access to long and beautiful pistes round to Marguns and off-piste runs down the Suvretta valley towards St Moritz Bad. There are easy connections to and from the Marguns bowl, which offers more varied skiing, with long runs both easy and challenging down from Trais Fluors and Glüna. The run down to Celerina is narrow and awkward in several places.

The **Corvatsch** area, similarly, is accessible from both ends at valley level and consists of a band of connected drag-lifts above the tree-line serving intermediate skiing, with a single cable-car climbing much higher. But the skiing is more varied and challenging – especially from the top to the middle station, where the snow is nearly always excellent and the views, across to the Piz Bernina and its own glaciers, even better. The direct piste is an exhilarating sustained slope, either bumpy or hard and very fast depending on conditions, with an extraordinary view back up to a sheer blue ice wall at the end. The easier, less direct route is manageable by most intermediates. Another great joy is the beautiful long run through the woods to St Moritz Bad, via a secluded mountain hut. There is good off-piste skiing; one reporter was pleased and surprised to find the various runs down to Champfér, Surlej and (more adventurously) into the Roseg valley so little used.

A piste down from Corvatsch mid-station connects with the **Furtschellas** skiing above Sils via a long chain of lifts stretching across rocky mountainsides. At the other end there are some excellent long runs from Furtschellas itself to the isolated base station. Although not precipitous, none of the runs on the lower half of the mountain is easy.

A single long cable-car goes up from beside the Bernina pass road to the magnificently situated hotel, restaurant and sun-terrace of **Diavolezza**, in the middle of marvellous glacier scenery. There is an easy open slope beside a drag-lift at the top, and a straightforward long intermediate run all the way down under the lift. The great attraction is the much-skied off-piste run over the back, across the Morteratsch glacier and through woods to Morteratsch itself. It involves some walking and there are narrow passages between big holes and an awkward icy drop to negotiate at the end of the glacier; these should not deter reasonably competent skiers from enjoying the pleasures of a beautiful tour for little effort.

Lagalp is a consistently steep conical mountain opposite Diavolezza which presents long runs from top to bottom – ranging from very challenging (the direct route, initially steep and usually very bumpy) to only moderately so. A run from the top station links up with a couple of drag-lifts at the Bernina pass.

Nursery slopes are not very satisfactory, there being very little available space on the valley floor except at Celerina at the foot of the Marguns gondola. Most St Moritz beginners start on slopes at Corviglia

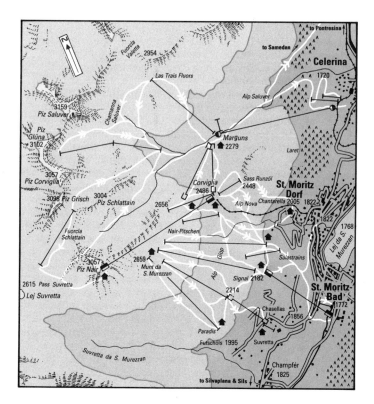

around Chantarella and Salastrains where there is a beginners'
merry-go-round; when snow conditions are good they can progress to
long easy runs in this sector, but often the transition is an awkward one.

Mountain restaurants on Corviglia are plentiful and varied, from
anonymous self-service cafeterias to very attractive chalets. On the
Corvatsch side only the Fuorcla Surlej and Hahnensee (Lej dals
Chöds) restaurants have any charm. Prices are high.

Lifts

Passes Oberengadin pass covers all
lifts and public transport. Available for 5
or 10 non-consecutive days. Also local
day, half-day and longer passes.

Cost 6-day pass SF175.
Beginners Two nursery lifts included in
ski school cost. Otherwise coupons.
Children 30% off, under 16.

Large areas of skiing depend on few lifts, especially the Corvatsch,
Diavolezza and Lagalp cable-cars, where there are often long queues.
The main season lasts from Christmas to the end of February, and
January is busier than in most Swiss resorts.

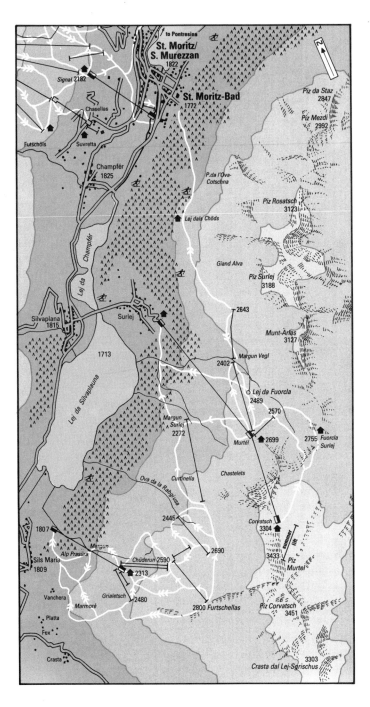

to Pontresina

**St. Moritz/
S. Murezzan**
1822

St. Moritz-Bad
1772

Signal 2182

Chasellas

Futschöls

Suvretta

Champfèr
1825

Lej dals Chöds

Giand Alva

P.da l'Ova-
Cotschna

Piz da Staz
2847

Piz Mezdi
2992

Piz Rosatsch
3123

Piz Surlej
3188

Lej da Champfèr

Silvaplana
1815

Surlej

1713

Lej da Silvaplauna

2643

Margun Vegl

2402

Munt-Àrlas
3127

Lej da Fuorcla
2489

2570

Margun
Surlej
2272

Curtinella

Ova da la Rabgiusa

Chastelets

Murtèl   2699

2755 Fuorcla
Surlej

2445

1807

Sils Maria
1809

Margun

Alp Prasüra

Chüderun 2590

2313

Vanchera

Grialetsch

Marmorè

2480

Platta

Fex

Crasta

2690

2800 Furtschellas

Corvatsch
3304

summer lift

3433

Piz
Murtèl

Piz Corvatsch
3451

3303
Crasta dal Lej Sgrischus

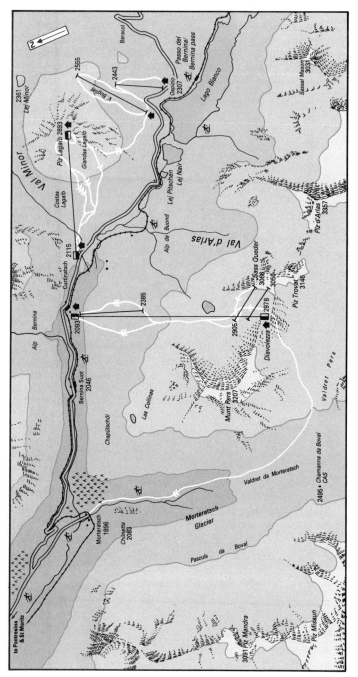

2898

The resort

St Moritz is a resort of parts. **St Moritz Bad**, the spa part, is spread out beside the lake on the valley floor without shape, style or sign of life. There are good although not especially smart shopping facilities. The cross-country track passes through, and there is direct access to Corviglia. **St Moritz Dorf** is tightly packed on the steep hillside to the north of the lake, beneath the ski slopes of Corviglia. This is fashionable St Moritz, more like a town centre than a village, and much less attractive than its beautiful sunny setting and its habitués. Bulky Victorian hotels loom over the lake as others do over British coastal links. These hotels are exclusive worlds of their own, at the heart of high society; outside them and the expensive shopping precincts, St Moritz is not particularly smart. Nor is it convenient – distances on foot are considerable and parking is difficult.

From the top of the resort a road winds down an attractive wooded slope, following the course of Cresta and Bob runs, which end beside hotels at the edge of the quiet, spacious village of Celerina.

Accommodation is spread out around the two component parts of town. 65% of St Moritz's hotel beds are in 4- and 5-star hotels. For ski-lift convenience the best locations are on the edge of Bad near the Signal lift – where the secluded Chesa Sur L'En (∅ 33144) is a luxurious old chalet, beautifully decorated and furnished – or high up in the centre of Dorf. The Steffani (∅ 22101) is one of the most attractive of the smaller hotels, with a pool; simpler, but still comfortable, b&b hotels in the centre are the Eden (∅ 36161), Languard (∅ 33137) and Rosatsch (∅ 33547). The Sonne in Bad (∅ 33527) is large, adequate, styleless and inconveniently located, but cheap by local standards.

Most of the smart **après-ski** is hotel-based, with formal dress requirements in several establishments – including the Palace Hotel's King's Club disco, where photographers and bouncers crowd the door. The Steffani is a popular, rather more casual and less expensive venue for drinking and dancing. There are a few simple, honest restaurants on the main square in Dorf, and in Bad. Do not be taken in by the 'Casino', which is a tacky bar with dancing and strip-shows.

Ski school

Classes 2hr morning and afternoon. Cost 6 days SF148. Private lessons SF40/hr.

Children Ski kindergarten, ages 3–12, 10.00–4.00, 6 full days SF120. Special courses Helicopter skiing.

We are not over-equipped with reports, but there is evidently no difficulty in finding English-speaking teachers.

Other activities

Cross-country Easy trails (19km) between St Moritz Bad and Maloja. Difficult trail (7.5km) between Bad and Pontresina. Medium trails (15km) above Pontresina to Roseg and Morterasch valleys. 1.6km easy trail at Bad is floodlit.

Not skiing Sleigh rides, ice rink, curling, swimming, sauna/solarium, toboggan run, hang gliding, riding, golf, tennis, bobsleigh/Cresta run, 120km cleared paths, museum, 'plane joy-rides, spa cures, English films, aerobics.

The frozen lakes and side-valleys make up one of the most famous and beautiful X-C areas in Europe, and the annual 42-km marathon attracts over 10,000 entrants. St Moritz is a spectacular destination for non-skiers both active and inactive. There are long and beautiful walks to restaurants in the skiing area (Corviglia) and up the Roseg and Morteratsch valleys, with only X-C skiers and chamois for company. In season, there are lots of spectator sports. The tonic effect of the high and dry 'champagne climate' is famous.

Travel

Airport Zurich; transfer about 3½hr. Air taxis to Samedan (4km).
Railway Main-line station in resort.

Road Via Zurich, Chur; chains often needed.
Reachable resorts None outside the Engadine.

The ski area is very scattered, and trips around St Moritz itself are long and steep. In general, trains and buses serve skiers well, but the bus service between Bad and Dorf is often oversubscribed. There is no evening service, and trains stop at about 10pm – so après-skiers need a car or taxis. Parking is difficult in Dorf – there is a multi-storey park. All approaches except that from Austria involve high passes – the Julier pass (from Chur) is kept open but is often snowy. The past lives on in the special train service from London to St Moritz, and rail is the best means of access apart from a private plane. St Moritz is also one terminus of the Glacier Express, which runs to Zermatt via Andermatt – a spectacular journey, as is the Bernina Express over to Italy.

Miscellaneous

Tourist office ✆ (82) 33147. Tx 74429.
Medical Doctor, dentist, chemist, fracture clinic in resort; hospital at Chur (78km).
Equipment hire 6 days skis SF90, boots SF40, X-C SF70.

Resort beds 6,000 in hotels, 6,200 in apartments.
Package holidays BL, CM, KU, MM, PS, SCG, SGW, SWT.

Pontresina 1800m
All the activity in St Moritz attracts most of the non-skiing and après-skiing custom from the other villages around – Celerina, Silvaplana and Sils – which are quiet resorts for families who come to the area (not all on high budgets) to ski or simply to enjoy the beautiful surroundings. Pontresina is much more developed, and does feel and look like a self-sufficient resort, albeit a sedate one. Although it is closer than St Moritz to some of the best skiing (Diavolezza and Lagalp) there is no significant skiing from the village itself. Many traditionalists return annually to the great comfort and considerable charm of Pontresina hotels, and appreciate being at a distance from the glitter and hubbub of St Moritz. The Steinbock (✆ 66371) and Engadinerhof (✆ 66212) are very comfortable and attractively traditional hotels on the single main street. It is one of the best locations in the region for cross-country skiers, and also has a good skating/curling rink and pool.
Tourist office ✆ (82) 66488. Package holidays CM, MW, SGW, SWT.

'To travel hopefully is a better thing ...'

Madesimo Italy 1550m

Good for   *Tough skiing*
Bad for   *Easy road access, short airport transfers, après-ski, not skiing, nursery slopes, easy skiing, Alpine charm*

Of all the remote Italian resorts hidden away near the Swiss border, Madesimo is one of the least accessible, but one of the most tempting for good skiers. Its skiing issues a challenge in the form of one of the most notorious descents in the Alps, the Canalone – not a reference to the pasta-like state of legs at the bottom of the run, but to its dauntingly steep, gun-barrel form. The vital statistics of the ski area (over 1300m vertical) show impressive length as well as pitch. But the reality is a disappointment. The skiing is steep enough to be challenging, and the Canalone itself is wild and beautiful as well as a stiff technical challenge. But one run doesn't make a skiing holiday. Skiers good enough to enjoy the Canalone find the area limited after a few days (it is not very suitable for off-piste skiing), and skiers not good enough for it find quite a lot of the skiing unpleasantly difficult.

Like many Italian resorts, Madesimo comes to life only at weekends. Italians drive up in their thousands despite (or perhaps because of) the hair-raising access road. On a Friday you may have to wait for a quorum before the cable-car will run (in January it may not run at all); next day you may face a 2½-hour queue for a drag-lift.

The village itself does not have much appeal. Despite claims to be an 18th-century health resort, it does not seem old, and most of the buildings are characterless apartment blocks around a large tower hotel. In the reports we have, the feature of Madesimo most consistently picked out as memorable is the beauty and drama of the coach transfer from Milan, which doesn't say much for the resort.

Motta, a tiny community on the open hillside above Madesimo, is reached only by snow-cat from the larger resort or directly by cable-car from the lower village of Campodolcino. Although very close to Madesimo and its skiing, Motta is not connected with it.

The skiing top 2890m bottom 1550m

Madesimo's skiing is spread along the west-facing flank of mountainside above the village, broadly skiable lower down but increasingly rocky and hostile higher up around the Pizzo Groppera, accessible only by cable-car and only just skiable. Behind Groppera are two more lifts opening up a friendlier north-east-facing mountainside which keeps snow late into spring.

At the north of the village is a series of parallel drags which have limited easy skiing but more importantly offer a way for those staying at

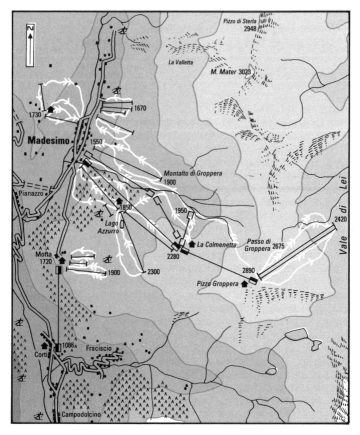

that end of the resort to get to the main lifts in the village centre. The final and longest drag is to Montalto, and from here you can with luck find a path across into the heart of the skiing – an attractive variety of good, long runs above and (in woodland) below Lago Azzurro (1850m). This area is accessible from the village by the main cable-car to La Colmenetta (2280m) or by a drag-lift beside it. This area suffers from its westward orientation and tends to ice in good weather, making many of the staple intermediate runs unpleasant. The last sections down to the bottom stations, where several runs converge, can be hazardous enough to put many people off skiing down.

From Lago Azzurro you can see across the open hillside to a huge gilt statue of the Madonna gesticulating as if imploring a snowfall on skiers' behalf, beside Motta's three short drag-lifts. Despite being very close to each other on the same slope, they serve runs varying from very easy (green) to moderately steep (black). Motta has the attraction of morning sunshine, but is quite a plod (an attractive walking or X-C trail) across from Lago Azzurro. The Colmenetta Est drag-lift above Lago Azzurro serves two pleasant, open intermediate runs.

The mid-station of the cable-car stands at the top of steep slopes which provide some tough skiing, especially beside the very steep Colmenetta Nord lift – not obviously a piste, as it is marked on the map.

The top cable-car section to Pizzo Groppera climbs over a very steep, very rocky and menacing mountain face which looks unskiable. But there is a very long, steep gully to one side which is almost permanently in the shade. This is the Canalone, a much feared run which is everything a famous black run should be – long, consistently steep (before the gentle run-out at the end, the run takes only 1.85km to drop 724m) and dramatic. A long funnel it is, but for most of its length not an unpleasantly narrow one, and in good snow conditions it is negotiable by many less-than-expert skiers. Being the only way down the mountain except by lift, lots of brave intermediates ski it.

The reverse of Groppera is a beautiful open side of the Valle di Lei, which drops steeply down to a reservoir. The drag-lifts give just under 500m vertical of varied intermediate pistes and off-piste skiing between them. Snow conditions are nearly always more pleasant on this side.

Nursery slopes (beside the Hotel Meridiana and far away at the northern end of the village) are not very extensive, and there are few runs for easy progression. Madesimo is not for beginners.

Mountain restaurants are few and not very attractive, except for the refuge at Lago Azzurro, a good sunbathing spot which gets very crowded when the resort is busy. As well as the main restaurants there are a couple of drinks stands in Valle di Lei and at Piano dei Larici.

Lifts

Passes Area pass covers all lifts including Motta. Day and afternoon passes available.

Cost 6-day pass L94,000.
Beginners Coupons.
Children No reduction.

The great problem with the Madesimo lift system is its reliance on the top section of the cable-car for access to the Valle di Lei and the Canalone. This (like the Vallei di Lei drag-lifts) gets very crowded at weekends, while during the week it may run infrequently or not at all. Several reporters commented on cable-car closure because of wind. Some drag-lifts close for lunch during the week.

The resort

Madesimo is set high up in a narrow valley at the top of an extremely steep climb through desolate rocky scenery from Chiavenna. The slopes round Madesimo are wooded but the overall impression is bleak and hostile, in winter at least. The village stretches thinly a long way (over half a mile) up the dead-end valley from the centre.

Although there aren't large numbers of British skiers in Madesimo, at off-peak times there are few others, so the impression is of a larger number. When we visited most recently there were lots of school-children. Several reporters commented favourably on the helpfulness, quality and cheapness of ski shops, both for hirers and purchasers.

Accommodation offered by UK operators is mainly in hotels, none very luxurious. Because of the arrangement of the lifts, being at the top end of the village isn't too much of an annoyance for skiing, but it is very inconvenient in the evening. Of the central hotels near the main cable-car and chair-lift departure stations, La Meridiana (∅ 53160) is an exception to the norm in being friendly, cheerful, and obviously decorated and looked after with pride; some bedrooms are small. The Cascata and Cristallo (∅ 53108) is a larger, convenient alternative with its own pool and sauna. The big tower hotel is the Grand Hotel Torre (∅ 53234), which is no longer modern or luxurious but is still spacious – almost eerily so out of season. Rather quaintly, it advertises reserved seats on the Groppera cable-car. Try that one on the Milanese.

Après-ski is limited to a couple of discothèques (very quiet during the week despite free entrance) and a few bars and restaurants, most of them cheap and simple. The Osteria Vegia (near the cable-car station) stands out (it dates from 1781 and looks its age) and is expensive. The Dogana Vecchia is a long way from the centre (further even than the Gran Baita Hotel), and also old and very attractive. The ice rink is open in the evening and tour operators may offer evening snow-cat rides and toboggan descents.

Ski school

Classes 2hr mornings only.	**Cost** 6 days L65,000. Private lessons
Children No kindergartens.	L19,000/hr.

We have mixed reports on the ski school – language difficulties on the one hand, helpful use of video on the other.

Other activities

Cross-country 5km trail at north end of village. 3.5km at Lago Azzurro/Motta. Instruction available.	**Not skiing** Natural ice rink (skating till 11pm), ski bobbing, bowling, 15km of cleared paths, cinema, swimming/sauna/ solarium, toboggan run.

Madesimo is not good either for X-C or non-skiers. The toboggan run, supposedly open morning, afternoon and evening, was not in evidence when we visited. Tour operators usually offer excursions to St Moritz, a long day-trip, and to Chiavenna – a delightful old town.

Travel

Airport Milan; transfer at least 4hr. **Road** Via Chamonix/Milan. The last 20km are difficult; chains often required.	**Railway** Chiavenna (20km); daily buses to resort. **Reachable resorts** St Moritz, though it's a fair distance away.

Madesimo is inconvenient to reach by car, and having a car is of little benefit. The coach transfer from Milan along Lake Como and up a very steep hairpin road through numerous single-track tunnels is long, beautiful and dramatic. Take tranquillizers.

Miscellaneous

Tourist office ∅ (343) 53015. Tx 312216. **Medical** Chemist, doctor and fracture clinic in resort, hospital and dentist at Chiavenna (20km).	**Equipment hire** 6 day skis L22,500, boots L10,500, X-C L22,500. **Resort beds** 700 in hotels, 1,500 in apartments. **Package holidays** BS, CI, GL, IT, SMW,] SPT, TH.

New into the arena

Flims Switzerland 1100m

Good for *Big ski area, sunny skiing, cross-country skiing, not skiing*

Bad for *Tough skiing, skiing convenience, late holidays, après-ski*

Linked resorts: Laax, Falera

Take a long-established, sedate, year-round resort, better known for its sunshine and woodland walks than for its skiing and little known at all in Britain, and graft on to its modest lift system a huge new network of mechanisation opening up a vast interconnected ski area, and you have the strange hybrid phenomenon that is Flims and Laax and the White Arena ski area which they share. Suddenly the skiing is extensive, varied, beautiful, intelligently conceived, and smartly equipped. Unfortunately the resorts aren't ideal bases for skiers, and don't fit in with the brave new image of the modern ski-circus. But, provided you don't mind the identity problem, the inconvenience, and the peculiar ugliness of the local place-names, Flims and Laax have a lot to offer skiers and non-skiers alike.

Flims lies on a wooded hillside near the foot of the mountains which form the northern wall of the Vorderrhein valley. Hundreds of metres beneath the wooded shelf on which the resorts stand, the river cuts through a rocky gorge. The railway follows it, but the main road runs through Flims. Although the mountains climb high they are not steep, and the valley is so wide that the setting is open, spacious and sunny. Flims is split into two separate parts – Dorf and Waldhaus.

Laax, 5km away, is smaller and more attractive, with a modern purpose-built satellite at Murschetg. The rustic farming hamlet of Falera adds yet another alternative style of base.

The skiing top 2981m bottom 1080m

The skiing area extends over a very broad section of the northern wall of the valley. It faces mainly south-east, but is broken up by a number of deep gullies and tributary valleys whose flanks face south-west and north-east. Most of the ski area is very sunny, and the runs down to the resorts cannot be relied upon. The terrain is varied, with long woodland runs on the lower slopes, open ground above and a small area of glacier skiing at the top. There are few very steep slopes around, but good skiers will enjoy many runs which make up in length what they may lack in technical difficulty – the World Cup Downhill course starts little more than half-way up the mountain.

The **Flims** entrance to the ski area is an old lift station on the edge of Flims Dorf which cannot cope with the demand for parking places, lift

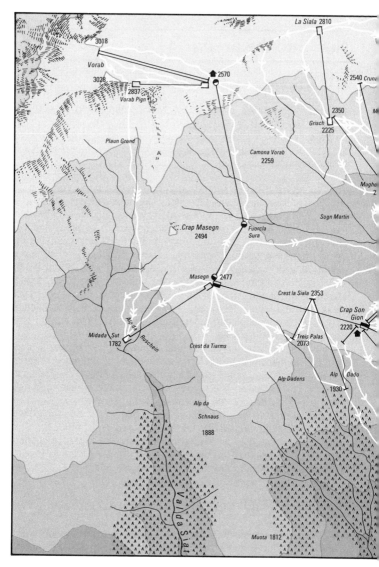

tickets, or space on lifts. Of the two main lifts, the more important for Flims's pistes is the chair. The runs beneath this lift and the gondola to Startgels are mostly easy, and even the run from Naraus marked black holds no terrors, apart from frequently inadequate snow cover. There are usually a lot of people around though, because the restricted Flims day-pass confines its users to this area.

For good skiers, the main attraction of Flims's skiing is the descent from **Cassons**, reached by cable car from Naraus up over the cliffs of the Flimserstein. There is an annoying walk up behind the top station,

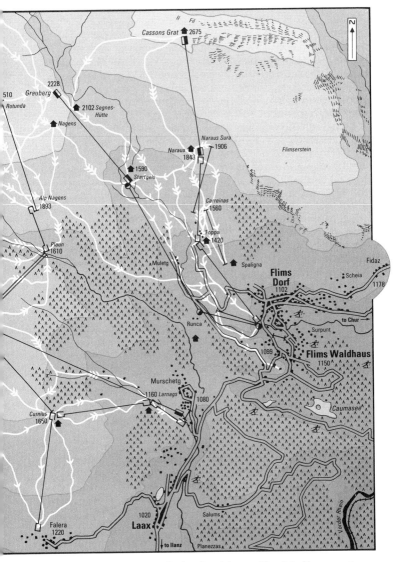

but the view is splendid, as is the direct descent back to Naraus – a fairly steep, wide open 800m face, paradise in good fresh or spring snow conditions. Only the gentler bottom half ever has a prepared piste. The alternative red run is less satisfactory, with one rather steep section near the beginning followed by a walk up to the Segnes-Hütte.

The cable-car from Startgels to Grauberg connects Flims skiing with the **La Siala** area, between Flims and Laax. The runs down to Startgels are good ones – short and tricky from Grauberg, long and beautiful round the back of the mountain from the top chair-lift – but most of the skiing on La Siala consists of long, open, featureless pistes.

From La Siala there are connections with **Laax** skiing either by traversing to (or from) the Vorab glacier restaurant, or via Plaun at the bottom of a steep-sided valley with lifts up either side. The awkward bumpy paths down to Plaun are categorised black, and lots of skiers take the chair down. The other side of the valley is much more satisfactory, with longer runs down from Crap Sogn Gion to Plaun – one black, two red, and often good off-piste skiing.

Crap Sogn Gion (St John's Hill) is where the vast (but still inadequate) cable-car from **Murschetg** arrives. Two chairs and a drag-lift make the same journey without queues, but usually not much more quickly. The run under the cable-car from Crap Sogn Gion is the downhill course where local hero Conradin Cathomen built up his skill and thighs. It is a magnificent trail, cutting a broad swathe through the woods, with a vertical drop of over 1000m. There are other gentler descents, through Curnius under the chairs, and down to Falera whose chair-lift is a useful back-door into the lift system.

The cable-car to **Crap Masegn** doesn't climb much but gives access to good, long, open runs down to Alp Ruschein, which are usually deserted and often good for off-but-near-the-piste skiing. In the other direction a gondola goes down into a gulley then up again to the bottom of the **Vorab** glacier, which offers gentle skiing with reliably flattering snow, accessible to all. For good skiers, and even strong intermediates, the great attraction of the Vorab is the run which drops over a saddle near the top down into an empty and beautiful valley. The run is marked black, but the short steep beginning is not as steep as all that, and the rest is mostly glorious, wide-open, fast cruising for over 1000m vertical to Alp Ruschein.

There are good wide **nursery slopes** beside Flims Dorf, and another nursery lift at the top of the Startgels gondola. There is a small nursery slope at Murschetg. Skiers with a few days' experience will find plenty of scope on the lower slopes above Flims Dorf.

The old part of the ski area, above Flims, is well provided with attractive old **mountain restaurants**, many of them accessible to walkers, and some of them outside the ski area altogether. On the Laax side there are just a few large, functional service areas, at obvious points. A happy exception is the piste-side chalet at Larnags.

Lifts

Passes Area pass covers all lifts and buses between resorts; available for all periods, including 8 non-consecutive days. Limited day-pass for lower Flims lifts (as far as Startgels and Naraus).
Cost 6-day pass SF190.

Beginners Passes or payment by the ride for Flims nursery lifts.
Children About 35% off, under 16.
Summer skiing Small area of about 400m vertical on Vorab glacier; 3 lifts; small summer X-C piste.

The two main lift departures, at Flims Dorf and Murschetg, are often seriously overcrowded at peak times, but once up the mountain there are rarely any significant queues. Get up, as they say round here, with the larks. The Falera chair-lift is the best way to avoid the queues at Murschetg. Startgels is another bottleneck; the cable-car is due to be relieved by a chair-lift.

The resort

Flims Dorf is the original village, long and spread out along a busy main road in a dull and characterless way. The base lift station is at the western edge of the village. Half a mile or so further south, Waldhaus, with no ski-lifts of its own, is the traditional resort – a large cluster of hotels among the trees and beside the main road. Waldhaus is quiet and comfortable, Dorf livelier, more like a small town than a ski resort. Both stretch down the hill below the road in a suburban, residential way with a few hotels mainly of interest to cross-country skiers.

Accommodation consists mainly of comfortable hotels and self-catering apartments in chalets. The best location for skiing accommodation is on the edge of Dorf, where a few medium-priced hotels are within easy walking range of the lift station – the lively, modern Albanasport (∅ 392333), Meiler (∅ 390171), Bellevue (∅ 393131), and the attractive new chalet-style Garni Curtgin (∅ 393566); small, quiet, friendly, and immaculately kept). The Crap Ner (∅ 392626) is the most comfortable hotel in Dorf; it is very inconveniently situated, but one reporter says it provided 'the best skiing food I've ever had'. In Waldhaus, the Parkhotel (∅ 390181) is a world of its own with a number of different buildings spread around the grounds – apparently the largest private park in Switzerland – and linked like airport terminals by tunnel. The hotel is hideous and the interior as dowdy as it is comfortable, but there is no shortage of entertainment – a beautiful pool, indoor tennis, organised bridge and lots more. There is also a regular bus shuttle to the lifts, and an easy piste through the woods home. The Waldeck (∅ 391228) is a smaller, smart new hotel by the main road, with neat and tidy rooms and a comfortable restaurant that prides itself on its fish. The hotel Surpunt (∅ 391169) is outstandingly well-placed for cross-country skiers. The Fidazerhof (∅ 391233) is remote (in a little community of chalets above Dorf), restful and comfortable.

Après-ski is generally muted. In Flims Dorf the meeting place for young people is the Albana hotel, which has a noisy pizzeria and a very pub-like pub at street level. Across the road, the Hotel Mailer offers a more conventional mixture of tea upstairs and dancing, in theory at least, downstairs (afternoon and evening). Most restaurants are in hotels; the Parkhotel has several of varying styles.

Ski school

Classes 2hr morning and afternoon.
Cost 6 days SF125. Private lessons SF45/hr.

Children 25% off. Ski kindergarten, ages 3–10, 9.00–5.00, 6 full days SF95. Non-ski kindergarten, ages 3–10, 9.00-5.00, 6 full days SF6.

Other activities

Cross-country Total length of trails 45km, from 2.5km to 20km. X-C centre and ski school at Surpunt.

Not skiing 50km of cleared paths, swimming/sauna in hotels, natural ice rink, tennis, riding school, sleigh rides, curling, sledging, ski-bob, bowling.

Both Flims and Laax cater very well for X-C skiers and non-skiers, with long walks and trails through beautiful woodland scenery, with plenty of bars. Of the two, Flims has more scope.

Travel

Airport Zurich; transfer about 3hr.
Railway Chur (17km); frequent buses.
Road Via Basel/Zurich ; chains rarely necessary.

Reachable resorts Lenzerheide-Valbella and Arosa are not far, Davos and St Moritz not out of the question.

The daytime regional post bus serves Flims, Murschetg and Laax well, and there are less frequent services to Fidaz and Falera. Depending on where you stay, and whether you want to wander after dark, a car can be useful. There are no access problems for drivers, except occasionally to Falera.

Miscellaneous

Tourist office ✆ (81) 391022. Tx 74328.
Medical Hospital at Chur (17km); doctor, chemist, dentist in resort.
Package holidays MM

Equipment hire 6 days skis SF80, boots SF40, X-C SF60.
Resort beds 2,200 in hotels, 5,500 in apartments.

Laax 1020m

Laax has emerged as a ski resort only recently. It is unaffected by the development of the ski area, mainly because the lifts are further than a walk away. Much the nicest hotel is the Posta Veglia (✆ 86 21415); old, very charming, a warm and lively atmosphere, and reasonable prices – for rooms and in the restaurant, the *stübli* and the piano bar. While old Laax has stayed as it was, Murschetg has grown a spanking new resort complex, most of which is at least convenient for the slopes (although a major element of it, the Happy Rancho complex, is a tiresome walk down the hill). At the foot of the pistes is the expensively neo-rustic Signina (✆ 89 390151). Like Flims, Laax is a good resort for walkers and cross-country skiers (Murschetg is linked to Flims by X-C trail), and offers free skating on the village pond as long as the ice holds.

   Of the other communities dotted around the sunny hillsides, **Falera** is the most important; it is a sleepy old village with farming smells and noises and just a couple of hotels, reached by narrow road. Although primitive, Falera has the great advantage of direct access to the main lift system; the Encarna (✆ 86 3334415) is the more central of two simple hotels.

   For skiing convenience and queue avoidance you can stay up the mountain in the modern and very well appointed Crap Sogn Gion Berghotel (✆ 81 392193; panoramic views, pool/sauna, bowling).
Laax tourist office ✆ (86) 21423. Tx 74836

Gemsstock gem

Andermatt Switzerland 1450m

Good for *Tough skiing, Alpine charm, off-piste skiing, rail access, resort-level snow, ski touring*
Bad for *Easy skiing, nursery slopes, skiing convenience, lift queues, mountain restaurants, not skiing*

Andermatt is full of character. It is one of the most important places in Switzerland for mountain military service, but retains a lot of simple Alpine charm, and the skiing on the mighty Gemsstock can be as exciting and challenging as anywhere. There is also some good skiing for near-beginners, but there is not a large network of lifts, and bad weather or heavy queues can make skiing practically impossible. Once much favoured by British skiers, Andermatt is now neglected by all but a faithful few. Over fine weekends and Christmas and Easter, it is very full of local Swiss and Italians, but most of the time the resort ticks over very slowly and seems to be threatening to stall.

The skiing top 2963m bottom 1447m

There are four ski areas along the flanks of the Urseren valley, between the Furka and Oberalp passes. The two main ones lie at either end of Andermatt, the two smaller and less popular areas south-west of Andermatt at the villages of Hospental and Realp.

The **Gemsstock** is Andermatt's big hill, climbing steeply from the south-western edge of the village to a peak over 1500m higher. The lift system is simple and incapable of accommodating large numbers of people: there is a two stage cable-car and a couple of lifts around the middle station (at Gurschen) where the mountainside flattens out a little to provide a small area suitable for intermediates. Above and below this the runs are moderately or very demanding. The steep slopes face north and keep their snow well; but avalanche danger can close large areas after snowfalls. From the top station, which gives magnificent views, you can traverse to a beautiful red run round the shoulder of the mountain, with a moderately steep section followed by a long path back to the middle station. Or you can tackle the runs down the front of the Gemsstock which offer 800m vertical, almost all of it severe. There are numerous variants down the one bowl. The snow sees almost no sun, and when it is fresh it is a good skier's dream. The top half is rugged terrain – some glacier, a lot of rocks (which can make off-piste excursions hazardous), no trees. It is too steep for piste machines. There is scope for skiing off-piste in the main bowl below glacier level, but also two very long off-piste descents in other directions – behind the Gemsstock down to the Gotthard Pass (the Guspis run), and down the Felsental to the main valley between Andermatt and Hospental; neither should be attempted without guidance. The bottom half of the main face is hardly more friendly than the top; there is a single long and challenging run, much less steep than the top section, but rightly categorised black. A reporter who has been to Andermatt more often and had less luck than us, has found this run is 'invariably in bad condition', which is not surprising considering the traffic it gets at the end of the morning and afternoon.

From Andermatt station, a short train ride up towards the Oberalp Pass, or a ride on the new chair-lift (sited beside the barracks, more for the convenience of soldiers than holiday skiers) brings you to **Nätschen**, where a small network of three drag-lifts serves an open area of easy, sunny, south-facing pistes. There are two ways down to Andermatt: the easy main piste mostly following the path of the road (closed in winter) and a direct descent (not pisted) more or less under the chairs. This starts gently, but becomes much steeper towards the village; difficult snow very often adds to the problems.

Above the village at **Hospental**, on the south side of the valley, there are just two lifts towards the Winterhorn – a chair with red runs down the steeper, scrub-covered lower half of the mountain, followed by a drag serving open blue runs. The lifts, which are long enough to give very worthwhile skiing, are rarely crowded. **Realp** (1538m), several miles further away, has just one little-used drag-lift, suitable for beginners and near beginners.

Andermatt has little in the way of **nursery slopes**, but for those beyond first steps the long run down from Nätschen to Andermatt is excellent and very civilised, served as it is by railway.

There aren't many **mountain restaurants** to tempt you to stay high for lunch – a fairly basic one near the Gemsstock mid-station and two sunnier, more agreeable restaurants near Nätschen railway station.

Lifts

Passes Area pass covers all Urseren valley lifts and the train. Passes for separate parts available.	**Cost** 6-day pass SF141. **Children** 22% off up to 16. **Beginners** Coupons or lift pass.

All lifts can be paid for by the ride. The Gemsstock cable-car is usually crowded at weekends; we have one report of two-hour waits at Easter. In low season, or if there is little demand, the top section runs infrequently. Trains from Andermatt to the Nätschen slopes run only every half hour.

The resort

Andermatt is the main settlement in the high, flat-bottomed Urseren valley. Although initial impressions of grim barracks, stony-faced guards and steep bare hillsides may be off-putting, closer inspection reveals Andermatt to be a very attractive village. It stretches along a single sharply bent main street between the two ski areas; the old compact heart of the village (which gets little sun) has little traffic and a mixture of buildings, some dilapidated hotels of faded grandeur, others

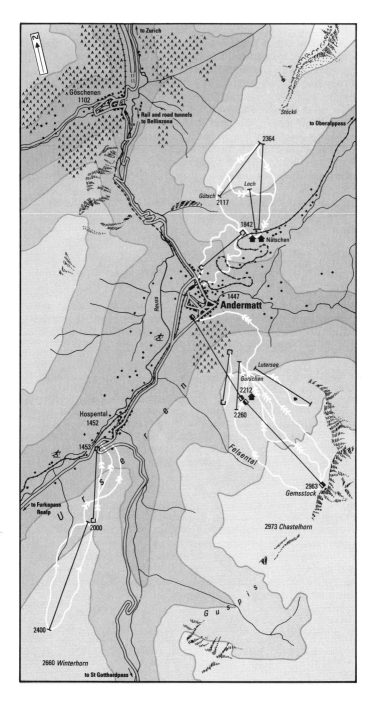

to Zurich

Göschenen
1102

Rail and road tunnels
to Bellinzona

Stöckli

to Oberalppass

2364

Loch

Gütsch
2117

1842

Nätschen

1447
Andermatt

Lutersee

Gurschen
2212

2260

Felsental

Hospental
1452

1453

2963
Gemsstock

2973 Chastelhorn

to Furkapass
Realp

2000

2400

Guspis

2660 Winterhorn

to St Gotthardpass

garishly colourful and some attractive old chalets.

Accommodation is nearly all in hotels (or barracks). Nowhere is ideal for all the skiing. For the Gemsstock, the Aurora is most convenient. Hotel Drei Könige und Post (∅ 67203) is a big, solid, chalet-style building in the centre without much atmosphere. The neighbouring Gasthaus zum Sternen (∅ 67264) is the most attractive old wooden chalet in Andermatt – cheap, fun, and a popular meeting and eating place. The Bergidyll (∅ 67455) is a comfortable chalet-style hotel near the station; friendly family management, good breakfasts.

Après-ski animation is mainly bar-orientated; some, like the Restaurant Tell and the Adler are packed with locals and soldiers – the bars suddenly empty at curfew. Others, like the bizarrely decorated Sternen and the Ochsen pub (hosted by a Swiss American ski freak) are popular with skiers. There are a couple of bars with more expensive drinks and some music and one disco. Restaurants, apart from the friendly Tell, are in hotels.

Ski school

Classes 2hr morning and afternoon.	**Children** Non-ski kindergarten, ages
Cost 6 days SF105. Private lessons	2–8, 6 full days SF240.
SF135/day.	**Special courses** Touring, off-piste.

Andermatt is a famous and favourite area for mountain touring, thanks in large part to the well-known veteran guide Martin Epp. He now has competition from another local skier and climber, Alex Clapasson, who runs weekly courses throughout the winter.

Other activities

Cross-country 20km of easy and	(with instruction), swimming (Hotel
medium trails along the valley floor.	Monopol), saunas, cinema (English
Not skiing Open air skating, curling	films), fitness centre, toboggan run.

The wide, flat valley makes an easy and not very interesting cross-country track which rises less than 100m over 9km. The trail is graded into green, blue and red loops – referring more to length than difficulty. Andermatt does not offer much for the non-skier.

Travel

Airport Zurich; transfer about 2hr.	**Road** Via Zurich; chains may be needed.
Railway Station in resort.	**Reachable resorts** None.

There is no public transport within the resort, and none is necessary. Having a car in the resort is no more than a luxury, saving some walking and a few train rides up and down the valley. Oberalp and Furka passes are closed in winter, but cars can be put on the train for access to resorts in south-east and south-west Switzerland. The famous Glacier Express train, running between Zermatt and St Moritz, calls at Andermatt.

Miscellaneous

Tourist office ∅ (44) 67454. Tx 868604.	**Equipment hire** 6 days skis
Medical Fracture clinic, doctor, dentist,	SF80; boots SF30; X-C SF85.
chemist in resort.	**Resort beds** 650 in hotels, 800 in
Package holidays MM, SCG.	apartments.

Titlis wonder

Engelberg Switzerland 1050m

Engelberg is a large, very traditional Swiss resort set deep in a wide and beautiful valley less than an hour south of Lucerne. Having grown up beside a famous and imposing monastery, it is now more of a town than a village but despite some ugly modern buildings the partly traffic-free centre has some charm – much more than most big Swiss resorts. The magnificent glaciated Titlis towers over 2000 metres above the valley floor and keeps the sun out of the centre for much of the day early in the season. There are some hotels in a more open setting on the west-facing slopes above the centre.

Engelberg attracts hordes of Lucerne weekenders for obvious geographical reasons. It attracts old folk, walkers and cross-country skiers because of the creature comforts and amenities of the resort and the secluded beauty of the wooded, narrow head of the valley, where a special cable-car runs at week-ends for non-skiers only. It may also attract a few demon skiers intrigued by the promise of exceptionally long, steep and beautiful runs (especially off-piste) from Titlis. These exist, but they are not reliable, and the piste skiing is disjointed and inconveniently arranged, making Engelberg a frustrating resort for most skiers, most of the time.

The Titlis base station is outside the resort centre and served by none-too-frequent ski buses. Weekend queues and travelling time have been cut by the installation of a new gondola up to a plateau at Trübsee (1800m). Beyond this there are still two stages of cable-car before skiers finally reach Titlis top station (3020m) via Stand (2450m). Below a small summer-skiing shelf of glacier, the only piste down to Stand is a black, and the off-piste routes are even sterner, notably the famous Laub, a wide, consistently steep north-east-facing wall from near Stand down towards Gerschnialp (1262m). There are limited areas of good stiff intermediate skiing between Stand and Trübsee and beneath the Jochstock (2563m), the starting point of another off-piste adventure trail down to Trübsee. These lifts are not well linked, and the plateau which separates the two sectors involves skiers in a tiresome plod to reach the entertaining runs down to base station.

On the sunnier side of the valley, and directly accessible from the resort, the much friendlier Brunni ski area is served by cable-car and two drag-lifts to Schonegg (2040m). There are enjoyable red runs beside the lifts on the open upper slopes, but the lower wooded ones are unreliable for snow, and the only run to the resort ends up on a road on the outskirts.

As well as beautiful walks and sleigh rides, Engelberg has a smart sports centre, with tennis and skating/curling rinks. There are kindergartens and two ski schools, one of which promises a maximum class size of six.

Tourist office ✆ (41) 94116. Tx 78566. **Package holidays** CM, IG, MM, SGW.

Jungfrau undefiled

Wengen 1270m Switzerland

Good for *Beautiful scenery, nursery slopes, easy skiing, big ski area, not skiing, family skiing, Alpine charm, rail access, chalet holidays, freedom from cars.*
Bad for *Tough skiing, short airport transfer, easy road access, late holidays*

Linked resort: Grindelwald
Separate resort: Mürren

According to the authorised (British) version of skiing history, this is the cradle of the recreational and competitive sport of today. It was at Wengen that British skiers hit on the idea of using the mountain railway to turn skiing into a 'downhill only' pastime, and at Mürren that Arnold Lunn organised the first slalom race, in 1922.

Wengen and Mürren have changed less than most of the famous early resorts. They are still small, car-free villages accessible only by railway (and cable-car, in Mürren's case), and the atmosphere is still crusty and cliquey. Families (including the Lunns) return year after year to the same comfortable hotels, chalets and drinks parties and treat the resorts as a second home, which is what they are for many. Each resort has its flourishing British racing club, and British skiers are still made to feel very welcome.

The regulars do not return purely out of nostalgia. The villages which face each other across the steep-sided Lauterbrunnen trench are among the most picturesque of Alpine resorts. Their setting is dramatic and the surrounding peaks are majestic, including the famous ascending trio of Eiger, Mönch and Jungfrau (4158m).

Tiny Mürren is the prettier, quieter and more private village. Keen après-skiers run the risk of jumping off the cliff out of boredom, and non-skiers must be satisfied by little more than the spectacular view. Mürren's separate ski area is limited in extent and most of it is difficult. It appears to lack variety, but many well-travelled skiers find it more satisfying than much larger areas. Wengen is more hotel-oriented, larger, livelier and more varied in its appeal. It shares a broad, mostly gentle ski area with neighbouring Grindelwald; the lack of cars, the good sunny village nursery slopes and guaranteed English-speaking instruction make Wengen ideal for beginners and children. Good skiers come hoping to find good snow off-piste in the shadow of the Eiger.

Grindelwald, the original climbing resort, is overshadowed by the mountains (it gets one hour of sun a day in midwinter) and by the special qualities of Mürren and Wengen, which make it seem ordinary. It is the largest of the three resorts, and the easiest access point to the Jungfrau skiing for motorists, local weekenders and skiers who commute from Interlaken or nearer villages.

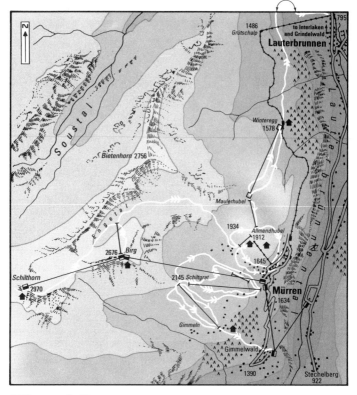

The skiing top 2971m bottom 943m

The skiing falls into three areas. The main one, Kleine Scheidegg/
Männlichen, is a rolling, partly wooded area of predominantly easy and
intermediate pistes shared by Wengen and Grindelwald. The slopes
above Wengen face west, those above Grindelwald mostly east. On
the opposite side of Grindelwald is First, a smaller area of mainly easy
south-facing runs, little used. On the other side of Lauterbrunnen is
Mürren's separate, mainly east-facing ski area. It goes much higher
than the rest of the Jungfrau skiing, and may provide skiing in good
conditions when Wengen is very bare.

A cog railway links both Wengen and Grindelwald with the col of
Kleine Scheidegg and another climbs from there to Eigergletscher and
on, by a tunnel through the Eiger, to Jungfraujoch, the highest railway
station in Europe. Eigergletscher is the top station for piste skiing
although there is an occasional off-piste excursion from Jungfraujoch
down the Aletsch glacier, the longest in the Alps, towards Brig. There
are challenging runs in many directions from **Eigergletscher** and some
good off-piste skiing notably on the Grindelwald side under the north
face of the Eiger ('White Hare') and down to Wixi by 'Oh God!'. This is
not really an area for the novice although the run from Fallboden (which

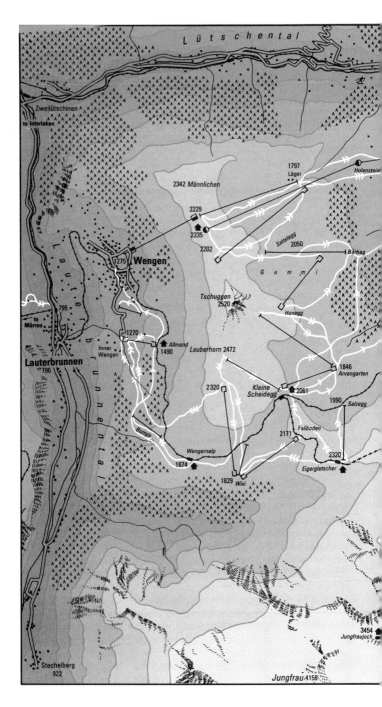

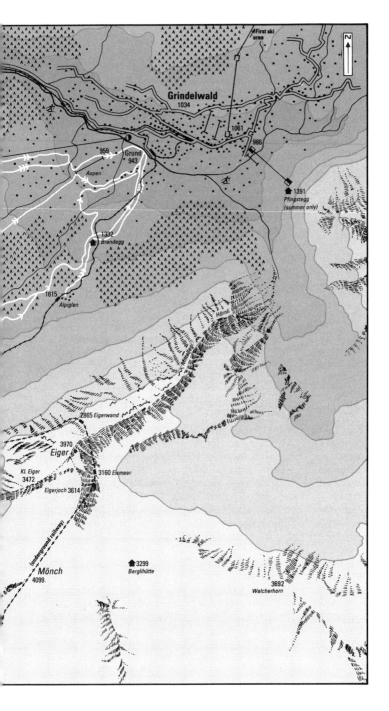

N

First ski area

Grindelwald
1034

1061

986

959
Grund
943

1391
Pfingstegg
(summer only)

Aspen

1332
Brandegg

1615

Alpiglen

Hörnli

2865 Eigerwand

3970
Eiger

Kl. Eiger
3472

3160 Eismeer

Eigerjoch 3614

(underground railway)

Mönch
4099

3299
Berglihütte

3692
Walcherhorn

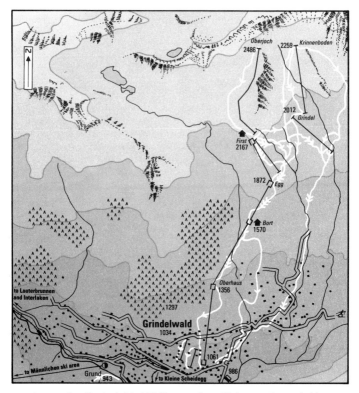

can be reached by train) to Wixi is popular with inexperienced skiers.

On the opposite side of Kleine Scheidegg is the Lauberhorn, which has given its name to the longest and most beautiful World Cup downhill course. The start and finish are easily identified but the actual course isn't, much to the disappointment of one reporter. The build-up to the race (in January) impedes skiing on the Wengen side of the mountain. At other times, it is a good intermediate area with runs back to the bottom of the drag-lift or on down to Wengen. The run back to Wengen is a mixture of open piste and path, the latter often very crowded. The Bumps drag, very popular with the ski school, and the Innerwengen chair, serve mostly easy slopes.

On the Grindelwald side of Kleine Scheidegg a series of lifts link up with the **Männlichen**, which can also be reached by cable-car from Wengen and gondola from Grund. There are good intermediate pistes here and some interesting off-piste skiing, particularly round the Gummi chair. The Arvengarten chair to Kleine Scheidegg and drag to Honegg give access to a lot of skiing but the chair suffers from being the only link back to Scheidegg. The Männlichen is mostly open and easy skiing with a few more challenging runs (notably the mogul slope on top) popular with piste-bashers as well as near-beginners.

There are several routes down towards Grindelwald from both Männlichen and Kleine Scheidegg, with open pistes on top and wooded areas further down. The piste gradings overstate difficulty and, provided snow is good enough, these very long, beautiful and easy runs (including a blue of 8.5km) are a leisurely skier's paradise. The main disincentive is the lift ride back – either crowded gondola or slow train. Runs finish at Grund, a short train ride away from Grindelwald.

The south-facing **First** area is awkward to reach for skiers based in Wengen, but provides plenty of amusement in good conditions. A very slow (25 minutes) side-saddle chair to First itself and several drags on the sunny slopes below Oberjoch serve flattering open skiing with a beautiful view of the Eiger. Good skiers make the journey for the spring snow on the upper slopes or for the 6km black run all the way down from First to Grindelwald, initially narrow but nowhere very steep. Unfortunately, snow conditions on the lower slopes are unreliable. There are easier indirect runs down, as well as the chair-lift route.

The original lift in **Mürren** was is the old railway, opened in 1912, from the top of the village to the **Allmendhubel**, with a small nursery area at the top. It still serves moderately easy runs down to the village and connections with the skiing on either side. Mürren's best gentle skiing is in the woods above Winteregg, where the station provides Wengen-based skiers with a direct way into and out of the skiing. When snow is good it is possible to ski down to Lauberbrunnen via a long tortuous path through the steep woods. This is the last leg of the famous Inferno course from the top of the Schilthorn. The race is run every January by over 1,000 skiers; the record time for the eight-mile course is 15¾ minutes, including some uphill skiing which holiday skiers can avoid by using the Maulerhubel drag. On the other side of the village, the steep Schiltgrat drag serves two very serious black runs of about 1.5km for 500m vertical, often huge moguls all the way. There is some easier, south-facing skiing down to Gimmeln and an easy run back across the mountain to the village, but snow conditions are often less friendly than on Winteregg, and the drag-lift can be treacherously icy.

The two-stage cable-car to Schilthorn adds over 800m vertical to Mürren's skiing. The ride up the cliff face to Birg and onward over a deep bowl to the famous round (and revolving) restaurant which crowns Piz Gloria, as seen in *On Her Majesty's Secret Service*, is one of the highlights of any trip to the region. The 360-degree views from the top are wonderful, and the run down is no less exciting; unfortunately there is no alternative to the difficult piste. Descent by lift is not covered by any lift pass – a deplorable incitement to foolhardiness. The first section of the run from the restaurant is steep, narrow, exposed and usually very bumpy or windblown. The run opens out into a beautiful, gentle, open bowl (the Engetal) with a drag-lift connection up to Birg and open skiing on the steep slope beside the lift. Beneath the Engetal the run becomes the Kanonenrohr (gunbarrel), an unnerving mixture of narrowness, rocks, moguls and a gaping precipice protected by nets, before running out gently towards Allmendhubel. There are off-piste variants of the Schilthorn descent, all of them difficult and often very dangerous.

Mountain restaurants are in most of the obvious places between

Wengen and Grindelwald. They all get crowded, particularly the ones at the railway stations which attract non-skiers as well as skiers. Reporters recommend the Jungfrau restaurant at Wengernalp 'for a warm welcome and excellent food at reasonable prices' and the Haunted House above Grund. Apart from their superlative views the restaurants at Birg and Piz Gloria have little to commend them.

Wengen is the best of the three resorts for beginners, and one of the best in the Alps. The excellence of its **nursery slopes**, sunny and well-placed, is one of the reasons. Provided snow is good the transition to the large expanses of easy piste skiing accessible by train is not too traumatic, but one reporter found the path down to Wengen 'formidable' because of the crowds of other skiers.

Lifts

Passes Jungfrau pass, available for 3 days and over, covers all three resorts' lifts and transport between Interlaken and Grindelwald, Lauterbrunnen and Stechelberg. Local passes available (including day passes) and daily supplements to cover other areas. **Cost** 6-day Jungfrau pass SF176; Kleine Scheidegg/Männlichen SF150. **Children** 35% off, under 16. **Beginners** Coupons.

Both the gondola and train at Grund can be horrendously crowded in high season and at week-ends. Other serious bottlenecks are Arvengarten, the main link to Scheidegg, and the Männlichen drag-lift. Wixi has been relieved by the addition of two new lifts. Several reporters commented wearily on the amount of poling needed to get from lift to lift, and one the high cost of the lift pass for an antiquated system – old T-bars as well as trains. Buying a pass at Lauterbrunnen on arrival can save a few francs for the trip up to the resort.

The resort

Set on an open shelf above the Lauterbrunnen valley and overlooked by the Jungfrau, Wengen is one of the most beautifully situated of Alpine resorts, surpassed for drama and views only by Mürren. Lots of wooden chalets are dotted about the hillside, and the centre consists of large, comfortable, traditional hotels. The train from Lauterbrunnen to Kleine Scheidegg runs through the resort and the station is the natural focus. All the activity is on or close to the main street, which is lined with hotels and shops (limited in range). There is an English church.

Accommodation consists mainly of hotels but there are lots of chalets with rooms and apartments to rent. Most of the UK operators offer hotel holidays, and reports suggest that standards are generally high. Although not a large resort, Wengen is long and hilly, and skiers not staying centrally can face walks of up to 15 minutes to the cable-car or station. The newly rebuilt Eiger (℘ 551131), right beside the station, is a friendly family-run hotel. In the main street the Victoria Lauberhorn (℘ 565151) is large and comfortable, the Sunstar (℘ 565111) is more modern and has its own swimming pool (with 'superb mountain views'), and the Bernerhof (℘ 552721) is an attractive hotel in traditional Alpine style. Reporters recommend the central Silberhorn (✆ 552241), the Alpenrose (✆ 553216), Schweizerheim (✆ 551112) – 'excellent value for money, comfortable rooms, good food in ample quantities' – and the Bellevue (✆ 551571) – 'welcoming, family-run, excellent tea, beautiful views'.

Après-ski is fairly quiet and unsophisticated. The most popular meeting place is the stube of Hotel Eiger by the station, not to be confused with the smaller Eiger Bar on the main street – also popular and always packed after skiing. At night the busy Gemstube has live music and a good atmosphere. There are a few tea-rooms, evening skating once a week, a night-club and a couple of discothèques. There is not much variety of restaurants.

Ski school

Classes 2hr morning and afternoon.
Cost 6 days SF125. Private lessons SF32/hr.
Special courses Helicopter skiing.

Children Ski kindergarten, ages 3–7, 9.30–4.30, 6 days with lunch SF95. Non-skiing kindergarten, ages up to 7, 9.00–4.00, 6 days with lunch SF90.

All we know of the school is that its instructors speak good English. Boy (and girl) racers can join the DHO (Downhill Only) club which trains in Wengen every Christmas and Easter.

Other activities

Cross-country 12km track in Lauterbrunnen valley.
Not skiing Skating/curling (artificial and

natural rinks), 20km cleared paths, swimming, sauna, solarium, toboggan runs, ski-bob, cinema, bowling.

Wengen is a splendid resort for non-skiers, and there are plenty of them, pottering around the delightful resort and trying their hands at curling. Long, beautiful mountain walks and the train make it possible to meet up with skiing companions; there's plenty of scope for longer excursions. It is no place for cross-country skiers.

Travel

Airport Bern is the closest, but most operators use Zurich or Geneva; transfers about 4hr.
Reachable resorts None outside the Jungfrau region.

Railway Station in resort.
Road Cars must be left at parks in Interlaken or Lauterbrunnen. Access via Basel; chains rarely needed.

There is no transport within the resort. The main access problem is the possibility of missing the last train up to the resort (about 11pm).

Miscellaneous

Tourist office (36) 551414. Tx 923271.
Equipment hire 6 days skis SF75, boots SF39, X-C SF68.
Resort beds 2,200 in hotels; 2,500 in apartments.

Medical Hospital Interlaken; doctor, chemist in resort; dentist in Lauterbrunnen.
Package holidays BL, CM, IG, JM, KU, MM, PS, SCG, SMW, SUP, SWT, TH.

Mürren   1640m

Mürren is a tiny village of 458 inhabitants and less than 2,000 guest beds, making Obergurgl seem positively urban. The train which climbs steeply from Lauterbrunnen arrives at one end of the village, and at the other end is the second station of the four-stage cable-car from the valley floor at Stechelberg (where there is a large car park) to Piz Gloria. Between the two is the tightly-packed village, mostly beautiful old chalets and narrow, steep streets (which means that most buildings share the beautiful views), with the old Allmendhubel funicular at the top. There are a couple of large, expensive hotels (the Mürren and the Eiger) and a smart new sports complex (swimming, sauna, skating/curling, squash, gym) by the station, and simpler ones in the centre, better placed for skiing. Among the less expensive hotels, the Alpenruhe (∅ 552738) is next door to the cable-car. The Bellevue (∅ 551531) near the Allmendhubel is recommended by a reporter for good food, and is attached to 'the best tea shop in the Alps'. The cheapest accommodation is in the large, central Regina (∅ 551421). Mürren is very quiet indeed in the evenings, with music in only one or two hotel bars. Evenings at Allmendhubel restaurant can be organised; they end perilously with a run down on skis or toboggan. It is hard to think of a more beautiful place to skate than on the ice rink near the station, and there are also some very pretty walks and expensive sleigh rides; but after a few days non-skiers are likely to find Mürren a bit too small and quiet.

Tourist office ∅ (36) 551616. Tx 923212.
Package holidays BL, IG, KU, MM, SUP, SUS, SWT.

Grindelwald   1040m

Grindelwald is a large and busy year-round resort spread along the valley floor between the magnificent peaks of Wetterhorn and Eiger on the the one side and the gentler wooded slopes of First on the other. The resort has lots of accommodation and leisure facilities including a good sports centre (skating, curling, swimming, sauna), long and beautiful walks high above the valley floor and (unlike the other Jungfrau resorts) long cross-country trails, totalling 45km. For skiers the place to stay is Grund, at the bottom of the main ski area or near Grindelwald station, for easy access to Grund by train. Several reporters recommend the Hotel Derby (∅ 545461) right on the station – 'excellent value, good varied food, noise not a problem' – but one case of overbooking is reported. The Bodenwald (∅ 531242) is also recommended – 'a comfortable small hotel with good food and skiing to and from the door' – but very remote for après-ski purposes. Après-ski in Grindelwald itself is more varied than in the other local resorts, but even here there is not much going on into the small hours. There is a good daytime bus service linking Grund, Grindelwald centre and the First chair-lift (each stage is about 15 minutes on foot). The buses are not covered by lift passes.

Tourist office ∅ (36) 531212. Tx 923217.
Package holidays IG, KU, MM, SHW, SUS, SWT, TH.

A house divided

Adelboden Switzerland 1360m

Linked resort: Lenk

Adelboden and Lenk are distinct but connected resorts a couple of valleys to the west of the famous Jungfrau region.

Adelboden is a charming old village, its long main street lined with overhanging wooden buildings. It has around it a considerable quantity and variety of skiing, but – and it's a big but – that skiing is split into no less than five widely separated areas (more if you count some of the baby lifts). The resort literature bravely tries to minimise the importance of this by treating the linking buses as just another form of ski-lift (eg No 22 – height gain 357m, length 7500m). There are ambitious plans for new lifts to improve matters, but at present the only area accessible directly from the village is Tschentenegg (1938m) – open intermediate skiing served by two chairs and a drag. In the rural suburb of Boden, there are nursery lifts and a drag going up to Kuonisbergli (1730m) and on to Höchsthorn (1903m); the blue/red/black gradings of the runs on the lower part exaggerate the variety of pistes. Across the valley, the drag to Fleckli (1862m) serves runs which are marked red and black but which hold no terrors other than poor marking. A minibus takes you 6km out to get to the next area, where a cable-car climbs steeply over 500m to the extraordinary Engstligenalp (1964m). Beyond the cluster of hotels and houses is a flat-bottomed bowl of mountains; it has only one lift of any significance, on the far side, which serves a short piste and is a launching point for off-piste skiing in the bowl and ski-tours outside it. There's a flat tow-drag across the bowl, but still a lot of plodding.

The area which connects with Lenk is another longish bus-ride away from Adelboden at Geils (1707m). Chairs up each side of a wide, open bowl (to 2080m and 2200m) serve intermediate and genuinely black runs but there are also links to the easier runs towards the centre. Lenk-bound skiers have the luxury of a gondola up to the col (1957m).

Lenk (1070m) is less appealing as a village than Adelboden – it has been more vigorously developed in recent years, primarily for the benefit of German cross-country skiers (there are good trails). Its skiing is not quite as spread out, but it still relies on 50-seat ski-lifts with four wheels to get from the village centre to its three separate ski areas. The skiing on this side of the dividing ridge and on Lenk's other mountain, Betelberg (served by a gondola and several drags and chairs), is uniformly easy with the exception of one black run towards the village.

Adelboden has extensive cross-country trails of easy and medium grades at Boden, Geils and Engstligenalp, artificial rinks for skating and curling, plenty of cleared paths, two hotel swimming pools, and horses for hire. There is a kindergarten.

Tourist office ✆ (33) 732252. Tx 922121. Package holidays IG, MM, SUS, SWT.

Catch a fallin' gstar

Gstaad Switzerland 1100m

Good for *Big ski area, easy skiing, cross-country skiing, mountain restaurants, not skiing, Alpine charm, rail access*
Bad for *Tough skiing, skiing convenience, late holidays, resort-level snow*

Linked resorts: Rougemont, Schönried, Saanenmöser, Zweisimmen, St Stephan
Separate resorts: Château d'Oex, Les Diablerets, Villars

The Gstaad area – Das Weisse Hochland or Le Blanc Pays d'en Haut, depending which side of the German/French language barrier you're on – could hardly be less appropriately named. The valleys between the Bernese Oberland and Lake Geneva have many attractions, but exceptional height and reliable winter whiteness are not among them. This is a pretty, medium-high region of charming villages dotted around wide, wooded valleys, with lots of little skiing areas between 1000m and 2000m linked fully by lift pass, post bus and the little Montreux Oberland Bernois railway, and partly by ski-lift and piste.

Gstaad is a picturesque, expensive village with an impressive list of famous visitors and part-time residents. This does not mean that it is a tremendously exciting place; it is genuinely exclusive, in the sense that celebrities go there to escape the consequences of celebrity – to live and party behind the closed doors of private chalets. Although Gstaad is not an old village, it is traditional in style of building. The few old buildings have been carefully maintained and form a charming nucleus, and the rest of the village is also attractive in a neat, solid way. It is traditional too in the style of affluent Alpine holiday it offers. Lots of people go there not to ski, and there is plenty for them to do. It is one of the few fashionable resorts where it really is more-or-less impossible to live economically; there are no inexpensive hotels.

But there is more to the area than Gstaad, and many Swiss families of no exceptional wealth use the other villages for simple family holidays or weekend skiing trips. Not far to the north-east of Gstaad is a large area of friendly skiing shared by Schönried, Saanenmöser, Zweisimmen and St Stephan. On the other side of the resort, Gstaad's skiing is linked to that above the unspoilt French-speaking village of Rougemont. And away at the western extremity of the region is the self-contained towny resort of Château d'Oex. The skiing is extended vertically by the Glacier Des Diablerets to the south. The glacier also forms part of the skiing of the small, spacious, chalet-resort of Les Diablerets (which, confusingly, is not part of the White Highlands region). The skiing of Les Diablerets is now linked with that of Villars, a long-established former British favourite which has been rather left behind by the changing tastes of keen skiers.

The skiing top 2275m bottom 975m

The White Highlands skiing is scattered widely around the mostly north-facing aspects of the Saane/Sarine Valley, and of the saddle which separates this from the Simmental. Gstaad, the main resort, has three small separate areas, all of them starting a rather inconvenient distance from the resort centre and railway station. The large ski area on the broad flank of the mountains between Schönried and St Stephan is not connected by piste. In the other direction, Gstaad's Eggli ski area links up with the Videmanette area above Rougemont. The Glacier des Diablerets, to the south is useful for late-season skiing.

Gstaad: Wasserngrat A double-stage mixture of open and closed chair-lifts serves an interesting and challenging range of slopes. The middle station is low down, giving fairly long runs down the top half of the mountain – useful in poor snow conditions. The blue/red/black gradings reflect real differences in steepness, with moguls under the top chair, open intermediate slopes served by a long drag-lift to one side, and gentle easy runs down to the bottom station.

Gstaad: Wispile A similar area to the Wasserngrat, served by a two-stage gondola. Runs on the top half are challenging, those down to the valley rather less so but still interesting. Pistes on both the Wasserngrat and Wispile cover only a small part of the round, steeply-sided wooded mountains. From both top stations there is scope for off-piste descents through the woods, steeply into the side valleys.

Gstaad: Eggli The Eggli plateau is a popular sunny rendezvous, good for beginners if snow is sparse lower down. There are some good, easy slopes served by short drags and chair-lifts above and below it, on down to Saanen. The direct black run underneath the gondola is not very steep but it often presents challenging off-piste or half-piste conditions. There is an easier way back to Gstaad from the mid-station of the lifts up from Saanen. Wide trails through woods go down into the very attractive and peaceful Chalberhöni valley with a connecting lift to the Rougemont skiing up the far side.

Rougemont: Videmanette The two-stage gondola from Rougemont starts quite a walk below the village centre and station. One regular visitor reports that this lift is frequently closed in bad weather or windy conditions, when skiers who go via Eggli can enjoy marvellously empty slopes. The top of Videmanette is impressively hostile; the run down the front of the Videmanette should not tempt many skiers, being steep and very narrow in parts, and skiable only infrequently. The main runs are behind the rock, with a wide-open, very gentle bowl served by chair-lift, reached from the top by a steep mogul field or an exposed path skirting it or by taking is a short shuttle lift down. Below the chair-lift, a good, long varied red run goes back to Rougemont. Towards Eggli there are several variants of the descent down a wide, wooded but spacious slope under the long chair-lift up from the Chalberhöni. The black run is not a severe one.

Schönried Schönried's skiing is on both flanks of the gentle saddle on which the village (1231m) sits. A gondola from close to the road goes

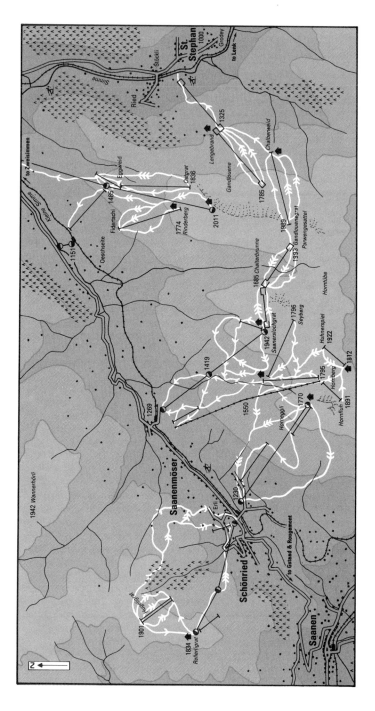

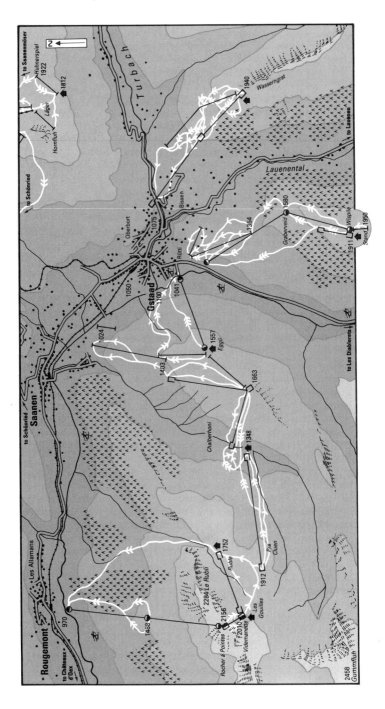

up to the top of the south-facing skiing at Rellerligrat (1834m). The most direct run, almost following the gondola, is graded black but is a straightforward intermediate run. A pair of short drags below the top serve worthwhile red slopes and give access to pleasant, long, easy blue and red runs to the village from Hugeligrat (1901m). From a point below and well away from the main road, a three-seat enclosed chair-lift has now replaced the drag-lift up to Horneggli, from which point black, red and blue pistes descend through another amiable wooded landscape. There is no great difference in the gradient of the pistes; we found that softer snow on the black made it the easiest.

Saanenmöser/St Stephan Although Saanenmöser is only a mile or two along the road from Schönried and they have lifts converging on the Hornfluh, their ski areas are for practical purposes separate. Saanenmöser's skiing is however shared with St Stephan, over the mountain in the Simmental, leading to Lenk. The skiing covers two valleys and the flank of the Simmental. From Saanenmöser a funicular railway goes to the right side of the first valley, and a gondola to the left. The valley is a network of pleasant easy and intermediate pistes, partly open and partly wooded, served by two drags starting from Lochstafel. The funicular links by drag and piste with a short run on the Huhnerspiel, facing south-west, which is the steepest bit of skiing in this area, but barely black. From the top of the gondola at Saanerslochgrat, pistes descend into the open bowl of the Chaltebrunne valley; except in poor snow conditions (which are not uncommon on these sunny pistes) the red and black runs hold no terrors. On both flanks of the valley there is scope for gentle off-piste exploration. Beyond the valley are the open slopes above St Stephan; this is an extensive area with the standard tri-colour set of runs on each of the top lifts providing good, fast intermediate skiing of no great difficulty and occasional moguls.

Zweisimmen Although surrounded by the skiing of Saanenmöser and St Stephan, the ski area of Zweisimmen is not connected to it by piste or lift; there are reputedly off-piste routes between the two areas. The long gondola from the village to the Rinderberg serves a glorious, gentle, north-facing slope with motorway blue runs on most of its length and fast intermediate pistes at the top and down the supplementary drag-lifts. The skiing is largely open, but with patches of forest around.

Glacier des Diablerets On our winter visits we have not found the Diablerets glacier open, so we have not experienced the apparently very worthwhile runs round the back of the Oldenhorn from the top station. Nor have we been able to sample the runs to the bottom stations. We can report that the remaining run from Cabane des Diablerets to Oldenegg (although scenically impressive and a distinctive high-mountain run) is hardly worth the effort involved in getting to it.

Mountain restaurants are generally attractive, adequately numerous in most of the obvious places, but expensive (we paid £6 for half a litre of the cheapest Italian wine). Particularly attractive restaurants on the way down from the Videmanette to the Chalberhöni, in the valley itself and around the Eggli.

Provided snow cover is adequate, the **nursery slopes** at the bottom

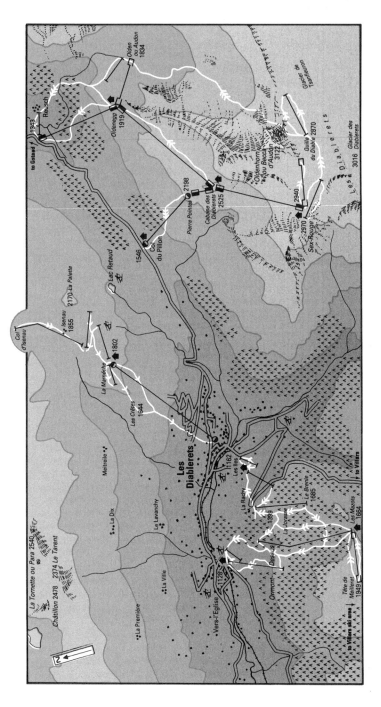

of the Wispile (Gstaad), Saanen, Schönried and Saanenmöser are all adequate and there is plenty of scope for progressing on to longer easy runs in the area.

Lifts

Passes Area pass covers all lifts in Gstaad, villages east to St Stephan and west to Château d'Oex, and the Glacier des Diablerets; also train, local buses and swimming pool. Day passes	available. **Cost** 6-day pass SF162. **Children** 40% off, under 16. **Beginners** Coupons or lift pass.

Around Gstaad the main complaint is the annoying distance of lifts from resort centre. The system is a bit old-fashioned, but crowds are not usually a problem except during Swiss holidays in February and at weekends. The notable lack of linking lift and piste between Zweisimmen and the surrounding skiing network is to be remedied.

The resort

There was very little to the village until the advent of the railway in the first decade of this century. The village centre is spacious but not awkwardly spread out, and is set in and around a wide U-bend in the railway line, mostly along a single, winding main street which is a busy through-route. There are dozens of luxury shops for furs, food, jewellery and clothes (Dior, Hermès, Piaget), and watchmakers by appointment to sheikhs who have winter branches in Gstaad.

One of the nicest things about the village is that its centre is not cluttered up with huge luxury hotels – most of these are spread round the edges of the village in their own grounds. Nearly all the **accommodation** is in hotels, nearly all expensive, especially in Gstaad itself. The famous and fantastic Palace dominates the resort from its hillside. It costs about £100 a head for half board unless you are someone's servant, in which you cost a mere £30, or a dog (£10 with food). For this, needless to say, there are plenty of facilities – fitness centre, pool, ice rink, nightclub and squash courts. Other large, very comfortable hotels around the town are quieter and, at about half the price of the Palace, still expensive. In the village centre, most of the hotels are along the main street. By far the most attractive are the Rössli (✆ 43412) and the Olden (✆ 43444), beautiful old chalets right in the middle of town, both comfortably modernised without losing their character. They are very popular places to eat and drink, with a lively atmosphere and a variety of bars and restaurants, as well as being comfortable and very friendly places to stay. The Olden is slightly smarter and has more comfortable bedrooms and is more expensive, especially its restaurant. There is almost no cheap accommodation in Gstaad, and even in the small villages in further corners of the ski area, the accommodation is mostly comfortable and far from cheap.

There is plenty of **après-ski** entertainment traditional and modern. Tea-rooms (Chez Esther), simple woody bars where locals gather for beer and cards (the Olden), smart restaurants with musical entertainment (the Chesery), discothèques (the Palace hotel's Green-Go), fondue evenings in various mountain restaurants. Among Gstaad restaurants the Olden is good, fashionable and expensive; the Curling-Restaurant and the Rössli are popular, friendly and less expensive. The Chlösterli is a magnificent 17th-century barn of a chalet about 3 km towards Gsteig; dancing to a live band in the central open-plan area and small dining rooms adjoining; expensive. Local youth fills the rather kitsch Harvey's Pub in Saanen. Much more commendable is the Reusch in Gsteig. Up-to-date films, many in English.

Ski school

Classes 10.00–2.30 with 45min for lunch.
Cost 6 days SF140. Private lessons SF34/hr.

Children Ski kindergarten, ages 3–6, 6 days SF140. Non-ski kindergarten, ages 2–6, 9.30–5.00, 6 days SF125.

Although this is mainly a medium-altitude skiing area, there are high mountains to the south and plenty of ski touring excursions are possible, notably to the Wildhorn, reached via Lenk. Guides can be hired – information from Hotels Rössli and Bernerhof in Gstaad.

Other activities

Cross-country Gstaad to Château d'Oex 15km, Gstaad to Gsteig 11km, 6km of loops in Launen Valley.
Not skiing Swimming (free with lift pass),

sauna, tennis, squash, skating, curling, fitness centre, 50km cleared paths, hot-air balloons.

Gstaad is a very attractive and popular place for a non-skiing holiday. Apart from good resort facilities, there are plenty of interesting excursion possibilities. X-C runs are long and attractive, but all at low altitude except at the recently developed Sparenmoos area above Zweisimmen. The tourist offices provide maps indicating approximate gradients. X-C skiers can catch buses back to Gstaad from Chlösterli (half way to Gsteig), and trains back from Château d'Oex and Rougemont. There are trails illuminated in the evening.

Travel

Airport Geneva; transfer about 3hr.
Railway Station in resort.
Road Via Lausanne or Bern; chains may

be needed.
Reachable resorts Leysin, Lenk.

The MOB railway and allied buses serve the skiing well enough. All the same, having a car is very handy. Parking can be a problem in Gstaad itself but not usually elsewhere. Access roads often congested at weekends (especially the Spiez road), but otherwise not difficult. The Col du Pillon (for Les Diablerets) is occasionally closed.

Miscellaneous

Tourist office ✆ (30) 45353. Tx 922211.
Medical Hospital, doctor, dentist, chemist in resort.
Equipment hire 6 days skis SF69-82, boots SF36, X-C SF62.

Resort beds 1,000 in hotels, 3,500 in apartments.
Package holidays BL, KU, MM, PS, SCG.

Minor resorts

Rougemont 870m

Only a few miles from Gstaad, this French-speaking village is in
another world of old chalets and barns. The Valrose (∅ 48146) is
adequately placed for the station and the Videmanette gondola, and
one of the cheapest places to stay in the whole area. Among the
attractions of the village is the warm, rustic and inexpensive Cerf
restaurant (excellent fondues to the accompaniment of saw-playing).
There is a rink for skating and curling.

Schönried 1230m

Schönried is a roadside straggle of a village, with no particular appeal
except that it is fairly centrally placed for the Weisse Hochland skiing,
and has some of it on its doorstep – or nearly so. It is also slightly higher
than neighbouring resorts, presumably to the benefit of its nursery
slopes. Hotels along the road include some fairly sumptuous ones in
the Gstaad mould, and simpler places. There is a swimming pool, a
squash court and a natural ice rink, and a cross-country trail to
Saanenmöser.
Tourist office ∅ (30) 41919.

Saanenmöser 1270m

Saanenmöser barely amounts to a village, but has a couple of hotels
well placed for access to the skiing – the Hornberg (∅ 44440) and the
less expensive Bahnhof (∅ 41506) – about the cheapest hotel in this
whole area. There is a natural ice rink.
Tourist office ∅ (30) 42222.

Zweisimmen 950m

Zweisimmen is an unexceptional village of no great charm, but with
abundant inexpensive accommodation well-placed for the ski-lifts, and
the station (for connections to other resorts). The very simple Derby
(∅ 21438) is right beside the Rinderberg lift. Two larger and more
comfortable hotels are the Rawyl zum Sternen (∅ 21251) by the
station, and the Krone (∅ 22626) in the centre.

Cross-country skiing is good, with very extensive trails along the
Simmental to Lenk, and a recently developed domain up on the
Sparenmoos (1640m–1790m). There are long cleared walks, toboggan
runs down from Sparenmoos, organised snowshoe outings, ski school
and kindergarten, natural ice rink, and some fairly unsophisticated
nightlife, including evening fondue parties in mountain restaurants. St
Stephan is a small, peaceful village a few miles up the valley towards
Lenk, with some attractive old hotels. Although it has the attraction of
skiing links with Saanenmöser, getting around by train to take
advantage of the lift pass is less easy than it is from Zweisimmen.
Tourist office ∅ (30) 21133.

Château d'Oex   1000m

Château d'Oex is a small established resort, pleasant enough but without much Alpine atmosphere. It has plenty of cross-country skiing on hand, and an artificial rink, but no pool. A cable-car from the centre climbs steeply to the base of the ski area (1225m), where a gondola goes up to La Braye (1630m). Supported by three drag-lifts, the gondola serves a friendly, wooded area of imprecisely defined easy and intermediate pistes facing roughly north-east – pleasant, but rather limited. Easy and intermediate pistes go on down to the valley in much the same vein, but arrive some way from the resort, at the foot of a chair-lift which will take you back into the skiing. Buses run to the resort.

Tourist office ✆ (29) 47788. Tx 940022. Package holidays GL, IT, SPT, STY.

Les Diablerets   1160m

Les Diablerets (the village) is a relaxed, spacious sprawl of chalets at the bottom of a broad U-shaped valley with the craggy crest of Les Diablerets (the mountain) at its head. The skiing, apart from that on the Oldenhorn and the Glacier des Diablerets (see above), is on lower, gentler mountains either side of the resort. There are two areas, both consisting entirely of easy-intermediate skiing. Isenau has open slopes facing south-west reached by gondola just above the centre. The Meilleret area starts further out and has a tedious chain of drag-lifts for access to the top, but its skiing holds more interest, with nicely varied runs among trees. There are adequate non-skiing amusements – swimming, 20km of cross-country, indoor and outdoor skating and curling. There are only a few hotels, mostly modern and anonymous. The central Auberge de la Poste (✆ 531124) is a cheap and cheerful exception.

Tourist office ✆ (25) 531358. Tx 456175. Package holidays PQ.

Villars   1300m

Villars perhaps deserves better than to be summarised in a paragraph, and it will be high on our agenda for fuller treatment in future. It is a long-established, all-round resort complete with mountain railway, very extensive cross-country trails and walks at high altitude, a modern sports complex and curling rinks. It enjoys a fine balcony setting, facing south-west across the Rhône valley. It is not a resort for the very keen skier who will soon tire of its rather limited ski-fields, wherein the more challenging runs are short and the long runs are gentle and inclined to run out of snow. The main area starts from Bretaye, a cluster of hotels and restaurants on a col at 1800m, and goes no higher than 2120m. Bretaye is reached directly by the railway from the centre or by gondola from the fringes of the resort. In good snow there is a link to the next mountain, Les Chaux, which is basically served by a gondola from the depths of the countryside. Bretaye is now also linked to the skiing of Les Diablerets.

Tourist office ✆ (25) 353232. Tx 456200. Package holidays CM, MM, NE.

Never on Sunday

Macugnaga Italy 1350m

Macugnaga is a small resort dramatically enclosed by the towering rock
and glacier of the eastern wall of Europe's second peak, the Monte
Rosa (4638m), not unlike Saas Fee's setting on the other side of the
mountain. There are two villages (Staffa and Pecetto) about half a mile
apart, both of them delightfully rustic and unspoilt by tourism. 'One of
the most beautiful villages I have ever seen,' wrote one otherwise
unimpressed reporter. Staffa is the busier of the two and more
important for most skiers, being more convenient for the two stage
cable-car which climbs steeply from the resort nearly 1500m towards
the Swiss border at the Passo di Monte Moro (2900m), where a statue
of the Madonna surveys the deep and beautiful valley and the majestic
array of peaks. There are a few nursery lifts at the bottom, two drags
serving the top 500m of the slope, and a couple of lifts at the top where
they once organised summer skiing, but the cable-car is what
Macugnaga's skiing is all about, and when it is shut (as it often is), there
is not much to be done. Variants of the single descent to Alpe Bill
(1700m) include a 6km red and a direct black of only 3km for the 1100m
vertical. There are no runs down from Alpe Bill and the bottom cabin is
small. Queues at peak times and especially on Sundays can be very
long indeed, uphill in the morning and downhill for lunch and in the
afternoon. During the week queues are rarely a problem. Slopes get a
lot of sun, and can be very icy.

Above Pecetto and beneath the Monte Rosa glaciers, the smaller
and less crowded Burky skiing is served by two chair-lifts from 1350 to
1900m. The east-facing skiing is gentle and wooded, much more
suitable for timid skiers than Monte Moro, but very limited in extent. A
third ski area on the other side of Staffa has been closed for over ten
years since an avalanche took out the cable-car. Monte Moro is a good
starting point for ski tourers who can cross the mountains to Saas Fee.

The very necessary ski bus is reported to work well in the morning,
but erratically after the driver has lunched. Paths through the villages
are often icy and at weekend the place is choked with cars. Reporters
agree that the people are as friendly as the resort is charming, and
several hotels in Staffa are recommended, notably the Zumstein
(✆ 4472): 'superb food and a friendly bar'. The small Cristallo (✆ 2129)
is in the centre of Pecetto, near the Burky lifts, and also recommended.
Après-ski is mostly in Staffa and bar-oriented, quiet but cosy. Tour
operators organise fondue evenings and dancing. There is very little for
non-skiers, except skating and the pleasure of wandering around. One
aspiring langlaufer was very disappointed.

Access is by narrow, long and avalanche-prone road from
Domodossola (39km) south of the Simplon tunnel. Transfers from Turin
and Milan take about five hours.

Tourist office ✆ (324) 65119. Package holidays GL, HM, PQ, TH

Pearl or plain?

Saas-Fee Switzerland 1800m

Good for *Alpine charm, late holidays, family skiing, nursery slopes, beautiful scenery, freedom from cars, resort-level snow*
Bad for *Après-ski, short airport transfers, skiing convenience*

Separate resort: Saas Grund

Saas Fee calls itself the pearl of the Alps. It is certainly set, pearl-like, in the pit of a tight, deep horseshoe of mountains; and in some eyes at least it is what might be called a pearl of a ski resort. Like neighbouring Zermatt, it is one of the very few resorts to be both old-established and traffic-free – but unlike Zermatt it has not developed into a noisy international resort; horse-drawn sleighs jingle along snowy paths, past beautiful old log cabins. The setting is dramatic and beautiful, though oppressive in midwinter when little sunshine reaches the village. The skiing has in the past disappointed some visitors, and the considerable extra skiing opened up by the new Metro Alpin underground railway only partly answers the critics. Although there are excellent nursery slopes beside the resort, and splendid, open, easy slopes up the mountain, much of the skiing is on the steep side – but there is not enough of it to keep eager piste-bashers happy for long, and experts are frustrated by the lack of off-piste skiing (which is limited by glacier danger). On the other hand, Saas Fee has enormous scope for ski-touring, for which it is a major point of departure. The resort is inconvenient for weekenders, but the skiing reached via the main cable-car is now sufficiently attractive to generate long queues late in the season.

The skiing top 3500m bottom 1800m

Saas Fee has skiing all year round thanks to the Feegletscher, hanging impressively on the mountainside south of the village. But at lower altitudes the glacier is a nuisance, dividing the north-facing skiing into two areas. Most obvious from the terraces of the village hotels are the mogul-fields of the Längfluh, embraced by two arms of the glacier. There are links (just) at the top of this area to the major Felskinn sector. The Plattjen area is a north-east facing slope, closer to the village and much used by the ski-school. Last, and distinctly least, is the Hannig on the opposite side of the village – low, little and south-facing.

The **Längfluh** area is consistently fairly steep, and well suited to intermediate skiers wanting a bit of a challenge. The gondola from the extreme edge of the village to Spielboden is surmounted not only by a cable-car (to 2870m) but also by a curious drag serving the shortest genuine black run we've encountered. Instead of going back down the reds and blacks from here, or playing on the middle-of-the-road reds

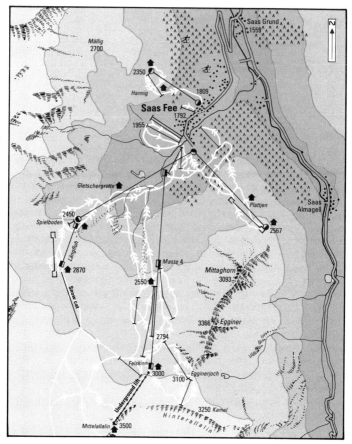

served by the top chair-lift, you can take the 'snow-cat', which serves a very gentle run back to Längfluh and connects with the Felskinn area.

The **Felskinn** skiing, normally reached by a cable-car which starts an annoying drag-lift-ride away from the edge of the resort, is more extensive. There is some very easy skiing on the top half (between 3000m and 2500m) served by drag-lifts; lower down it becomes steeper and bumpier, and inexperienced skiers can join the cable-car in mid-air at Maste 4 – though the easiest runs down are not intimidating. The Metro to Mittelallalin (3500m) has opened up more glorious open skiing, and makes it possible to ski across to Längfluh. At the top of the Metro, those up to a few metres of steep black run can put on their skis almost immediately, but the red starts an exhausting hike up the mountain and the blue starts higher than we were prepared to trudge. The bottom station of the Metro is regained via a short drag to a hole in the mountainside or via the drags to Egginerjoch and Kamel (3250m). This is the pre-Metro summer skiing, and is often closed early in the winter season; the lower drag serves a broad, easy red, the upper one a pair of short but worthwhile blacks. The black run to the Metro involves a tiring walk but is nowhere steep. In the opposite direction are steep east-facing off-piste runs, when conditions are right.

The **Plattjen** gondola runs (from the same building as that for Längfluh) up to 2567m. Its skiing is of easy-intermediate difficulty, with a slightly awkward start at the top. The main slope, above the trees, is served by a chair where moderate queues tend to form; there are easy and more difficult runs down from there through woods to the village – the black justifying its grading because of lumpy terrain rather than steepness. It is possible to ski directly across to the Felskinn cable-car.

The gondola to **Hannig** (2350m) serves short runs which are little skied except early in the season when other areas are cold or closed. New lifts to Mällig (2700m) are planned, not only improving the skiing down to Saas Fee, but also opening up new skiing to Saas Grund.

The **nursery slopes** are excellent – broad, gentle and well-placed for lunches and meeting up with other skiers; but the bottom, flat parts are not very sunny in midwinter.

All the main lift stations have **mountain restaurants** which are adequate but rarely charming; that at the top of Plattjen is particularly dire, but there is an atmospheric Berghaus half-way down the hill which compensates. The Gletschergrotte, hidden among trees off the piste down from Spielboden, is worth seeking out. There are superb close-up views of the glacier from Längfluh – worth a trip for non-skiers.

Lifts

Passes One pass covers all lifts but not the Längfluh Felskinn snow-cat. Day, afternoon and local passes available.
Cost 6-day pass SF180
Beginners Coupons for nursery lifts.

Children 30% reduction, up to 16.
Summer skiing Extensive runs from 3500m (Mitelallalin) and 3250m (Kamel) to Felskinn mid-station (2550m). Instruction available. Open all year.

Recent reports suggest that the skiing is now too attractive for the access lifts, at least in late season: huge queues build up for the Felskinn cable-car, morning and afternoon, forcing the ski school to adopt staggered class timing. Once up the mountain, no problem.

The resort

Although a small resort in a confined setting, Saas Fee is by no means compact enough to suit idle or weary ski-booted pedestrians: it spreads for over half a mile along a couple of narrow, car-free, rather hilly streets, through something like a resort centre where streets converge, along over a river to the bottom of the north-facing ski slopes, where skiers' hotels have grown up. There are depots here where you can leave your skis and boots at not exhorbitant cost. Shopping facilities are adequate, with food shops at both ends of the village.

Accommodation is mostly in traditional-looking hotels, comfortable but not luxurious, and self-catering chalets. The bulk of the resort is near the entrance car parks. Hotels over the river at the far end are much more convenient for skiers, and this is the main consideration –

there are no outstandingly attractive or unpleasant hotels. Two typical chalet-style hotels which are ideally placed for the lifts are the Waldesruh (✆ 572295) and the Derby (✆ 572345) – both medium-sized, comfortable but slightly dull.

Après-ski is limited to live bands in a couple of hotels, and one or two discos. No restaurants or bars linger on the palate or in the memory. There is floodlit night skiing once a week on the Hannig.

Ski school

Classes 2hr morning and afternoon. **Cost** 6 days SF125. Private lesson SF35/hr. **Special courses** Touring weeks (March, April, May and June).	**Children** Ski kindergarten, ages 5–12, adult hours, 6 days SF90, lunch available. Hotel du Glacier non-skiing kindergarten, ages 3–6, 9.00–5.00, 6 days with lunch SF113.

The ski school touring weeks involve several nights spent in refuges and a trip to Zermatt. Monte Rosa, Europe's second highest peak (4634m), is nearby, and a ski touring proposition.

Other activities

Cross-country 7½km loop, starts near entrance to village. Instruction available. **Not skiing** 20km cleared walks, swimming, natural ice rinks for skating,	curling, sleigh rides, tennis, fitness centre (sauna, solarium, massage), ski-bob runs, cinema.

Saas Fee is not a good resort for cross-country. Non-skiers should enjoy the attractive walks, and the village itself, but it is a bit claustrophobic. The leisure/sports centre is 'suberb'.

Travel

Airport Geneva; transfer 3½hr. **Railway** Brig; frequent buses. **Reachable resorts** Zermatt and Crans-Montana are within range for day-trips.	**Road** Via Geneva or Basel/Bern. The 28km drive from the main road near Visp is slow and may require chains.

Cars aren't much help – they have to be parked (at a charge) on the edge of the village. Within the village there are pricey horse-drawn sleighs (when it's snowy) or pricey electric carts (when it's not).

Miscellaneous

Tourist office ✆ (28) 571457. Tx 38230. **Resort beds** 2,200 in hotels, 5,800 in apartments. **Package holidays** BL, BS, BT, IG, KU, MM, SCB, SGW, SMW, SUS, SWT.	**Medical** Hospital at Visp (28km); fracture clinic, doctor, chemist, dentist in resort. **Equipment hire** 6 days skis SF90, boots SF45, X-C SF70.

Saas Grund

Saas Grund is a dull place, 250m lower, on the approach road to Saas Fee. Its own skiing is on the south- and west-facing slopes on the far side of the village from Saas Fee, the main lifts being gondolas from the village at about 1550m to Kreuzboden (2400m) and on to Hohsaas (3098m). There are a couple of short, easy runs at sunny Kreuzboden, but otherwise all the pistes are marked red or black. Above Hohsaas is the Laquinjoch; the name spells danger, and it was on the slopes around Kreuzboden that an April avalanche engulfed a party of skiers.

Which side of the Horn? It matters.

Zermatt Switzerland 1620m

Good for *Tough skiing, off-piste skiing, ski touring, beautiful scenery, mountain restaurants, big ski area, rail access, Alpine charm, freedom from cars, après-ski, late holidays, chalet holidays*
Bad for *Skiing convenience, easy road access, short airport transfers, nursery slopes*

Cervinia Italy 2005m

Good for *Nursery slopes, easy skiing, big ski area, sunny skiing, ski touring, resort-level snow, late holidays*
Bad for *Alpine charm, not skiing, lift queues, tough skiing, mountain restaurants, skiing convenience*

Although their skiing is linked, Zermatt and Cervinia are very different and separate destinations, and the only skiers who are likely to want to make much use of the link (which is expensive and very time-consuming) are those who have chosen the wrong resort.

Few resorts can rival Zermatt for skiing excitement, scenic beauty or village charm. For a combination of the three it is way out in front, and it can also boast plenty of nightlife, luxury hotels, and history. But don't expect a small unspoilt Alpine village. Zermatt is big business, catering for big-spending American and Japanese tourists as well as for the usual European skiing public. The village itself is large, with luxury shops and areas of rather anonymous modern buildings.

New lifts have done much to relieve the notorious queuing problem, but Zermatt is never going to be a convenient resort. Long and often icy walks are unavoidable. The two halves of the ski area are not linked and it still takes a long time to get around the mountains.

On the sunny side of Il Cervino (as the Matterhorn is known in Italy) is an ageing modern resort, once the showpiece of Italian ski resort development. The old climbing base of Breuil became new Cervinia, with cable-cars spanning vast glacial wastelands up to the unprecedented height of 3500m, opening up enormously long, very sunny ski runs and bringing the smart set to Cervinia's new grand hotels. Things have changed. Cervinia's lifts are exceedingly inefficient by modern standards and its skiing lacks challenge. The smart set has decamped and, with one or two exceptions, its hotels are now far from grand.

But Cervinia is still a lively and popular international resort, with plenty of British visitors. The skiing is still very high, sunny and reliable for snow, and there is nowhere in the world where beginners and timid but enthusiastic skiers can cover so much ground in scenery of such grandeur with complete confidence. Several of our most enthusiastic reporters are elderly; 'Such marvellous geriatric skiing!,' explained one.

The skiing top 3820m bottom 1620m

Zermatt

Zermatt's skiing divides naturally into three sectors covering about half of the deep, steep horseshoe of mountains which enclose the resort. On the eastern side are the two linked sectors of Blauherd and Gornergrat, both providing a mix of easy intermediate and seriously steep skiing, much of it north-facing. To the south of the resort the Schwarzsee and Klein Matterhorn lifts climb over steep north-facing slopes to the glaciers, where Europe's highest lifts provide a huge area of easy skiing, summer and winter.

The **Gornergrat/Stockhorn** skiing starts with a 40-minute train ride to Gornergrat, passing an area of excellent, very easy runs above Riffelberg – Zermatt's main nursery area, with plenty of sun and beautiful views of the Matterhorn. The run down to Zermatt has some steep sections but in good conditions is not difficult. There is a tough intermediate run towards Gant and Findeln, and some steep off-piste slopes. Beyond Gornergrat a two-stage cable-car to Stockhorn via Hohtälli stretches along a narrow, rocky crest, not climbing much but serving the wide, north-facing slopes above the Findeln glacier. This area, rarely open before February, is one of the premier tough skiing areas in the Alps, with huge mogul fields and late powder (beware crevasse and rock danger off-piste).

The **Blauherd** sector is now served by the three-minute Sunegga Express underground. There are easy, very sunny slopes between Blauherd and Sunegga and down to Findeln, and easy runs winding around the steep, wooded mountainside to the resort. There are also much steeper descents, notably the famous National downhill course, often crowded and bumpy. The **Unterrothorn** cable-car gives access to an excellent, long, steep, open face with an easier, sheltered intermediate run behind the ridge. From Unterrothorn there are also some not-very-steep, little-used south-facing runs down to Gant, for access to Stockhorn.

The **Klein Matterhorn/Schwarzsee** lifts start a brisk 15-minute walk from the centre. Cable-car and gondola climb gently over the often rocky lower slopes to Furri, where three cable-cars fan out. That to Trockener Steg is surmounted by Zermatt's flagship, the Klein Matterhorn cable-car, spanning ice falls and an almost vertical face to the highest cable-car station in Europe. A long tunnel leads to easy glacier slopes with just one moderately steep pitch in the long run down to Trockener Steg via Testa Grigia on the Italian border. Several long drag-lifts serve an enormous area of very easy skiing here, on top of the world. Unfortunately the lifts are often closed or very unpleasant in bad weather. A very beautiful off-piste run in this sector heads gently west across crevassed glacier from just below the Furggsattel towards the Matterhorn and from there either sharply round and back to Furgg or up to the top of the Hörnli lift, which involves a short climb.

Intermediates can ski down to Furgg, to the top of the second cable-car from Furri. There are some more difficult pistes and

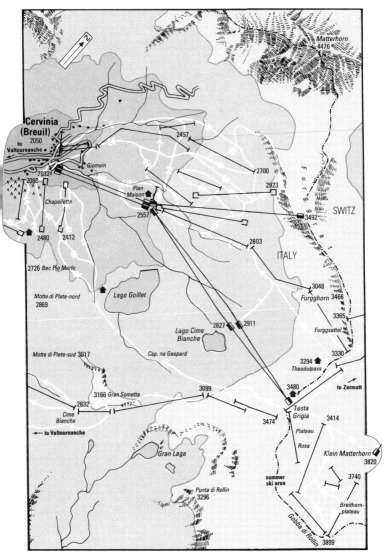

hazardous off-piste runs served by the bent Garten drag-lift and the run down from Furgg to Furri is an awkward reddish-black. In general, good skiers find the runs down from Schwarzsee more satisfying. There are several black ones plunging down towards the woods and through them to Furri, including the tough and narrow Tiefbach. The Hörnli drag-lift serves interesting north-facing gullies. Very often skiers take lifts down to Zermatt either from Schwarzsee or Furri because of poor snow cover and the difficulty of the runs, though there is a long and fairly gentle zigzag route.

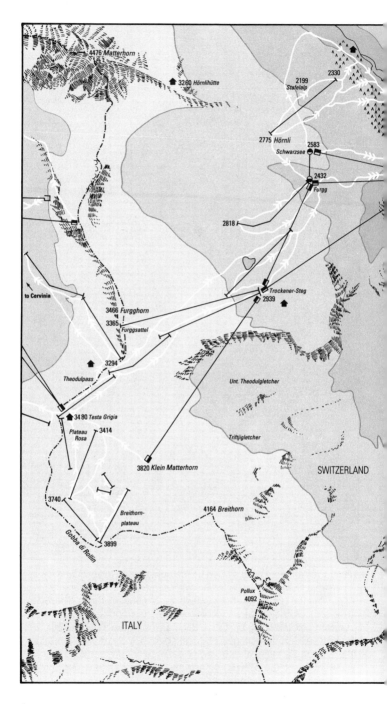

4476 *Matterhorn*

3260 *Hörnlihütte*

2330

2199
Stafelalp

2775 *Hörnli*

2583
Schwarzsee

2432
Furgg

2818

to Cervinia

Trockener-Steg
2939

3466 *Furgghorn*

3365 *Furggsattel*

3294

Theodulpass

34 80 *Testa Grigia*

*Plateau
Rosa* 3414

Unt. Theodulgletcher

Triftjigletcher

3820 *Klein Matterhorn*

SWITZERLAND

3740

*Breithorn-
plateau*

4164 *Breithorn*

Gobba di Rollin

3899

*Pollux
4092*

ITALY

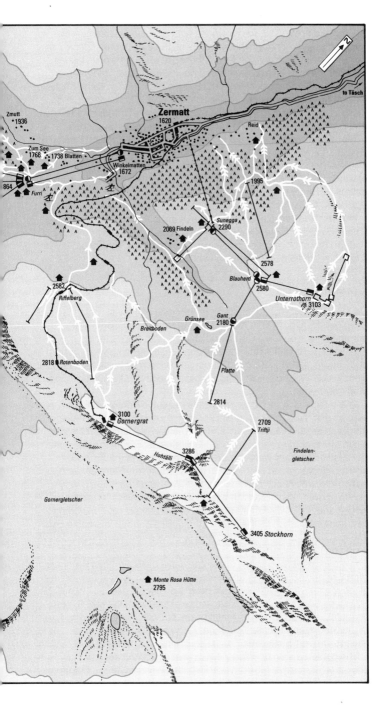

Zmutt
•1936

Zermatt
1620

Reid

Zum See
1766 •1738 Blatten

Winkelmatten
1672

1995

864 Furri

Sunegga
2290
2069 Findeln

2578

Blauherd
2580

Unterrothorn
3103

2582

Riffelberg

Breitboden

Grünsee

Gant
2180

Platte

2818 Rotenboden

2814

2709
Triftji

3100
Gornergrat

Findelen-
gletscher

Hohtälli

3286

Gornergletscher

3405 Stockhorn

Monte Rosa Hütte
2795

to Täsch

We have not visited Zermatt in the right conditions to sample the off-piste skiing. Although the slopes (with the exception of Stockhorn) do not consist of wide open faces, there are enormous possibilities, many of them steep and dangerous (rocks, crevasses and avalanches). Information is not difficult to obtain locally. Beneath the 29 local 4000-metre peaks there are vast areas of skiable glacier and thanks to the new heights reached by the lift system (Klein Matterhorn and Stockhorn) day tours do not have to be particularly arduous.

Mountain restaurants are greater in number, charm and privileged view than anywhere else in the Alps. As well as the smart, characterless new restaurants at the main lift stations there are dozens of little huts spread around the wooded slopes which make skiing a delight – skiing home at the end of the day can be a very protracted business. A worthwhile guide booklet is on sale in the resort.

Nursery slopes are few – a spacious area above Riffelberg and a small one at Sunegga. Despite the existence of very easy runs on Plateau Rosa, beginners are likely to find Zermatt a very inconvenient, expensive and probably unnerving place to ski.

Cervinia

On the Italian side of the Matterhorn the head of the valley climbs much more gently. It too is very rocky terrain and only a section of the horseshoe surrounding Cervinia is skiable, with slopes facing south and west. It is a remarkably open, sunny skiing area between 2000m and 3500m, shelving gently in steps, and broken up by clefts and lakes. Nearly all the skiing is easy and we have had few enthusiastic reports from good skiers.

The main lifts from the resort are the old cable-cars up to Plan Maison and the Cretaz drag-lifts up from the lower part of the village to the same area, a vast nursery and sunbathing plateau. The **Cretaz** chain of lifts continues on up to the Theodulpass. From the top of the lifts it is an awkward walk across to the beginning of the run down across the glaciers to Zermatt. On the Cervinia side there are long, easy motorways back down to Plan Maison, and from there a very gentle, roundabout green run back down to the resort. On the lower slopes above Cervinia there are several more direct runs, including two, shown as black on the map, in the gullies beneath the cable-cars. We saw no signs of these runs being open or skied, despite good snow conditions.

From **Plan Maison** a little cable-car with a big build-up of warnings climbs nearly 1000m over an awesome cliff to Furggen at the shoulder of the Matterhorn. A tedious walk down an internal staircase of nearly 300 steps brings you to the broad ledge at the top of the cliff. It is a beautiful, isolated, long run, mainly easy but with a couple of short, moderately steep sections near the beginning. There are some adventurous off-piste variants, not obvious to the uninitiated.

The cable-cars up to Plateau Rosa give direct and easy skiing access to Zermatt (all lifts beyond Plateau Rosa are Zermatt territory). The main run back to Cervinia is the famous Ventina, an uninterrupted run of nearly 8km for 1500m vertical. There is no great difficulty involved, apart from keeping up your momentum on the flat bits. A short way down this run there is a left fork for the run to Valtournenche, sometimes claimed as the longest piste in the Alps (starting at the Klein Matterhorn). As it happens, the run is punctuated by a short drag-lift ride up to the col (2896m) which divides Cervinia's skiing from that of **Valtournenche**. This consists of only a narrow chain of lifts and runs beside them, but provides a change of scenery and still more long, mostly easy runs down to Salette (2245m) and in good snow down through the woods, on piste or among the trees nearby, to the bottom of the Valtournenche gondola at 1610m.

Above and to the south-east of Cervinia are the **Carosello** lifts – little-used chair- and drag-lifts starting from the high part of the resort (each of the two luxury hotels has a lift outside the front door), accessible from the Ventina run. The slopes face west and north-west, are fairly steep and often unprepared, with scope for exploring between the pistes. There are runs back down to the cable-car station and, near the bob-sleigh run, down to Lago Blu below the resort.

Mountain restaurants are inadequate in number, expensive by Italian standards, and insanitary.

Nursery slopes are splendid. Enormous areas of the skiing are nursery-ish in gradient, and sporty beginners can be roaring down very long runs at the end of a week. The best nursery area is the Plan Maison plateau, but there are also slopes beside the resort.

Lifts

Passes Zermatt pass covers all Swiss lifts in network. Various partial coverage passes for different sectors. Cervinia general pass covers all Italian lifts in network, except Valtournenche gondola before 11.30. Cervinia passes of over 5 days valid for one day a week in Courmayeur. International day pass or daily supplement to Cervinia/Zermatt passes available; Zermatt supplement not valid on all Cervinia lifts.

Cost Zermatt 6-day pass SF206. Cervinia 6-day pass L110,000. International supplement SF23/L18,500, may fluctuate with exchange rates.

Children Zermatt: 50% off under 15.

Beginners Coupons or payment by the ride

Summer skiing Extensive; 8 lifts, 2935m to 3899m, accessible from both resorts.

Considering the constraints of the landscape Zermatt's lift system is impressive, despite its antiquated railway. The very swift Sunegga underground railway has done much to relieve the awful scrums for and on the Gornergrat railway, and several reports express relieved surprise at an absence of queues, even in February. Even so, it takes a long time to travel around the ski area – about an hour and a half to the Klein Matterhorn, and a long time to get across from the Sunegga Express to the skiing on Stockhorn (quicker than approaching via Gornergrat).

Cervinia's lift system, heavily dependent on small cable-cars, is not at all good. Despite doubling up of the lifts there are still very long queues at weekends and at holiday times, and it can take over two hours to Plateau Rosa; queues at Plan Maison are often worse than at the bottom. When the resort is not full the double-up lifts do not operate and there are still long waits between rides. One of the cable-cars to

Plateau Rosa has only one cabin and a trivial capacity. The cable-cars (notably Furggen) are often closed by wind, at very short notice. Cabins are filled stiflingly full. We have reports of long queues for lift passes at weekends.

The trouble with the link between the resorts is that it is so high, which makes closure (because of wind or bad visibility) frequent, at very short notice. Information is available at the bottom of the Zermatt and Cervinia lift systems, but it cannot be relied upon for the whole day. A lot of time is needed for the return journey in either direction, and the amount of skiing day trippers can do in the other resort is limited. From Zermatt it is possible to do most of Cervinia skiing in a day (in low season), whereas from Cervinia to Switzerland it is not possible to get more than a taste of what Zermatt skiing is like.

The resorts

Zermatt

Zermatt is a large, close-knit village which has grown to fill the limited space available at the foot of a steep ring of very high mountains, the Matterhorn outstandingly beautiful among them. Mountain streams rush down to fuel the thick torrent which runs through the village centre on its way down to the main Rhône valley. Officially, Zermatt is German-speaking, but locals speak a rough patois, and there are many Italian immigrant workers.

Zermatt is a world of its own, naturally cut off from Täsch and the valley below by a narrow, steep-sided pass which is prone to avalanche blockage. Cars are not admitted to the village, which is accessible only by train or taxi, and the centre is a delightful maze of snowy paths. The entire resort is built in chalet style, except for the large luxury hotels, old and new, in the centre. The very picturesque old quarter above the church is a neglected backwater, and most of the resort is new. The busy main street is lined with new hotels, expensive shops and banks. The centre is flat, and walking around is not difficult, apart from the considerable hazards of taxis and icy paths. It takes about 15 minutes to walk from the station to the bottom of the Matterhorn lifts. When there's enough snow, people ski along the village streets.

Because of the Matterhorn and its neighbours, Zermatt became a busy climbing resort in the mid 19th-century, and like Chamonix it still does as much summer as winter business. It is a fascinating place for anyone with an interest in Alpine history. In the early days, the British were prominent, and there is still a sizeable minority contingent of traditionalists in the old hotels and a new generation of keen young skiers and après-skiers. But even in winter there are three times as many Americans as British, and three times as many Germans as Americans. The style of the village is increasingly plush and expensive, and for Americanisation it comes second to St Moritz in the Alps. There is an English church.

Accommodation is mostly in hotels, new, luxurious and very expensive or simple and slightly less expensive. A few companies offer staffed chalet holidays and self-catering in chalet apartments. The least inconvenient location is probably in the middle near the river, the most inconvenient up in the old village. For up-to-the-minute facilities the luxury hotels to choose are the Zermatterhof, the Schweizerhof, the Alex or the Mont Cervin, but for style there is no beating the elegantly modernised Monte Rosa ($\emptyset$ 661131), the original Zermatt hotel, with its Alpine club mementoes and its Whymperstube bar. Most of the simpler hotels are clean and comfortable in a typically Swiss way: reporters were well pleased with the Gornergrat ($\emptyset$ 671027), near the stations. The Sport is a popular British haunt, but inconvenient.

Après-ski is very varied, with bars, restaurants and dance spots to cater for most tastes and full pockets. Youth gathers in the plastic neo-ranch-style Broken Bar/Brown Cow for drinking, pasta and disco (in separate rooms). For a more civilised atmosphere, there is Elsie's bar for snails and hock, the Alex for cocktails, or the Whymperstube, recommended by one reporter for cheaper Swiss food. The Stockhorn is recommended for meat fondue, the Tenne for 'Haute cuisine at London prices'. More than one reporter subscribes to the view (which we are inclined to share) that most restaurants serve 'honest, anonymous Swiss-American food at dishonest Swiss prices'. There is a tea-dance at the Hotel Bristol. The cheapest place to dance is the Walliserkanne – 'a bit grubby and jammed full'.

Ski school

Classes 2½hr morning and afternoon.	kindergarten, ages 6–12, 9.30–4.00, 6
Cost 6 days SF120. Private lessons	full days SF160 with meals. Non-skiing
SF90/half day (1 or 2 people).	kindergarten, ages 2–8, 8.30–5.00, 6 full
Children 33% off, under 13. Ski	days SF170 with meals.

Zermatt's ski school has a poor reputation for large classes and high prices, but we have no reports. Certainly the skiing is best suited to skiers who have done a lot of learning elsewhere. Day tours and the Haute Route to Chamonix can be arranged, as can helicopter drops if booked well in advance.

Other activities

Cross-country Winkelmatten to Tuftra	Täsch.
(3km), Furri to Schweigmatten (4km).	**Not skiing** Curling, sauna, tennis,
More extensive trails (up to 15km) to	skating, swimming, museum.

Zermatt is a skiers' resort in winter, and non-skiers tempted by the scenery and the old village should visit it in summer. Winter walks are limited, and so is the cross-country skiing (Täsch is more suitable). A visit to the graveyard will reward anyone who has a sense of history.

Travel

Airport Geneva; transfer about 5hr.	Lausanne; chains may be needed.
Railway Station in resort	**Reachable resorts** Saas Fee, Crans-
Road Access only to Täsch (5km). Via	Montana.

There is a vast car park by the station at Täsch, where someone makes a living resurrecting dead car batteries. The train runs frequently to the centre of Zermatt, where the only transport is electric and horse-drawn taxis for which there are fixed prices. Zermatt is one terminus of the spectacular Glacier Express, which runs to St Moritz via Andermatt. Zermatt is one of the few resorts which is still most conveniently reached from Britain by train.

Miscellaneous 66 11 8 1

Tourist office ✆ (28) 671031. Tx 472130
Medical Hospital at Visp; fracture clinic, dentist, doctor, chemist in resort.
Equipment hire 6 days skis SF82, boots SF42, X-C SF68.

Resort beds 6,600 in hotels, 10,800 in apartments.
Package holidays BL, IG, JM, KU, MM, SCh, SGW, SUP, SWT, TH.

Cervinia

Cervinia is a styleless collection of ageing modern buildings set very high in a bleak, open setting beneath the massive granite bulk of the Matterhorn (which was designed to be seen from Switzerland). In the centre at the foot of the slopes is a couple of lively streets of bars and shops at the foot of the slopes. Some of it is reserved for pedestrians, the rest a one-way circuit, plagued with weekend traffic. Above the cable-car station, buildings (mostly the smarter hotels) stretch on up the hill towards the Carosello lifts, with the two luxury hotels at the top enjoying the best views of the Matterhorn and glaciers. Apart from this upper part, it is a compact resort, easily enough negotiated on foot although the climb up to the cable-car station is tiresome. its clientèle consists of local weekenders and the British. Despite its unlovely looks, several reporters assure us that it is a friendly place. Shopping is adequate for skiing and self-catering purposes.

Except for some new apartment development on the lower slopes near the cable-car, most **accommodation** is in simple hotels. Most of the hotels used by UK operators are in the main centre of the village, within walking distance of the Cretaz drag-lifts. We had few enthusiastic reports of accommodation and several very unenthusiastic ones. The more comfortable hotels are more spaciously set above the cable-car station, beneath the Carosello lifts. Only the smartly modernised, expensive Grand Cristallo (✆ 948125) is at all luxurious and cosmopolitan. One regular visitor to the resort recommends the Fosson (✆ 949125), 'simple, friendly, popular with Italians', and well placed for the drag-lifts. The Al Piolet (✆ 949161) and the Edelweiss (✆ 949078) are relatively attractive and cheerful; the first is well-placed for the cable-car station. Just above it, the Hermitage (✆ 948998) is a quiet, comfortable hotel beside the road up to the Cristallo.

Après-ski is not very varied, consisting of hotel bars without much character, except for the Dragon Pub in the Hotel Pelissier, a favourite British haunt with British beer on tap. There are several discothèques, and occasionally evening bob-sleigh to watch. Eating out is not very cheap, but there is no shortage of restaurants and we have good reports, especially of the Copa Pan which describes itself as 'naif-elegante'.

Ski school

Classes 3hr, mornings only.
Cost 6 days L85,000. Private lessons
L20,000/hr.

Children No kindergarten facilities.
Special courses Heli-skiing, touring.

We have mixed reports of the quality of instruction. There are one or two native English-speakers at the ski school, available for private lessons.

Other activities

Cross-country Two 5km trails (graded medium), one of them near the resort, one a mile or two out on the way to

Valtournenche, at Perreres.
Not-skiing Natural ice rink (until March), hotel pools/sauna, bowling.

Cervinia is not recommended for either cross-country skiers or non-skiers.

Travel

Airport Turin; transfer about 2½hr.
Railway Châtillon (27km); several buses daily.
Road Via Lyon/Annecy or Geneva, Mont

Blanc Tunnel; chains may be needed.
Reachable resorts Zermatt (linked by lift), Courmayeur (covered by lift pass).

Coach excursions are organised to enable skiers to make use of the reciprocal arrangement with Courmayeur, about an hour and a half away in good conditions. Not many reporters thought the trip worthwhile. Having a car in the resort is not much help – parking is difficult, especially near the cable-car, and there are traffic problems around the resort. There is no public transport within the resort.

Miscellaneous

Tourist office ∅ (166) 94136.
Tx 211822.
Medical Hospital at Aosta (52km); fracture clinic, doctor, chemist in resort.
Equipment hire 6 days skis L30,000,

boots L20,000, X-C L25,000.
Resort beds 2,150 in hotels, 3,000 in apartments.
Package holidays BS, CI, EN, HA, HO, IT, MV, PP, TH.

Plaine Morte resort

Crans-Montana Switzerland 1500m

Good for *Sunny skiing, beautiful scenery, big ski area, family skiing, cross-country skiing, nursery slopes, après-ski, not skiing, rail access*
Bad for *Alpine charm, resort-level snow, tough skiing, late holidays*

Separate resort: Anzère

Crans and Montana, once separate, have now merged to form the largest resort in Switzerland – a vast suburban sprawl whose main quality is a splendid south-facing balcony setting, high above the Rhône Valley on a wooded ledge broad enough for a golf course (which hosts the Swiss Open). On a fine day in December the resort gets eight hours of sun, when Grindelwald gets one. As they have grown together the distinction between simple Montana for skiers and smart Crans for furs, bridge and golf has become less and less noticeable. Both parts of the resort lack village atmosphere, with residential outskirts, traffic jams and one-way systems, parking meters, and concrete shopping precincts not obviously geared to wintersports. The building style is mostly urban and undistinguished. The resort has characterless comfort and the multiple amenities of a conference town, with all the dullness of Switzerland at its worst and none of the charm of Switzerland at its best. Despite the many smart shops in Crans (Cartier, Gucci, caviar, furs) the resort as a whole is expensive without being stylish and its skiing is extensive without being particularly interesting.

And yet we have reports from satisfied customers. What they tell us is that the comfortable hotels and all the off-slope facilities (including beautiful walks and cross-country trails) count for less than the broad area of south-facing, panoramic, intermediate skiing; no doubt it is very agreeable when the sun is strong enough for sunbathing satisfaction, but has not yet managed to do serious damage to the snow.

The skiing top 2927m bottom 1500m

There are three well-linked areas accessible from four base stations along the broad south-facing mountainside. There are one or two difficult runs and some off-piste skiing for early risers lucky with snow conditions, but in general the skiing is much more suitable for leisurely than adventurous skiers. Virtually all of the skiing is between 1500m and 2500m and is evenly split between open and wooded terrain; the exception is the Plaine Morte glacier and the single run down from it.

The main lifts out of Crans and Montana meet up at **Cry d'Err**, at the heart of the western sector of the ski area – the one most used by holiday skiers and the most suitable for the timid. Most of the skiing nearby is easy, and the run to Chetseron is flat enough for

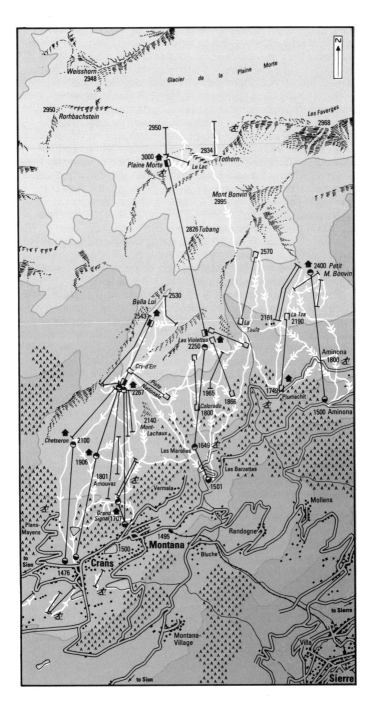

near-beginners. The area above Grand Signal, reached by short gondola from Montana, is a crowded junction of lifts and pistes which serves as the nursery area. Runs down to Crans and Montana are pretty paths, not always easy to distinguish from roads and footpaths. The woods below Chetseron sometimes provide some good off-piste skiing. There is some tougher skiing from Bella Lui, notably the excellent Nationale downhill course to Les Barzettes, and several off-piste runs, down to Les Violettes and beside the Nationale lift.

The **Violettes** area, accessible by easy piste from the Verdets lifts as well as by the Nationale, provides some tougher intermediate runs down to Les Barzettes, with a big mogul-field by the Colorado lift. The great attraction of the area is the Plaine Morte cable-car, which adds a spectacular new dimension to the skiing, climbing to the edge of an oceanic expanse of flat glacier with a breathtaking panorama of peaks to the south. There is a little skiing at the top, open in summer, and a single long run down, manageable for most intermediate skiers. It roughly follows the course of the first Kandahar downhill race in 1911, subsequently transplanted to Mürren. Adventurous off-piste skiers occasionally venture down into the steep, dangerous valley below Les Faverges and round behind Petit Bonvin to Aminona.

The end of the serious part of the Plaine Morte run is at **Toula**, at the bottom of a steep-sided valley which provides the toughest skiing in the region, genuinely black. Neither of the black runs is a necessary part of the route to or from **Aminona**'s skiing. This consists of open, easy runs at the top between La Tza and Petit Bonvin, and some tougher slopes in the woods above Aminona, with some off-piste in the trees, and an easy alternative from the bottom of the Barmaz chair-lift.

Nursery slopes are excellent at Crans. There is flat skiing, with baby lifts, on the golf course, and easy runs around Cry d'Err. Montana's Grand Signal area is crowded and a bit steep, but has the advantage of being part of the main ski area.

Mountain restaurants are in all the obvious places, but there are few in the Violettes and Aminona sectors. Apart from the excellent restaurant at the mid-station of the Crans gondola, they are unremarkable, but many are easily accessible to walker and cross-country skiers as well as downhillers.

Lifts

Passes General pass covers all lifts and ski bus. Available for all periods including 'hourly' passes giving a refund when handed in early.
Beginners Coupons.

Cost 6-day pass SF147. 8% off in lowseason. 10% off families of four plus.
Children 40% off, under 16.
Summer skiing Small area from 2800m to 2950m. 2 lifts. 12 km X-C trail.

Reporters are generally satisfied with the lift system. The main queuing is at ski school time for the Cry d'Err gondolas from Crans and Montana, for the the Verdets lifts and for the Plaine Morte cable-car in fine weather. The Toula and Nationale lifts are now chairs.

The resort

Crans stretches up through the woods to Plans Mayens (1620m). Montana's upper suburb is Vermala (1600m), a string of residential chalets and a couple of tall hotel blocks. East of Montana the road along the mountainside is built up as far as Les Barzettes, a convenient skiing access point with some hotels but no resort life. Aminona is a long way from the rest of the resort and consists of no more than a large car park for local skiing day-trippers and a cluster of tall modern apartment blocks.

Accommodation is mostly in apartments and comfortable hotels, some of them modern and very expensive, others long-established and old-fashioned. Staffed chalet holidays are also available. The resort is large and the lift departures are a long walk from some hotels in the centre of Crans and at the eastern end of Montana near the Sierre funicular station. Among the expensive hotels, the Parc ($\emptyset$ 414101), opened in 1892 and set beside the water in Montana, is handsomely traditional. The Hauts de Crans ($\emptyset$ 415553) is brand new, a luxury chalet-style development in the woods above Montana, well-placed for skiers and walkers. The Etoile ($\emptyset$ 411671), National ($\emptyset$ 412681) and Robinson ($\emptyset$ 411353) are simple hotels within easy walking distance of the Crans lifts; the Robinson is friendly and has a good restaurant. The very friendly old Mont Blanc ($\emptyset$ 412343) is particularly beautifully set above Plans Mayens, a long way from the resort but beside the pistes down from Chetseron and excellent for walks and cross-country.

Après-ski includes discos, lots of bars and tea-rooms, a cinema in each centre, and a casino in Crans. There is no shortage of expensive restaurants, with much more variety than in most Swiss resorts. Montana has a wider range of inexpensive places to eat and drink, including a pizzeria and a noisy, crowded pub.

Ski school

Classes 2hr mornings, all day excursion on Fridays.	Children Ski kindergarten, ages up to 12, 20% off adult cost. Non-ski kindergarten, ages 3–6, 8.30–4.30, 6 days with lunch SF210.
Cost 6 days SF76, including Friday excursion. Private lessons SF35/hr.	

Although lifts have taken most of the touring out of Crans-Montana skiing, it is still a good place for tours, notably up to the Wildstrubel and Wildhorn from Plaine Morte and over the other side towards Gstaad, Lenk and Adelboden. The ski school has guides.

Other activities

Cross country 40km in three areas. 15km (easy) around Crans; 13km (more difficult) across the mountain between Plan Mayens and Aminona via Grand Signal; 12km trail at Plaine Morte, open in summer.	Not skiing Skating, curling, swimming (hotel pools), tennis, toboggan run, ski bob, fitness centre, bowling, 50km walks, indoor golf, bridge, hot-air balloon rides, squash.

Crans-Montana is an excellent resort for X-C and non-skiers. There are long, sunny and beautiful walks, many of them beside the X-C tracks, punctuated by restaurants with sun terraces on the lower slopes of the Alpine skiing area. The Hotel Aïda Castel in Montana has weekly bridge tournaments, and there are frequent curling tournaments.

Travel

Airport Geneva; transfer about 3hr.
Railway Sierre (15km); funicular or bus to resort.
Road Via Pontarlier, Lausanne; chains may be needed.
Reachable resorts Saas Fee, Zermatt, Verbier (via Super Nendaz), Champéry.

The ski-bus is an invaluable complement to the lift system, running regularly to a time-table between Crans and Aminona, serving all the main lift departures. There is no evening service. The resort is easy to reach by car, and having a car is a considerable asset given the extent of the resort and skiing. Parking centrally is difficult and restricted.

Miscellaneous

Tourist office Crans ✆ (27) 412132. Tx 473173. Montana ✆ (27) 413041. Tx 473203.
Medical Hospital at Sierre (15km); fracture clinic, doctor, dentist, chemist in resort.
Equipment hire 6 days skis SF96, boots SF41, X-C SF70.
Resort beds 5,000 in hotels, 25,000 in apartments.
Package holidays BL, BT, IG, IT, JM, KU, MM, SCG, SPT, SWT, TC, TH.

Anzère 1430m

Anzère is a small modern resort just along the hill from Crans-Montana but with a quite separate ski area. It consists mainly of apartment buildings, cleverly disguised to look like chalets, with a car-free commercial precinct in the centre, where there are a couple of hotels. The village is built on a slope (1430m to 1550m) but there are lifts from both top and bottom, so location of apartment is not critical.

The skiing area (up to 2420m) is small and very sunny, with mostly easy and intermediate skiing above the tree-line, including a good nursery area at the top of the mountain, with restaurant at hand. There are longer runs through the woods to the village offering more variety and challenge – changing snow conditions through the day can create treacherous ice mogul-fields which may prompt the most accomplished skiers to go down by lift. At the bottom of the long, gentle, east-facing Combe de Serin run down to Les Rousses (1780m) you can grill your own lunch at the restaurant. Anzère is small (about 6,500 beds) and the lifts are hardly ever crowded.

The resort is quiet after dark, but there are a couple of discos and some good restaurants. There are two cross-country trails (total 15 km) and marked walking paths through the woods at resort level. Other facilities include an artificial skating and curling rink, and a swimming pool with sauna. There are skiing and non-skiing kindergartens. A lift pass for seven non-consecutive days is available – attractive for visitors with a car wanting to branch out.

Tourist office ✆ (27) 382519. Package holidays MM, PS, TC, TH.

Jobs for the girls

Verbier 1500m

Good for *Off-piste skiing, tough skiing, big ski area, ski touring, après-ski, easy road access, beautiful scenery, sunny skiing, rail access, chalet holidays, self-catering holidays*
Bad for *Skiing convenience, lift queues, easy skiing, not skiing*

Linked resorts: Haute Nendaz, Thyon 2000

Lots of smart young Britons go to Verbier for social reasons. It offers a wider range of chalet accommodation (staffed and self-catering) than any other resort, which means lots of winter job opportunities and a good social life for the seasonal immigrants and their house guests. Lots of keen skiers of all ages go for the skiing – a varied and beautiful ski area which provides some formidable black runs and tremendous off-piste skiing. But there is a lot wrong with Verbier's skiing. There are lift bottlenecks where big queues are common; the main ski area around Les Attelas is small, and too congested for the good of the pistes or skiers; the only piste out of this area is a long tough black; and, not least, the lift pass is the most expensive in Europe.

The resort is a vast sprawl of chalets and chalet-style hotels, spacious to a fault and devoid of character. Although fashionable in its way, it is loud rather than stylish, with none of the glitter of traditionally grand resorts. The après-ski is lively but casual, and there are no sumptuous hotels or inviting shop windows.

There are quieter and smaller resorts in the neighbouring valleys with access to Verbier's skiing, in theory at least. Haute Nendaz is the main alternative, better placed for skiers who want to explore the whole region. It is a large and amorphous apartment resort, and the lift queues and layout make it best suited to skiers with a car. Veysonnaz and Thyon 2000 are much smaller modern self-catering resorts at the eastern end of the ski area. Thyon is high, open and convenience-oriented, and well suited to families and timid skiers. Veysonnaz (1230m) is set below it among the trees, at the bottom of some splendid woodland runs.

The skiing top 3328m bottom 821m

Verbier's local skiing takes place in two separate areas, with lift departures at opposite ends of the resort. The two are linked by off-piste runs which are often skied into a piste-like state.

The smaller area is **Savoleyres**, nearly always pleasantly quiet, and reached by lifts starting high above the centre. The runs down on the sunny Verbier side of the mountain are mostly open and intermediate, and there may be excellent spring snow skiing beneath the Pierre Avoi.

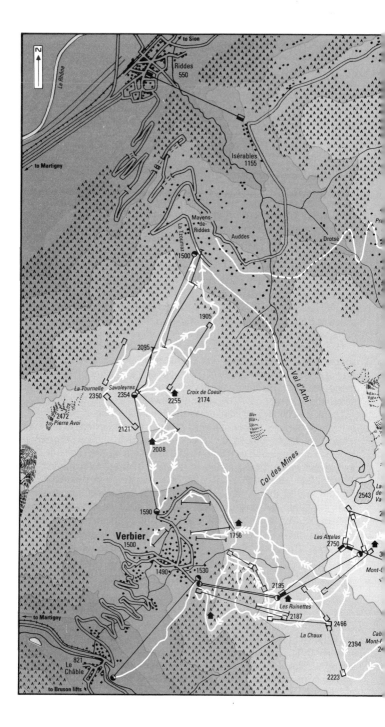

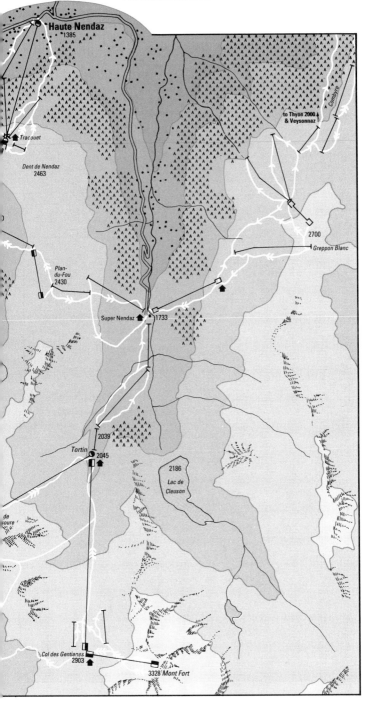

Haute Nendaz
1385

Tracouet

Dent de Nendaz
2463

to Thyon 2000
& Veysonnaz

2700

Greppon Blanc

Plan-
du-Fou
2430

Super Nendaz 1733

2039

Tortin 2045

2186
Lac de
Cleuson

de
soure

Col des Gentianas
2903

3328 Mont Fort

Combyre

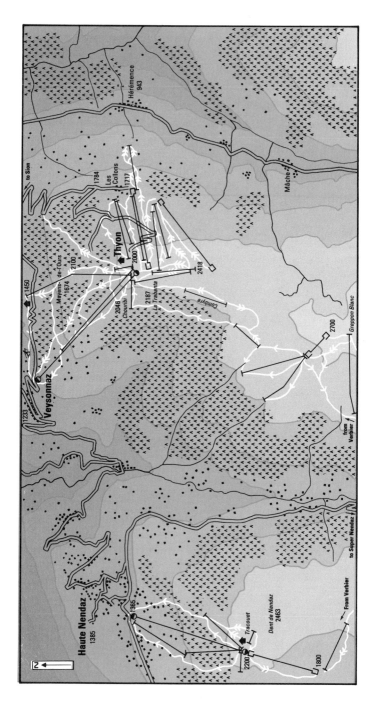

Snow conditions on the lower slopes are particularly unreliable and difficult. On the other side of Savoleyres there are long north-facing trails, none of them very difficult, through the woods to La Tsoumaz, little skied and usually with good snow.

At the other end of the village various alternative lifts go up to the heart of Verbier's skiing on the slopes beneath the ridge of **Les Attelas**. The skiing in the sheltered Lac des Vaux bowl covers a wide range of intermediate difficulty and the area is popular with ski school classes just off the nursery slopes. Skiing down towards Ruinettes is tougher, with a mogul-field near the top which may persuade many timid skiers that the best way down to the resort is by lift. From Ruinettes to Verbier there is a good variety of runs, with a blue path as well as tough runs directly down through the trees for keen mogul skiers. These wooded slopes are very useful in bad weather. A much-used way home from Lac des Vaux is the attractive Col des Mines off-piste route which runs round from the bottom of the lifts before crossing over the ridge to the south-facing slopes above the nursery lifts. Although not difficult, this slope is often unsafe. An alternative off-piste run is the Val d'Arbi, prettily down through the woods to La Tsoumaz.

The cable-car from Les Attelas to Mont Gelé is small and short but serves some of Verbier's most famous skiing – all of it off-piste. There are very extreme couloirs down to Les Attelas which are occasionally skied, but the main runs are the longer steep and open ones behind Mont Gelé, ending up at Tortin or La Chaux. The slopes are rocky and exposed, and require good snow cover for safety.

The main link with the eastern half of the skiing is the chair-lift from Lac des Vaux to Col de Chassoure at the top of the notorious **Tortin** black run – a dauntingly long, wide and steep mogul-field which may or may not be a piste. It is a splendid run for skiers who like that kind of thing, but is often congested by skiers who don't. The two-stage **Mont-Fort** cable-car from Tortin plateau has added enormously to the available skiing. The run from the top (where there are spectacular views) starts with a short steep mogul-field where, in contrast to Tortin, the danger is caused by hot skiers going too fast. Around the mid-station there are some splendid, open, very easy runs served by drag-lifts, but the only run down to Tortin is a long, not too tough black, with some excellent off-piste variants. The long run down from Col des Gentianes to La Chaux is much less difficult (a lot of it is path) and provides splendid views of the Grand Combin and neighbouring glaciers. In good snow it is possible to ski to Le Châble, on an off-piste run where vineyard terraces provide abrupt drops. From Mont-Fort the run is said to be 18km for the exceptional 2500m drop.

From Tortin there are easy runs down to the Super-Nendaz skiing service station where lifts branch east for Thyon 2000 and Veysonnaz, and west for Haute-Nendaz. A long chain of short lifts and easy runs along the upper slopes of the mountainside leads to the high modern resort of **Thyon 2000**, where there are broad nursery slopes and some excellent long runs down through the woods to Veysonnaz and Mayens-de-l'Ours. On the other side of Super Nendaz two steep drag-lifts to **Plan-du-Fou** give access to an off-piste run (not difficult) to

Prarion and on down through woods past Drotsé to Auddes, where a special bus links up with La Tsoumaz/Savoleyres lifts.

Haute Nendaz skiing is a simple arrangement of long intermediate north-facing runs above the resort, served by the long Tracouet gondola or alternative drags, and shorter south-facing slopes behind Tracovet down to Prarion. The new Plan-du-Fou cable-car makes it possible to get to Super-Nendaz and Tortin on skis.

Above Le Châble at **Bruson** there is a quiet skiing area, between 1000m and 2300m described by a reporter as surprisingly interesting and extensive, and very pleasantly uncrowded. The lift pass also encourages excursions to other resorts in nearby valleys, notably **Champex** and **La Fouly** in the beautifully secluded Val Ferret, which is very well suited to cross-country skiing as well as having some small but far from boring Alpine ski areas. There is also some excellent high skiing, on piste and off it, above the entrance to the **St Bernard** tunnel, around the pass (between 1900 and 2800m) and down into the Italian sun on the other side.

Verbier's **nursery slopes**, between Ruinettes and Savoleyres, have been somewhat encroached upon by the growth of the resort, but they are still good – sunny and gentle. The ski area is not suitable for skiers progressing from nursery to piste.

Mountain restaurants are not very plentiful, and the one at Tortin is very inadequate and expensive. The Carrefour restaurant at the top of the nursery slopes and the bottom of the pistes down to the resort is friendly and very popular throughout the day and evening. Particularly attractive, out-of-the-way restaurants are at Clambin (on one of the indirect runs from Ruinettes) and the Cabane de Mont-Fort.

Lifts

Passes One pass covers all the lifts and ski buses in the four valleys, and lifts in several other nearby ski areas (Bruson, Val Ferret). Day and half-day passes, 10 days non-consecutive, and passes excluding Mont-Fort available.
Cost 6 days SF224 (inc Mont-Fort), SF198 (exc Mont-Fort). Mont-Fort supplement SF10/day. Super St Bernard supplement SF10/day. Reductions for families.
Children 50% off, up to 16.
Beginners Day and half-day passes for nursery lifts.
Summer skiing Small area at Mont-Fort 2700m to 3300m.

Verbier has an unenviable reputation for lift queues. The new 6-seater gondola has doubled capacity to Ruinettes and relieved queues in the resort greatly, but there are still long queues at weekends for the 4-seater gondola which gives direct access from Le Châble to Les Attelas, with few spaces for skiers who want to join at Verbier. A high-season report tells of 'horrific' queues at Haute Nendaz – for the lifts out of the resort in the morning and the bus and lifts back to it in the afternoon. The new Plan-du-Fou cable-car from Haute Nendaz has revived the old problem of long queues for the Tortin gondola. Usually, but not reliably, Tortin and La Chaux lifts stay open past the official closing time to clear any backlog. The top section of Mont-Fort is often very crowded in good weather from mid-morning onwards. Passes are only very occasionally inspected: if you're caught without one they take your skis away.

The resort

Verbier is splendidly set on a wide, sloping, sunny ledge high above Le Châble, with beautiful views of the mountains which separate Switzerland, Italy and France. A central square is the focal point of the resort, surrounded by a complicated one-way system of busy streets, often congested at weekends, when all the second-home owners pour into town. Most of the shops, bars and hotels are on, or close to, the square and the street up to the Medran lifts. Below it there is still a bit of an old village backwater, but most of Verbier's continuing expansion has taken place across the broad slopes between Ruinettes and Savoleyres, now a vast suburban chalet-town, where it is very easy to get lost among so many identical chalets. Shopping is good but not spread widely around the resort.

Accommodation offered by British operators is mostly in chalets, of which there is a huge variety. Location matters a lot – the top of the resort is good for skiing but very tiring for après-ski and especially inconvenient for self-caterers who face long walks to and from shops. Most of the hotel accommodation is central: we had good reports of the small Les Chamois ($\emptyset$ 76402) 'comfortable, good food, convenient for Medran'. Other central, comfortable hotels include the large, friendly Hotel de la Poste ($\emptyset$ 75681) and its less expensive modern annexe L'Auberge ($\emptyset$ 575272). There is some much cheaper accommodation in Le Châble for budget skiers with no care for the bright lights and British voices.

Après-ski is livelier than in many chalet resorts. As well as all the chalet-party parties there are loud and popular bars, notably the Nelson, a typical plush Continental pub with draught bitter. Of the discos, the Farm Club is the smartest and very expensive, the Scotch cheapest and very crowded. There is a wide range of restaurants, from very expensive to simple pizzas at the crowded Fer à Cheval. Booking is essential for most restaurants on Friday and Saturday evenings. Reporters recommend Robinsons and Le Caveau, the second specialising in fondue and raclette.

Ski school

Classes 2¼hr mornings.
Cost 6 consecutive half-days SF73.
Private lessons SF35/hr.
Special courses Cours de Godille (wedel courses) and ski tours.

Children Ski kindergarten, ages 3–10, 9.00–4.30, 6 days with lunch SF175. Non-ski kindergarten, ages 18mth up, 8.30–5.30, 6 days with lunch SF180.

A second ski school, L'Ecole du Ski Fantastique, doesn't take beginners and specialises in off-piste skiing, adventure skiing, heli-skiing, and tours. Verbier is on the Haute Route between Chamonix and Zermatt, so tourers can find plenty to do.

Other activities

Cross-country 4km trail at Verbier, 20km at Le Châble, 4km at Bruson.
Not skiing Skating, curling, swimming, sauna, fitness centre, cinema, ski-bob, 15km cleared paths.

Verbier is not generally suitable for cross-country or non-skiers, but several reporters enjoyed the facilities at the smart new sports centre (squash, swimming, artificial ice rink). Ski-bobbing is popular on Savoleyres (instruction is available), but not permitted elsewhere.

Travel

Airport Geneva; transfer 2½hr.
Reachable resorts Champéry, Crans-Montana, Anzère, Chamonix (some distance, over the Col des Montets).

Railway Le Châble (15km); bus or gondola to resort.
Road Via Pontarlier, Lausanne; chains may be needed.

Regular but not very frequent buses link Savoleyres and Medran lifts with the Place Centrale from about 8.30am to 7.30pm. They are free to lift pass holders and get very crowded at peak times. Verbier is one of the most accessible of the big Swiss resorts, from which it suffers at weekends. There is lots of traffic in the centre and parking is difficult and vigorously policed. There's a multi-storey car park at the entrance to the resort. Having a car is useful for saving evening walks, and exploring the fringe areas covered by the lift pass.

Miscellaneous

Tourist office ✆ (26) 76222. Tx 473247.
Medical Clinic, doctor, dentist, chemist in resort; hospital in Martigny (20km).
Equipment hire 6 days skis SF64, boots SF37, X-C SF64.

Resort beds 2,200 in hotels, 22,000 in chalets and apartments.
Package holidays AT, BL, BS, BT, BV, CW, EN, JM, MM, NE, PS, SCG, SKW, SMG, SMW, SUP, SUS, TH.

Haute Nendaz 1350m

High up on the southern wall of the Rhône Valley above Sion, a steep sprawl of second-home and resort development climbs from the old village of Nendaz to the north-facing ski slopes of Tracouet. At the top, Nendaz Station and Haute Nendaz have merged to form a long, hilly hairpin resort, with most of the accommodation a 15-minute walk below the lifts. It is a large, quiet, self-catering place without much village atmosphere. Unfortunately its lift system is inadequate and inconvenient, and for many skiers the day starts with a queue for the bus up to **Super-Nendaz**, no more than a cluster of service buildings at the foot of lifts up to Tortin, but genuinely convenient: the hotel Siviez (✆ 882458) is very cut off in the evening, but good for skiers, who can be at Mont-Fort long before the crowds from Verbier. There are a few hotels in the main resort; Le Déserteur (✆ 882455) is friendly, simple and lively, and not too inconveniently placed (there is a bus stop outside). There is a lift pass for the Nendaz/Veysonnaz half of the ski area as well as for the whole region, but it is not much cheaper than the pass including Verbier. There are 20km of cross-country trails, an artificial ice rink, swimming, squash, long walks and an all-day kindergarten.

Tourist office ✆ (27) 881444. Tx 38643. Package holidays IG, SKW.

Portes du Soleil: open invitation

Avoriaz France 1800m

Good for *Big ski area, nursery slopes, skiing convenience, family skiing, freedom from cars, short airport transfers, resort-level snow, self-catering holidays*
Bad for *Not skiing, Alpine charm, après-ski, mountain restaurants*

Linked resorts: Champéry, Les Crosets, Champoussin, Morgins, Châtel, Morzine

If 'Portes du Soleil' doesn't tempt you, the promoters of this huge Franco-Swiss ski area have a ready supply of other slogans. How about 'Ski sans frontière'? Or 'Le plus grand domaine skiable du monde'? This last may sound familiar, because the rival French ski area of the Trois Vallées has for years been awarding itself the very same distinction. The fact that neither area has established its superiority over the other should not be taken to mean that they are indistinguishable. Whereas the Trois Vallées is four adjacent, densely mechanised ski areas efficiently linked together, the Portes du Soleil is a looser network of skiing in as many as 15 resorts, some of them linked up in only twos and threes. And although there is a core circuit of skiing linking the resorts of Avoriaz and Châtel in France with Morgins and Champéry in Switzerland, that circuit cannot be compared to the Trois Vallées. Nevertheless, it is the linked skiing of these resorts (and one or two smaller Swiss ones) which draws people back. The skiing in Avoriaz caters well for most standards of skier, and the circuit can be done by early intermediates with a sense of adventure.

Avoriaz is much the most popular resort with British skiers. It is one of the most individual of French purpose-built resorts, built on a steep slope, in a bold architectural style which fits in with the high, craggy surroundings better than most such developments. It has adopted neither the monolith approach nor the multiple hamlet approach, but is basically a village made up of apartment blocks. There is skiing below it, above it, beside it, through it; but it is not quite as convenient as it sounds, because most of the skiing ends up at the foot of the village and you often need to take a lift to get home. It is predominantly a family self-catering resort, and is not fashionable or smart, but has more après-ski life than many other such places. The apartments in which you cater for yourself are unlikely to be the high point of your holiday.

The main alternatives for British skiers are Champéry and Morgins in Switzerland. Champéry is an atmospheric old mountainside village, its long main street lined by wooden chalets; it is not ideally placed for skiing, whether on the circuit or off it. Morgins is a pleasant, spacious, chalet-style resort, mainly of recent development, which itself forms a link in the circuit, between Champéry and Châtel.

The skiing top2275m bottom 1100m

The skiing covered by the Portes du Soleil lift pass embraces hundreds of miles of piste. We are limiting ourselves to the main circuit, where most British visitor spend their time.

Avoriaz The skiing around Avoriaz itself can be divided into four areas. Above the village is an upward extension of the main nursery slopes, Le Plateau, with a variety of drags serving runs from green to very green – a splendid though rather exposed area for confidence-building. At the bottom of the village there are essentially three alternative directions.

Directly south of the village is the main Hauts Forts sector, which

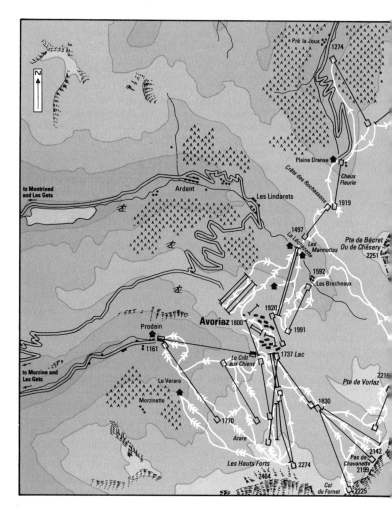

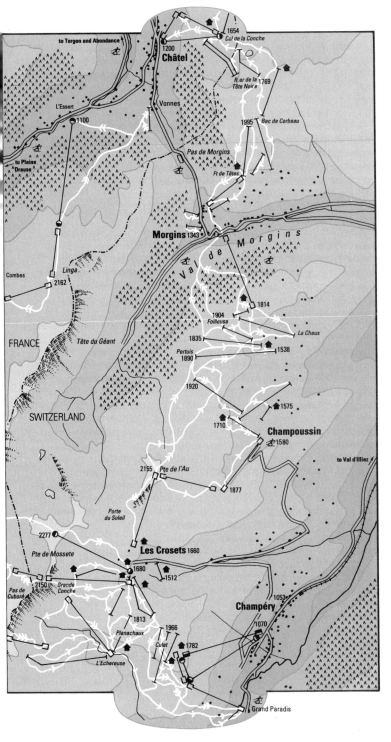

to Torgon and Abondance

Châtel
1200
1654
Col de la Conche

R. er de la 1769
Tête Noire

L'Essert
1100
Vonnes

1995 Bec de Corbeau

to Plaine
Drause

Pas de Morgins

Ft de Têtes

Morgins 1343

Val de Morgins

Combes
2162 Linga

FRANCE Tête du Géant

1814
1904
Foilleusa
1835 La Chaux
1538
Pertuis
1890

SWITZERLAND

1920

1575

1710 Champoussin
1580

to Val d'Illiez

2155 Pte de l'Au

1877

Porte
du Soleil

2277

Pte de Mossete

Les Crosets 1660

1053

2150 1680
Grande 1512
Conche

Champéry
1070

Pas de
Cuboré

1813

1966

Planachaux

1782

Culet

L'Echereuse

Grand Paradis

from Avoriaz looks steeper than it is. There are some trees towards the bottom, but the skiing is mainly above the tree-line; there are several marked pistes but the whole bowl becomes a piste as skiers stray all over it. The runs are all easy, getting a little more difficult towards the bottom. Unfortunately, they get very crowded; the ski school comes up here and so do the fledgling racers, who occasionally close off part of the piste for practice.

A long chair starting on the left but veering right from the same area at the bottom of the village takes you to the most challenging skiing in Avoriaz. There are several routes descending all or part of the way towards Prodain, 650m below Avoriaz, and over 1300m below Les Hauts Forts. The mogulled pistes become narrower as you descend into the trees, with an easier variant via the Le Crot chair-lift. The runs are crowded in the late afternoon, and dodgy for snow, but very valuable in bad weather.

The third direction is by chair and drag to the north-east-facing bowl between Pas de Chavanette and Col du Fornet. Here there are several marked runs but it is another area of wide open, intermediate skiing above the tree-line where you can ski virtually wherever you want; there is an easy trail back to the bottom of the village. An alternative way back from Chavanette for adventurous intermediates is over into the next valley – a lovely, easy run after the top mogul-field – down to Les Brochaux and Les Marmottes. Lifts up either side take you to Avoriaz or set you off on the clockwise circuit to Châtel.

Champéry-Les Crosets-Champoussin Chavanette is where the skiing of Avoriaz meets the big, open ski-fields of these three Swiss resorts. It starts with the notorious 'Swiss Wall' – a long, steep mogul slope of about 300m vertical, easily covered in a single fall when snow is hard. Severity and danger depend critically on the very variable snow conditions – the slope gets a lot of sun. You can take the chair-lift down instead, and it is no disgrace. There is acres of open easy skiing served by the drags either side of the Chavanette chair, connecting with the Planachaux slopes above Champéry, and with the adjacent bowl of Les Crosets. Planachaux is reached from Champéry by gondola or cable-car, or by chair-lift from Grand Paradis. The pistes down to the valley end at this point, having wound their way through hamlets and across the river – an interesting route, and not difficult, but hard work. There are minibuses from and to Champéry.

Les Crosets sits above the tree-line surrounded by abundant, wide open pistes – good easy to intermediate skiing, some of it north-facing but most of it sunny. There are lifts up to points on the French border, that to Cubore serving a steep unprepared (and often uncovered) black slope at the top which mellows as it descends. Via the Pointe de l'Au, a series of linked drags and easy-intermediate pistes makes the connection first with Champoussin and then with Morgins. The mountainside above Champoussin is broad and sunny, with little variety of terrain. This whole area is ideally suited to the beginner to intermediate skier; for good skiers the main interest will be in the plentiful opportunity to venture off-piste. (The marking in this area is so poor that sticking to the piste is in any case very tricky in poor visibility.)

Morgins/Châtel Morgins does not have much skiing on the side reached from Champoussin, but it includes a splendid north-facing intermediate trail through tall pine forest to the village. Skiers bent on the Soleil circuit then face a tedious uphill walk across the village to the nursery slopes and the lifts for Châtel. The area between Morgins and Châtel is a pleasant contrast to the bleak ski-fields of Avoriaz and Planachaux – a series of short drags and winding pistes, largely among thin woods, eventually takes you over the border to the open slopes of Super-Châtel, in France.

It is at Châtel that the Soleil circuit breaks down. Whichever way you are travelling, the link cannot be made on skis; if going anti-clockwise, a substantial bus-ride is needed to the gondola up to Linga, the first of a long chain of lifts and pistes towards Avoriaz. The skiing in this sector offers more variety than other major legs of the circuit, and includes a long, challenging but not severe black beside the Linga gondola (for skiers going anti-clockwise or with the time to play about en route). You eventually find yourself at Les Marmottes, along with a lot of other skiers wanting a lift up to Avoriaz.

At Avoriaz the **nursery slopes** run alongside the top half of the village to Le Plateau; it is an excellent area, convenient for the bars and restaurants of the village, high and sunny. Champéry's slopes are at Planachaux – a cable-car ride from the village – and are a bit on the steep side. Morgins has broad, gentle sunny slopes right in the village. Châtel has large slopes inconveniently located outside the village, and big open areas up the mountain at Super-Châtel.

Mountain restaurants are not a strong point of the area as a whole, and the French sections in particular. You need to plan your breaks, rather than hoping to find yourself happening on a suitable hut at just the right time. There is a charming little refuge on the way down to Grand Paradis from Planachaux, but most restaurants are purpose-built and not particularly pleasant.

Lifts

Passes Portes du Soleil pass covers all lifts. Local, day and half-days passes available. Sharing arrangement with Flaine and Argentière.
Cost 6-day Portes du Soleil pass

FF561/SF133. Avoriaz pass (for 7 days) FF470.
Children 30% off.
Beginners Special passes.

There is a fundamental problem with the Avoriaz lifts – nearly all skiers need to take a lift up to the resort at the end of the day, and queues form at the two obvious places – the bottom of the village (skiers returning from Hauts Forts and Champéry) and Les Marmottes (skiers returning from Châtel). The latter are a powerful argument for doing the circuit clockwise – though you miss some good skiing that way. Reporters are unanimous in finding the Portes du Soleil piste maps unhelpful, despite their apparently careful attempts to make clear the lift and piste connections on the circuit. Geneva is close, and weekend skiers add to the crowds. The Prodain cable-car is often crowded in high season and when lower nearby resorts are short of snow.

The resort

Avoriaz is reached from the valley either by a narrow, winding road or cable-car from Prodain, near Morzine. It is set on a long south-facing slope which steepens towards the bottom. Cars must be left in parks at the top of the slope; you have to take a horse-drawn sleigh or ratrac to get you and your luggage to your accommodation. There are also public lifts within buildings to help you get about when you're not on skis. The busiest part of the resort is the middle section, around the foot of the nursery slopes; there are lots of bars and restaurants lining the slopes, and shops for ski gear, clothes and food. The shopping is more varied than in some modern resorts, but the main supermarket is expensive and overcrowded. What used to be an entirely open area beside the nursery slopes has now had an extravagant Maison du Tourisme placed in the middle of it, rather spoiling the view from the chairs which appear outside the cafés on a sunny day. The lack of cars and the specially enclosed nursery area suits children well, but with skiers and sleighs cutting through the resort it is hardly hazard-free.

Nearly all **accommodation** is in apartments; there are a couple of hotels, too, but they're indistinguishable from the apartment blocks. None of the accommodation used by reporters has been impressive, and some of it has been distinctly poor. Apartments in Alpages II are described by one reporter as 'quite disgracefully cramped'; another reporter went without hot water for a week. Several of the blocks are said to be getting generally tatty. Location in the resort is not very important for skiing purposes, but if you stay right at the top it can be rather a hike back after a night out.

Après-ski is fairly lively and varied by the standards of purpose-built resorts. There are lots of bars and all are fairly crowded in the evening; reporters felt they were generally expensive. There are more relaxed cocktail and piano bars with even higher prices, and three discos. There are lots of restaurants, including pizzerias and several Asian/Oriental ones as well those doing serious French food, and reporters generally enjoyed their eating out.

Ski school

Classes 2hr morning, 3hr afternoon.	**Children** Ski kindergarten, ages 3–14,
Cost 6 full days FF496. Private lessons	9.30–5.30, 6 days with lunch FF750.
FF110/hr.	**Special courses** Touring, racing.

Reports on the ski school are divided, with some highly complimentary comments and some quite scathing; one reporter changed classes twice in search of the right standard and a caring instructor, which is an indictment of the school but may offer a valuable model for others who don't like what they are first given. Opinions are divided, too, about the children's village; in principle, it seems a splendid facility, with games rooms as well as specially contrived slopes. But one or two reports suggest that there is a lack of sympathy towards children who don't like wearing ski boots all day, and perhaps towards non-French children.

Other activities

Cross-country There are three circuits totalling 23km on the way into the resort, of which 1km is for beginners.

Not skiing Swimming, sauna, squash, aerobics, cinema.

We lack informed reports on the rewards of the X-C trails, but they are quite lengthy and at high altitude. The resort cannot be recommended for non-skier, although the cable-car (and then bus) offers a means of escape to less hostile surroundings in Morzine, and thence further afield. There is very little to do or to watch apart from skiing.

Travel

Airport Geneva; transfer 2hr.
Road Via Geneva; chains may be needed. Cars must be left in open parks on the edge of the resort. (Alternatively you can leave your car at Prodain, and take the cable-car up.)

Railway Cluses; bus and cable-car to resort.
Reachable resorts Apart from the many resorts in the Portes du Soleil, it is possible to get to Flaine (most easily via Samoëns) or Chamonix.

You are unlikely to make any use of a car while in Avoriaz, and you may spend your time wondering whether it will start on departure day after sitting on an exposed col at 1800m for a week or two. The road up to the resort is long and tortuous, and expeditions are better organised around the cable-car to the valley. Bus connections into Morzine, however, are reported to be infrequent and erratic.

Miscellaneous

Tourist office ✆ (50) 740211.
Tx 385773.
Equipment hire 6 days skis FF300, boots FF170, X-C FF280.
Resort beds 450 in hotels, 11,000 in apartments.

Medical Hospital in Morzine; dentist, medical centre, dentist, chemist in resort.
Package holidays BL, BS, CHA, CM, EN, FL, FT, GL, HA, IG, IT, MM, NE, SKW, SPT, STC, SUP, TC.

Minor resorts

Champéry Switzerland 1050m

Champéry is a pretty and rather sleepy traditional Alpine village set in attractive surroundings on the side of a valley facing the savage peaks of Dents du Midi. The main street, mainly closed to traffic, runs the length of the village, climbing gently from the station to the ski-lifts at the opposite end. Most of the hotels, restaurants and shops are to be found along its length, although there is some new development down the hill on the valley road which skirts the village. The sports centre is also in the valley bottom, with good facilities for skating, curling, swimming and bowling. There are cleared walks, and a short cross-country course up the valley at Grand Paradis.

Food shopping is good – in addition to the supermarkets there are small specialist shops; there are also shops selling clothes and souvenirs as well as ski equipment (a clue to the village's summer popularity). There is not much après-ski – a couple of discos and some live music, and several bars and restaurants. Le Farinet is the most

lively and sophisticated venue for both dining and dancing. Most of the
other restaurants are rather anonymous Swiss neo-Alpine in style.
Hotels range from the fairly simple to the moderately plush. The lifts are
a stiff climb above the end of the main street, so a long walk as well is to
be avoided (though there is a ski-bus). The Beau-Séjour (∅ 791701) is
ideally placed, and has been comfortably refurbished. The Hotel de la
Paix (∅ 791551) is a friendly, cheaper alternative.
Tourist office ∅ (25) 791141. Tx 456263.
Package holidays BL, BS, KU, MM, PS, SCB, SUS.

Morzine France 1000m
Morzine is an old resort on a busy cross-roads, inconveniently situated
half an hour by bus away from the Les Prodains cable-car station, for
access to the heart of the Portes du Soleil. Out of season it is an
attractively quiet and ordinary small holiday town with an interesting
range of shops and restaurants and a great many hotels and
guest-houses, all at valley rather than mountain prices. At holiday time
and at weekends it becomes horribly choked with through-traffic and
motorised skiers, who also pack the car parks and cable-car to Avoriaz.
Morzine has some skiing of its own, with intermediate runs linking up
with Les Gets and some tougher ones runs beneath the Pointe de
Nyon. None of the skiing is easily accessible on foot from the centre of
town. There is a big artificial skating rink where ice-hockey is staged,
curling, riding and swimming.
Tourist office ∅ (50) 790345. Package holidays EN, FL, FT, SCG, SUS, TC.

Morgins Switzerland 1350m
Morgins is a spacious residential resort spreading across its valley just
below the pass separating it from French Châtel. Almost all the
accommodation is in chalets and apartments, and the resort is fairly
quiet and relaxed. There are a handful of hotels; most reporters have
stayed in the big, token-chalet-style Bellevue (∅ 772771) which looks
over the resort from its hillside, and have generally approved. La Forêt
is reportedly 'a glorified youth hostel'. There is a reasonable range of
shops, and a few bar-restaurants, but it is not a resort for keen
après-skiers. There is indoor tennis and a natural ice-rink with curling,
but apparently no swimming in winter. Cross-country loops amount to
12km.
Tourist office ∅ (25) 772361. Tx 456261.
Package holidays KU, SCB, SCP, SDO, SUS.

Les Crosets Switzerland 1660m
Les Crosets is a ski station in the heart of the open slopes on the Swiss
side of the Portes du Soleil circuit. It is a tiny place, with a couple of
hotels and a handful of restaurants, all fairly functional and with no
great appeal. For sporting facilities or a bit more life, it's a two-hour walk
into Champéry according to our one reporter, who 'didn't see a bus all
week'.
Tourist office ∅ (25) 791423. Package holidays HM.

Champoussin Switzerland 1580m

Champoussin represents more of an attempt to create a mini-resort than Les Crosets. Its new buildings, in rustic style, are almost all apartments under the skin, but most of our reporters have stayed in the main hotel, the Alpage (∅ 772711), and have been impressed by everything except the inadequately heated pool. It also has a sauna, and a disco – but the resort is 'death to apre's-skiers'. There is a skating rink.

Tourist office ∅ (25) 772727. Package holidays GL.

Châtel France 1200m

Châtel is an old village which has been thoroughly overwhelmed by its recent development as a ski resort. It now sprawls along the road running through towards Morgins, down the hillside and along the valley towards the Linga lift which is its connection with the skiing of Avoriaz. At weekends, particularly, the centre is choked with cars and buses – it's the kind of resort where transport figures largely in skiers lives. There are lots of hotels, and hundreds of chalets and apartments to rent, 20 ski shops, a dozen restaurants – all buzzing when the French are in town.

Tourist office ∅ (50) 732244. Package holidays HM, VF.

Happy families on the moon

Flaine France 1600m

Good for *Family skiing, nursery slopes, big ski area, skiing
convenience, short airport transfers, freedom from cars, late holidays,
self-catering holidays, easy skiing, resort-level snow*
Bad for *Alpine charm, not skiing, tough skiing, mountain restaurants*

Linked resort: Les Carroz

Le Grand Massif is a loosely linked ski area spread over what is indeed
a large, although not outstandingly high, group of mountains. At its
heart is Flaine, the modern French ski resort without a difference. It is
all new, and grey. It is also ideal for what the tourist office calls careless
skiing: hardly any footslogging, hardly any cars, excellent nursery
slopes and facilities, a wide range of intermediate runs, reliable snow,
not much queuing. Add very short transfers from Geneva, and its
popularity with British families is explained. The link with Samoëns,
Morillon and Les Carroz extends Flaine's skiing greatly and adds
missing ingredients – long runs through a wooded, inhabited landscape. (Unfortunately, the exposed link lifts are often closed in bad
weather, when these sheltered slopes are most appealing.)

Les Carroz is the most attractive of the minor resorts as a base for
skiers. It is a sharp contrast to Flaine – inconveniently arranged on the
road up, in a beautiful setting with good cross-country trails.

The skiing top 2480m bottom 690m

The Grand Massif skiing divides into several sectors, each linked to the
next at only one or two points. Most of **Flaine's** skiing is spread around
the north-facing half of the basin in which the resort lies, with several
lifts climbing to different points around the rim at nearly 2500m, giving a
vertical range of some 900m. Most of the skiing is above the tree-line.
The main lift is the cable-car to Grandes Platières, a broad high
plateau, flat enough for cross-country skiers and walkers, with a
panoramic view including the magnificent spikes, glaciers and domes
of Mont Blanc. There is a large number of intersecting runs down to the
resort from all sides, most of them easy red or stiff blue. For timid skiers
there are less direct, open blue runs. The most difficult descents are in
the middle of the ski area, where the terrain is very fragmented. This
means tricky sections in the middle of otherwise uncomplicated runs –
the black run under the cable-car would otherwise be red.

The off-piste routes in the main bowl are very often skied into a
piste-like state, and exploration in search of virgin snow is likely to end
abruptly at the brink of a cliff or a pot-hole. But there is good off-piste
skiing newly opened up by the long Gers drag-lift – reached with some
difficulty from Grandes Platières. It is a steep, deep coomb, prone to

avalanche; the lift opens late in the season, and closes early in the afternoon. The much shorter Véret lift serves a similar, fairly steep, often dangerous bowl, mainly of interest to off-piste skiers.

The rest of the Grand Massif skiing is reached via the valley of the Lac de Vernant, which is often very crowded with commuting skiers. The Tête du Pré des Saix on the far side is the central point of the whole system. North-facing runs descend steeply down towards **Samoëns** far below. The top section offers some of the best, albeit short, tough runs in the area (bumpy piste and off-piste). The skiing is interrupted by a short chair-lift at the Plateau des Saix, then there's a further 800m vertical down to the outskirts of Samoëns; the steeper black option is a splendid sweeping course through the woods, but is soon scraped bare. On the other side of a wide valley, the parallel **Morillon** runs are long, gentle, woodland trails – less varied than the piste map suggests – punctuated by clearings with restaurants. The runs down to **Les Carroz** are shorter but offer a broader network and greater variety of trails (all below the tree-line), with distinctly blackish sections at the top of some of the red runs, and some good off-piste slopes. There are some very gentle runs around the top of the gondola, but the blue run to the village is often in poor condition and crowded.

Flaine's **nursery slopes** are excellent – spacious and absolutely central, and ranging from the gentle to the flat, but the slopes and lifts are used by lots of other skiers on their way to and from the main runs.

There are only two **mountain restaurants** above Flaine; both have sunny terraces and the one at the top of the cable-car serves as one of the most spectacular sun-bathing and picnic spots in the Alps.

Lifts

Passes Grand Massif pass covers all lifts and gives right to day pass in La Clusaz, Argentière and Avoriaz. Local Flaine pass also available – can be extended once only to cover Grand Massif; available for day and half-day. **Cost** 6-day Grand Massif pass FF460. **Children** About 20% off, under 12. **Beginners** Several free lifts, limited day pass FF40.

The main problems are weekend crowds and queues for the cable-car, where a wait of over half an hour is not uncommon. There are crowds and fast skiers on the nursery slopes and lifts, and commuter traffic leads to queues for the lifts at Lac de Vernant. Reporters considered the lift pass arrangements rather inflexible, and found the advertised low-season discount was not available for the Grand Massif pass.

The resort

Flaine is a tiny place, 200m below the point at which the road in breaches the rim of a wide, desolate basin. It has been built in two parts – Flaine Forêt (mostly apartment buildings) is on a shelf above Flaine Forum, which is a square at the heart of the resort, with most of the bars, restuarants, shops and hotels. There is a free lift shuttle between the two, day and night. Front de Neige is simply a piste-side extension of Forum. The resort is extremely compact, and you can get to most

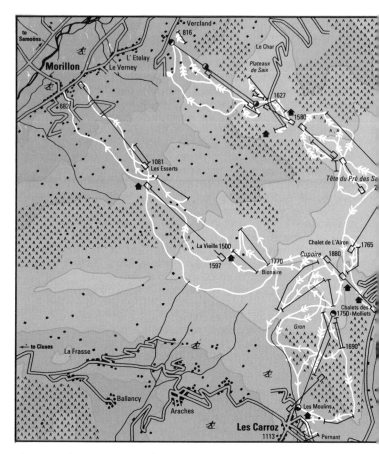

places staying under cover. Shops are no more than adequate, except the food shop which prepares dishes for lazy gourmet self-caterers.

Most of the hotel **accommodation** is in Forum, with self-catering flats – at least as far as UK packages are concerned – mostly in Forêt. Reporters express frustration at having to queue for a lift down to the cable-car in the morning. The hotels are very similar – bright, modern, and adequately comfortable, with small bedrooms and spacious public rooms. Reports are generally favourable, especially of Le Totem (∅ 908064). Les Lindars (∅ 908166) is outstandingly caring for young families, with a nursery and electronic babysitting. Apartments in Front de Neige are well placed for skiing from and to your door.

Après-ski is very muted; few people bother to use the two discothèques, and confine themselves instead to various restaurants and bars. They are expensive – even the lively White Grouse Pub, with its darts and bitter and happy hour. Most tour operators organise evenings out (meal and dancing) in the Bissac nursery slope restaurant.

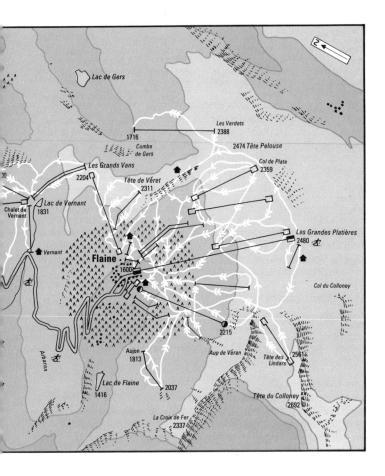

Lac de Gers

Les Verdets
1716 2388

Combe
de Gers 2474 *Tête Pelouse*

Les Grands Vans Col de Plate
2204 2359

Tête de Véret
2311

Chalet de Lac de Vernant
Vernant 1831

Les Grandes Platières
2480

Flaine
1600 Col du Colloney

Vernant

Col du Colloney

2215

Arbaron Aujon Aup de Véran Tête des 2561
1813 Lindars

Lac de Flaine Tête du Colloney
1416 2037 2692

La Croix de Fer
2337

Ski school

Two schools: Ecole du Ski Français and Ski Ecole International.
Classes 2hr morning and afternoon.
Cost 6 days ESF FF432 (24 hrs), SEI 402 (22 hrs). Private lessons FF95/hr.
Special courses Competition, off-piste, touring, excursions, freestyle private lessons, monoski, cross-country.

Beginners Ski evolutif on request.
Children Ski kindergarten, ages 3–7, (both schools); timetable as for adults, lunchtime care/food available. 6 days all inclusive ESF FF710, SEI FF725. Non-ski kindergarten, ages 3–7, at Hotel Les Lindars, 9.00-6.00, 6 days FF435.

Flaine is where the Ski Ecole International was started 15 years ago to shake up ESF ski teaching. The differences between the schools are not great. The SEI are reputedly stronger on languages, and have many more English than French pupils, but the ESF can provide English-speaking instructors. Reports are generally favourable, but include a children's class size of 25, an adult abandoned half-way down the mountain because he was too slow, and changes of instructor during the week.

Other activities

Cross-country 700m loop at Flaine; 8km off-piste trail at Grandes Platières (cable-car from Flaine), 8 km of trails at Vernant and Col de Pierre Carrée (bus from Flaine). Longer trails near Les Carroz, and much longer ones around Morillon and Samoëns. **Not skiing** swimming/sauna, natural ice rink, snow-shoe excursions, hang-gliding, ice driving, art/crafts gallery.

Flaine cannot be recommended for non-skiers. Cross-country skiers have to be prepared to take buses or lifts to the trails, which is hardly ideal; Les Carroz is much more suitable. There is a vast extent of very low cross-country trails around Morillon and Samoëns.

Travel

Airport Geneva; transfer about 1½hr. **Railway** Cluses 30km; several buses daily. **Road** Via Geneva or Lyon/Annecy; chains often needed. **Reachable resorts** Avoriaz, Chamonix, La Clusaz and Megève

One of Flaine's attractions is that it is close to Geneva. But the climb up from the valley is a slow, tortuous 30 km, and often snowy beyond Les Carroz. Good skiers may find a car valuable for the odd day's skiing in Avoriaz or the Chamonix valley.

Miscellaneous

Tourist office ✆ (50) 908001. Tx 385662. **Resort beds** 1,100 in hotels; 5,000 in apartments. **Package holidays** BS, EN, FT, HO, IG, JM, MM, SCG, SKW, SUP. **Medical** Doctor, chemist in resort; dentist at Les Carroz (16km), hospital at Cluses (30km). **Equipment hire** 6 days skis FF185, boots FF95, X-C FF180.

Les Carroz 1160m

Last outpost of civilisation on the road to Flaine, Les Carroz is an attractive, spacious village, spread broadly across a sunny, sloping shelf high above the steep-sided Arve valley. It attracts few British visitors, but lots of cross-country skiers, families and weekend day-trippers whose cars strangle the resort. The gondola and chair-lift station is a steep walk above the commercial centre of the resort, but within easy reach of some attractive, simple old hotels – Airelles (✆ 900102), Bel Piste (✆ 900017) and the charming Croix de Savoie (✆ 900026). Most of the self-catering accommodation is much less conveniently placed. Even if staying centrally, keen skiers may be glad of a car – for avoiding the gondola queues and making the most of Flaine's skiing. Cross-country skiing is very good; the trails (35km) are not immediately by the village. The ski-bus serves them as well as the lift station. Les Carroz is quiet in the evenings except during school holidays. There is a single discothèque, outside the village, and several friendly bars and restaurants. The chance to go riding in the snow is apparently 'une des dernières expériences inoubliables'.

Tourist office ✆ (50) 900004. Tx 385281.
Package holidays BS, EN, FT, HO, IG, JM, MM, SCG, SKW, SUP.

Juggernaut withstanding

Courmayeur Italy 1230m

Good for *Mountain restaurants, beautiful scenery, après-ski, off-piste skiing, ski touring, easy road access, short airport transfers, cross-country skiing, not skiing*
Bad for *Skiing convenience, nursery slopes, tough skiing, easy skiing*

The British love Courmayeur, despite its highly inconvenient layout and despite the loss of much of its Alpine village charm since the Mont Blanc road tunnel forced heavy through-traffic upon it. Its ski area is not very big; there is no very challenging skiing, not much that is very gentle, and few very long runs. But it is an attractive and remarkably varied area, with lots of restaurants and beautiful changing views, and with some wilder and higher runs served (not very reliably) by the top cable-cars. Lift queues are not now the problem that they used to be. The resort is stylish without being exclusive, lively without being rowdy – still one of the most attractive of Italian resorts.

The skiing top 3452m bottom 1293m

Most skiers start and end the day on the vast cable-car which spans the river valley, linking the edge of the village with the plateau of **Plan Checrouit**. Alternatives are to drive or catch a bus either across the valley for the old gondola to Plan Checrouit, or out to the new Val Veny cable-car, near Entrèves. The east-facing Checrouit bowl has a large number but hardly a great variety of moderately difficult to moderately easy runs, none of which is very long. The pistes are often crowded, especially near the bottom where they meet. There are surprisingly steep, narrow passages even on some of the variants graded blue.

The wooded north-west-facing **Val Veny** side of the mountain, linked in a couple of places with the Checrouit bowl, has beautiful, longer and more varied runs, with some challenging bumpy trails taking the hillside fairly directly and an easy, wide winding path. In places, there are dangerously steep slopes beside the pistes (notably piste 19).

The cable-car above Lago Checrouit opens up a deep and sheltered bowl, usually keeping good snow, and with plenty of space for short off-piste excursions from the single uncomplicated run back down. A further short cable-car gives access to the serious off-piste skiing, principally a long and very popular run (1500m vertical) down a secluded valley which ends up at Dolonne.

The lift pass also covers the three-stage **Mont Blanc** cable-car which climbs over 2000m to Punta Helbronner, giving easy access to the famous Vallée Blanche run to Chamonix – see page 302. There is an afternoon bus back from Chamonix. The run down the Italian side of the Massif is very steep at the top and often dangerous. By contrast the run down the bottom stage of the cable-car is a long, straightforward, and rarely skied piste. The Punta Helbronner is a excellent point of departure for ski touring excursions, and has a few summer ski-lifts.

Nursery slopes at Plan Checrouit are cramped by all the buildings and milling skiers. The progression to the rest of Courmayeur's skiing is also not an easy one.

Mountain restaurants are, to quote one satisfied reporter, 'a point of special commendation', and remarkably numerous. Plan Checrouit is a proper little Hochcourmayeur, with accommodation and ski shops as well as a number of bars and restaurants. There are lots of mostly very welcoming chalets and converted cow-sheds dotted around.

Lifts

Passes All lifts covered by lift passes of more than two days' validity. Mont Blanc lifts excluded from shorter passes. Passes for 6 or more days include a day in Cervinia (Zermatt lifts not covered). No buses covered.

Cost 6-day pass L12,6000. About 12% off in low season.
Children No reduction.
Beginners Free nursery lifts at Plan Checrouit and top of Val Veny cable-car (which can be paid for by the ride). Otherwise general pass needed.

The Checrouit cable-car is a long walk from the centre, but fairly free of queues except at weekends; queues elsewhere are rare. The top cable-cars are very often closed. Ski and boot depots at Plan Checrouit take a lot of the unpleasantness out of getting to and from skiing.

The resort

Courmayeur is a long village which now merges with its neighbouring hamlets Verrand, Villair and La Saxe, all of them quiet and prosperous second-home areas with some beautiful old rough-stone buildings. Some haphazard and unbecoming expansion has taken place along the Verrand road near the cable-car, about half a mile from the old centre – now just an open space beside the main busy road. On Wednesdays the vacuum is filled by a large and lively market, where reporters have found bargains. The heart of the old village is nearby, a delightful maze of cobbled alleys partly reserved for pedestrians.

There is a great variety of **accommodation**. Few hotels are well situated for the main lift. Accommodation on the hill up to Verrand or Villair is very picturesque, but quite a slog after a day's skiing. The Pavillon (∅ 842420) is the best situated of all Courmayeur's hotels, and one of the most comfortable and expensive; it has a very good pool and sauna. A reporter recommends the Cresta et Duc (∅ 842585), also well-placed and comfortable. The Edelweiss (∅ 841590) on the edge of the old centre is friendly, cosy, and less expensive. Reporters have recommended the Scoiattolo (∅ 842274) despite its poor location at the Entrèves end of town. The central Bar Roma (∅ 843040) and Turistica (∅ 842563) are very cheap and basic. Near the gondola station, the Dolonne (∅ 841260) is a comfortable b&b place.

Après-ski resides mainly in the many bars and restaurants. The Bar Roma with its comfy sofas and armchairs is the most popular and lively

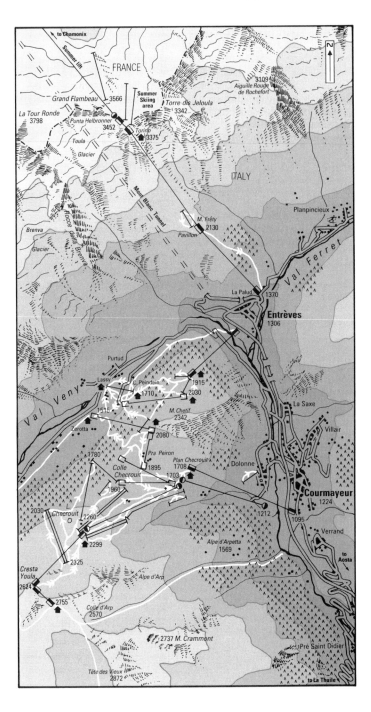

place in the early evening. There are a few discos of which the Abat-Jour is usually the fullest ('all the charm and style of a Butlins Holiday Camp'). There are lots of restaurants, including cheap places to fill up with pizza or pasta, nowhere cheaper or heartier than the Turistica. Of the more ambitious restaurants the most famous are the Maison de Filippo in Entrèves, a splendid place for an empty stomach and an unfussy palate, and K2 in Villair. There are also some restaurants and discos at Dolonne and Verrand. The ice rink is open every evening until midnight, with disco music and lights.

Ski school

Classes 3hr mornings only.
Cost 6 days L85,000. Private lessons L20,000/hr.

Children Ski kindergarten, ages 5–10, 9.00–4.00, 6 days with lunch about L200,000.

The ski school and the local mountain guides run programmes of off-piste skiing and helicopter skiing. Courmayeur is a famous mountaineering centre, and the scope for ski touring is vast.

Other activities

Cross-country Several trails of between 3km and 20km in Val Ferret starting at Planpincieux, accessible by bus from Courmayeur. 5km difficult and 3km easy at Dolonne. 4km at Entrèves.

Not skiing Swimming/sauna at Pré St Didier (5km), artificial ice rink, Alpine museum, tennis, cinema, bridge, walking paths in Val Ferret and Dolonne.

The main cross-country trails are far from the resort and Alpine skiing areas, but in other respects excellent – long, varied and very beautiful. For non-skiers there are plenty of interesting excursions, and good walks around the resort and in secluded side valleys. In fine weather the cable-car ride to Punta Helbronner is spectacular.

Travel

Airport Geneva; transfer about 2hr. Turin almost as convenient.
Railway Pré St Didier (5km); frequent buses.
Road Via Geneva or Lyon, and Mont

Blanc Tunnel; chains rarely needed.
Reachable resorts Despite the lift-pass deal, Cervinia is not close; the Chamonix valley makes a much better day-trip.

The main resort bus service, serving cable-cars and cross-country area, runs about every 15 minutes. There are less frequent buses to Dolonne. Having a car is not necessary (the resort is vigorously policed) but is a great advantage for skiing and non-skiing excursions.

Miscellaneous

Tourist office ✆ (165) 82060. Tx 215871.
Medical Hospital at Aosta (36km); doctors, dentists, chemists in resort.
Equipment hire 6 days skis L30,000, boots L20,000, X-C L30,000.

Resort beds 2,600 in hotels, 13,800 in chalets/apartments.
Package holidays B., BS, CI, SCG, SKW, SNP, TC, TH.

The price of excellence

Chamonix France 1035m

Good for *Tough skiing, off-piste skiing, beautiful scenery, late-season holidays, ski touring, short airport transfers, easy road access, rail access, après-ski, self-catering holidays*
Bad for *Skiing convenience, nursery slopes, easy skiing, timid intermediates, lift queues, resort-level snow, mountain restaurants*

Separate resorts: Argentière, Les Houches, Le Tour

Chamonix Mont-Blanc can boast some of the most beautiful scenery in the Alps and some of the longest, most beautiful and demanding descents. The price of such superlatives is high. France's largest ski resort in terms of beds is small in terms of lift capacity, and the queues can be terrible. The skiing is in several separate areas and the only lift which is not a stiff walk from the centre is the once-in-a-holiday Aiguille du Midi cable-car. There is very little skiing for the novice, the timid or the unfit skier. The mountains are avalanche-prone, and crevasses pose a threat on many of the finest runs. Weather is volatile and when it's bad much or all of the skiing is closed. But good skiers who are lucky with the conditions will forgive all this – and find skiing elsewhere just a little tame.

Chamonix is a large, noisy, and not very pretty town, but it has history and great character, and is full of all sorts of people from all over the world – from furry-booted pensioners profoundly inhaling the mountain air to hordes of young Swedish holiday-makers. It attracts numbers of Real Mountain Men, many of them from America. The number of British visitors is small but growing. Many, ill informed by holiday brochures, are disappointed by what they find.

The main alternative to Chamonix is the old village of Argentière, only five miles up the valley but in another, simpler world. It has excellent difficult skiing, but not much else. Several other villages and hamlets in the valley offer accommodation and, in some cases, skiing. Les Houches is the most important of them – an old farming village which has become a sprawling, characterless village with limited skiing – but often the only place to ski in bad weather.

Le Tour, at the head of the valley beyond Argentière, is another old, attractive village, at the foot of its own glacier. There is some open, mostly easy skiing above the village, but it is not a good place to be based, and may be cut off in bad weather.

Chamonix is most suitable for late-season skiing, when the high glacier runs and the area's enormous ski touring possibilities are reliably accessible. In January, too, the resorts are quiet, and in fine weather the skiing is magnificent; even the Vallée Blanche is occasionally open. But the risk of disappointment and forced marches to Megève and Courmayeur is high.

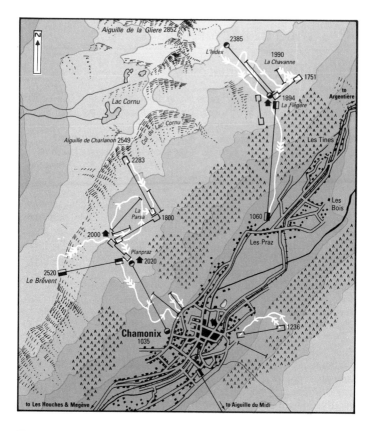

The skiing top 3790m bottom 980m

The Chamonix valley skiing is split up into six separate areas along the two valley walls and at its head. The best of the scenery and skiing is on the enormous, steep, mostly north-facing slopes of the mountains lined up at the shoulder of Mont Blanc, served by cable-cars from Argentière and from Chamonix. Until recently the second of these – to the Aiguille du Midi – was Europe's highest cable-car; it is still the most spectacular. The famous Vallée Blanche run from the top is one of the highlights of any visit. The skiing on Argentière's Grands Montets is where most good skiers will want to spend most of their time. Chamonix's own ski areas are the south-facing Brévent and Flégère.

Chamonix's original skiing fame was based on **Brévent**, now reached by a 6-seater gondola starting a steep walk from the centre and an exciting cable-car over an abyss to the top station, which gives marvellous views of Mont Blanc. Apart from a few short lifts serving easy runs near mid-station, and a new chair-lift up to the Col Cornu which will one day develop into the connection with Flégère, Brévent is

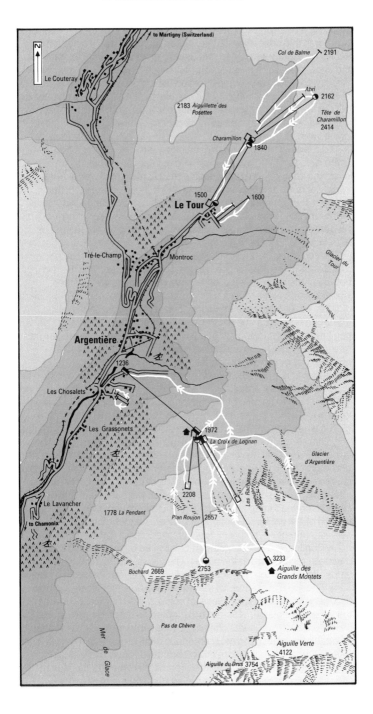

basically a one-run ski area. It is quite a run. The top half to Planpraz is an impressive descent with an exposed, bumpy wall. The bottom section is slightly less steep, but usually more demanding because of the snow conditions and because it is much longer. A long, narrow gully is followed by a wider, bumpy section, which goes on and on and on until you arrive jelly-limbed at the bottom station. All in all, a relentless 1500m vertical. The mountain gets a lot of sun, and the lower piste is a natural avalanche path; an early-season slide may close it for the rest of the year.

The **Flégère** skiing, a few ridges along the mountainside from Brévent, is similar in many ways. The top section, served by an enclosed chair-lift, is less awesome than Brévent, but has a greater variety of runs, mostly tough blue to tough red in difficulty. As at Brévent, there is only one run down from the mid-station, and that is black, and also very often closed. Snow conditions permitting, La Flégère has better possibilities than Brévent for off-piste skiing; it is especially good for spring snow.

The cable-car at **Argentière** sees some of the worst queuing marathons in the Alps. It goes up to Croix de Lognan, which is the bottom of the main skiing – there is only one run down the steep, wooded slope to the valley, a long and tiring red, not in itself particularly difficult, but often in poor condition, and very crowded in the late afternoon. The area above Lognan may seem limited, and certainly you can tire of always taking the same lifts, eating in the same restaurant, seeing the same faces and standing in the same (considerable) queues. But with the right conditions and the right guidance, good skiers can find more satisfaction and even more variety here than in far more extensive ski areas.

Most of the main face of the mountain between about 2000 and 2600m is a wide open area of ridges and bowls, mogul-fields and gullies where the distinction between piste and off-piste usually means very little. Apart from the top section of the cable-car there are only three lifts, and only two of the pistes are prepared: one short blue (the only easy run on the mountain) and the long, challenging and busy red served by a gondola/chair-lift hybrid. The same lift gives access to a beautiful off-piste descent to Le Lavancher, the better half of which may soon be opened up to piste skiers. The chair-lift underneath the top section of the cable-car, serving a shorter, steeper mountainside, serves a number of different descents including a stiff mogul-field.

The top section of the cable-car is followed by an exposed 200-step metal staircase down to the pistes. The views from here are stupendous, and the runs long and steep, 4km and 5km for the 1260m vertical to the mid-station. Of the two runs, the longer is more scenic and gives some awesome views of some of the choppiest sections of the Argentière glacier. The red run marked on maps is rarely open. The various off-piste descents offer a choice of grandiose glacier scenery or steep, open slopes. The most notorious of all Argentière's runs is the Pas de Chèvre (Goat's Hop) down an often dangerous west-facing slope, all the way from the top of the Grands Montets to the Mer de Glace glacier, where it joins the Vallée Blanche run to Chamonix.

Not the least of the pleasures of skiing at Argentière is the sight of the other skiers. Nowhere else this side of the Atlantic is there such a congregation of rubber-legged experts and bone-headed maniacs putting on a constant display of the state of the art, from monoski freestyle with wings to mogul-bashing on cross-country skis.

Le Tour's skiing is open, gentle (at least by local standards), sunny and uncomplicated. As well as the long, easy intermediate runs (easier above the gondola mid-station than below it), there are a couple of drag-lifts at the bottom, with the best nursery slopes in the valley. There is also scope for interesting off-piste skiing to different points along the road to Switzerland. You catch the little train home.

Les Houches' skiing is served by a small cable-car and a gondola lift from either end of the village over very steep, wooded slopes to either side of the Col de Voza (1653m). Skiing consists of runs back down from both these points (Bellevue, 1812m; and Prarion, 1966m) to Les Houches – splendid long, wide trails through the woods with little to choose between them. The run down from Prarion is the official downhill course and is categorised black – although named La Verte. Apart from these runs there is a small network of drag-lifts between the Col de Voza and Prarion, serving an open slope of about 300m vertical, and some small drag-lifts with slopes suitable for beginners. There is also a wide blue run down to Les Houches. Behind the Col de Voza it is possible in the right conditons to ski down to St-Gervais. In any other context Les Houches would seem a perfectly agreeable little skiing area. In these surroundings, however, it is overshadowed, and the skiing seems second-rate. And when the weather dictates that this is the only skiing open, you may have an hour's queue for a lift.

The Chamonix Valley cannot be recommended for beginners, but there are **nursery slopes**. The best ones are at Le Tour – spacious and open. There is a small nursery area near the bottom station of the Grands Montets cable-car, which is rather confined and sunless. At Chamonix there are some nursery lifts at the bottom of the Brévent where snow is often poor late in the season.

Chamonix is a place for mint-cake and survival rations rather than leisurely lunches, and **mountain restaurants** are few, uninteresting, and expensive, except at Les Houches. When queues are bad the shortage of sunny terraces is disappointing, and off-piste picnics are called for; pick your spot with great care when on a glacier.

Lifts

Passes Mont Blanc pass covers all valley lifts and buses and a number of resorts outside the valley. Day and half-day passes available only for individual areas, most economically bought via transferable coupons. All major lifts can be paid for by the ride.
Cost 6-day pass FF555.
Children No reduction.
Beginners Day passes or cash for nursery lifts. Limited passes at Argentière.

Lift queues can be enormous. At Argentière you may have to fight to get a numbered card for a ride in two hours' time. Tour operators bus their numerous clients to the station before the public bus service starts, and lift queues start earlier every year. The Aiguille du Midi is even worse late in the season at weekends (people start queuing before dawn), but if you hire a guide he'll queue for you. On Brévent and Flégère, the problem is queuing to get down when the lower runs are closed. The lift pass system is complicated; because of the risk of lift closures in bad weather, many skiers prefer the coupon-for-day-pass formula to the area lift pass. Argentière levies large supplements for rides on the top section of the cable-car if you buy a pass with cash instead of coupons.

The resort

Chamonix has been one of the Alps' leading resorts, summer and winter, for two centuries since Mont Blanc was first climbed. Traditional and old-fashioned as its centre is, Chamonix is no longer pretty. The centre is crowded, busy, noisy, and full of traffic. Modern blocks stand around the edge of town, and Chamonix merges with neighbouring hamlets and villages.

Most of the **accommodation** on offer to British package tourists is in (or near) Chamonix. There are a few expensive, comfortable hotels and many simple, old, cheap ones. There is plenty of self-catering accommodation in recently-built complexes and also in privately-owned chalets around the valley. There is no ideal location for accommodation, except perhaps near the bus terminal in Chamonix or in the centre of Argentière for those who want to concentrate on the Grands Montets. Unless taking a car, avoid accommodation located downstream of Chamonix – you'll have to change buses in the centre of town to get to Flégère and Argentière. The Auberge du Bois Prin (℘ 533351) is the most attractive hotel for skiers who have a car; small, comfortable, and expensive, not far from the Brévent lift. The Mont-Blanc (℘ 530564) is absolutely central, large and comfortable, has a heated open-air pool, and is expensive. The Albert Premier (℘ 530509) is comfortable and has a long-established gastronomic reputation; it is not too far from the centre of town, and there is a bus-stop nearby. The Eden (℘ 531843) is a small, simple, inexpensive hotel serving good food at honest prices; its situation at Les Praz is not central, but not inconvenient.

Après-ski is varied and lively, although not particularly smart apart from the Casino and a few expensive restaurants. Most of the custom goes to the numerous bars (with and without music), self-service canteens, pizzerias and crêperies, and cinemas (including skiing films at the Alpine museum); there are a few discothèques.

Ski school

Classes 2hr morning and afternoon.	25% off school prices. Three non-ski
Cost 6 days FF359. Private lessons	kindergartens, ages up to 8.
FF94/hr. Mountain guide about FF700/	**Special courses** Guided ski tours, off-
day.	piste courses, mono-ski courses and
Children Ski kindergarten ages 4–12,	lessons, race training.
9.00–5.00, 6 days with lunch FF638.	

Guides can be hired from Argentière and Chamonix, both excellent points of departure for late-season ski tours, and from Les Houches. The famous Haute Route goes from Argentière to Saas Fee via Zermatt and takes three to seven days. The Compagnie des Guides in Chamonix organises weekly departures in April and May. There is also an independent association of mountain guides in Chamonix.

Other activities

Cross-country Trails at Chamonix and Argentière with 2km (black) trail linking the two networks. Chamonix (from Les Praz): 10km green, 6km blue, 4km red. Argentière: 3km green, 3km blue, 6km red. No runs at altitude. Also 14km trails at Les Houches.

Not skiing Artificial indoor and outdoor ice-rinks, tennis, swimming, fitness centre, saunas, Alpine museum (school holidays), coach and aeroplane excursions, snowshoe outings.

The valley is too built-up near Chamonix for cross-country skiing, but interlinked woodland loops of different grades further up the valley are excellent. For non-skiers there is plenty to do – beautiful cable-car excursions (although there are no walking possibilities from any of them), good coach excursions, an excellent modern sports centre. The valley is not an ideal place for mountain walkers.

Travel

Airport Geneva (83km); transfer 1½hr.
Road Via Lyon/Annecy or Geneva; chains rarely necessary, except higher up the valley.

Railway Station in resort.
Reachable resorts Megève and neighbouring resorts close, Flaine and Courmayeur (in Italy) easily reached.

Public transport around the valley consists of buses linking Les Houches and Chamonix, and Chamonix and Le Tour via Argentière. Services are just about adequate for skiing purposes, but stop at about 7pm. There is also a small railway which runs from Le Fayet (below St Gervais) to Martigny in Switzerland via Chamonix and Argentière. It is an enormous advantage to have a car – you can get around in the evening, you don't have to queue and push to get on buses during the day, and other resorts are easily reached. Verbier can just about be added to the list of reachable resorts, provided the unpredictable Col des Montets is open (chains often needed). Parking is subject to the usual town-centre problems.

Miscellaneous

Tourist office ✆ (50) 530024. Tx 385022.
Medical Hospital, chemists, doctors and dentists in resort.
Equipment hire 6 days skis FF170–220, boots FF90–135, X-C FF180.

Resort beds 4,900 in hotels, 9,200 in apartments and chalets.
Package holidays BL, BS, CHA, CM, FL, FT, IG, SDO, SUS, TC, TH.

Argentière 1240m

Argentière is a small but strung-out village, beautifully set beneath the local glacier, its onion-domed church outlined against the ice-falls and jagged peaks in a natural post-card scene. Chalet development and some ugly modern blocks are spread up and down the valley on either side of the old village centre. The main street is the Chamonix to Martigny road; although no major route and often closed in winter, this means quite a lot of traffic. A further hazard to pedestrians is the large and unruly dog population.

In the evening you can eat and drink in congenial surroundings, and occasionally dance; during high season the few establishments are very crowded. Hotels are mostly simple. The Grands Montets

(✆ 540666) is best-placed for the cable-car; it has no restaurant and is more expensive than most. The Savoie (✆ 540013) is cheap, cheerful, and a perfectly manageable walk from the cable-car. Argentière has a ski school (a way of beating the queues), its guides and off-piste skiing tuition (aimed at strong skiers) run by a celebrated local precipice-skier.
Tourist office ✆ (50) 540214. Package holidays BL, IG, SCG.

The Vallée Blanche

The Vallée Blanche is probably the most famous ski run in the world, some 18km long, with a vertical drop of 2770m – impressive statistics which immediately suggest one of its characteristics: that it is not at all steep. Many good skiers expect a technical challenge, and are disappointed – all you need is control over your speed and direction on a moderate slope. The run gives intermediate skiers the chance to enjoy grandiose glacier scenery normally reserved for a hardy minority of adventurous off-piste skiers and ski tourers. It is a sightseeing excursion on skis, to be done on a good day and at a gentle pace. Naturally, the run is extremely popular, and on a fine day at Easter there are enormous queues for the lift and at bottlenecks on the way down. Although usually easy to follow, the Vallée Blanche is not a piste, and it makes sense to ski it in a group with a guide; apart from the obvious benefits, a guide can also queue for your lift tickets.

Not the least spectacular part of the experience is the astonishingly engineered two-stage cable-car to the Aiguille du Midi from the edge of town. At the top, a tunnel cut in the ice leads to a long, steep, narrow ridge with terminal drops on either side; you have to clamber down this ridge, usually with the help of makeshift steps and a rope, before putting on skis, and for most non-mountaineers it is an uncomfortable few minutes. A guide can provide useful advice, help carry skis and even rope groups together. Courmayeur-based skiers can enjoy the Vallée Blanche without having to submit to this ordeal – see page 292.

From the bottom of the ridge, the long run cruises off through a white wilderness of ice, snow and rock, with long stretches where the most difficult thing is keeping up momentum. The most awkward section is a junction of glaciers known as the Salle à Manger, where steeper terrain breaks up the ice like a frozen waterfall, with huge crevasses gaping beside the narrow path where queues of skiers build up. Even here the skiing is not technically difficult. The glacier section of the run ends with a walk uphill off the Mer de Glace on to terra firma; again queues can be a problem. From here, it is a long ski down round the mountain to Chamonix, mostly a path across the steep hillside, where progress is often impeded by an abundance of stones, mud and tree roots.

For those who want greater excitement than the normal Vallée Blanche run can offer, there are several severe and perilous crevasse-hopping descents from the Aiguille du Midi. Those who just want to get away from the beaten track can take ski touring equipment and branch off (under guidance) from the main trail to explore other facets of this vast area of glacier.

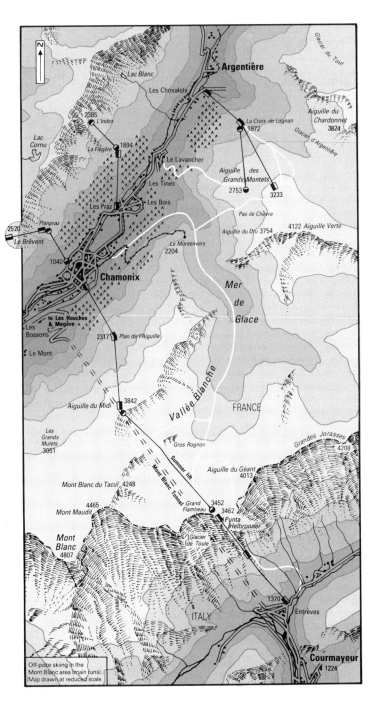

N

Glacier du Tour

Argentière

Lac Blanc

Les Chosalets

Aiguille du
Chardonnet
3824

2385 *L'Index*

La Croix de Lognan
1972

Glacier d'Argentière

Lac
Cornu

La Flégère 1894

Le Lavancher

Aiguille des
Grands Montets
2753   3233

Les Tines

Les Praz

Les Bois

Pas de Chèvre

Planpraz

4122 *Aiguille Verte*

2520

Le Brévent

Aiguille du Dru 3754

1040

Le Montenvers
2204

Chamonix

**Mer
de
Glace**

**to Les Houches
& Megève**

Les
Bossons

2317 *Plan de l'Aiguille*

Le Mont

Vallée Blanche

FRANCE

3842

Aiguille du Midi

Les
Grands
Mulets
3051

Gros Rognon

Grandes Jorasses
4208

Summer lift

Aiguille du Géant
4013

Mont Blanc du Tacul 4248

Mont Blanc Tunnel

4465
Mont Maudit

Grand
Flambeau

3452
3462

Punta
Helbronner

**Mont
Blanc
4807**

*Glacier
de Toule*

1370

Entrèves

ITALY

Courmayeur
1224

Off-piste skiing in the
Mont Blanc area (main runs).
Map drawn at reduced scale.

French skiing with a human face

Megève France 1100m

Good for *Easy skiing, big ski area, mountain restaurants, beautiful scenery, cross-country skiing, not skiing, Alpine charm, après-ski, short airport transfers, easy road access, sunny skiing*
Bad for *Tough skiing, skiing convenience, late holidays, resort-level snow*

Linked resorts: St-Gervais, St-Nicolas-de-Véroce, Combloux

Megève, an old village in a beautiful, sunny setting at medium altitude, became France's fashionable ski resort in the early days of the sport. Many keen skiers have come to demand more of a challenge than the gentle surroundings of Megève can supply, but the resort has not lost its popularity. There is still a lot of wealth around and starlets in need of publicity still come in their furs to pose for the resort gazette. Megève has the traditional charm of a resort where, in the words of the tourist office, wood has not given way to concrete, and where the variety of wintersports has not been lost. Horses and (wheeled) sleighs wait in the square, beneath a fine old church; carefully restored rough old buildings and an open-air ice rink add to the scene. The narrow central streets are car-free most of the time, and lined by very attractive and expensive shop windows.

Megève's skiing is not enormously varied, but there is a lot of it. It is mainly friendly skiing, mostly below the tree-line but with open pastures giving long, gentle runs for near-beginners and intermediate skiers, lots of sun and superb views. Old restaurants and even hotels are spread round the ridges at the top of the lifts, and much of the area is as easily enjoyed by walkers and cross-country skiers as by downhillers. The cross-country skiing, like the downhill, links up with the skiing of St-Gervais, a dull 19th-century spa town which also has a lift link with Les Houches in the Chamonix valley.

The skiing top 2350m bottom 900m

The skiing is in three widely separated areas. The least busy is reached by gondola starting some way north of the town and going over open slopes to the sunny, wooded knoll of **Le Jaillet**. To the west, beyond a dip, is the bald high-point of Le Christomet. To the north, drags take you into the skiing above Combloux. The skiing in this area is as a whole friendly and easy, though there are more challenging runs under both the gondola and the Christomet chair. On the other side of the resort there is much more skiing, mostly facing west and north, on the two sides of the wide horseshoe of mountain slopes curving round beneath the gentle peak of Mont Joly.

Megève's original cable-car, to the plateau of **Rochebrune**, starts a long way from the centre, but is now duplicated by a gondola and chair-lift from the centre of town. There are then a couple of short lifts up to the Alpette, the top of the sector and of Megève's famous downhill course (named after local hero Emile Allais), which runs steeply down behind the mountain to Cassioz; unfortunately, this run is often not open to the public. None of the other pistes is particularly difficult, and intermediate and inexperienced skiers will particularly enjoy the length of them (up to 760 metres vertical). The chair-lift back up to Rochebrune makes it possible to avoid the flat nursery fields at the bottom of the cable-car. Two long drag-lifts now make a link across the wide mountainside to the **Côte 2000** lifts, where two drags serve good, sustained, fairly challenging runs, including the women's downhill course. The area is sheltered from the sun, and usually holds its snow well. The two new lifts themselves serve good, long red runs.

Megève's most famous skiing mountain is the rounded end of the easterly arm of the horseshoe. The cable-car and drag-lift to the **Mont d'Arbois** both depart from high above the resort. **Princesse** is the north-facing side of the mountain, served by a long, two-stage gondola starting way out of town at Demi-Lune – very convenient for day-trip visitors. On the crest where these lifts meet the cable-car and gondola from Le Bettex (an outpost of St-Gervais), there are lots of little link runs, a few hotels and restaurants, and panoramic walking paths. The runs down to Megève are mostly open and easy, and include a long green. There is some more challenging skiing around the Mont Joux, the next peak along from Mont d'Arbois on the ridge which climbs towards Mont Joly, with increasingly steep slopes around the bowl. The scope here has been greatly increased by the opening of a new chair-lift the top altitude in the area. Both this and the nearby Epaule chair-lift give access to challenging pistes down on the Megève side, and some particularly good skiing down to St-Nicolas-de-Véroce (1200m) – mostly red runs and wide, rarely exploited east-facing off-piste slopes. For good skiers this is some of the best terrain in the whole area. From Mont Joux and the Epaule lifts there are long, fairly easy runs, mixed open and woodland terrain, down to Les Communailles near Le Bettex and St-Gervais.

The slopes on the north-facing Princesse side of the mountain are wooded and rather more challenging than the runs down to Megève from the Mont d'Arbois, but the black labels on the piste map overstate the difficulty. There is often some good off-piste skiing among the trees underneath the top half of the gondola. The lower slopes of the Princesse are gentle and often lack snow.

Nursery slopes at the bottom of the major lifts are good but not very reliable for snow. In good conditions most first-year skiers will soon be able to handle Le Jaillet.

Mountain restaurants are good, but generally rather expensive. Attractive old restaurants and hotels easily accessible to skiers and non-skiers alike stand at the top of the Mont d'Arbois/Mont Joux area. The restaurant at the top of the Rochebrune cable-car is shoddy, but the chalet hotel restaurant at Alpette is very attractive.

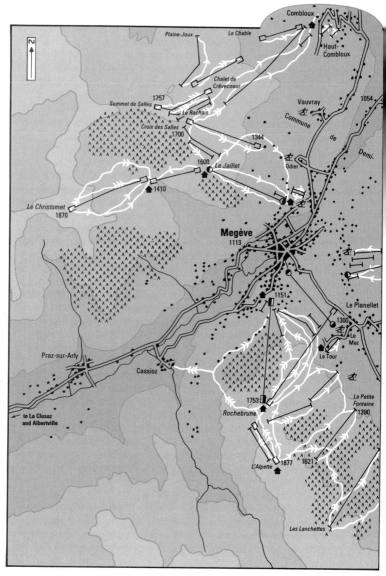

Lifts

Passes Mont-Blanc lift pass (4 or 6 days) covers all the lifts and resort buses, as well as those of St-Gervais, St-Nicolas, Les Contamines, the Chamonix valley and several other small resorts. Various other passes are available for any number of days. All lifts can be paid for individually.

Cost 6-day Mont Blanc pass FF555.

Beginners Local pass or cash.

Children About 10% off local passes, under 10.

When the resort is full, expect queues for the main access lifts.

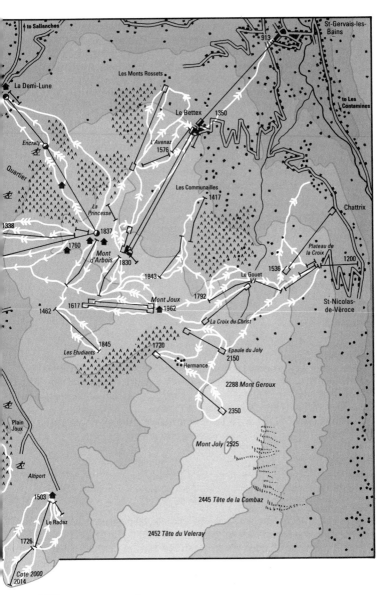

The resort

As Megève has grown to become one of the largest in France, it has
spread far in all directions from the centre. The style of the hotels and
chalets is not very picturesque, but nor is it ugly.

Accommodation is in a wide range of hotels and private chalets let out for self-catering holidays. The resort centre is the best compromise location. Outstanding luxury hotels are the Mont Blanc (℘ 212002), in the centre, murals by Jean Cocteau, and the Chalet Mont d'Arbois (℘ 212503) near the cable-car. The comfortable Ferme-Hotel Duvillard (℘ 211462) is very convenient for the Mont d'Arbois lift. The Castel Champlat (℘ 212549) is central and comfortable; it has no restaurant. The simpler Mont Idéal (℘ 212416) is next door to the Mont-Blanc.

Après-ski is lively and smart, at least until the end of February, when Megève starts to wind down. There are scores of restaurants in a great variety of styles. There is some smart nightlife in the disco/cabaret/ casino and the Club des Cinque Rues (a jazz club). There isn't much cheap, informal après-ski, except for a few simple bars and a bowling alley. Sometimes there is ice hockey.

Ski school

Classes 2hr morning and afternoon. **Cost** 6 days FF316. Private lessons FF109/hr (1 or 2 people). **Children** 25% off. Several ski and non-ski kindergartens, ages 2–8, 9.00–5.00.

6 days with lunch FF600–1,300. **Special courses** Competition classes in school holidays. Guides available for off-piste excursions.

Other activities

Cross-country Three areas, each with green, blue and red loops: bottom of Jaillet (total 17 km); bottom of the Mont d'Arbois cable-car to Princesse mid-station (total 8km); beyond Le Mas in valley between bottom of Rochebrune

and Côte 2000 lifts (total 33km) **Not skiing** 50km cleared paths, skating (outdoor and indoor), curling, swimming, riding, sleigh rides, judo, dance classes, bridge, aeroplane excursions, tennis.

The resort is very large and no tranquil Alpine backwater, but X-C trails are in varied and attractive surroundings. The Mont d'Arbois/Princesse trails link up with the St-Gervais ones. There is plenty for non-skiers to do, with particularly good walks in the ski areas, all of which give marvellous views. Walks are graded from easy to off-piste (there are no black walks). Annecy makes an attractive excursion.

Travel

Airport Geneva; transfer about 1½hr. **Railway** Sallanches (13km); frequent buses. **Road** Via Geneva or Lyon/Annecy;

chains rarely needed **Reachable resorts** Chamonix, Flaine Courmayeur, La Clusaz all within range.

Reasonably frequent daytime bus services link the centre to Rochebrune and Mont d'Arbois; less often to Jaillet, Princesse and the Côte 2000 lifts. Sleigh rides are so organised that they form an effective (and expensive) transport system. Although the resort isn't easy to negotiate by car, a car is very handy for skiers with a Mont Blanc lift pass and a sense of adventure.

Miscellaneous

Tourist office ℘ (50) 212728. Tx 385532. **Medical** Hospital at Sallanches (13km); doctors, dentists, chemists in resort. **Equipment hire** 6 days skis FF200,

boots FF85, X-C FF185. **Resort beds** 3,500 in hotels, 22,500 in apartments. **Package holidays** FL, JM, MM.

Cuisine classique

La Clusaz France 1100m

Good for *Cross-country skiing, easy road access, short airport transfers*
Bad for *Skiing convenience, late holidays, tough skiing*

La Clusaz is a large, long-established summer and winter resort just up the road from Annecy – in style, as in location, mid-way between the small, old-fashioned family resorts of the Mont Blanc area and the big, modern sporty ones of the Tarentaise. The layout of the resort is messy and inconvenient, but its atmosphere is very French and unfussy and, for a resort which has escaped the attention of the international package industry, it has a lot of skiing. Most of the skiing is below 2000m and consists of broad runs through woodland, but there is also some high, open skiing with good off-piste runs – making it a very flexible resort, capable of amusing almost all categories of skier in almost all weather conditions. In some ways its all-round appeal is very like that of nearby Megève, but with a big difference of emphasis: La Clusaz is less self-consciously fashionable and has more challenging and more varied skiing. It fills up with local youth at weekends and holiday times, when it is very lively; out of season it is almost too quiet, as old couples and young families on tight budgets while away their evenings playing cards in simple hotels.

The skiing top 2490m bottom 1100m

There are four areas, spread round the sides of two valleys facing north, east and west. Two are reached by lifts from the resort centre, the other two from points along the valleys. Despite roads and rivers, all four areas are linked by lift or piste – though some of the links are green pistes which involve as much walking as skiing.

Beauregard, served by a single cable-car from the bottom of the resort, is a gentle wooded mountain with very attractive easy skiing in pastoral surroundings at the top (1650m) – good for beginners, walkers and cross-country skiers – and a couple of longer runs back down to the resort. The black starts quite steeply but is otherwise not very black. The green run round the mountain to join up with the Etale skiing is better suited to cross-country than Alpine skiers for most of its length.

L'Etale is a taller, steeper mountain, also served by a single cable-car from bottom (1250m) to top (1960m). Skiing is limited to one flank of the mountain (facing north-west), open and fairly steep at the top, with several drag-lifts serving the gentler and more spacious slopes at the bottom. From the bottom station, beside the Croix-Fry road, the Transval cable-car shuttles skiers to and from the Juments chair-lift which serves one side of the Aiguille area.

L'Aiguille is the largest area, directly accessible from the village by chair-lifts. There are several sections. The Crêt du Merle is a half-way station with a small nursery area, ski school assembly point and restaurants. There are several ways back down into the village through the woods, none of them particularly difficult. Above Crête du Merle there are some fairly stiff red runs from Crêt du Loup, with plenty of room for a gentler course to be taken. The west-facing run from Crêt du Loup to the bottom of the Juments chairlift is marked blue, but is long (over 600m vertical) and in places fairly steep; it will challenge most skiers and bore none. Provided there is enough snow to cover the tree stumps, off-piste skiers can have fun underneath the chairs. Skiing above Crêt du Loup is in a mostly fairly gentle bowl, but the lifts give access to some of La Clusaz's most interesting off-piste skiing – the Combe du Borderan down to the bottom of the Juments chair-lift (west-facing), and the Combe du Fernuy, which is the first of a series of about a dozen long, steep gullies facing north-west, cut like furrows in the wall of the long Chaîne des Aravis.

The north-west-facing **Balme** slopes provide La Clusaz's highest and most challenging skiing, with fine, long runs down two more of the Aravis coombs giving skiing of over 1200m vertical. Although you can ski and plod across from the Crêt du Loup, most people go to and from this area by bus. The main black run is steep enough to serve as a speed-skiing course.

There are small **nursery slopes** beside the resort and at the bottom of each sector. The best nursery areas are at the Crêt du Merle and on the top of the Beauregard, which is delightful. There is plenty of skiing for beginners and timid intermediates as long as the snow conditions on the lower slopes are good.

Mountain restaurants are not very numerous, but attractively old-fashioned (especially the hotel at the top of Beauregard).

Lifts

Passes Area pass covers all La Clusaz lifts but not ski-bus; available for day or half-day, four days and longer; weekly pass valid one day at Le Grand Bornand and Flaine

Cost 6-day pass FF450. Small reduction in low season.
Children About 20% off, under 12.
Beginners Cash or lift pass.

We have no information about queues at peak times. Piste marking is somewhat indeterminate, especially around Beauregard. Many of the links between the various skiing areas are laborious.

The resort

The setting of la Clusaz is a rather enclosed one beside a river at the meeting point of several steep-sided wooded valleys. The village has grown and no longer fits comfortably into its narrow slot, and the sprawl of buildings along the valley and up its sides is complicated by a series of road junctions and roundabouts; it is a somewhat confusing and traffic-ridden place. Downtown La Clusaz, or La Clusaz Sud as it is

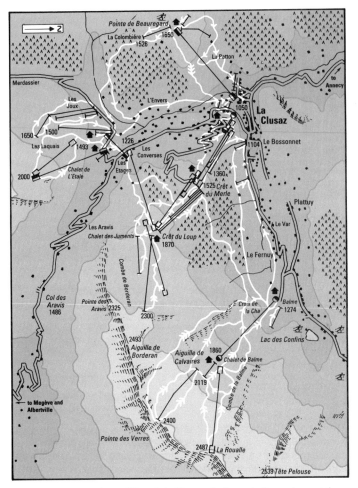

signed, is pleasantly traditional, built round a large bulbous-towered church (you don't need an alarm clock if you're staying centrally), with a stylish modern shopping precinct beside it and a fast-flowing stream below. Shopping is attractively varied, and there are the very ordinary cafés you find in every French village but in few French ski resorts.

La Clusaz is very much a weekend resort for inhabitants of Annecy and Geneva, and most of the **accommodation** is in private chalets dotted around the hillsides, many of which are available for rent. In the centre of the resort there are lots of simple, reasonably priced hotels. The Christiania (✆ 026060), the Hotel des Aravis (✆ 026031) and the Montagne (✆ 026161) are all centrally placed, quiet family hotels. The very welcoming Lac des Confins (✆ 024171) is in a remote and beautiful but not particularly inconvenient setting, ideal for cross-country skiers and escapists.

Après-ski is lively at weekends and peak holiday period, otherwise quiet. The skating rink is open every evening, snow-shoe excursions to mountain restaurants for a fondue are organised once a week and there are about four or five discothèques. There are lots of restaurants, both in the resort centre and around the valleys. Le Foly is a particularly attractive log cabin up in the Les Confins valley, more expensive than most.

Ski school

Classes 2½hr morning and afternoon. Cost 6 days FF430. Private lesson F90/hr (1 or 2 people). Children 25% off, under 12. Ski kindergarten, ages 3½–6, 8.30–6.00, 6 days with lunch FF767. Non-ski kindergarten, ages up to 4½, 8.30–6.00, 6 days with lunch, FF563. Special courses Off-piste, ski touring by the week or day. Competition classes in school holidays only

Other activities

Cross-country 4km green, 4.5km blue, 9.5km red, 7km black in Les Confins valley; 1km green, 3km blue, 6km red, 13km black at Beauregard/Croix-Fry. Ski school in each sector. Not skiing Walks and snowmobile rides in X-C areas, plane joyrides, artificial outdoor ice rink, outdoor pool (February onwards).

The X-C trails are varied and beautiful although not immediately accessible from the resort. For X-C skiers going up to Beauregard, there is no alternative to paying for the cable-car trip by trip. Excursions to Annecy are easy. The attractive old market town of Thônes is also worth a visit.

Travel

Airport Geneva; transfer 2hr. Railway Annecy (32km); frequent buses. Road Via Lyon/Annecy; chains rarely needed. Reachable resorts Megève, Chamonix, Flaine, Valmorel

The Col des Aravis (1486m) for access to Megève and Albertville is occasionally closed in winter and often snowy. There is a bus shuttle service (not covered by the lift pass) running along two lines, linking the various ski areas with the resort centre. There is no service after 7pm. The bus service to Le Grand Bornand is free for holders of weekly lift passes. Having a car in the resort is handy but not really necessary. Parking in the resort centre can be a problem at weekends. There is an underground car park.

Miscellaneous

Tourist office ✆ (50) 026092. Tx 385125. Medical Hospital at Annecy (32km); doctors, dentist, chemist in resort. Package holidays AT, FL, MM, VF, WM. Equipment hire 6 days skis FF200, boots FF110, X-C FF175. Resort beds 1,800 in hotels, about 15,000 in apartments

Disneyland in the snow

Valmorel France 1400m

Good for *Nursery slopes, family skiing, skiing convenience, freedom from cars, Alpine charm, lift queues, resort-level snow*
Bad for *Tough skiing, not skiing, après-ski, mountain restaurants*

Linked resort: St-François-Longchamp

Valmorel is a brand-new resort at the west of the Tarentaise region. Like many others, it is an apartment resort planned to cater for families. But its architects have contrived to imitate a traditional village, deliberately introducing the variety that normally develops over time. The result, especially the colourful toytown shopping street, is refreshing, and the layout is so ingenious that little convenience is sacrificed. The ski area is small by local standards. There are splendid high-level easy motorways, but most of the skiing is intermediate, and more difficult than the gradings suggest – though good snow usually helps. Old St-François (1450m) and new Longchamp (1650m) are separate villages over the Col de la Madeleine sharing a small, sunny skiing area, newly linked to Valmorel.

The skiing top 2403m bottom 1250m

Valmorel sits at the foot of a deep horseshoe of ski-fields with slopes facing north, west and east. In a number of places gullies and cliffs break up the bowl, but lift and piste connections work smoothly enough.
   A long chair-lift from the centre of the village goes up to the rounded Tête de Beaudin, where drag-lifts serve long, very easy runs on top and down into the Celliers valley. The Montagne de Tête, on the morning-sun side of the resort, can be reached by drag-lift from here, or by chair from the resort. It provides good scope for off-piste skiing, a genuine black run and some tough intermediate ones down to the resort. There is also a very long green trail though the woods to Combelouvière. From the Celliers valley a new 3-seater chair-lift goes up to the Col de la Madeleine (1933m); the run down to Longchamp is easy and involves some poling; the blue run back starts with a narrow, steepish section, properly marked red on the mountain.
   Lifts from the top of the village give access to the Col du Gollet. This is a fine open slope with off-piste or black and red runs, and is also the starting point of the great Nine Valleys adventure, with an open off-piste descent towards Les Menuires. Beyond the Col de Mottet, the high point of the Valmorel system, is the start of an exhilarating long black run down behind Riondet into the Celliers valley.
   The dense network of indistinguishable blue and red pistes just above the village gives inexperienced skiers no easy options. But there

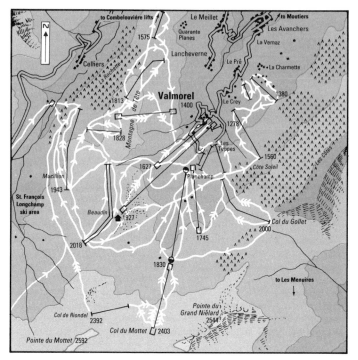

are good **nursery slopes** with three lifts on the east side of the resort, away from the main pistes. The runs are specially contoured to assist the learning process.

There are only three **mountain restaurants** in the whole ski area, at Beaudin, Montagne de Tête and the Col de la Madeleine. These have good sun terraces and loos, but are cramped.

Lifts

Passes Cheval Noir pass covers all Valmorel and St-François-Longchamp lifts. Local pass also available.
Cost 6-day pass FF508.

Children 20% off, under 13.
Beginners Coupons or limited day passes.

There is very rarely any queuing even at peak holiday times. Ski school priority can lead to short hold-ups. St-François-Longchamp is more crowded during school holidays, and the return trip can be slow.

The resort

Valmorel has runs and lifts reaching down into the very centre and down both flanks and tentacles of road reaching up – so drivers can park close to their accommodation, but the pathways of the resort are car-free. At the base of the resort is Bourg-Morel, its commercial centre – a single pedestrian street full of restaurants, shops and bars, with café terraces at the foot of the main pistes. Most apartments are in small blocks grouped into several 'hamlets' – two of them served by a cable-car (Télébourg) from Bourg-Morel. Nearby is the children's village, Saperlipopette, the spiritual heart of the resort.

Nearly all the **accommodation** is apartments, well liked by our reporters. La Fontaine, on the east side, is the least attractive location, not served by the Télébourg and not close to the nursery slopes. There are three hotels, rather expensive and functional. The Hôtel du Bourg (∅ 098666) in Bourg-Morel is the only one which offers terms other than weekly board. Skiers with cars can stay much more cheaply outside the resort at the little Cheval Noir in the delightful hamlet of Les Avanchers (∅ 098190), or in the valley.

Après-ski is very limited. There are several satisfactory restaurants where you can get cheap snacks or sophisticated cuisine, quite lively bars, and a disco. We have reports of fireworks and street entertainers.

Ski school

Classes 3hr morning (advanced) or afternoon (inexperienced).
Cost 6 days FF353. Special beginners' course including lifts FF634. Private lessons FF132 for 75min.
Children Flexible arrangements for children up to age 13, including play, ski

school, lunch, tea as required, 8.45–7.15. Typical cost: 6 days with lunch FF675. All-day classes possible; 25% off adult prices, under 13.
Special courses Off-piste (various formulae), Nine Valleys tours via Méribel to La Plagne and Val d'Isère.

The kindergarten and play areas are very attractive. Reports on the ski school are very favourable, except that English-speaking instructors are not always easy to secure. The Nine Valleys tour is more ski tourism than ski touring; there are variants of different standards.

Other activities

Cross-country Trails totalling 17km, starting 3km from resort beyond le Pré nursery area (transport provided free for those taking X-C ski school).

Not skiing Organised snow-shoe outings, toboggan run, aerobics, fitness training, sauna.

Valmorel is not suitable either for X-C or for non-skiers. There are few cleared walks, no swimming pool, and few excursion possibilities.

Travel

Airport Geneva; transfer about 3hr.
Railway Moûtiers (18km); frequent buses.
Road Via Lyon/Chambéry; poor road

from Aigueblanche; chains may be needed.
Reachable resorts Trois Vallées resorts, Champagny, La Plagne, Les Arcs.

The free Télébourg shuttle lift runs from 8.30 to 11.30; it gets very crowded at ski school time in the morning. Having a car in Valmorel is of no use, except to ski in nearby resorts.

Miscellaneous

Tourist office ∅ (79) 098555.
Tx 980321.
Equipment hire 6 days skis FF200, boots FF80, X-C FF150.
Resort beds 280 in hotels, 6,000 in apartments.

Medical Chemist and doctor in resort; dentist at Aigueblanche (12km), hospital at Moûtiers (18km).
Package holidays FT, MM, NE, SCB, SCP, SCG, STC, TH, WT.

Les Trois Vallées: big is beautiful

Courchevel France 1300 – 1850m

Good for *Nursery slopes, easy skiing, big ski area, skiing convenience, après-ski, resort-level snow, chalet holidays*
Bad for *Alpine charm, short airport transfers, easy road access, not skiing*

Méribel France 1450 – 1700m

Good for *Big ski area, lift queues, sunny skiing, chalet holidays, self-catering holidays*
Bad for *Après-ski, short airport transfers, nursery slopes, easy road access, not skiing*

Linked resorts: Les Menuires, Val Thorens

'Le plus grand domaine skiable du monde' is the rather nebulous catchphrase of one of the skiing industry's biggest conglomerates. Four important resorts share an enormous linked ski area (to be imprecise, some 175 lifts and 450km of piste) which in one holiday many skiers can barely come to terms with, never mind exhaust.

Parisians who can afford it fly with their poodles to Courchevel, stay in comfortable hotels, and dine and dance without counting the centimes. For them, Courchevel is one of the best equipped of all French resorts; and for skiing gourmets it is without doubt the best resort in the world (which is not saying much). Its slopes offer enormous scope for beginners and timid skiers, enough variety of difficulty and terrain to satisfy experts, and better snow than in Méribel or Les Menuires. The major drawback is that it is difficult for Courchevel-based skiers to make much use of the high-altitude skiing in Val Thorens, at the far end of the domaine skiable. Courchevel is split into several parts, usually referred to by numbers approximating to altitude. The resort centre is at 1850, the highest part.

Méribel is a British favourite. Its attractions are that it occupies the central valley, from which you can make the most of the enormous skiing, and that it is the prettiest of the resorts; it does not have much competition. It may be a very convenient or an extremely awkward resort, depending on where you stay in which of the two resort villages – Méribel-les-Allues (which we're calling Méribel) or Méribel-Mottaret (Mottaret) higher up the valley. Neither has much après-ski.

Budget-conscious French skiers go to Les Menuires, fail to swing a cat in their apartments, and congratulate themselves on getting expensive skiing on the cheap (which of course they are not). Rejected moonshot candidates, and those who believe that the key to good skiing is altitude, go to Val Thorens, the highest resort in Europe.

The skiing top 3200m bottom 1270m

The Méribel and Courchevel valleys are well linked by a simple arrangement of lifts up to a single point on the mountain dividing the two. Les Menuires and Val Thorens are not nearly so well connected to Méribel because they are much further up their valley.

The **Courchevel** skiing is spread widely across the mountainside with a great variety of terrain and orientation. The shape of the mountains is concave, with the steeper runs around the rocky rim dividing Courchevel from Méribel, and a huge area of gentle slopes just above the resort which gives rise to the idea that the skiing consists entirely of nursery slopes. This is far from the truth.

From the big central station in Courchevel 1850 the left-hand gondola goes up to Verdons, where a vast new cable-car climbs to the top of the skiing at Saulire. This is the only lift from Courchevel which gives access to the three notorious couloirs dropping from the mountain crest – scoffed at by connoisseurs as being neither long nor steep nor narrow, but as graded pistes indisputably severe.

All the other runs served by the cable-car can also be reached from the alternative gondola from Verdons. There are several steepish red and genuinely black alternative ways back to Verdons; other pistes lead over to Méribel; more still round and down into the beautiful wide Vallée des Creux and from there either down to 1550 (a tediously flat trail) or, via linking lifts, back to 1850 or over to 1650. These are long runs with plenty of opportunity for exploration (by no means always safe) near the pistes on the top half.

Each of the three chair-lifts from Lac des Creux serves interesting, challenging skiing. The new Creux Noirs lift opens up an off-piste run to Mottaret. The Chanrossa lift serves an impressive, wide slope of about 500m vertical; the black piste is only moderately steep but the heavily skied off-piste area is steeper. Chanrossa gets a lot of afternoon sun and the snow deteriorates. Behind Chanrossa harmless red runs lead into the extensive Courchevel 1650 skiing – wide open and easy, with a choice of green and blue motorways leading to the bottom.

The right-hand gondola from 1850, and several drag-lifts nearby, serve the skiing below the Col de la Loze. Long black trails, not steep but consistently challenging, go down through thick woods to Le Praz, giving 900m vertical. There
is plenty of off-piste scope. There is some less demanding skiing in this sector – easy runs in the morning sun down to 1850 and 1550. From the Col de la Loze itself, an attractive piste – not difficult but often with poor snow – leads to Méribel Altiport.

The skiing of the **Méribel** valley spreads across both flanks, facing roughly east and west – ideal for sunny skiing morning and afternoon. There is no difficulty in getting across from one side to the other or making the links along the mountainsides above the two resorts. The slopes are open, and wooded only above Méribel. Most of the runs are intermediate, with blue runs that are often unpleasantly difficult, and black runs which are mostly not.

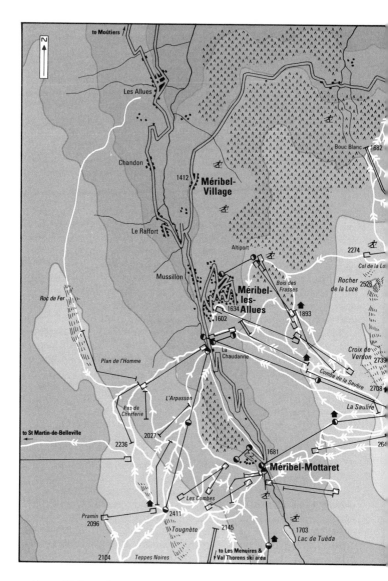

Above Mottaret there are many variants of the open runs directly down from Saulire, mostly stiff red but with some winding routes which are just about blue. The slopes face south-west and snow conditions are often treacherous. Artificial snow machines have recently been installed on the lower slopes. In good conditions, the little-used Grande Rosière run is a splendid sustained black. The excellent black race-course down to Méribel is rarely open to holiday skiers.

The runs in the Burgin sector immediately above Méribel are mostly

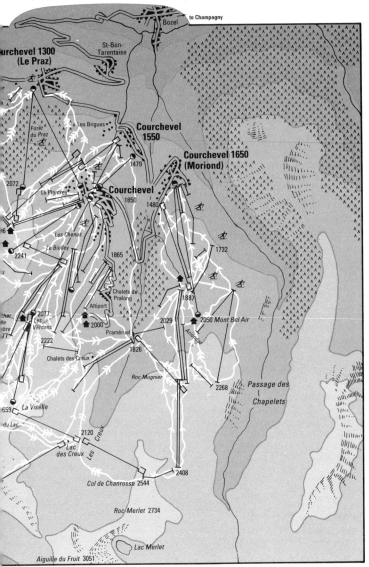

shorter and easier and have more reliable snow. Above the Altiport is a particularly fine green run for near-beginners. From Rond-Point at the top of the village a piste runs down beside the resort to the Chaudanne lift station. This run gets badly worn.

The east-facing slopes are more varied and fragmented, with little bowls and ridges out of the way of the piste network. Above Méribel the long two-stage gondola to Tougnète serves a long black run back down to the base station – a short steep mogul field at the top, an easy middle

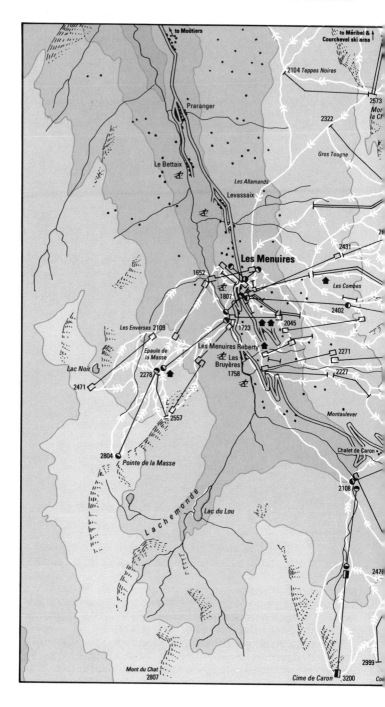

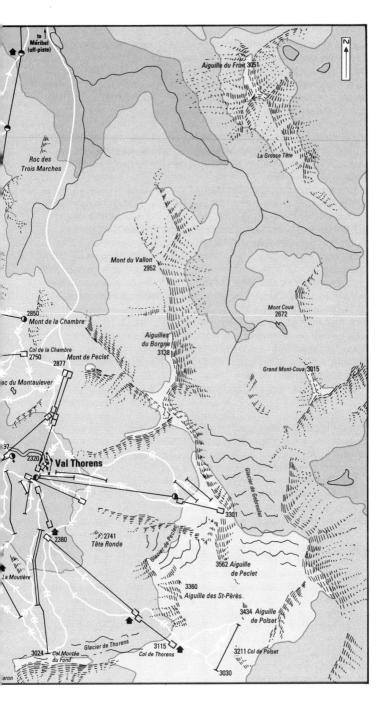

section with connections to Mottaret, and a steeper run down through the woods under the bottom section of the lift, often short of snow. There is a large, uncrowded area of easy and intermediate runs in the newly opened Roc de Fer/Pas de Cherferie sector. The new Plattières gondola towards Les Menuires has a wide, easy blue trail beneath the first two sections, and a short, unprepared black pitch under the top one. The easy black and enjoyable red runs served by the Mont de la Challe drags often provide good snow when it's in short supply. From the Roc de Tougnes and Roc des 3 Marches there is plenty of scope for finding off-piste ways down between the runs; some of these slopes are often dangerous. Mottaret and Méribel are linked directly by a very easy, wide green run.

Les Menuires's skiing, like Méribel's, is spread over two sides of a valley, but here connections from one side to the other are awkward. Above the resort are various long runs, facing south-west, of about 1000m vertical from the Roc des 3 Marches and the Mont de la Chambre (the main links with Méribel). The many variants are stiff intermediate runs, often made more difficult and unpleasant by poor snow and crowds of skiers in transit. The lifts on the upper slopes to the north provide links with Méribel rather than interesting skiing. A more adventurous route to Meribel is the often piste-like itinerary behind Mont de la Chambre down a wide, empty and beautiful valley, followed by a long path through woods beside the river to Mottaret. The runs, of which there are several variants including one from the top of the Val Thorens chair-lifts, are steep only in a few places, but involve a fair amount of poling or skating, and the negotiation of narrow and boulder-strewn passages.

Opposite Les Menuires, La Masse is a much more tempting mountain for good skiers. Its slopes face north-east and usually have much better snow; the runs are long (again about 1000m vertical) and tough, including some genuine blacks, and are not busy with transit crowds. The main off-piste run to La Châtelard and St-Martin-de-Belleville runs high along the crest of the mountains. Another run drops down into the valley between La Masse and the Cime de Caron.

Val Thorens is set at the head of the Belleville valley and is tightly enclosed by a horseshoe of mountains with slopes facing south, west and north. Most of the lift departures are below the resort, and the lower slopes are gentle; streams (and associated ice) are a hazard.

The big Cime de Caron cable-car climbs swiftly to the highest point in the Trois Vallées winter skiing, and opens up some magnificent runs. An easy track runs round the back of the peak with a long off-piste run down into the valley between Caron and La Masse. The black north-facing piste is a long, wide, open, steep slope – couloirs apart, the most challenging piste in the Trois Vallées. The red runs on the shoulder of the mountain are often closed.

The rest of Val Thorens skiing seems rather ordinary after Caron, though the drags to the east of it serve north-facing slopes which are enjoyable for their reliably good snow. Runs on the glacier from the Col de Thorens are wide and easy. Those on the other side of the rocky Aiguille de Péclet are slightly more challenging, and this area is reported to be good for off-piste. The chair-lifts on the Mont de Péclet are used mainly for access to Les Menuires and Méribel (see above).

Courchevel has very good **nursery slopes** – both 1850 and 1650 have huge areas of very green skiing immediately above the resort. 1650's pistes are much-less crowded. The slopes at both Méribel and Mottaret are too steep and busy for comfort. Les Menuires' nursery area is broad, gentle, convenient and sunny, but hideously crowded and often icy. Val Thorens's nursery runs are spacious but much used by other skiers.

Mountain restaurants are more numerous than in many modern resorts, though few are particularly attractive. Fortunately, there are lots of good and easily accessible restaurants in the resorts.

Lifts

Passes Three Valleys lift pass covers all lifts of Courchevel, Les Menuires, Val Thorens and St-Martin-de-Belleville but not bus services. Each valley has a variety of local passes, of which the more extensive ones can be extended to cover the Three Valleys by the day. Main pass available by the day, six days or longer including ten non-consecutive days, valid all season.

Cost 6-day Three Valleys pass FF618. 10% off in low season.
Childen 10% off, under 13 – more on most local passes.
Beginners Coupons valid for limited areas of lifts in Courchevel, Méribel and Les Menuires. Two free lifts in Val Thorens, and limited-area lift pass.
Summer skiing Extensive at Val Thorens, 2800 to 3300m.

The Trois Vallées lift system copes with the enormous numbers of skiers remarkably well. Rapid and regular improvements have been made in recent years. The main queue black spots are the major lifts out of Courchevel and Les Menuires at peak periods. Mottaret also gets crowded by skiers are returning to Courchevel, though the new alternative via Méribel has halped. Closing times are very rigidly enforced, and the taxi rides home are long and expensive.

The resorts

Courchevel

Courchevel consists of a string of communities along the road which winds up one flank of the wide Bozel valley. 1300, 1550, and 1850 are stacked up the same hillside, with lift and piste connections between each other; 1650 is out of the way on the other side of a river gorge.

1300 (Le Praz) is an attractive hamlet with a few hotels and a couple of restaurants at the bottom of the skiing, handy for the cross-country trails. 1550 is more of a resort, but a characterless one – a dormitory suburb, by-passed by the road, by most skiers and by all serious après-skiers. It has some inexpensive hotels and restaurants. Both 1300 and 1550 have ways up the mountain, and over to Meribel, avoiding the 1850 bottleneck. 1650 (Moriond) is no more than a straggle of roadside apartment blocks and hotels with a few shops.

1850 is the main focus; it is an ugly place, built without much style in the early days of French purpose-building in the late 40s, and much added to since with no advance in aesthetic achievement. It is now a large resort spread between 1700m and 1900m, above and below the original site on a wide shelf about on the tree-line. The hub is a huge lift-station complex known as La Croisette. Either side of it there are lively and very smart shopping streets; cars can be a nuisance. The centre is reasonably compact, but chalets and hotels are spread far and wide across the hillsides, mostly on or near an easy piste.

Accommodation is in staffed chalets, apartments in chalets, and lots of hotels. Most chalets used by UK operators are on the east side, if not in the centre. In general, standards of accommodation are high, and hotel prices are high too. In the comfortable category no less than four hotels have restaurants with Michelin rosettes; the Carlina (∅ 080030) is one of them, well placed above the centre towards the altiport. Also very comfortable and expensive is the more central Grand Hotel Rond-point des Pistes (∅ 080269). Of the less expensive hotels, the Albaron (∅ 080357; no restaurant) and the Dahu (∅ 080118) are both quiet and central. In 1550, the Chanrossa (∅ 080658) is friendly and well-placed for lifts.

When the French are on holiday there is a lot of expensive, chic, late **après-ski**. At the smartest places, with cabaret – the Grange and the New St-Nicolas – you should expect to pay about £7 to get in and have a drink, and refills are no cheaper. One reporter summed up the discos as 'the best I've ever encountered – expensive, stylish and yobbo-free'. There are places with a more Alpine atmosphere, relaxing piano bars, and many good restaurants, including the two down in Le Praz. Out of French holiday periods the resort is quieter, and the après-ski depends more on the not-so-big-spending British.

Ski school

Classes 2½hr morning, 2hr afternoon. Cost 6 days FF434. Private lessons FF103/hr (1 to 4 people). Children About 25% off, under 12. Ski kindergarten (1850), ages 5 up, 9.00–5.00, 6 days with lunch FF640. Non-ski kindergarten (1850 and 1650), ages 2–5, all day with lunch, FF175/day.

Reports indicate rather undesirably frequent changes of instructor, but are otherwise generally favourable.

Other activities

Cross-country Ten trails totalling 30km; mostly easy, in woods above Le Praz and at 1650. Not skiing Artificial ice rink for skating/ curling, bridge and chess and le Scrabble, 'plane excursions, parachuting, aerobics.

Courchevel is not a very attractive resort for non-skiers (except full-time après-skiers). Interesting excursion possibilities are few. Although it is not really a natural choice for cross-country skiers, our one X-C reporter was well pleased with the woodland trails and the possibility of skiing up by the Col de la Loze (reached by lift).

Travel

Airport Geneva; transfer 3½hr plus. Daily direct flights to altiport from Paris. Railway Moûtiers (25km); frequent buses. Road Via Lyon/Chambéry; chains may be needed. Horrific peak weekend jams. Reachable resorts La Plagne, Les Arcs, Valmorel, Val d'Isère, Tignes.

A bus shuttle service (not covered by the lift pass) links the different parts of the resort, and there are regular buses to the altiport during the day. There is an hourly service until about 10pm, not a lot of help to serious après-skiers. If you go up to Courchevel 1850 from the lower stations you can always toboggan, slide or ski back down the pistes if the moon is out. For après-ski excursions a car is of value.

Miscellaneous

Tourist office ✆ (79) 080029.
Tx 980083.
Medical Hospital at Moûtiers (25km); doctors, chemists and dentist in resort.
Equipment hire 6 days skis FF250,
boots FF120, X-C FF240.
Resort beds 11,000 in hotels, 17,000 in apartment/chalets.
Package holidays JL, FL, JM, MM, SCG, SKW, SMG, SNP, SVP, WT.

Méribel

Méribel-les-Allues (Méribel) is built in something like traditional village style. It spreads steeply from about 1400m, beside the river, up the west-facing side of the valley to about 1650m, with large chalet-style buildings all along the road which winds up the hillside and continues past the top of the resort (Rond-Point, where the ski school meets) on through the woods to the Altiport. Commercial and social life revolves around the hectic little square at the bottom of the village, now by-passed by the main valley road. In general Méribel is a quiet residential resort, a favourite place for secluded luxury chalets.

Accommodation is mostly in apartments and staffed chalets, of which there is an enormous choice. Because Méribel stretches across the hillside as well as up it, there can be long walks to and from skiing unless you are based close to the village piste. Of the several hotels, the Orée du Bois (✆ 005030) is conveniently placed at Rond-Point, and is straightforwardly comfortable. Hotels apparently close to the gondola station are less convenient than they seem – you have to walk to the lifts. The Adray (✆ 086026) is isolated but very conveniently on-piste. The Altiport Hotel (✆ 005232) is comfortable, expensive and isolated.

Après-ski is quiet. There are a few tatty bars and restaurants in the centre, and a teenies' disco half a mile down the valley. There are smarter restaurants up the hillside, of no great culinary distinction.

Mottaret is higher up the valley, better placed for skiing links with Courchevel and (especially) Les Menuires. Like Méribel it climbs high up the side of the valley – in this case the east-facing side, up to 1850m – and again there is a piste down the southern side of the resort to the centre; access to the piste is much less of a problem here.

Accommodation is nearly all in apartments (though there are several hotels) generally favourably reported upon. Most reporters stayed at the top of the resort (Le Hameau) where many of the apartments have balconies with splendid views. There is not much après-ski here – just a few restaurants and a big, anonymous congregation area and bar. Reporters commented on high drinks prices in the British-run bar – 'kept us in the apartment drinking duty-free.' There are more stylish restaurants and bars at the bottom of Mottaret, but it's a steep 20-minute walk back.

Ski school

ESF and international school.
Classes ESF 2½hr morning, 2hr
afternoon. International school morning
or afternoon.
Cost 6 days FF433 (25½hr) ESF.
International school FF450 (15hr).
Private lessons FF104/hr.

Children About 33% off (ESF), under 12.
Ski/non-ski kindergarten at Méribel,
ages 2–8, 9.00–5.30, 6 days with meals
FF577. At Le Hameau (Mottaret) ages
3–8, 9.00–5.00, 6 days with meals
FF620.
Special courses Competition, free-style.

The international section of the ski school guarantees instruction in
perfect English except during the February holidays. The price is high.
We have favourable reports of the Pingouins kindergarten at Le
Hameau; children in ESF ski classes at Mottaret can have lunch at the
Pingouins and stay there after ski school has finished.

Other activities

Cross-country 4.5km blue track and
2km green track at Mottaret; 10km red,
5km blue, 1.5km green track near
Altiport, above Méribel and itinerary from
Altiport to Courchevel.
Not-skiing Artificial ice rink, swimming,

flying lessons and excursions, hang-
gliding, ice/snow driving (Mottaret),
bridge, squash (Mottaret), about 10km
walks (Méribel and Mottaret). Fitness
centre with sauna, jacuzzi, fitness room
above Le Hameau in Mottaret.

The cross-country trails in the woods around the Altiport are in beautiful
surroundings and suit not very ambitious cross-country skiers well.
Méribel does not have a lot to offer non-skiers, Mottaret even less.

Travel

Airport Geneva; transfer 3½hr plus.
Railway Moûtiers 18km; 5 buses a day.
Road Via Lyon, Chambéry; chains may

be needed. Horrific peak weekend jams.
Reachable resorts Valmorel, Les Arcs,
La Plagne, Va' d'Isère, Tignes.

Having a car is a considerable advantage, especially for those who
want to go out in the evening to eat, drink or dance. There is a bus
service running between 8.30am and 7.30pm between Mottaret and
Altiport via Méribel. Rides can be paid for individually or by weekly
abonnements. The Mottaret/Le Hameau gondola is covered by the lift
pass only until 5.30. If there is sufficient demand, there may be buses in
the late afternoon between Courchevel and Méribel.

Miscellaneous

Tourist office ✆ (79) 086001.
Tx 980001.
Medical Hospital at Moûtiers (18km);
chemist and dentist in Méribel, doctors
in Méribel and Mottaret.
Equipment hire 6 days skis FF250,

boots FF130, X-C FF240.
Resort beds 1,400 in hotels, 17,600 in
apartments and chalets.
Package holidays BL, BV, CW, FL, JM,
MM, NE, SDO, SKW, SMG, SMW, SNP,
SNT, STC, SUP, SUS.

Les Menuires 1850m

Les Menuires is one of the ugliest blots on the Alpine landscape – a
cheerless, functional scattering of apartment blocks, shopping blocks
and lift pylons. But it serves a purpose, providing many ordinary French
families with economical apartment accommodation conveniently
placed for access to the enormous skiing of the Trois Vallées. There is
not much nightlife, and not much to do except ski.
   The resort has four neighbouring components, all of them above the

valley floor. The centre is La Croisette, a crescent of linked blocks with cars and road outside and an open, snowy plaza of lifts, pistes and café sun terraces inside. Nearly all the entertainment (numerous bars and restaurants, and three discos) and shopping facilities are here. Reberty, about 1km south, is the satellite most often offered by British operators. It gives easier and less crowded access to Val Thorens, but we have reports of very cramped accomodation, crowds in the supermarket, and annoyance at having to walk to La Croisette for evening entertainment. (The free shuttle bus stops about 7.30, and the piste across often lacks snow.) The gondola from the lower satellite of Preyerand up to La Croisette runs until midnight.

At La Croisette there is an all-day nursery for children up to age 12, with skiing for those of age 4 or more. Good English is reportedly rare in the ski school. There are 16.5km of cross-country trails, through a landscape of no great beauty, along the valley in both directions.

Tourist office ∅ (79) 082012.
Package holidays BS, CHA, CM, FL, GL, MM, SCB, SCP, SKW, TH.

Val Thorens 2300m

The highest resort in the Alps is remotely set in an unrelieved white and grey wilderness. The resort is not very large, two loosely-grouped clusters of tall, white-and-wood blocks with pistes on all sides (and through the middle), most of them broad and easy; skiing to and from most residences is possible, and snow conditions at resort-level are almost always very good. Although no more picturesque than Les Menuires, the resort seems less of an eyesore and aims to sell not just on price but on quality of facilities. It attracts lots of young Germans and Swedes as well as a few British skiers. At the lower end of the resort is a very smart sports complex with tennis and squash, a pool, saunas and a popular bar. Below the resort in a rather isolated position is another smart new development, the imaginative Temples du Soleil residential complex.

Convenient apartments and sure resort-level snow attract many families. Nursery slopes are good (but often crowded) and there are all-day ski and non-ski kindergartens, and special classes for teenage skiers, with an emphasis on acquiring racing skills. The main risk for children, as for adults, is bad, very cold weather.

All accommodation is convenient for skiing and shopping. We had very mixed reports about the quality of apartments and the service provided by the rental agencies. Few reporters stayed in hotels, but one recommended the well-placed and comfortable Val Chavière (∅ 000033). An expensive new hotel near the sports club, the Val Thorens (∅ 000433), is due to open for 1985–86. There are a few enticing food shops, but when the resort is full there is not enough supermarket space. Après-ski is very limited.

Val Thorens offers skiing for most of the year. The summer ski-fields on the two glaciers are extensive (2800m to 3300m) and include some challenging skiing on the Glacier de Péclet.

Tourist office ∅ (79) 000808.
Package holidays AT, BL, BS, FL, FT, HO, JM, MM, SCG, SKW, STC, SVP, TH.

Ski yourself to sleep

La Plagne   France 1800 – 2100m

Good for *Nursery slopes, easy skiing, big ski area, skiing convenience, family skiing, late holidays, off-piste skiing, resort-level snow, self-catering holidays, freedom from cars*
Bad for *Après-ski, not skiing, tough skiing, Alpine charm, short aiport transfers, easy road access, mountain restaurants*

Linked resorts: Montchavin, Les Coches, Champagny

La Plagne represents the state of the art of resort-building. It is a large and very fragmented place, confusing at first, but very straightforward in its appeal. The skiing is enormous in extent and vertical range; few of the pistes are challenging, but the off-piste skiing is excellent. Snow conditions are reliable except at the lower extremes of the network. Nursery slopes are abundant and immediately accessible, and child-care facilities are excellent. Nearly all accommodation is in modern apartments, conveniently placed for getting to and from skiing. And there you have it – apart from some lift bottlenecks which manifest themselves in the peak holiday season, a perfect recipe for a rather limited winter holiday which suits many skiers very well indeed.

There are bits of La Plagne on the gentle slopes above the tree-line dominated by the enormous monolith of Aime 2000, a great castle in the Alpine sky, where thousands of skiers can be pigeon-holed and processed under one roof. There are also smaller resort components much lower down, some of them modified old villages, others new developments. These low resorts are not directly below La Plagne, but are reached by taking lifts high up to the rim of the wide bowl above the resort centre. This makes the low skiing less valuable in bad weather, and complicates travel between sectors.

The skiing   top 3250 bottom 1250

The core of La Plagne's skiing is a central area above Plagne Centre and its close neighbours Plagne Villages, Bellecôte and Belle Plagne, all of them set between 1900m and 2050m. The western side of this basin is dominated by the single building of Aime 2000 (actually at 2100m), from which it is easy to ski down to Centre. Below it is Plagne 1800, or Plagne Lauze, the newest of the resort units. There are three other facets to the skiing: down into the woods behind Aime 2000 as far as Montalbert; south-facing slopes above Champagny, on the side of an entirely different valley; and, at the eastern end of the skiing area, a high area of glacier skiing and a low area of woodland runs towards Montchavin and Les Coches. From the glacier to Montchavin gives an enormous descent of 15km and 2000m vertical, but there are no pistes down, and no lifts back up to the glacier.

The central basin above the five residential units provides timid skiers with a very extensive range of not very long, not at all steep runs with a vertical range of about 500m. There are slightly longer descents from Roche de Mio and a greater scope for a challenge (bumps under the chair and open off-piste areas). The basin is split up by broken ground, and you have to be constantly on your guard against losing your way. One neglected and exceptional feature of this area is the long runs directly down from Aime 2000, through woods past Plagne 1800 – far enough (to 1400m) to give a long and challenging run (the black Emile Allais).

Behind the Le Biolley lifts above Aime 2000 there are some stiff runs, initially west-facing and liable to be icy and very difficult in the mornings. After this steep open slope a gentle trail through woods links with the Emile Allais run or with the Les Adrets lift for a gentle run through the woods to **Montalbert**.

The south-facing slopes above **Champagny** can be reached from several points above the central resort units without any great difficulty. For good skiers the toughest skiing and usually the best snow is in the area beside the long, steep Verdons drag-lift, with a splendid off-piste excursion all the way down to Champagny from the Mont de la Guerre. Unfortunately the Verdons drag-lift is often closed. The rest of Champagny's skiing is easy, sunny and not very extensive.

The **Bellecôte** glacier is the ace in La Plagne's hand. Unlike many glacier skiing areas it opens up plenty of challenging skiing, with long and wide black runs of nearly 1000m vertical and even longer off-piste runs down to Les Bauches, where there are lifts back towards Bellecôte and an easy piste on down to Montchavin. There are more adventurous things to be done from Bellecôte with a guide, including very long runs down towards Peisey and the Champagny valley, and there is also a moderately easy red run back from the glacier to the Col de la Chiaupe. Unfortunately the lifts are often closed, particularly early in the season.

The **Montchavin/Les Coches** runs, reached by chair-lift from Plagne Bellecôte as well as by off-piste run down from the glacier, provide plenty of variety of woodland skiing, most of it intermediate, with a drop of over 1000m vertical from the Arpette chair-lift to Montchavin. One reporter recommends the off-piste skiing among the trees between the pistes in this sector. Getting back to the Arpette is a slow business, involving a chair and three drag-lifts. From Montchavin there are buses down to Peisey-Nancroix for access to Les Arcs.

Nursery slopes are generally very good with playgrounds for children on the doorsteps of most of the resort units. Plagne Centre, Plagne Villages, Belle Plagne and Bellecôte are the most suitable of all, with gentle surrounding slopes, very reliable for snow.

Mountain restaurants are not very many and not very special, although the distinction between resort restaurants and mountain restaurants is hardly valid. Several reporters mention the boisterous warmth of the lunchtime atmosphere and excellent value for money at Chez Thérèse in the Hotel Bouquetin at Champagny.

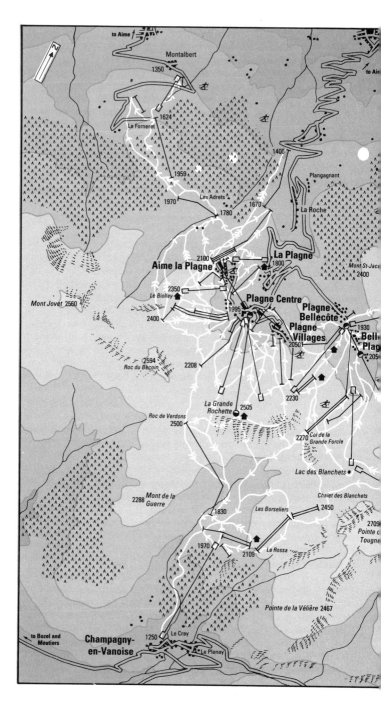

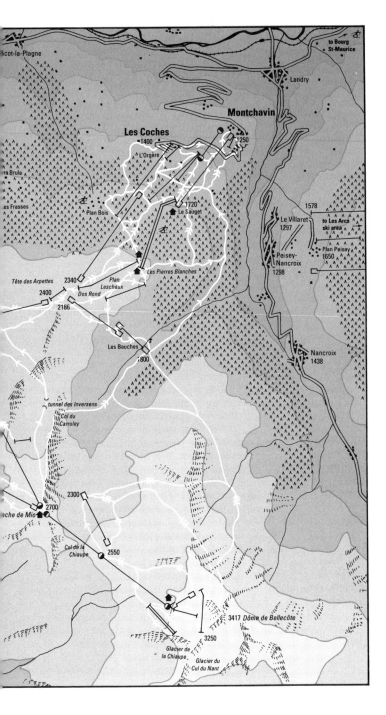

icot-la-Plagne

to Bourg
St-Maurice

Landry

Montchavin

Les Coches
1400

1250

L'Orgère

ra Brula

1578

es Frasses

Le Villaret
1297

to Les Arcs
ski area

Plan Bois

1720

Le Sauget

Plan Peisey
1650

Peisey-
Nancroix
1298

Tête des Arpettes   2340

Plan
Leschaux

Les Pierres Blanches

2400

Dos Rond

2186

Les Bauches

1800

Nancroix
1438

tunnel des Inversens

Col du
Carroley

2300

2700

oche de Mio

Col de la
Chiaupe

2550

3417 Dôme de Bellecôte

3250

Glacier de
la Chiaupe

Glacier du
Cul du Nant

Lifts

Passes La Plagne pass covers all La Plagne and Les Arcs lifts (but not bus shuttles) and is also valid one day a week in Val d'Isère and Tignes. Half-day and day passes available. A few main lifts can be paid for by the ride.
Children No reduction. Free pass for children under 7 in January and early February.

Cost 6-day pass FF590.
Beginners Limited passes for inexperienced skiers in each of the four main areas (Central La Plagne, Champagny, Montchavin and Montalbert) available by the day.
Summer skiing small area on Bellecôte glacier (3000m to 3250m) served by 4 lifts.

In general the system runs smoothly, even if you do spend a very long time on lifts getting around the large and not at all steep ski area. But during the February holidays, queuing can be a serious problem. About 80% of the resort's 25,000 beds are in the central area, which means lots of skiers leaving it in the morning and crowding the lifts back in the afternoon. The main bottleneck is Bellecôte; Centre is not much better, and queues of at least half an hour for the Grande Rochette and Roche de Mio lifts are common.

The resort

The original 1960s development is Plagne Centre, still the main centre for shopping, entertainment and après-ski. The buildings are big, square blocks, many of them linked by covered walkways. The hub is a dark and dank underground commercial precinct with lots of shops, bars and restaurants in little cubicles. The other units are all predominantly colonies of self-catering **accommodation**. Aime 2000 and Bellecôte consist of large blocks; Bellecôte is recommended by several reporters, and convenient for skiing. Belle Plagne, Plagne Villages and Plagne 1800 (Plagne Lauze) all have smaller buildings less densely concentrated; they have less shopping and entertainment, but are linked to Bellecôte and Centre. The most popular unit with British skiers (including our reporters) is Belle Plagne, which has a more colourful and fanciful design than the others; it is convenient for skiing, especially for Roche de Mio, and has adequately comfortable and quiet apartments. Although rather out of the way, Plagne 1800 is the newest development and the standard of the apartments is reported to be high. Of the lower villages, Les Coches is an entirely modern development, similar in style to Belle Plagne. Nearby Montchavin is a customised old hamlet, although without much village life of its own.

There is some staffed chalet accommodation in Centre, as well as a few functional hotels. The Graciosa (⌀ 090018) is small and friendly and its restaurant, the Etoile d'Or, highly reputed.

Après-ski activity is very limited. There are bars and restaurants in all the residential units and a few discothèques, the greatest selection being in Centre, but not many places with any character or animated atmosphere. The Grande Rochette gondola is sometimes open in the evening, with fondues and braserades served at the mountain restaurant at the top.

Ski school

Classes 4hr or 5hr per day depending on location, with extra classes over lunchtime in holiday periods.
Cost 6 days (4hr daily) FF415. Private lessons FF104/hr (up to four people).
Beginners *Ski évolutif* available.

Children Classes, ages 6–13, 6 days FF293. Ski kindergarten, ages 3–7, 9.00–5.00, 6 days with lunch FF790. Non-ski kindergarten, ages 2–6, at all main centres, 6 days with meals about FF790.

Facilites for children are generally excellent with nurseries and kindergarten playgrounds in all the main resort units. One reporter mentioned a shortage of English-speaking instructors in Montchavin.

Other activities

Cross-country 26km trail from Montalbert to Peisey Nancroix. Short trail at Plagne Villages. Extensive trails (15km, 10km, 8km, 5km and 4km) and off-piste itineraries in the valley above Champagny.

Not skiing Swimming (Bellecôte), skating (Bellecôte), 20km marked walks, squash (Plagne 1800), sauna/solarium (Centre, Plagne 1800).

In general, the high units of La Plagne are suitable only for downhill skiers. Montalbert and Champagny are better for X-C.

Travel

Airport Geneva; transfer 4hr plus.
Railway Aime (18km); frequent buses.
Road Via Lyon or Geneva; chains often necessary. Horrific peak weekend jams.

Reachable resorts Les Arcs, Val d'Isère, Tignes, Courchevel, Méribel, Les Menuires, Val Thorens, La Clusaz, Valmorel.

All five main bits of La Plagne are linked by bus or lift from 8am until 1am but the Plagne 1800–Centre bus operates only until early evening. Buses have to be paid for by all. Buses from Bellecôte to Centre are often crowded late in the afternoon. Cars are not much use in La Plagne, but useful for getting to Val d'Isère or the Trois Vallèes.

Miscellaneous

Tourist office ✆ (79) 090201. Tx 980043.
Resort beds 4,500 in hotels, 20,500 in apartments.
Package holidays BL, BS, CH, EN, GL, HO, IG, IT, JM, MM, NE, NT, PS, SCG, SKW, STC, SUP, TH, TX, WT.

Medical Hospital at Bourg-St-Maurice (35m), doctors at Centre and Bellecôte, chemist at Centre, dentist at Aime (18km).
Equipment hire 6 days skis FF250, boots FF125.

Champagny 1250m

A peaceful collection of hamlets, some of them old, in a secluded valley. The main community (Champagny le Bas) is linked to the La Plagne ski area by a chain of lifts starting a stiff walk above the village centre. The simple Les Glières (✆ 220446) is the larger of Champagny's two hotels, and convenient for the chair-lift. Beyond the village the mountains form a narrow gateway into a beautiful lonely upper valley (Champagny le Haut, 1450m). This is an excellent place for cross-country skiing and is also the end of off-piste downhill runs from Bellecôte glacier.

Tourist office ✆ (79) 220953.

Learn to ski fast – 200km/hr

Les Arcs France 1600–2000m

Good for *Ski évolutif, tough skiing, big ski area, off-piste skiing, skiing convenience, lift queues, beautiful scenery, family skiing, freedom from cars, rail access, late holidays, resort-level snow, sunny skiing, self-catering holidays*
Bad for *Alpine charm, mountain restaurants, après-ski, not skiing, short airport transfers, easy road access*

Les Arcs is a fifteen-year-old, predominantly self-catering resort consisting of three units; Arc 1600 (or Arc Pierre Blanche) and 1800 are close neighbours on the broad flank of the main Isère Valley above Bourg-St-Maurice, Arc 2000 is in a secluded high bowl of its own at the heart of the skiing.

Thanks to new lifts at the top and bottom, the skiing is extensive, interesting and suitable for all grades of skier, with plenty of easy runs above Arc 1800 and Arc 2000, and more than enough challenge on the slopes of the Aiguille Rouge for most skiers. The lift system is well thought-out and queues are rarely bad; and accommodation is nearly all conveniently placed for skiing. For après-ski and non-skiing facilities the resort scores very low marks, and prices are high. One of Les Arcs' greatest selling points is *ski évolutif* (see 'A Skiing Primer') which was introduced to Europe here. Opinions and members' reports on this method of learning to ski vary widely; it suits many people, but it is not so attractive that you should disregard all else to come here.

In holiday periods, when the French are in residence *en masse*, Les Arcs may be smart, but off-season it isn't – the noisy, young British presence is very obvious. The resort has hit a vein of demand in Britain for self-catering holidays among budget-conscious skiers, many of whom are surprised by the very high cost of everything in Les Arcs.

Les Arcs has a cable-car link with Bourg-St-Maurice, a real town with a good Saturday market, real locals and reasonable prices. There are also plenty of good value restaurants and hotels.

The skiing top 3226m bottom 1100m

The broad north-west facing mountain flank above Arc 1600 and Arc 1800 is well served by chairs and drag-lifts to a ridge of rocky peaks with skiing up to about 2400m. On the other side is a wide bowl with Arc 2000 in the pit, lifts up from it to over 3000m, and ski runs on down below the new resort buildings to Villaroger, a hamlet beside the road up to Val d'Isère.

The runs above **Arc 1800** are open and relatively easy, even those marked red. These slopes, on which many inexperienced skiers rely, get a lot of afternoon sun, and late in the season tend to be icy in the

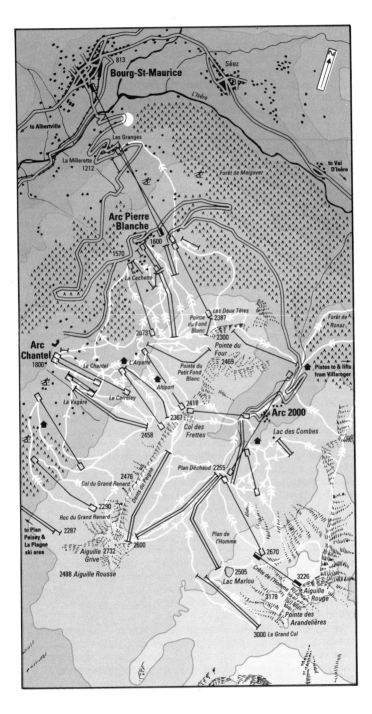

morning and slushy in the afternoon. The skiing connects with lifts up from Plan Peisey (1600m), between Les Arcs and La Plagne. This is an excellent area for skiing in bad weather, with plenty of good runs on and off the piste in woodland.

The skiing above **Arc 1600** is steeper and more wooded. There are some excellent broad, fairly steep trails, and there is some good off-piste skiing between them. Timid intermediate skiers can take a blue run down from top (Les Deux Têtes) to bottom or over to Arc 1800, but even this run has a few awkward passages. In good conditions it is possible to ski down towards Bourg-St-Maurice.

The bowl above **Arc 2000** has easy runs down into it from several points along the ridge reached from Arc 1600 and Arc 1800. It is a splendid area for inexperienced skiers to enjoy a lot of space and beautiful scenery. The far side of the bowl is dominated by the Aiguille Rouge, served by a number of lifts and Les Arcs' only cable-car. The Aiguille Rouge is what makes Les Arcs special. It is one of the few lift-served mountains in the Alps which is entirely of black steepness. Unfortunately it is often closed when conditions are not good. From the exposed open peak there are magnificent views across to the glaciers of the Mont Pourri (3782m). Off-piste slopes are in many places so steep and rocky that they are skiable only by very expert skiers; pistes are long and challenging. The Villaroger run, giving a vertical drop of over 2000m, has an enormous variety of terrain, and for much of its course is dark red to black.

The face of the Aiguille Rouge above Arc 2000 is the setting of the fastest European speed-skiing run. This track starts off extremely steeply (about 45 degrees) and then levels out gradually into a huge open runout down to Arc 2000, which is just what the competitors need, along with high altitude for low air resistance. When the speed-skiers are at it, in their rubber suits, streamlined helmets and 240cm skis, the spectacle is very impressive; 200km/hr is the going rate these days. You may even catch a ride on a chair-lift with the world's fastest skier. There are plenty of challenging runs not served by the cable-car. Underneath the chair-lift to the bottom cable-car station there are usually some formidable bumps. Exciting off-piste runs start from the top of the drag-lifts at the Grand Col, and beside the Aiguille Grive (behind the Aiguille Rouge to Villaroger), and in the other direction to Nancroix and Plan Peisey. These runs are a long way from pistes and should not be attempted without guidance.

It is perhaps just as well that *ski évolutif* does not involve long days spent on **nursery slopes**, for Les Arcs is not ideally provided with these, although there are suitable open spaces on the upper edge of Arc 1800 and Arc 1600. Areas are roped off near the resort for the first stages of *ski évolutif* and for children's ski playgrounds (*ski évolutif* is not taught to those under 12).

Mountain restaurants are generally inadequate. Most people return to their apartments or restaurants in the resort complexes. In the Arc 2000 valley there is a very attractive old chalet beside the river near the bottom of the Comborcière drag-lift. There is an attractive rustic restaurant at the bottom of the pistes down to Villaroger.

Lifts

Passes Area pass covers all lifts of Les Arcs, Plan Peisey and La Plagne including cable-car to Bourg-St-Maurice, but no bus services. Weekly passes valid for one day in Val d'Isère/ Tignes. Coupons available for some lifts (notably Bourg-St-Maurice cable-car). **Cost** 6-day pass FF575. **Children** 15% off under 13, free under 7. **Beginners** Inclusive package covering ski school, lift pass and ski hire.

For a new French ski resort Les Arcs' lift system is surprising: it is all chairs and drags except for the single cable-car at the top. The lifts work well – multiple routes out of the resorts and lots of triple chairs up to the dividing ridge. Getting back from Arc 2000 in the afternoon can involve longer waits for the two main linking lifts, especially the awkward Comborcière drag-lift. There are often queues for the Aiguille Rouge cable-car. Queues in 1800 to buy lift passes at weekends can be worse than queues for the lifts; if driving, buy the lift pass at the Bourg-St-Maurice cable-car station.

The resort

The two important parts of Les Arcs are Arc 1600 and Arc 1800. Both command magnificent views north-west across to Mont Blanc, and west along the valley into the setting sun. They are both compact clusters, with curving forms hugging the mountain, designed to give a large number of apartments and hotels sunny terraces and balconies. Wood has been widely used, but the buildings were poorly finished and are now beginning to look distinctly tatty.

Of the two main units, Arc 1800 is bigger and has most of the bars and shops, restaurants and apartment blocks. It is itself split into two sectors – Le Charvet and Les Villards – each with a supermarket in easy reach of all the apartments. We have mouthwatering reports of good take-away cooked dishes taking the sweat out of self-catering. No cars are allowed into Arc 1800, and you may have a 10-minute walk across the village with your luggage.

Arc 1600 is smaller and quieter, and although the standard brochure term 'villagey' is misleading, the bars and restaurants are smaller and more personal. Most of 1600 consists of a horseshoe of buildings around the Hotel La Cachette with sunny terraces in front of the shops and restaurants. Arc 2000 is for the moment no more than a couple of large, squarish dull blocks (including the Club Méditerranée) and a very limiting place to stay – though there are ambitious plans for its development into the major Arc.

Most reporters took self-catering **accommodation** in Arc 1800 and one or two were disappointed at having to walk up from the lower blocks to the slopes. The standard of apartments varies little – most are tight on space and unluxurious, and cooking facilities are limited. There is a widespread use of bunk beds and the usual sofa beds in living areas. Plenty of apartments get a lot of afternoon sun, but promises of day-long balcony sunbathing should be treated sceptically. People not wanting a self-catering holiday should consider Bourg-St-Maurice.

There are a number of small hotels near the cable-car station offering cheap rooms or half-board. The cable-car arrives on the edge of Arc 1600, a bit of a walk from resort and skiing.

Après-ski is very limited. There are bars, restaurants and discothèques in Arc 1600 and Arc 1800, none of them with much atmosphere. The Hotel du Golf is probably the best nightspot.

Ski school

Classes 2hr, morning and afternoon.
Cost 6 days FF990 including lifts and equipment hire. 6 days for non-beginners FF418. Private lessons FF108/hr.
Children Ski kindergartens, ages 4–8, 6 days with lunch and equipment hire FF1060. Non-ski kindergartens, ages 1–6, 8.30–6.00, 6 days with lunch FF740.
Special courses Intensive race training, powder skiing weeks or guided day excursions, ski extrême weeks, mono-ski lessons or courses, speed-skiing.

For adult beginners, ski school means *ski évolutif*. There is a theoretical class size limit of 10 people, but one reporter says that even in January this was disregarded and that there was no control over what standard people in a given class were. If you want to have a go at speed-skiing, apply at Arc 2000. Equipment is provided; starting from the very top of the run is not recommended.

Other activities

Cross-country 4 and 7km trails, accessible from 1600 and 1800.
Not skiing Natural ice rink (1800), saunas in hotels (1600 and 1800), organised snowshoe outings, and 10km cleared walks (1800 and 1600), solarium, cinema, chinese gymnastics (1800), keep-fit sessions; gym music sessions (1800), bridge (1800 and 1600), hang-gliding.

Les Arcs is not recommended either for X-C skiers (one reporter found trails and school oversubscribed and the instructor uninterested) or non-skiers. Several members regretted the lack of a swimming pool. Skating may not be available late in the season.

Travel

Airport Geneva, transfer 4hr plus. Horrific peak weekend traffic jam.
Railway Bourg-St-Maurice; frequent buses and direct cable-car to resort.
Road Via Lyon/Chambéry; chains often needed from Bourg-St-Maurice.
Reachable resorts La Plagne, Val d'Isère/Tignes, Trois Vallées resorts, Valmorel.

Having a car isn't much help in Les Arcs (cars have to be parked at the edge of each complex). Frequent daytime buses run between Arc 1600 and Arc 1800, and occasionally to Arc 2000, which run until 8pm. The cable-car to Bourg-St-Maurice runs until about 6pm.

Miscellaneous

Tourist office 1600: ✆ (79) 077373. Tx 980016. 1800: ✆ 074800. Tx 980303. 2000: ✆ 073255. Tx 980417.
Medical Hospital in Bourg-St-Maurice, doctor, dentist, chemist in Les Arcs
Equipment hire 6 days skis FF320; boots FF180; X-C SF300.
Resort beds 960 in hotels, 8,830 in apartments.
Package holidays BL, CM, EN, FL, FT, HA, HO, MM, NE, NT, SCB, SCP, SDO, SFA, SKW, SLV, SMG, SNP, SVL, TH, WT.

Le ski rules, OK?

Val d'Isère France 1850m

Good for *Big ski area, easy skiing, tough sking, off-piste skiing, nursery slopes, late holidays, resort-level snow, après-ski, lift queues, summer skiing, self-catering holidays, chalet holidays*
Bad for *Alpine charm, mountain restaurants, short airport transfers, easy road access, not skiing*

Tignes France 2000m

Good for *Big ski area, off-piste skiing, late holidays, resort-level snow, lift queues, skiing convenience, self-catering holidays, family skiing*
Bad for *Alpine charm, après-ski, not skiing, easy road access, short airport transfers, mountain restaurants*

These two very different resorts share only a lack of charm and an almost inexhaustible, high-altitude ski area which has established itself as one of the world's premier destinations for keen skiers. Opinions about the relative merits of the two resorts vary, but our scores of reporters were unanimous in their approval of the skiing; nearly all would return for further exploration of its enormous off-piste potential, some of the easiest slopes any skier could ask for on top of the world at over 3000 metres, and mile upon mile of motorway ideally suited to the Great British piste-basher. Crowds are rarely a problem except in bad weather, when there is very little skiing to be done, especially at Tignes. Perhaps most important of all (especially after the experience of the last few years), snow conditions are reliable until late April.

Val d'Isère and Tignes are skiers' ski resorts; you don't have to be an expert, but you do have be keen. Anyone with more varied requirements of an Alpine winter holiday than to ski, drink, eat, dance and sleep, all in characterless surroundings, should not be tempted.

Tignes is the very model of a modern French resort, built up rapidly and not at all prettily from nothing at over 2000m in the pit of a huge treeless horseshoe of mountains, beneath the glaciers of the Grande Motte, one of Savoie's highest and most shapely peaks. It is a large, mostly self-catering resort split into three parts round a small lake. It is quiet after dark, and by day there is almost nothing to do except ski. Most of the resort is ideal for convenience skiing.

There is more to find fault with in Val d'Isère; the resort is a styleless straggle, the lifts aren't central, and the runs down to the valley are difficult. But at least it feels like a village. There is also more variety – of accommodation (style and cost), and of après-ski. Young enthusiasts from all over the world fill the resort, and it has livened up enormously. The British tour operators have moved in en masse, and their staff and clients are everywhere.

The skiing top 3488m bottom 1550m

Val d'Isère/Tignes divides naturally into at least six separate sectors. On the Val d'Isère side the Le Fornet/Iseran, Solaise, and the Bellevarde/La Daille sectors are strung in a row along the curving road up from Bourg-St-Maurice to Le Fornet served by efficient ski-buses through the resort (Train Rouge). The first two sectors are linked by lift at altitude; Solaise and Bellevarde only at valley level just beside Val d'Isère. Bellevarde/La Daille links up over the Tovière ridge with Tignes, which has skiing around all sides of a horseshoe, in three main sectors – Tovière, Grande Motte (going up to the glacier), and Palet/Palafour/Aiguille Percée. Behind the Aiguille Percée there is still more skiing down to the hamlets of Les Brévières and Les Boisses. These lower runs are the most important examples of what many reporters consider a general feature of the area – pistes graded to appear easier than they are.

The **Solaise** cable-car was Val d'Isère's first lift, installed in 1943. Under it and the parallel chair-lift there are some steep, awkward and often bare runs through the trees. Above the tree-line, underneath the top half of the cable-car, and served by its own drag-lift is Val d'Isère's most famous run: the Plan, or simply the Bumps, a wide mogul-field, not particularly long steep, but a cult. Bumps are left to grow to very impressive dimensions. Descending to the left of the cable-car, missing out most of the bumps run, Piste S is one of the most difficult in the area, very often just as bumpy as the Plan but longer, steeper and narrower: a run to sort out real skiers from Solaise swanks. Beyond the Tête de Solaise, a high, long, gentle bowl provides a lot of long, easy runs (green and blue) complicated only by piste crossroads. Around the steep rims of the bowl there is a lot of off-piste skiing, often dangerous. The long Cugnai chairlift gives access to a beautiful back bowl off-piste area, often including a semi-piste and quite often out of bounds because of avalanche danger. The pistes down from Cugnai join up with the Arcelle/Manchet area – open slopes with good, fairly long intermediate skiing beside the lifts.

From behind Tête de Solaise there is some particularly beautiful, uncrowded skiing down to Le Laisinant, between Le Fornet and Val d'Isère, where you pick up the bus. The runs are marked red and blue, but the blue is not as easy as the blues higher up, and long. This is another area for excellent off-piste skiing of varying degrees of difficulty, in the right conditions.

At the top of the bowl behind Solaise there is a short, steep drag-lift with a run beside it, and a tunnel near the top through the Crête de Lessières which separates the Solaise and Le Fornet ski areas. The run down the other side from the tunnel, to the gentle pistes around the Col de l'Iseran is awkward at the best of times, and most skiers opt for the dramatic chair-lift ride over the ridge and down the other side.

The **Le Fornet** skiing starts with a cable-car (often the least crowded way of getting into the skiing) up over steep, wooded slopes – in this case only 400m vertical – above which the ground flattens out, giving a

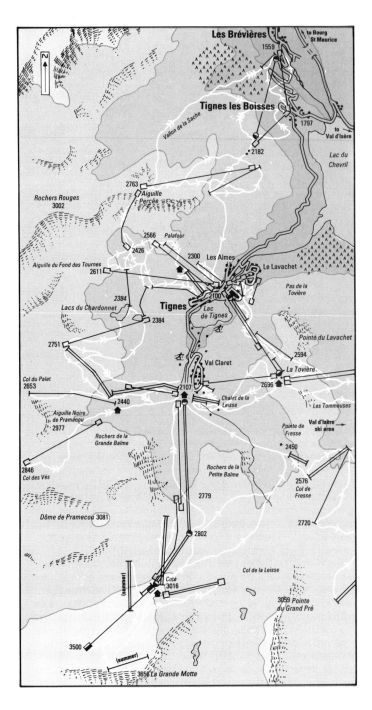

Les Brévières

to Bourg
St Maurice

1559

Tignes les Boisses

1797

to
Val d'Isère

Lac du
Chevril

Vallon de la Sache

• 2182

2763 Aiguille
Percée

*Rochers Rouges
3002*

2566 *Palafour*

2426

2300 Les Almes

Le Lavachet

Aiguille du Fond des Tournes

2611

Pas de la
Tovière

2384

Tignes

*Lac
de Tignes*

Lacs du Chardonnet

2384

Pointe du Lavachet

2751

2594

*Col du Palet
2653*

Val Claret

La Tovière

2696

2107

*Chalet de la
Leisse*

Les Tommeuses

2440

*Aiguille Noire
de Pramecou
2977*

Pointe de
Fresse

Val d'Isère
ski area

*Rochers de la
Grande Balme*

• 2450

2846
Col des Vés

*Rochers de la
Petite Balme*

2576
*Col de
Fresse*

2779

2720

Dôme de Pramecou 3081

2802

Col de la Leisse

(summer)

Coté
3016

*3059 Pointe
du Grand Pré*

3500

(summer)

3656 La Grande Motte

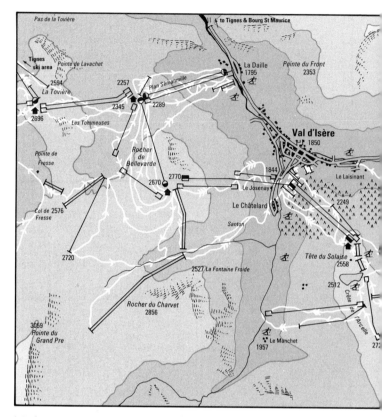

lot of very easy motorway skiing. From the Col de l'Iseran lifts continue round the corner, up on to the Pissaillas Glacier which offers open, extensive, easy skiing, winter and summer. For good skiers the attraction of Le Fornet is the off-piste skiing among the trees and above all the off-piste runs from the glacier. The so-called Col Pers run from the glacier is long and beautiful, but not difficult and a great favourite for giving piste skiers a taste of adventure. The off-piste skiing behind the Signal drag-lift is much more open, and much steeper. There is a blue run marked down under the Fornet cable-car – although it is mostly traversing, there are some awkward passages.

The Rocher de **Bellevarde** rises steeply and impressively on the western side of Val d'Isère, and a long cable-car climbs quickly from the same station as the Solaise lift on the edge of town to near the peak, over 900 metres above the resort. As in so many parts of the area an alternative chair-lift route makes it possible to get up without too much of a queue. From La Daille the other, more gentle side of the mountain is served by a long two-stage gondola (or a series of chains) to a sunny plateau below the top cable-car station. The runs directly down from Bellevarde to Val d'Isère, under the cable-car, are long, steep and demanding – about the most difficult piste skiing in the area. There is

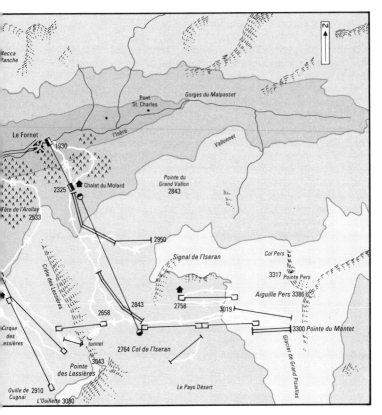

also some very good off-piste skiing. Bellevarde gets a lot of sun, and snow tends to deteriorate quickly.

There are easier ways to the village, but a narrow gunbarrel on the blue Santon run makes it more difficult than most people expect. Near the Santon is a black run (the Epaule) which is more open, and has fewer people on it. Though no match for the face of Bellevarde in terms of sustained challenge, it certainly deserves its grading. The long twin drag-lift round the back of the Rocher du Charvet gives access to an off-piste run called the Tour du Charvet, similar in appeal to the Col Pers – beautiful and not too difficult although often dangerous. The many runs from the top of Bellevarde down to the middle station above La Daille are spread around a wide area, and nearly all very easy except for the splendid downhill race course (the OK run) underneath the gondolas hugging the Bellevarde rock. It is quite often closed, either for races or because of avalanche danger. The bottom half of this area mostly consists of runs and off-piste runs through trees, which are the main characteristic and attraction of the area, along with splendid views northwards to Mont Blanc. The runs to La Daille are the easiest runs down to the valley but often unpleasantly crowded and icy. An interesting excursion is the so-called Piste Perdue, more or less following the course of a river, down a gully.

From the La Daille middle station the main connection with Tignes is a double triple-chair to **Tovière**. Despite the impressive capacity of this link, there are still queues and the alternative Col de Fresse route is usually a short cut for skiers heading for the Grande Motte area. There is a good open off-piste area down from Tovière to La Daille, keeping left of all the lifts and the Piste Perdue.

From Lac de Tignes the old gondola lift up to Tovière, and thus linking with Val d'Isère, has now been supplemented by a system of chair-lifts. The run straight back down under the gondola is a very good one – black with a steep mogul field at the bottom – and there is the possibility of an even steeper variant on the top section (the Mur de Paquerettes). Less severe runs (blue and red) lead to Val Claret, joining up with the fairly straightforward run down from the Col de Fresse and merging, to the discomfiture of beginners, with the Val Claret nursery lifts.

The **Grande Motte** is served by a notorious old double gondola lift, which always seems to be overcrowded or breaking down. A two-stage chair-lift now runs in parallel, and is a more reliable and less crowded way to the main Grande Motte congregation area at about 3,000m. Here there is a splendid new restaurant with a wide sun terrace; the views are superb.

The Grande Motte cable-car, which is rarely open early in the season, serves a run which is easy, but more interesting than most of the pistes on the Iseran glacier; there are lots of warnings about crevasse danger off the pistes – and a reporter tells us that that a piste machine fell into a crevasse *on* the piste. From the bottom of the glacier, at around the mid-station of the gondola, there are two long pistes down to Val Claret. One is a long and not too difficult red, often extremely crowded; the other is a fairly straightforward blue connecting with the Col de Fresse lifts – usually a much quicker way of getting back to Val d'Isère than going to down to Val Claret and up to Tovière. The run for good skiers to tick off is the Wall, which is just what it sounds like: a short, but very steep drop over the end of the glacier, near the piste. A particularly fine off-piste run crosses the glacier high up, involving a bit of a climb and drops behind the Rocher de Grande Balme to join up with the skiing below the Col du Palet.

The **Col du Palet/Aiguille Percée** area above Val Claret and Lac de Tignes is probably the least exciting skiing in Tignes, but there is a lot of it. It is very sunny and rarely crowded, with lots of runs which do not differ greatly – nearly all in the blue or easy red category, with a few steeper pitches. There is a superb, very long and beautiful red run down from Aiguille Percée to Tignes Les Brévières (La Sache). There is also a blue via Tignes les Boisses, which at the bottom may be icy and not as easy as a blue run should be. This area is attractive, and Les Brévières itself is a pleasant place for lunch. The Col du Palet is the starting point of long off-piste runs down to Champagny (between la Plagne and Courchevel) and Plan Peisey (between Les Arcs and La Plagne), not difficult on firm late-season snow, according to one report.

Val d'Isère's main **nursery slopes** are conveniently located (between the old village and the Solaise cable-car station), open and gentle, with plenty of bars and restaurants nearby. La Daille has a smaller area with a couple of free lifts for beginners. There is enormous scope for near-beginners way up on the Iseran glacier, and on the slopes above La Daille and Solaise. Tignes' nursery areas are very reliable for snow, but tend to be crowded – especially at Val Claret.

Val d'Isère and Tignes score very low for **mountain restaurants**, with a particular black mark for sanitation – in some cases there is none. The number of restaurants is simply inadequate for the size of the area, and most of them are unpleasant, unwelcoming, overcrowded and expensive. Only two are to be recommended – the chalet at the top of Tovière, and the brand new Panoramique on the Grande Motte. Not surprisingly, many skiers come down to the bottom (Val d'Isère, Lac de Tignes, Les Brévières) for lunch. At Les Brévières the obvious restaurant at the bottom of the pistes is the least pleasant in the village, except for sunbathing.

Lifts

Passes Area pass covers Val d'Isère and Tignes, swimming pool and resort buses and gives one free day a week in La Plagne and Les Arcs. Day passes available.
Cost 6-day pass FF590.
Children 40% off, under 13.

Beginners Two free lifts at La Daille; limited beginners' pass FF50 per day.
Summer skiing Very extensive, both at Tignes (2700 to 3500m, open all year) and at Val d'Isère (2700 to 3300m, open July to Sept).

The system is well conceived and energetically improved every year, so that when everything is working queues are not a problem. A greater problem is often congestion on the piste, especially on the Grande Motte, Solaise and runs down to La Daille. There are often queues for the Grande Motte cable-car. When the weather is bad the valley lifts tend to come under greater pressure, especially the La Daille gondolas. Among off-piste skiers this is a pilgrimage resort thanks to the sheer extent of the skiable region and the number of open slopes you can reach by lift. The area has a reputation for avalanches, but this may have a lot to do with the numbers of people who go off-piste skiing. The resorts take the dangers very seriously and work very hard, not only to make the mountains secure, but also to inform skiers about off-piste as well as piste conditions. The radio service (with information in English) in Val d'Isère is particularly useful in this respect.

The resorts

Val d'Isère

Val d'Isère is set in a remote steep-sided valley, beyond the reservoir which drowned the old village of Tignes some 30 years ago. The road emerges from a series of tunnels into the valley at La Daille, little more than a cluster of modern apartment buildings at the foot of the pistes. Val d'Isère proper starts half a mile or so up the road, a gathering density of mostly ugly blocks and a few chalets. The road becomes a main street, with shops, bars, hotels and residences on either side of the river, with concrete banks to curb the spring floods. The centre of the resort is a wide 'T' junction where the Isère valley is joined by the small Le Manchet valley which is the site of the main lift departure stations. A fine old 11th-century Savoyard church and some rough old buildings huddled around it are all there is to old Val d'Isère. Beyond the village, the road up to the Col de l'Iseran, Europe's highest road pass, is open in winter only as far as the old hamlet of Le Fornet.

Val d'Isère is not a huge resort, despite the fact that it serves one of the largest linked ski areas in the world. It has only about half the capacity of Chamonix or Megève. Its development as a resort happened after the war, and there is nothing planned about the look of the place. It is long and strung-out, so nowhere is very far from the main road bus route; it is also flat, so walking is no great hardship. Although the road in winter goes nowhere, there are always lots of cars and buses around. The shopping isn't very exciting, but there are a few excellent shops for gourmet self-caterers, and a delightful dairy.

There is a much wider choice of **accommodation**, and many more hotels, than in most purpose-built resorts.

Central hotels and residences are within easy walking range of the main cable-car station and nursery slopes; from other places you either face longer walks or the bus. There are no really luxurious hotels and plenty of small, simple ones offering good value. At the top end of the range the rather soulless Sofitel (⌀ 060830) is central and the Grand Paradis (⌀ 061173) is even better placed for the main lifts. Of the other hotels, we have favourable reports of the Aiglon (⌀ 060405) – good food, French atmosphere but not a very convenient location; and of the central Squaw Valley (⌀ 060272). The Bellier (⌀ 060377) is another welcoming, traditional French family hotel with good food; it is quietly but not inconveniently located and the views are splendid. The Savoyarde (⌀ 060155) has been revamped after a fire; we await confirmation that the food is still excellent. Of the several well-placed, adequately comfortable b&b places, the Henri Oreiller (⌀ 060845) is more attractive than most.

La Daille is perhaps the most convenient place to stay from the skiing point of view; blocks of flats at the bottom of the easiest of Val d'Isère's home runs, with nursery slopes free for beginners and ski school, and only two lift rides away from the Tovière divide, for access to Tignes. Après-skiers without cars will find La Daille dull.

Après-ski is plentiful and varied, with more excellent restaurants than you are likely to need, even for a holiday of great indulgence. Several are more distinguished than the Bar Jacques, which stays open until 4am, but none is friendlier. Hotels offer excellent fixed-price meals and you can get very good traditional Savoyard meals in La Daille and Le Fornet. The variety and entertainment value of bars is as good, some totally British, others hardly at all (and more expensive). Dick of Dick's Tea-Bar (a joke) doesn't need, but deserves, a special mention, as one of the originals of a thriving breed – the ex-pat ski resort publican/DJ, who provides a forum for piste-chat and entertains large numbers of Brits much more effectively and cheaply than French nightclubs and piano bars can do.

Ski school

ESF (Val d'Isère and La Daille), and Snow-Fun (English section at Hotel Solaise).
Classes (Both schools) 2½ or 3hr morning, 2½hr afternoon.
Cost ESF 6 days FF496, rises to FF552 after February. Private lessons FF110/hr. Snow-Fun 6 days FF425. Private lessons

FF80/hr.
Children 30% off adult ESF prices. ESF ski kindergarten, ages 3–10, 9.00–5.00, 6 days with meal FF661. Non-ski kindergarten same hours and cost.
Special courses ESF: mono-ski, race training, off-piste, tests. Snow-Fun: off-piste, ski extrême.

Guides are available in both schools, and there is huge potential for day-trip ski tours. Val d'Isère is full of freelance instructors, including two off-piste specialist teams – 'Top ski' for experts, by the session or week, and 'Clé des Neiges', weekly packages only. Heli-skiing on nearby Italian mountains can be arranged at Killy Sport.

Other activities

Cross-country 17km of easy trail around the resort and towards La Daille.
Not skiing Walks in Le Manchet valley.

Swimming (free with lift pass), natural ice rink (free), dance/aerobics, hang-gliding, sauna/massage, solarium, gym.

Despite these provisions for X-C and non-skiing activity, serious practitioners of either should not be tempted to Val d'Isère.

Travel

Airport Geneva; transfer 4hr plus.
Railway Bourg-St-Maurice (33km); four buses daily.
Road Via Lyon/Chambéry; chains often

needed. Horrific peak weekend traffic jams.
Reachable resorts La Plagne, Les Arcs.

There is a free and frequent ski-bus service along the valley is invaluable, although a terrible crush at peak times (skis have to be taken inside). There is a less frequent evening service to La Daille. Buses to Tignes are occasional and expensive.

Miscellaneous

Tourist office ✆ (79) 061083. Tx 980077.
Medical Fracture clinic, doctor, dentist and chemist in resort; hospital in Bourg-St-Maurice (33km)
Equipment hire 6 days skis FF200,

boots FF100, X-C FF155.
Resort beds 3,000 in hotels, 12,400 in apartments.
Package holidays BL, CM, CMW, FL, JM, MM, SDO, SCG, SKW, SMG, SUP, SVL, TH, WT.

Tignes

The setting of Tignes is austere, with no woodland to relieve the bare mountain scenery. Its high and open situation makes it a good place to ski late in the season, but not a good place in bad weather. The centre is Lac de Tignes, beside the lake, already rather shoddy but at least with some variety of building style and the usual selection of bars, restaurants and shops. There are some sunny restaurant terraces. Le Lavachet is a nearby but inconvenient satellite which is linked by ski-lift shuttle. Val Claret, the third unit making up Tignes is a cluster of tall, modern blocks on the other side of the lake and at the foot of the Grande Motte lifts. From here there is easy access to all skiing areas, and reporters found they were able to satisfy all their material requirements within the one building where they were staying.

Accommodation, at least that offered by UK operators, is largely self-catering or staffed apartments. Most of the hotels are in Lac de Tignes and are neither attractive nor luxurious. One exception in all respects is Le Ski d'Or ($\oslash$ 065160), an expensive, very comfortable modern chalet hotel in Val Claret. Most of the self-catering accommodation is in Val Claret and Le Lavachet, and is modern and planned with the usual economical use of space. Les Brévières is attractive, but best enjoyed on excursions from Tignes.

Après-ski is generally quiet, but there are plenty of restaurants and a few nightclubs in all sectors. Of the restaurants, Le Ski d'Or is outstanding in cost and quality and the degree of attentiveness verges on the precious. Harry's Bar in Le Lavachet is a pale imitation of the originals, but nevertheless a fairly cheap place to drink, with musical accompaniment; it rarely merits the term discothèque. The Hotel 2100 on the edge of Lac de Tignes has dancing and bar-priced drinks, and there are a couple of more expensive discothèques in both Le Lac de Tignes and Val Claret. Le Palaf (Lac) is usually the most lively of them.

Ski school

ESF (Lac de Tignes, Val Claret)
Classes 2½hr morning and afternoon.
Cost 6 days FF662. Private lessons FF106/hr.
Children 40% off classes, under 12. Ski kindergartens: Lac, ages 4–10, 8.45–5.00, 6 days with meals FF676. Val

Claret, ages 5-10, 8.30–5.00, 6 days FF680. Non-ski kindergartens: Lac ages 2½–4, 8.45–5.00, 6 days FF620. Val Claret ages 18m–3, 8.30–3.00, 6 days FF790.
Special courses Freestyle, tests, racing, off-piste.

Guides can be hired for the excursion to Champagny or Plan Peisey via the Col du Palet, and will arrange transport back; the trip is very attractive now that the Les Arcs and La Plagne lifts are covered.

Other activities

Cross-country 9km of easy trails around Lac de Tignes and at Les Boisses. Summer X-C trail on the glacier.

Not skiing Natural ice rink; dance classes; occasional 'soirées animations' at the leisure centre in Val Claret.

We have reports of reports of weekly duplicate bridge. Even more emphatically than Val d'Isère, this is no place for X-C skiers or non-skiers.

Travel

As for Val d'Isère, except that having a car is much more of an asset for après-skiers. Like Val d'Isère, Tignes has a resort shuttle bus service which runs until midnight and is free. There is also a bus service from Les Boisses and Les Brévières to Tignes, which is much less reliable. There are few buses to Val d'Isère.

Miscellaneous

Tourist office $\oslash$ (79) 061555. Tx 980030.
Medical Doctor, fracture clinic, dentist, chemist all in resort; hospital in Bourg-St-Maurice (25km).
Equipment hire As Val d'Isère.

Resort beds 1,200 in hotels, 20,100 in apartments.
Package holidays AA, BL, CH, CM, EN, FL, HO, MM, SDO, SCG, SKW, SLV, SMG, STC, SUP, SVL, TX.

Military two-step

Valloire France 1400m

Valloire is an old village tucked away in a secluded bowl high up above the Maurienne valley, beside the road up to the very high Col du Galibier (closed in winter), where the *département* of Savoie meets Hautes-Alpes. It has developed gradually as a resort over the sixty years since skiing became popular with the local military; although not a strikingly picturesque village, it has retained the atmosphere and appearance of a real community.

The skiing is spread over five sides of two neighbouring mountains and gives plenty of variations of terrain and landscape, and long runs of nearly 1000m vertical. There is no very difficult skiing (the black runs are not steep). Both areas are served by lifts only a few minutes' walk from the centre and going up to almost 2500m, but most of the skiing is below 2000m. Each mountain has a small nursery area at the bottom and another beside a restaurant half-way up.

The major sector is **Setaz**, reached by a slow series of lifts over a narrow north-facing slope, more of a mountain-end than a mountainside. A 6-seater gondola is planned for 1985–86. Various descents go through the woods to the resort or down the steeper sides of the mountain – easy ones from the restaurant, tougher ones starting higher up. The downhill race-course starts near the top – a 3.8km run for 920m vertical. The west-facing slope goes down to Les Verneys, beside the Galibier road (1563m); beyond it, on the Crey Rond massif, is a small nursery area and a chair-lift up to 1912m opening up a very worthwhile expanse of off-piste skiing. The east-facing slope of Setaz is linked at Pragontier (1750m) to the **Crey du Quart** sector – a broad, open, sunny hillside, lightly scrub-covered lower down. There is some excellent easy skiing on the gentle, spacious top half; there may also be some more demanding slopes on the bottom half, but on our visits they were unskiable. Conditions are more reliable on the north-facing runs towards Valmeinier – again, satisfying length and varying difficulty from easy blue to toughish red, graded black.

Cross-country trails climb south from Valloire to Les Verneys and on to Plan Lachat (1961m); this gives a maximum of 20km return, including sections of varying difficulty, blue to black, with several restaurants along the route. The setting is rather enclosed. The easiest loops are at Les Verneys, which can be reached by bus from Valloire.

There are several modest, inexpensive hotels and unobtrusive apartment buidings. The most attractive hotel is the Christiania (✆ 560057), a simple but adequately comfortable and spacious chalet building, conveniently placed on the main shopping street between the two lift departures. Although there is a fair range of bars and restaurants and two discothèques, the evening ambience is subdued. There are kindergartens and an artificial ice rink.

Tourist office ✆ (79) 560396. Package holidays SCG, SMD.

Resort of extremes

Alpe d'Huez France 1850m

Good for *Nursery slopes, easy skiing, big ski area, tough skiing, off-piste skiing, late holidays, resort-level snow, family skiing, sunny skiing, easy road access*
Bad for *Skiing convenience, not skiing, Alpine charm, mountain restaurants*

Linked resorts: Auris, Villard-Reculas

Alpe d'Huez is a bleak, grey modern resort spread widely across a treeless hillside in an open, sunny setting high up on the northern wall of the Romanche valley east of Grenoble. 'If it isn't sunny at Alpe d'Huez it must be night-time' is the resort's silly catchphrase. The skiing is well-suited both to beginners, with green runs at low level, and to experts, with the world's longest black run and some very long, exciting off-piste runs; it caters less well for the intermediate majority.

Like Les Deux Alpes, a close neighbour as the helicopter flies but emphatically separated by the deep, wide valley, Alpe d'Huez is an early post-War development, which means it has grown up piecemeal, and has hotels as well as apartments, and animated après-ski – at least at holiday times, when it has quite a chic French clientele. It attracts few non-French visitors, and in January is a bit like a ghost town.

The skiing top 3320m bottom 1450m

There are three distinct areas, two of them accessible from the top of the resort. The third is separated from the resort by the Sarenne gorge, but can be reached by catching a lift down or indirectly on skis.

Most of the skiing takes place on the **Grandes Rousses**, reached by a two-stage gondola followed by cable-car to Pic Blanc. The first section climbs only very gently over the enormous area of green runs; above it the rocky massif climbs increasingly steeply. The second gondola serves little skiing of its own and if the top cable-car is not open, the chair-lifts up to Clocher de Mâcle offer more interesting runs. These include a beautiful, long black down past Europe's highest disused coalmine (the Combe Charbonnière) and from there either round to the resort or down into the Sarenne Gorge. A more direct descent is the downhill race-course.

Behind the Pic Blanc cable-car station is the south-facing Glacier de Sarenne which starts steeply and is free of crevasses. The view is enormous and so are the runs – only blacks, of which two are notorious. One is the steep mogul-slope under the cable-car, reached via a tunnel through the mountain. The second is the 16km run all the way down the glacier and into the Sarenne Gorge, the longest black run and possibly

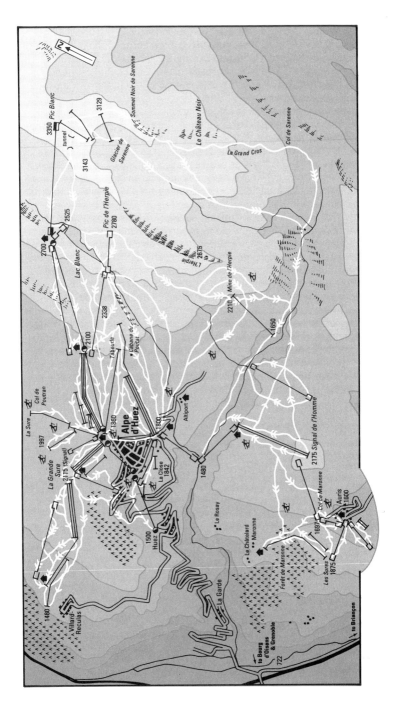

the longest piste in the Alps. It is a superb trail, wild and beautiful, of over 1800m vertical. Most most of the run is not at all steep; a few black passages punctuate long, fast-cruising stretches.

Pic Blanc is also the point of departure of a number of very long off-piste runs via other peaks (Etendard, Pic Bayle). Some of the runs involve precipitous walks and some involve skiing very steep and often dangerous slopes; others are just enormous descents in various directions ending up in valleys far from Alpe d'Huez – hence the local helicopter taxi service. For all these adventures guides are essential.

The **Signal** climbs to a rounded peak not very far above the top of the resort with easy, open runs beside the lifts. Behind the Signal, longer runs drop down the west-facing mountainside towards Villard-Reculas, including a black (La Forêt) which exaggerates the density of the scrub as well as the steepness of the run.

On the other side of the resort, the **Signal de l'Homme/Auris** sector is not very large, but offers plenty of variants on the north-facing runs down to the river gorge, increasingly steep near the bottom (there is an easy path). The short intermediate runs served by chair-lifts above the new part of Auris were very short of snow when we visited. There is also some challenging skiing in the Forêt de Maronne, including an unmaintained black run beside the steep Le Châtelard drag-lift.

Nursery slopes are exemplary: very spacious, very extensive, very gentle and adjacent to the resort. The Signal and Auris areas provide a fair range of blue runs for progress from the nursery area, but the main Grandes Rousses system has no very easy runs above 2200m.

Mountain restaurants are few and dull, notable exceptions being the chalet at the bottom of the Villard-Reculas lifts (which has a ski-in outdoor bar where you can sit down to drink without taking skis off), and the Forêt de Maronne hotel/restaurant at Le Châtelard.

Lifts

Passes Area pass covers all the lifts, ski-bus, pool and ice rink. Passes of over 5 days give a free day in Les Deux Alpes, Serre-Chevalier, Puy-St-Vincent, Milky Way resorts. Various limited day passes available.
Cost 6-day pass FF485.
Children 10% off, under 13.
Beginners Two free lifts, payment for others by the ride or by limited day pass.

We have no information on queues; when we visited the resort it was not at all full and there was no problem. No doubt when all the apartments are full in February, the main Grandes Rousses gondolas and especially the cable-car do get crowded. The latest refinement to the Alpe d'Huez lift system is helicopters – for trips to Les Deux Alpes and retrieving off-piste skiers from the end of long off-piste runs.

The resort

Alpe d'Huez is a large resort on a very sunny ledge high above Bourg d'Oisans. It is a quite exceptionally open and spacious setting, sunny all day but sheltered by mountains to the north and east. Although modern the resort is not at all new or stylish architecturally and has spread over a large area of steepish hillside in a triangular shape with the main lift departure at the top.

Accommodation is in apartments and plenty of small and medium-sized hotels, none of them particularly luxurious. Outstandingly the best location for skiing purposes is right at the top of the large resort near the lift station, especially for skiers on full-board terms. The Christina (∅ 803332) is the friendliest and most charming and one of the few attractive, chalet-style buildings in Alpe d'Huez. The nearby Chamois d'Or (∅ 803132) is a bright, functional, comfortable modern hotel with a highly reputed, expensive restaurant. Après-skiers may prefer to be nearer the bottom of the resort. The comfortable Vallée Blanche (∅ 803051) is well-placed and has its own disco.

Après-skiing is lively and varied but very seasonal (New Year, February and Easter holidays). The resort is generally reckoned to come second to Courchevel for good restaurants. There are several stylish piano bars and several hotels have live bands or discothèques. Also a few fast food counters and one or two simple, inexpensive bars.

Ski school

ESF and SEI (Ski Ecole International).
Classes 2hr morning and afternoon.
Cost 6 days, ESF FF440, SEI FF580.
Private lessons FF100/hr.

Children Ski kindergarten, ages 4–12, 6 days ESF FF300, SEI about FF495.
Special courses Off-piste, competition, mono-ski.

The SEI offers *ski évolutif* for adult beginners and has a maximum class size of 8. Both schools run extra classes at lunchtime and school holiday periods. The Youth Hostel has its own ski school.

Other activities

Cross-country Beginners' loop, 6.3km and 8.2km blue loops, 16.4km red loop above resort.

Not-skiing 30km cleared paths, artificial ice rink (skating/curling), heated open pool, clay pigeon shooting, boules, hang-gliding.

Despite its attempts to cater for cross-country skiers and non-skiers Alpe d'Huez is not recommended for either category.

Travel

Airport Geneva; transfer 2½hrs.
Railway Grenoble (65km); daily buses.
Road Via Lyon/Grenoble; chains may

be needed
Reachable resorts Les Deux Alpes, La Grâve, Serre-Chevalier, Montgenèvre.

We noticed no bus service around the resort, although the tourist office mentions a mini-bus. A daytime lift shuttle runs frequently up and down, with a stop in the middle. Alpe d'Huez is much more easily reached by road than many more famous resorts to the north. There are motorways all the way to Grenoble and a good valley road as far as Bourg d'Oisans.

Miscellaneous

Tourist office ∅ (76) 803541. Tx 320892.
Medical Hospital Grenoble (65km); doctors, dentists, chemists in resort
Equipment hire 6 days skis approx

FF240, boots FF130, X-C FF230.
Resort beds 2,500 in hotels, 15,000 in apartments.
Package holidays FL, STY.

Fresh pastures

Les Deux Alpes France 1650m

Good for *Tough skiing, off-piste skiing, big ski area, resort-level snow, late holidays, après-ski, summer skiing, easy road access*
Bad for *Alpine charm, mountain restaurants, not skiing*

Linked resorts: Bons, Mont de Lans, Venosc

Separate resort: La Grâve

Les Deux Alpes is a messy modern resort strung out across a high saddle on the southern side of the Romanche valley, opposite Alpe d'Huez. Originally two communities (the summer pastures of Mont-de-Lans to the north and Venosc to the south) it has merged into one over the last twenty years as the development of a very large, very high ski area has made it a major resort. It offers an excellent range of intermediate runs, enough tough and off-piste skiing for the more adventurous and a magnificent area of gentle glacier skiing.

The resort is less inconvenient than it looks, for skiing purposes at least. It is also much more friendly than it looks, and, once you get used to the shambles, it is even possible to grow fond of the place: there are plenty of simple, inexpensive hotels and bars and the local people are mostly relaxed and welcoming. It attracts a few non-French skiers.

The skiing top 3423m bottom 1270m

As far as skiing goes, Une Alpe et Demie would be a more appropriate name. The western side of the skiing climbs only a few hundred metres above the resort and is little used, despite the attraction of a long north-facing run down to the small village of **Bons**. This run is not maintained and the snow may be difficult or lacking. Most of the runs to Les Deux Alpes are gentle, and the mountain is never crowded.

The skiing that matters is on the eastern side of the resort. The lower slopes are broad and steep, the upper ones on the glacier broad and gentle; between the two, from 2200m to 3200m, is a large area of narrower middle slopes where the ground is too broken up to provide a network of runs, although some good north-facing slopes have been opened recently. This area is a bottleneck in the long lift system up to the glacier and in the pistes back down.

The first section of skiing immediately above the resort, with main access lifts from the central complex and from Alpe de Venosc, is a broad, steep, open, west-facing mountainside, terraced for safety. There is little variety in the runs, but all are difficult except for a green run along a road at the northern end of the mountain, from which it is possible to traverse to most parts of the resort. At the Venosc end, the

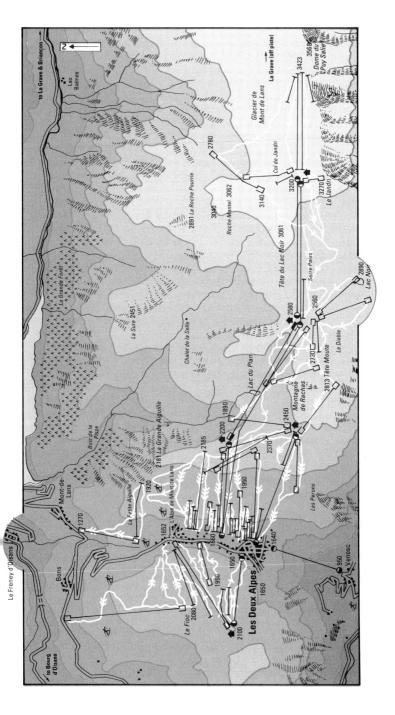

black run from the Tête Moute is not a very special one but does give an uninterrupted 1200m vertical descent. At the other end of the slope, the run down to **Mont de Lans** is similar to the one to Bons.

The top of this broad mountainside is a spacious open ridge with very easy runs and a number of lifts along it. Behind the ridge and the Tête Moute, a deep coomb interrupts the ski area. The installation of the Combe du Thuit chair-lift has opened up some good off-piste skiing here, and a stiff red run under the chairs. It also provides an alternative to the narrow, crowded track round the bowl which is the main way home. From Tête Moute there is an easy run across to the top of the cable-car. There are also some stiffer north-facing runs between the rocks, down to the Lac du Plan and onward to the Thuit chair.

The top section of the gondola to the Col de Jandri spans a slightly more open area of long blue and red runs with shorter, north-facing runs served by the Lac Noir and Toura chair-lifts. There are splendid views from the top of both these lifts, steeply down into the Vénéon valley. Although there is not a very wide network of lifts, the skiing in this area is long (over 1000m vertical).

The Glacier de Mont de Lans above the Col de Jandri is one of the best summer skiing areas in Europe: a wide expanse of long, easy runs between 2780m and 3423m in winter (3568m in summer). This is a lot of open, easy skiing with magnificent views and totally reliable snow conditions. Naturally the glacier area is often closed by bad weather. The drag-lift to the Dôme de la Lauze is usually closed in winter, which means a gentle half-hour walk for good skiers embarking on the magnificent and popular off-piste excursion across the glaciers to **La Grâve**, where there is a variety of beautiful, steep, north-facing, off-piste runs to the resort 1700m below. It is strongly advisable to join a guided group for this excursion. Les Deux Alpes' very long and narrow lift system gives plenty of other opportunities to go off-piste, but not many of the runs end up anywhere near the resort. Many come into the category of ski mountaineering, and guides are essential.

Nursery slopes are at the foot of the steep slopes on the west-facing side of the village beside Alpe de Venosc. Although not a very extensive area these serve the purpose. **Mountain restaurants** are few, uninteresting and expensive.

Lifts

Passes Area pass covers all lifts, swimming pool and ice rink, and gives a reduction at the fitness centre. Available for all periods from half-day. Three other more limited passes are available. Passes of over 5 days give one free day in Alpe d'Huez, Serre-Chevalier, Puy-St-Vincent, Montgenèvre and Sansicario.

Passes of over 11 days give two free days in each centre.
Cost 6-day pass FF457.
Children 10% off, under 13 years.
Beginners Two free lifts plus limited pass for 18 lifts near the resort.
Summer skiing Extensive area with 5 lifts, 2780m to 3568m.

In the past the great problem has been the time taken to reach the glacier, with long lift rides and queues at each stage. The new 20-seater gondola to the Col de Jandri will no doubt help, although morning queues at Alpe de Venosc may still be a problem. There may be queues for the gondola down when snow conditions are poor.

The resort

The setting of Les Deux Alpes is a remarkably symmetrical one, with steep drops to the north and south of its plateau and steep walls climbing evenly to the east and west. Of the two parts, Alpe de Venosc is the more compact and lively, and is splendidly set on the ledge above the very steep Vénéon Valley. Distances on foot are long.

Accommodation is mostly in apartments but there are also lots of small hotels, mostly simple and friendly. The best location is either in the centre near the main Jandri lift station. The Meije (∅ 805063) is a very friendly, small chalet-style hotel with an open fire in the sitting room. Le Cairn (∅ 805238) has less charm and is marginally less convenient but is similar in style. Attractive hotels (also simple and inexpensive) at the Venosc end are the Chalet Mounier (∅ 805690), Pied Moutet (∅ 805021) and Neiges (∅ 805202).

Après-ski is plentiful, lively and varied, with a number of interesting and good restaurants, entertaining bars, a couple of discothèques at Alpe de Venosc, and one at Alpe de Mont de Lans.

Ski school

Classes 3hr morning or 2hr afternoon.
Cost 6 days (18hr) FF391. Private lessons FF95/hr (1 or 2 people).
Children 30% off in classes. Ski kindergarten, ages 4–6, 9.00–5.00, FF57 for 3-hr session. Non-ski kindergarten,
ages 2–6, 9.00–5.00, FF750/week including lunchtime care/meal. Evening babysitting also provided.
Special courses Off-piste/touring day excursions, competition classes, weekly adventure courses.

A local ex-champion freestylist runs the courses of adventure skiing, including freestyle, mono-ski and off-piste.

Other activities

Cross-country 1km, 2km, 3km and 8km loops, northern end of resort (Petit Alpe and La Molière). 4km and 8km trails at Venosc (reached by gondola) with links to Bourg d'Oisans.
Not-skiing Skating (artificial rink), open-air heated pool, sauna, fitness centre with facilities for body-building, dance classes and Turkish bath, squash, cinemas.

The resort is not ideal for X-C or non-skiers. Venosc (reached by gondola) is the best place for X-C (given good snow).

Travel

Airport Geneva; transfer 3hr.
Railway Grenoble (75km); several buses daily.
Road Via Lyon/Grenoble; chains may be needed.
Reachable resorts Alpe d'Huez, Serre-Chevalier, Montgenèvre, La Grâve.

There is no local bus service: for a resort over a mile and a half long this is annoying. There is a helicopter shuttle service to Alpe d'Huez.

Miscellaneous

Tourist office ∅ (76) 792200.
Tx 320883.
Medical Hospital Grenoble (75km); doctors, dentists, chemists in resort.
Equipment hire 6 days skis FF220,
boots FF110, X-C FF130.
Resort beds 5,000 in hotels, 15,000 in apartments.
Package holidays AT, FL, GL, SMD, SMG, SUP.

Skiing suburb

Serre-Chevalier France 1350m – 1500m

Good for *Big ski area, nursery slopes, off-piste skiing, cross-country skiing*
Bad for *Not skiing, Alpine charm, easy road access, resort-level snow*

Serre-Chevalier is not a village but a mountain, which stands above Briançon, the highest town in Europe, privileged in the amount of good skiing on its doorstep. The ski-slopes of Serre-Chevalier have been a playground for local skiers for over half a century, and both resort and ski area have developed in a messy, unplanned way. It still has the atmosphere of a place for locals, and although the resort is not at all picturesque it does offer the chance to enjoy something of everyday provincial France. Visitors from further afield bring cars and use the area as a base for exploring accessible resorts in France and Italy. Lift pass arrangements are complicated and liable to change but generally allow visitors to divide their time between many different resorts.

The three components of the resort are styled as Serre-Chevalier 1350, 1400 and 1500 but they are separate and rather different villages, normally known by their proper names. Each has accommodation and varying resort facilities, but only Le Monêtier (1500) has any village atmosphere. Unfortunately it is the least convenient.

The skiing certainly deserves to be more widely known. As well as a large area of mostly intermediate pistes there is a huge amount of unpisted, skiable north-facing mountain within striking range of the lifts.

The skiing top 2780m bottom 1350m

Most of the lifts and pistes are concentrated above the neighbouring villages of **Chantemerle** and **Villeneuve**, in a linked network covering two adjacent bowls of open, mostly intermediate skiing between 2000m and 2500m, with longer runs of varying difficulty down through thinly wooded lower slopes, dotted with chalets and farm buildings and with rough roads which make easy alternatives to the direct descents to the valley floor. There are no outstandingly difficult runs.

Above **Grand Alpe** is an open basin of rather featureless intermediate runs with a good but congested nursery area at the top of the gondola. The double Prorel drag-lift serves quieter pistes and several off-piste runs, including one (after an initial climb) down to Briançon. Slightly stiffer, woodland trails run down from Serre-Chevalier itself to Serre-Ratier including an excellent fast race-track.

The **Fréjus/Echaillon** sector above Villeneuve provides more interesting runs for good skiers, with short, fairly steep unprepared pistes beneath the crest of the mountain chain. There are splendid views southwards into the Vallouise and a beautiful run (L'Isolée, well

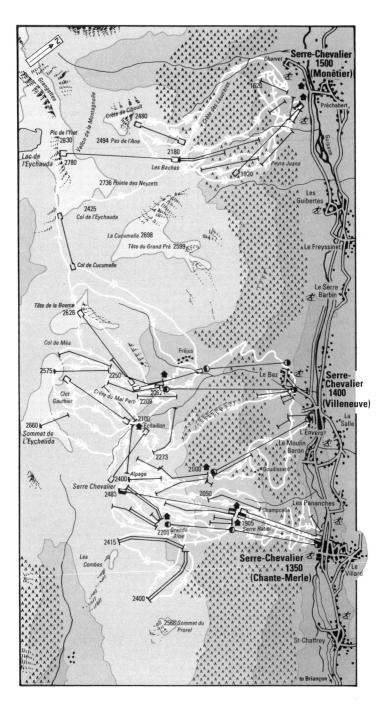

Serre-Chevalier
1500
(Monêtier)

Charvet

1620

Préchabert

Crête de Ciboult 2480

Pic de l'Yret
2830

Vallon de la Montagnolle

2494 Pas de l'Ane

2180

Les Bachas

Peyra Juana

1920

Lac de
l'Eychauda 2780

2736 Pointe des Neyzets

Les
Guibertes

2425
Col de l'Eychauda

La Cucumelle 2698

Tête du Grand Pré 2599

Le Freyssinet

Col de Cucumelle

Le Serre
Barbin

Tête de la Boeme
2626

Col de Méa

Fréjus

2575

2250

Le Bez

Serre-
Chevalier
1400
(Villeneuve)

Clot
Gauthier

Crête du Mal Parti

2062

2209

La
Salle

L'Envers

2660

2100
Echaillon

Le Moulin
Baron

Sommet de
L'Eychauda

2273

2000

Goudissard

Alpage

2050

2400

Serre Chevalier
2483

Champcella

Les Pananches

1905

Serre Ratier

2200
Grande
Alpe

2415

Serre-Chevalier
1350
(Chante-Merle)

Le
Villard

Les
Combes

2400

2566 Sommet du
Prorel

St-Chaffrey

to Briançon

Grangettes

Guisane

named) along the narrow ridge from Eychauda towards Echaillon. Inexperienced skiers can enjoy very long runs to the valley.

Le Monêtier's previously limited network of lifts is now linked to the Fréjus sector by a series of chair-lifts and has been extended upwards by the Yret chair-lift, the highest point in the lift system, giving runs of 1300m vertical to the valley. The link run itself, is not difficult, but it is high and exposed – unpleasant or impossible in bad weather. The wide and beautiful east-facing bowl above Fréjus has now been opened to piste skiers; other favourite off-piste runs have simply been made more accessible, notably the descents from Yret behind Cibouit. Most of the piste skiing down to Le Monêtier is challenging. The vast extent of larch woods, up to 2200m, makes good off-piste skiing.

Nursery slopes are good, with open areas at the foot of Villeneuve and Le Monêtier slopes, and higher up at the top of the Fréjus and Grand Alpe gondolas.

Mountain restaurants are at most of the main lift stations, and not very special. The old chalet-hotel Serre-Ratier is a welcome exception to the general mediocrity.

Lifts

Passes Grand Serre-Che pass covers all local lifts, entrance to Villeneuve pool, but no buses; available for all periods from half day, also 8 non-consecutive days; passes of 5 days and over give right to one day pass in each of Les Deux Alpes, Alpe d'Huez, Puy-St-Vincent, Milky Way resorts from Montgenèvre to Sansicario. Various limited passes available; also Briançon

region pass (6 or 7 days) covering Serre-Chevalier, Puy-St-Vincent, La Grâve, Montgenèvre/Sansicario. Cost 6-day pass FF490. 20% off in low season. Beginners Free lift at Chantemerle, beginners' day passes for valley lifts at Villeneuve and Monêtier. Children About 40% off, under 12.

Crowds are a weekend phenomenon, and confined to Villeneuve and Chantemerle, each of which now has three access lifts from the valley. As a result main pistes around Grand Alpe and Fréjus can be very congested. Streams and hillocks make it difficult or impossible to traverse across the natural balcony at around 2000m.

The resort

Chantemerle (1350) is only 5km out of Briançon and serves mainly as a service area for skiing commuters; space between main road and river is limited and parking facilities are inadequate. **Villeneuve** (1400) is more spread out, with a narrow, noisy and dangerous main-road high street on one side of the river and more spacious resort development (commercial centre and apartment buildings) at the foot of the slopes on the other side. If there is any centre of Serre-Chevalier, this is it. Near the Fréjus lifts the old hamlet of **Le Bez** has been converted to serve as a resort community without losing all its charm. **Le Monêtier** (1500) is a quiet old rural spa village with some delightful huddles of old buildings between road and river. The lift departure is on the other side of the river, quite a walk from the centre.

Accommodation consists of apartments and a few hotels in

Chantemerle and Villeneuve, and some simple hotels in Le Monêtier. Villeneuve is the best location for skiing convenience, provided roadside hotels are avoided. The Christiana (∅ 247633) is a simple, friendly and reasonably priced hotel between the two main lifts. The Aigle du Bez (∅ 247224) is a clean and functional new woody hotel at Le Bez, very convenient for the Fréjus lifts. In Le Monêtier the simple Alliey (∅ 244002) is very charming and central. Skiers with cars and wanting to explore other resorts may prefer to stay in Briançon. The Mont-Prorel (∅ 202288) is a quietly situated and attractive skiers' hotel with inexpensive rooms and a good restaurant.

Après-ski is quiet except at weekends. There are plenty of restaurants (the Serre and the Marotte in Villeneuve are recommended) and a few discothèques, of which the Baita (Villeneuve) and Serre-Che (Chantemerle) attract most of the local young.

Ski school

Ecole de Ski Français in all three villages, Ski Ecole International in Villeneuve and Chantererle.
Classes 3hr morning, 2hr afternoon; Le Monêtier, 2hr morning and afternoon.
Cost 6 days mornings only ESF FF300, SEI FF400; 6 days mornings and

afternoon ESF FF504. Private lessons F91/hr (1 or 2 people).
Children 30% off. Ski and non-ski kindergartens in all centres, typically for ages 2–6, 9.00–5.00, FF720/week.
Special courses Off-piste, freestyle.

The ski schools are very active in organising day excursions.

Other activities

Cross-country About 80km of trails along valley floor between Briançon and Le Casset (west of Le Monêtier).
Not skiing Most facilities at Villeneuve,

natural ice rinks (all centres), riding, 20km cleared paths, ice driving, sleigh rides, fishing (from early March).

The X-C skiing is good, especially west of Le Monêtier (the best base) where the valley is less built up; long off-piste excursions towards the Col du Lautaret are possible. Despite the various facilities, Serre-Chevalier is not appealing for non-skiing holidays.

Travel

Airport Grenoble; transfer about 2½hr. Also Turin.
Reachable resorts Montgenèvre, Sestriere, Sauze d'Oulx, Bardonecchia, Puy-St-Vincent, Risoul, La Grâve, Alpe d'Huez, Les Deux Alpes.

Railway Briançon (5 km); frequent buses.
Road Via Grenoble/Col du Lautaret (occasionally closed) or Chambéry/Fréjus Tunnel; chains may be needed.

Local transport consists of seven buses a day from Briançon along the valley, serving all main resort centres and lifts. Having a car is extremely useful for skiers keen to make the most of the region.

Miscellaneous

Tourist offices Villeneuve ∅ (92) 247188; Chantemerle ∅ 240034, Tx 400152; Le Monêtier ∅ 244198, Tx 244004.
Medical Doctor and chemist in resort; hospital and dentists in Briançon (5km).

Equipment hire 6 days skis FF200, boots FF100, X-C FF200.
Resort beds 30,000, mainly in apartments.
Package holidays FL, SPT.

No carte blanche

Sauze d'Oulx Italy 1500m

Good for *Après-ski, big ski area, mountain restaurants, sunny skiing*
Bad for *Skiing convenience, not skiing, Alpine charm, resort-level snow, late holidays*

Sestriere Italy 2040m

Good for *Nursery slopes, resort-level snow, big ski area, skiing convenience*
Bad for *Alpine charm, tough skiing, mountain restaurants, not skiing*

Montgenèvre France 1850m

Good for *Big ski area*
Bad for *Not skiing, après-ski, late holidays*

Linked resorts: Sansicario, Clavière, Jouvenceaux, Cesana Torinese

From Sauze d'Oulx it is possible to ski via Sestriere, Sansicario, Cesana Torinese and the French border at Clavière to Montgenèvre; and it is possible to ski all the way back, weather (and the customs) permitting. This, roughly anyway, is the Milky Way (Voie Lactée/Via Lattea). It was also the Carta Bianca ski region until until Sauze and Sestriere pulled out of the shared lift pass arrangement. This is no great tragedy: the Milky Way is not so much a single ski area, ripe for sharing, as an excursion which skiers may take repeatedly, occasionally or not at all, depending largely on which of the resorts along its length they stay in.

For many years Sowzy has been one of the most popular resorts in the Alps with young British skiers. The resort has some real attractions – extensive and interesting skiing, a delightful old village core, and some very convivial mountain restaurants; it also has faults – steep, icy streets between hotels and lifts, very casual piste maintenance, an inefficiently arranged lift system. But the cheap and extremely cheerful nightlife is the main attraction, for those who like that sort of thing; it is also the main drawback, for those who don't. Sauze has an erratic snow record, over recent years at least. On our January inspection visits in 1984 and 185, the lower nursery slopes were pastures brown, and many higher runs which were open should have been closed.

Sestriere, over the hill, could not be more different. It was the first purpose-built ski resort, created by Mussolini and Fiat mogul Agnelli on a high, wide pass near racy Torino. Cable-cars up to peaks above the pass gave Sestriere a splendid, open ski area which at the time must

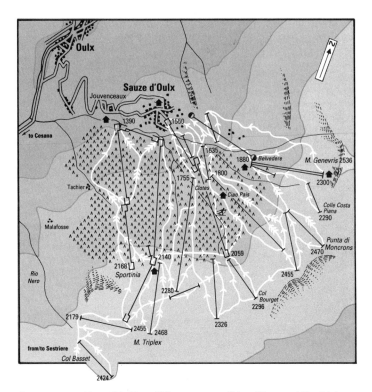

have seemed breathtaking. Fifty years on, it is still one of the highest resorts in the Alps, but the skiing no longer seems so exceptionally extensive and the drawbacks of the bleak setting are all too apparent. Sestriere is still quite a fashionable place for Torinese weekenders, but most of the time it is pretty dead, and most of the older buildings have grown rather tatty.

A border village on a high pass is an unpromising specification for a resort. But Montgenèvre, just inside France, is a surprisingly attractive, real old village, popular with local weekend skiers. It is quiet and inexpensive by French standards; the skiing is mostly easy but links well with that of Clavière. It would attract the 'family resort' label but for the main road running between the village and the ski slopes.

It is often easier to make the most of the Milky Way resorts by driving than by travelling between them on skis, particularly starting from the resorts at the extremes of the chain. Having a car also makes it possible to visit a variety of French resorts, and there are lift pass arrangements which encourage this. Montgenèvre is a the best base, with Serre-Chevalier only a few miles west, and Alpe d'Huez, La Grave and Les Deux Alpes within reach on the road to Grenoble. In the other direction from Briançon are Puy-St-Vincent, Risoul and Vars. The area is reached via Chambéry and the Fréjus tunnel, or Grenoble and the Col du Lauteret; chains are often needed.

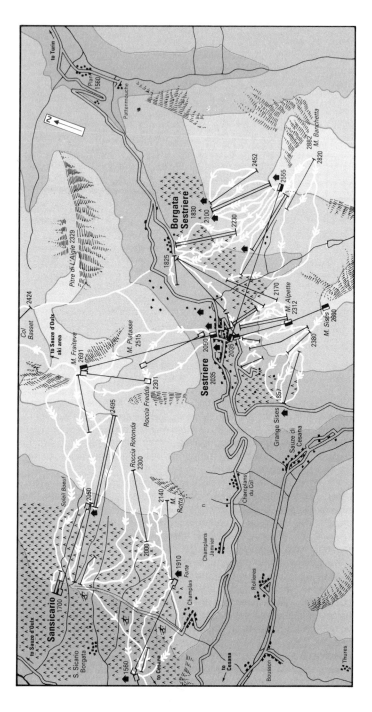

The skiing

The skiing of **Sauze d'Oulx** is on a quarter-circle of mostly wooded mountainsides facing west and north. Lift departures are awkwardly sited, and the ski area is broken up by river gullies and a lack of co-operation between different lift companies. The main division is between the main Sportinia/Clotes system and the Genevris lifts, only recently covered by the same pass as the bigger area, and still relatively neglected.

The sunny plateau of **Sportinia** is at the heart of the skiing. It has a couple of hotels, a small and crowded nursery area, and a circle of restaurants. Above it there is some good open skiing around the top of Triplex, with a couple of lifts behind giving access to Col Basset and the off-piste run down to Sestriere. The steep slopes down from the top of Fraiteve can be reached only from Sestriere, but the Rio Nero run can be joined part-way down. Below Sportinia there are excellent wide runs back through the woods – marked blue, red and black, steep in places but never really difficult. There is also a green run which traverses across the mountain and back, but which is not entirely trivial skiing.

The **Genevris** lift departs a long way from most hotels. From the Belvedere mid-station there are drag-lifts serving gentle runs below Monte Genevris; below Moncron are Sauze's most challenging pistes, where the difficulty is often accentuated by lack of maintenance.

Sauze is linked over Monte Fraiteve with **Sestriere** (but not with Sansicario). The slopes face south-east, and are very exposed – so they often lack snow and the lifts are often closed by wind. The bulk of Sestriere's skiing is on the other side of the resort, on Monte Sises and Monte Banchetta. A two-stage cable-car from the resort to 2600m serves the **Sises** area. There are a number of short drag-lifts with short and quite steep runs down from the half-way station, Alpette. From the top, there are challenging off-piste descents (given good snow) to the steep, north-facing gorge which divides Sises from Banchetta and intermediate pistes (mostly red) to Sestriere and over west-facing slopes to Grangesises. A cable-car from the resort crosses the river gorge to **Banchetta**. The drag-lift above it opens up some challenging pistes and an excellent red run into the dividing valley and on through woods to the roadside mini-resort of Borgata. Below the cable-car station there is a wide expanse of red and blue pistes and some entertaining off-piste hollows and ridges above the sunny Amfiteatro. From Borgata there are drag-lifts up to Sestriere and very easy runs down – ideal for near-beginners.

From the top of the **Fraiteve** cable-car there are intermediate runs back down to Sestriere. One of the best runs in the region for good skiers is over on the Sauze side of the mountain, down the steep Rio Nero gully. Snow permitting, the valley can be skied down to the Oulx–Cesana road – a magnificent, varied descent of some 1400m vertical. The normal skiing route from Sauze via Col Basset is an unmarked off-piste run, not particularly steep.

The open slopes above **Sansicario** can be reached from Sestriere's

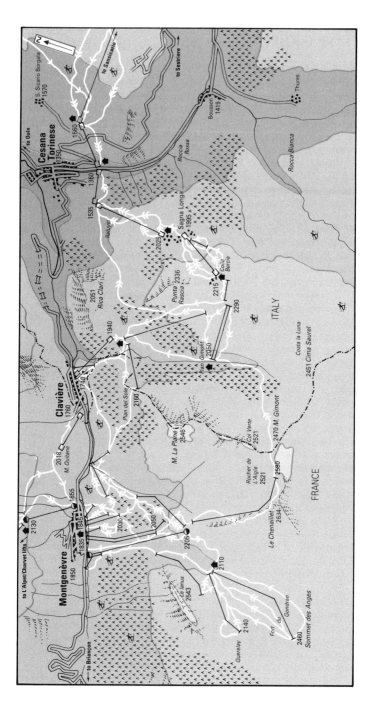

lifts; they are fairly steep at the top, and the run all the way down to
Sansicario, starting off black or red, is a challenging and satisfying
descent. Most of the rest of the west-facing skiing is wide, intermediate
to easy woodland trails. There are some good long off-piste runs to
points along the Cesana–Oulx road. Runs to La Combe, beside
Cesana, get progressively steeper as they go down; the section below
the bottom chair-lift is never easy and is often too bare to be skied.

Montgenèvre has ski slopes on both flanks of the pass on which it
sits. The south-facing side, Chalvet, is marginally higher (up to
2,600m), and usually less crowded than the north-facing slopes which
form the connection with the other Milky Way resorts – Claviere, then
Cesana and Sansicario.

The gondola for **Chalvet** starts a few minutes' walk east of the
centre. A trio of long drag-lifts then serves treeless, mostly easy runs
with more difficult runs down either side of the Chalvet and off-piste
skiing down to Montgenèvre from the Bélier drag (2365m). There is
only one piste down to Montgenèvre, a fairly easy red. A chair-lift from
Clavière serves a short, awkward black run and a more roundabout
blue back down, and a very gentle link run across to Montgenèvre.

The **Charmettes** gondola from the west end of the resort and
drag-lifts from the centre serve mostly easy runs through woods to an
open nursery area. From the top of the gondola there is a choice of
three skiing areas. The wide, sheltered bowl of Querelay/Les Anges
has eerie ruined fortress buildings around the crests and some red and
black runs beneath them; but there is really no difficult skiing except
off-piste over the back. The Brusset drag-lift serves some challenging
skiing in the woods. The long, dogleg drag-lift through beautiful rocky
scenery to the Rocher de l'Aigle has a good red run beside it, and
serves a very good off-piste run to the foot of the Brusset drag. It also
leads to Italy, via a traverse around the mountain then an easy run to
the Gimont drag-lift; the runs down to La Combe just outside Cesana
provide some of the most challenging skiing in the Milky Way, both on-
and off-piste among the trees. The bottom section is often bare. From
La Combe a series of no less than six lifts is needed to reach the point
where the skiing of Sansicario meets the skiing of Sestriere.

Nursery slopes at Sauze are adequate – the main slope is at
Sportinia, where there is a lot of open space, though it gets very
crowded. There are also nursery areas at Belvedere on the Genevris
side, and in the village (if there's snow). There are good slopes all
around Sestriere, especially between the resort and Borgata.
Montgenèvre's slopes are on a good wide open, sometimes
windswept, area immediately beside the resort, with the possibility of
skiing all the way down from Les Anges on green runs. They get get
crowded, especially at weekends.

The distribution of **mountain restaurants** is patchy. There are few
mountain-top restaurants, but lower down there are some excellent
places for lunch above Sauze, Borgata, Sansicario, and Clavière/
Cesana – these last 'incredibly cheap,' says one report.

Lifts

Sauze/Sestriere

Passes Area pass covers all lifts in these two resorts and gives one free weekday in Alpe d'Huez, Les Deux Alpes, Serre-Chevalier and Puy-St-Vincent. Supplements are payable for Sansicario/Montgenèvre lifts.
Cost 6-day pass L105,000. 20% more at Christmas and Easter.
Children No reduction.
Beginners Coupons.

Montgenèvre

Passes Pass covers lifts as far as Cesana and gives two free days at Alpe d'Huez or Les Deux Alpes, but supplements are payable for Sansicario/Sestriere/Sauze lifts. 7-day Briançon regional pass also covers Serre-Chevalier, Puy-St-Vincent and La Grâve.
Cost 6-day pass FF370.
Children 35% off, under 12.
Beginners Day passes for limited area. A few lifts can be paid for by the ride.

There are very often long queues for the lifts from Sportinia above Sauze, with no easy way to avoid the bottleneck. At weekends lifts out of Montgenèvre become crowded. Lifts in Italy close for lunch.

The resorts

Sauze d'Oulx

Sauze stands on the sunny west-facing flank of a wide valley junction. It is built on a steep slope; it is also large, and growing, and almost everywhere seems to be a long, steep walk from everywhere else – including the three widely separated lift stations. Sauze is an undistinguished mess of modern buildings – though not the monstrosity that many more 'carefully' planned resorts are. The large central square is a car park most of the time, and the site of a market once a week – good value, reports say.

Accommodation is mostly in hotels, basic to simple, without charm, and cheap. By far the best location is around Piazzale Miramonti, between Clotes and Sportinia lifts. The only attractive hotel in this area is the new and small Hermitage (∅ 85385), in a sunny open situation overlooking the village nursery slopes. The San Giorgio (∅ 85162) is far from luxurious and badly placed, but very friendly and very inexpensive. The Palace (∅ 85222) is the biggest, the most comfortable and the most expensive hotel, but not at all stylish. The Capricorno at Clotes (∅ 85273) is expensive and attractive, but isolated after the lifts close. You can be first on to the nursery slopes by staying at Sportinia – the Monte Triplex (∅ 85015) or even the old Capanna Kind (∅ 85206). The Ciao Pais (∅ 85280) also offers cheap, very simple accommodation.

Après-ski in Sauze is very lively ('Force 8 varying gale force 10 at times'), very British, and very inexpensive. It is not to everyone's taste – we have bitter reports of holidays spoilt by the rowdiness. The bar in the Hotel Derby is a long-established favourite.

Ski school

Two schools, at Sportinia and Genevris.
Classes 3hr mornings only (afternoon classes can be arranged).
Cost 6-days L88,000. Private lessons
L20,000.
Children Ski kindergarten at ski school. Non-ski kindergarten, ages up to 8, 9.00–5.00.

Other activities

Cross-country X-C skiers can use the green run to Pian della Rocca.

Not skiing Natural ice rink, tennis, bowling.

Sauze is not good for cross-country or for non-skiers. Walking around is no a great pleasure, and there are few non-skiing facilities. If it snows, the ice rink is apparently not cleared promptly.

Travel

Airport Turin; transfer 2½hr.
Railway Oulx (30min); frequent buses.

Road See page 363.
Reachable resorts See page 363.

There is a ski-bus service until 6pm, via the centre.

Miscellaneous

Tourist office ∅ (122) 85009.
Medical Doctor, chemist in resort; dentist in Oulx; hospital in Susa (29km).
Equipment hire 6 days skis L30,000, boots L1500, X-C L45,000.

Resort beds 1,800 in hotels, 8,200 in apartments.
Package holidays BS, CI, CL, EN, HA, IG, NE, NT, SPT, STY, TH.

Jouvenceaux 1380m

This small and charming hamlet is just below Sauze d'Oulx, and is growing up the road from Oulx to meet it. At the bottom of the lifts which link the two villages is a delightfully unspoilt maze of crumbling alleys with old fountains and medieval paintings on the wall of the church. Most of the Jouvenceaux accommodation is quite a walk or a bus ride from its lifts, and does not share the charm of the old village.

Tourist office ∅ 122-85009. Package holidays IG.

Sestriere

Sestriere is a bleak place, spread around the wide col with a scattering of thin larches around the bottom of the mountain flanks. The great landmarks are the tall, round towers of the Torre and the Duchi d'Aosta hotels, now occupied by Club Med. Lifts depart from central positions.

   Accommodation is in the form of hotels, apartments and Club Med. Among the hotels, the only luxurious one is the new low-rise business-style Sestriere (∅ 76576), which is expensive. The Savoy Edelweiss (∅ 7040) is simple and central, as is the Olympic (∅ 7344) near the bottom of the Fraiteve cable-car. The Miramonti (∅ 7048) is not very well situated, but very friendly, attractive and good value.

   Apres-ski depends critically on the time of the season: it is moderately lively when the Italians are in evidence.

Ski school

Classes 3hr, mornings only.
Cost 6 days L88,000. Private lessons L20,000 per hour (one person).

Children No kindergarten arrangements.

Other activities

Cross-country There is a small loop at the resort.

Not-skiing Ice driving, swimming, ice rink, cinema.

An ice driving course can be included in the hotel-plus-lift-pass formula. The resort is not an appealing place for X-C or non-skiers.

Travel

Airport Turin; transfer 2½hrs.
Railway Oulx; frequent buses.

Road See page 363.
Reachable resorts See page 363.

Buses run to/from Borgata, Grangsises and the end of the Rio Nero run (on the Oulx–Cesana road).

Miscellaneous

Tourist office ✆ (122) 76045.
Medical Doctors, chemist and fracture clinic in resort; hospital Pinerolo (60km), dentists in Grangesises.
Equipment hire 6 days skis L30,000,

boots L15,000, X-C L45,000.
Resort beds 1,400 in hotels, 12,600 in apartments.
Package holidays CM.

Sansicario 1700m

Sansicario is a small modern resort in a sunny position half-way up a west-facing mountainside. It consists mainly of apartment buildings below a neat commercial precinct to which it is linked by a shuttle lift. The whole place is rather stylish in a clinical way and patronised almost exclusively by Italians. It is well placed for exploring all the Milky Way resorts. Facilities are generally good for beginners, especially children (a good skiing and non-skiing kindergarten providing all-day care and lunch if required). Cross-country skiers are reasonably well catered for, with a 10km loop across the hillside from the resort. Non-skiing and après-ski facilities are good, but there is little variety – a discothèque, a smart restaurant, a cheap restaurant, swimming, sauna, massage, gym, riding and even ski-jöring. Accommodation is of a high standard, mostly in apartments, but with a few comfortable, expensive hotels, of which the most attractive is the Rio Envers Gallia (✆ 811313), a bit of a walk along the hill from the centre.

Tourist office ✆ (122) 811212. Tx 211495.

Montgenèvre

The village is spread along the north side of the busy main road across the high col, now also the main street. Immediately on the other side of the road are open, north-facing ski slopes, with lifts spread out along the hillside.

Accommodation is in mostly fairly simple hotels and apartments spread along the main road and behind it in the old village. Access to skiing is not a problem from most places, and the Italian end of the village is relatively more convenient. There is no very luxurious accommodation and prices are reasonable. The Napoléon (✆ 219204) and the Rois Mages (✆ 219264) are both well-placed on the main road. The Valérie (✆ 219002) is more attractively set in the old village behind the main road.

There is not much **après-ski** activity, especially during the week, but there is a good choice of inexpensive restaurants and a couple of them have nightclubs attached. The Ca del Sol is a popular bar in the centre.

Ski school

Classes 2½hr morning, 2hr afternoon. **Cost** 6 days FF450. Private lessons FF105 1hr, one or two people. **Children** Ski kindergarten, ages 5–12, 6 days without meals FF360. Non-skiing kindergarten, ages 18 mth–6, 6 days without meals FF300. Babysitting can be arranged.

The ski school organises a few excursions, for example to La Grâve.

Other activities

Cross-country There are several loops among woods on either side of the pass, and a route to Clavière.

Not-skiing Natural skating rink, open until 11pm, curling.

Montgenèvre is better than other resorts in the Milky Way for X-C skiing. There is very little for non-skiers to do in the village.

Travel

Airport Turin; transfer 2½hr. **Railway** Briançon (10km) or Oulx (17km).

Road See page 363. **Reachable resorts** See page 363.

Miscellaneous

Tourist office ✆ (92)219046 **Medical** Doctor and chemist in resort; hospital and dentist at Briançon (10km). **Equipment hire** 6 days skis FF140, boots FF70, X-C FF110.

Resort beds About 140 in hotels, 5,900 in apartments. **Tour operators** CL, HM, MM, SMD, SPT, TH.

Clavière 1750m

Clavière is very much a border village, with the customs post in the middle. There are a number of quiet and not unattractive hotels along the road. The village is tightly enclosed by wooded slopes on either side, but there is a small nursery lift, and access to the skiing above Montgenèvre and Cesana, with easy runs back from both. There is a cross-country trail up to Montgenèvre and back.
Tourist office ✆ (122) 8856. Tour operators CL, HM, SMD.

Cesana Torinese 1350m

Cesana is an attractively dilapidated old village at a road junction. It is confined and sunless, and accommodation is limited. More holiday-makers go to the hotels and chalets dotted around the ski slopes (mainly at Sagna Longa, 2000m). The chair-lifts up from La Combe to the skiing above Clavière and Sansicario are a long walk from the centre.
Tourist office ✆ (122) 76698.

Hutch; not just for rabbits

Puy-St-Vincent France 1600m

Unlike most French Alpine developments well-known in Britain, but like several other resorts in the southern Alps and most of the Pyrenean ones, PSV is small, cheap and unsophisticated. It was the first resort of its kind to be launched in Britain by a coach operator, and it has attracted a sizeable minority following, mainly because of low prices. The British presence is now an important and very noticeable one. The atmosphere is the gregarious joviality of a holiday camp. PSV's popularity has recently been boosted by its spectacular giant-killing coup in playing host to World Cup races moved from Val d'Isère because of a lack of snow.

PSV is a split-level place with a split personality. At 1400m is the old community – just an attractively messy mountain village with a couple of simple hotels which is linked by lift with the new complex at 1600m. This isolated, unsightly, modern (but already shoddy) hulk of an apartment complex is what most brochures mean by PSV.

From upper PSV at 1600m the skiing extends up the mountain to 2750m, and down it to 1400m, giving a very respectable total vertical drop for a small resort. There is an attractive mixture of woodland skiing, on and off the piste, up to about 2000m, and a bowl of open snowfields above it, which gives access to an occasional, long, initially steep off-piste run into the beautiful Vallon de Narreyroux. This is a good little skiing area, mostly facing north and east, with some tough runs near the top, and plenty of skiing to suit beginners and timid intermediates. Queues are rarely a problem, there are easy slopes around and between PSV 1400 and 1600, and the two ski schools usually feature some native English-speakers. But it is little, and offers less scope than its less well-known neighbours of Les Orres and Risoul/Vars. After a few days most piste-bashers will be keen for a change of scenery and should consider organising day-trips to other resorts in the Briançon area (Serre-Chevalier and Montgenèvre are the most convenient) covered by the local lift pass.

The single building at 1600m consists mainly of flatlets, but there are also hotels. The complex has a single supermarket, which gets more crowded than the lifts at peak times, an occasional bank, some surprisingly smart ski and clothes shops, pinball machines, a few bars and restaurants, but no chemist. Après-ski is very limited, with the notable exception of the parties regularly organised by the UK operators. Apart from this, evening activities consist of organised outings to restaurants. PSV is very convenient; the ski-lift is just in front of the building, where there is also a kindergarten play area. At lunchtime or after skiing you pop straight out of your ski bindings into your flat. Cross-country skiers can tackle a reputedly difficult 15km trail in the woods beside the resort; there are no non-skiing sports facilities.

Tourist office ✆ (92) 233580. Tx 403404. **Tour operators** SCB, SCP, SMD.

Not so splendid isolation

Isola 2000 France 2000m

Good for *Family skiing, nursery slopes, skiing convenience, resort-level snow, freedom from cars, short airport transfers, self-catering holidays*
Bad for *Not skiing, Alpine charm, après-ski, easy road access*

Isola 2000 is the most southerly major ski resort in the Alps, and one of the highest of the purpose-built, apartment-based, family-oriented resorts of which the French have made a speciality. It claims an exceptional record of both snow and sunshine, and to reinforce the point offers a 'Sun and Snow Guarantee'. The terms of the guarantee make it of negligible value to most British visitors, but what is clearly of considerable value is the basic formula the resort offers: hotels and apartments looking directly on to a gloriously long, gentle, sunny nursery slope, with cars safely confined elsewhere. The merits of the rest of the compact, densely exploited ski area are secondary – though it has considerable attractions for every grade of skier. Also secondary, for most visitors, are the drawbacks of the resort itself.

In its original form, Isola was the ultimate purpose-built resort – designed so that you could step from the front door of your hotel or apartment block into your bindings and schuss off down the nursery slope, and in the afternoon reverse the process. Everything you might want access to during the evening was provided under the one roof, so that you didn't need to stray outside. The purity of this original concept has been lost in recent years by the construction of Le Hameau – a group of small apartment blocks slightly above and to the north of the main complex. This presumably reflects the realisation that the main resort building has very little to be said for it, apart from its convenience and safety. It is uncompromising and charmless outside, claustrophobic and charmless inside; what's more, it is now showing its age, and becoming tatty.

Isola does not rely entirely on self-catering families for its custom: on good weekends, there is a jet-set invasion from the Côte d'Azur (only one and a half hours' drive away) which fills the three hotels and ensures hefty queues for some of the lifts. The main flaw in the lift system is that a lot of the best skiing is served by a few lifts of low capacity, which are easily accessible to day visitors.

The skiing top 2610m bottom 1800m

The resort's piste map employs a sensible division of the skiing into three areas, though all are linked – the south-west-facing slopes of Domaine du Levant, and the north-east-facing slopes split by the Tête de la Cabane into the Domaine du Pélevos, immediately above the

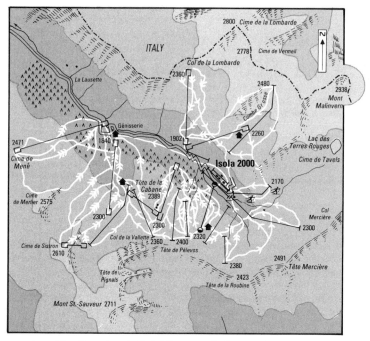

resort, and the Domaine du Saint Sauveur, further west.

The **Pélevos** area is densely equipped with pistes and lifts, the major one being a gondola which departs directly from the resort building. From the top (2320m) there are satisfyingly varied easy and intermediate runs back down through the patchy trees, and links in both directions to drags which go slightly higher. If you go east, you can get to a long green run, well away from the lifts, which is splendid for near beginners in the right conditions, but hard work if there is new snow. If you go west, a drag gives access to further varied runs to the resort and makes the link with the Saint Sauveur area. Skiing down to the big car park at 1900m (the main way into the skiing for day visitors, below the resort) brings you to a chair which forms another link with the Saint Sauveur area as well as serving its own worthwhile red and black runs.

Saint Sauveur is the serious sector, with satisfying skiing for intermediates and experts. A drag and short chair take you to the high point of Isola's skiing, the Cime de Sistron (2610m), on the flank of Mont Saint Sauveur. The three long black runs off the back of the summit were closed when we visited, but the lower section which runs parallel to the blue and reds down through the woods to Génisserie certainly justifies the rating. There would appear to be considerable scope for off-piste variants on these runs. The chair back from Génisserie is crucial for getting back to the Sistron skiing and thus back to Isola. The queues for it can be considerable, and are predicted by an electronic bulletin board at the point where you commit yourself to its care. The point of going down is to take the long alternative chair to

Mont Mené (2471m), from where parallel blue, red and black runs depart – very exposed at the top (and often closed), more sheltered and wooded lower down. When we visited the piste signing and closure on this mountain was in complete chaos (not typical of the resort at a whole).

Once safely back up the vital Génisserie chair, a choice of lifts takes you back over la Cabane to the Pélevos slopes, and runs either to the resort or down to 1900m, where the main chairs go up to the Levant area – the Col de la Lombarde and Combe Grosse. These serve south- and south-west-facing slopes which are distinctly gentler than those opposite, mainly on open mountainsides above the trees. Easy traverses from this area link with drag-lifts at the head of the valley serving long, flat green runs which are an uphill extension of the nursery slopes.

The **nursery slopes** are superb, running the length of the resort, and the progression to real pistes is so gradual as to be imperceptible. Skiers who have been distressed by fouling of the nursery slopes at other French family resorts (notably Avoriaz) will be encouraged to hear that dogs are banned from the slopes here.

Mountain restaurants are few, but adequate for a small ski area with good lifts out of the resort, permitting trouble-free lunching at base. The Génisserie restaurant (at the bottom of the Saint Sauveur skiing) is stylishly rustic.

Lifts

Passes One pass covers all lifts. **Cost** 6-day pass FF415. 15% off in low season (including most of March).

Beginners Coupons, or limited-area Mini-Pass. **Children** 30% off, under 12.

The lift system works well enough except at weekends, when the under-endowed Saint Sauveur sector cannot take the strain of the crowds, particularly at Génisserie. There are elaborate systems for informing skiers about lift and piste conditions, including 24-hour TV (you can hire sets); we didn't find the information very reliable.

The resort

The meandering spinal corridor will convey you to wherever you want to go within the main complex, including a few shops which are sufficiently flashy to betray Isola's second role as a venue for weekend sprees from the Côte d'Azur. Residents of Le Hameau are dependent on the mother ship for everything other than sleeping space, and to get to and from it are provided with something which no self-respecting convenience resort should need – a shuttle bus.

Accommodation is mainly in apartments, though there are three hotels spaced along the building, arranged in price order from up-piste, down-market Le Druos (✆ 231220) via the Pra du Loup (✆ 231171) to down-piste, up-market Le Chastillon (✆ 231060). Reporters recommend paying the premium for south-facing balcony rooms. The resort brochure contains detailed plans of apartments in both the main building and Le Hameau. Le Hameau is well placed for the Levant skiing but less so for the main slopes.

Après-ski in the early evening revolves around bars, one or two crêperie-style restaurants and the supermarket, and is quite lively. Later on there are two discos; whether you will find them animated other than at weekends is another question. For dining out there is a restaurant symbolically detached from the complex in the middle of the nursery slope – the Cow Club, recommended by one reporter – and you can get to the Génisserie by car. There is a babysitting service, but you can't expect English to be spoken.

Ski school

Two schools: Ecole de Ski Français and Ski Ecole International.
Classes ESF 2hr to 2½hr, mornings only; SEI 4½hr/day.
Cost 6 days ESF FF282, SEI FF650. Private lessons FF99/hr.
Beginners *Ski évolutif.*

Children 6 days SEI FF360. Ski kindergarten, ages 3–12, 9.00–5.15, 6 days with lunch FF786. Non-skiing kindergarten, up to age 8, 9.00–5.00.
Special courses Various, from both schools – including mono-ski, artistic, slalom skiing, ski touring.

We do not have recent reports on the ski schools. As elsewhere, the SEI sets out to capture non-French business, and the ESF claims that nearly all its instructors are bilingual – so there should be no langauge problems. Advance booking is recommended for the kindergarten.

Other activities

Cross-country One trail of 4km.
Not skiing Natural ice rink, swimming pool (outdoor, from February), sauna, cinema, ice driving.

People who are not interested in downhill skiing should not contemplate a holiday in Isola unless planning to read (or write) lots of books. The skating rink is positioned, logically but depressingly, in the shade of the main building.

Travel

Airport Nice; transfer 2hr.
Railway Nice; two or three buses daily.
Reachable resorts Auron.
Road Via the Côte d'Azur; chains often needed.

The roads approaching Isola directly from the north-west are difficult and much slower than sticking to the motorway round to Nice. A car is of no use while you're there, except for excursions to the Côte d'Azur or Auron. The shuttle bus serving Le Hameau runs from 8.30am to midnight. No other transport around the resort is necessary.

Miscellaneous

Tourist office ℘ (93) 231050.
Medical Medical centre in resort, with doctor and chemist.
Package holidays FL, MM, NE, WT.
Equipment hire 6 days skis FF270,

boots FF110, X-C 213.
Resort beds 460 in hotels, 6,140 in apartments.

Embrun solaire

Les Orres France 1600m

Les Orres is a small modern resort beautifully set above the handsome old town of Embrun and the Serre-Ponçon reservoir east of Gap. It deserves to be better known than it is, for the skiing is high, beautiful and varied, the resort is user-friendly without being a concrete blot on the landscape, and the people are unusually cheerful and welcoming. In good conditions (which are reputed to be unreliable) there is plenty of scope for an entertaining and inexpensive week.

The resort is a scattering of apartment buildings and chalets across a steep, lightly-wooded hillside a few miles beyond the old hamlet of Les Orres. Although it's a long way up to the nucleus of the resort from its lower fringes, there are pistes through the resort, lifts from top and bottom, and a shuttle cable-car from the car park at the entrance to the resort to the centre. Most rented accommodation (flats) is in the buildings immediately surrounding the central concourse, a small plateau with a shopping precinct and sunny café terraces at the foot of the pistes, pleasant and animated at lunchtime (there are no mountain restaurants). Bar prices are reasonable and the evening atmosphere is very chummy. There is one discothèque and outings to restaurants in old Les Orres and Embrun can be arranged.

The ski area extends across a broad north-west-facing mountainside which rises to a crest between two peaks with a top lift station at 2720m. All the lifts are chairs or drags, so there is no escaping cold weather. Early in the season the sun does not stay long on the slopes. Good skiers have a choice of several long and satisfying runs down to the resort and below (1170m vertical), or alternatively a series of tough runs on the open upper slopes. All the skiing above 2000m is red or black, and one or two of the red runs ought to be black. A particularly beautiful run drops behind a ridge into a wide neighbouring bowl, one day to be equipped with ski-lifts, according to the plans. Immediately above and beside the resort there is an area of gentler skiing served by chair-lifts, but the runs are short and used by other skiers speeding down to the resort. There are a few nursery lifts, but in general the terrain is not ideal for beginners. Queues are rarely a problem except over the February school holiday period. Even then, skiers neglect the lifts at the northern side where there is some good off-piste skiing in the woods as well as long red pistes.

There are two ski schools, and all-day ski and non-ski kindergartens. In the recent past most British ski school pupils in Les Orres have used instructors employed by their tour operator.

Les Orres has little to offer non-skiers, and the advertised total of 50 km of X-C trails includes a large proportion of 'itineraries'. There are a few hotels in the resort, and a greater range of accommodation, some of it very cheap, in Embrun.

Tourist office ✆ (92) 440161. Package holidays FL.

Short-circuit skiing

Risoul, Vars France 1850m

Risoul and Vars are two very different resorts sharing an extensive ski area above Guillestre, south of Briançon. Vars, which attracts a chic French clientele but few foreigners, is the longer established and larger of the two and has more skiing. Unlike most neighbouring resorts, it has more to it than ski-fields and apartments – varied shopping, lively après-ski, some attractive hotels, good walks and cross-country trails, and mountain restaurants. Its drawbacks are that it is ugly, set in a rather enclosed position in a narrow valley, and very strung out along the road up to the Col de Vars, between 1650m (Vars Ste Marie) and 1850m (Vars les Claux, the main resort). The most attractive hotel is Les Escondus (∅ 455035), small, friendly and very convenient.

Risoul is a new resort in a beautiful open situation with splendid views over a once strategic junction of valleys (complete with fortifications) towards the highest peaks of the southern Alps. It is built on a normal village plan, with large wood-clad buildings grouped loosely around a main street, and an annoying amount of traffic. At the top of the village is a broad, sunny plateau at the foot of the pistes, with an arc of apartment buidings and café terraces. The mountains above do not keep the sun out. Risoul is small but less claustrophobic and better equipped with bars and restaurants than many similar places. There is skating, and long cross-country trails round the mountain.

The Vars/Risoul ski area consists mainly of two broad bowls above the two resorts facing east and north respectively. They are nearly back-to-back, but the neighbouring peaks at the top of the two areas are separated by a saddle which is not equipped with lifts. This makes skiing from Risoul to Vars and back a roundabout business, but the whole area is not enormous and it is easy to ski the whole circuit in a leisurely day. Neither area is very large, neither offers very much difficult skiing, and few of the runs are long – the resorts are high and the top of the runs not much higher (nearly 2600m); but, provided the links are open (when we visited the top runs had been swept bare by wind), there is plenty of scope for energetic intermediate skiers. Most of the Risoul side is gentle and particularly suitable for inexperienced skiers, with an excellent sunny beginners' area out of way of the rest of the pistes. When snow is abundant it is possible to ski down to old Risoul (1071m) on a piste graded red which carries on from the beautiful run along the easternmost rim of the bowl. Vars also has some attractive woodland runs on the opposite side of the valley.

The weekly lift pass on sale in Risoul covers all lifts; Vars skiers can choose between a local pass or one covering both resorts. Day passes are local, with a supplement payable for skiing both areas. There are kindergartens in both resorts.

Tourist offices Risoul ∅ (929 450260; Vars les Claux ∅ (92) 455131.
Package holidays Risoul SMD; Vars SCG, STY.

White heather club

Scotland

Like Sicily, Cyprus, the Lebanon, Australia and the Massif Central, Scotland has mechanised skiing areas which attract hardly any skiers from abroad. Aviemore, the main resort, tries hard to appeal more widely than to local weekenders. But most skiers living south of Hadrian's Wall can get to major Alpine resorts almost as quickly, easily and cheaply as they can to the Highlands, so Scottish ski resorts must compete on equal terms with the Alpbachs, the Verbiers, the Selvas, the Méribels and even the Soldeus for the custom of the English, Welsh and Irish. It is an uphill struggle.

As our maps shows, Aviemore's ski area, on Cairngorm, has less skiing than the smallest Alpine resorts mapped in this *Guide*, which themselves mainly appeal to people who don't take their skiing too seriously – people attracted by the charm of Alpine villages which make Aviemore in winter look very bleak and unwelcoming, and by the thought of log cabins on the mountainside serving spiced *Glühwein* and *Apfelstrudel* at all hours of the day, putting to shame the unlicensed Cairngorm cafeterias with their coffee and cling-film sandwiches. There are resorts in the Alps which lack to some extent this sort of appeal – but they tend to compensate by having ski areas which are hugely extensive or superbly designed for convenience, or both.

But the greatest disadvantage of Scottish skiing is the weather. Skiing often takes place in extremely unfriendly conditions, with no shelter provided by trees or enclosed lifts. At other times skiing does not take place at all, except on the dry slope at Aviemore Centre. All the same, Scottish skiing is a serious business taken seriously by many excellent skiers who would scoff at the idea of spending much time in tiny Austrian or Italian resorts. This is rugged outdoor country, and the Scots revel in the hard Highland winter as part of the mountain experience. Hard as the winter is, snow is unreliable, and weather conditions extremely volatile. Storms and high winds may not only close lifts for long periods but also affect the quality of the snow; piste conditions are rarely as flattering as Alpine piste-skiers expect.

Skiing in Scotland does have some advantages – the advantages of not being abroad. People speak something at least closely related to English, and in ski school this is a great advantage. Lift queues are as orderly as only British queues can be. Shop prices are much the same as at home and so is the cost of evening entertainment. There is a great sense of camaraderie, and the après-ski ambience is warm and friendly.

If you are a keen skiing Scot, you no doubt ski in all of the three main centres (Glencoe and Glenshee as well as Cairngorm) and most often in the one which is most easily accessible from home. You will probably have found that on weekends when conditions are good, you are not alone in wanting to exploit them. If you are a holiday skier from south of the border, used to Alpine resorts, you should not contemplate Scotland for your once-a-year skiing holiday. As a supplement to an Alpine skiing holiday though, a weekend or week late in the season may provide some excellent skiing. In general, conditions are at their best in March, April, and well into May. (Fences beside the pistes and lift tracks cause snow to accumulate there and to persist long after it has disappeared from most of the mountain.) Daylight hours are longer and conditions on the mountain are more likely to be bearable than in the depth of winter. And as spring advances it is increasingly possible to enjoy a non-skiing Highlands holiday, with some skiing thrown in almost as a bonus.

Aviemore is the only developed resort, with comfortable hotel accommodation and good facilities for non-skiing entertainment. Glencoe and Glenshee are more often used by day-trip skiers, but there is cheap and friendly accommodation within striking range, and many skiers prefer these areas precisely because of the absence of modern development. Their lift systems are smaller and their lift passes cheaper than Cairngorm's, but weekend queues are usually worse.

Aviemore

Aviemore lies in the broad Spey valley between Perth and Inverness, about three hours by coach from Edinburgh or Glasgow. The main road along the valley is a good one, but occasionally blocked. The Cairngorm ski area is nearly ten miles away, to the east. There is a bus service to the slopes, hourly from 9.30. Most of the local ski school arrangements fit in with the bus, but one reporter was frustrated at being unable to reach the ski area before 10.30 in the morning, being unable to hold skis upright in the bus, and having to hitch back (there was no relief bus when the last bus back at 4.30 was full).

There is not much of an old village, just a few shops, hotels and guest-houses near the station, and the place largely consists of the modern resort development – the Aviemore Centre. The facilities available at the Centre include bars and discos, a dry ski slope, swimming, skating and curling, squash, snooker, a fitness centre, a craft centre, amusement arcades, and the Santa Claus Land children's park. The main activities are covered by non-skier's abonnement or 'rover' ticket for three days or a week. Undoubtedly these facilities do a lot, especially for children, to reduce the risk of boredom when skiing is not possible.

Reporters agree that Aviemore après-ski is very jolly, with live entertainment and reasonably-priced drinks in hotel bars. There is a disco and skating disco in the Centre, a cinema, and several restaurants, from the Happy Haggis fish and chips to the Winking Owl's medium-haute cuisine. Après-ski shopping is limited by the conventional opening hours of the shops.

Many people may prefer to be in a quiet hotel with a supply of whisky and good books. There are several other villages and towns in the Spey Valley, less obviously affected by tourism but offering good accommodation, ski school and hire shops. In good weather there are beautiful walks and excursions in the neighbourhood, including

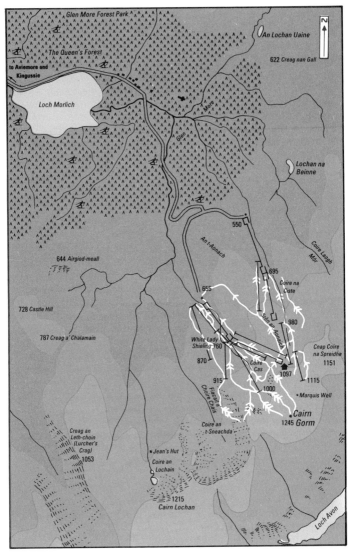

Loch-an-Eilean with its picturesque ruin and Loch Garten where ospreys come to nest in spring. Other activities which can be combined with skiing in spring are pony-trekking, fishing, watersports, golf and reindeer-spotting.

There are several hotels and a self-catering chalet motel in Aviemore Centre itself; the Post House (☎ 810771) is comfortable in typical Trusthouse Forte style. There are several simple b&b houses in the village. The Coylumbridge hotel (☎ 810661) is large, comfortable, expensive and self-contained, outside Aviemore on the way to the ski area; it has a cosy log-cabin bar and dancing in the evening, and its own ice rink and pool.

The Cairngorm ski area consists of four chair-lifts and ten drag-lifts serving a broad area of open mountainside with runs giving a maximum of about 450m vertical, or 600m for those prepared to walk up from the top station to the summit. There are two car parks at the bottom of the slopes, and four main access lifts. The runs offer reasonable variety; there are easy nursery slopes at the top, and easy longer runs down to Shieling and the car park and beside the Fiacaill tows. The White Lady chair and tow serve stiffer intermediate runs, nearly always mogulled, and there are tough narrow gullies below the West Wall chair. The Headwall runs down from Cairngorm summit are genuinely steep.

Apart from snack bars near the two car parks there are two facilities on the hill: the licensed restaurant at the Shieling, with an often overcrowded picnic room, and the Ptarmigan snack bar at the top. About the only claim that can be made for this is that it is the highest eating place in Britain.

Weekend queues are a problem, particularly when the higher lifts are closed; if all lifts are open, waits are not usually longer than 15 minutes. Queuing is conducted in a uniquely orderly way, in ranks so that piste-space is not wasted. Piste maintenance and marking is lacking, and when the mist comes down it is very easy to get lost. Exposed rocks are not flagged, and the snow fences beside piste and lift tracks are a further hazard. As one reporter put it, 'pistes short but of varying difficulty, with interesting obstacles – heather, boulders, reindeer etc.' When we visited, the information board at the bottom of the car park chair-lift (purporting to describe snow conditions on the diferent runs) was very inaccurate.

There is a variety of different lift passes available, including a limited day pass designed to permit inexperienced skiers to ski around the Ptarmigan area, and vouchers which can be exchanged for five day passes over the course of several seasons. Day passes at just under £10 seem expensive compared with weekly ones at about £35, but the longer passes are very risky because of the frequent closure of all or most of the lifts.

There are several ski schools in Aviemore and many others based in nearby villages. We have a few reports, and they are generally very favourable. All the ski schools offer packages of equipment hire, tuition and lift pass, costing about £60 to 70 a week. The Strathspey and Post House hotels have nurseries with resident nannies all year.

When there is a lot of snow, the forest land around Glenmore provides plenty of scope for cross-country skiing, as the mountains do for nordic ski touring and winter climbing. Dangers resulting from the unpredictability of the weather should not be underestimated. Access to the cross-country trails is opposite the Cairngorm Whisky museum at Inverdruie, just outside Aviemore.

Tourist office ✆ (0479) 810363. **Snow report** ✆ 031-246 8031.

Southern comfort

The Pyrenees

The Pyrenees are as high as all but the highest Alps, and have plenty of skiing above 2000m. They are undoubtedly the second-best skiing mountains in Europe, and have certain advantages (mainly cost) over the Alps for skiers who don't mind the limitations of the skiing, and of the snow – it is not very reliable, and whole seasons of poor conditions are not rare. As far south as this, the spring sun is hot; March is late for Pyrenean skiing, and snow conditions vary enormously during the day. Even in January, when the sun shines it is very pleasantly warm. We have reports of good Easter skiing holidays in Andorra but, as late as this, new snow deteriorates very quickly once the sun comes out.

France

The French Pyrenees attract local weekenders, student groups, lots of local school-children even during the week, and families on tight budgets. There are very few British or other foreign skiers and not much English is spoken in the ski schools. Unfortunately none of the resorts is at all charming: in general they are rather colourless and the atmosphere flat. Access from Tarbes airport is easy.

Provided there is snow, the skiing in the best resorts is fine for beginners and intermediate skiers who have not acquired a taste for big ski areas. Perhaps because of the unreliable conditions, surprisingly little development has taken place, despite persistent talk of grand plans. The largest area is the linked systems of **Barèges** (1250m) and **La Mongie** (1800m), where the link consists of very long and dull runs beside and along summer roads – the resorts stand either side of the Col du Tourmalet (2114m). Barèges is a dreary late-19th-century spa with a small area of attractive woodland skiing; although inconveniently placed, the Hotel Richelieu (✆ 62 926811) is recommended by two reporters. La Mongie is a bleak purpose-built roadside station with higher open skiing (up to 2350m) and a few challenging runs.

St Lary (830m) is the other French resort where you can get package holidays. It is a pleasant ordinary village – 'stone-built, complete with farms... real people live there' writes one reporter, who warmly recommends the Hotel Mir (✆ 62 394003). Skiing starts at **Pla d'Adet** (1680m) – a dull, modern ski-station with some accommodation, reached by cable-car from St Lary. There are queues for the cable-car at peak times, and also for the lifts on the gentle slopes at Pla d'Adet. The skiing extends in a chain of up-and-down lifts and runs, some of them long by Pyrenean standards (over 700m vertical); the scenery is open and beautiful but it is difficult to ring the changes on the long trip from one end to the other and the skiing lacks variety.

Gourette (1400m) is a lively, small, modern resort 50km south of Pau with interesting and varied skiing up to 2400m, including some stiff north-facing slopes.

Spain

The appeal of Spanish skiing is the cheapness of it and the friendliness of the local people. It is said that great progress has been made to raise the notoriously low standards of equipment, lifts and instruction, but equipment for hire is still not of very high quality, lifts are still not very reliable, and lots of instructors still confine their advice to 'follow me' – quite useful in the absence of reliable piste maps, grades or signs, but hardly a complete service. The ski areas are small and do not satisfy the adventurous, with the possible exception of **Baqueira-Beret** (skiing from 1500m to 2500m), the only smart, not-cheap resort in the Pyrenees, by appointment to King Juan Carlos.

The largest of the Spanish areas is **Super Molina/Masella** – or it could be, if the Super Molina system were not so very fragmented; it is particularly unreliable for snow, key lifts are often closed because of wind (or the effects of wind on snow cover) and it suffers from large influxes from Barcelona, not only at weekends. Masella has the longest and most interesting runs (between 1600 and 2550m), but the resort consists of nothing more than one large, unfriendly hotel. Super Molina is slightly less depressing, but is also small, modern and characterless.

Formigal (1500m) is a small, remote, unattractive, purpose-built resort, with a considerable extent of open, intermediate skiing above it up to 2350m. Getting to the skiing often involves a bus ride, and the lift system is notoriously vulnerable to closure because of high winds. The evening atmosphere in the hotel bars along the resort's single street is reported to be extremely convivial. Formigal shares a lift pass with **Panticosa** – nearby, but not easily reached except by car. It is an old farming village with a small one-hill skiing area. Skiers return, Thomson say, because of the friendliness of the local people, and we can offer no other explanation.

Cerler (1500m) is a very handsome old village with a small new resort development (including the comfortable hotel Monte Alba) about 15 minutes' walk away at the foot of a small but interesting skiing area (up to 2364m). Here too, wind is reported to be a problem.

One of the disadvantages of the Spanish Pyrenean resorts is access. Cerler is about five hours from Zaragoza airport, Panticosa and Formigal about four hours. Super Molina/Masella and Baqueira are more easily accessible, from Barcelona.

Andorra

Andorra differs from the Spanish Pyrenees in being even cheaper (lifts, lessons and equipment are cheap, as well as meals and drinks), and in being very popular with British skiers and après-skiers, who have the benefit of an English-speaking ski school, by all accounts very well run. The British influence runs deep, with lots of British and colonial expatriates in the principality, living there in retirement or running hotels, bars, restaurants, development companies and ski schools. Everyone seems to know everyone else and there is a very easy-going, friendly atmosphere which sets Andorra apart.

None of Andorra's ski areas is very large or challenging, but that doesn't seem to matter. You don't go there for tough skiing – or for comfortable accommodation, haute cuisine, charming surroundings, ice rinks, snowy paths, smooth-running bus services or comfortable sheltered gondola lifts. You go for sun, fun, and a cheap holiday. The recipe suits lots of young skiers (and lots of not so young ones) well.

Andorra is a small duty-free principality with French and Spanish co-rulers. Spanish language (Catalan) and currency prevail, except in the north-east around Pas de la Casa, where skiing and supermarkets serve French weekenders. The single main road (42km long) carries heavy traffic from the Spanish border (850m) through the capital, Andorra La Vella, over the Port d'Envalira (2408m) to the French border at Pas de la Casa (2095m). The road is lined by a succession of very ugly, shoddy modern villages – 'all the same, like abandoned building sites,' wrote one reporter. One of them is Soldeu, the main skiing area and resort. Most British operators send their clients to hotels there or in Encamp (which has no skiing), about 20 minutes down the road. The side valleys north of La Vella have been more recently developed, with much more acceptable results. The main skiing here is near Arinsal. There is some accommodation in the village, and apartments within walking range of the lifts, but most packages to Arinsal use accommodation in La Massana a few miles towards La Vella. There is also skiing at Pas de la Casa and at two new developments, Pal and Arcalis, in the valleys beyond La Massana.

For all skiers not staying in Soldeu, transport is vital. Those with a car can reach all the skiing from a single base, but most skiers rely on tour operators' shuttle services which do not allow much flexibility. There are public buses, but they are unreliable and infrequent and of most use to skiers based in La Vella. There is one general pass, valid for 10 days and covering Soldeu, Arinsal and Pas de la Casa.

Soldeu's skiing starts with a tiresome walk across a rickety bridge from the village ('I was exhausted before I started'). It features a broad area of mostly easy open skiing between 2100m and 2560m, and a variety of runs down through the woods to Soldeu and its neighbour El Tarter (1700m), an alternative access point beside the main road up from Encamp and La Vella. There are some tougher runs, and some off-piste skiing, through the woods. The slopes are mostly north-facing and in good conditions Soldeu provides excellent skiing for beginners and leisurely intermediates, including a 6km green run from top to bottom. There is a children's ski school and a good kindergarten. At the top of the main chair-lift is a wide, sunny nursery area: the main complaint seems to be that it is too hot. The skiing organisation as a whole seems to be of a higher standard than in the Spanish resorts.

The most convenient access point for the **Pas de la Casa** skiing is Grau Roig (2040m), a collection of buildings near the main road. Ski-lifts climb up to the high ridge from both sides, providing a simple arrangement of open runs (about 500m vertical) facing west above Grau Roig, and north-east above Pas de la Casa (2095m). Snow is reliable, scenery is bare and severe, there is little variety of terrain, but plenty of space across the mountainside.

Arinsal's skiing is at present much more confined, a narrow east-facing coomb with variants of a single descent from about 2500m to a congregation area with ski deposit and hire shops at 1950m, at the top of the chair-lift from the valley (1550m). There is also a black run under the bottom chair, and an indirect blue route down.

New **Pal** is a smartly equipped skiing area ('the only civilised skiing loos in Andorra, and a good restaurant') in prettier scenery than most, from 1810m to 2350m. There are attractive nursery runs on woodland clearings and a few gentle longer runs, most of them wooded. The area extends across a north-facing hillside, and involves a lot of traversing from lift to lift. In the far north **Arcalis**, difficult to reach even at the best of times, is in an even more embryonic state. It already provides some interesting skiing between 1940m and 2550m round a rugged north-facing bowl.

Après-ski revolves around bars, restaurants and discos. As well as ski-school celebrations, tour operators organise fancy dress parties, fondue outings, and bar crawls. Most of the quality restaurants are difficult to reach without a car, and in the resort hotels and restaurants food is cheap but indifferent. Bar prices are very low, with huge lethal cocktails for about £1. Skiers used to Alpine resorts, especially big French and Swiss ones, are amazed at how friendly and relaxed the atmosphere is, with free drinks flowing at the slightest excuse and lots of entertaining characters on both sides of the bar. Discothèques rarely get going much before midnight; entrance is often free, and the price of drinks not much higher than in the bars.

Shopping is Andorra's main industry and tourist attraction. La Vella is a supermarket city where well-known brands of gin can be found for £2 to 3 a litre, whisky for about £3. New ski equipment costs 30% to 50% less than usual.

Accommodation used by British operators is mostly very basic, and some of it primitive. We looked at most of the hotels and particularly liked the Rossell in La Massana, the Naudi in Soldeu, and the Prats Sobirans apartments close to the Arinsal lifts. We saw few preferable hotels not used by tour operators, except for the altogether remarkable Residencia Belvedere in Encamp, a small guest-house very well run by a British couple, mostly for British visitors (✆ 31263). Hotels we liked least were the Encamp, Riu Blanc and La Mola in Encamp, and the Font in La Massana.

Access for air travellers is most convenient from Barcelona. Twice-daily 'service taxis' cost about £10 a head between four. Transfer time is about 3½ hours. Transfers from Toulouse (about 4 hours) and coach trips from Britain are vulnerable to closure of the road from France; our inspector endured a 17-hour journey to Toulouse via a rail-only tunnel. There are overnight trains from Paris to L'Hospitalet, with connecting buses.

Tourist office phone numbers: **France** St Lary (62) 395081 Barèges (62) 926819 Gourette (59) 051217. **Spain** Cerler (974) 551012 Formigal/Panticosa (974) 488125 Baqueira-Beret (973) 645025 La Molina (972) 892175. **Andorra** Soldeu 51151 Encamp 31405 La Massana 35693.

Package holidays Thomson (TH) is the main operator to the French and Spanish Pyrenees – they go to all resorts except Gourette and Baqueira-Beret. Other operators: Barèges FL; Super Molina IG; Cerler IT; Baqueira-Beret SML; Arinsal AH, BV, SNC; Encamp FR, RA, SNW; Soldeu FR, SFA, SML.

Resort index

Resorts are grouped into chapters, usually because they share a skiing area, and are arranged in a geographical sequence going from north-east Italy anti-clockwise to southern France; then come Scotland and the Pyrenees. The page references take you to the start of the chapter in which the resort is described or mentioned. In general, multi-part resorts such as La Plagne or Les Arcs are indexed only once.

The contents of the resorts section of the Guide are listed in chapter order on page 64; that's where you should look if you know roughly where you want to go, but don't know the names of the resorts in that region. A comparative summary of all the major resorts in the Guide starts on page 72; that's where you should look if you know what your holiday needs are but don't know which resorts will meet them. (For help in getting clear what you do want in a resort, see 'Choosing your resort', page 51.)

Resort names starting with Le, La or Les are not indexed under L, but under the initial of the main part of their name. Those named after Saints are indexed as under Saint, not San, St or whatever.

MAKING THE MOST OF YOUR SKIING

Up to this point, the Guide has been devoted more-or-less to one end: helping you decide where to go skiing. But in our 'Skiing Primer' we took newcomers to skiing on a guided tour of the other considerations involved in a skiing holiday. And in this final section of the Guide we go back over much of that same ground – but in more detail, for the benefit of experienced skiers as well as novices.

Getting equipped

As anyone bitten by the skiing bug finds out all too soon, kitting yourself out for skiing is something of a nightmare. Not only is the equipment and clothing expensive, but also it's virtually impossible to know which brands or models will meet your needs; whether the new, improved product that everyone else seems to be using is actually any advance on what you're using at present; whether your apparent inability to make any progress towards perfect parallel turns can or cannot be attributed to your inferior skis/boots/thermal underwear.

It's tempting to spend huge amounts of money rather than have doubts like these gnawing away at whatever shreds of confidence you possess. In this chapter, we aim to help you find a cheaper strategy. We assume you're familiar with the basics of ski equipment and clothing; if not, turn first to 'A Skiing Primer' – which includes a section on the vital question of whether to rent or buy.

Choosing boots

Beginners, intermediates and experts require different things of their boots. Racers, who want the ultimate in control, use boots with high, stiff shells and custom-moulded inners to get a tight grip on the foot: the stiffer the shell and the harder the inner padding, the more directly any leg movement is transmitted to the ski. If you're an advanced skier, you might well use boots much like the ones racers use. But for most skiers, precise transmission of leg movements is much less important than comfort; and in the very early stages, when you're grappling with the basics of walking, standing, stopping and turning, some freedom of movement within the boot is positively desirable.

So boots for ordinary skiers are 'de-tuned' versions of the ideal ski boot; the further down the makers' ranges you look (which normally means the further down in price), the more you will find boots designed to be comfortable and accommodating. They will have shells which don't reach so far up your leg, they will flex forward more easily as you bend your knees, and the inner padding will be softer.

It isn't easy to find a boot which will be comfortable throughout a seven-hour skiing day and at the same time give you the degree of control you need. There is in the end no substitute for trying boots out on the slopes; but you make success in picking a boot in the shop more likely if you understand the different parts of the boot, and how they vary between models. These days there are two basic types of outer **shell** – the conventional *front-entry* type, and the newer *rear-entry* sort – and a wide range of **adjustments** to give a close fit to your foot. There are some variations in type of **inner** boot, too.

Boot features

Boot shells vary in **height**. Experts' boots reach high up the leg; beginners' boots should not reach nearly so high.

Front-entry boots have a tongue, and open like an everyday laced boot. They are normally closed and tightened with a row of three to five clips. **Rear-entry** boots have a hinged flap behind the calf which opens to let you get your foot in, and pushes the foot forwards into the shell when closed. There are no hard and fast rules as to which type provides a better fit. Rear-entry boots are easy to get into. But the majority of ski racers, who need a particularly close fit, continue to ski in front-entry boots.

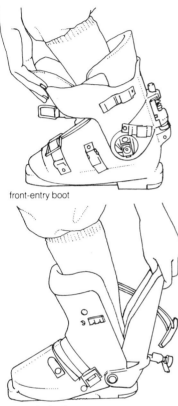

front-entry boot

The boots you choose must fit your foot comfortably to start with. But when you're skiing it's equally important that you're able to **adjust** the boot, reducing its volume around the foot. On a front-entry boot, there will usually be two, three or four clips to tighten the fit around the foot, ankle and lower leg. The fit of a rear-entry boot is normally tightened by an internal plate, cable or inflatable air bladder which presses against the instep. There may be only one such device, or more.

All boots have a built-in **forward lean**, which means that the shell above the ankle is angled forwards (usually by 10 to 15 degrees from vertical). Avoid boots with the most pronounced forward lean unless you want to ski aggressively. Some boots can be switched from forward lean to vertical to make walking easier. Some boots for experts allow adjustment of the forward lean.

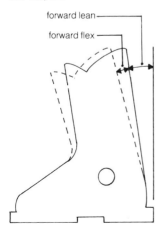

rear-entry boot

forward lean —————
forward flex ———

Boots are also designed to **flex**, so that you can press your shin forwards without a great deal of force. Ideally the shell should be hinged at the ankle. Some boots have a flex control so that you can adjust the boot's flexibility to suit your weight and strength and the amount of forward pressure you want to apply to the ski – useful for advanced skiers.

Some boots now have a built-in **cant control** to alter the angle of the upper boot to the sole, thus compensating for bow-legs or knock-knees.

A **non-skid heel** makes boots safer for walking; they wear out – buy replacements when you buy the boots.

adjustments on
advanced boots

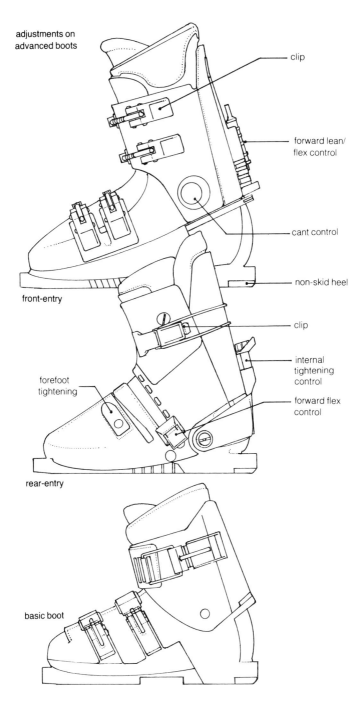

clip

forward lean/
flex control

cant control

non-skid heel

front-entry

clip

internal
tightening
control

forefoot
tightening

forward flex
control

rear-entry

basic boot

Getting the fit right

Finding a good comfortable pair of boots should be your clear priority when buying equipment. A hurried purchase could be a disaster, so allow plenty of time to try different models in different shops. Here are some guidelines to help you.

• Try boots at specialist ski shops where there are likely to be staff who can help with specific fitting problems – first by working out what your problem is and then if necessary making modifications to the shell or inner boot. Ask whether these services are available. Avoid Saturdays and the busy pre-Christmas rush if you can.

• Consider going to the Ski Show in November at Earls Court (Glasgow also holds one) in order to draw up a short-list of boots. This is an ideal place to visit a number of retailers, all under one roof, with a large selection of boots – though it's rather too hectic to evaluate a boot thoroughly. Go to the Show on a weekday: weekends are much too busy to get good service.

• Take along the socks you will be skiing in, and wear them (one pair only) when trying out boots.

• Start with your normal shoe size but expect to move up or down a half size or more, as necessary. Salomon rear-entry boots have their own sizing system for which you need to be specially measured in the shop. Your toes should be free to wiggle inside the boot. Lean back in the boot (get someone to hold the front down) and your toes should lightly touch the front of the boot if the size is about right.

• Ask to try the boots out with some skis, or bindings fixed to dummy skis. Then you'll be able to ensure that your heel is firmly held down: put all your weight on one foot, and push that knee forwards and downwards, with your shin pressed against the front of the boot. There should be no upward movement of your heel. If you find the pressure on your shin painful you may be better off with a softer boot.

• The boots should also hold you firmly around the calf and around the instep but without causing cramp, numbness or pressure.

• If a pair of boots seem comfortable at first, sit around wearing them for a further 20 to 30 minutes to check for discomfort.

• Try boots from different manufacturers. They can vary appreciably in fit since the inner boots are modelled to different lasts. Try different boots on your left and right feet to compare fit.

• Try operating the clips and other fitting controls while you wear the boots – and preferably while wearing gloves. Are they convenient and easy to use?

• Once you've bought the boots, wear them at home or ski on them at a plastic slope to identify any problems before your holiday.

Some shops offer a 'comfort guarantee' or commit themselves in some other way to taking the boots back if you find them uncomfortable when you actually go skiing. You won't get your money back, but you will get a credit note for the price you paid, less a rental charge. The amount of this charge varies, but will be around a quarter to a third of the original price. Whether this represents good value will depend on how much skiing you get out of the boots: if you use them for three weeks but on the whole are not happy with them, you'll have done quite well; but if the boots turn out to be hopelessly uncomfortable you'll have to hire replacements in the resort – so you'll effectively have hired two pairs for the duration of your holiday.

Some shops take a different approach, and undertake to modify the boots you buy so as to make them fit comfortably – or to exchange them for another pair. Again, this arrangement is fine as long as you don't find the boots too painful to use when you arrive on the slopes.

Problem feet

The majority of skiers find boots that fit 'off-the-shelf', and you should certainly try out all available brands and models before concluding that you're a special case. If and when you reach that conclusion, you can have a pair of standard boots specially modified – either by having the inner or shell of a standard boot altered, or by fitting orthopaedic insoles moulded to your feet.

The most common problems are these:

Wide foot If you find your boots exert pressure on the bones at the widest part of the foot, the first thing to try is modification of the inner boot. A moulded inner can be ground away at the pressure points; with a stitched inner you can try padding the area around the pressure points – a less sure remedy. In more extreme cases the shell of the boot can be stretched by heating the plastic to soften it – though there are limits to how far this can be taken.

Flat foot Various problems can arise if your feet don't have the normal arched instep. If you feel pressure on the back of the heel, try fitting arch supports or heat-moulded orthopaedic insoles. If the pressure is on the ankle bones, you can fit C-shaped pads to the inner boot, ahead of the outer bone; a moulded inner can be ground away at the pressure point if pads don't solve the problem.

High instep If the arch of your foot is exaggerated, you may feel pressure on top of the instep or underneath the arch. First, try removing any arch-support insole from the boot. If the problem remains, a moulded inner can be ground away over the instep.

A good ski shop will be able to carry out the modifications. Orthopaedic insoles, made by Sidas, are heated and pressed to the shape of the foot sole with additional arch support. The cost is around £12 per pair and you may have to search for a shop which offers the service. (The distributors are Europa Sport, Ann Street, Kendal, Cumbria, LA9 6AB; ✆ 0539 24740.)

The alternative to modifying standard boots is to buy boots which are specially designed to cope with difficult feet. Some models made by Dachstein, Dynafit and Koflach have an inner which can be filled with foam to fit your foot. The process involves standing inside the boot while bladders inside the inner boot are injected with a rubbery plastic foam. This sets to shape around the foot. Successful foaming requires considerable expertise on the shop's part but can be a useful way of dealing with unusual bone protrusions etc.

Lange have developed a system called Thermofit which achieves a similar result in a different way. The inner boot is made of a material which softens when heated. Inside the padding are electric heating elements which heat up the inner while you stand in it. When the elements are disconnected, the padding moulds to fit while it cools around the foot.

Problem legs

People with bow-legs or knock-knees tend to encounter special difficulties in skiing. If you have either problem (and it shows up as uneven wear of your normal shoe soles) you will probably find it hard to keep your ski soles flat on the snow and turn with a good parallel technique. If you have bow-legs, in particular, you'll tend to catch the outside edge of your skis on the snow in a gentle turn, with disastrous consequences.

When this problem was first tackled in the 1970s the cure was to fit angled wedges between the bindings and the skis, so that the soles of the skis were parallel to the snow even if your boot soles weren't. Although some shops still undertake this work, it's more common now to try to compensate with the boot. Some expensive boots (eg Nordica NR980, Lange ZR/ZS/ZT, Dynafit 3F Competition, Salomon SX91 Equipe) have a cant control which changes the angle of the boot's upper part relative to its sole. In most boots it is also possible to fit an angled plate under the inner boot. And some compensation can be introduced if you have a boot foamed to fit your foot (see above).

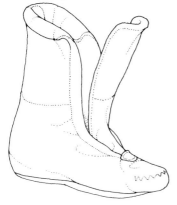

There are two basic varieties of **inner boot**. *Moulded* inners (which are generally seamless) have the advantage over the *stitched* type that they can, if necessary, be shaved or ground to eliminate pressure points where they exist. The hardness of the foam padding in either type varies from soft, for beginners' boots, to firm, for experts' boots.

Choosing skis

When it comes to choosing skis it's all too easy to be blinded by choice and pseudo-scientific jargon. Well over a hundred models are available in British ski shops and the more shops you visit the more brand names you'll find. Unfortunately, once you put the names, graphics and other gloss to one side, there are few immediately apparent differences between models. Boots you can to some extent evaluate in the shop; it's not so simple with skis. You can easily find yourself at the mercy of a very enthusiastic salesman who probably skis much better than you and has very firm ideas on what is This Year's Ski.

So how do you avoid buying the wrong ski, and make some attempt at narrowing the choice towards one which will suit your needs? The first step is to resolve to spend as little as possible. It's easy to spend a lot of money on skis in the hope that they'll transform your skiing technique; but they won't – a course of good instruction would be a better buy. While it's worth spending on boots and bindings, which can markedly affect your control and safety, the best that an expensive pair of skis can do is to make your skiing a little faster, a little more stable and a little more accurate. (Expert skiers, capable of appreciating subtle differences in ski performance, may well want to choose skis which are not only expensive, but specially designed for particular sorts of skiing – moguls, or powder; what we are concerned with here is the intermediate skier who wants a compromise ski for all sorts of skiing.)

The next thing is to make sure you're looking at skis that will suit your standard of skiing. Ski manufacturers produce different models for different groups of skiers, according to ability. Beginners' and intermediates' skis are deliberately 'de-tuned' to cope with imperfect technique on the part of the user and to handle easily at low speeds. Experts' skis are designed to give precise control at high speeds, when the pressure being exerted on the ski in turning is very high; an inexpert skier going more slowly would find such skis hard work.

Sorting out which skis will suit you isn't always easy. Standard 'target groups' of skiers were devised some years ago by the German and Austrian standards institutes, and on some skis you'll find a symbol which identifies the target group(s) the ski is made for – see below. But on most skis you won't, and your best be then is to try to get hold of catalogues produced by the ski makers or by retailers (which draw on the makers' ones).

Using the definitions below you can easily assign yourself to one of the three target groups. (This will help you to determine what length of ski you need as well as in finding the right models.)

Target Group L – Beginners or those who can ski parallel on easy slopes only, and at slow speeds.
Target Group A – Intermediates who can ski parallel on moderate gradients and easy snow conditions at medium speeds.
Target Group S – Experts who can ski all types of slope, snow and gradient at higher speeds.

What length of ski?

Once upon a time, the length of skis you should use was determined by how high above the ground you could reach – the 'hands-high' formula. The rule has a certain common-sense appeal – a very short person would certainly have trouble manoeuvring very long skis – but it is fundamentally wrong: it doesn't take account of the way skis work, which is by bending in response to the forces the skier subjects them to. These days, it's recognised that factors other than height need to be taken into account – that is, your weight and your standard of skiing; but height still receives more attention than it deserves.

It's easy to get confused by the apparently simple matter of the length of a ski. The confusion arises because different skis of a given length – 185cm, say – are designed to suit various sorts of skier. If designed for a big, heavy skier, a 185cm ski will be called a short or compact ski; if for a small, light skier, it will be called a full-length ski. Thus it is possible for one person's 'short' ski to be longer than another's 'full-length' one.

Short skis were all the rage a few years ago, when their advantage of easy turning attracted all the attention – not surprising, because the alternative then was the much more unwieldy full-length ski. Short skis are still the best bet for beginners, but ski makers now flatter intermediate skiers by insisting that they need something which is quicker and holds its direction better – the mid-length ski. Manufacturers have coined all sorts of names for their mid-length models: sport, stretch, Elite, Lite and Performance, for example.

Some manufacturers, recognising that height alone is not a good guide to the correct length of ski, have made length selection easier by marking on their skis a tiny chart which shows the length you need according to which of the L-A-S target groups you fall into (see previous page). But the lengths these markings give still relate to your height; for example, the marking shown below means that a skier in group A should use that ski in a length which reaches 15cm to 25cm above head height, a skier in group L in a length which reaches 5cm to 15cm above head height.

This is an improvement on going by height alone, but it still ignores the important question of weight. Two skiers of the same height would be led to buy the same length of ski, but a relatively heavy skier may overload the ski and bend it too much, making it slow and difficult to keep running straight, while a relatively light skier will find it difficult to turn. *Guide* contributor David Goldsmith has come up with a simple formula which makes proper allowance for weight. On the facing page we explain how to calculate your ski length the Goldsmith way.

Ski length

Deciding what length of ski you need is not easy for most skiers.

Beginners renting skis should be mainly concerned to avoid skis which are too long to be easily managed in the slow, clumsy manoeuvres they'll be doing at first. For them, choosing skis by height is not a bad thing, and they should be aiming for skis reaching to eye height or lower.

It's for the intermediate skier (even more than the expert, who can be expected to have learnt from experience) that the choice is particularly complicated. The basic problem is that the correct length of ski will depend not only on the skier's weight, height and standard of skiing, but also on the design of the model of ski under consideration. This means that you're very dependent on the maker and retailer of the ski to tell you in simple language how to choose the right length for you – and that we can't give any general rules which will apply to all skis.

But when you go to buy skis it's exceptional to be given clear and sensible guidance about the length of ski you need. Normally, you'll be advised simply in terms of your height and the style of ski you're looking at, without reference to your weight or standard of skiing. The best thing we can do in these circumstances is to balance that advice with a calculation of ski length which does take those factors into account – even if it ignores subtle differences between skis.

If you follow through the calculation set out below, you'll arrive at a ski length which is appropriate to an average intermediate skier using typical brands of ski. If you don't consider yourself an average intermediate skier – in other words that you don't fit into Target Group A – you can subtract from or add to the basic length this calculation produces. A a timid or slow intermediate skier could knock off as much as 15cm, while an aggressive, relatively advanced skier could add as much as 15cm.

Allowing for weight
1 Write down your weight in pounds
2 Subtract 100 from that figure
3 Divide the result by 8
4 Call the final result W

The correct length of ski cannot simply be judged by your height – it depends on several other factors, explained here.

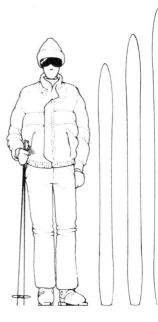

Allowing for height
1 Write down your height in cm
2 Subtract 150 from that figure
3 Divide the result by 4
4 Call the final result H

Your basic ski length
Work out the sum: W + H + 175
The result, rounded to the nearest 5, is your basic ski length in cm.

Note If you're very light or very short, these sums may give a negative result meaning that you need skis shorter than 175cm. Adult skis are rarely sold in lengths of less than 170cm, but you can get children's skis of any length, and thereby save worthwhile amounts of money.

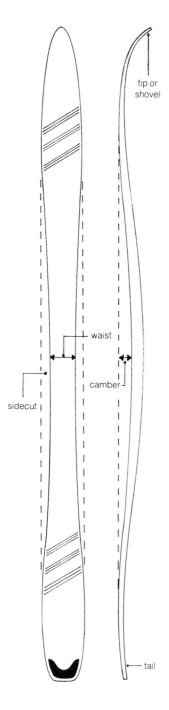

tip or shovel

waist

camber

sidecut

tail

Ski characteristics

As we've stressed elsewhere, what's most important when choosing skis is not to get carried away by the glossy brochures and the sales pitch. You may find it easier to see through all that if you understand a bit about the theory of ski performance – and you'll also be better able to evaluate skis as you use them.

A top-down view of a ski shows that it is not the same width all the way along. The ski's *sidecut* – the degree to which it is waisted in the middle – affects its turning ability: the more pronounced the sidecut, the more the tip of the ski will tend to bite when the ski is tilted on to its edge, and the more easily the ski will perform a turn.

A side view shows that the thickess of the ski varies, too – it's thicker and stiffer in the centre than at the tip and tail – and that it has a definite curved shape. When put on a flat surface, the centre of an unweighted ski stands higher than the tip and tail; the purpose of this *camber* is to distribute the skier's weight along the length of the ski.

To show how a ski responds to the loads put on it, we've shown a ski on the facing page supported by a set of springs, like the springs in a mattress. The natural shape of the ski is visible only when the ski is unweighted (1). On hard pistes, a uniform distribution of weight (2) is what you need to keep the whole edge of the ski in contact with the snow – and this means you need a relatively stiff ski. When skiing deep, soft snow, contact is not the problem since the whole ski will be immersed; what you need then is a softer-flexing ski so that the tip tends to float (3). If you use a ski which is too short and too flexible, it will be inclined to flex too much; your weight will be concentrated beneath your boots, and the ski will not turn properly on hard snow (4). If on the other hand you use a ski which is too long and stiff, your weight will be concentrated at the tip and tail, making it difficult to swivel the ski on the snow (5).

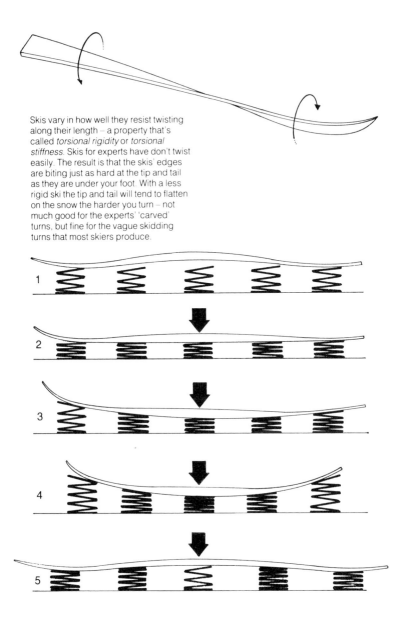

Skis vary in how well they resist twisting along their length – a property that's called *torsional rigidity* or *torsional stiffness*. Skis for experts have don't twist easily. The result is that the skis' edges are biting just as hard at the tip and tail as they are under your foot. With a less rigid ski the tip and tail will tend to flatten on the snow the harder you turn – not much good for the experts' 'carved' turns, but fine for the vague skidding turns that most skiers produce.

Looking after skis

Skis will perform at their best only if the soles and edges are kept in perfect condition. Unfortunately, it's all too easy to damage a ski by hitting the occasional exposed rock. You can often avoid the worst of them by keeping to the side of the piste. If you see a rock ahead and can't avoid it, try to take it straight rather than skidding across it – a groove cut down the sole is easier to repair than a gash across the edge. If the snow is wearing really thin, it's best to rent skis, in spite of the cost. Any serious damage you do to your skis may be irreparable or involve re-soling – an expensive business.

The ski's **edges** need to be sharp in order to give you control on hard snow or ice – though at the extreme tip and tail of the ski it's advisable to have slightly dulled edges. Check your edges regularly for sharpness by drawing the face of a fingernail across them. A well sharpened edge will produce wide shavings. Edges should be sharpened to a right-angle (or a little more acute). This is a possible DIY job – a special edge-sharpening tool from a ski shop is best but if you have an appropriate file already you can make do with that.

Shallow notches down the middle of the ski's **sole** don't markedly affect the performance of the ski, but are easily repaired. You can repair them yourself using a special 'candle' of plastic material (the common brand is P-tex) which drips molten plastic into the notch; once it has set you scrape the repair smooth with a rectangular steel scraper. Any deep holes which expose the layer underneath the sole, or notches along the edge of the ski, should be repaired professionally. The latter can seriously affect the turning power of the ski in some circumstances.

Even if you manage to avoid conspicuous damage to the soles of your skis, in time they will wear down in the middle, and become concave. The middle of the sole cannot be built up (unless you have the ski completely re-soled); the edges of the sole must instead be reduced until they are level with the middle. A slightly concave sole can be filed flat by hand using a single-cut file – get one around ten inches long, with a handle. Hold the file in both hands flat against the sole, with your thumbs pressed downwards over the ski edges; file in one direction, from tip to tail. The grooves of the file will become clogged with plastic during use; clear them regularly with a fine wire brush or a special file 'card'.

For flattening more seriously worn soles most shops use a large belt-sanding machine, but it is not a wholly satisfactory approach. Unless the ski is drawn smoothly over the belt by a skilled operator, uneven grinding takes place. A belt also tends to grind the sole rather coarsely to a slightly lower level than the edges – it's then vital that the edges be cut back by hand filing. A better result is achieved with a high-speed stone grinding wheel. Regrettably, very few shops have these machines – one of the few we've seen is installed at Alpine Sports, 215 Kensington High Street, London W8; tel: 01-938 1911.

Skis run best with a thin film of **wax** on the soles. This also helps protect the soles. You can apply wax by rubbing a solid block along the sole, or you can buy it in aerosol or paste form – more convenient, but more expensive. But the best solution is to apply hot molten wax, which will form a bond with the sole and last much longer.

Most ski shops use a special machine for this job: the ski is pushed over a roller which picks up molten wax from a small reservoir and leaves a fairly even coating along the sole. Some shops carelessly leave it at that; but the wax coating should then be scraped down and the centre groove cleared – most of the wax should end up on the workshop floor. If the wax film is proud of the steel edges, the effect of the edges will be reduced. The soles should be smooth and polished, with the film of wax no thicker than paper.

You can hot-wax your own skis satisfactorily with a few pieces of uncomplicated equipment. You can get special waxing irons, heated by a small butane gas cylinder, but an ordinary non-steam electric iron is fine for the job – provided you take a socket adaptor with you or fit a local plug to the flex. The wax is melted and dripped on to the ski by holding a block against the surface of the iron. You then spread it quickly over the sole with the iron, taking great care to avoid overheating the sole, which is easily damaged. You'll need a rectangular steel scraper to smooth the wax down. Unfortunately it's not always a practical proposition to tackle this work in a hotel or chalet – be prepared to clear up a fairly messy residue of wax shavings afterwards.

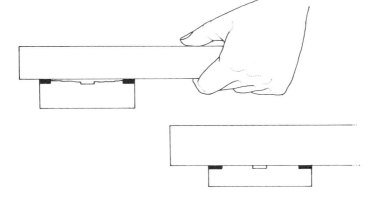

Check that your ski soles are flat from edge to edge by holding a ruler across the sole. If you can see light under the ruler (apart from the groove, of course) the sole needs filing, sanding or grinding flat – a concave sole will make the ski difficult to pivot on the snow.

Choosing bindings

You'll find that buying a pair of bindings is pretty straightforward after searching for a boot that fits or a ski that suits. Most bindings are suitable for most people – they have a wide range of adjustment. If you weigh between 45kg and 90kg (7st and 14st), more-or-less any binding sold for adults will do; but check the recommended weight ranges for specific models before you buy.

Satisfy yourself that a binding has been tested and approved by one or more of the Continental test institutes. If it has been approved, the manufacturer is entitled to use the appropriate institute's logo on its products or packaging – look out for the initials TUV, IAS or GS (Germany), BFU (Switzerland), ISO (International) or ONORM (Austria).

Bindings of the following brands are generally approved and available in the UK: Ess, F2, Geze, Look, Marker, Salomon and Tyrola. Each manufacturer produces a range of models with varying degrees of mechanical sophistication. The advantages of buying the top models are usually over-stated, even for advanced skiers. Anyone except a racer or very aggressive skier will get satisfactory performance from one of the cheaper models.

What all bindings have in common is some way of triggering the release by hand (or with your ski pole) – it's worth finding out how convenient this is – and screw controls to set the point at which the toe and heel units will release in a fall. Modern bindings show the setting on an internationally standard scale (see inset). Ski brakes are now a standard feature of most bindings.

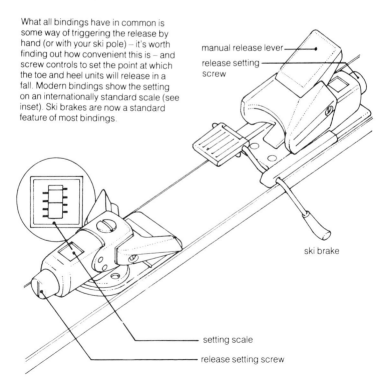

manual release lever

release setting screw

ski brake

setting scale

release setting screw

Most brands of binding have very much the same overall form; the Salomon model shown here is just one example. But there are brands which aim to be a bit more clever. The 'turntable' bindings made by Look are designed so that when the toe is released the boot pivots around the line of your leg and not around the extremity of the boot heel – perhaps imposing less of a strain on the leg.

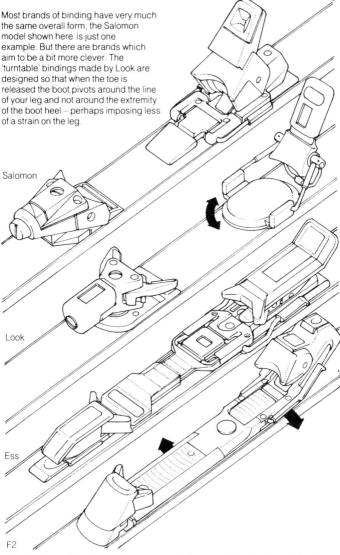

Salomon

Look

Ess

F2

Two bindings which differ radically from convention are the Ess VAR and the F2. The Ess has toe and heel units connected by a flexible steel band. The whole assembly can be shifted forwards and backwards along the ski, about an inch either side of the normal position. This is meant to have advantages in controlling the way the ski behaves: when the binding is shifted forwards the ski should turn more quickly; when the binding is shifted backwards the ski should run straight more easily. Sophisticated stuff. The F2 binding holds the boot in a plate. The heel release works in much the same way as a conventional heel unit. In a twisting fall, however, the whole plate holding the boot pivots until it reaches a certain point, where the heel unit releases. Thus the usual friction between boot and toe unit is supposed to be cut out.

Bindings safety

It's very important that bindings are properly set to suit you and your boots. In principle, the best way to make sure of this is to leave it to a competent, conscientious ski-shop mechanic. But not all mechanics fall into that category, and there is a lot to be said for understanding how to adjust your bindings yourself.

● Get your supplier to demonstrate the adjustments and (if you're buying) give you a detailed instruction leaflet.
● Check that the bindings are adjusted to the size of your boots – if they're not, the boot may wobble in the bindings, or be jammed by excessive friction. The heel unit will incorporate an indicator to show whether the two units are the right distance apart, and the toe unit must be set at a height above the ski which holds the toe-piece of the boot precisely but not tightly.
● Mark your skis left and right and ensure that each set of bindings is adjusted to suit the correct boot – there may be slight differences between the soles of your two boots; if you want to swap your skis over so that they wear evenly, do so only occasionally, and re-adjust the bindings accordingly.
● Check that the release settings are right for you. If the bindings have the new internationally agreed setting scales, you should be able to work out from the instructions what setting to use; ideally, you should then have the bindings tested to see that the scale setting is accurate. The alternative (which you'll have to resort to if you don't have information on what the scale means) is to adjust the settings by trial and error. You can start out on the slopes with low release settings and gradually adjust them upwards until you're no longer coming out of the bindings when you don't want to; or you can set the bindings before you start out. Put your boots on and follow the steps set out below for each ski. In each case, start with the release settings at the minimum, so that the binding will open easily; turn up the release setting a bit and try again; repeat the exercise several times, turning up the release setting each time, until it takes all your strength to open the binding.
To check heel release Put the skis on the floor with their tips against a wall. Step into one set of bindings; get someone to stand on the back of the ski; simulate falling forwards by leaning towards the ski tip, pressing your knee forwards and pulling up at the heel.
To check toe release Step into one set of bindings on a carpeted floor (not one that's very precious). Lean forwards, pushing your weight down at the ball of your foot; grip your knee with both hands and tip the ski on to its outside edge (right edge on right ski, left edge on left ski). Twist your whole body towards that same edge (clockwise on right ski, anti-clockwise on left ski) while putting your weight on the ski.
● Whenever your skis have been left exposed to the elements, check by hand that the bindings are not iced up.
● Before stepping into the bindings, always scrape snow, ice or dirt from the soles of your boots. They can dangerously jam up the toe unit.

Choosing poles

The most important thing about ski poles is that they should be the right length. Poles for adults vary from 110cm to 135cm, in 5cm steps. When choosing a pole in the shop you have to allow for the few inches of shaft which digs into the snow when skiing – see drawing. If you are unsure of your pole length, always take the next size up. If necessary, a pole can be cut down to size by removing the handle and cutting off an inch or two of the shaft with a hacksaw.

The quality of alloy used in making a pole's tubular shaft is crucial to its strength. Look for poles conforming to DIN 7884. Avoid heavy poles, which can be tiring.

Handles vary widely in design. It's important that you're comfortable when gripping the handle. Moulded finger grips help a lot as does a good platform under the hand for support. Most handles come with a strap, which not only makes it less likely that you'll lose the poles but also allows you to put your weight on the pole without having to grip the handle tightly. Strapless or 'swordgrip' handles have a flexible shield around the back of the hand which holds the pole on to your hand in normal circumstances but allows it to be pulled away in a fall. They were developed originally for racing; they have the advantage for ordinary skiers that they're less fuss to get in and out of – but most people seem to prefer handles with straps.

If you're buying handles with straps make sure that they are of the type which releases in an emergency. This will ensure that your arms and wrists don't suffer if your pole gets caught in something and you continue moving, or if you get seriously tangled up in a fall.

When you plant your pole in the snow, your forearm should be just about horizontal. To check the length of a pole in the shop, you have to allow for the two or three inches at the bottom which will be sticking in the snow. Do this by holding the pole upside down, with your hand immediately under the basket.

Be sure that you're happy with the way the straps are adjusted, and that they are designed to release in a serious fall.

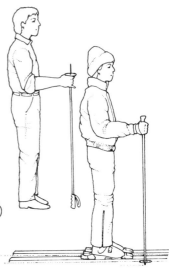

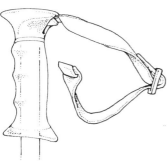

Choosing clothes

As we explain in 'A Skiing Primer', ski clothes are more often designed to look good than to work well. It's difficult to give clear guidance on what to buy, when the effectiveness of a garment can depend on small details of its construction – and when fashion demands that each season's range should be different from the last. But there are definite practical considerations to be borne in mind as you grapple with the temptation to junk last year's boiler suit for this year's parka; and even quite experienced skiers might be grateful to be reminded of those considerations – and for some demystification of the 'miracle materials' you'll find in the shops.

Insulation

The basis of insulation is trapped air; the more air that's trapped in the material of a garment, and the less that air is able to move around, the warmer it will keep you. Jackets are usually padded with either an artificial fibre filling or natural down. These fillings vary both in thickness and weight; and there are now special versions of fibre meant to give better thermal insulation for the same amount of material.

Ordinary artificial *fibre* filling is the cheapest and most common, and works adequately provided there's enough of it; it doesn't absorb water, so even when wet it retains much of its insulating power. The new improved fibres trap air more effectively in two different ways. *Thinsulate* is made up of microfibres that are one tenth the thickness of typical synthetic fibres; the result is that air trapped within the filling has more difficulty moving around. *Dacron Hollofil* is made up of hollow fibres which trap air within themselves as well as in the spaces in between.

Down is the fluffy, not-quite-feathery undercoating of birds, usually waterfowl; it puffs up in use, making the garment bulky. When not in use, the garments can be squeezed up into small bundles. Down is light and very warm when dry, but can become heavy and lose some of its effect when wet. You need to make sure that it's encased in a water-resistant material.

Fabrics

Most materials of which ski clothing might be made are either impervious to water (in which case you get moisture evaporating from the body condensing on the inside of the garment) or not (in which case you get soaked by rain or wet snow). Fabrics can be waterproofed, which in theory means that big drops of water will be kept out, while water vapour will be allowed to escape; but it is rarely completely successful. There are now several materials which have been specially developed to tackle this problem, which skiing shares with mountaineering and other similar pursuits:

Gore-Tex is now quite long-established, and increasingly common; it's a laminated fabric with a membrane sandwiched in the middle which does the vital job of discriminating between water drops trying to get in and water vapour trying to get out.

Stormbeta is a more recently introduced fabric made by a special process which is used to coat the fabric with a 'synthetic wax treatment'. The makers claim a waterproof and highly flexible finish, high tear strength, increased wind and abrasion resistance, plus a surface which repels dirt and grease. This process has been applied to polyester/cotton materials which, in the past, have not proved receptive to coatings.

Mecpor is also a recent development, and again involves the application of a surface coating to a fabric – in this case a layer of resin.

Seams and stitching are extremely important and you need to look at these aspects carefully. No matter how waterproof the actual fabric is, if the seams are loosely stitched or made from a non-waterproof fabric there's always the possibility that water will get in through them. The same thing applies to wind – a garment will not be windproof unless all the seams are airtight.

It's important that your ski clothes should not be too slippery – when you fall on a steep slope, you want to come to a halt as soon as possible rather than sliding until you hit something or somebody. Some years ago, ski clothes were made which were dangerously slippery; once the lesson had been learnt, fabrics which weren't so slippery appeared on the market with the tag 'anti-gliss'. As the slippery fabrics have disappeared, so has the need to label other fabrics in this way.

Jackets

Insulation Ordinary fibre filling is the norm, and there's no particular reason to pay for the more expensive alternatives unless you particularly want to look slim (when the fancy fibres are what you need) or fat (when down will achieve the desired effect).

Room to move? Does it give you plenty of room to move around and stretch, particularly round the shoulders? Jackets which come with either stretch inserts or pleats in the shoulders provide a greater range of movement. When you raise or move your arms, the bottom of the jacket should stay at (or below) the waist, and sleeves should stay at the wrist. A close-fitting waist prevents snow going up your back, and close fitting cuffs do the same for your arms.

Durable shoulders? How will the shoulders stand up to the wear and tear of carrying skis? It's a good idea to have extra protection on the shoulders, preferably in a dark colour so that the dirt won't show.

Effective collar? Will the collar be any good for keeping the wind and snow at bay on a cold day? A high collar that you can zip right up to your nose is best.

Good hood? Some jackets have an attached hood zipped into the collar, which is particularly useful if you find yourself skiing in a blizzard; a drawstring is needed to pull the hood tight around your face, leaving only your eyes, nose and mouth exposed.

Window pocket? A window pocket, usually on the front or the sleeve, can save you digging in your pockets for your lift pass every time you have to produce it – unless you have to put the pass through a computerised machine to get on the lift (which is now quite common).

Zips   Does the zip look as if you could work it with your thick ski-gloves on – not only unzipping but engaging the two bits?

Warm waist?   You need to consider jackets along with trousers – one or other of them must take responsibility for keeping you warm and dry around the middle.

Trousers

Insulation   Fibre filling is the norm in salopettes. You don't need as much insulation as you do in a jacket, and pants made of other, less well-insulating materials are worth considering if you don't like the baggy look of fibre-insulated ones – stretch nylon and cord pants are usually much more close-fitting, but cord is not always waterproof. You can buy loose, and light, water- and wind-proof overtrousers to wear over ski pants and they will keep you warmer.

Room to move?   Can you squat and touch your toes without distressing either the garment or yourself?

Warm waist?   Dungaree-style trousers are what you need if you plan to wear a short jacket.

Warm ankles?   It's important that the trouser leg has an effective arrangement (usually an elasticated cuff) to go over the top of your boot and keep the snow out.

Durable ankles?   The part of your trouser leg which goes over the top of your boot gets a lot of wear on the inside from the other ski; it needs a patch of tough material which won't be cut or easily worn by the ski edge.

One-piece suits

Most of the same considerations apply. Suits with the jacket attached to the trousers by a zip are more practical than those which are indivisible; but unaccountably they are very rare in the shops. The most important part of these suits is the zip; make sure it's sturdy and easy to use. It's very important to have plenty of room to manoeuvre – it will be uncomfortable if your suit is too tight and there's always the possibility that it will rip when you fall over. You can buy suits without any insulation, called 'shells'. They can be very useful if you are likely to go skiing at different times of the year and don't want to buy more than one outfit – they enable you to wear several extra thin layers underneath when the weather's cold.

Surviving the experience

Going skiing is a bit different from most other ways of spending a holiday – and from most other outdoor activities that the averagely indolent person gets up to. First, it's physically quite demanding. Downhill skiing can be a relatively relaxed business if you ski well and gently; but the less well you ski, the more effort everything takes, and the better you ski the more you're likely to want excitement out of your skiing – which means speed, and harder work. More importantly, skiing taxes muscles which at other times may barely be used – in particular, of course, in the legs. It uses those muscles for long periods each day; and it imposes all sorts of sudden shocks and strains on the body. Preparing for all these unusual demands on your body by doing exercises beforehand makes very good sense.

Skiing is also different because it exposes you to dangers which are unfamiliar, and easy to ignore. You could ski for years without appreciating quite what these dangers are – thinking of snow simply as friendly white stuff, of cold winds as no more than an irritant when you're standing in a lift queue. It may take a shock – perhaps a scare in bad weather, or a real tragedy witnessed at close quarters – to bring home the fact that the mountains in winter are basically a hostile place, where you need to have your wits about you. Once off the nursery slopes, every skier needs some understanding of snow and of mountain weather in order to keep the risk of a mishap to a minimum, and some idea of how to react if the worst comes to the worst.

Getting fit to ski

It's easy to convince yourself that going out of your way to get fit before going skiing is a waste of time. After all, you say to yourself, the skiing itself will soon loosen up any reluctant muscles; and, in any case, those twice-weekly sessions of squash/swimming/darts are already keeping you in good shape. And it is certainly true that the majority of skiers have happy holidays without doing any training beforehand. But it is equally true that to get the most out of your skiing you need to prepare for it. If you don't, you risk:

- wasting valuable (and expensive) skiing time getting fit
- feeling stiff and achey in the process of getting fit
- being too weary to ski as many runs as you would like
- finding that your skill deteriorates as your muscles get tired
- being unable to build up a rhythm because of too-frequent rests
- not having the muscle power to put in as many turns as you should
- being more prone to injury.

What sort of exercise?

Being fit for squash, tennis, rugby, football or whatever is not the same as being fit for skiing. Different sports make different demands on the body, and skiing is no exception – so to be really fit for skiing you've got to train specifically for skiing. But there's no denying that other forms of exercise do help in some ways.

One of the main requirements of skiing is *stamina* – the ability to keep on exerting yourself. As your muscles get tired you become increasingly unable to use your skills and perform the movements involved. Stamina is one aspect of fitness which can be improved by any form of exercise. By exercising regularly and for an increasing length of time, you will develop your muscle fibres and increase the efficiency of your breathing and circulation. Jogging (either on the spot or over a distance) is simple and effective – do it for a short time at first, gradually increasing the minutes as your system becomes more efficient. When 5 minutes is easy, run faster but for only 3 minutes, then increase the duration again as your stamina continues to improve. Other forms of strenuous exercise – cycling or swimming, for example – make good substitutes if jogging doesn't excite you. The kind of exercises we explain later in the chapter can help with stamina, if you work at them; aim to do several exercises consecutively. As it gets easier, take shorter rests and increase the length of each exercise.

Your muscle **endurance** determines how many times you can repeat the same movement, or how long you can maintain a given position. The old party-trick of sitting against a wall is an example of an exercise which increases the endurance of your thighs (as well as measuring it) but it doesn't give you power of movement.

The **strength** of your muscles is important too. You need strong muscles to make powerful turns, and to react to the unexpected or the undesirable – 'fighting the fall'. And strong muscles give good support to the bones – if fighting the fall has failed. Training for strength is to do with increasing the number and efficiency of muscle fibres, so that they can work harder for longer.

Increased **suppleness** of your joints and muscles – an increased range of movement – helps to cut down the risk of injury to either muscles or bones. You encourage this by using your joints through their full existing range of movement, and stretching your muscles.

When to exercise

Start exercising at least six weeks before your holiday, doing a 15-minute session each day – after all, you'll be skiing every day. If you normally lead a completely inactive life, start earlier. If you need to break yourself in gently, regard four sessions a week as a minimum. Do it at whatever time of the day suits you. Maybe you can spare a quarter of an hour at lunchtime; or you might choose to exercise when you finish work – although initially this takes some self-discipline at the end of a long day, lots of people find that it does give them quite a boost for the evening. If you do your exercises first thing in the morning (and then, at least, you've got them out of the way), it is particularly important that you warm up properly when you start – remember, your body has been on a go-slow for several hours.

You don't have to jump around in a leotard to do your muscles some good – and you can minimise the amount of time you need to devote specifically to exercising by interspersing your day with occasional exercises. You can make valuable use of those vacant minutes during the day – when the iron is heating, the watched kettle not boiling, the bath running or even when making a telephone call. And you can build exercise into other activities – for example by doing five knee-bends every time you pick something up off the floor.

Spare-moment exercises should never be strenuous – leave that for the serious sessions when you have time to warm up first. Over the page we show several gentle exercises that can be done any time, any place (though some are perhaps better not done in public).

One useful exercise that can be done absolutely anywhere is simply to tighten up your muscles without moving. It is particularly valuable to work your thigh muscles in this way. Nobody in the bus queue will ever know you're shortening your quadriceps to pull up your patellae (knee caps). This is an excellent exercise for those with knee problems. Another not-too-strenuous exercise, although slightly more likely to attract attention, is to swivel your joints (particularly wrists, shoulders and hips) through the biggest circles you can manage.

Never do difficult and energetic exercises until you have done a series of gentler, easier ones first, to work all the parts of your body through their natural ranges of movement. We show a set of suitable **warming-up exercises** on page 415. Do these exercises (mixed up to give a bit of variety) for at least 3 minutes; some people may need longer to loosen up. After the initial warm-up it's good to get the heart pumping a little faster by running on the spot. Aim to do 3 minutes, starting with a minute's very relaxed jogging, then start to raise your knees further – about half as far as the highest you could manage. Every 20 seconds vary the height of your knees and/or the speed at which you run. Revert to the gentle jogging when you need to.

Starting on page 416 we explain and illustrate 11 individual exercises which can form the basis of **serious exercise** sessions. If you're going to embark on this or any other series of serious exercises, bear these points in mind:

- if you are in any doubt about the wisdom of starting an exercise programme, consult your doctor first
- don't eat for an hour before your exercise sessions
- put on your favourite music with a beat to exercise to
- before you do any exercise, pull in your stomach muscles
- never do more exercise than you feel you want to do; it is *not* true that if it hurts it must be doing you good
- similarly, never do any individual exercise which you can't manage without hurting yourself; train, don't strain
- after you've done something energetic take in some good deep breaths; your muscles need a good oxygen supply
- as you get fitter, increase the number of times you do an exercise in a single session.

Spare-moment exercises

Knee-bends Whenever you pick something up from the floor, squat down several times in quick succession

Stretch A Feet apart and stomach in, relax forward towards the floor and gently bounce as far as you can

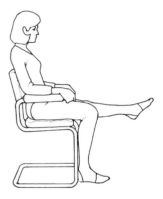

Wall-sitting Slide down the wall until your thighs are horizontal, your shins vertical; stop when your thighs quiver

Thigh-building Sit up straight and hold your leg out horizontally, taking the weight on your thigh muscles

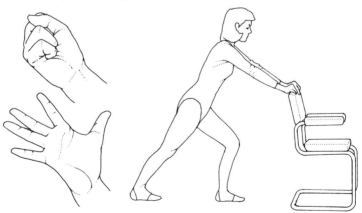

Finger-flicking Clench your fist, then flick your fingers open and stretch your palm as far as you can

Stretch B Stretch one leg out behind you and bounce the heel of that leg towards the ground, stretching your calf

Warming up exercises

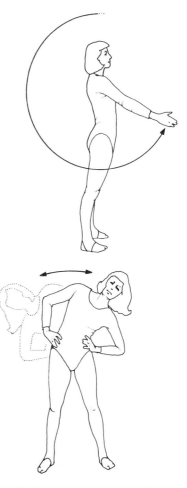

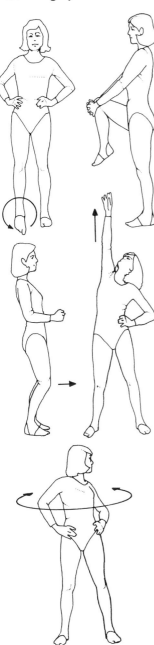

Start by swinging your arms and legs forward and back in opposition – ie left arm and right leg at the same time. Swing them out to the sides as well as to and fro. Follow the swings by:

1 circling your ankles
2 pulling your knees to your chest
3 circling your arms
4 bouncing gently on tip-toe
5 stretching as high as you can
6 bending to one side then the other
7 twisting at the waist

After a gentle warm-up, and before going on to the main exercises, do some jogging on the spot to get your heart pumping – see page 413.

Arm circles Good for strengthening your arms and shoulders and, like all standing exercise, good for your abdominal muscles. With your arms straight to the sides at shoulder level, palms up, do 10 quick, football-size arm circles each way. Repeat with palms down.

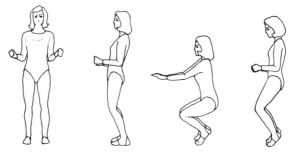

Knee bounces Not only excellent for strengthening your thighs and calves but also for building up your endurance. Stand with your feet parallel and hip-width apart. Hold your arms in a ski-pole position – elbows in, forearms horizontal. Bend your knees forward over the line of your toes, then straighten. Do 10 of these quick knee bounces. Crouch. Keeping your heels off the floor come up half way, hold this semi-crouch for the count of 4, bounce twice then stand straight. Use your arms to help you balance.

Press ups Particularly good for the pectorals and abdominal muscles. The exercise should be adapted to suit your strength. Lie face down, with your hands flat on the floor next to your shoulders. If you lack strength in the shoulders, upper arms and abdomen, keep your legs and hips on the floor and push only your chest off the ground. Start with 5, gradually build up to 20; when that's easy try a couple of real press-ups – tighten your stomach and bottom muscles and lift your whole body, pivoting on your toes.

Lean backs Especially good for the inner side of the knees but they must not be over-done. You will be able to feel your thighs working. Kneel with your feet together and knees hip-width apart. Squeeze your bottom muscles, pull in the paunch. Lean back for the count of 2, pull forward. It is important to keep your body, from your knees to your head, absolutely straight.

Side leg flings Will improve the flexibility of your hips and help strengthen some of the muscles involved in side-stepping. Lie on one side, head supported by your hand, other hand on the floor. Point both feet, and raise your upper leg towards the ceiling 8 times. Pull up the toes of both feet and repeat the exercise. Point both feet again, take the lower leg back about a foot, swivel your upper hip towards the floor, and repeat the exercise again (you won't be able to get the leg quite so high this time). Finally, bring the top leg forward until almost at right angle to your body, pull up your toes and repeat the exercise again. Roll over and do the other side. Don't forget to pull in your stomach muscles all the time.

Twisty jumps Will improve your stamina while strengthening your calf and thigh muscles. Put your feet firmly together, go up on your toes; put your arms in a ski-pole position. With your shoulders forward (down the mountain) all the time, jump a couple of inches off the floor, twist from your waist so that your knees go to the left and then the right. These are quick jumps – aim to do 20, on the spot. Then, with the same lower body twist, bend your knees a bit more and jump higher. These jumps are half as quick as the little ones so do half the number.

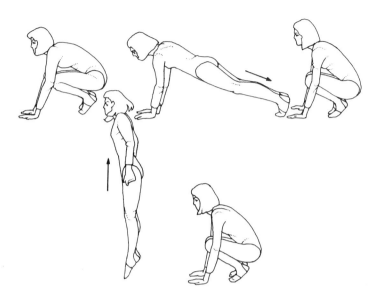

Burpees A quick series of movements that builds up your stamina whilst strengthening your calf, thigh, abdominal, shoulder and arm muscles. Quite an exercise! You may have seen the Superstars doing these on TV. They're really two exercises in one – squat thrusts with a small jump up in between. Start with the squat thrust and when you feel fit enough add the jump. From standing, crouch down. Put your hands flat on the floor; taking your weight on your hands, thrust both feet straight back behind you, and then immediately pull them back in, and jump up. Repeat this for 10 seconds at first and aim for 30 seconds.

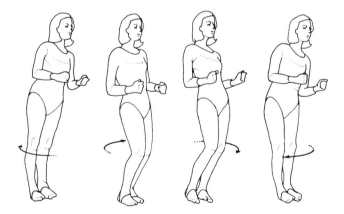

Knee circles Good for the whole leg, especially for extending the movement of your knee and hip. Do these as often as possible. Stand with your feet flat and together, arms in a ski-pole position. Roll over on the sides of your feet to start the knee circle, push your knees forward and circle them round to the other side. Do 5 of these smooth circles each way before repeating with your legs shoulder-width apart. These circles come from your hips.

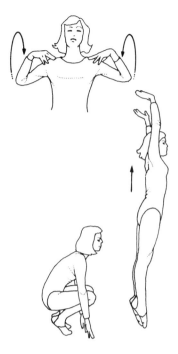

Shoulder rolling Obviously good for the flexibility of your shoulders. Stand with a firm base for your feet and your hands on your shoulders. Quickly rotate your shoulders to make very large circles with your elbows – start with 10 and aim for 50. Repeat the same number in the opposite direction.

Power jumps Will improve your stamina and strength, not to mention endurance. They are particularly good if you intend skiing off-piste but you should include them anyway. Crouch down. Spring up off the floor, straightening your legs. Fling your arms up in the air as you jump. Land on your toes as you return to the crouch. Jump up again straight away. Do them for, say, 10 seconds and after the last jump come up half way from the crouch, heels off the floor, your thighs close to the horizontal, and hold for as long as you can.

Snowplough sequence Very good for calf and knee strength and movement. It will also work your thighs. If you are at all doubtful about the strength of your knees don't do the last part of the exercise. Stand with your heels shoulder-width apart and toes together, arms in a ski-pole position. Push your knees forward over the line of your toes and don't let your feet roll over. Straighten your legs. Do 8 of these knee bounces. Finish with your knees bent. Push them as far forward as you can. Keeping your feet flat, straighten your left leg; count to 8. Shift your weight on to the right leg, bending that one and straightening the left one. Lift the left leg a few inches off the floor. Hold this position for the count of 4. Straighten then bend that knee twice (as you get fitter, increase this number to a maximum of 8). Now start again on the other leg.

Staying safe on the mountain

Skiing isn't the 'dangerous sport' that it once was. Modern boots and bindings, properly adjusted, make it very unlikely that you'll come back from your holiday with a broken leg. And, in a properly organised resort, serious accidents of any kind are kept to a minimum by close monitoring of snow and weather conditions. But the evident efforts of the resort authorities – the constant ski patrols and piste grooming, the closure of the top lifts in bad weather, the detonation of avalanches – are not a guarantee of safety, even for the skier who sticks entirely to the piste. It's well worth acquiring a grounding in what the dangers of the mountains are, and how to deal with them.

Weather and exposure

Skiers are interested in weather not only because it determines the quantity and quality of snow available to ski on, but also because (to one degree or another) anyone out on a mountain in winter is at the mercy of the elements.

The mountains themselves greatly influence the conditions. They tend to generate their own weather, or at least to exaggerate the weather that is being experienced in the lowlands – if rain is expected in general, there'll be snow (or rain) in plenty in the mountains. If high winds are forecast, they will be much stronger at 3,000m than at lower altitudes – much stronger, even, than at ski-resort altitude. Temperatures are almost always lower the higher you go, by appreciable amounts – as much as a degree Celsius for every 100m of altitude. Thus, the higher lifts in a resort can be closed because of hundred-mile-an-hour winds and temperatures of twenty degrees below freezing, when in the valley there is little more than a frosty breeze blowing.

Although it is hard to predict weather patterns accurately weeks in advance, day-to-day forecasting is not the black-magic art many people take it to be. Weather follows patterns which, when understood and recognised, produce reasonably accurate forecasts.

The better-organised resorts display daily (or even twice daily) a local weather forecast including a *synoptic chart*. These charts use lines (similar to contour lines on a map) called *isobars* to show variations in atmospheric pressure over a region. As a general rule, a low-pressure area (a 'depression') indicates bad weather and a high-pressure area (an 'anti-cyclone') good weather. The spacing between the isobars gives an indication of wind speed – isobars close together mean high winds, isobars far apart mean calm weather.

These charts also show *fronts* – junctions between moving masses of warm air and cold air. An approaching front can often be recognised by characteristic and definite changes in the clouds in the sky; a warm front normally brings rain clouds.

The impact the weather has on skiers exposed to it depends on the temperature, the wind speed and the precipitation (weatherspeak for rain or snow). For many skiers, the most important direct result of bad weather is poor visibility, either because of mist or blowing snow. But it's also mostly – though by no means only – in circumstances like these that the effects of cold on the body are likely to become serious. The rate at which you lose heat from the body rises considerably with the speed of the wind. (Not for nothing do car engines have cooling fans.) This effect is known as windchill, and the measure of it is the chill factor – the difference between the actual air temperature and the lower temperature you sense; this difference can amount to tens of degrees Celsius. If your clothes get wet through, heat loss will again be increased considerably. So it's important to have on clothing which is both wind- and water-resistant. Exposure to cold and hostile climates can be more than just unpleasant – if protracted it can result in frostbite or hypothermia.

Frostbite is the excessive cooling of small areas of the body – usually of the fingers, toes, nose, cheeks or ears; it can be the result of extremely low temperatures, or of ordinarily low temperatures coupled with inadequate clothing – if you lose a glove, say. The affected tissue first goes white and numb; this first-degree frostbite can be dealt with simply by immediate re-warming – by putting your hands under your armpits, for example. Warming should be gentle, not involving anything hot or rubbing the skin – least of all with snow. It's only in the most extreme conditions, rare in skiing, that frostbite develops to its second or third-degree stages, which can eventually result in tissue loss.

Hypothermia is the condition resulting from a drop in the temperature of the body as a whole. It is a result of exposure to cold, wet weather with insufficient food and clothing. It is difficult to diagnose, as the symptoms are often similar to those of exhaustion, and indeed it is by no means certain how much of the condition is in part due to tiredness. But the distinction between the two is important: tiredness can't kill, hypothermia can.

Some of the more obvious symptoms of hypothermia are out-of-character behaviour, physical or mental lethargy, slurring of speech, sudden unexpected spurts of energy, and abnormality of vision. It is important to realise that not all of these symptoms will manifest themselves; and that if one member of a party is hypothermic, the rest of the party are also probably suffering to some degree as well.

Hypothermia is better prevented than treated. In very cold conditions, as well as wearing proper clothing, you need to eat lots of high-energy food throughout the day. If you're feeling cold, it may be that all you need do is put a hat on – in doing so you may be reducing by as much as a half the total heat loss from your body. If someone does show signs of hypothermia, the obvious priority should be to get them out of the weather into somewhere warm, preferably with a supply of warm drinks. Until then they should be kept as warm as possible – add more warm clothes (don't remove those already being worn). Do not give alcohol, which will simply increase the rate at which heat is lost. If for some reason the person is unable to carry on skiing, remember that you can conserve a lot of body warmth by huddling together. In extreme conditions, evacuation by stretcher may be essential. In any case, seek medical help as soon as possible.

Accident procedure

When an accident occurs, it's important to know how to act quickly and efficiently in order to preserve life and minimise suffering. If you are armed with some basic knowledge of first aid and with common sense, you can accomplish a great deal at the scene of the accident – and to do so may be vital if the accident is serious.

Someone whose injury is clearly superficial should be helped to carry on skiing down the mountain and then to seek medical help. If the injury is too serious or painful for the casualty to move, first of all mark the accident site by placing crossed skis about ten metres uphill of the casualty; this will warn others of the obstruction, and so prevent multiple pile-ups, and will attract help either from other skiers, ski instructors or ski patrols.

If the bindings have not released, you can usually help to make the casualty comfortable by carefully removing their skis. If the injury is to the lower leg *do not* remove the ski boot – it has the effect of a splint, and leaving it on will generally help to minimise discomfort until the breakage can be given proper attention. Keep the casualty warm, comfortable and set about contacting the ski patrol, who will effect the evacuation. Send a *competent* skier down the piste in search of the nearest SOS point or lift station, armed with all the relevant information – what sort of injury the patrol will have to treat, as well as the precise location of the casualty (referring to piste marker numbers if they exist). Expect a wait of around half an hour, and devote yourself to keeping the injured person cheerful and warm, and watching for signs of deterioration in their condition. Anyone who shows signs of shock – going pale, cold and faint – should be encouraged to lie with their head lower than their feet; don't give any food or drink.

Although it's unlikely, except after an avalanche or a very long fall, it's not impossible that the injured skier will be in a more serious condition. The first priority is to check that the person is breathing, and if not to administer artificial respiration – the kiss of life, or whatever other method you know about. More lives can be saved by attending speedily to breathing than by any other single measure. If artificial respiration is necessary, make sure that no foreign bodies are lodged in the mouth or throat – for example vomit, broken teeth or, in the case of avalanche victims, snow. Continue with respiration until the patient breathes normally again, or until medical help arrives, or until the casualty is presumed to be dead (a very serious presumption for unqualified people to make). Someone who is breathing but unconscious (or seems likely to become unconscious) can vomit and choke, so it is best to turn them on to their side. But first it's important to try to establish the extent of their injuries: a fractured limb will need to be protected against movement, while an injury to the back or spine makes any movement extremely risky.

The next priority is to deal with any severe bleeding. Bleeding is best stopped by applying direct pressure to the site of the wound, using some sort of cloth pad if possible. If bleeding continues, do not remove the pad but place another pad on top of the first and continue applying pressure to the wound .

Safety on the piste

Skiing is a lot like driving. There are 'rules of the road', which may be applied with legal force just as in driving; they're fairly obvious, and simple; and skiing would be a lot safer if everyone obeyed them. You'll see the rules presented in various ways, but what they amount to is this:

- ski in control, so that you can stop within your range of vision
- take a course which will not interfere with any skier ahead of you
- don't block the piste unnecessarily
- don't disregard signs closing runs or warning of dangers.

You'll be personally safer if you always assume that no one else is obeying these rules – that every other skier is out of control, and that around every bend and over every bump is a huddle of people or a Ratrac bashing the piste. This is not a difficult assumption to make, since there are always plenty of people who are evidently oblivious of the rules.

Three other rules which increase your own chances of avoiding accidents are these:

- don't assume that the snow ahead of you will behave like the snow you're on – particularly late in the season, when the effects of sun and shade can be profound
- don't start skiing without doing some gentle exercises to warm up cold muscles – see the earlier part of this chapter for some ideas
- don't be tempted to have 'just one more run' when you finish your 'last' run of the day and find the lift is still going; you'll be tired, and liable to make mistakes; and deserted pistes can be very lonely places once the sun has gone down.

Safety off-piste

Most people start skiing off-piste in a small way – maybe even accidentally – by straying on to virgin snow next to a piste. The main thing to be wary of then is having to ski in very heavy, sticky snow: a fall in such snow is likely to be a slow, twisting affair which even the best bindings don't deal with as effectively and safely as a more abrupt fall on the piste.

When soft snow develops a hard crust on its surface – usually as a result of wind, or snow during the day and extreme cold at night – it can provide a very good skiing surface, provided it can support the skier's weight. But it may support only a flat ski, not a ski on its edge. Every time a turn is made on this *breakable crust*, the ski punches through the surface layer and sinks into the softer layer beneath. This again makes unpleasant falls likely. The best solution is to try to ski with both skis evenly weighted or to resort to slow snowploughs.

But serious off-piste skiing, well away from the beaten track, can have many dangers – avalanches, crevasses on glaciers, the possibility of losing your way, for example. Only skill and experience keep these risks down to a reasonable level. If in doubt, don't go off-piste without a guide. In any event:

● never go alone
● always ski in control; an injury no more serious than a twisted ankle can have very serious consequences off-piste
● use safety straps when skiing in deep snow, otherwise it may take hours to find a lost ski after a fall – if you find it at all
● always assess the risk of avalanche – and if it's significant, be sure that you know how to minimise the risk on particular slopes
● if possible, carry an avalanche cord and an avalanche transmitter to steer rescuers towards you if you are buried
● carry a map and compass *and* know how to use them; navigation is a skill which takes time and practice to master, and it is the only way to find your route in bad visibility
● be wary of slopes where the run-out is not obvious from the start.

If an accident happens off-piste, the first aid priorities are exactly the same as on-piste, but evacuation is usually a much more difficult, serious and lengthy procedure. If possible the ski patrol should be summoned, but you should remember that they are not responsible for the help and rescue of off-piste skiers. You may have to be rescued by helicopter. This can be very costly, and so it is essential that you have adequate insurance – see page 448. Since the rescue is liable to take much longer, it is particularly important that the casualty is kept warm to reduce the chances of hypothermia (see Weather). It is also best to send two skiers for help, and they should ideally have a map grid reference giving the exact site of the accident. A casualty who is in a dangerous position, exposed to avalanche for example, should if possible be moved to a safer location.

Avalanches

To most skiers, snow is simply the solid, low-friction material on which you ski; it's sometimes hard, sometimes soft, sometimes light and dry, sometimes heavy and sticky, sometimes wet and sloppy. Whatever condition it's in, you necessarily adapt to it and think no more about it. But ask a mountaineer about snow and he will paint a different picture, because he knows that snow can hold all kinds of dangers and that he has to rely on his own judgement of those dangers. What the mountaineer is worried about, above all else, is the risk of avalanche – the sudden movement down the mountainside of a huge mass of snow, sweeping away anything and everything in its path. Off-piste skiers obviously need to be similarly concerned; but avalanches are not only dangerous to off-piste skiers, they can sweep down pistes as well – as incidents in recent winters have served to demonstrate. Never disregard avalanche warnings signs; see our 'Skiing vocabulary', page 472, for translations of the vital words.

Whatever the truth of the claim that no two snow crystals are alike, there is certainly a great variety of types of crystal, and their properties vary widely. Perhaps the two clearest examples are the perfect Christmas-card star crystal and the hailstone – the one mainly air, the other mainly ice. The type of crystal is dependent upon atmospheric conditions prevailing at the time of formation – and upon subsequent weather. Falls at different times will accumulate as a series of layers of snow which may or may not be easily distinguished. What determines the chances of avalanche is the degree to which these layers have become bonded together, and the degree to which they remain separate.

In cold, still conditions snow falls as a dry powder which lies on the ground (if it is the first fall of the winter), or more probably on the surface of the existing snow pack. If the existing snow surface is hard and icy, any slope steeper than about 20 degrees presents ideal conditions for an avalanche: the new snow will build up until the mass is too great for its grip on the slippery mountainside, and then it will slide, starting at a point and spreading in a fan shape. Powder-snow avalanches are usually easy to predict – they follow heavy falls (more than 20cm) of light, dry snow, usually on a hard base. ('Sunballs' may be apparent – naturally occurring snowballs caused by snow melting in the sun, which leave trails in the snow as they run off.) Only a rise in temperature, allowing the new snow to settle and bond with the old, will render the slope safe. If the weather stays cold and dry, the danger of avalanche will remain. North-facing slopes, which don't receive much direct sunlight, may be dangerous for many weeks.

If a wind is blowing when the snow falls, the result will be quite different. The wind picks up the falling snow and sweeps it across the ground to be deposited on lee slopes – slopes which are sheltered from the prevailing wind. This snow then forms a slab, which is very dangerous; it gives the appearance of being firm and safe, but it is not – it is liable to break off across the whole width of the slope, and this breaking off is particularly likely to be triggered by the slicing action of a skier's traverse. This 'windslab' has a characteristic chalky appearance and tends to squeak when walked on or when a ski stick is pushed into it. The wind strength at the time of deposit will determine the hardness of the slab formed. Strong winds can strip the snow from windward slopes and deposit it on lee slopes as windslab in much the same way as they do falling snow.

There is a third type of avalanche, which occurs particularly in spring – the wet-snow avalanche. This is triggered by a pronounced rise in temperature, usually in the afternoon. Wet-snow avalanches often follow well defined tracks, and are most common on south-facing slopes, where the snow faces the midday sun.

So basically the danger periods for avalanches are: after heavy snow falls; after strong cold winds; and on warm afternoons. The old rule of thumb, that snow is safe 24 hours after it has fallen, is not true. Snow is not rendered safe until it has been through a rise and subsequent fall in temperature which causes the new snow to consolidate.

If you are unfortunate enough to be caught in an avalanche, current theory says that you should discard your skiing equipment to make movement easier; attempt to move to the side of the avalanche; try to stay on your feet for as long as possible – the more snow that passes by, the less there is to bury you; once swept off your feet, keep your mouth shut and save your strength for the the last few seconds of the avalanche, as the snow is coming to rest – and then attempt to get as near the surface as possible and try to maintain an air space around your face. The difficulties of translating this theory in practice seem considerable.

If you see someone else being buried by an avalanche, mark the spot where they were hit by the avalanche and the spot where you last saw them; then make an immediate search below that point – the longer a person is buried, the less their chance of survival. Use a ski-pole with the basket removed to probe the snow. Only after this initial search has been completed should you go off in search of help (unless of course there are enough of you around to divide these tasks).

Variations on the theme

This *Guide* concentrates on skiing as most people in Britain understand it – skiing downhill, using heavy, stiff boots attached firmly to heavy, stiff skis. But downhill (or Alpine) skiing is only one form of the sport. Cross-country skiing (or Nordic skiing, *langlauf* in German, *ski de fond* in French) is very different: you use long, light skis and relatively light boots which are barely attached to the skis at all, and you ski downhill only as much as you are prepared to ski uphill.

Cross-country developed as a sport about a century ago in Scandinavia, where skis had long been used as means of everyday travel across snow-covered fields and woods. They are still a standard way of getting around in winter there, whether for shopping, going to school or hunting. More recently, cross-country has seen explosive growth in other European countries and in North America. There are now millions of cross-country skiers in Europe's Alpine countries alone.

Cross-country skiing naturally evolves into ski-touring, in which you may travel considerable distances on ski, often going from hut to hut or from hotel to hotel, and possibly skiing off the beaten path, in untracked snow. However, Alpine skis are also used for ski-touring of a rather different sort, with special boots and bindings and detachable 'skins' to enable the skis to grip going uphill. They come into their own on the steep terrain and fast descents encountered in the high mountains, though suitable Nordic skis may also be used there. Alpine ski-touring has about it an air of intrepid mountaineering; but, as we explain later in this chapter, you don't have to be a mountaineer (or an exceptionally good skier) to go touring, and enjoy it.

Cross-country skiing

Cross-country skiing should appeal to anyone who likes snow, walking or jogging, and is not exclusively addicted to downhill skiing. It is easy to learn to a reasonable standard (though in its more advanced form it is just as technical as Alpine skiing); it is less hazardous than Alpine skiing, and less expensive (because the gear costs less and lift tickets do not have to be bought); and many people who live near moorland or hilly country can practise it not far from home for at least some days each winter.

Its essence is its freedom and grace of movement, using the glide of the skis to maximum effect. It is not like plodding along on snow-shoes; and it often requires a varying rhythm as your route takes you up and down over undulating terrain. The downhill sections are usually gentle, but give an exhilarating sensation of speed; a good sense of balance, and elementary techniques like the snow-plough and the stem and skating turns will see you through.

Skiing cross-country you rely very little on artificial help such as ski-lifts, and get a marvellous sense of being close to nature and of peace and quiet. It is also a very healthy sport, involving the use of legs and arms, and also lungs and heart, though not in any excessive way except during competition. It gives well-earned enjoyment through your own efforts; and for its devotees it is a way of life, leading them to health and fitness year-round – if you're to be really fit when the snow arrives, you have to do some training in the summer (for example with roller skis).

Photographs of cross-country skiers often show an advanced racing style, giving the impression that you really need to be in hard training if you are to ski properly. But, like walking, jogging and running, cross-country can be done at any speed, depending on your own inclination; it can vary from the equivalent of a gentle stroll on a Sunday afternoon to that of a marathon run or longer.

Like downhill skiers, most cross-country skiers these days stick to prepared trails; these are not simply flat paths, but have distinct grooves in which you aim to keep your skis – like tramlines. In Scandinavia, these tracks range for many miles; from your mountain hotel or chalet you might do a 10km trek in the morning and perhaps a shorter one in the afternoon; if you're more energetic you might do the 20km or the 50km track instead. In Alpine ski resorts, the tracks may be as short as 3 or 5km (some are even shorter), so that it would become repetitive to go too far.

It is thus a sport for all the family, with both the youngest and the oldest well able to enjoy it at whatever pace suits them best – though teenagers may prefer Alpine skiing, with its greater speed and excitement. But there's no doubt that you will enjoy cross-country most if you are reasonably fit – for example if you also enjoy hill- or mountain-walking. Fitness means that you can keep going without tiring; and this in turn helps you to ski better and with less effort, and in turn to get more enjoyment out of your skiing and your surroundings.

Many of the people who ski cross-country do so to avoid the technicalities and the general hurly burly of Alpine skiing; it gets them out and about on the snow when the other members of the family are skiing downhill, for example. It is perfectly possible to combine the two sports in a single holiday. Many Alpine resorts now cater for cross-country, and in some the terrain lends itself well to cross-country tracks – for example in Pontresina or St Moritz in Switzerland, or Seefeld in Austria. Some people even find it pleasant to ski Alpine for half of the day and Nordic for the other half.

You can hire the equipment you need for cross-country skiing, and it would be normal to do so if you are combining cross-country with a downhill skiing holiday; this is probably the best course anyway until you have decided to commit yourself to the sport. But when you are clear that you will want to continue with cross-country skiing, it would be best to buy at least shoes or boots, and preferably also skis and sticks, so that you have equipment which really suits you and so that you can take any opportunities to go skiing near your home.

Equipment

You will need shoes or **boots** specially made to fit into the bindings on the skis. The weight of the shoe or boot will depend on the type of cross-country skiing: very light shoes are used for racing, but quite heavy and robust boots for mountain skiing off-piste, where a strong control is needed to give the necessary stability and edging in icy conditions. For everyday recreational skiing, you need something which comes between these extremes.

As the drawings over the page show, there are three main types of **binding**; each connects only the toe of the boot to the ski, in a fairly flexible way. Each of them also comes with a heel grip, to help control the skis when turning – either a serrated plate or a plastic fitting which slots into the heel of the boot.

Your sticks (or poles) are an important means of propulsion. They need to be longer than Alpine ones – they should come up to your armpits, or to between your armpits and your shoulder for an extra long push. They need a sharp point for gripping on ice, preferably inclined forwards so that it comes out from the snow easily when you have moved ahead of it.

Cross-country **skis** are rather longer than Alpine skis – 190cm to 210cm is the normal range. The length helps to give the even spread of pressure on the snow necessary for a good glide (compensating for the narrower width of the skis), and also improves your stability in bumps and dips. For track skiing, the edges may be quite straight, but some waisting will help them to turn when off the track. They are made in three widths: 48mm (at the centre) for racing; 52 to 55mm for normal use; and 58 to 65mm (possibly with metal edges) for wilderness skiing, off the track (including mountain ski-touring). The narrower skis, combined with lightweight boots and narrow bindings, give the best glide on tracks if only because there is the least friction against the sides of the track.

The skis need to glide well so that you can travel with the least effort and most grace; but they also need to grip, without sliding back, when you drive forward off your foot – so that you transmit all your energy to the forward movement. The ability to both glide and grip has traditionally been obtained with Nordic **waxes** applied to the sole of the ski, to suit the particular snow conditions and temperature. It may sound surprising but it is in fact quite possible, within a fairly narrow temperature range, for a wax to be soft enough to let the snow grip into it when stopped for the forward drive, yet glide over the snow as it moves on. The question of temperature is particularly important around the melting point as the hardness and crystalline strength of the snow reduces when it warms, and it needs correspondingly softer waxes to match it.

For the novice, in particular, waxing is a bit intimidating, and a welcome development in recent years has been the various 'waxless' skis, which get the necessary grip and glide from a textured sole. They don't work quite so well as a really good waxed ski, but are fine to start with and get the feel of cross-country. You can then progress to waxing if you think that rather better performance justifies the bother.

The two main movements in cross-country skiing are the double-pole push, in which you use both poles and your arm strength to drive the skis forward (most useful when you are already travelling at speed) and the alternating or **diagonal step**, shown (not very athletically executed) below, in which the drive off one foot is counterbalanced and assisted by a swing forward of the opposite arm and stick.

Cross-country skis, like Alpine skis, have an arch or **camber** to spread your weight along the whole length of the ski. The fastest skis have an arch which is deep and rigid, so that the section under your foot presses on the snow only as you drive forward off that ski – it is this centre section which gives the grip needed for the forward drive, while the rest of the ski sole can be smooth to give the least friction for gliding.

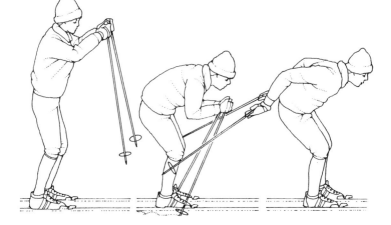

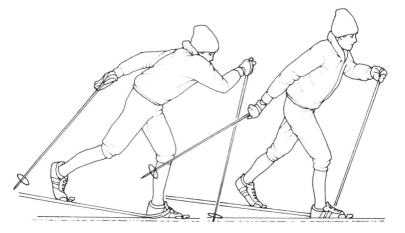

There are several different types of **waxless skis**:

● stepped or fishscale, where the sole has slight but distinct sloping 'teeth' to grip the snow one way but not the other – the best all-rounder

● mica-sole, in which slivers of mica are embedded at an angle in the plastic base material – a microscopic version of the fishscale sole, giving excellent grip, but a bit slow

● mohair strips stuck to the sole – also a bit slow, and the most easily damaged.

The three sorts of **bindings** you're likely to come across are these:

● the 'Nordic norm' – a three-pronged binding on the ski and a boot with a matching extension on the toe; there are variants of different widths, so make sure boots and bindings match

● narrower bindings designed to minimise friction with the snow at the side of the ski – the link between boot and binding tends to vary from make to make, so it's vital to be sure that the two are compatible

● the traditional cable or Kandahar binding, which is still used by some ski-tourers.

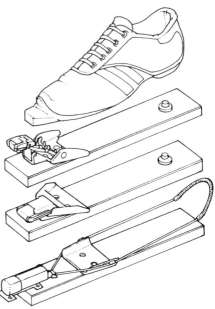

There is a considerable range of waxes (both hard waxes in sticks and klister waxes in tubes) to suit the range of temperatures and types of snow; but to start with the complexities can be avoided by using the two wide-ranging waxes now available, one for below-freezing and one for above-freezing temperatures. You rub the below-freezing one on to the soles of your skis and get the best possible spread and smoothness with a rubbing cork. Then if the weather turns warm and you find that the skis are not gripping, you add some of the above-freezing wax (being softer, it will hold on to the other wax), increasing the area covered until the ski grips satisfactorily. When it gets colder, you reverse the process by scraping off the above-freezing wax which may otherwise tend to ball up as the snow gets stronger and sticks in it.

Clothing

The cross-country skier wears clothes rather similar to those of a walker or jogger – free-moving and wind-resistant, but not heavy or bulky. They must both conserve heat when moving slowly and allow you to get rid of heat when going strongly; hence plenty of zips are needed. It will pay to have several thin layers, rather than one or two thick ones, so that you can adjust the amount more readily.

Your jacket should be windproof. Below it have a thin sweater and a thin thermal vest, with possibly a shirt as well. Generally, you should not expect the clothes you ski in to keep you warm when standing still, and should carry an extra sweater for this purpose. A scarf can help to keep you warm before you have really got started. A wool hat, or a peaked cap, may sometimes be needed. For your hands, anything from windproof mittens (with thermal pile) to lined leather gloves will do; but they should not have any rough internal stitching as this would cause discomfort when gripping your ski sticks hard to push yourself along.

It's normal to wear breeches, often supplemented by thermal long johns; but any loose fitting wind-proof trousers will do. Knee-length stockings complete the outfit, preferably with some form of cloth gaiter to protect them (and the boots) from snow.

How to do it

It is easy to learn to ski cross-country to a moderate standard, since the basic techniques are not at all difficult – most of the movements will come fairly naturally once you get moving on cross-country skis, and develop the necessary balance, agility and rhythm on which everything else depends.

But you can now get tuition in many resorts, including ones very much dominated by Alpine skiing, and it's worth having some instruction in the early days if at all possible. There is quite an art in transferring your weight from one ski to the other in the most efficient way – with the aim of keeping your skis really gliding. These movements can best be developed by imitating a good Nordic skier; but a worthwhile trick is also to ski without sticks for half an hour or so in order to get your foot positions correct.

Where to do it

Cross-country skiing is best done in Scandinavia, where virtually everyone learns to ski as a child, and where most families go to the open country for cross-country skiing, especially at Easter. The Norwegian uplands to the west and north of Oslo have hundreds of miles of ski-routes, giving plenty of scope for day trips from mountain centres; for example from the British lodge at Kvitavtn Fjellstuge which has a very extensive programme (and would be a good place to start cross-country). There is also enormous scope for long journeys from hut to hut, possibly even with dog sledges. And there are vast areas suitable for cross-country in Sweden and Finland too.

For a normal cross-country holiday, you would be based in one place, either a hotel or a mountain lodge (sometimes it is difficult to tell the difference as the lodges are so comfortable). You then do day trips out from there, or may even return for lunch and go out again. This has the advantage that you ski lightly laden and do just as much or as little as you wish. You also have all the other attractions of a comfortable hotel, including possibly some nightlife.

As cross-country skiing can be done wherever there is rolling terrain with good snow cover, the scope elsewhere in Europe is also very considerable. And with the increasing popularity of the sport the number of places where it is practised is correspondingly growing. Areas with extensive cross-country skiing include many parts of Austria, the Dolomites (eg the Trento area) and other parts of northern Italy (eg the Aosta valley), Bavaria (eg Mittelberg and Oberammergau), the Black Forest, the Jura and many other parts of France including the pre-Alps, the Massif Central and the Pyrenees.

While a number of the Alpine resorts have cross-country ski-schools and tracks suitable for learning the techniques, few give sufficient scope for the long journeys which are the particular attraction of cross-country skiing. Instead they may be short circuits of only about 3km or 5km, sometimes with steep sections, strenuous at that altitude. So if you want to enjoy some cross-country as an adjunct to an Alpine skiing holiday, it is necessary to choose your resort carefully. There should be extensive tracks and, to ensure a reasonable chance of good snow in the period December to March, these need to be at about 1000m altitude. They are most likely to be found in wide valleys running east–west, where the south side will be in shadow; or alternatively on plateaux off the main valleys. Avoid steep-sided narrow valleys with a lot of habitation if you want to get the true feel of cross-country. Examples of Alpine resorts with good potential for cross-country are St Johann and Seefeld in Austria; Pontresina/St Mortiz, Klosters/Davos, Kandersteg and Lenk in Switzerland; and La Clusaz in France. There is very extensive cross-country in North America, notably throughout the eastern states of the USA and in Canada.

In Britain there are usually quite a number of days each winter when it is possible to take cross-country skis on to moorland or hilly country, such as the Pennines (sometimes even the South Downs!); while in Scotland there can be good possibilities, for example in the Cairngorms and Glenshee.

Cross-country touring

Cross-country touring, involving a continuous journey lasting several days or a week, with nights in different hotels or cabins, is a natural extension of cross-country skiing. It gives a challenge, as difficult or easy as you wish according to the choice of tour; and the opportunity to get away from one area and feel that you have achieved a real journey. To enjoy touring, you need to be able to ski cross-country without fatigue and to be able to carry a rucksack with essential gear, weighing perhaps 10kg to 15kg – food and spare clothing, and possibly a sleeping bag. For anything but the simplest tours the party must include someone who is experienced in map-reading and navigation and who has an understanding of winter survival in case something goes wrong. The alternative is to join an organised tour, with an experienced leader and possibly a guide.

A good plan when starting touring is to spend some of the first week at a fixed base, getting to know each other, and improving fitness and skill, before starting your tour from hut to hut.

In Norway, excellent touring may be found in the whole upland area between Oslo and Trondheim. Areas with good chains of huts include the Hardangervidda and areas to the north of Finse (on the Oslo–Bergen railway); the Jotunheim; and the Rondane. Sweden has Lappland (notably the Abisko-Kebnekaise area) as well as areas further south. Tours are possible in the other areas of Europe which lend themselve to cross-country, of which perhaps the best are those in the Jura, with its very attractive combination of hills, farms and quiet, peaceful villages.

Organised holidays

A few of the major tour operators include cross-country holidays within their programmes. The main specialist operator in Britain is Waymark Holidays, which has a wide range of holidays, including tours and competitions. Travellers (The Watermill, Kendal) arranges cross-country tours in remote areas such as Lappland.

Organised tours are arranged by some of the clubs (particularly the Eagle Ski Club) and national organisations (notably the DNT – the Norwegian Touring Federation – and the Club Alpin Français).

Competition

At top international level, Nordic racing is one of the most demanding of sports. But there is also plenty of competition at Citizen, regional or club level which is there to be enjoyed by those who like to test and improve themselves in this way.

The shortest distance is 5km and the longest international distance is 50km (taking only about 2 hours), but the Citizen races may go up to 85km or 90km. The Citizen races may be likened to the marathons for runners or joggers; and attract thousands of participants of all ages and standards. The most famous, forming the world Loppet series, are: Dolomitenlauf; Marcialonga; König Ludwig Lauf; Gatineau; Transjurassienne; American Birkebeiner; Finlandia Hihto; Vasaloppet; Engadin Skimarathon; and Birkebeinerrennet. But there are many other Loppets, including even one in Iceland. To enter, you will normally need to be a member of a club within the national ski organisation and may have to have a racing licence and a medical check-up. Waymark Holidays organise parties to train for and race in some of these competitions.

A particularly demanding variation is the Biathlon where cross-country racing is combined with rifle shooting. This tends to be a military preserve because of the standard of training required – both physical and with weapons.

Clubs and associations

In Britain, in addition to the touring clubs mentioned above, there are many cross-country ski clubs, particularly in the Midlands and north of England and in Scotland. It would be worth joining one in order to meet fellow cross-country enthusiasts and find out about cross-country skiing opportunities; to share transport; and possibly to enter competitions. Lists may be obtained from the English Ski Council or the Scottish National Ski Council respectively.

Alpine ski-touring

Quite apart from Nordic or cross-country ski-touring is the much less widely practised sport of Alpine ski-touring, which takes place on the steeper ground of the Alps, the Pyrenees and other mountains. Although it bears some similarity to cross-country touring, this form of touring derives from Alpine skiing (using very similar equipment) and may be linked also with Alpine mountaineering. It involves travelling over steep mountains on skis, using bindings which allow the heel of the boot to lift for walking uphill, and fabric 'skins' on the soles of the skis to grip the snow.

The really good tourer, or ski-mountaineer, will be able to climb big mountains on skis, such as the Wildspitze in Austria, Monte Rosa in Switzerland and Mont Blanc in France; but much of the fun of ski-touring comes from travelling over cols and on glaciers well below the summits, or even at much lower levels, near the tree-line. A main attraction of Alpine ski touring is just to travel through such high mountain country, and experience the magnificent solitude and beauty of the mountains, with their steep faces and glaciers, which it is normally impossible for anyone else, other than Alpine mountaineers, to know. Although you do not have to be a mountaineer, for the easier tours at least, you do need some love of the mountains to get the most satisfaction from it. And unless your party includes really experienced mountaineers you will probably need a guide.

From many resorts, it is possible to undertake day-tours, usually starting from the top of a lift and involving some climbing uphill to a col or ridge to get access to fresh country outside the scope of the piste system. There is a great deal of pleasure to be gained from such excursions – the technical satisfaction of using skis whatever the snow conditions, ranging from good spring snow to breakable crust or icy snow; and there is the physical pleasure of climbing uphill on skins, and the health and fitness which come with it. But the best touring comes from travelling from hut to hut, over the high cols and glaciers, and including suitable peaks from time to time. Then there is the comradeship of the group, where everone relies on each other to some degree, and you share a communal life 24 hours a day. A particular pleasure is the long, lazy afternoon at the hut, following a good ski-tour that morning – working out and savouring the prospects for tomorrow, or just reading or sleeping.

The main qualification you need to go touring is the ability to stay upright on your skis in all conditions. Falling is physically tiring, delays the party and can also of course cause injury in the normal way; falling in the wrong place (eg near a crevasse or above an icy slope) can be dangerous. Ski-tourers therefore tend to ski very steadily and reliably, often forsaking parallel turns for stem-swings where these are more effective – for example in difficult snow or where it is important to save energy (eg with a heavy sack or at high altitude). But it also helps if you're a good enough skier to be able to concentrate on the route-finding and on enjoying the day, rather than on skiing technique.

Ski-touring can be physically demanding, but is rarely exhausting. It is much more a question of rhythm and steadiness than of dashes of speed and lung-bursting activity. You will need to be fit enough to walk uphill with skis, skins and a pack; and to ski downhill without getting tired. You must be acclimatised to the altitude for the higher tours; but otherwise the question of just how fit you need to be really depends on how strenuous the tour is. For a first tour, it should be possible to find something which has a gentle first few days, without excessive uphill climbing, which will allow you to acclimatise.

You must have the right equipment to go touring. In some resorts where ski-touring is customary, you can hire skis with touring bindings and skins; and this would certainly be advisable for day tours. But for serious touring – going from one valley to another, which may be some distance away – it's more convenient to own your equipment.

Equipment

Ski-tourers need **boots** which are a cross between conventional ski boots and mountaineering boots – with a ridged rubber sole, and some flexibility for the ankle to move forward without discomfort; but for a short tour, ordinary ski-boots can be used, with the top clips undone for going uphill. Most of the main manufacturers make touring **skis** which are flexible in the tip, light in weight, easy in difficult snow, grip well on ice, and may have a groove in the heel to take the rear clip of the **skins**. For ease of carrying, lightness and manoeuvrability, you may wish to choose rather shorter ones than you would use for downhill skiing. The **bindings** need to have all the normal release functions since it is particularly important not to hurt yourself when far from help.

For steep, icy ground, or on summit ridges, it may be necessary to climb on foot, possibly even roped up. An **ice-axe** may then be a considerable help, and a necessary safeguard against falling; it's important to know how to use it. **Crampons** (sets of spikes which fit

Uphill progress when ski-touring depends on having fabric *skins* (so called because sealskins were originally used) strapped or glued to the sole of the ski to give grip on the snow; for icy snow you need snow blades (*harscheisen*), which may be part of the touring binding or clipped into special fittings on the side of the ski, below the boot.

Touring *bindings* allow your heels to lift from the ski when going uphill – and some have a special device to make climbing more comfortable by supporting the heel at an angle to the ski. When skiing downhill, the boot is clamped to the ski in the normal way. Safety straps are better than bindings, since it's important not to get separated from your skis if your bindings release in a fall.

beneath your boots) will also give you a very much better footing than boots alone. Before going on an alpine ski-tour, check with the leader as to whether you are likely to need them.

Clothing

Clothing needs to be warm and windproof, but it is important also to be able to get rid of excess heat: so good ventilation (plenty of zips) is vital. Ski-tourers tend to use mountaineering clothing (breeches, gaiters over the boots, an anorak or cagoule, and a warm hat, possibly supplemented with a down jacket); but for a day tour in good conditions, or for a moderate longer tour, ordinary Alpine ski clothing would be satisfactory, provided it can be ventilated.

Touring skills

Touring on moderate ground (for example below the upper tree-line), like cross-country touring, requires little more than common sense and the ability to move on skis without falling. Most ski resorts have gentle untracked terrain nearby, often on summer paths away from the main pistes, and there is everything to be said for starting to find your way around on these as early as possible – provided they are genuinely moderate, there is no avalanche risk and you always go with someone else. But any more difficult terrain requires both care and skill; for example anyone starting to tour at moderate altitudes away from resorts would need the ability to:

● ski reliably off-piste, carrying a rucksack; this requires a sound stem Christie (or stem swing) turn
● walk up-hill on skis, using skins
● halt a fall by rolling over or by using ski sticks
● read a map and compass
● recognise avalanche conditions and know the main rescue procedures.

To safely embark on high Alpine ski-touring you would need, in addition, an adequate understanding of:

● use of *harscheisen* – blades fitted beneath the boot to give grip when walking uphill on hard or icy snow
● glacier touring technique including simple rope handling, crevasse formations and crevasse rescue
● elementary snow and ice climbing, including the use of ice-axe and, if possible, crampons
● elementary rock scrambling or climbing, including methods of belaying
● Alpine weather.

An introduction to these skills can be obtained on various touring meets of the main British clubs (see below). The leaders of touring parties, especially ones without guides, bear a heavy responsibility and must have not only these skills but also the more general skills of mountain leadership, which come only with considerable experience.

Where and when to do it

There are quite a number of regular tours such as the round tours of the
Stubai or the Oetzal, traverses of the Silvretta or Ortler, or the Haute
Route of the Valais (Chamonix to Saas Fee) or the Bernese Oberland
(Les Diablerets to Meiringen). In addition there are many single day
tours, for example in the Bernina, or the Vallée Blanche on Mont Blanc.

In deciding what to undertake, the main considerations are:

- the competence, experience and fitness of the party
- the availability of guides
- the time of year – the lower areas tend to be in condition early
(March) while the higher ones come in later (April or May)
- the recent and forecast weather and snow conditions, with their
implications for avalanche risk
- the technical difficulty and magnitude of the tour, taking account of
the state of the glaciers
- the intervals between huts; their dates of opening; whether or not
they have a guardian; and whether or not they provide food and fuel
- rescue arrangements.

It is essential to get to know the route as accurately as possible before
embarking on it. You can do this by studying very closely the various
guidebooks and maps, from reading accounts in journals and other
publications, and by talking to club members and others who have done
it. Allow plenty of time in case of bad weather or other problems.

Clubs and associations

The main ski clubs with Alpine ski-touring activities are the Ski Club of
Great Britain, the Eagle Ski Club, and the Scottish Ski Club. The Ski
Club of Great Britain runs and subsidizes several tours each year
including some for beginners, in addition to arranging day tours at
certain centres, through the SCGB resort representatives. The Eagle
Ski Club has a major touring programme, which includes a high Alpine
training course.

The Association of British Mountain Guides can provide details of
guides specialising in Alpine ski touring.

Waymark Holidays and Travellers arrange parties for the Haute
Route, in addition to their cross-country tours.

The Alpine countries have their own national Alpine clubs which own
huts, publish guidebooks, journals and newsletters and arrange many
other facilities for their members. These facilities usually include
preferential treatment in almost all the Alpine huts, cheap rates on the
mountain railways and cable-cars in each club's own country and,
usually at extra cost, insurance against the often very high cost of a
rescue party. The British Ski Federation, in association with the British
Nountaineering Council, runs a ski-touring leaders' course – as do
some of the Continental clubs. The British ski clubs sometimes award
scholarships to assist British skiers to attend one of the ski-touring
courses.

Most British ski tourers undertaking high mountain tours join one of the Continental clubs, though of course this is not necessary for lower level touring. It is not only pleasant to be a member, but also, over a fortnight or so, it may save you more than the cost of the subscription through the preferential rates in huts. The UK branch of the Austrian Alpine Club (OAV) is the most popular, and has ski-touring activities for its members. Alternatively, the British Mountaineering Council can provide a reciprocal rights card which entitles the holder to reduced rates in huts. The Council also runs training courses.

Star turn

Like the history of so many sports, the story of Alpine ski racing is one of Great British invention followed by consistently greater foreign achievement in performance. Considering that we are a predominantly snowless and non-mountainous nation, the modest achievements of our national ski teams are hardly a matter for despondency; after all, the Swiss and Austrians don't turn out champion yachtsmen. On the contrary, what is surprising is that it took the sporting enthusiasm of Britons, graduating from their formative playing-fields to the Public Schools Alpine Sports Club, to exploit the competitive potential of downhill skiing. At the time (in the early 1920s), the skiing establishment consisted of Scandinavians, and official competitive skiing consisted solely of Nordic events (cross-country marathons and ski jumping). Downhill, or Alpine, skiing was not considered a pastime for real men, and it took ten years of increasing enthusiasm in Europe for unofficial Alpine races before they were officially recognised.

Ski jumping champions in Norway and downhill racing champions in Austria are gods. To be in Austria after the 1984 Olympics (when the country's medal haul in the Alpine skiing events was one bronze) was to witness national mourning. Even in Britain, millions of non-skiers spend their winter Sunday afternoons watching ski races from the Alps. Some of them are armchair experts, well versed in the intricacies of compressions, tucks, pre-jumps, chicanes and gliding technique; others are simply revelling in the brilliant spectacle of the mountains and of athletes taking very considerable risks to limb, and even life; very few are watching because of an attachment to any of the participants. But once in a while a British skier emerges who, at least for a while, manages to compete on equal terms with the best racers from the Alpine countries and North America. One such racer is *Konrad Bartelski*, whose second place in a World Cup downhill race in the 1981-82 season earned him the respect of the skiing world and a place among the top seeds for the next season. Who better, we thought, to guide us through the contemporary racing scene?

Ski races straight and narrow

Ski racing has come a long way since the days when racers set off all at once (the expressively named geschmozzle start) in a first-past-the-post race with no prescribed course, and plenty of spills for winners as well as the also-rans. For obvious reasons of safety, the old horse-race soon gave way to the lesser excitement and greater precision of individuals competing against the clock down a narrowly defined course – planned within internationally agreed guidelines, landscaped for variety, groomed for safety and, yes, watered for speed. The three main alpine races are Downhill, Slalom and Giant Slalom. In all of them skiers compete one by one down a set course, and the man or woman with the fastest time wins. The different disciplines use different kinds of course, which test different qualities in the racer.

The longest, straightest and fastest race is the **Downhill**. Men's courses are set on hills giving between 850 and 1,000 metres of vertical drop, women's between 500m and 700m. The course length is two to three miles for men, up to two miles for women. Racers take something less than two minutes on the course, which means average speeds of 50 to 60 miles an hour for women, and 65 to 70 miles per hour for men. Skiers are allowed a series of practice runs before each race, which consists of a single descent. In normal conditions the course deteriorates and gets slower as more and more racers go down, and usually the winner is one of the early starters; the first fifteen to run, in randomly selected order, are the seeds, based on recent performance. Still, a late starter can come up with a surprise victory, especially when a downhill race is run after a lot of fresh snow which tends to give later skiers an advantage.

Courses for **Slalom** races are set on short, steep and usually (indeed preferably) icy slopes, giving only about 200m vertical drop for men, 180m for women. In this relatively short space men have to ski through 55 to 75 gates, women through 45 to 60; they are laid out on the hill in such a way as to test turning ability and control more than speed alone. No practice runs are allowed, and the race is run over two legs on different courses (in the early days of racing it used to be one leg on hard snow, the other on soft). Racers ski the second leg in the order they finished the first, except that the first five go in reverse order – so the leader skis fifth. Most courses take about a minute.

The **Giant Slalom** consists of about the same number of gates as a slalom, but spaced out more widely over a course of about a mile, giving a vertical drop of 300m to 400m for men, and 300m to 350m for women. The race is run like a slalom, with each leg taking about 90 seconds. For reasons to do with the organisation of ski racing competitions, a new discipline has recently been introduced; this is the **Super Giant Slalom** or Super-G, where gates are spread over an even longer, wider course designed to give the Downhill racers more of a chance of winning. It's too early to say whether this event will catch on or not, but so far top racers have been distinctly cool in their reaction to the new discipline.

The circuit

All the course regulations are laid down by the FIS (Fédération Internationale du Ski) which organises a circuit of races every winter, starting in Europe in December, ranging from Bulgaria and Sweden to Furano in Japan, before finishing in North America several long, hard months later. Racers score points for finishing in the first fifteen of any race, and these points over the season decide placings in the annual **World Cup** Championship. At the end of the season the highest scorer in each discipline wins the World Cup for that event. There is an overall World Cup title for the best performer in all disciplines, with a limit placed on the amount of points which can be amassed in any one, and extra points for combined performance in Downhill and a Slalom event at a particular race meeting. It's an extremely complicated scoring system which is often changed, usually to the disadvantage of specialists like Sweden's Ingemar Stenmark, and the advantage of all-round skiers who enter and score points in downhill races as well as winning slaloms.

As far as men's skiing is concerned, the Giant Slalom has proved to be much closer to the Slalom than to the Downhill, and since skiers have become specialists it's the slalom skiers, notably Stenmark, who have dominated the Giant Slalom. This has given them a commanding advantage in the overall competition, designed to reward all-round achievement, even if, like Stenmark, they don't compete in downhill races; so the Super-G was conceived to suit downhillers and redress the balance. In the early days of the World Cup, when Killy and Schranz walked off with all the prizes in all the events, things were much simpler! Killy won the first overall World Cup in 1967 with maximum points – three victories in all of the three disciplines. It's hard to imagine any skier doing that now – although the outstanding achievements of the young Swiss Pirmid Zurbriggen in the World Cup and World Championships in 1985 immediately gave rise to talk of a second Killy.

Specialisation hasn't been so pronounced among women. A number of Downhill racers have been consistent Giant Slalom winners, outstandingly Austria's Anne-Marie Moser-Pröll, who dominated women's racing in the 1970s. Liechtenstein's Hanni Wenzel and the German Rosi Mittermaier each won two golds and a silver medal in the 1980 and 1976 Winter Olympics respectively.

So every year the World Cup produces several champions based on consistent performance throughout the season. These aren't the only champions around, though. Every Leap Year, attention shifts from the World Cup circuit to the **Winter Olympics**, where all the laurels go to the best skier on the day in a single race in each discipline. The **World Championships** are an Olympic-style race meeting organised by the FIS, and are now to be held every two years. The gold medallists in each discipline reign as World Champions for two seasons. So it can happen that a skier who hasn't won a race for two years and who hasn't done at all well in the World Cup is still the World Champion in a particular discipline. One odd feature of the World Championships is the Alpine Combined title, which goes to the best performer in a shortened Downhill and one of the slalom events. At the Schladming World Championships in 1982 none of the three combination medallists finished in the first ten places of any of the three races, which shows how specialised men's racing has become, and arguably makes rather a nonsense of the combined and overall titles. Skiers compete to win races, not accumulate points, and that's why the Olympics and World Championships mean more to many skiers than the World Cup.

The business angle

World Cup racers are technically amateurs and most fulfil the requirements of the Olympic Committee, but all the top racers earn a living from the sport out of commercial sponsorship; so-called 'broken time' payments are allowed, enabling the athlete to be compensated for not having the time to work because of competition and intensive training. Rules of eligibility for the Olympics, or at least the interpretation of them, are in practice stricter than for the World Cup and World Championships, which has meant that a few of the world's top skiers have been unable to compete for Olympic medals. It happened to Karl Schranz at Sapporo in 1972, and in 1984 at Sarajevo the absentees included the near-invincible Stenmark, Hanni Wenzel – both of these two ruled out because of semi-professional status – and the brilliant young slalom skier Marc Girardelli, disqualified because he skis under a flag of convenience (Luxembourg) instead of representing his true nationality (Austria).

There is some professional racing, mostly in North America, where the parallel slalom is the great spectator sport. Two racers battle it out together side by side on parallel courses, swapping sides for the second leg to even out the inevitable differences. Ironically, the prize money for pro racing isn't as good as the money the top World Cup racers can attract, and as a result the pro circuits tend to attract the less successful amateur racers.

Racing skills and thrills

Among Alpine ski races Downhill is the ultimate test of commitment and guts, and that's what makes it so exciting to watch and to perform. In the Downhill it's man against mountain, rather than man against contrived difficulty. Within the two minutes of the race, skiers accelerate up to 90 miles an hour; they fly off ridges for up to 50 yards in the air, and their legs have to contend with crushing forces in a compression (where the course flattens out), and through every inch of a tight bend. There's no need to be an expert technical observer to enjoy watching this kind of race, and it comes across well on television, where you benefit from cameras positioned at different points on the mountain, although you'll never really appreciate the speed until you stand on the sidelines and watch the racers flashing past. Part of the drama of the Downhill race stems from the risks the racer has to take to stand a chance of winning. The man who completes the course elegantly and in perfect control from start to finish rarely turns in the fastest time – as illustrated by the example of the great Franz Klammer, who on so many of his greatest winning runs has seemed to be out of control and courting disaster. Downhill racing, of course, is also the discipline which sees the most spectacular crashes, and although we racers like to think that people don't watch for that reason, there's no doubt that the spills add to the thrills.

The appeal of the Slalom is rather more subtle. Unlike the Downhill racer, who can hardly hope to win if he doesn't push himself right up to and even beyond his normal capabilities, the Slalom skier has to make the tactical judgement about when to ski with a safety margin, hoping others will force too hard and miss a gate, and when to let rip. Where many skiers would choose to go all out on the first leg, in the hope of establishing a margin for a safety-conscious second run, Ingemar Stenmark made a speciality of skiing unspectacularly in the first leg and then coming from behind to annihilate the field with a blistering second run. The Slalom can be a dramatic struggle in its own way, and for the spectators on the hill it's much easier to follow the race as a whole than it is with a Downhill race on its much longer course. On television the dominant impression is of an indecipherable maze of red and blue poles. What never seems to come out is how steep slalom courses are, and what an achievement it is simply to hang on to the icy mountain and negotiate the awkward, twisting course.

The modern style of slalom skiing gives the impression that racers devote more energy to knocking down poles than to controlling their skis. This is because all they have to do is make sure that both their skis pass on the required side of the pole; from the hips up, the body takes a much straighter line down the hill than the feet, which means that poles get knocked all over the place. Fortunately, they are flexible and unbreakable these days, and the risk of skewering yourself on a broken slalom pole isn't great.

While the two extreme disciplines of Downhill and Slalom make greatest demands on a skier's resilience and courage on the one hand, and his agility and lightning reflexes on the other, the Giant Slalom is a test of the precise application of technique at high speed, and demands a combination of smoothness and strength.

Downhill courses

The required vertical drop for the course means that any resort hosting a World Cup Downhill has to have at least one substantial mountain; there are no World Cup courses in Scandinavia, and one in Eastern Europe (Sarajevo) has to start from the roof of a mountain restaurant to be high enough. All the same, it isn't safe to assume that because a resort features on *Ski Sunday* it must have magnificent, really tough skiing. Most are not in themselves outstandingly difficult descents for any fairly competent skier, and a consistently steep 'black' run would be too dangerous for a Downhill race; bends are often put in to keep speeds down as well as to provide a test. Few of the world's famous Downhill courses are in particularly high resorts. Some resorts have very little skiing apart from the racing hill itself – Igls, near Innsbruck, for example, and Les Houches, near Chamonix – and the courses themselves are frequently closed to holiday skiers; some, indeed, are rarely opened. Naturally, many very small resorts with limited skiing can host Slalom and Giant Slalom events, so when it comes to picking a holiday resort you shouldn't be influenced at all by prominent mentions of FIS race courses in their promotional literature.

Very few ski-runs are long and varied enough to make for a good Downhill race – providing tight turns, jumps and alternating steep and gentle sections (which are technically just as demanding as the more hair-raising parts of the course); the most exciting are famous annual venues. The famous Hahnenkamm at Kitzbühel probably presents the greatest challenge to character, commitment and, some would say, sanity. The wooden starting hut is the launch-pad into the most demanding 30 seconds of ski racing in the world; when you're standing at the top poised to go, it's like your first jump off the top diving board.

Perhaps the most gratifying race is the longest, the Lauberhorn at Wengen. It starts in the shadow of the north face of the Eiger and packs into its 2½ miles every aspect of Downhill racing – long bends and tight hairpins, broad open stretches and narrow chicanes, taking the racer over cliffs and under railway lines; and all of this in the spectacular wrapping of the Bernese Oberland at its most beautiful. To win these two races in the same year is every Downhill racer's dream.

Behind the scenes

Of course, there's much more to ski racing than what you see on the course on the day, although the racer gets all the glory for a victory. Each national squad has its back-up team of technical experts who have the great responsibility of cooking up the right blend of ski-wax for snow conditions on the course; these can change hour by hour, and usually vary over different parts of the course. Just as important is the fact that during training (for Downhill) there are groups of coaches and technicians stationed all the way down the mountain to amass as much information as possible about the racer training on the course – the Austrians and the Swiss will have up to 15 observers on the hill, giving them a big advantage over smaller teams. With only three or four training runs, this in-depth analysis is essential to establish the fastest line and select the optimum equipment. There are video cameramen filming all the top racers, as well as lines of electronic timing equipment to establish who is gaining time at which point on the course.

Ski racers train long and hard. As soon as one season is over in April, preparation for the next one begins with the racers hardly having time for a breather before they have to head off to the weight training rooms, wind tunnels (to perfect aerodynamic posture), running tracks, and snow – some of them to the summer snow-fields on Alpine glaciers, others crossing to the other end of the world to ski in Australia and New Zealand. Long hours of race training are designed to simulate, wherever possible, true racing conditions. As well as building up agility, strength and stamina for the duration of a race, the skier has to be prepared mentally to maintain form through the long winter with all the travelling it involves. So when you're reaching for your beach towel, think of the poor World Cup skiers loading their huge ski bags into vans and aeroplanes for another heavy summer's training!

If ski racing still sounds attractive, the best way to approach it is to join one of the racing clubs at your nearest dry ski slope, or to sign up with one of the long-established race training clubs which organise trips to the Alps in the winter holidays; the Ski Club of Great Britain can give information about these. Either way gives you the opportunity to compare your ability with others of your age and, equally important, to enjoy a new aspect of skiing – you don't have to be a World Cup champion to get an enormous amount of fun out of ski racing. If you do aim for the top then you'd better grit your teeth and start working hard right now. But don't forget still to enjoy your skiing!

Travel facts

In this final major chapter of the *Guide* we bring together all the names and numbers you're likely to need when you get down to arranging the practical details of your holiday – whether you take your car, buy a package or travel independently by public transport. It isn't just facts; in particular, the major section on insurance has clear buying guidance, and that on motoring has advice on how to deal with the extreme road and weather conditions you'll meet in the mountains. The chapter is broken down into the sections, some quite short, some quite substantial, listed below.

Insurance

As we explain in 'A Skiing Primer', if you're set on a particular package holiday you may not have much choice about the insurance you get. And these days the obvious differences between one policy and another may not seem huge. But the less obvious differences are not trivial – they may matter enough to steer you away from the tour operator you first thought of, or to make you decide to buy your insurance independently. In this section we outline the variations, so that you can weigh up the policies which are thrust at you. We take in turn each of the kinds of cover you can expect to find.

First, a bit of key terminology. Under many sections of a policy, the amount that's paid out in settlement of a claim will be less than the amount you've lost. The difference, called an *excess*, varies between policies and between sections, but is usually £10 to £25 per claim. Every separate incident is considered to be a separate claim. For example, if your ski bag is damaged on the journey out and you lose your ski poles at a later stage of the holiday, you will be making two claims, and you will have to bear two excesses; if your ski bag is damaged and your ski poles are lost as a result, the result is one claim.

We divide policies into those offered by tour operators and those sold separately – 'independent' policies. Where we say 'all policies', we mean all those we've looked at, which strictly speaking is not all but a great many. It's unlikely that you will come upon policies which do not follow the usual pattern, but it's vital to check that the policy you're about to buy suits **you**.

As well as setting out the reasons for which you'll be able to claim, a policy will have *exclusion clauses* – these tell you about circumstances in which the insurance company won't pay up. You should carefully check these exclusions before buying a policy in case there are any which might catch you out. You'll often find that you won't be covered if you take part in very risky sports – for example, ski-jumping, racing in major events, ice hockey or bob-sleigh riding. Other things to watch out for are exclusions relating to illnesses you've suffered from or for which you've been treated recently.

Although everyone should read policies carefully, there are two groups who should be particularly wary – those who are over 65 and those for whom pregnancy is a possibility. Some policies have an age limit, usually 70 or 75 years; others have an age exclusion in respect of medical and cancellation expenses only. Where pregnancy is concerned policies vary a lot. Some have no exclusions at all, others provide cover only if the pregnancy starts after the policy is taken out or is in the early stages when the holiday is to be taken. A few exclude all claims.

Claims for loss or theft of money (sometimes belongings as well) will normally be met only if the incident has been reported to an appropriate authority (usually the police) within 24 hours. Claims involving expenditure should always be supported by receipts. And claims must always be submitted within a reasonable time of your return.

Cancellation

What it's for To repay money you've paid in advance for a holiday you're unable to go on.

Do you need it? Yes, unless you're making no advance bookings.

Who offers it? All policies.

When it applies Most policies pay up if you are prevented from travelling by your own illness, or the illness or death of a close relative of yourself or of another member of your holiday party. Most pay if any member of the party is called for jury service or is required to appear in court as a witness. Some pay if you have to cancel because a close business associate or someone you plan to stay with while on holiday is ill, if you're made redundant or if your home is made uninhabitable by fire, flood or burglary. Look for a policy giving the widest possible cover and the fewest worrying exclusion clauses.

What you can claim Whatever you have paid out – minus an excess if you have paid the whole bill. (You don't get your insurance premium back of course.)

How much cover? Tour operators policies generally cover the cost of the holiday; others set a limit – often £1,000. Obviously you need to make sure that the limit is high enough to meet the full cost of your holiday.

Curtailment

What it's for To repay a proportion of money you've paid for a holiday you have to cut short, and extra costs arising from an early return home.

Do you need it? Yes, unless you're making no advance bookings.

Who offers it? All policies.

When it applies If you have to come home early for the kinds of reason set out under Cancellation.

What you can claim A proportion of the pre-paid cost of the holiday, according to the length of time on holiday you've lost, and reasonable additional expenses for travel and accommodation to get you home. Most policies have an excess.

How much cover? Generally, the same limits apply here as under Cancellation. With tour operator policies, a limit equal to the cost of the holiday may be too low if you have to fly back soon after you arrive. Narrow cash limits may be similarly inadequate – look for a limit of at least twice the holiday cost.

Medical expenses

What it's for To meet costs arising from illness or injury.

Do you need it? Yes, even in countries where there are good reciprocal health care agreements (see over the page).

Who offers it? All policies.

When it applies If you fall ill or injure yourself during the holiday, either on or off the slopes, or require emergency dental treatment.

What you can claim All treatment expenses – doctors' fees, hospital bills, prescription charges etc – plus any additional accommodation and travel costs resulting from your illness or injury, including mountain rescue in normal circumstances (see over the page). Most policies will not pay the additional cost of private-room accommodation in hospital unless your doctor thinks it is necessary.

In the event of death all policies will meet 'reasonable' costs for burial or cremation locally or for reasonable cost of transport of the body or ashes to the place of residence in the UK.

Some policies will not cover surgery or treatment which can reasonably be delayed until you return to the UK, where you can be treated under the NHS or your own medical bills insurance. Some policies, on the other hand, provide for any expenses incurred up to 12 months after the time when you are injured or fall ill – so whether you're treated on the spot or privately in Britain makes no difference.

How much cover? Anything from £10,000 to an unlimited amount. The smaller amounts of cover on offer will deal with the great majority of cases in Europe, but may not be enough for the few really nasty ones involving air ambulances staffed by high-powered medical teams. To be on the safe side (which is after all what insurance is about) we would recommend cover of £50,000. If you're going to North America you should have at least £500,000 – but since unlimited policies are available, why not take one? If you don't have sufficient cover, you will simply become personally liable for any costs incurred.

The limit on claims in the event of death is normally £1,000.

Hospital benefit

What it's for To cheer you up.

Do you need it? Not really.

Who offers it? Several policies.

When it applies If you have to spend at least 24 hours in hospital as a result of an injury or illness outside the UK.

What you can claim? A specified amount (usually £10, sometimes more) for every 24-hour period in hospital.

How much cover? Most policies set a limit to what they will pay – often £200.

Personal accident

What it's for To compensate you for disablement, or to compensate your heirs for your death.

Do you need it? Not as part of a skiing policy. If you think you need insurance against disability or death, you should have a policy which gives you this cover all the time.

Who offers it? Most policies, although with some it's an optional extra.

When it applies In the event of death, loss of a limb or an eye, or permanent total disablement. Most policies will pay compensation for disablement occurring up to twelve months after the date of the accident. Some also offer a weekly benefit for temporary total disablement.

What you can claim A fixed lump sum, according to the injury you suffer.

How much cover? The size of the lump sum varies considerably; it's usually at least £5,000 but can be as much as £25,000. Compensation for children (and in some policies, for elderly people) is much lower.

Mountain rescue

If you are caught in an avalanche, or lost on the mountain, the resort authorities will normally meet the cost of finding and resuing you. If it is your own fault, however, you will be liable for the very considerable costs incurred and these are not recoverable under insurance.

If a rescue team judges it necessary for you to be transported off the slopes by helicopter, you don't have much alternative, even if your policy won't cover the cost (of around £10 a minute). They are used fairly frequently in Switzerland, less often elsewhere because of environmental laws. You can buy helicopter insurance in most Swiss resorts if your own policy excludes it.

Free treatment abroad?

If you are in a country which is a member of the European Community you can get the same health treatment as a national of that country. This isn't necessarily free as it is in the UK – in France, for example, you have to pay any bill and claim back a proportion of it from the local sickness insurance office. To take advantage of these 'reciprocal' health agreements you'll need to take a form E111 with you – apply on the form in the DHSS leaflet SA30 around a month before you go away. Once you get your E111 it'll be valid for two years. If you don't have an E111 you can claim from the DHSS when you get back home so keep all your receipts and be prepared for a long wait.

In some other countries, both inside and outside Europe, you are entitled to free or cheap treatment on production of your British passport and/or NHS medical card. DHSS leaflet SA30 has details.

Reciprocal care agreements should not be regarded as a substitute for insurance – most ski-resort hospitals are privately run, and you've still got rescue and other costs to provide for. But taking the necessary documents to plug you in to the local health care scheme has the advantage that if you happen upon a public hospital you may be able to get treatment without having to produce much (or any) cash.

Personal liability

What it's for To meet claims made against you by others for damage to themselves or their property for which you are legally liable.

Do you need it? Yes and no: this sort of insurance is valuable at any time, so you really should have a permanent policy. Household contents insurance normally provides it.

Who offers it? All policies.

When it applies If an individual successfully makes a claim against you for damages. Many policies won't cover claims made by members of your own family or by someone you employ. And watch out if you hire a car – a skiing policy won't cover you for liability arising out of the use of a vehicle, so you must make sure you are adequately covered under the insurance you get with the rented car.

What you can claim Any damages awarded against you (and legal costs of disputing the claim), but not the costs of defending yourself in criminal proceedings.

How much cover Usually £500,000 but sometimes £250,000 or £1,000,000. We recommend that you have at least £500,000 of cover.

Personal money

What it's for To replace lost or stolen money, and other things which can be used in exchange for goods or services.

Do you need it? Yes, unless you have an existing policy which covers you all the time for such risks.

Who offers it All policies – though some include it within the Baggage and personal effects section.

When it applies If your cash, travellers' cheques, credit cards are stolen, lost or destroyed. Such things as air and other travel tickets, petrol coupons and vouchers will also be covered. Some specialist winter sports insurance policies specifically cover the loss of your lift pass, but this would otherwise be dealt with as a specialised form of travel ticket.

What you can claim The value of whatever you have lost.

How much cover? The limit of cover varies from £100 to £500, but most are in the £150 to £250 range. While this may not sound much, remember that there are special arrangements to replace travellers' cheques or credit cards if you lose them, so they should not need to be taken into account.

Baggage and personal effects

What it's for To replace lost or damaged belongings.

Do you need it? Probably, though many of your possessions may be already covered if you have a house contents and/or an all risks policy.

Who offers it? All policies.

When it applies If any of your possessions are lost, stolen or damaged – with certain exceptions. Contact lenses and documents are excluded by virtually all policies, and some won't pay if unattended baggage goes missing.

What you can claim Usually the actual value of what you lose (ie its second-hand value, not the cost of replacing it with something new).

How much cover? It's usually between £500 and £1,000. It's important to work out how much it would cost to replace your belongings should the whole lot be lost – it may be more than you think, particularly if you're relying on the holiday policy to cover such things as your jewellery and cameras as well as clothes and suitcases. And many policies also cover ski equipment in this section. Most policies have a limit on what will be paid for any one item, often somewhere in the £200 region. A pair of skis and ski sticks is usually counted as one item as is a camera together with its lenses, flash unit and so on. Some policies also have a limit to what they will pay out in total for valuables such as jewellery, watches, cameras and so on.

Delayed baggage

What it's for To tide you over until your delayed bags turn up.

Do you need it? It can certainly help.

Who offers it? Most policies.

When it applies If your baggage is delayed for 12 hours or more.

What you can claim The cost of essential items. If you have a tour operator policy, the rep should give you the necessary cash; if your baggage never turns up, the money you've been given will be deducted from your claim for the loss. If you have an independent policy, you will have to use your own money and claim it back on your return to the UK. If your skiing equipment is delayed you will be entitled under some policies to the cost of hiring replacements until it shows up.

How much cover? The limit on what you can claim ranges from £50 to £100.

Ski equipment

What it's for To replace lost or damaged ski equipment.

Do you need it? Yes, if ski equipment is excluded from cover under Baggage and personal effects; hired equipment is likely to be excluded even if your own equipment is not.

Who offers it? Some tour operators and specialist skiing policies; some have a separate ski equipment section, others include it as a subsection of Baggage and personal effects.

When it applies If your skis, ski sticks, bindings or ski boots are lost, stolen or damaged. Some policies which cover loss or theft of hired equipment will not cover *breakage* of hired skis.

What you can claim Some companies pay the cost of replacement, or repair if that is practicable, others pay only the market value, allowing for wear and tear. Some companies insist you bring broken skis home with you, so that they can satisfy themselves that they are not repairable. Although some companies say they will pay only for the one broken ski, in practice this is often not the case – you will be covered for the pair. If it's your own equipment that's lost or broken some policies will cover the cost of hiring replacements for the remainder of your holiday (as well as paying for a replacement set); if not you have to bear the cost of rental yourself – or buy new equipment out of your own pocket.

How much cover? Cover is usually limited to between £200 and £300. This is more than enough for a cheap set of equipment, but not for a flashy set. If you're taking your own skis it's worth looking for a policy which will pay for hire of replacement skis. If you're hiring skis make sure you won't have to pay for any damage or loss yourself.

Ski pack

What it's for To repay a proportion of what you have paid a tour operator in advance for a 'ski pack' (a package of equipment hire, lessons and lift pass) if you become unable to make use of it.

Do you need it? Worth having if you're buying a ski pack.

Who offers it? Some tour operators.

When it applies If you fall ill or are injured during the holiday.

What you can claim A proportion of the cost of the ski pack, depending on how long you spend out of action.

How much cover? Look for cover of at least the cost of the ski pack.

Travel delay

What it's for To compensate you for big delays in your journey.

Do you need it? It's less fuss than seeking compensation in other ways.

Who offers it? Most policies, although with some it's an optional extra.

When it applies If you're delayed for more than twelve hours – often only if the delay is for a specified reason – usually including strikes, mechanical breakdown and bad weather.

What you can claim A specified daily amount during the delay or, if you wish to cancel your holiday, the total cost of it.

How much cover? Usually £20 for the first 12 hours, £10 for each subsequent 12 hours, up to a maximum of £60. If you cancel your holiday, the limit of cover in the Cancellation section will apply.

Missed departure

What it's for To meet the costs which arise if you miss the flight out.

Do you need it? Seems worthwhile.

Who offers it? Mostly tour operator policies, and a few independent ones.

When it applies If public transport fails to deliver you to the airport or other departure point in time to join the booked trip – provided you allowed a reasonable time to get there. Some policies also cover you if you miss the flight because of a car accident or breakdown.

What you can claim The cost of extra transport to get to your resort, and accommodation if necessary.

How much cover It varies a lot and could be from as little as £150 to £500.

Interruption of transport

What it's for To compensate you if you're marooned in your resort.

Do you need it? Doubtful; it's the tour operator's responsibility to get you home once they've got you out to a resort.

Who offers it Several policies have variations on the same theme.

When it applies There are policies which will cover you for hi-jacks, avalanches, landslides, riots, strikes or civil commotions provided that they occur within the period of insurance. Some tour operators have a *weather extension* which covers you only if the difficulties are attributable to the weather. Several tour operators include something under other policy sections.

What you can claim What you have to spend while marooned, up to a limit.

How much cover? The cover limit varies from £100 to £300.

Tour organiser failure

What it's for Refund of advance payments if your operator goes bust.

Do you need it? No. The insurance applies only to circumstances in which you would get your money back anyway – though you may get it back more promptly from an insurance company.

Who offers it A few independent policies.

When it applies If the holiday you've booked has to be cancelled or cut short because the tour operator goes out of business – provided that you've booked with an ABTA member or a licensed operator (which means that the insurance company will get its money back in the end).

What you can claim Whatever you have paid out – or a proportion if you are already on holiday when the collapse occurs.

How much cover? Up to £1,000.

Withdrawal of services

What it's for To compensate you for a lack of services in your accommodation.

Do you need it? It's less fuss than suing your tour operator.

Who offers it? A few policies.

When it applies If there is no water or electricity in your room; no waiter service at meals; no hot meals are served; no chambermaid services.

What you can claim A daily amount, usually of £20, for as long as the services are missing.

How much cover? There is usually a maximum total payment of £200.

Snow guarantee

What it's for To meet the cost of getting to snow or lifts if your resort lacks either, or to compensate you for their absence.

Do you need it? Not essential. You can claim only in extreme conditions.

Who offers it? Only a few policies but many tour operators now have a separate snow guarantee.

When it applies If all the lifts in the resort are shut and it's impossible to ski – either because of the weather or because of a shortage of snow.

What you can claim The cost of getting to a nearby resort – in practice your operator will probably arrange for transport, ski school (where appropriate) and lift pass for a nearby resort, and no money changes hands. If that's not possible, some will pay compensation – often £15 a day.

How much cover? Unlimited.

National tourist offices

The national tourist office of a foreign country may be able to give you a lot of information, or only a little. The best will have full lists of accommodation, and detailed literature on individual resorts.

Andorran Delegation in Great Britain
63 Westover Road, London SW18 2RS;
✆ 01-874 4806.
Austrian National Tourist Office
30 St George Street, London W1R 9FA;
✆ 01-629 0461.
Canadian High Commission
Canada House, Trafalgar Square,
London SW1Y 5BJ; ✆ 01-629 9492.
French Government Tourist Office
178 Piccadilly, London W1V 0AL;
✆ 01-491 7622.
German National Tourist Office
61 Conduit Street, London W1R 0EN;
✆ 01-734 2600.

Italian State Tourist Office
3rd Floor, 1 Princes Street, London W1R
7RA; ✆ 01-408 1254.
Norwegian Tourist Board
20 Pall Mall, London SW1Y 5NE;
✆ 01-839 6255.
Scottish Tourist Board
23 Ravelston Terrace, Edinburgh EH4
3EU; ✆ 031-332 2433.
19 Cockspur Street,London SW1Y 5BL;
✆ 01-930 8661/3.
Spanish Tourist Office
57 St James's Street, London SW1A
1LD; ✆ 01-499 0901.
Swiss National Tourist Office
Swiss Centre, 1 New Coventry Street,
London W1V 8EE; ✆ 01-734 1921.
United States Travel and Tourism
22 Sackville Street, London W1X 2EA;
✆ 01-439 7433.
Yugoslav National Tourist Office
143 Regent Street, London W1R 8AE;
✆ 01-734 5243.

Public transport

Going by rail
You can travel directly to quite a number of ski resorts by rail – mostly long-established resorts; some in Austria are on a direct line from Calais, so you can get there without leaving the train except to cross the Channel. The new high-speed TGV trains make it possible to leave Paris after an early breakfast and get to many French resorts in time for lunch.

We list major resorts with railway stations, and give approximate journey times from London and the number of changes of train involved.

Andermatt One change, 19hr
Arosa One change, 18hr
Aviemore Direct, 10hr
Badgastein Direct, 21½hr
Chamonix One change, 21hr
Champery Two changes, 20½hr
(including TGV)
Davos One change, 18hr
Grindelwald Two changes, 17½hr
Gstaad Two changes, 18hr
Kitzbühel One change, 24hr
Klosters One change, 17½hr
Les Arcs One change, then cable-car
from Bourg St Maurice, 13hr

Mayrhofen Two changes, 24½hr
Mürren Three changes, 17½hr
St Anton Direct, 20hr
St Moritz One change, 19hr
Verbier One change, then cable-car
from Le Chable, 18½hr
Wengen Two changes, 17hr
Zell am See One change, 24hr
Zermatt One change, 19hr

Going by coach
Several of Europe's major coach companies have been brought together under one organisation, Supabus, which connects with National Express services from all over the UK. Destinations include several from which you could launch off into the Alps – eg Grenoble, Chamonix, Geneva (all with 3 services a week) and Aosta (one service a week). Adult fares to the closer destinations are just over £40 single, single, around £75 return; children go for half price. Tickets, single or return, can be bought from Supabus offices in London (Victoria), Birmingham, Bristol, Cardiff, Leeds, Liverpool, Manchester, Newcastle, Nottingham and Sheffield; or at any one of 3,300 National Express agents.

Going by air

Quite apart from the fact that most package holidays employ air transport, there are many ways in which an independent traveller can fly out to ski. There are scheduled air services to many airports within striking distance of the skiing regions, and provided you look for 'promotional' fares (which have inconvenient conditions attached – advance booking for example) the cost need not be prohibitive. But it will almost always be cheaper to buy a seat on a charter flight from a tour operator – many firms listed in the Package Holidays section of 'Travel facts' sell seats on their flights with no accommodation strings attached, making use of loopholes in the regulations which are meant to prevent this. Some of these firms offer what amounts to a scheduled service, with several flights a week to their major destination airports.

UK airports

When departure day arrives, it's always worth giving your departure airport a call to check that your flight is not delayed. We give the phone number of the information service, and an outline of the public transport links.

Belfast Aldergrove ✆ (0232) 229271 Airport buses run from Great Victoria Street Bus Station.
Birmingham ✆ 021-767 5511 Airport buses run from High Street and Bull Ring Bus Station, and from Coventry. New passenger transit system links airport with Birmingham International railway station.
Bristol ✆ (027587) 4441 Buses from Temple Meads railway station and the bus station, and from Weston-super-Mare.
Cardiff-Wales ✆ (0446) 711211 Airport buses from Llantwit Major and Cardiff bus stations.
East Midlands near Derby ✆ (0332) 810611 Buses from many places including Nottingham, Loughborough, Derby, Leicester.
Edinburgh ✆ 031-333 1000 Airport buses from Waverley Bridge.
Glasgow ✆ 041-887 1111 Airport buses from Buchanan and Anderston bus stations.
Leeds and Bradford ✆ (0532) 503431 Buses from Bradford Interchange and Harrogate bus station.
London: Gatwick ✆ (0293) 28822 Fast trains from Victoria station, and normal ones from London Bridge; Greenline buses from Victoria coach station. Buses from many points in the south.
London: Heathrow Terminal 1 (British Airways and UK flights) ✆ 01-745 7702; Terminal 2 (other European airlines) ✆ 01-745 7115; Terminal 3 (inter-continental flights) ✆ 01-745 7412, departures ✆ 01-745 7067 On the London Underground system (Piccadilly Line); Railair coach link from railway stations at Reading, Woking. Airport buses from central London railway stations – Victoria (A1), Paddington (A2), Euston (A3); Greenline buses from Victoria coach station.
Luton ✆ (0582) 36061 Bus services from London: St Pancras, Victoria; St Albans, Luton railway station, Luton bus station.
Manchester ✆ 061-437 5233 Airport buses from Manchester: Victoria railway station, Chorlton Street bus station, Piccadilly railway station; also buses from Stockport and other towns.
Newcastle ✆ (0632) 860966 Airport buses from Newcastle Central station and Eldon Square Bus Concourse.

Foreign airports

We list the transport links you're likely to want to use if you're travelling independently. On a package you'll normally be transferred to the resort by your operator. Even going independently, you may be able to arrange a seat on a package transfer coach going to your resort.

Bern Bus connection to Bern railway station.
Geneva: Cointrin Airport buses to Geneva and Lausanne stations. Bus links with several ski resorts in the Savoie.
Lyon Airport buses to Lyons Perrache station, and buses to Tarentaise towns and resorts.
Milan Airport buses from Linate, buses from Malpensa; both to town centre.
Munich Airport bus to Munich railway station, and buses to Kitzbühel, Innsbruck and the Dolomites.
Nice Airport buses to Menton, Monte Carlo, Nice, Cannes, and buses direct to Isola 2000 and other resorts.
Salzburg Airport buses to Salzburg railway station, and buses to Kitzbühel.
Turin Airport buses to town centre.
Venice Airport buses to town centre.
Zurich Train to Zurich railway station, and buses to western Austrian resorts.

Going by car

Whenever you're planning to take your car on the Continent there are a number of things to bear in mind:

- always carry official documents including driving licence, vehicle registration document, insurance certificate and passport
- make sure you are fully insured; to be sure that you are covered as fully abroad as at home, you need a Green Card from your insurance company
- display an approved GB sign on the back of your vehicle
- remember that seat belts are compulsory in many countries on the Continent, and that children are not allowed in front seats in many countries
- carry an advance warning triangle – either compulsory or recommended for most Continental countries
- adjust or adapt your headlights for driving abroad
- carry a good map or road atlas
- get your car serviced well in advance of departure
- carry a first aid kit in Austria – it's compulsory
- fit an exterior rear view mirror on the left hand side of the car – valuable anywhere on the Continent, compulsory in Italy.

Preparations

When going to the mountains in winter, the weather and road conditions you're likely to meet make special preparations necessary:

- if your car engine is water-cooled, make sure the anti-freeze is strong enough; this is particularly important if the car is going to be left outside at night, when the temperature may drop as low as –30 degrees C
- don't forget you'll need a strong solution of winter screenwash, too
- if you have any doubts at all about the condition of your battery, have it tested before you set off; and consider equipping yourself with thick copper 'jump leads' so that you can start your engine from another car's battery
- check the car handbook to see whether thinner oil is recommended for very low-temperature conditions, and whether you need to adjust the engine air intake

- if you can arrange it, get some experience on a skid pan before you go – on snow-bound roads in the Alps, your car will spend a good part of its time skidding in one way or another
- if your car's headlights throw a lot of light upwards (rather than having a very sharp top edge to their beam) consider fitting special fog lamps – night driving in falling snow is a nightmare without good lights
- take a small shovel for getting out of roadside drifts; if you have a tow rope, take that, too.

Snow-chains

If you expect to find snow on the pistes in your resort, it's reasonable to expect snow on the roads as well. And if there is snow on the roads you'll need chains for the car's driving wheels – not only to keep going on hills but also to satisfy the local laws. (In Austria, the police have a habit of obliging chainless motorists to buy chains from them, at punitive prices.) Chains tend to be expensive in Britain; in and around the Alps they're easy to find at much lower prices (at least in common car sizes) in hypermarkets and service stations. You can hire chains from the AA.

You should put your chains on before they become absolutely necessary; if you wait until the car slithers to a standstill you may find yourself putting them on in an acutely inconvenient and dangerous place, perhaps blocking the road. It helps if you practise putting them on as soon as you buy them – not only to make sure that you know how, but also to make sure that you've got all the bits.

You can keep chains on while driving on ordinary roads, but only for short periods and at very low speeds – the limit should be specified in the instructions. People who live in or near the Alps avoid the tedious and messy business of repeatedly applying and removing chains in one of two ways. The first is by fitting special winter tyres with chunky treads and often with metal studs; these are meant to be used at higher speeds on normal roads, but aren't a practical (or economic) proposition for a trip across the Continent. The second is by owning a four-wheel-drive car (normally also fitted with chunky tyres); four-wheel-drive is a huge advantage, making chains unnecessary in all but the most extreme circumstances and giving much more control when going downhill, where chains don't help all that much – particularly on a rear-wheel-drive car. If you have a choice of front- and rear-wheel-drive cars, take the front-wheel-drive.

In the mountains

Once you've arrived there are several ways in which you can diminish the risk that you'll be caught out by the cold or the road conditions:

● when parking the car overnight, try to leave it in a place where it (or at least the engine) will be sheltered from the wind, and where you can safely leave the handbrake off (so that it doesn't get frozen on); leave the car with first or reverse gear engaged
● pull the wipers away from the windscreen so that they don't get frozen in position
● don't disregard road closures: a closed road which looks passable may be closed because of avalanche danger
● don't be tempted to drive in après-ski boots unless your car has agricultural pedals
● drive at about half the speed you reckon would be safe – especially downhill
● when starting off or going uphill on snow, use the highest possible gear to minimise the risk of the driving wheels spinning.

Alpine passes

Many Alpine passes are blocked by snow during the winter months, but some are kept open by snow-ploughs; we list below major passes which are normally kept open.

Aprica (Italy), Bayard (France), Bracco (Italy), Brenner (Austria–Italy), Brunig (Switzerland), Bussang (France), Croix-Haute (France), Faucille (France), Fern (Austria), Forclaz (Switzerland), Fugazze (Italy), Gerlos (Austria), Ibaneta Roncesvalles (France–Spain), Jaun (Switzerland), Julier (Switzerland), Katschberg (Austria), Loibi (Austria–Yugoslavia), Maloja (Switzerland), Mauria (Italy), Mendola (Italy), Monte Croce di Comelico (Italy), Montgenèvre (France–Italy), Mosses (Switzerland), Ofen (Switzerland), Peyresourde (France), Port d'Aspet (France),

Potschen (Austria), Resia (Italy–Austria), Restefond (France), Seeberg (Austria–Yugoslavia), Semmering (Austria), Sestriere (Italy), Somport (France–Spain), Tenda (Italy–France), Thurn (Austria), Tonale (Italy), Toses (Spain), Turracher Hohe (Austria), Wurzen (Austria–Yugoslavia) and Zirer Berg (Austria).

Tunnels

There are several tunnels which help you avoid making a detour or travelling over a mountain pass. Some but not all charge a toll. We list below the major tunnels, together with the one-way toll, where relevant.

Frejus France–Italy FF72.
Mont Blanc France–Italy – wheel chains occasionally required for the approaches to the tunnel during winter FF72.
Grand St Bernard Switzerland–Italy – wheel chains may be needed in the winter SF22.50
St Gotthard Switzerland – wheel chains needed for the approaches but are not allowed within the tunnel.
San Benardino Switzerland.
Arlberg Austria AS140.
Felbertauern Austria AS100 in winter.
Glelnalm Austria AS120.
Katschberg Austria AS120.

In addition there are the following rail tunnels; cars are transported through the tunnel on a train.

Lotschberg Kandersteg–Goppenstein SF28; Kandersteg–Brig SF40.
Simplon Brig–Iselle – SF37.
Lotschberg + Simplon Kandersteg–Iselle SF67.

Motorway tolls

You have to pay tolls on most motorways in France, Italy and Spain, and on sections in Austria and Yugoslavia. These can add up to quite an amount over a long journey (particularly in France) so it's worth doing your sums. It may be cheaper (but take longer) to drive on non-toll roads and stay the night on the way. If you are using toll roads make sure you have some of local currency – toll booths don't accept travellers' cheques. In Switzerland, foreign motorists using motorways must display a toll disc which costs SF30 at the border (also available from motoring organisations in the UK).

Continental ferries

When planning winter crossings to the
Continent, bear in mind the possibility of
bad weather. If there are heavy seas,
hovercraft services are more liable to
interruption than conventional ferries;
while long ferry crossings can seem (or
even *be*) interminable. Return fares in
winter 1984–85 for two adults in a typical
saloon are £80 to £120 on the short and
medium-length crossings to France and
Belgium. We list addresses, phone
numbers and routes for companies
operating ferry and hovercraft services
to the Continent. *Holiday Which?* usually
reports on ferry fares in its March issue;
in 1984 and 1985 the reports covered
quality of service as well.

Sealink British Ferries PO Box 29,
Victoria Station, London SW1V 1JX; ✆
01-834 8122. Dover–Calais; Dover–
Dunkerque; Dover–Oostende;
Folkestone–Boulogne; Harwich–Hoek;
Newhaven–Dieppe; Weymouth–
Cherbourg.
Townsend Thoresen Russell Street,
Dover, Kent CT16 1QB; ✆ (0304)
203388. Dover–Boulogne; Dover–
Calais; Dover–Zeebrugge; Felixstowe–
Zeebrugge; Portsmouth–Cherbourg;
Portsmouth–Le Havre.
Brittany Ferries The Brittany Centre,
Wharf Road, Portsmouth PO2 8RU;
✆ (0705) 827701. Portsmouth–St Malo;
Plymouth–Roscoff; Plymouth–
Santander.
Hoverspeed International Hoverport,
Ramsgate, Kent CT12 5HS; ✆ (0843)
594881. Dover–Calais; Dover–
Boulogne.
Norfolk Line Atlas House, Southgates
Road, Great Yarmouth, Norfolk NR30
3LN; ✆ (0493) 856133. Great Yarmouth–
Scheveningen.
North Sea Ferries King George Dock,
Hedon Road, Hull HU9 5QA; ✆ (0482)
795141. Hull–Rotterdam; Hull–
Zeebrugge.
Olau Line Olau-Line Terminal,
Sheerness, Kent ME12 1SN; ✆ (0795)
666666. Sheerness–Vlissingen.
Sally Line 54 Harbour Parade,
Ramsgate, Kent CT11 8LN; ✆ (0843)
595522. Ramsgate–Dunkerque.
DFDS Danish Seaways Scandinavia
House, Parkeston Quay, Harwich, Essex
CO12 4QG; ✆ (0255) 554681. Harwich–
Esbjerg; Harwich–Gothenburg;
Harwich–Hamburg; Harwich–Cuxhaven;
Newcastle–Esbjerg/Gothenburg.

Motorail services

You can get your car to the Alps by
putting it on a car-carrying train, but
getting to the starting point may involve
quite a bit of driving; few routes begin at
the Channel ports (see below). It's
advisable to book as early as possible –
up to six months in advance – to be sure
of getting on. Below we list some typical
services. In brackets we give the
number of services per week, where it is
regular. Then we give second-class
return fares for winter 1984–85; there is a
supplement of £6.10 per person (one
way) for a couchette, about £15.90 per
person for a berth in a three-person
sleeper. All our examples, with the
exception of the Düsseldorf and Köln to
Munich routes (which are day services)
have couchettes and sleepers. For more
information on these and other routes,
contact British Rail.

Route	Couple	Family
	£	£
Köln–Munich (3–4)	157	184
Hamburg–Innsbruck (1)	347	390
Düsseldorf–Villach	345	387
Paris–Milan	237	263
Hamburg–Chur (1)	363	405
Amiens–St Gervais (1)	140	195
Paris–St Gervais (7)	115	160
Paris–Moutiers (3)	112	155
Paris–Grenoble (3)	110	153
Paris–Narbonne (1)	147	205
Calais–Nice (7)	377	452
Paris–Nice (7)	184	256

Road maps

We list below the maps recommended
by *Holiday Which?*. We list them in price
order (cheapest first) and give the scale.

THE ALPS
Kümmerly + Frey: Alpine Countries 1:1
million, Alpine Roads 1:500,000

FRANCE
national maps (all 1:1 million)
Recta-Foldex, Michelin, IGN,
Geographia International, Hallwag.
regional maps
Michelin 1:200,000, Recta-Foldex
Cart'Index 1:250,000, IGN Red Series
1:250,000

note *The Holiday Which? Guide to
France* is an indispensable aid to
making the most of a journey across the
country.

ITALY
national maps
Michelin 1:1 million, Freytag & Berndt 1:650,000, Shell-Mair Special 1:750,000, TCI Carta Stradale 1:800,000, Kümmerly + Frey 1:500,000
regional maps
TCI Carta Automobilistica 1:200,000 £3.95
TCI Carta Turistica 1:400,000 £3.70

AUSTRIA
national maps
Michelin 1:400,000, Freytag & Berndt 1:500,000
regional maps
Freytag & Berndt: Grosse Strassenkarte 1:300,000, Touring Atlas 1:250,000

SWITZERLAND
national maps
Kümmerly + Frey/Swiss Touring Club 1:300,000

Motoring organisations

The two main motoring organistions – the AA and RAC – offer various services to members (eg advice on route-planning and road conditions). They and several other organisations also offer insurance against some of the cost and inconvenience of breakdowns and accidents abroad.

Breakdown insurance is an expensive way of buying peace of mind, but you may feel it's worthwhile – particularly in winter, when roads are at their most dangerous and cars at their least reliable. Some of the breakdown insurance deals on offer can (or must) include personal insurance for medical expenses and so on.

Most of the following are included in all the policies we looked at, though the amounts you can claim vary from company to company:

● assistance if you break down either in the UK or abroad including towing to, and storage in, a garage
● emergency labour charges
● the cost of despatching any spare parts, including communication expenses but not the cost of the parts themselves
● additional hotel and travel expenses
● hire of replacement vehicle
● all necessary costs to bring your vehicle home but not including cost of repairs or sea passage
● chauffeur to drive vehicle home if only driver is medically unfit

● legal cover, including bail bond

In addition, both the AA and RAC offer emergency credit vouchers.

Below we give addresses and phone numbers of companies offering breakdown cover, with premiums.

Automobile Association (AA), Fanum House, Basing View, Basingstoke, Hampshire; ✆ (0256) 20123. Their 5 star service costs £18.50 for 31 days. There's an extra charge of £2.50 for non-members.
Royal Automobile Club (RAC), RAC House, Landsdowne Road, Croydon, Surrey; ✆ 01-686 2525. They have a Travellers' Bond; the Vehicle Protection costs £20.50 for standard cover (31 days), £27 for de luxe (3 months). There's an extra charge of £2.50 for non-members.
Europ Assistance, Europ Assistance House, 252 High Street, Croydon, Surrey CR0 1NF; ✆ 01-680 1234. Their Motoring Emergency Service costs £24 for 13–23 days, plus £3.30 for each additional week or part thereof.
National Breakdown Recovery Club, Cleckheaton Road, Low Moor, Bradford, West Yorkshire BD12 0ND; ✆ (0274) 671299. They offer vehicle protection as part of an insurance package – you have to take out their medical cover as well. For a vehicle and two passengers it costs £21 for 10–17 days, £24.50 for 18–23 days, £27.50 for 24–31 days, plus £4 for each additional week.
Mondial Assistance, 3 Church Road, Croydon, Surrey CR0 1SG; ✆ 01-686 2444. Their Motorists Emergency Service costs £23.20 for 11–17 days, £26.40 for 18–31 days.
Red Rovers Motorists Association, 55–57 Albert Street, Rugby, Warwickshire CV21 2SG; ✆ (0788) 74391. Their Motorsafe Emergency Service costs £21.50 for 18 days, £26 for 31 days.
The Caravan Club Ltd., East Grinstead House, East Grinstead, West Sussex RH19 1UA; ✆ (0342) 26944. Their Red Pennant Foreign Touring Service (from £35 for up to 31 days) is available only to members.

Virtually all these organisations charge an additional fee (£4.00 to £8.00) if you are towing a caravan or trailer.

Package holidays

The resorts section of the *Guide* contains lists of companies offering package holidays to each resort. The lists consist of two- and three-letter codes, and the operators are set out here in code order.

We have listed only those operators whose holidays are bonded, so that clients' pre-payments are without doubt protected in the event of the financial failure of the company. The letters ABTA after the name and address signify that the operator is a member of the Association of British Travel Agents, which means that their holidays are available through high-street travel agents. The letters ATOL signify that the operator has a licence from the Civil Aviation Authority to run air package holidays using charter flights.

Many operators sell flight seats without the other components of a package holiday, and indeed this list includes a number of companies which do not sell proper packages at all – their business is selling charter flight seats which formally count as packages.

Many operators whose business is holidays by air or coach will give you a reduced price if you drive out in your own car.

There are many agencies which have self-catering accommodation to let independently rather than as part of a package holiday. We list the major ones in the ski market after the tour operators.

At the end of this whole section, on page 470, is an alphabetical index of operators and their codes.

AA Alpine Adventure Club
91 Wembley Park, Middlesex HA9 8HF
✆ 01-200 6080 / 903 4447
Telex 916196 ADLIB
ATOL, ABTA
Recent off-shoot of Ski Val, operating holidays for schools, groups and clubs. Their prices include instruction and equipment hire. **Resorts** Only one: Tignes les Boisses, France. **Accommodation** Hotels which are run along the lines of staffed chalets. **Travel** Air, coach. UK Airports: Gatwick, Glasgow, Manchester. Coach departures: London. **Ski guides** No.

AH Andorra Holidays
PO Box 2, Dalbeattie
DG5 4NT, Scotland
✆ (038778) 684 Telex 776146 BARBND
ATOL
First offered a programme during 1983–84. Also sell flight seats. **Resorts** Arinsal in Andorra. **Accommodation** Hotel, chalet and self-catering. **Travel** Air, coach. UK airports: London, Manchester. Coach departures: London. **Ski guides** No.

AT Activity Travel
12 Raeburn Place, Edinburgh EH4 1HN
✆ (031) 332 9457/8
Telex 72165 TELEX G ATT ACTIVITY
ATOL
Started operating holidays in Scotland but now offer the Alps too. They also sell flight seats. **Resorts** La Clusaz, Les Deux Alpes, Val Thorens in France, plus Verbier in Switzerland. **Accommodation** Hotels, self-catering apartments, staffed chalets. **Travel** Air, coach. UK airports: Edinburgh, Gatwick, Manchester. Coach departures: Scotland. **Ski Guides** Yes.

AU Austro Tours
10 Spencer Street, St Albans,
Herts AL3 5EG
✆ (0727) 38191 Telex 298822 AUSTRO
ATOL, ABTA
Part of the St Albans Travel Service Group. Also sell flight seats. **Resorts** 29, all in Austria – in all mountain areas. **Accommodation** Hotels, pensions, self-catering apartments. **Travel** Air. UK airports: Gatwick, Heathrow, Luton. **Ski guides** No.

BL Bladon Lines
56 Putney High Street
London SW15 1SF
✆ 01-785 2200 Telex 295221 SKIBLT
Personal callers: 309 Brompton Road,
London SW3 2DY
ATOL, ABTA
Sell 'a la carte' tailored holidays and flight seats as well as packages. **Resorts** Many in France, Switzerland and Austria, plus Courmayeur in Italy, Aspen and Vail in USA. **Accommodation** Mainly staffed chalets, club-style hotels, budget chalets; also hotels, pensions, self-catering apartments. **Travel** Air. UK airports: Gatwick, Glasgow, Luton, Manchester. **Ski guides** Yes.

BS Blue Sky Holidays
Blue Sky House, London Road,
East Grinstead, West Sussex
RH19 1HU.
✆ (0342) 28211 Telex 95227 BLUSKI
Glasgow: ✆ 041-248 2791
Manchester: ✆ 061-834 2791
ATOL, ABTA
Part of the British Caledonian Travel
Group; they also sell flight seats.
Resorts Many in Austria, Italy, France
and Switzerland, plus Liechtenstein.
Accommodation Hotels, pensions, self-
catering apartments. **Travel** Air. UK
airports: Gatwick, Glasgow, Manchester.
Ski guides Yes.

BT Best Skiing Holidays
31 Topsfield Parade, London N8
✆ 01-341 7171 Telex 25302 GRECIA
ATOL, ABTA
Part of the Grecian Holiday group. Also
sell flight seats. **Resorts** Seven in
Austria, three in Switzerland.
Accommodation Hotels, pensions,
rooms, self-catering apartments and
chalets; staffed chalets in Switzerland.
Travel Air. UK airports: Gatwick, Luton,
Manchester. **Ski guides** No.

BV Beach Villas
8 Market Passage,
Cambridge CB2 3QR.
✆ (0223) 311113 Telex 817428 BCHVLA
ATOL, ABTA
Established operators of summer villa
holidays who have been offering skiing
holidays for several years. They also sell
flight seats. **Resorts** Arinsal in Andorra,
Meribel in France, Verbier in
Switzerland. **Accommodation** Staffed
chalets, plus self-catering apartments,
hotel in Verbier and Meribel. **Travel** Air.
UK airports: Gatwick, Manchester. **Ski
guides** No.

CA Cavalier Holidays
39 Greenwich Church Street
London SE10 9BL
✆ 01-858 8233
ATOL
Sell flight seats to Milan and Munich.
Travel UK airports: Gatwick, Luton.

CB Canterbury Travel
248 Streatfield Road, Kenton, Harrow,
Middlesex HA3 9BY.
✆01-206 0411 Telex 923062 CANTRV
ATOL, ABTA
Sell flight seats as well as packages.
Resorts Seven, all in Austria.
Accommodation Hotels. **Travel** Air,

coach. UK airports: Heathrow. Coach
departures: Birmingham, Dover,
London, Wolverhampton. **Ski guides** No.

CC Club Continental
219 South Street, Romford,
Essex RM1 1QL
✆ (0708) 752222 Telex 8956938 XIIISL
ATOL, ABTA
Specialists in holidays for 18- to 32-year-
olds, who offered skiing for the first time
in 1984–85. They also sell flight seats.
Resorts La Massona in Andorra.
Accommodation Hotels. **Travel** Air,
coach. UK airports: Gatwick,
Manchester. Coach departures:
Birmingham, London, Manchester. **Ski
guides** Yes.

CH Crystal Holidays
Alexandra House, 138-140 Alexandra
Road, Wimbledon, London SW19 7JY
✆ 01-879 0555 Telex 265284 CRYHOL
ATOL, ABTA
Resorts Several in Austria, plus La
Plagne, Tignes and Villard de Lans in
France. **Accommodation** Hotels, club
chalets, self-catering apartments. **Travel**
Air, coach. UK airports: Gatwick, Luton.
Coach departures: London. **Ski guides**
No.

CHA Car Holidays Abroad
13A Bull Plain, Hertford,
Herts SG14 1DY
✆ (0992) 554355/7
Telex 817460 CAHOL
ABTA
Resorts Chamonix, Avoriaz and Les
Menuires in France. **Accommodation**
Hotels, self-catering apartments. **Travel**
Own car or they can arrange flights. **Ski
guides** No.

CI Citalia Holidays
Marco Polo House, 3 Lansdowne Road,
Croydon, Surrey CR9 1LL
✆ 01-686 5533 Telex 8812133 CITCRO
ATOL, ABTA
Italian state-owned company; will tailor-
make holidays as well as selling
packages. **Resorts** Ten, all in Italy.
Accommodation Hotels, self-catering
apartments. **Travel** Air. UK airports:
Gatwick, Heathrow. **Ski guides** No.

CL Club 18-30
Academic House, 24-28 Oval Road,
London NW1 7DE
✆ 01-485 4141/ 267 4311
Telex 295440 CLUB A
Bradford: ✆ (0274) 760077

ATOL, ABTA
Part of the Intasun group; operate cost-conscious holidays for 18- to 30-year-olds. **Resorts** Eight in Austria and three in Italy, plus Montgenevre in France, Sol Y Nieve in Spain and Sinaia in Rumania. **Accommodation** Hotels, pensions, staffed chalets. **Travel** Air, coach. UK airports: Gatwick, Heathrow, Luton, Manchester. Coach departures: Birmingham, Bristol, Leeds, London, Manchester. **Ski guides** No.

CM Club Mediterranee
106-108 Brompton Road, London SW3 1JJ
✆ 01-581 4766 Telex 299221 CLBMED
ATOL, ABTA
A French-owned company, based in Paris. Their holidays are all-inclusive, covering most things from full-board accommodation to lift passes and ski instruction. **Resorts** Six in France and eight in Switzerland, plus Sestriere in Italy and Copper Mountain in USA. **Accommodation** Hotels with twin, 3- or 4-bedded rooms. Few singles. **Travel** Usually air to Paris, then train; some flights to Geneva. UK airports: Gatwick, Heathrow. **Ski guides** No (but instruction included in cost of holiday).

CR Cresta Holidays
Six Acre House, Town Square, Sale, Cheshire M33 1SN
✆ 061-962 9226 Telex 667171 CRESTA
ATOL, ABTA
Sell flight seats to Basel, Geneva, Grenoble, Lyons, Milan, Munich, Nice, Rome, Turin, Venice, Zurich. **Travel** UK airports: Gatwick, Heathrow, Manchester.

CW Club Mark Warner
20 Kensington Church Street, London W8 4EP
✆ 01-938 1851 Telex 24304 SKIMWT
ATOL, ABTA
Resorts St Anton in Austria, Meribel and Val d'Isère in France, Selva in Italy and Verbier in Switzerland. **Accommodation** Club-style hotels, staffed chalets. **Travel** Air. UK airports: Edinburgh, Gatwick, Manchester. **Ski guides** Yes.

DE DER Travel Service
15 Orchard Street, London W1H OAY
✆ 01-486 4593 Telex 21707 DERLDN
ATOL, ABTA
In addition to their packages, they 'tailor-make' holidays and also sell flight seats. **Resorts** Three in Germany, three in Austria. **Accommodation** Hotels, pensions, private houses. **Travel** Air. UK airports: Heathrow. **Ski guides** No.

ED Edwards Ski Holidays
861 Green Lanes, Winchmore Hill, London N21 2QS
✆ 01-360 9241 Telex 27606 EDWARD
ATOL, ABTA
Sell coach seats as well as packages. **Resorts** Four in Austria, one each in Italy, Liechtenstein. **Accommodation** Hotels, pensions, private houses. **Travel** Air, coach. UK airports: Gatwick, Heathrow. Coach departures: Birmingham, Coventry, Dover, London, Manchester. **Ski guides** No.

EN Enterprise Wintersports
1 Wardour Street, London W1V 3HE
✆ 01-439 7611 Telex 299738 FLAIR
ATOL, ABTA
Operated by British Airways. Sell flight seats as well as packages. **Resorts** Many in Austria, six in France, four in Italy, plus Switzerland, Spain, Bulgaria. **Accommodation** Hotels, pensions, self-catering apartments. **Travel** Air. UK airports: Gatwick, Heathrow, Luton, Manchester. **Ski guides** Yes.

FH Falcon Holidays
190 Campden Hill Road, London W8 7TH
✆ 01-221 0088 Telex 22535 WESELL
Manchester: ✆ 061-831 7000
Glasgow: ✆ 041-204 0242
ATOL, ABTA
Sell flights to Basel, Berne, Geneva, Lyons, Milan, Munich, Nice, Rome, Turin, Venice, Zurich. **Travel** UK airports: Birmingham, East Midlands, Edinburgh, Gatwick, Glasgow, Heathrow, Manchester.

FL French Leave Ski France
21 Fleet Street, London EC4Y 1AA
✆ 01-583 8333 Telex 24438 TULPNT
ATOL, ABTA
Under same management as Maeva (see Letting agencies). **Resorts** 23, all in France. **Accommodation** Hotels, self-catering apartments. **Travel** Air, coach, rail. UK airports: Gatwick, Heathrow. Coach departures: London. **Ski guides** No.

FR Freedom Holidays
224 King Street, London W6 ORA
✆ 01-741 4471 Telex 892928 FREDOM
Manchester: ✆ 061-236 0019
ATOL

Sell cost-conscious holidays direct to the public. They also sell flight seats. **Resorts** Encamp, Soldeu in Andorra. **Accommodation** Hotels, self-catering apartments. **Travel** Air. UK airports: Gatwick, Manchester. **Ski guides** Yes.

FS Flair Savers
1 Wardour Street, London W1V 3HE
℘ 01-434 2451 Telex 299738 FLAIR
Glasgow: ℘ 041-248 3191
ATOL, ABTA
Operated by British Airways. They sell flights to Geneva, Milan, Munich, Rome, Turin, Zurich. **Travel** UK airports: Gatwick, Luton, Manchester.

FT French Travel Service
Francis House, Francis Street
London SW1P 1DE
℘ 01-828 8131/ 9152
Telex 919354 FTSLON
ATOL, ABTA
Resorts Eight, all in France.
Accommodation Hotels, self-catering apartments. **Travel** Air, rail. UK airports: Gatwick. **Ski guides** No.

GB Good Buy/Transac
246 Kensington High Street,
London W8 6NF
℘ 01-602 5044 Telex 8813076
TRANSAC
ATOL, ABTA
Sell flight seats to Bern, Geneva, Lyons, Milan, Nice, Rome, Salzburg, Turin, Zurich. **Travel** UK airports: Gatwick, Heathrow.

GL Global Ski
Glen House, 200 Tottenham Court Road, London W1P OJP
℘ 01-323 3266/ 637 3333
Telex 21446 GLOBAL
ATOL, ABTA
Belfast: ℘ (0232) 244038
Cardiff: ℘ (0222) 390261
Glasgow: ℘ 041-204 0181
Manchester: ℘ 061-236 0209
Now part of the Intasun Leisure Group. They sell flight seats as well as packages. **Resorts** Many in Austria, plus Italy, France, Switzerland, Spain, Bulgaria. **Accommodation** Hotels, pensions, staffed chalets, self-catering apartments. **Travel** Air, coach. UK airports: Belfast, Gatwick, Luton, Manchester. Coach departures: London, Dover. **Ski guides** In Avoriaz and Livigno.

GT German Tourist Facilities
184/186 Kensington Church Street,
London W8 4DP
℘ 01-229 2474 Telex 263696 GTFL
ATOL, ABTA
Sell flight seats to Bern, Geneva, Munich, Salzburg, Zurich as well as packages. **Resorts** Four in Germany. **Accommodation** Hotels. **Travel** Air. UK airport: Gatwick. **Ski guides** No.

HA Hards Wintersports
20-24 High Street, Solihull, West
Midlands B91 3TB
℘ 021-704 5222 Telex 338276 HARDS
ATOL, ABTA
Sell holidays aimed at the cost-conscious skier. **Resorts** Seven in Austria, three in Italy, two in France. **Accommodation** Hotels, pensions, chalets, self-catering apartments, private houses. **Travel** Air, coach. UK airports: Birmingham, Gatwick, Manchester; Lydd (air/coach). **Ski guides** No.

HM Hourmont Total Ski
Brunel House, Newfoundland Road,
Bristol BS2 9LU
℘ (0272) 426961 Telex 44817 HOURMT
ATOL, ABTA
Have a large programme of holidays for school parties. In 1983–84 they introduced a second programme, budget skiing for groups, under the banner Hourmont Total Ski. Instruction, equipment hire and lift passes are included in the cost of all holidays. **Resorts** Austria, Italy, France, plus Les Crosets in Switzerland. **Accommodation** Hotels, pensions, catered apartments. **Travel** Air, coach. UK airports: Bristol, Gatwick, Glasgow, Luton, Manchester. Coach from schools. **Ski guides** No (but instruction included in cost of holiday).

HO Horizon Holidays
Broadway, Edgbaston, Five Ways,
Birmingham B15 1BB
℘ 021-632 6282
Telex 335641 HORIZON
ATOL, ABTA
Sell flight seats in addition to their package programme. **Resorts** Many in Austria, five in France, four in Italy. **Accommodation** Hotels, pensions, self-catering apartments, private houses. **Travel** Air. UK airports: Birmingham, Bristol, East Midlands, Gatwick, Glasgow, Luton, Manchester. **Ski guides** No.

IG Inghams Travel
329 Putney Bridge Road,
London SW15 2PL
✆ 01-785 7777 Telex 25342 INGHAMS
ATOL, ABTA
Inghams now incorporates Swans, and
is part of Hotelplan – the tour-operating
subsidiary of giant Swiss company
Migros. They sell flight seats as well as
packages. **Resorts** Over 20 in Austria;
14 in Switzerland, 6 in Italy, 5 in France,
plus Spain, Bulgaria, Romania,
Yugoslavia. **Accommodation** Hotels,
pensions, self-catering apartments,
private houses, catered chalet in
Chamonix. **Travel** Air. UK airports:
Birmingham, Edinburgh, Gatwick,
Glasgow, Heathrow, Luton, Manchester,
Newcastle, Stansted. **Ski guides** No.

IS Intasun Skyworld
52 Grosvenor Gardens,
London SW1W OAU
✆ 01-730 0299
Telex 8950133 SKYWOLD
ATOL, ABTA
Sell flight seats to Geneva, Milan,
Munich, Turin. **Travel** UK airports:
Gatwick, Luton, Manchester.

IT Intasun Skiscene
Intasun House, 2 Cromwell Avenue
Bromley, Kent BR2 9AQ
✆ 01-290 0511 Telex 896089 INTASN
Bradford: ✆ (0274) 736403
ATOL, ABTA
Sell flight seats as well as packages.
Resorts Many in Austria, five in Italy, plus
France, Switzerland and Spain.
Accommodation Hotels, pensions, self-
catering apartments, private houses.
Travel Air. UK airports: Gatwick, Luton,
Manchester. **Ski guides** No.

JH James Hill Travel
1 Duckworth Lane, Bradford, West Yorks
BD9 5ER
✆ (0274) 491151 Telex 51634 JHTRAV
ATOL, ABTA
Sell flight seats to Basel, Geneva, Lyons,
Milan, Nice, Rome, Turin, Venice. **Travel**
UK airports: Heathrow; Manchester
(Milan only).

JM John Morgan Travel
Meon House, College Street
Petersfield, Hampshire GU32 3JN
✆ (0730) 68621 Telex 86181 MEON
London: ✆ 01-499 1911
ATOL, ABTA
Now part of the Meon Travel group.

Resorts Seven in France, four in
Switzerland, plus Austria and Italy.
Accommodation Staffed chalets/
apartments, self-catering apartments,
hotels. **Travel** Air. UK airports:
Edinburgh, Gatwick, Heathrow,
Manchester. **Ski guides** Three days a
week in some resorts.

KU Kuoni Travel
Kuoni House, Dorking, Surrey RH5 4AZ
✆ (0306) 885044 Telex 859445 KUODK
ATOL, ABTA
An established Swiss-owned company
which has only recently entered the
wintersports market. They also sell flight
seats. **Resorts** Fifteen, all in Switzerland.
Accommodation Hotels, self-catering
apartments in Wengen and Lenzerheide.
Travel Air. UK airports: Gatwick,
Heathrow. **Ski guides** No.

MM Made to Measure Holidays
PO Box 40, Chichester, West Sussex
PO18 8HA
✆ (0243) 574333
Telex 869205 MTMHOL
ATOL
Originally specialising in tailor-made
holidays, Made to Measure now offer
ready-made packages too, selling direct
to the public. **Resorts** Switzerland,
France, Austria. **Accommodation** Hotels,
pensions, self-catering apartments.
Travel Air, coach. UK airports: Gatwick,
Heathrow, Manchester. Coach
departures: London. **Ski guides** No.

MY Magic of Italy
47 Shepherds Bush Green,
London W12 8PS
✆ 01-743 9555 Telex 296761 MAGIC
ATOL, ABTA
Sell flights to Milan, Rome, Turin, Venice.
Travel UK airports: Gatwick, Heathrow,
Luton.

NE Neilson Holidays
International House, 125 Granby Street,
Leicester LE1 6FD
✆ (0533) 554646 Telex 342427 NEILSN
ATOL, ABTA
Specialists in low-cost holidays aimed at
the younger end of the market. Also sell
flight seats. **Resorts** Many in Austria and
France, plus Bormio, Santa, Caterina,
Sauze D'Oulx in Italy, Verbier, Villars in
Switzerland. **Accommodation** Self-
catering apartments, hotels, pensions,
private houses. **Travel** Air, coach. UK
airports: Birmingham, Edinburgh,
Gatwick, Glasgow, Luton, Manchester,

Newcastle. Coach departures: Birmingham, London, Manchester. **Ski guides** in some resorts.

NH National Holidays Skiing

Mill Street East, Dewsbury, West Yorks WF12 9AG

✆ (0924) 453611 Telex 55335 NATHOL
Also offices in most major cities.
ATOL
Part of the National Bus Company. **Resorts** Six, all in Austria. **Accommodation** Hotels, pensions. **Travel** Coach from several departure points; or you can join ski coach at London or Dover using National Express services at no extra charge. Planning air holidays for 1985–86. **Ski guides** No.

NT Nat Holidays

Holiday House, Domestic Road
Leeds LS12 6HR

✆ (0532) 434077 Telex 557435 NATUK
ATOL, ABTA
Sell packages aimed at the cost-conscious skier. They also sell flight seats. **Resorts** Twelve in Austria, two each in France and Italy, one in Switzerland. **Accommodation** Hotels, pensions, self-catering apartments, chalets, private houses. **Travel** Air, coach. UK airports: Birmingham, East Midlands, Gatwick, Glasgow, Manchester. Coach departures: 27 different points. **Ski guides** No.

PA Pilgrim-Air

44 Goodge Street, London W1P 1FH

✆ 01-637 5333/ 5311
Telex 267752 SPESER
ATOL
Glasgow: 041-248 7302
Manchester: 061-798 8228
Sell flight seats to Milan, Turin, Venice. UK airports: Birmingham, Bristol, East Midlands, Gatwick, Glasgow, Luton, Manchester.

PH Peter Holden Holidays

Clare House, 166 Lord Street
Southport, Merseyside PR9 0QA

✆ (0704) 37456 Telex 67243 PHHOLS
ATOL, ABTA
Resorts Arinsal in Andorra. **Accommodation** Aparthotel. **Travel** Coach. Departures from various points in NW England. **Snow guarantee** No. No.

PQ Pegasus Gran Slalom

24a Earls Court Gardens,
London SW5 OTA

✆ 01-370 6851 Telex 8952011 SAINTA

ATOL, ABTA
In addition to their regular holidays, Pegasus Holidays have a separate programme for schools and sell flight seats. **Resorts** 10 in Italy, Les Diablerets in Switzerland, Les Houches and Les Carroz in France and Zell am Ziller in Austria. **Accommodation** Hotels, self-catering apartments in Marilleva. **Travel** Air. UK airports: Gatwick, Heathrow, Luton. **Ski guides** No.

PS Peter Stuyvesant Travel

35 Alfred Place, Store Street,
London WC1E 7DY

✆ 01-631 3278 Telex 25257 PSTLON
ATOL, ABTA
As well as conventional packages, they sell 'club' holidays, mainly direct to the public; some prices include tuition (video, too) with a qualified, English-speaking instructor/guide, and ski pass. They run the Ali Ross Ski Clinics in Wengen and La Plagne. They also sell flight seats. **Resorts** Seven in Switzerland, four in Austria and La Plagne in France. **Accommodation** Hotels, self-catering apartments, club in La Plagne. **Travel** Air. UK airports: Gatwick. **Ski guides** In some resorts.

RA Ramblers Holidays

13 Longcroft House, Fretherne Road,
Welwyn Garden City, Herts AL8 6PQ

✆ (07073) 31133 Telex 24642 RTOUR
ATOL, ABTA
Specialists in holidays for cross-country skiers. **Resorts** Five in Austria, two in Switzerland, one in Andorra. **Accommodation** Hotels, pensions. **Travel** Air. UK airports: Gatwick, Heathrow. **Ski guides** No.

SCB Schools Abroad

Grosvenor Hall, Bolnore Road,
Haywards Heath, West Sussex
RH16 4BX

✆ (0444) 459921
Telex 877156 SCOARD
ATOL, ABTA
Specialists in holidays for school groups; prices include equipment hire and instruction. **Resorts** Many in Italy, Switzerland, France, Austria; also Bulgaria, Spain. **Accommodation** Hotels, pensions. **Travel** Air, coach. UK airports: Belfast, Gatwick, Glasgow, Heathrow, Luton, Manchester, Newcastle, Stansted. Coach departures: from schools. **Ski guides** No (but instruction included in cost of holiday).

SCG Ski Club of Great Britain

118 Eaton Square, London SW1W 9AF
01-245 1033 Telex 291608 SKIDOM
The Ski Club of Great Britain does not
sell package holidays, but in conjunction
with ATOL-holding tour operators it
organises 'Skiing Parties' for members.
All parties have at least one leader per
eight members, and they often hold
BASI (British Association of Ski
Instructors) qualifications. The parties
fall into specific categories; for instance
you can learn to ski off-piste; take British
ski tests; ski with groups of your own
age; go with other families; or send your
children on one of the special teenage
parties. Most of the resorts offered are in
France and Switzerland, a few in Italy
and Austria, and one in Scotland.
Accommodation Usually in hotels
although they do offer some staffed
chalet and self-catering holidays as well.
Travel Mostly by air. UK airports: usually
Gatwick (occasionally Heathrow and
Luton) though on certain dates
Manchester and Glasgow are available
at a small extra cost.

SCP Skiscope

Grosvenor Hall, Bolnore Road,
Haywards Heath, West Sussex
RH16 4BX
✆ (0444) 459921
Telex 877156 SCOARD
ATOL, ABTA
Part of the Schools Abroad group selling
holidays for individuals and small groups
direct to the public. They also sell flight
seats. **Resorts** In Italy, Austria, France,
Bulgaria, Switzerland, Spain.
Accommodation Mostly hotels, some
self-catering apartments (breakfast
provided). They stress the fact that their
hotels are sometimes modest. **Travel** Air.
UK airports: Belfast, Gatwick, Glasgow,
Luton, Manchester, Newcastle,
Stansted. **Ski guides** Yes.

SDO Ski an Do Holidays

14 Stafford Street, Edinburgh EH3 7AU
✆ 031-226 6626 Telex 727846 SKIDO
ATOL
Sell direct to the public; also sell flight
seats. **Resorts** Five in France, and
Morgins in Switzerland. **Accommodation**
Hotels, self-catering apartments,
catered chalets. **Travel** Air. UK airports:
Edinburgh. **Ski guides** Yes.

SFA Skifare

Ski MacG Ltd, 260a Fulham Road,
London SW10 9EL
✆ 01-351 5736 Telex 262209 SUNLON
ATOL, ABTA
Revived for 1984–85, selling packages
for the cost-conscious skier, direct to the
public. **Resorts** Les Arcs in France,
Soldeu in Andorra. **Accommodation**
Mostly self-catering, hotels. **Travel** Air,
coach. UK airports: Gatwick, Glasgow,
Manchester. Coach departures: Dover,
London, Manchester. **Ski guides** No.

SGW Ski Gower

30 High Street, Studley, Warwickshire
B80 7HJ
✆ (052785) 4546
Telex 335540 WEMMAS
ATOL, ABTA
Specialists in holidays for school groups;
prices include instruction and
equipment hire. **Resorts** Eight, all in
Switzerland. **Accommodation** Hotels,
youth centres. **Travel** Coach, rail from
schools. **Ski guides** No (but instruction
included in cost of holiday).

SKW Ski West

Westfield House, Westbury,
Wilts BA13 3EP
✆ (0373) 864811 Telex 449628 WESTRA
ATOL, ABTA
In addition to their main package
programme they sell holidays for
groups, and flight and coach seats.
Resorts 10 in France, 4 in Austria, 2 in
Switzerland and Courmayeur in Italy.
Accommodation Self-catering
apartments, staffed chalets, hotels,
pensions. **Travel** Air, coach. UK airports:
Gatwick, Glasgow, Heathrow,
Manchester. Coach departures: Dover,
London. Birmingham, Manchester can
be arranged for large groups. **Ski guides**
No.

SLD Slade Travel

Slade House, 15 Vivian Avenue,
London NW4 3UT
✆ 01-202 0111 Telex 23425 SLADE
ATOL, ABTA
Sell flight seats to Bern, Geneva, Lyons,
Milan, Munich, Nice, Rome, Turin,
Venice, Zurich. **Travel** UK airports:
Birmingham, Gatwick, Heathrow, Luton,
Manchester.

SLV Ski Lovers

20 Craven Terrace, London W2 3QH
✆ 01-258 0177 Telex 22359 WALKAB
ATOL, ABTA
Specialists in holidays for 18–35 age
group. **Resorts** St Johann im Pongau,
Waidring, Fugen, Kirchdorf in Austria,
Les Arcs, Tignes in France.
Accommodation Hotels, club-style
hotels, pensions, staffed and self-
catering apartments. **Travel** Air, coach.
UK airports: Gatwick. Coach departures:
London. **Ski guides** No.

SMD Ski Sunmed

4-6 Manor Mount, London SE23 3PZ
✆ 01-699 5999
Telex 894977 SUNOPS
Manchester: ✆ 061-834 7011
Belfast: ✆ (0232) 796565
ATOL, ABTA
Sell holidays aimed at cost-conscious
skiers. **Resorts** Les Deux Alpes,
Montgenèvre, Puy St Vincent, Risoul,
Valloire in France, Clavière in Italy.
Accommodation Hotels, apartments
(catered and self-catering), staffed
chalets. **Travel** Air, coach. UK airports:
Gatwick. Coach departures: Dover,
London. **Ski guides** Yes.

SMG Ski MacG

260a Fulham Road, London SW10 9EL
✆ 01-351 5446 Telex 262209 SUNLON
Birmingham: ✆ 021-643 2752
Glasgow: ✆ 041-552 1312
Manchester: ✆ 061-833 9195
ABTA, ATOL
In addition to selling packages direct to
the public, they offer special ski weeks,
including some for unaccompanied
children, and sell flight seats. **Resorts**
Six in France, Verbier in Switzerland.
Accommodation Staffed chalets/
apartments, hotels, self-catering
apartments. **Travel** Air, coach. UK
airports: Gatwick, Glasgow, Manchester.
Coach departures: London. **Ski guides**
In some resorts.

SML Ski Miquel

12 Tib Lane, Manchester M2 4JB
✆ 061-832 2737/ 3773
Telex 667664 SHARET
ATOL
Sell packages and flight seats direct to
the public. **Resorts** Soldeu in Andorra,
Baqueira in Spain. **Accommodation**
Hotels, self-catering apartments. **Travel**
Air. UK airports: Gatwick, Manchester.
Ski guides Yes.

SMW Small World

850 Brighton Road, Purley,
Surrey CR2 2BH
✆ 01-660 3999 Telex 23487 VILLAS
ATOL, ABTA
Specialists in staffed chalet holidays.
Resorts Six in Italy, four in Switzerland,
two in France. **Accommodation** Staffed
chalets. **Travel** Air. UK airports: Gatwick.
Ski guides In some resorts.

SNC Snowcoach Holidays

Holiday House, 146-148 London Road
St Albans, Herts AL1 1PQ
✆ (0727) 66177/ 33141
Telex 8814162 CANTAB
ATOL, ABTA
A subsidiary of Club Cantabrica, selling
low-cost holidays. **Resorts** Achenkirch,
Kirchbichl, Kirchdorf, Söll in Austria, Le
Collet d'Allevard, Puy St Vincent in
France, Arinsal in Andorra.
Accommodation Hotels, pensions, self-
catering apartments. **Travel** Coach from
London and many regional connections.
Ski guides Yes.

SNP Snowplan

Woodleigh Leisure Ltd, 84 High Street,
Prestwood, Gt Missenden, Bucks
✆ (02406) 4745/ 2634/ 5978
ATOL, ABTA
Specialists in holidays for school groups;
prices include instruction and
equipment hire. **Resorts** Austria, France,
and Courmayeur in Italy.
Accommodation Hotels, pensions.
Travel Air, coach. UK airports: Gatwick,
Luton. Coach departures: from schools.
Ski guides No.

SNT Snowtime

23 Denmark Street, London WC2H 8NA
✆ 01-836 3237 Telex 267707 SNOWT
ATOL
Sell packages and flight seats direct to
the public. **Resort** Méribel in France.
Accommodation Mainly staffed chalets,
a few self-catering apartments, hotels.
Travel Air. UK airports: Gatwick; limited
availability from Glasgow, Manchester.
Ski guides Yes.

SNW Snow World

PO Box 99, 29 Queens Road, Brighton
BN1 3YN
✆ (0273) 202391/ 23397
Telex 877593 ASLINK
ATOL, ABTA
Sell packages geared towards cost-
conscious youngish skiers; they also sell

flight seats. **Resorts** Encamp, Soldeu in Andorra, Livigno in Italy.
Accommodation Hotels, self-catering apartments. **Travel** Air, coach. UK airports: Gatwick. Coach departures: London. **Ski guides** Yes.

SPT Schoolplan Tours
Schoolplan House, 77 Grand Parade, Brighton, Sussex BN2 2JA
✆ (0273) 697411
Telex 87374 SCHPLA
Glasgow: ✆ 041-332 0506
ATOL, ABTA
Part of the Intasun Leisure Group; specialists in schools parties – instruction, equipment hire and lift pass are included in the cost of their holidays. **Resorts** Italy, Austria, France, Switzerland. **Accommodation** Hotels, pensions, apartments – some self-catering. **Travel** Air, coach. UK airports: Belfast, Gatwick, Glasgow, Luton. Coach departures: from schools. **Ski guides** No (but instruction included in cost of holiday).

STC Ski TC
161 Reepham Road, Norwich NR6 5NZ
✆ (0603) 483543 Telex 975379 CENTRE
ATOL, ABTA
Sell flight seats as well as packages. **Resorts** Seven, all in France. **Accommodation** Self-catering apartments, some hotels. **Travel** Air, coach. UK airports: Gatwick, Luton. Coach departures: Dover, London. **Ski guides** In some resorts.

STY Ski Travelaway
Tudor House, 71 Park Road, Sutton Coldfield, West Midlands B72 1QE
✆ 021-355 3681 Telex 338654 TRAVEL
ATOL, ABTA
Specialists in holidays for groups. They also sell flight seats. **Resorts** In France, Italy, Austria, Switzerland. **Accommodation** Hotels, catered apartments. **Travel** Air, coach. UK airports: Belfast, Bristol, Gatwick, Luton, Manchester. Coach departures as arranged. **Ski guides** No.

SUP Ski Supertravel
22 Hans Place, London SW1X OEP
✆ 01-584 5060 Telex 263725 SUPTVL
ATOL, ABTA
Specialists in chalet holidays. They also sell flight seats. **Resorts** Nine in France, four in Switzerland, Lech and St Anton in Austria. **Accommodation** Staffed chalets, also hotels, self-catering apartments and

a few special parties. **Travel** Air, coach. UK airports: Edinburgh, Gatwick, Heathrow, Manchester. Coach departures: Dover, London. **Ski guides** In most resorts.

SUQ Sunquest Holidays
Aldine House, 9-15 Aldine Street, Shepherds Bush, London W12 8AW
✆ 01-749 9911 TELEX 23619 SUNQST
ATOL, ABTA
Sell flight seats to Geneva, Lyons, Milan, Munich, Turin, Venice, Zurich. They also have a small programme to Rumania. **Travel** UK airports: Gatwick, Heathrow, Manchester.

SUS Sun & Ski Travel
14a East Street, Havant, Hampshire PO9 1AQ
✆ (0705) 453434 Telex 86638 SHORES
ATOL
In addition to selling packages direct to the public, they arrange ski parties and sell flight seats. **Resorts** Eight in Switzerland, four each in Austria and France. **Accommodation** Hotels, pensions, self-catering apartments. **Travel** Air. UK airports: Most, including Gatwick, Heathrow, Luton, Manchester. Coach can be arranged for groups or large parties. **Ski guides** Only for organised groups or parties.

SVL Ski-Val
91 Wembley Park Drive, Wembley Park, Middx HA9 8HF
✆ 01-200 6080/ 903 4444
Telex 916196 ADLIB
ATOL, ABTA
Sell holidays mainly direct to the public. **Resorts** Val d'Isère, Tignes and Les Arcs in France, Kitzbühel in Austria. **Accommodation** Specialise in staffed chalets and clubs (small hotels), some hotels and self-catering apartments. **Travel** Air, coach. UK airports: Edinburgh, Gatwick, Manchester. Coach departures: London. **Ski guides** Yes.

SWS Swiss Airtours
63 Neal Street, London WC2H 9PJ
✆ 01-836 6751/ 240 1416
Telex 295356 BRITAV
ATOL
Sell flight seats to Geneva, Zurich. **Travel** UK airports: Gatwick.

SWT Swiss Travel Service
Bridge House, Ware, Herts SG12 9DE
✆ (0920) 3971 Telex 81633 BRIDGE
Personal callers: 54 Ebury Street,

London SW1
ATOL, ABTA
Resorts Switzerland only – a good cross-section. **Accommodation** Mostly hotels, some self-catering apartments. **Travel** Scheduled air. UK airports: Gatwick, Heathrow, Manchester. **Ski guides** No.

TC Thomas Cook Holidays
PO Box 36, Thorpe Wood,
Peterborough, Cambs PE3 6SB
✆ (0733) 502200 Telex 32581 THCOOK
Birmingham: 021-236 0439
Leeds: (0532) 449306
London: 01-437 9080
Manchester: 061-228 1768
Newcastle: (0632) 615145
ATOL, ABTA
In addition to their skiing programme, their Adventure Holidays include skiing in Lapland. They also sell flight seats.
Resorts Seven in Austria, three in France, two in Switzerland, plus Sol y Nieve in Spain, Courmayeur in Italy.
Accommodation Hotels, pensions, self-catering apartments. **Travel** Air. UK airports: East Midlands, Gatwick, Heathrow, Manchester. **Ski guides** Yes.

TH Thomson Holidays
Greater London House, Hampstead Road, London NW1 7SD
✆ 01-431 0518 Telex 261123 THGLH
Also offices in Birmingham, Bristol, Cardiff, Glasgow, Leeds, Leicester, Manchester, Newcastle.
ATOL, ABTA
Sell flight seats as well as packages.
Resorts Over 50, in Austria, France, Italy, Spain, Switzerland. **Accommodation** Hotels, pensions, private houses, self-catering apartments, chalets. **Travel** Air. UK airports: Birmingham, Gatwick, Glasgow, Luton, Manchester. **Ski guides** In many resorts.

TK Twickenham Shekel Savers
84 Hampton Road, Twickenham, Middx TW2 5QS
✆ 01-898 8681 Telex 922889 TTTRAV
ATOL, ABTA
Sell flight seats to Geneva, Munich, Nice, Zurich. **Travel** UK airports: Gatwick, Heathrow, Manchester.

TT Tentrek Holidays
152 Maidstone Road, Ruxley Corner, Sidcup, Kent DA14 5HS
✆ 01-302 6426/ 7828
Telex 897497 TENTRK
ATOL, ABTA
Sell holidays geared towards the cost-conscious skier. They also sell flight and coach seats. **Resorts** Seven, all in Austria. **Accommodation** Hotels, pensions, private houses. **Travel** Air, coach. UK airports: Gatwick. Coach departures: London; some connecting regional departures. **Ski guides** Yes.

TX Trax Leisure
6 Comeragh Road or PO Box 578, West Kensington, London W14
✆ 01-385 5864/ 4187
Telex 947083 ASTIR
ATOL
Sell sell packages and flight seats direct to the public. **Resorts** Tignes, La Plagne in France, Schnalstal in Italy.
Accommodation Hotels, self-catering apartments. **Travel** Air, coach. UK airports: Gatwick. Coach departures: London. **Ski guides** Yes.

UJ Unijet
Sandrocks, Rocky Lane, Haywards Heath, West Sussex RH16 3QS
✆ (0444) 458181 Telex 87677 VIKING
Birmingham: 021-236 3050
Glasgow: 041-204 0505
London: 01-660 8079
Manchester: 061-833 0055
ATOL, ABTA
Sell flight seats to Geneva and Munich.
Travel UK airport: Gatwick.

UK UK Express
Whitehall House, 41 Whitehall, London SW1A 2BY
✆ 01-839 3303 Telex 8956029 EXPRES
ATOL, ABTA
Sell flight seats to Geneva, Milan, Munich, Salzburg, Zurich. **Travel** UK airports: Gatwick, Heathrow.

VF Vacances Franco-Britanniques
1 St Margarets Terrace, Cheltenham, Glos GL50 4DT
✆ (0242) 526338 Telex: 43574 VFB
ATOL
Sell packages direct to the public.
Resorts La Clusaz, Châtel in France.
Accommodation Hotels, self-catering apartments. **Travel** Air. UK airports: Gatwick. **Ski guides** No.

VX Valexander Tours
24 Crawford Place, London W1H 1TE
✆ 01-402 4262/ 723 6964
Telex 892352 VALEX
ATOL, ABTA
Sell flight seats to Geneva, Milan, Munich, Turin. **Travel** UK airports: Gatwick, Luton.

WM Waymark Holidays
295 Lillie Road, London SW6 7LL
✆ 01-385 5015
ATOL
Specialists in cross-country skiing, both
from centres and on tour. **Resorts**
Austria, Germany, Norway, Switzerland,
two in Italy, one each in France, Sweden.
Accommodation Hotels, pensions, (huts
on tours). **Travel** Air. UK airports:
Gatwick, Heathrow, Manchester,
Newcastle. **Snow guarantee** No. **Ski
guides** Yes.

WT Welcome Tours
Air France Holidays and Welcome
France Holidays
Georgian House, 69 Boston Manor
Road, Brentford, Middlesex TW8 9JQ
Air France: ✆ 01-568 6981
Welcome France: ✆ 01-568 6985
Telex 8953196 AFHOLS
ATOL, ABTA
The two holiday programmes run by
Welcome Tours offer the same
accommodation. **Resorts** Seven, all in
France. **Accommodation** Hotels, self-
catering apartments. **Travel** Air with Air
France, own car with Welcome France.
UK airports: Heathrow. **Ski guides** No.

Letting agencies
The companies listed here are major
agencies for the letting of self-catering
accommodation independent of
package holidays.

European Holiday Homes
Unit 12B, Lansdown Industrial Estate
Cheltenham, Glos GL51 8PL
✆ (0242) 41808 Telex 437244 CMINTL
Offer self-catering accommodation in
Europe including France, Switzerland,
Austria and Italy. Their brochure lists
accommodation in twenty of the more
popular ski resorts but others can also
be arranged.

Interhome
383 Richmond Road,
Twickenham TW1 2EF
✆ 01-891 1294 Telex 928539 IH GB
A Swiss company which is Europe's
biggest holiday-home and hotel agency.
They have properties in hundreds of ski
resorts in Austria, Switzerland, Germany,
Italy, and France. You can book direct
with them or through a travel agency. It's
mainly accommodation only but they
offer 'skiing holidays by car' to some
Swiss resorts.

Maeva
21 Fleet Street, London EC4Y 1AA
✆ 01-583 8383 Telex 24438 TVLPNT
ATOL, ABTA
Operated by French Leave. Offer self-
catering apartments in many French ski
resorts.

Perrymead Properties (Overseas)
55 Perrymead Street, London SW6 3SN
✆ 01-736 4592/ 5331
Telex 943763 CROCOM REF PER
Properties to let in six resorts in
Switzerland and Italy.

Operators in name order

The main tour operators are in code
order; use this index to find operators by
name.

What to pack

We have listed on this page all the things you *might* want with you on a skiing trip – not just the things we think you *should* take. The first thing to do with the list, therefore, is to go through it crossing out the things you don't possess or don't want with you; you're then left with a checklist that you can tick off as you do your packing. There's space at the end for your own non-skiing clothes list. (In 'A Skiing Primer' we give advice on what clothes first-timers should think of taking.)

Packing checklist

GENERAL
☐ hip-flask (and funnel)
☐ passport
☐ travel tickets
☐ accommodation papers
☐ foreign cash (for ski-pass)
☐ British cash (to get home)
☐ cheques
☐ credit cards
☐ first aid kit
☐ sewing kit
☐ Swiss Army penknife
☐ lip salve
☐ sun-screen
☐ après-sun cream
☐ camera, film
☐ detergent (for clothes)
☐ sunglasses
☐ contact lenses
☐ contact lens kit
☐ alarm clock
☐ small torch
☐ GSG resort checklist

FOR SKIING
☐ skis
☐ safety straps
☐ boots
☐ socks
☐ poles
☐ ski repair kit
☐ tools for bindings
☐ gloves
☐ inner gloves
☐ hat

☐ scarf
☐ goggles
☐ ski trousers
☐ ski jacket
☐ shirts
☐ pullovers
☐ warm underclothing
☐ bumbag/rucksac
☐ photo for ski-pass
☐ personal stereo/tapes
☐ compass
☐ avalanche bleeper

FOR NOT SKIING
☐ swimsuit
☐ moonboots
☐ wellingtons
☐ slippers/house-shoes
☐ corkscrew
☐ books
☐ games
☐ jewellery
☐ make-up
☐ hairdrier
☐ iron
☐ clothes (write your own list)

Skiing vocabulary

We translate words and expressions of particular value on a skiing trip. Many are also included in our Glossary and Index on page 476.

English	French	German	Italian
ambulance	ambulance	Krankenwagen	ambulanza
ankle	cheville	Knöchel	caviglia
antifreeze	antigel	Frostschutz	antigelo
area	région	Gegend	zona
avalanche danger	danger d'avalanches	Lawinengefahr	pericolo di valanghe
back (body)	dos	Rücken	schiena
bandage	bandage	Verband	benda/fasciatura
bindings	fixations	Bindung	gli attacchi
– toe-piece	– butée	– Zehenteil	– pezzo della punta
– heel-piece	– talonnière	– Fersenteil	– pezzo posteriore
blanket	couverture	Decke	coperta
blister	ampoule	Blase	vescica
blizzard	tempête de neige	Schneesturm	tormenta
blocked (road)	barré	blockiert	bloccato
blood wagon	traineau	Rettungsschlitten	slitta
bone	os	Knochen	osso
bruise	contusion	blauer Fleck	ammaccatura
bumbag	banane	Gürteltasche	borsa-marsupio
burn	brûlure	Brand(wunde)	scottatura
cable-car	téléphérique	Seilbahn	funivia
caution	attention	Achtung	attenzione
chains (snow)	chaines	Schneeketten	catene
chair-lift	télésiège	Sessellift	seggiovia
clinic	clinique	Klinik	clinica
clip (on boot)	boucle	Schnalle	clip
closed	fermé	geschlossen/ gesperrt	chiuso
col	col	Sattel	valico
cold	froid	kalt	freddo
collision	collision	Zusammenstoss	scontro
compass	boussole	Kompass	bussola
cornice	corniche	Wächte'	cornice
crampons	crampons	Steigeisen	ramponi da ghiaccio
crevasse	crevasse	Gletscherspalte	crepaccio
cross-country	ski de fond	Langlauf	sci di fondo
crutches	béquilles	Krücken	grucce
cut (on skin)	plaie	Schnittwunde	taglio
danger	danger	Gefahr	pericolo
dangerous	dangereux	gefährlich	pericoloso
descent	descente	Abfahrt	discesa
downhill ski	ski aval	Talski	ski a valle
drag-lift	téléski	Schlepplift	skilift/traino
edges (of skis)	carres	Kanten	gli spigoli
exit	sortie	Ausgang	uscita
first aid	premiers secours	erste Hilfe	pronto soccorso

English	French	German	Italian
fog	brouillard	Nebel	nebbia
forbidden	interdit/ défendu	verboten	vietato
fracture	fracture	Bruch	frattura
freestyle	ski acrobatique	Freestyle	stile libero
gaiters	guetres	Gamaschen	gambali
glacier	glacier	Gletscher	ghiacciaio
gloves	gants	Handschuhe	guanti
goggles	lunettes protectrices	Skibrille	gli occhiali
gondola	télécabine	Gondelbahn	telecabina
guide	guide	Führer	guida
gully	couloir	Schlucht	canalone
helicopter	hélicoptère	Hubschrauber	elicottero
helmet	casque	Schutzhelm	casco
herring-bone	montée en ciseaux	Grätenschritt	salita a spina di pesce
hill	colline	Berg	collina
hire, for	à louer	zu vermieten	da noleggio
hospital	hôpital	Krankenhaus	ospedale
hut (mountain)	cabane	Hütte	rifugio
ice	glace	Eis	ghiaccio
icy road	chaussée verglacée	Glatteis	strada ghiacciata
information	renseignements	Auskunft	informazioni
instructor	moniteur	Skilehrer	maestro/istruttore
jacket	veste	Jacke	giacca
knee	genou	Knie	ginocchio
left (hand)	gauche	links	sinistra
leg	jambe	Bein	gamba
lessons, ski	leçons de ski	Skistunden	lezioni da sci
lift pass	forfait/ abonnement	Liftausweis	abbonamento
lift coupons	coupons	Punktekarte	abbonamento a punti
ligament	ligament	Band	ligamento
map	carte	Karte	carta
mittens	moufles	Fausthandschuhe	manopole
mogul	bosse	Buckel	gobba
mountain	montagne	Berg	montagna
mountain restaurant	restaurant d'altitude	Berggaststätte	ristorante del rifugio
muscle	muscle	Muskel	muscolo
neck	cou	Hals	collo
no entry	accès interdit	kein Eintritt	vietato accesso
nursery	garderie d'enfants	Kindergarten	asilo
nursery slope	piste pour débutants	Ubungshang	pista 'baby'
off-piste	hors piste	abseits der Piste	fuori di pista
open	ouvert	offen/geöffnet	aperto
out of order	derange	ausser Betrieb	guasto
overtrousers	surpantalon	Überhose	sopracalzoni
pass	col	Pass	passo
pelvis	bassin	Becken	bacino
piste	piste	Piste	pista
plaster	plâtre	Gips	gesso
pool, indoor	piscine couverte	Hallenbad	piscina coperta
queue	queue	Schlange	coda
rent (verb)	louer	mieten	affittare
repair	réparer	reparieren	riparare
rescue service	service de secours	Rettungsdienst	servizio soccorso
rib	côte	Rippe	costola
ridge	arête	Kamm/Grat	spigolo
right (hand)	droite	rechts	destra

English	French	German	Italian
rucksack	sac à dos	Rucksack	zaino
safety strap	lanière	Fangriemen	cinghia di sicurezza
salopette	salopette	Lifthose	tuta
screwdriver	tournevis	Schraubenzieher	cacciavite
skating rink	patinoire	Eislaufplatz	pista di patinaggio
ski (noun)	ski	Ski	sci
ski (verb)	faire du ski/skier	skilaufen	sciare
ski boots	chaussures de ski	Skisschuhe	scarponi da sci
ski brake	stoppeur	skistopper	freno
ski-flying	vol à ski	Skifliegen	volo da sci
ski instructor	moniteur	Skilehrer	maestro di sci
ski-jumping	saut à ski	Skispringen	salto da sci
ski lift	téléski	Ski lift	ski lift
ski pants	pantalon de ski	Skihose	pantaloni da sci
ski patrol	pisteurs	Pistenwart	pattuglia sciistica
ski pole	bâton de ski	Skistock	rachetta da sci
ski resort	station de ski	Wintersportort	localita sciistic
ski run	piste	Abfahrt/Piste	pista
ski school	école de ski	Skischule	scuola sci
ski-touring	ski de randonnée	Skitour	sci alpinismo
skier	skieur	Skilaufer/ Skifahrer	sciatore
skins (touring)	peaux de phoque	Felle	pelli
slide (verb)	glisser	rutschen	scivolare
sling	écharpe	Schlinge	bendaggio ad armacollo
slope	pente	Hang	pendio
slush	neige fondue	Schneematsch	neve sciolta
snow	neige	Schnee	neve
snow-blindness	cécité des neiges	Schneeblindheit	accecamento da neve
snow-drift	congère	Schneeverwehung	cumulo di neve
snowfall	chute de neige	Schneefall	nevicata
snowplough	chasse-neige	Schneepflug	spazzaneve
snow-slabs	plaques de neige	Schneebrett	lastre di neve
splint	attelle	Schiene	stecca
sprain	entorse	Verstauchung	storta/strappo
stop (noun)	arrêt	Haltestelle	fermata
stop (verb)	arreter	anhalten	fermare
strained	froissé	gezerrt	teso
stretcher	brancard	Tragbahre	barella
summer skiing	ski d'été	Sommerskifahren	sci estivo
sun	soleil	Sonne	sole
suncream	crême solaire	Sonnencreme	crema da sole
ticket	billet	Fahrkarte	biglietto
toboggan	luge	Rodelschlitten	toboga/ slittino
tourist office	office de tourisme/ syndicat d'initiative	Verkehrsbüro	ufficio turismo/ turistico
traverse (verb)	traverser	traversieren	traversare
turn (verb)	tourner	wenden	girare
turn (noun)	virage	Drehung	girata/curva
twisted	foulé/tordu	Verrenkt	slogato
uphill	en amont	bergauf	a monte
valley	vallée	Tal	valle
visibility	visibilité	Sicht	visibilita
waistcoat	gilet	Weste	panciotto
wax	cire/fart	Skiwachs	sciolina
wedel	godille	wedeln	serpentina
weight	poids	Gewicht	peso
wind	vent	Wind	vento
X-ray	radio	Röntgenbild	radiografia
zip	fermeture éclair	Reissverschluss	chiusura lampo

Reporting to the Guide

This first edition of the Guide has been greatly strengthened by the hundreds of reports we have had from people about their own skiing holiday experiences. We hope you will help future editions, too, by sending in further reports on the resorts you visit; whether or not you agree with what we've said in this edition, this is your opportunity to influence what we say in future. The only incentive we can offer is that when the next edition emerges, we shall again give free copies of the Guide to 25 randomly chosen reporters.

Rather than provide cramped tear-out report forms, we've prepared the checklist below. If you use the items in the list as headings for your reports, the job of analysing the reports will be greatly simplified. You'll also be sure to cover subjects on which we need help, and not subjects which are more easily covered by other means: the information we need above all from holiday-makers is about aspects of a resort which it is difficult to judge on a brief inspection visit. Under *Prices*, please aim to be general in your judgements ('wine outrageously expensive by French standards') but specific in your evidence ('ordinary Cotes du Rhone FF32 a bottle in most places, FF45 at Le Dahu'). Be sure to distinguish mountain restaurants from village restaurants and bars.

Send reports to The Good Skiing Guide, Holiday Which?, 14 Buckingham Street, London WC2N 6DS. Please write as clearly as you can, or type your reports if at all possible. Include your name, address and phone number, and give us some idea of the skiing skills and interests of yourself and your companions.

Resort report checklist

BASICS
☐ Resort name
☐ Date of visit

SKIING
☐ Snow and weather
☐ Weather information
☐ Piste maintenance
☐ Mountain rescue
☐ State of nursery slopes
☐ Lift closures
☐ Lift queues
☐ Ski schools
☐ Ski kindergartens
☐ Ski hire shops
☐ Mountain restaurants
☐ New lifts or runs
☐ Planned lifts or runs

RESORT
☐ Road access
☐ Non-skiing activities
☐ Restaurants and bars
☐ Après-ski
☐ Non-ski kindergartens
☐ Food shops
☐ Medical facilities
☐ Accommodation
☐ Clientele / atmosphere
☐ New facilities

PRICES
☐ Restaurants
☐ Bars
☐ Nightclubs / discos
☐ Ski / boot hire
☐ Food shopping

Glossary / Index

This combined glossary and index covers general skiing terminology, and a few people who figure prominently in the general chapters of the *Guide*.

Resort reports have their own index on page 387, and are not included here.

Italic type is used throughout for cross-references to other entries.

A

Aerials *Freestyle* discipline involving acrobatic jumps
Alpine skiing Skiing downhill (as opposed to *cross-country*) 10
Angulation Zigzag posture necessary for *carved turns* and in a *traverse* on a steep slope
Anticipation Positioning of upper body to assist ensuing turn
Anti-friction pad Slippery pad behind toe-piece of *binding* to ensure efficient release of boot 404
Anti-gliss Type of fabric used in ski clothing, designed not to be too slippery in case of fall 409
Après-ski Late-afternoon and evening ski resort entertainment 22
Artificial slope *Dry slope* 42
Avalanche Slide of *snow* down a mountainside, often extremely destructive 420
Avalement *Compression turn*

B

Ballet *Freestyle* discipline involving dance-like movements
Banana *Bumbag* 38
BASI British Association of Ski Instructors
Basic swing Long-radius *parallel turn* taught by *BASI*
Basket Disc near bottom of *pole* to limit penetration into *snow* 407
Biathlon Competition combining *cross-country* racing and target shooting
Binding Means of attaching *boot* to *ski*, designed to release in fall 32, 404
Bird's nesting *Off-piste* skiing among trees (deliberately)

Black run Steep, difficult marked run, usually left unprepared 25
Bleep Signal-emitting device carried by *off-piste* skiers to assist rescue after an *avalanche*
Blood wagon Stretcher-sledge used by *ski patrol* for carrying injured skiers down mountain 44
Blue run Easy marked run, in some resorts the easiest there is 25
Bob sleigh Armoured toboggan for teams of two or four riders
Boot Instrument of torture not made for walking 31, 391
Brake Spring-loaded prongs attached to *binding* which prevent runaway ski after fall on piste 32, 404
Breakable crust Hazardous *off-piste* snow condition 423
Bubble *Gondola* lift 27
Bucket Cage-like lift with no seat and no advantages
Bumbag Small pack worn as belt around waist 38
Button lift One-person *drag-lift* 28

C

Cable binding Simple kind of *binding*, obsolete and dangerous
Cable-car Lift with large cabin without seats, suspended from cable 27
Camber Arched shape of *ski* when no weight on it 400
Canting Altering angular relationship between *boots* and *skis* to compensate for knock-knees or bow-legs 396
Carved turn Turn in which ski moves in its own track, with minimal skidding
Chair-lift Lift with series of chairs suspended from cable, each carrying one to four skiers 16, 28
Chalet Uniquely British style of skiing accommodation 47
Chalet girl One who cooks for and cleans up after holiday-makers staying in a *chalet* 47
Chalet tea High carbohydrate event: bread and jam – and crumbs of the cake consumed by those who quit skiing at 3pm 47
Chicane Narrow passage in *Downhill* race-course 446

H

Harscheisen Blades beneath boot designed to provide grip on icy slopes when ski touring 436

Heli-skiing Skiing with the aid of helicopter uphill transport

Herringbone Method of climbing on skis, like *snowplough* in reverse

High season Opposite of *low season*

Hip flask Essential aid to morale

Hockey stop *Uphill christie*

Hot-dogging *Moguls*

Hypothermia Dangerous lowering of body temperature 421

I

Ice bar Mountain bar serving naturally chilled drinks

Inner boot Usually detachable, cushioned lining of *boot* to ensure insulation and snug fit 396

Inner glove Silk or similar glove worn inside ski glove for extra warmth 36

Inner skiing Unconventional ski teaching method which aims to exploit natural learning ability

Insurance Don't go without it 448

Intermediate Skier who is off the nursery slopes but neither happy nor expert on the most difficult runs

J

Jet turn *Parallel turn* initiated by sharp braking action

Jump turn *Parallel turn* in steep or difficult conditions

K

Kangaroo turn Trick *turn* involving exaggerated sitting position

Kick turn Turn executed at a standstill; invaluable in moderately awkward spots; impossible in really awkward ones

L

Langlauf *Cross-country* skiing 428

Lift pass 'Rover' ticket giving unlimited rides on lifts for period of validity 30

Loipe *Cross-country* ski run

Long ski Ski of full, orthodox length – roughly 10 to 20cm above head height, depending on weight 398

Low season Periods of winter in which package holidays are cheaper than in *high season*, and other prices may or may not be 20

Luge *Skeleton toboggan*

M

Mid-length ski Ski meant to be ideal compromise for *intermediate* skiers between *long* and *compact* skis – usually just above head height 398

Mogul Large bump in ski-run caused by skiers being sheeplike 26

Mogul field Section of ski-run consisting entirely of moguls 26

Moguls *Freestyle* discipline involving acrobatic skiing through *mogul field*

Monoski Single broad ski with room for both feet side by side

Moon boots Fat, warm, snow-proof après-ski boot (major brand) 37

Motorway Broad, easy *piste*

N

Nordic skiing *Cross-country* skiing and ski jumping 428

Nursery slope Gentle slope used by beginners 24

O

Off-piste Area and technique of skiing away from marked, prepared and patrolled ski runs 24

P

Parallel Slalom Alpine racing discipline

Parallel turn *Turn* executed with skis parallel throughout

Piste Ski run marked, patrolled, usually prepared, and virtually always graded according to difficulty 24

Piste basher Tracked bulldozer used to compact and smooth snow on runs 26; derogatory term for someone who displays apparent competence on the piste, but never ventures off it

Pisteur Member of resort *ski patrol*

Plastic slope *Dry slope* 42

Points card Similar to *coupons* 30

Pole Essential aid to balance 32, 407

Pole plant Action of planting ski pole in snow, ingredient of most parallel turns

Poma *Button lift* (brand name) 28

Porridge Sticky, lumpy *snow*

Powder Light, newly-fallen *snow* 26

Q

Queues Necessary prelude to riding most lifts in *high season* 27, 57

R

Racing pants Tight-fitting elasticated skiing trousers 34

Raclette Related to *fondue*, but substituting potatoes for bread

Ratrac *Piste basher* (major brand)

Red run Medium-tough ski run 25

Roller skiing Simulation of *Cross-country* skiing on tarmac, using roller-skate-like ski

Rope tow Primitive form of *drag-lift* 28

Rotary binding *Turntable binding* 404

Rotation/counter rotation Shoulder movements once fashionable as ingredients of *parallel turns*

S

NOTE Many terms normally prefaced by 'ski' are to be found not here but under their own initial letter – eg 'ski-pole' is under 'pole'

Safety strap Leash attaching *boot* to *ski* to prevent runaway ski after fall on *piste* and loss of ski in *powder snow* 32

Salopettes Skiing dungarees 34

Schuss Descent sufficiently gradual or short not to require a *traverse* or *turns*

Scorpian Brand of very short ski without tail, broader in the middle

Self-catering Affordable way for families to go skiing 46

Short ski *Compact ski* 398

Short swing Short-radius parallel turn taught by *BASI*

Shovel Front *tip* of *ski*

Sidecut Narrowing of *ski* between *tip* and *tail* 400

Sideslip Controlled sideways slide down slope on skis, invaluable on steep slopes

Side step Stepping sideways up or down ski slope on skis

Skating turn Turn involving exaggerated transfer of weight from one ski to another, as in ice skating

Skeleton toboggan Basic frame toboggan for single rider

Ski Expensive plastic plank 31, 397

Ski birding Skiing with wing-like flaps for extra uplift

Ski bob Small bicycle-like conveyance with skis instead of wheels

Ski bum Person (m or f), usually good-looking and young, who will do anything for a season in a ski resort 41

Ski Club of Great Britain 12

Ski evolutif Method of teaching beginners using gradual progression from short skis to longer ones, and immediate learning of *parallel turns* 42

Ski flying Competition judging ski jumps according to length alone

Ski guide Tour operator employee, meant to show you the slopes but not how to ski 45

Ski jumping Competition judging length and style of ski jumps

Ski-lift Any form of lift which carries skiers up (or down) mountains; more specifically, a *drag-lift* 28

Ski-mountaineering Climbing up mountains and skiing down them 435

Ski pass *Lift pass* 30

Ski patrol Team employed to supervise safety of pistes 44

Ski route Ski run marked on mountain but not prepared or patrolled

Ski school Most common and most reliable source of skiing tuition 40

Ski stopper *Brake* 32, 404

Ski-touring *Alpine skiing* without recourse to lifts

Skins Artificial fur stuck or tied to base of skis for walking uphill on snow (when ski-touring or mountaineering) 436

Slalom/Special Slalom Alpine racing discipline with tightly-spaced *gates* 442

Snow Atmospheric vapour frozen into ice crystals and falling to earth in light white flakes, or spread on it as a white layer after falling (Concise Oxford Dictionary 6th edition) 25, 422

Snowcat/Snowmobile Vehicle capable of negotiating snowy mountain terrain

Snow-chains Means of keeping cars going on snowbound roads

Snowplough Basic method of controlling speed and turning by forming skis into a V, tips together

Snow shoes Broad, round webbed footwear for walking on soft *snow*

Sole Smooth base of *ski*, which slides on *snow* 31

Speed skiing Pursuit of speed records

Spring snow Hard but granular crust formed by thawing of snow by day and freezing overnight 26

Star turn Turning round on flat ground

Stem Half-snowplough used in transitional turns (stem turn/stem christie) between *snowplough* and *parallel turns*, and in difficult snow

Step-in binding Typical modern *binding*

Step turn Parallel turn initiated by step uphill

Studio/duplex Small compartments to let in large blocks in French Alps, in which you can eat and sleep but not live

Super-G Alpine racing discipline coming between *Downhill* and *Giant Slalom* 442

T

T-bar Two-person *drag-lift* 28
Tail Back part of ski 400
Target group Classification of skiers and skis to simplify ski selection 397
Telemark Method of turning when skiing downhill with *cross-country* equipment
Tip Front part of *ski*
Touring binding Adjustable *binding* enabling heel to be secured to ski for downhill skiing and detached from it for climbing 436
Trail North American terminology for *piste* 24
Transfer Journey (usually by coach) from airport to ski resort 54
Transformed snow *Spring snow* 26
Traverse Skier's course across slope of hill, terminated by a *turn*
Tuck *Egg* position
Turn What learning to ski is all about
Turntable binding *Binding* with rotating heel piece 404

U

Unweighting Method of briefly taking skier's weight off skis as an aid to turning
Uphill christie Method of turning uphill and stopping with skis parallel

V

VSOP Not what you should fill your *hip flask* with

W

Waist Narrow part of ski 400
Wall Steep, wide descent
Wax Applied to ski sole for lubrication and protection 402, 429
Wedel German term for succession of linked short-radius turns
Wedelkurs Package of intensive ski instruction and accommodation offered at beginning of season 51
Wedge *Snowplough*
Wedging *Canting*
White-out Skiing conditions in which falling snow, fallen snow and cloud merge, and all sensation of direction is lost; not to be confused with black-out (après-skiing conditions)
White week Package offered by resort, usually in low season, including accommodation, lift pass and instruction
Windslab Dangerously unstable and invisible patches of *crust* caused by wind over surface of snow 423
Winter stick Broad ski used (off-piste) like surfboard (brand name)

X

XC American term for *cross-country* skiing 428

Y

Yodel Time-honoured Austrian way of emptying bars at closing time; or even earlier

Z

Zdarsky, Mathias Father of *Alpine skiing* 11
Zip Means of closing jacket which becomes inoperable on *chair-lifts* at sub-zero temperatures 409

For full **resort**

index see pages

387–8